ROUTLEDGE INTERNATIONAL HANDBOOK OF HUMAN TRAFFICKING

According to the UNODC (2015), human trafficking (HT) is the fastest growing means by which people are enslaved, the fastest growing international crime, and one of the largest sources of income for organized criminal networks. It profoundly impacts the physical and mental health of victims, their families, and entire communities and is recognized as a crime against humanity.

Despite burgeoning interest, education, research, and advocacy efforts, a pinnacle handbook devoted to human trafficking and modern-day slavery – with global focus and multidisciplinary scope – does not currently exist. The *Routledge International Handbook of Human Trafficking* was created to fill this resource gap. Divided into four sections, the *Handbook* offers the reader a comprehensive and fresh approach via (a) in-depth analyses and opportunities for application (through case studies, critical thinking questions, and supplemental learning materials); (b) multidisciplinary linkages, with disciplinary overlap across each of the four sections acknowledged and highlighted; and (c) content experts representing multiple segments of society (academia, government, foundation, law enforcement, and practice) and global vantage points (Australia, Finland, Germany, Netherlands, South Africa, Thailand, and the United States).

Written by expert scholars, service providers, policy analysts, and healthcare professionals, this *Handbook* is an invaluable resource for those already working in the field, as well as for students in any discipline who want to learn (or learn more) about HT and modern-day slavery.

Rochelle L. Dalla, PhD, is Professor of Family Studies at the University of Nebraska–Lincoln (UNL). Her research focuses on marginalized and hard-to-reach populations of sex trafficking survivors in the United States and India. She is Editor in Chief of the *Journal of Human Trafficking* and has been honored with multiple research and teaching awards, including the *Distinguished Research and Creative Career Award* (2018), the *Distinguished Teaching Award* (2017 and 2001), the *Swanson Award for Teaching Excellence* (2007), and the *Charman Outstanding Professor Award* (2004).

Donna Sabella, MEd, MSN, PhD, PMHNP-BC, is the former Seedworks Endowed Associate Professor of Social Justice at the University of Massachusetts–Amherst College of Nursing. Dr. Sabella is a co-founder and Associate Editor of the *Journal of Human Trafficking*, as well as founder and Contributing Editor of the *American Journal of Nursing*'s Mental Health Matters column. She is also a co-founder and the first program director for Dawn's Place, a residential recovery program for trafficked women in Philadelphia. She has numerous presentations and publications about human trafficking and is considered a pioneer in nursing for her work in this area.

ROUTLEDGE INTERNATIONAL HANDBOOKS

THE ROUTLEDGE HANDBOOK OF TEACHING LANDSCAPE
Edited by Elke Mertens, Nilgül Karadeniz, Karsten Jørgensen, Richard Stiles

THE ROUTLEDGE INTERNATIONAL HANDBOOK OF SPIRITUALITY IN SOCIETY AND THE PROFESSIONS
Edited by Laszlo Flanagan and Bernadette Flanagan

THE ROUTLEDGE INTERNATIONAL HANDBOOK OF LANGUAGE EDUCATION POLICY IN ASIA
Edited by Andy Kirkpatrick and Anthony J. Liddicoat

ROUTLEDGE INTERNATIONAL HANDBOOK OF MIGRATION STUDIES, 2E
Edited by Steven J. Gold and Stephanie J. Nawyn

ROUTLEDGE HANDBOOK OF CONTEMPORARY FEMINISM
Edited by Tasha Oren and Andrea Press

ROUTLEDGE HANDBOOK OF THE BELT AND ROAD
Edited by Cai Fang and Peter Nolan

ROUTLEDGE HANDBOOK OF LANGUAGE ACQUISITION
Edited by Jessica S. Horst and Janne von Koss Torkildsen

ROUTLEDGE HANDBOOK OF IDENTITY STUDIES, 2E
Edited by Anthony Elliott

ROUTLEDGE INTERNATIONAL HANDBOOK OF POVERTY
Edited by Bent Greve

ROUTLEDGE INTERNATIONAL HANDBOOK OF NEW DIGITAL PRACTICES IN GALLERIES, LIBRARIES, ARCHIVES, MUSEUMS AND HERITAGE SITES
Edited by Hannah Lewi, Wally Smith, Dirk vom Lehn and Steven Cooke

ROUTLEDGE INTERNATIONAL HANDBOOK OF HUMAN TRAFFICKING
A Multi-Disciplinary and Applied Approach
Edited by Rochelle L. Dalla and Donna Sabella

For more information about this series, please visit: www.routledge.com/Routledge-International-Handbooks/book-series/RIHAND

ROUTLEDGE INTERNATIONAL HANDBOOK OF HUMAN TRAFFICKING

A Multi-Disciplinary and Applied Approach

Edited by Rochelle L. Dalla and Donna Sabella

LONDON AND NEW YORK

First published 2020
by Routledge
2 Park Square, Milton Park, Abingdon, Oxon OX14 4RN

and by Routledge
605 Third Avenue, New York, NY 10017

First issued in paperback 2020

Routledge is an imprint of the Taylor & Francis Group, an informa business

British Library Cataloguing-in-Publication Data
A catalogue record for this book is available from the British Library

Library of Congress Cataloging-in-Publication Data
Names: Dalla, Rochelle L., editor. | Sabella, Donna, editor.
Title: Routledge international handbook of human trafficking : a multi-disciplinary and applied approach / edited by Rochelle L. Dalla and Donna Sabella.
Description: Abingdon, Oxon ; New York, NY : Routledge, 2019. | Series: Routledge international handbooks | Includes bibliographical references and index. | Provided by publisher.
Identifiers: LCCN 2019027103 (print) | LCCN 2019027104 (ebook) | ISBN 9781138244269 (hbk) | ISBN 9781315277035 (ebk)
Subjects: LCSH: Human trafficking—Handbooks, manuals, etc.
Classification: LCC HQ281 .R79 2019 (print) | LCC HQ281 (ebook) | DDC 364.15/51—dc23
LC record available at https://lccn.loc.gov/2019027103
LC ebook record available at https://lccn.loc.gov/2019027104

ISBN 13: 978-0-367-72671-3 (pbk)
ISBN 13: 978-1-138-24426-9 (hbk)

Typeset in Bembo
by Apex CoVantage, LLC

CONTENTS

List of Figures *viii*
List of Tables *ix*
List of Images *x*
List of Contributors *xi*
Preface *xxi*
List of acronyms and abbreviations *xxiii*

Introduction 1

SECTION I
Public policy **5**

1 The roles of past slaveries in contemporary anti-human trafficking discourse: implications for policy 7
Karen E. Bravo

2 What we talk about when we talk about trafficking: a reflection on the first 20 years of the modern anti-slavery fight 36
Ambassador Luis C.deBaca (Ret.)

3 International policies to combat human trafficking 71
Natalia Ollus and Matti Joutsen

4 Narratives of human trafficking in international issue arenas with implications for policy formation 103
Niina Meriläinen

SECTION II
Criminal justice **133**

5 Where is the justice in criminal justice? 135
Marie Bussey-Garza, Michelle M. Dempsey, Christian Martin, and Shea M. Rhodes

6 Combating human trafficking: challenges to the criminal justice system and what practitioners need to know 159
Katharine Bryant, Jacqueline Joudo Larsen and Elise Gordon

7 The law of human trafficking: from international law to domestic codification in the U.S. and abroad 189
Nicole J. Siller

SECTION III
Healthcare **213**

8 The complex mental health consequences of human trafficking: what every provider needs to know 215
Sandra L. Bloom and Susan Brotherton

9 Syncope and malnutrition in an adolescent girl 240
Kanani E. Titchen and Hanni M. Stoklosa

10 Human trafficking and public health 262
Anita Ravi

11 Trafficking in persons for the purpose of organ removal 286
Ana Manzano

SECTION IV
Social work **313**

12 Training social workers in anti-trafficking service 315
Jacquelyn C.A. Meshelemiah

13 Unique contributions of social work in combating human trafficking 342
Melissa I.M. Torres, Maura Nsonwu, Laurie Cook Heffron, and Noël Bridget Busch-Armendariz

14 How to work across multiple sectors to respond to human trafficking: values, leadership, alliances, and program models 364
Celia Williamson and Dominique Roe-Sepowitz

Index *389*

FIGURES

3.1 The steps of the National Referral Mechanism 97
4.1 Policy formation process 123
6.1 Modern slavery through the lens of Situational Crime Prevention theory 161
6.2 Modern slavery as an umbrella term 168
9.1 Duluth Model Power and Control Wheel 246
10.1 Power and Control Wheel 263
10.2 Socioecological framework contextualizing and conceptualizing commercial sexual exploitation of children 265
10.3 Bay Area Regional Health Inequities Initiative's Public Health Framework for Reducing Health Inequities (BARHII) 268
12.1 Anti-trafficking training model 323
12.2 Anti-trafficking model 335
13.1 Continuum of cultural competency 355
14.1 Eight elements of the PATH Model 376
14.2 Movement along continuum of mental health 379
14.3 Ten critical pathways for restoration 380
14.4 Phoenix 1st Step Drop-In Center 385

TABLES

2.1 Administration legacies 43
2.2 Tier placement, criteria and examples 54
3.1 International conventions on trafficking 73
3.2 Comparison of main international hard-law instruments on trafficking in persons 76
3.3 Comparisons of victim assistance by the three main international conventions 90
4.1 Comparison of NGO and EP narratives: 2011–2012 115
4.2 NGO narrative comparisons 2011–2012 and 2016–2017 119
4.3 EP narrative comparisons 2011–2012 and 2016–2017 121
4.4 Comparison of NGOs and EP narratives: 2016–2017 122
7.1 Defining the "acts" in trafficking in persons 194
7.2 Defining the "means" in trafficking in persons 196
7.3 Defining the types of exploitation in trafficking in persons' "purpose" element 199
8.1 Risk factors for sex trafficking 216
8.2 Indicators of human trafficking 217
8.3 Signs and symptoms of trafficking 222
8.4 Assessment of trauma: key questions 230
8.5 Stages of change 232
9.1 Salient points from the case study indicate possible human trafficking 242
9.2 Important questions to ask the potentially trafficked patient 250
9.3 A 12-step approach to human trafficking in the healthcare setting 251
9.4 Resources 255
10.1 Typology of sex trafficking 266
10.2 Typology of labor trafficking 266
10.3 Adverse childhood experiences (ACEs) 269
10.4 Major U.S. climate trends 275
11.1 Organ trafficking terminology 290
12.1 Human rights and human trafficking 317
12.2 Multi-site placement 327

IMAGES

3.1 Screenshot of the UNODC PSA "Work Abroad" campaign 79
3.2 Poster on labour trafficking from the TIP Office of the U.S. DHHS 80
3.3 Poster for the IOM Jamaica campaign for safe migration 80

CONTRIBUTORS

Sandra L. Bloom is a Board-Certified psychiatrist, graduate of Temple University School of Medicine, and Associate Professor at the Dornsife School of Public Health, Drexel University. From 1980–2001, she served as Founder and Executive Director of the Sanctuary programs, inpatient psychiatric programs for the treatment of trauma-related emotional disorders and President of The Alliance for Creative Development, a multidisciplinary outpatient practice. Between 2005 and 2016 over 350 social service, juvenile justice, and mental health organizations have been trained in the Sanctuary Model. For the past 30 years, she has pioneered work in the field of traumatic stress studies. In 1998, she and a colleague published the first book connecting traumatic stress studies, violence, and public health practice in *Bearing Witness: Violence and Collective Responsibility*. She is author or co-author of a series of books and articles on trauma-informed care that include *Creating Sanctuary: Toward the Evolution of Sane Societies*, published in 1997 with a second edition in 2013; *Destroying Sanctuary: The Crisis in Human Delivery Service Systems*, published by Oxford University Press in 2010; and *Restoring Sanctuary: A New Operating System for Trauma-Informed Systems of Care*, published by Oxford University Press in 2013. She and colleagues developed and applied a trauma-informed psychoeducational curriculum known as "S.E.L.F." that has been widely distributed. Her latest contribution is through "P.R.E.S.E.N.C.E.," an online training and consultation program for organizations. She co-chairs CTIPP (The Campaign for Trauma-Informed Policy and Practice), whose goal is to advocate for public policies and programs at the federal, state, local, and tribal levels. CTIPP is being award the Distinguished Service Award for 2019 from the American Psychiatric Association.

Karen E. Bravo is Vice Dean and Professor of Law at the Indiana University Robert H. McKinney School of Law. A well-known international law scholar, and expert in the study of human trafficking, her research interests include regional integration, labor liberalization, business and human rights, slavery, and human trafficking. She teaches business and international law, including Illicit International Markets (concerning the transborder traffic in people, money and drugs). Her publications include *Exploring the Analogy between Modern Trafficking in Humans and the Trans-Atlantic Slave Trade; Free Labor! A Labor Liberalization Solution to Modern Trafficking in Persons; Interrogating the State's Role in Human Trafficking*; and *Interrogating Everyperson's Roles in Today's Slaveries*. She has lectured on human trafficking and slavery around the world and is the founder and leader of the Slavery Past, Present and Future project, an interdisciplinary initiative that brings together scholars of slavery from a multiplicity of disciplines. She is a graduate of the University of the West Indies (B.A); Columbia University School of Law (J.D.); and New York University School of Law (LL.M.).

Susan Brotherton, MSW, is Director of Philadelphia Social Service Ministries for The Salvation Army of Greater Philadelphia where she oversees a variety of residential programs, anti-human trafficking services, and other social services. She has been an employee of the Salvation Army for 24 years, previously serving as the director of the trauma-informed Red Shield Family Residence. She has represented The Salvation Army presenting promising practices in trauma-informed care, creating trauma sensitive cultures, serving families and youth experiencing homelessness, and meeting the unique needs of survivors of commercial sexual exploitation. She is an adjunct professor in Temple University's social work program, in the School of Public Health, instructing both BSW and MSW students. Prior to her work with the Salvation Army, she worked in the behavioral health field, where she managed a residential program for adults whose lives have been affected by mental illness, worked as a clinical case manager, and a psychotherapist serving individuals and families.

Katharine Bryant is an international development specialist and Manager of Global Research at the Walk Free Foundation. She has been co-author of the Global Slavery Index since 2014 and oversees Walk Free's research program on "what works?" to combat modern slavery. This includes an assessment of government responses released as part of the Global Slavery Index and the promising practices database, which collates evaluations of the impact of anti-slavery and counter trafficking programming. She has worked in counter-trafficking and anti-slavery programming and research for the past ten years, including at the International Organization for Migration, Save the Children, and UNICEF.

Noël Bridget Busch-Armendariz is a nationally recognized expert in sexual assault, human trafficking, and domestic/dating violence. She is co-author of the first textbook on human trafficking, *Human Trafficking: Applied Research, Theory, and Case Studies.* As a principal investigator, she has led research externally sponsored by the NSF, Department of Justice, Texas Office of the Attorney General, and the Governor of Texas. In 2016, she visited with Department of Defense Secretary Ash Carter to discuss integration of research findings and recommendations in sexual assault policies regarding the military. Members of the Pentagon have invited her as a consultant and trainer on workplace harassment and sexual harassment. She and IDVSA research institute staff developed a blueprint with the University of Texas System Police to provide guidance on improving law enforcement's response to campus sexual assault. She also provided expertise to the White House Task Force to Protect Students From Sexual Assault. She serves as the Principal Investigator of the Cultivating Learning and Safe Environments (CLASE), one of the most comprehensive studies on the issues protected under Title IX. It has been nationally recognized for its innovative methodological approaches, comprehensiveness on topics that impact student's lives across diverse ecosystems, and its ground breaking programmatic and policy implementation strategies. She has worked as shelter for survivors, support group facilitator, program director, and registered lobbyist. In addition to her interpersonal violence work, she has previously served as principal investigator for a program providing intensive health and mental health services to refugees, victims of trafficking, asylees, and other immigrants in Central Texas. Over the past 25 years, she has traveled and lived extensively throughout the world including Northern Ireland, the Republic of Ireland, Romania, Albania, South Korea, Dubai, and the United Arab Emirates. She serves on the board of directors for SAFE, served for five years on the board of directors for American Gateways, and served on the policy committee of the Texas Council on Family Violence. She is a returned Peace Corps volunteer. She has been recognized for her contributions to social work as the Recent Most Distinguished Contributions to Social Work Education by the Council on Social Work Education and has been recognized by her students and colleagues with teaching and service awards. She is happily married to Larry Armendariz and is most proud to be Daniel's mother. She is a sexual assault survivor.

Marie Bussey-Garza, J.D., Esq., is an associate in the Philadelphia office of Akin Gump Strauss Hauer & Feld LLP. She concentrates her practice on complex commercial litigation, with an emphasis on class action defense. She has substantial experience litigating cases in federal and state courts, as well as in arbitration, for clients in a wide range of industries, including retail, communications, insurance, and nonprofit. She has defended class actions involving claims of false advertising, consumer fraud, unfair competition, data privacy violations, and violations of the Telephone Consumer Protection Act. She also counsels clients on contract enforceability and compliance issues. Additionally, she maintains an active pro bono practice, with an emphasis on assisting survivors of commercial sexual exploitation with their complex and varied legal needs. She received her J.D. summa cum laude from Villanova University Charles Widger School of Law in 2017. During law school, she served as managing editor of *Tolle Lege* for the *Villanova Law Review* and was selected to the Order of the Coif. Additionally, she interned for the Honorable Michael M. Baylson, Senior U.S. District Judge for the Eastern District of Pennsylvania. She received her B.S. in enology from California State University, Fresno in 2009 and her B.B.A., with highest honors, in management information systems and business honors from The University of Texas at Austin in 2002.

Ambassador Luis C.deBaca is a diplomat and manager who has investigated and prosecuted cutting-edge cases, negotiated national security and human rights advances, and managed multimillion-dollar grant portfolios combating modern slavery and sexual abuse. In the Civil Rights Division of the U.S. Justice Department, he became one of the country's most decorated Federal Prosecutors, investigating and prosecuting cases of involuntary servitude, police misconduct, racial violence, money laundering, and immigration violations. He served as the Justice Department's Involuntary Servitude and Slavery Coordinator and helped to establish both the Clinton-era Worker Exploitation Task Force and the Bush administration's Human Trafficking Prosecutions Unit, of which he was the inaugural Chief Counsel. He played key roles in the drafting of the Trafficking Victims Protection Act of 2000 and negotiating the United Nations' Trafficking in Persons Protocol. As Counsel to the House Committee on the Judiciary, he negotiated immigration, Civil Rights, and national security legislation. During the Obama administration, as Ambassador-at-Large for the Office to Monitor and Combat Trafficking in Persons, he coordinated U.S. activities against contemporary forms of slavery, launching initiatives on supply chain transparency, victims' rights, and survivor input, as well as overseeing the annual *Trafficking in Persons Report* which assesses the efforts of over 190 countries. As Director of the Office of Sex Offender Sentencing, Monitoring, Apprehending, Registering, and Tracking, he spearheaded innovative research into adult and juvenile offender behavior, streamlined federal information systems, supported Indian Tribes in their efforts against sexual violence, and successfully negotiated methods of preventing child sex tourism by sex offenders. He retired from federal service at the conclusion of the Obama administration. He is currently the Robina Fellow in Modern Slavery at Yale University's Gilder Lehrman Center for the Study of Slavery, Abolition, and Resistance. In his consulting practice, he is working to ensure exploitation-free supply chains and financial flows, to support innovation in law enforcement, and to establish information-sharing that makes communities and industry safer. He speaks regularly to business, academic, and law enforcement audiences, and is a life member of the Council on Foreign Relations.

Michelle M. Dempsey is the Harold Reuschlein Scholar Chair and Professor of Law at Villanova University Charles Widger School of Law. Previously, she was a CUF Lecturer in Law at the University of Oxford and Tutorial Fellow at Worcester College and Brasenose College, where she taught Jurisprudence and Criminal Law. A former criminal prosecutor, her book, *Prosecuting Domestic Violence: A Philosophical Analysis* (Oxford University Press), was awarded second prize in the UK's Society of Legal Scholars Peter Birks Award for Outstanding Legal Scholarship. Her scholarly interests focus on the state's response to violence against women, as explored through the intersections of law and philosophy. She received her D.Phil. (Ph.D.) from the University of Oxford, her LL.M. from the London School of Economics, her J.D. from the University of Michigan Law School, and her B.A. from the University of Illinois. She is an elected member of the American Law Institute, currently serves as co-Editor-in-Chief of the multidisciplinary, international journal *Criminal Law & Philosophy*, and served as the co-director of the Criminal Law Theory Program at the Robina Institute for Criminal Law and Criminal Justice at the University of Minnesota Law School from 2009–2016. Her scholarship regarding prostitution, sex trafficking, and commercial sexual exploitation has been published in *Criminal Law Review* (UK), *University of Pennsylvania Law Review, Social & Legal Studies, Qualitative Inquiry, Emory International Law Review, Journal of Catholic Social Thought, Criminal Law & Philosophy, American Criminal Law Review*, and *Journal of Human Trafficking*.

Elise Gordon is a Research Analyst at the Walk Free Foundation. She is one of the co-authors of the 2018 Global Slavery Index, a global study of prevalence, vulnerability, and government responses to modern slavery published by the Walk Free Foundation. Her work involves both quantitative and qualitative research of modern slavery, including producing national estimates of modern slavery from representative surveys undertaken in a range of international contexts and, through qualitative methods, broadening the research base on the nature of modern slavery around the world. She has qualifications in health sciences from Curtin University, Western Australia and experience in quantitative alcohol research, with a focus on the epidemiology of alcohol-related harm.

Laurie Cook Heffron, Ph.D., LMSW, is an Assistant Professor in the School of Behavioral and Social Sciences at St. Edward's University in Austin, Texas, where she teaches undergraduate students and directs the Social Work Field Education Program. She joined the faculty of St. Edward's University after having served as Post-doctoral Fellow in Immigration and Violence Against Women at The University of Texas at Austin and as former Associate Director for Research at UT-Austin's Institute on Domestic Violence and Sexual Assault. Her research and expertise focus on domestic and sexual violence, human trafficking, and the experiences of, and relationships between, violence against women and migration. She also draws from direct social work practice experience with a variety of communities, including refugees, asylum-seekers, trafficked persons, and other immigrants. Blending her research and practice experience, she regularly provides assessments and serves as an expert witness in immigration cases of women and children seeking T visas, U visas, and asylum based on domestic violence. She studied Linguistics and Spanish at Georgetown University and earned a Master of Social Work (MSW) and Doctorate in Social Work from The University of Texas at Austin.

Matti Joutsen, Ph.D., is Special Advisor at the Thailand Institute of Justice (2017–). Previously, he served as Director of the European Institute for Crime Prevention and Control, affiliated with the United Nations (HEUNI). He has also served for example as a lower court judge in Finland, as the Director of International Affairs at the Ministry of Justice of Finland and as the interregional adviser for the UN crime prevention and criminal justice programme. His research interests cover the broad spectrum of crime and criminal justice. His many publications and papers deal among others with victim policy, prosecutorial decision-making, corruption, economic crime, organized crime, juvenile delinquency and non-custodial sanctions. His focus since the 1990s has been on transnational police and judicial cooperation, in particular within the context of the United Nations, the European Union and other international structures. He served as Rapporteur-General at the Tenth UN Congress on the Prevention of Crime and the Treatment of Offenders (Vienna, 2000), and as vice-chairman at the three subsequent UN Congresses (Bangkok, 2005; Salvador de Bahia, Brazil, 2010; and Doha, April 2015). He also served as Rapporteur-General at the Fourth Session of the Conference of the States Parties to the United Nations Convention against Corruption (Marrakesh, Morocco, 2011) and has otherwise been actively involved in the work on review of the two United Nations Conventions, on corruption and on transnational organized crime. He has received the degree of Doctor of Laws (J.S.D.[hab.]) at the University of Helsinki.

Jacqueline Joudo Larsen is a criminologist and Head of Global Research for the Walk Free Foundation, with a technical role leading their survey program. During a 15-year career in research, she has focused on social justice and human rights issues, with a particular interest in unpacking the causes of crime, understanding vulnerability and resilience, and using that information to drive policy change. She previously led research on human trafficking, victimization of international students, sexual assault, and violent extremism at the Australian Institute of Criminology.

Ana Manzano, Ph.D., is an applied social scientist working mostly with healthcare disciplines, bringing methodological expertise in the research of complex healthcare issues, policies and interventions. She is interested in the relationship between research methods, evidence and policy making particularly at the health-social interface. She collaborates with health professionals, other social scientists and health service researchers to develop evaluations of complex interventions using qualitative and mixed-methods approaches. She is a world-leading realist methodologist and who works with policy and academic stakeholders in multidisciplinary projects in the national and international health field. As such, she has researched and written widely on research methodology and the social aspects of organ donation and organ trafficking. This builds on her longstanding interest in the social aspects of healthcare, healthcare user decision-making, and the interface between crime, welfare and health inequalities. She has over ten years of experience teaching these subjects at university. Since 2015 she has been an *Expert member for Transplant Tourism and Paid Donation Group at* ELPAT – the European expert platform on "Ethical, Legal and Psychosocial Aspects of organ Transplantation."

Christian Martin is a former student intern at The Villanova Law Institute to Address Commercial Sexual Exploitation. In addition to working on "Where Is the Justice in Criminal Justice?" (Chapter 5, this volume), he has also assisted in research projects on state and federal statutes related to commercial sexual exploitation, helped organize the survivor led symposium hosted by the Institute, and learned a great deal about what it means to be a survivor advocate from the Institute's founder and faculty advisor.

Niina Meriläinen, Ph.D., is a post-doctoral power-relations and human rights researcher from Tampere University, Finland, the Faculty of Management and Business. Currently she works in ALL-YOUTH-research project which is funded by the Strategic Research Council (SRC). Her main research focus areas are multidisciplinary communication, power-relations, narratives and human rights research from various perspectives. She combines multidisciplinary theoretical frameworks to empirical case studies. She has published all her papers in international journals and handbooks. During her career, she has worked in applied science universities and NGOs in Finland, Germany and the Netherlands.

Jacquelyn C. A. Meshelemiah, Ph.D., is a licensed social worker (LSW) who has earned her Bachelor of Science in Social Work (BSSW), Master of Social Work (MSW) and Doctorate (Ph.D.) from the College of Social Work at The Ohio State University. Dr. Meshelemiah has taught numerous courses across the curricula, but now exclusively teaches Assessment & Diagnosis in Clinical Social Work Practice as well as Human Trafficking. She is the author and co-author of numerous publications, presentations, and trainings at the university, local, national and international levels. Her primary research agenda centers on social justice, human rights and anti-trafficking work. Professional travels have taken her to over half of the United States as well as to Africa, Europe, Asia and Central America.

Maura Nsonwu, PhD, MSW, LCSW, is a professor of Social Work at North Carolina State University. She has practiced as a clinician, educator, and researcher in refugee resettlement, human trafficking, healthcare, child welfare, and social work education over 30 years. She has received external funding and produced numerous publications in these areas of inquiry which often intersect with one another. She has recently co-authored the textbook *Human Trafficking: Applying Research, Theory and Case*, released in 2018. She is a research fellow with the Center for New North Carolinians (CNNC) at the University of North Carolina at Greensboro serving refugee/immigrant communities as an advocate/scholar. In this work, she has partnered closely with resettlement agencies as well as the United Nations High Commissioner for Refugees (UNHCR). She also serves as the president of the Association for Immigration and Refugee Service Professionals (ARSP), a national organization to support professionals who work in immigration and refugee related fields and those they serve. She specializes in qualitative research often conducting community-based participatory research (CBPR) with refugee and immigrant communities (African, Montagnard, and Latino). One of her CBPR grant-funded projects delivered culturally relevant mental health services to the local Latino community. Many CBPR projects include interdisciplinary collaboration with a variety of faculty and students from other disciplines and universities. Her work with the Interprofessional Health Education program partnered undergraduate and graduate level social work students with nursing, physician assistant, physical therapy, and pharmacy disciplines to cultivate collaborative healthcare practice to better serve patient-centered care. She has enjoyed serving in a number of administrative positions throughout her career. However, her real joy is teaching (and learning from) her students; she has been fortunate to work with undergraduate, graduate, and doctoral students.

Natalia Ollus, Ph.D., is Director of the European Institute for Crime Prevention and Control, affiliated with the United Nations (HEUNI), situated in Helsinki, Finland. She has been engaged in the prevention of human trafficking since 1999, when she started working with NGOs in Northern Europe, assessing their capacity to support victims of trafficking. At the United Nations Office on Drugs and Crime (UNODC) in South Africa, she was responsible for training legal practitioners on the obligations of the UN Trafficking Protocol. She has also worked as an anti-trafficking adviser at the Organisation for Security and Cooperation in Europe (OSCE) in Vienna and as an adviser on good governance at the Permanent Mission of Finland to the UN in New York. Having worked in international, governmental and non-governmental organizations, she has a broad understanding of policies related to human trafficking. She has engaged with and trained law enforcement officers, border guards, prosecutors, government representatives, civil society, businesses and trade unions on how to counteract human trafficking. She has also been involved in the development of national and regional anti-trafficking policies and programmes. Her research interests focus on the exploitation of migrant workers and trafficking for the purpose of forced labour, anti-trafficking policies, violence against women as well as the rule of law. She has written articles on the exploitation of migrant workers, arguing that it should be seen as a form of corporate crime. She has also published studies assessing legislation and policies governing the assistance to victims of trafficking. Her recent work includes exploring the economic crimes related to human trafficking as well as collaborating with companies so as to include the prevention of exploitation into corporate social responsibility policies. She holds a Doctor of Laws (LL.D) degree from the University of Turku. Contact: natalia.ollus@om.fi

Anita Ravi, M.D., is a board-certified family physician, assistant professor at the Icahn School of Medicine at Mount Sinai and the founder and medical director of the PurpLE Clinic at the Institute for Family Health. Her vision for the PurpLE (Purpose: Listen and Engage) Clinic was simple but pioneering: a community health center-based clinic targeted to the needs of people who have experienced human trafficking and individuals impacted by other forms of trauma, including sexual assault and domestic violence. Today, PurpLE has served over 300 people and has been recognized as a Health Resources and Services Administration "Promising Practice" in the care of people who have experienced domestic violence and human trafficking. She received the 2016 Family Medicine Education Consortium's "Emerging Leader" Award and she regularly draws, writes and speaks at events across the country on how the healthcare system must radically adapt to meet the needs of survivors of trafficking and other forms of gender based violence. Her advocacy work includes serving as an elected member of the American Medical Association's Women's Physician Section Governing Council and as a board member of the New York State Academy of Family Physicians. She also conducts forensic examinations for people seeking asylum and facilitates health education workshops in correctional settings and in collaboration with community-based organizations for people who have experienced homelessness, incarceration and/or trafficking. She is a graduate of Washington University in St. Louis, received her Medical Degree from the University of Michigan School of Medicine, her Master's in Public Health from Yale University and her Masters in Health Policy research from the University of Pennsylvania School of Medicine/Robert Wood Johnson Foundation Clinical Scholars Program.

Shea M. Rhodes, Esq., has dedicated her career to combating violence against women, protecting the rights of those who are oppressed or exploited, and championing human rights. As the Co-founder and Director of the Institute to Address Commercial Sexual Exploitation (CSE Institute) at Villanova University Charles Widger School of Law, she works with and on behalf of victims and survivors of commercial sexual exploitation and human trafficking. The CSE Institute promotes survivor-oriented, trauma-informed legal responses to commercial sexual exploitation and human trafficking. She is a member of several anti-trafficking initiatives, locally and internationally, including Philadelphia's Anti-Trafficking Coalition, the Pennsylvania

Anti-Human Trafficking Advocacy Work Group (PAHTAWG), Shared Hope International's JuST Response Council, and sits on the Executive Committee for World Without Exploitation (WorldWE). She also sits on the Board of Directors for Dawn's Place, a residential treatment program for women who are victims of commercial sexual exploitation and sex trafficking. Prior to forming the CSE Institute in 2014, she served the Philadelphia community as an Assistant District Attorney for nearly ten years. She began her career as a staff attorney for the Crime Victim's Law Project, providing legal assistance and advocacy to adult and child victims of rape, sexual assault, and stalking. She is a graduate of Villanova University Charles Widger School of Law and the University of Kansas.

Dominique Roe-Sepowitz, MSW, Ph.D., is an associate professor in the School of Social Work at Arizona State University and she is the Director of the ASU Office of Sex Trafficking Intervention Research. She has her Master's degree and Ph.D. in social work and is a researcher, professor and a forensic social work practitioner. She teaches in the clinical track of the masters of social work program as well as provides clinical intervention groups focused on abuse and trauma in the community to women and men exiting prostitution. Her expertise includes sex trafficker profiles, establishing a prevalence of sex buyers, and sex trafficking victim prevention and intervention design. She works very closely with community groups including the Phoenix Police Department, the Phoenix Prosecutor's Office and Catholic Charities DIGNITY programs. Her research work spans the prevention, detection, identification and trauma-focused treatment of sex trafficking victims. Recent projects include estimations of online sex buying demand, estimating the prevalence of sex trafficking victims within the juvenile delinquency and adult probation systems in Arizona, surveying Arizona's homeless young adults about their sex trafficking experiences (Youth Experiences Survey), studying patterns within arrest cases of traffickers, exploring sex ads and demand response around the Super Bowl in 2014 and 2015, and evaluating interventions for sex trafficking victims. Community partnerships for developing new knowledge about sex trafficking include the Las Vegas Metropolitan Police Department, the Phoenix Police Department, and the Tucson Police Departments. She has conducted research with partners including Thorn: Digital Defenders of Children, Shared Hope International, and Demand Abolition. Community interventions that Dominique has helped to develop includes the Phoenix 1st Step Drop-in Center, projectstarfish.education, and Phoenix Starfish Place. She has been invited to provide expertise to human trafficking specific work groups for federal agencies including DOJ, SAMHSA, OVW, and the White House. She has participated in conference presentations at the United Nations and as an international expert speaker for the U.S. Department of State.

Nicole J. Siller, Ph.D., is a Senior lecturer in law at Deakin University. From 2008–2013, she served as an Assistant District Attorney in Philadelphia, Pennsylvania. In 2017, she successfully defended her doctoral thesis: *Trafficking in Persons under International Law and Its Incorporation within Enslavement as a Crime against Humanity.*

Hanni M. Stoklosa, M.D., MPH, is Executive Director of HEAL Trafficking, an emergency physician at Brigham and Women's Hospital (BWH) with appointments at Harvard Medical School and the Harvard Humanitarian Initiative. She is Director of the Global Women's Health Fellowship at BWH, Connors Center. She is an internationally recognized expert, advocate, researcher, and speaker on the well-being of trafficking survivors in the U.S. and internationally through a public health lens. She has advised the United Nations, International Organization for Migration, U.S. Department of Health and Human Services, U.S. Department of Labor, U.S. Department of State, and the National Academy of Medicine on issues of human trafficking and testified as an expert witness multiple times before the U.S. Congress. Moreover, she has conducted research on trafficking and persons facing the most significant social, economic, and health challenges in a diversity of settings including Australia, China, Egypt, Guatemala, India, Liberia, Nepal, Kazakhstan, the Philippines, South Sudan, Taiwan, and Thailand. Among other accolades, she has been honored with the U.S. Department of Health and Human Services Office of Women's Health Emerging Leader award, the Harvard Medical School Dean's Faculty Community Service award, has been named as an Aspen Health Innovator and National Academy of Medicine Emerging Leader. Her anti-trafficking work has been featured by the New York Times, National Public Radio, Glamour, Canadian Broadcasting Corporation, STAT News, and Marketplace. She published the first textbook addressing the public health response to trafficking, *Human Trafficking Is a Public Health Issue, A Paradigm Expansion in the United States.*

Kanani E. Titchen, M.D., FAAP, is an Adolescent Medicine physician at St. Barnabas Hospital and an Assistant Professor at the City University of New York and Albert Einstein College of Medicine. She is a member of the American Academy of Pediatrics Council on Child Abuse and Neglect, the Advocacy Committee for the Society for Adolescent Health and Medicine, and a member of the North American Society for Pediatric and Adolescent Gynecology. She has authored numerous articles for medical journals and for the lay press about U.S. child sex trafficking and physician education. She has advocated for human trafficking survivors at the New York City Mayor's Office to End Domestic and Gender Based Violence, at the U.S. Department of Health and Human Services, and at the United Nations. She has spoken at multiple academic institutions, hospitals, and on TEDˣ and public radio about the need for a trauma-informed approach for working with victims and survivors of human trafficking. She is a graduate of Sidney Kimmel Medical College of Thomas Jefferson University in Philadelphia, PA. She stayed on as a pediatric resident at Thomas Jefferson University/A.I. duPont Hospital for Children and completed her fellowship in Adolescent Medicine at the Children's Hospital At Montefiore. During her tenure as the 2013–2014 President of the American Medical Women's Association National Resident Division, she created an online video tutorial (www.doc-path.org) to educate doctors about human sex trafficking. She is a Co-Chair of AMWA's Physicians Against the Trafficking of Humans and Co-Creator of the SUSTAIN and LIFT CME-accredited training initiatives.

Melissa I. M. Torres, Ph.D., is Director of the Human Trafficking Research Portfolio at the Institute for Domestic Violence and Sexual Assault at the University of Texas at Austin's Steve Hicks School of Social Work. She developed and taught a class on human trafficking at the University of Houston, where she is co-founder of the Latin American Initiative. Her social work career includes HIV testing and counseling, managing community education and prevention for a domestic violence and sexual assault service agency, and legislative research for a public policy organization. She served as Subject Matter Expert on the U.S. Department of Health and Human Services' healthcare professional's response to human trafficking program, an initiative of the Federal Strategic Action Plan on Services for Victims and she developed the first national training on outreach and service provision with vulnerable and immigrant populations during disaster for the American Red Cross. She serves as the human trafficking expert for various academic studies in the U.S. and Latin America, has partnered with schools of social work and human rights advising on exploitation and irregular migration throughout the Americas, and has conducted trainings and workshops on forced migration and exploitation for legislators, investigators, healthcare professionals, advocates, and social service providers in the U.S., Mexico, El Salvador, Bolivia, Colombia, the Netherlands, and Ghana. She is Vice President of the

International Board of the Women's International League for Peace and Freedom (WILPF), the world's first and oldest feminist peace organization, and consulting NGO to the United Nations. She has served as co-faculty for the United Nations Practicum on Advocacy in New York City, a program of WILPF U.S., and as the delegate for the Universal Periodic Review on Human Rights of the United States at the UN, Geneva. She was a doctoral fellow of the Council on Social Work Education's Minority Fellowship Program and a fellow of the Global Freedom Exchange, a Vital Voices program for women leaders and human rights defenders around the world in the fight against human trafficking. She has received a Certification of Congressional Recognition by the U.S. Congress for her work with the U.S. Department of Labor Women's Bureau and recognition from the American Red Cross for her service to the Houston immigrant community during the Hurricane Harvey disaster response. She is a native of the Rio Grande Valley of Texas and was raised along the U.S.-Mexico border.

Celia Williamson, Ph.D., is a professor in the Social Work department at The University of Toledo and Executive Director of the Human Trafficking and Social Justice Institute. Her research focus has been in the area of human trafficking, with particular attention to domestic minor sex trafficking. She has published numerous articles, has delivered over 200 presentations and been the keynote speaker at more than 20 conferences. She also studies prostitution, vulnerable women, and drug abuse. She founded the first anti-trafficking program in Ohio in 1993. She has completed nine studies, 19 articles/reports, and edited two books on sex trafficking; and she has received federal funding from 2002 to 2012 to conduct research in this area. Additional accomplishments include founding the annual International Human Trafficking and Social Justice Conference and founding the Lucas County Human Trafficking Coalition. She is Chair of the Research & Analysis Subcommittee for the Ohio Attorney General's Human Trafficking Commission and is a founding member of the Global Association of Human Trafficking Scholars.

PREFACE

Human trafficking. Not all that long ago most people were, in all likelihood, unfamiliar with the term and probably knew very little about what it meant. Early public introduction and exposure to human trafficking overwhelmingly highlighted sex trafficking, which was often incorrectly associated with prostitution, and did not offer much about labor trafficking and other forms of human exploitation. The common public perception of prostitution as being a victimless crime and one in which those being prostituted entered into willingly created more confusion than anything else – but the attention paid to sex trafficking guaranteed people would pay attention – always a good thing for media ratings. But those were the early days when we were just beginning to connect the dots and realizing what we had been looking at was just the tip of the iceberg. That was then.

Today, while we still have more to learn and do, we have made advances in what we do know. We know that human trafficking is a global occurrence; that sex trafficking is but one form of human trafficking; that it involves people of all ages, backgrounds, and circumstances as victims and victimizers; and that it is indeed a complex phenomenon requiring interdisciplinary efforts to understand and combat it. And just as the public is becoming more knowledgeable and informed about what human trafficking is, there is increased interest among students and faculty in various educational settings to learn more about this universal exploitation of men, women and children. This book, the *Routledge International Handbook of Human Trafficking: A Multi-Disciplinary and Applied Approach*, grew out of an awareness of the need to provide students with evidence-based information about the important and timely issues surrounding human trafficking by those actively working in the field and knowledgeable about its complexities. The *Handbook* is targeted to upper-level undergraduate and graduate students and offers a comprehensive and multidisciplinary overview of human trafficking and modern-day slavery across four fields of inquiry: public policy, criminal justice, healthcare, and social work.

While no one book can do justice to the big picture of this global and horrific crime, we have aimed at creating a work that provides readers with a solid understanding related to the basic foundation and components of human trafficking as seen through the lens of four disciplines that are key in combating human trafficking. Readers are also encouraged to complement this work with the many other excellent sources of information available to you, especially online. It is our hope that this handbook leaves readers better informed and more aware of what is meant by the term human trafficking than they were before they picked it up. And it is our hope that what doesn't get lost in all the words contained within is that once all is said and done, we never forget those who have been victimized and trafficked. The knowledge we gain is meant to be used. It is our hope that it will be used to help others, in whatever way is possible and relevant to your situation.

Rochelle L. Dalla, PhD, CFLE
Donna Sabella, MEd, MSN, PhD, PMHNP-BC
March 15, 2019

ACRONYMS AND ABBREVIATIONS

4-Ps	Protection, Prevention, Prosecution, and Partnerships
ANITP	National Agency Against Human Trafficking (Europe)
APHA	American Public Health Association
ASEAN	Association of Southeast Asian Nations
CEDAW	UN Convention on the Elimination of All Forms of Discrimination Against Women
CoE	Council of Europe
CPS	Crown Prosecution Service (Europe)
CSEC	Commercial Sexual Exploitation of Children
DEVAW	UN Declaration on the Elimination of Violence Against Women
DMST	Domestic Minor Sex Trafficking
ECCAS	Economic Community of Central African States
ECOWAS	Economic Community of West African States
ECPAT	End Child Prostitution, Pornography and Trafficking of Children for Sexual Purposes
EFTA/EEA	European Free Trade Association/European Economic Association
EU	European Union
EUROPOL	European Union Agency for Law Enforcement Cooperation
GAATW	Global Alliance Against Trafficking in Women
GRETA	Europe's Council Group of Experts on Action Against Trafficking in Human Beings
ICCPR	UN International Covenant on Civil and Political Rights
ICE	U.S. Immigration and Customs Enforcement:
ICESCR	UN International Covenant on Economic, Social and Cultural Rights
ICRMW	UN International Convention on the Protection of the Rights of All Migrant Workers and Members of Their Families
IDP	Internally Displaced People
IDMC	Internally Displaced Monitoring Council (Africa)
ILO	International Labour Organization
ILO-IPEC	International Labour Organization-International Program for the Elimination of Children Labour

IMF	International Monetary Fund
IOM	International Organization for Migration
INGO	International Non-Governmental Organization
INTERPOL	International Criminal Police Organization
LEA	Law Enforcement Authorization
LSI	La Strada International
MOU	Memorandum of Understanding
NAM	National Academy of Medicine
NGO	Non-Governmental Organization
NRM	National Referral Mechanism
NHTRC	National Human Trafficking Resource Center
OAS	Organization of American States
ORR	U.S. Office of Refugee Resettlement
OSCE	Organization for Security and Cooperation in Europe
OTIP	Office of Trafficking in Persons
OVC	Department of Justice Office of Victims of Crimes (U.S.)
PITF	President's Interagency Task Force (to Monitor and Combat Human Trafficking)
SIMEV	National Integrated System for Monitoring and Assessing Victims of Trafficking in Persons (Europe)
THB	Trafficking in Human Beings
TIC	Trauma-Informed Care
TIP	Trafficking in Persons
TVPA	Trafficking Victims Protection Act
TWAIL	Third World Approaches to International Law
UCSE	Underground Commercial Sex Economy
UN	United Nations
UNDP	United Nations Development Programme
UNECE	United Nations Economic Commission for Europe
UNHCR	United Nations High Commissioner for Refugees
UNICEF	United Nations Children's Fund
UNESCO	United Nations Educational, Scientific, and Cultural Organization
UNICRI	United Nations Interregional Crime and Justice Research Institute
UNIFEM	United Nations Development Fund for Women
UNODC	United Nations Office on Drugs and Crime
UNOHCHR	United Nations Office of the High Commissioner for Human Rights
UN.GIFT	United Nations Global initiative to Fight Human Trafficking
UNTOC	United National Convention against Transnational Organized Crime
UN Women	United Nations Entity for Gender Equality and the Empowerment of Women
VoT	Victim of Trafficking

INTRODUCTION

The *Routledge International Handbook of Human Trafficking: A Multi-Disciplinary and Applied Approach* was born from the realization that having a handbook that presented information about the basic foundation and components of human trafficking was needed. More and more educational and training programs are introducing students to human trafficking in a variety of ways, including adding talks or lectures into existing courses to developing courses solely devoted to the topic and in some cases to creating a certificate on human trafficking. Essential to whatever approach is used is having resources that provide students with rich content from experts in the field. We hope that this handbook is such a source. The handbook was created with the desire to provide readers with information from a variety of disciplines as the approach to understanding and combating human trafficking involves a team effort. While numerous disciplines have a seat at the table, this work focuses on four areas that play an important role on a number of levels. A brief summary of each section is provided below.

Section I: public policy

Public policy – the dynamic, complex, and interactive system through which public problems are identified and countered[1] – is the driving force by which trafficking in persons (TIP) will be eradicated. As such, Section I of this *Handbook* is devoted to its examination. Chapter 1 situates human trafficking (HT) within a historical context and draws attention to the similarities and differences between it and the trans-Atlantic slave trade. Deep analysis into the legal definition of human trafficking coupled with its origins in the anti-trafficking fight are, according to Karen E. Bravo, necessary for the creation of more effective policy enactments. Historical trends that shape the current anti-trafficking fight continue in Chapter 2 with author Luis C.deBaca's framing of the Trafficking Victims Protection Act (TVPA), the United Nations Trafficking Protocol (the Protocol), and U.S. leadership efforts in the global fight to combat human trafficking. Noting limitations of the modern anti-trafficking frame due to "unresolved cultural and legal legacies," retired Ambassador Luis C.deBaca argues for global instruments and policies embedded in a rights-based, survivor-centered perspective; contemporary and historical examples provide rich context.

International policy arenas are central to Chapters 3 and 4. In Chapter 3, Natalia Ollus and Matti Joutsen provide in-depth analysis of the evolution of international policy to prevent and respond to human trafficking. Identification of critical international frameworks and assessment of their impacts with particular attention to victims' rights versus state interests are highlighted. Niina Meriläinen completes Section I with a description of empirical research to explore narratives of human trafficking presented by three gatekeepers: Amnesty International (AI), Human Rights Watch (HRW), and the European Parliament (EP). The results, she argues, "suggest that the formation of various human rights policies in the international arenas are deeply affected by selective narratives that include the dynamic interrelatedness between various human rights violations, and other political and social issues, actors and events."

Section II: criminal justice

As human trafficking is universally acknowledged as a crime, it is imperative that we pay attention to the domestic and international laws and how they determine what constitutes criminality and justice as well as how they impact what happens to victims and possible consequences for traffickers. Chapter 5 begins the discussion by asking where is the justice in the criminal justice system, especially in regard to how justice is served as it relates to sex trafficking. Authors Bussey-Garza, Dempsey, Martin, and Rhodes walk us through six categories of criminal justice as they answer this question and explain where the weaknesses lie in each conception of justice when it comes to ensuring justice for victims.

While both Chapters 5 and 6 focus on the criminal justice system, the former focuses mostly on the U.S. justice system, and the latter examines criminal justice responses to human trafficking on international, regional, and national levels. In Chapter 6, Bryant, Joudo Larsen, and Gordon also examine a number of challenges the criminal justice system faces when confronted with human trafficking, and what practitioners need to know in order to overcome the obstacles confronting them in their efforts to combat human trafficking. The final chapter in this section, Chapter 7 by Siller, shifts the focus from the criminal justice system to what the author refers to as the law of human trafficking. The chapter provides information about international law concerning human trafficking and describes the elements of the crime of human trafficking as defined under U.S. federal law.

Section III: healthcare

It is well-known that being trafficked, regardless of the type of trafficking an individual is subjected to, can and does lead to numerous health problems, both physical and behavioral. Bloom and Brotherton's Chapter 8 presents information on the complex mental health consequences and needs of victims of human trafficking, providing information about risk factors, trauma bonding, and complex PTSD. In Chapter 9, Titchen and Stoklosa combine elements of behavioral and medical issues through a case study of a young girl with the goal of preparing healthcare professionals to correctly recognize the signs of human trafficking and appropriately support identified victims.

The extent to which human trafficking occurs worldwide has clearly raised it to the level of a public health issue, as Ravi notes in Chapter 10. The author presents information about how the socioecological model can be used to conceptualize human trafficking as a public health issue and discusses how several areas important to and related to human trafficking can be understood through a public health approach. Finally, while sex trafficking is talked about frequently, Manzano's Chapter 11 affords us a look into a lesser publically acknowledged form of trafficking, the trafficking in persons for the purpose of organ removal. Organ transplantation abroad is a global business, and the need for organ donations exceeds the number of organs available to those in need. This chapter clarifies what is meant by organ trafficking, details the numerous complexities of this phenomenon, and defines key terms and concepts. It also presents some of the legislative challenges surrounding attempts to regulate organ transplantation as well as what motivates some individuals to buy and/or sell human organs.

Section IV: social work

Social work is a human rights profession which promulgates the belief that all individuals, regardless of race, creed, sexual orientation, religious affiliation, or any other defining demographic, deserve to be viewed and treated with dignity and worth and afforded access to basic necessities of life. Social work is therefore a profession deeply ingrained in the anti-trafficking fight. Author Jacquelyn Meshelemiah provides a comprehensive overview of the training of social workers in Chapter 12, charging the profession to adopt a human rights approach in anti-trafficking service. Chapter 13 expands upon the context set by Meshelemiah with deep assessment of the unique contributions of social work in addressing both international and domestic human trafficking. Here, authors Torres, Nsonwu, Cook Heffron, and Busch-Armendariz apply social work theory and international practice through an ecological lens using a case study. In this manner, the intersection of systems of care is highlighted in addressing human trafficking survivors' needs. Section IV concludes with Celia Williamson and Dominique Roe-Sepowitz – experts in harnessing the energy, voice, and resources of multi-sector teams for successful programmatic outcomes – who describe necessary components for coalition building in addition to strategies for avoiding common pitfalls and barriers. Description of two successful multi-sector anti-trafficking programs allows for application and deeper analysis of presented concepts.

Note

1 John, P. (1998). *Analyzing public policy*. New York: Continuum.

SECTION I

Public policy

1

THE ROLES OF PAST SLAVERIES IN CONTEMPORARY ANTI-HUMAN TRAFFICKING DISCOURSE

Implications for policy

Karen E. Bravo

Abstract

According to contested sources, 40 million people worldwide are enslaved, and hundreds of thousands are trafficked across international borders. In response, anti-trafficking activists, academics, and others have sought to use the trans-Atlantic slave trade and slavery to understand and combat this contemporary form of exploitation. However, those who have invoked the trans-Atlantic slave trade have failed to explore it other than superficially or to adequately map out the similarities and differences between the trans-Atlantic trade and human trafficking. As a consequence, the ability to effectively combat modern human trafficking has been undermined both internationally and domestically. The analogy is underutilized as currently deployed because it does not illuminate the essential similarities or differences in the two forms of exploitation. Analysis of the trans-Atlantic slave trade and of white slavery offers a richer understanding of human trafficking that can be used to more effectively combat modern trafficking than do current efforts.

Learning Objectives

At the end of the chapter, readers will be able to:

1 Understand the background of the legal definition of "human trafficking" and the origins of the anti-trafficking fight;
2 Identify types of uses of the word "slavery" and understand the purposes and effects of those uses;
3 Interrogate their own and society's reaction to those uses;
4 Understand and critique the discourse regarding human trafficking, and identify the contradictions between the discourse/rhetoric used and the types of actions taken by states;
5 Understand the historical context of human trafficking and its linkages to past forms of human exploitation;
6 Illustrate the role, use, and potential misuse of history in understanding and addressing modern challenges;

7 Compare and contrast trans-Atlantic slavery, white slavery, and human trafficking to identify differences and similarities among the three forms of exploitation and foster critical reflections on policy approaches to human trafficking; and
8 Map the relationship (including gaps) between rhetoric and policy creation and implementation.

Key Terms: human trafficking; slavery; trans-Atlantic slave trade; white slavery; the United Nations Protocol to Prevent, Suppress and Punish Trafficking in Persons, Especially Women and Children; Convention Against Transnational Organized Crime; Trafficking Victims Protection Act (TVPA); U.S. Trafficking in Persons (TIP) Report.

Introduction

The focus of late nineteenth- and early twentieth-century activists on sex and the protection of white women has continued to limit understanding of the fundamental similarities among the trans-Atlantic slave trade, white slavery, and contemporary human trafficking. (As used herein, the term "trans-Atlantic slave trade" also includes trans-Atlantic slavery, in which the trade itself was embedded and of which it formed a part.) It was the exploitation and enslavement of whiteness that, together with the threats to state borders and authority, stimulated coordinated international action by state entities against modern human trafficking. But it is the image of enslaved Africans that arouses and harnesses visceral public outrage and support for anti-trafficking efforts.

Analysis of the trans-Atlantic slave trade and of white slavery offers a richer understanding of human trafficking that can be used to more effectively combat modern trafficking than do current efforts. Trans-Atlantic slavery was a centuries-long international trade in people and their labor, spanning the early 1500s to the 1880s (Davis, 2006). It coexisted with and surpassed in scope trans-Saharan slavery and the trade of slaves from the East Coast of Africa to the Gulf States. Following the end of trans-Atlantic slavery in 1888,[1] nation states and international institutions legally recognized and committed to protecting fundamental rights of human beings.[2]

Given the legal prohibition, an apparent resurgence in the enslavement of human beings might have seemed impossible. However, that resurgence has been documented worldwide in the form of "human trafficking" (see U.S. TIP Report, 2018). Indeed, analysis of the economic roots and structure of the two forms of exploitation indicates that modern trafficking in human beings is as interwoven with and central to contemporary domestic and global economies as were the trans-Atlantic trade and white slavery to their contemporaneous economic systems (Bravo, 2007).

This chapter examines some uses of the trans-Atlantic slave trade in modern anti-human trafficking efforts and discourse and the impact of those uses, and it identifies the role of the late nineteenth- and early twentieth-century efforts against white slavery in the modern discourse. I focus on the analogy to trans-Atlantic slavery, even though a majority of the users of the term do not explicitly refer to trans-Atlantic slavery. It is my claim that the power of the emotional impact and lasting structural legacies of trans-Atlantic slavery in contemporary society has embedded the image in all contemporary references to "slavery." Permutations such as "modern slavery," "contemporary slavery," and "contemporary forms of slavery" attempt to piggyback on that emotional power, while simultaneously avoiding in-depth structural comparisons or acknowledgement of the legacies of trans-Atlantic slavery. The chapter is organized as follows:

1 An overview of human trafficking, and international and domestic U.S. responses to it;
2 Examination of the uses made of trans-Atlantic slavery and the slave trade in anti-trafficking discourse and efforts;
3 Discussion of the ways in which white slavery frames the perceptions of and responses to human trafficking;

4 A claim that these two forms of exploitation could play more meaningful potential roles in current anti-human trafficking efforts; and
5 I conclude that, to be successful, anti-trafficking efforts must target the economic incentives and structures that facilitate the trade in human beings.

Human trafficking

How do you feel when you hear the word "slavery"? What mental image do you have? What is your definition of "slavery"?

Separated from the trans-Atlantic slave trade by more than 100 years and a seeming eternity in human development, human trafficking today might appear to be an aberration, a dreadful anomaly in the march of human progress. In reality, human trafficking has re-emerged only in the sense that it has re-entered public consciousness. Slavery has *always* been a part of human existence and was *not* eliminated by the nineteenth-century abolition of trans-Atlantic slavery (Miers, 2003). In the early 2000s, according to varied and frequently *conflicting* sources (see Wong, 2005), 27 million people worldwide were enslaved (Bales, 2004); either four million or 600,000–800,000 (or some unknown number of) individuals are trafficked annually across international borders (Kapstein, 2006; U.S. Dept. of Justice (2006); Richard, 2000); and each year 14,000–17,500 people are trafficked into the United States (U.S. TIP Report, 2006). By 2016, the International Organization for Migration (IOM) estimated that 40 million persons are enslaved worldwide (IOM Global Trafficking Trends, 2006–2016).

The modern trade[3] in human beings – their purchase, sale, and distribution – has significant ramifications for international human rights, international criminal law, and the global economy. The modern "re-emergence" of trafficking in human beings and of slavery is said to be linked to the deepening interconnection among countries in the global economy, overpopulation (with its consequent production of disposable people) (see Bales, 2004), and the victims' economic and other vulnerabilities. Despite the expenditure of a great deal of intellectual, legal, social, and other resources to prevent and punish human trafficking, there is little or no evidence of effective, systemic impact on the size and operations of these activities (U.S. TIP Report, 2018).

The UN Working Group on Contemporary Forms of Slavery first raised the issue of sex tourism in its 1978 report (Miers, 2003), and the existence of international sex markets became generally known through media reports and other information channels (see, for instance, Handley, 1989; Erlanger, 1989; Simons, 1994; Kempadoo, 2005). However, it was not until the 1990s that modern human trafficking began to fully engage the consciousness of Western legislators and the public in general (see, for example, *Man Pleads*, 1999; Connolly, 1999; Crecente, 1999; Chen, 1999; Barry, 1998; Nicholson & Wheeler, 1998; Triads, 1997). A perceived growth in the buying and selling of human beings followed the collapse and dissolution of the Soviet Union (Wong, 2005). Media and other reports disseminated frightening statistics and horrific reports of the purchase and sale of women and young girls from republics of the former Soviet Union, in particular, into Western Europe (Caldwell, Galster, & Steinzor, 1997).

Is human trafficking "slavery"?

The dominant perception of modern human trafficking is that it is an abnormal parasitic appendage to global and domestic economies and the product of the greed of particularly monstrous individuals and groups. The images of forced sexual slavery on a large scale was alarming and created concern that spread throughout the globe. According to dominant narratives, growing numbers of victims were enslaved by modern-day traffickers: tricked by schemes offering employment abroad or other prospects of fruitful economic opportunity – or simply sold by parents or other authority figures – countless men, women, and children around the world were being subjected to sexual or other exploitation without compensation. Victims were deprived of freedom of movement, raped, beaten, and violated in various ways through mechanisms of violence, force, psychological abuse, coercion, and fraud. By the late 1990s, conventional knowledge held, based on varying statistical sources, that up to four million people were trafficked annually across national borders (see USAID, 1999). In addition, the trade in humans was said to be a $5–7 billion per year illicit industry – less profitable than only the traffic in illegal drugs and arms (Tiefenbrun, 2002).

Confronted with evidence of the increase in the traffic and exploitation of human beings and violations of state borders and laws, scholars, policymakers, non-governmental organizations (NGOs), and legislators came together in both the international and domestic U.S. arenas to combat human trafficking. The United Nations Protocol to Prevent, Suppress and Punish Trafficking in Persons, Especially Women and Children, Supplementing the United Nations Convention Against Transnational Organized Crime (2001) (hereinafter the Trafficking Protocol) United Nations, 2001a was adopted and ratified as a protocol to the more wide-ranging Convention Against Transnational Organized Crime (2001) (hereinafter the UN Convention) (for analysis of international legal tools see Ollus and Joutsen, Chapter 3, this volume). One of the principal achievements of the Trafficking Protocol is the creation of the first international definition of trafficking. The Trafficking Protocol defines trafficking in persons as:

> The recruitment, transportation, transfer, harbouring or receipt of persons, by means of the threat or use of force or other forms of coercion, of abduction, of fraud, of deception, of the abuse of power or of a position of vulnerability or of the giving or receiving of payments or benefits to achieve the consent of a person having control over another person, for the purpose of exploitation. Exploitation shall include, at a minimum, the exploitation of the prostitution of others or other forms of sexual exploitation, forced labour or other services, slavery or practices similar to slavery, servitude or the removal of organs.
>
> *(United Nations, 2001a)*

The U.S. domestic statute, the Trafficking Victims Protection Act (TVPA) of 2000 (United States, 2000), was adopted a mere month before the UN Organized Crime Convention and Trafficking Protocol were opened for signature.[4] Together, the international instruments and the U.S. legislation have been influential in the fight against and interpretation of modern trafficking in humans. In addition to the obligations voluntarily undertaken by state parties under the Convention and Protocol, the series of U.S. State Department reports issued pursuant to the mandates of the TVPA have vastly increased public and institutional awareness of, and knowledge about, human trafficking (see C.deBaca, Chapter 2, this volume for analysis of U.S. domestic policies). For example, the U.S. State Department has issued annual reports each year from 2001 through the present. Each successive report reflects an increase in the depth and breadth of coverage of human trafficking and the efforts against it.

Two contrasting accounts illuminate the emergence of broad public awareness around trafficking and the subsequent development of an international consensus to combat it. Commentators such as Kelly Hyland (2001) pointed to growing international concern regarding the scope, complexity, and criminality of modern trafficking in humans as the impetus for the development and adoption of the United Nations' anti-trafficking treaty in 2000. In contrast, other scholars have highlighted states' growing realization of the threats that modern trafficking poses to their sovereignty and national security. According to Wong (2005),

> The conjunction of trafficking and illegal immigration materialized into the political consciousness of Europe at the 11th International Organization for Migration (IOM) Seminar, devoted to the theme of "Global Human Trafficking" in 1994. In an influential paper presented to that conference by a leading European scholar on international migration, the emergent model of the new unholy trinity threatening the borders of Europe – trafficking, illegal immigration, and organized crime – was introduced and authoritatively quantified.
>
> *(pp. 74–75)*

Wong located European alarm about human trafficking that arose in the period following the fall of the Berlin Wall within broader European fears of being inundated by migrants from the former Soviet Bloc. Similarly, Gallagher (2001) noted: "While human rights concerns may have provided some impetus (or cover) for collective action, it is the sovereignty/security issues surrounding trafficking and migrant smuggling which are the true driving force behind such efforts" (p. 975). Gallagher pointed to a widespread state concern regarding the threat of illegal and unregulated immigration. "Wealthy states are increasingly concerned that the actions of traffickers and migrant smugglers interfere with orderly migration and facilitate the circumvention of national immigration restrictions" (p. 976).

I offer four additional potentially complementary interpretations of activity leading to the international instrument adopted in 2000.

- First, the reported human rights violations and victimization of women and children offended the world's conception of where, what, and who human beings had become in the post–World War II and post–Cold War era.
- Second, the attainment of a level of human progress and acceptance of the norm against slavery led to the determination to stamp out the continuing exploitation.
- Third, the perceived sharp increase in illicit traffic, together with the types of victims (Eastern Europeans who are identified as white) and the importation of trafficking into the very heart of the West, aroused a visceral sense of invasion and violation.
- Fourth, the end of the Cold War briefly facilitated international consensus about the threat of transnational criminal enterprises to state borders and freed state resources to combat a previously identified crisis for which resources and international cooperation theretofore had been unavailable.

While intergovernmental efforts proceeded on the international level, other fighters against human trafficking have looked to earlier periods of human enslavement for insight into the trade and for weapons to fight against it. Two examples of enslavement that appear to be particularly relevant are the trans-Atlantic slave trade and the white slavery of the late nineteenth and early twentieth centuries. Comparisons of modern human trafficking and the trans-Atlantic slave trade reveal fundamental similarities in their economic roles and the ways in which both systems of exploitation formed and form part of the dominant "legitimate" economic systems of their times. Analysis and comparisons of white slavery and the responses against it add depth to the understanding of modern efforts against human trafficking and the potential drawbacks of abolitionist methodologies.

How is trans-Atlantic slavery similar to and different from human trafficking today?

Historians estimate that, from the 1400s until Brazil ended its slave trade in 1888 (Davis, 2006), 9.5 million Africans were shipped from Africa to the Americas and elsewhere (see Rawley, 2005). The trans-Atlantic slave trade arose amid the rush of European powers to exploit the "New World" "discovered" by Christopher Columbus (see Davis, 2006; Mintz, 1985).[5] The Portuguese and Spanish (Davis, 2006) introduced African enslaved persons to replace the indigenous inhabitants of the Americas who were quickly falling prey to the colonists' depredations, diseases, and labor demands. The trans-Atlantic slave trade and African slavery played an integral role in European exploration and settlement of the hemisphere (Kolchin, 2003). Although the majority of the enslaved Africans and their New World descendants were destined for agricultural labor on the plantations of the Caribbean, Central and South America, and the United States, slave labor was used in and essential to all aspects of the New World economies (Davis, 2006).

Following hard-fought political battles in Britain, the African slave trade was outlawed in the British Empire in 1807, effective January 1, 1808 (Davis, 2006). Enshrined in and protected by the U.S. Constitution,[6] the slave trade officially ended in the United States by congressional legislation that same year (United States, (1810); see also Finkelman, 2001). Nevertheless, illicit slave trading from Africa and a newly resurgent internal trade in black enslaved persons continued in the continental United States, and the importation of enslaved persons across the Atlantic to the Americas continued until 1850 (Finkelman, 2001). The United Kingdom abolished slavery in 1838, paying out millions of pounds of compensation to slaveholders in its colonies. In the United States, slavery was ended by the Thirteenth Amendment to the U.S. Constitution only after the devastating internecine conflict of the Civil War.

Uses of trans-Atlantic slavery and the slave trade in anti-trafficking discourse

Much of the material describing and analyzing modern human trafficking – academic scholarship, opinion writers, legislators, and government officials – invokes and analogizes to the trans-Atlantic slave trade. Such invocations and analogies occur in many venues and are widespread in media reports, scholarly literature, legislative history and policy, and NGO reports, as well as pronouncements from world leaders such as the president of the United States, the prime minister of the United Kingdom, and the pope. The content of these references and analogies varies with the intent of their users. The "old slavery" may be compared to the "new slavery" in order to distinguish the new slavery from the old: the egregiousness of the exploitation of enslaved persons, the estimated number of victims of the old and new slaveries, or the race or ethnicity of victims are all categories that make use of this old-new comparison. Often, the implicit or explicit hypothesis is that modern trafficking in humans is more widespread and horrifying and involves greater victimization and human degradation than did the trans-Atlantic slave trade (see Vatican official, 2006). In other uses, no or little reference is made to "old" slavery except, implicitly, through the modifier "modern" or "contemporary" in conjunction with the word "slavery." New incoherent definitions are offered – a wish list of anti-exploitation, coexisting uneasily with ignorance and lack of understanding, or discounting of trans-Atlantic slavery and its legacies.

Why and how is the word "slavery" used to refer to human trafficking? What is the effect of that use on efforts to fight human trafficking?

The use of analogies is fundamental to human reasoning and analysis, allowing the comparison of new experiences to old, categorization of the new, and decisions about and examples for how to deal with the newly encountered experience. Those references are pervasive and wide-ranging in the anti-trafficking discourse but have been superficial, counterproductive, and harmful to the fight against human trafficking. Analysis of the usage of the trans-Atlantic slave trade analogy exposes trends strongly infused with appeals to emotions rather than to the intellect. The trends may be identified as (1) the emotional exhortation to action, (2) the diminution of the horror of trans-Atlantic slavery, (3) the assumption of the mantle of righteousness, (4) distancing of our (enlightened) time from theirs or "how far we've come," and (5) the mythic slaying of the dragon or the perception of human trafficking as an entirely new form of exploitation.

Several of the examples reproduced and analyzed below fall within more than one of the trends identified. The intertwining of these categories of uses demonstrate the deep-seated nature of the perceptions of and emotional reaction to the trans-Atlantic slave trade and the variety of ways in which it can be rhetorically deployed.

Emotional exhortation to action

In the most common use of the trans-Atlantic slave trade analogy, users compare human trafficking to the earlier slavery in order to stimulate the audience to action. Trans-Atlantic slavery is used as an emotional and historic touchstone – the blueprint against which this "new" traffic is measured. The more immediate the access to visceral imagery and emotions that this touchstone evokes, the more the new system of exploitation is said to resemble the trans-Atlantic slave trade. As a result, the analogy user's call to action becomes more powerful, and the audience is more likely to support the mechanisms suggested by the analogy user in their crusade against the modern traffic.

President George W. Bush illustrated the methodologies used to exploit references to the trans-Atlantic slave trade while speaking about trafficking to the UN General Assembly on September 23, 2003. In his speech, the president boldly referenced slave trade and slavery:

> We must show new energy in fighting back an old evil. Nearly two centuries after the abolition of the transatlantic slave trade, and more than a century after slavery was officially ended in its last strongholds, the trade in human beings for any purpose must not be allowed to thrive in our time.

The identification of human trafficking as "an old evil," coupled with the martial tone of the call to arms, appeals to the emotions of the listener while giving direction to the revulsion that the language evokes.

Another example of the emotional exhortation to actions comes from a speech by Ambassador John Miller (2006), then director of the U.S. State Department's Office to Monitor and Combat Trafficking in Persons:

> We have to make sure that we get our language straight. There are a lot of euphemisms. I head up an office that is called the Office of Monitoring and Combating Trafficking in Persons. Trafficking in persons is the euphemism; what we are really talking about is the slave trade. Back in the nineteenth century, when people talked about slavery, they did not talk about slaves. They talked about field hands or house boys. It made it sound better. Today we talk about forced laborers or sometimes the phrase sex worker – as if

one could describe it as a normal form of work. . . . it is important to call it by its real name: slavery.

By explicitly invoking the trans-Atlantic slave trade, then Director Miller attempts to arouse the revulsion and rejection of his audience to the existence of the "new" trade.

In this excerpt from his *New York Times* video blog, journalist Nicholas Kristof (2006) exemplifies the use of emotional exhortation to action. Here, he invokes the image of the trans-Atlantic slave trade to illustrate the horrors of modern sex trafficking in Cambodia.

> [Audio Narration:] To us slavery seems a remote part of history but it is not. . . . They had been sold into slavery by their parents or kidnapped by neighbors. The problem here isn't prostitution, as such, and the real problem isn't trafficking, it is slavery. Every year worldwide 700,000 people are ensnared by human trafficking across international borders. I found it stunning that [*simultaneous depiction of black enslaved persons with the following scrolling text*: It seems almost certain that the modern slave trade is larger in absolute terms than the Atlantic slave trade in the 18th and 19th centuries] scholars estimate that the slavery trade today is probably larger than it was in the 18th or 19th centuries. At its worst the trafficking system takes innocent village girls and imprisons them in brothels to be raped repeatedly. . . . Now the talk about sex slavery may sound like hyperbole, but it is not. And the shame lies not with the girls but with our own failure to respond as firmly to slavery today as our ancestors did in the 1860s.

The depiction of black enslaved persons serves to invoke the horror of trans-Atlantic slavery and invites the listener to compare it to modern traffic in human beings. Kristof further states that "the shame lies . . . with our own failure to respond as firmly to slavery today as our ancestors did in the 1860s," implying that the modern traffic in human beings is the same as or worse than was trans-Atlantic slavery. However, as is typical of such comparisons, while the image of trans-Atlantic slavery is used, the user does not attempt an in-depth comparison of the two forms of exploitation. In addition, this is tantamount to hagiography of the Western role in slavery and its legal abolition: it grossly misrepresents Western creation of and response to trans-Atlantic slavery and its abolition or, at the very least, views it through rose-colored glasses.

In a 2016 op-ed extolling the efforts of the United Kingdom against "modern slavery," Prime Minister Theresa May makes savvy use of the emotional power of the language and images of slavery. She described the Modern Slavery (UK) Act as having "delivered tough new penalties to put *slave masters* behind bars" (May, 2016, emphasis added). May later describes an independent reviewer of the legislation as "a barrister with a proven track record of successfully prosecuting *slave drivers*" (emphasis added). She thus blurs the boundaries between "slavery" as a legal concept with emotion-inducing rhetorical flourishes.

Diminution of the horror of trans-Atlantic slavery

What criteria should be used to compare human trafficking and trans-Atlantic slavery?

In this category, the user builds upon the emotional exhortation to action. Here, the analogy user once again evokes the touchstone of trans-Atlantic slavery and takes for granted the audience's agreement that trans-Atlantic slavery must be condemned and rejected. However, unlike with the call to action, this analogy user implicitly or explicitly diminishes the horror of that historic and still-influential system of exploitation. The purpose of the user is to magnify modern human trafficking, whether with respect to the extent of the human rights violations committed or the scope of the exploitation (usually the absolute number of victims or number of countries involved). That diminution also serves to arouse both emotional reaction and action in the listener-reader. The message, in effect, is "as horrible as you know the trans-Atlantic slave trade and slavery to have been, an even greater horror is full-fledged in our time, in our country, in our lives." Some typical examples follow:

> There are more slaves alive today than all the people stolen from Africa in the time of the transatlantic slave trade.
>
> *(Bales, 2004, p. 9)*

> Two hundred million people are victims of contemporary forms of slavery. Most aren't prostitutes, of course, but children in sweatshops, domestic workers, migrants. During four centuries, 12 million people were believed to be involved in the slave trade between Africa and the New World. The 200 million – and many of course are women who are trafficked for sex – is a current figure. It's happening now, today.
>
> *(Specter, 1998)*

> Contemporary forms of slavery include bonded labour, trafficking, the worst forms of child labour, forced marriage and the abuse of domestic migrant workers. *These now involve many times the number of people the transatlantic slave trade ever involved.* Although reliable statistics on contemporary slavery are hard to come by due to its illegal nature, Kevin Bales estimates that 27 million people are contemporary slaves (Bales, 1999). *Some international NGOs have put the number as high as 200 million.*
>
> *(van den Anker, 2004, p. 18, emphasis added)*

> Whatever the exact number is, it seems almost certain that the modern global slave trade is larger *in absolute terms* than the Atlantic slave trade in the eighteenth and nineteenth centuries was.
>
> *(Kapstein, 2006, p. 105, emphasis added)*

In analyzing the preceding examples, several trends are worthy of note. First, in the authors' use of the trans-Atlantic slave trade as a comparator to human trafficking, they imply that modern trafficking is worse than the historic slavery, even as they make use of this emblematic, readily accessible image of slavery. Second, the authors' use of absolute versus proportional numbers as comparators is misleading, saying (E.g. Kapstein, above). A meaningful analysis would refer to the proportion of the existing human population that was enslaved at the time of the trans-Atlantic slave trade versus the proportion of the contemporary human population that is enslaved. For example, a comparison could be drawn to the proportion of Africa's then population that was enslaved during the slave trade versus the proportion of source country populations that are now enslaved. Another worthwhile calculation would be a comparison of the individual country's or region's proportion of export earnings or economic activity represented by the trade in enslaved persons at the time of the trans-Atlantic slave trade and in the present. Third, the numbers referred to – whether 9 or 12 million – are limited to first-generation enslaved persons exported in chains from the shores of Africa.

That number does not engage with the numbers of their descendants and other later-born generations who were enslaved through laws of birthright enslavement during the four centuries of the trans-Atlantic slave trade and who continue to be subordinated through legal, cultural, economic, and other measures. Fourth, the speaker-writers make no reference to other severe forms of exploitation that were contemporaneous with the trans-Atlantic slave trade and slavery. These include serfdom, indentured servitude, impressment, Barbary slavery, and other forms of exploitation practiced by and against European populations. Finally, references to statistics presented by other authors evidence the struggle by academics, activists, NGOs, and officials to understand the scope of human trafficking. Unable to definitively pin down the scope of human trafficking, they repeat numbers offered up by prior authors – even while sometimes noting their potential inaccuracy – until those numbers gain the aura of hard fact (U.S. Government Accountability Office, 2006) (hereinafter 2006 GAO Report).

Running throughout is an inherently contradictory view of trans-Atlantic slavery: it is both (a) the ultimate in evil that never should have existed but is being repeated, and (b) not as bad as the modern traffic in human beings – either because more persons are *now* victimized or because human trafficking is happening *today*.

Assumption of the mantle of righteousness

With this category of usage, the analogy user assumes the mantle of righteousness by invoking her or her country's (or ancestors') past actions against and continued condemnation of trans-Atlantic slavery. The mantle of righteousness confers authority upon the individual spokesperson or country and delays or avoids questioning of the mechanisms against modern trafficking proposed or deployed by that individual or country. After all, who would (and why would they?) question the activities of a country or person with such an impeccable anti-slavery lineage and proven methods?

In addition to the first excerpt under "Emotional Exhortation to Action" above, some typical examples include the following:

> People of conscience have fought against the different manifestations of slavery for centuries. This anti-slavery legislation is in the tradition of William Wilberforce . . . who [was an] ardent abolitionist.
>
> *(U.S. 146th Congress, 2000)*

> The right to be free from slavery and involuntary servitude is among the inalienable rights recognized in the U.S. Constitution. Acknowledging this fact, the United States outlawed slavery and involuntary servitude in 1865, recognizing them as evil institutions that must be abolished. Yet, current practices of sexual slavery and human trafficking are similarly abhorrent to the principles upon which the United States was founded.
>
> *(U.S. 2000, Purposes and Findings)*

> More than 140 years ago, the United States fought a devastating war to rid our country of slavery and to prevent those who supported it from dividing the nation. Although we succeeded then in eliminating the state-sanctioned practice, human slavery has returned as a growing global threat to the lives and freedoms of millions of men, women, and children.
>
> *(U.S. TIP Report, 2004)*

> Just as it was Britain that took an historic stand to ban slavery two centuries ago, so Britain will once again lead the way in defeating modern slavery and preserving the freedoms and values that have defined our country for generations.
>
> *(May, 2016)*

> President Abraham Lincoln and the abolitionist movement gave America a unique inheritance: a principled commitment to fight slavery in all its pernicious forms. This administration is continuing the fight to end modern slavery and using every tool at its disposal to achieve that critical goal.
>
> *(Ivanka Trump, 2018)*

A more in-depth and objective analysis of the preceding examples would reveal that the analogy user's affiliated country was (1) not so committed in its opposition to trans-Atlantic slavery (and/or enslavement in general) and (2) that abolitionist mechanisms deployed in the past (versions of which are now advocated) were not as successful as is implied (Bravo, 2007, pp. 240–43). That is, both the United Kingdom and the United States (including through its predecessor colonies) played crucial roles in and benefited from the growth of the trans-Atlantic slave trade; and the slave trade and slavery continued for more than 400 years and were incorporated into the U.S. Constitution. Only through a violent internecine war was slavery legally abolished in the United States. In addition, as discussed in "The Mythic Slaying of the Dragon" below, state-supported slavery and enslavement continued in other guises, including in the United States. Both denial of any complicity in *and* avoidance of appearing to be involved in slavery's re-emergence are also implicit in the statements regarding the United States' and the United Kingdom's staunch historical and contemporary opposition to the practice, ignoring the roles of states in severe forms of contemporary exploitation (Bravo, 2014).

Yet another theme is the condemnation of developing countries, which are identified as complicit in or not working hard enough against modern trafficking. If country X (for example, the United States or the United Kingdom) successfully eliminated slavery so long ago, why hasn't country Y (for example, Ghana or Thailand) done the same? According to Kempadoo (2005),

> The dominant international approach to trafficking primarily identifies foreign-originating international gangs and "source" countries as the main culprits, criminals, and beneficiaries in the trafficking business. Given that the majority of "destination" countries are claimed to be Western, postindustrial countries, this creates an international divide around nationality and race. . . . The narrow lens of the state anti-trafficking approach and the skewed representation of migration are particularly evident for the United States. . . . Thus, the first U.S. government report to document trafficking in the country identifies Mexican, African, and Middle Eastern families; Thai and Latin American men; Russian, East European, and Italian organized crime groups and syndicates; Asian, Mexican, and Nigerian smuggling rings; the Canadian "West Coast Players"; Chinese Triads; Hmong gangs, etc., as the primary agents who profit and benefit from trafficking.
>
> *(p. xvii)*

This use therefore turns the tables so that the historically victimized – African countries whose territories were sources of trans-Atlantic slaves – are recast as the contemporary exploiters.

Assumption of the mantle of righteousness serves to hide from the listener-reader (and perhaps from the analogy user herself) that the structural apparatus that facilitated chattel slavery remained in place after its legal abolition. In so doing, the similarity in economic rationales and incentive structures and the participation of "legitimate" enterprises and institutions in both trans-Atlantic slavery and modern trafficking in humans are obscured. As Kempadoo (2005) states:

> The crediting of trafficking to the foreign "Other" who is configured as a threat to Western societies and civilization, serves thus as a scare tactic to corral racist, nationalist sentiments and to obfuscate the interaction between the state, corporate capital, and underground sectors. . . . The few cases of corporate corruption and use of trafficked labor that have come to light – such as Walmart and Tyson Foods in the U.S. . . . suggest that there are indeed multiple parties who benefit from criminal activities.
>
> *(p. xix)*

Distancing our enlightened times, or "how far we've come"

In distancing our enlightened times from the centuries of the trans-Atlantic slave trade (or "how far we've come"), the analogy user assures the contemporary listener-reader of her own virtue and "hides the ball" so that the listener-reader does not perceive the structural and systemic similarities between human trafficking and the trans-Atlantic slave trade. So unlike the average individual and consumer of the past for whom slavery was a well-known and open aspect of her existence, today's listener-reader may believe that she is not complicit in or a beneficiary of the modern traffic in humans. In addition, because the modern traffic in humans is presented as an aberration in our enlightened times, the listener-reader does not understand that she should question the systemic exploitation embedded in foundational structures of our societies, economies, or political systems (Bravo, 2017). By positing a dichotomy of "either slavery or freedom" and ignoring or rejecting the connections between the two forms of exploitation, and by assuring the listener of her lack of complicity, the analogy user makes it easier for the listener-reader to accept the dominant neo-abolitionist law enforcement paradigm as potentially effective for ending the repellent modern trade (Bravo, 2007, pp. 224–29). Deeper inquiry into contemporary global and domestic legal, economic, social, and political organizations and institutions seems to be unnecessary.

An example of this trend includes President George W. Bush's September 23, 2003, address to the United Nations that was excerpted earlier. Note that President Bush refers to the "ending" of the trans-Atlantic slave trade two centuries ago (the United States ended its slave trade in 1807) and to the "end" of slavery. (The "end" and "ending" of slavery and the slave trade are in quotation marks to refer to the viability of the argument that there was no such historic end to the practice(s)). However, he skates over the reality that the country's internal slavery and slave trade did not "end" until the Civil War and the Thirteenth Amendment to the U.S. Constitution. Also ignored is the question whether the conditions endured by the formerly enslaved persons and their descendants (including peonage, Jim Crow laws, and other legal, economic, and political limitations on their freedom and autonomy) might fit within the definitions now used to delineate "modern slavery" (see Binder, 1996 p. 2101–03; McKee, 2005 p. 15; Blackmon, 2008). Ultimately, the effect of the tone of this speech is to enshroud the United States in righteousness – it is the crusader against the modern scourge – without acknowledgement of the historic participation and complicity of the United States or its contemporary role in either human trafficking or the subordination and exploitation of the contemporary descendants of enslaved Africans. Another example is provided by commentator Ethan Kapstein:

> Just as the British government (after much prodding by its subjects) once used the Royal Navy to stamp out the problem, today's great powers must bring their economic and military might to bear on this most crucial of undertakings.
>
> *(2006, p. 104)*

This distancing from ancestral wrongs facilitates an approach to trafficking that glosses over or ignores essential similarities between the trans-Atlantic slave trade and modern human trafficking. Those similarities might point to a fundamental problem with modern civilization's system of organizing itself. After all, as Kapstein cautions:

> Just as the brutal facts of the Atlantic slave trade ultimately led to a reexamination of U.S. history . . . so must growing awareness of the modern slave trade spark a recognition of the flaws in our contemporary economic and governmental arrangements.
> *(2006, p. 103)*

Similarly, Ivanka Trump's (2018) op-ed excerpted earlier betrays an inability to connect contradictory U.S. policy with the human trafficking whose elimination she claims is critical to U.S. policy. According to Trump,

> The Trump administration, in collaboration with the resilient survivors who serve on the U.S. Advisory Council on Human Trafficking, is prioritizing efforts to ensure law enforcement, immigration authorities and customs officials have the training and resources to identify victims of trafficking at U.S. ports of entry and in local communities.

Yet her op-ed was published even as the Trump administration used tear gas to prevent self-identified refugees from seeking asylum in the United States (see Sherman, 2018) and was detaining children separated from their families in expanding migrant detention centers (Burke & Mendoza, 2018).

The mythic slaying of the dragon

In the myth of the slaying of the dragon, the speaker, using triumphalist language, acclaims the historic abolition of trans-Atlantic slavery. The speaker-writer then declares the wisdom of abolitionist techniques as the path to eradication of modern trafficking in persons. The previously reproduced examples excerpting the September 23, 2003, speech of U.S. President George W. Bush, the 2016 op-ed of UK Prime Minister Theresa May, and the Purposes and Findings of the TVPA (2000) fall within this category. In each, the speakers and drafters state that trafficking has appeared despite successful efforts to abolish slavery.

However, this trend denies the reality that trans-Atlantic slavery did not end with abolition. As a result of the continued profitability of securing cheap labor and the legacies of the racial hierarchy that sustained trans-Atlantic slavery, the much vaunted and celebrated abolition of the slave trade in the British Empire was followed by the introduction of a system of indentured servitude. During this time, various alternative forms of slavery arose: the indentured servitude of Chinese and Indian laborers in the Caribbean colonies of the British Empire (Williams, 1984), the "blackbirding" of the inhabitants of the South Pacific to the Queensland colony of Australia (Grenfell Price, 1972), and the forced labor of native inhabitants in many of the newly colonized territories of the dismembered African continent. As Lowell J. Satre (2005) noted:

> All European powers in the nineteenth and early twentieth centuries sought regular and inexpensive labor for their colonies. . . . The ending of slavery and the slave trade in the nineteenth century forced employers to look elsewhere for labor. Indentured labor was one alternative, leading to the transfer of millions of people throughout the

> world. . . . Natives were drafted by governments to build roads, haul goods, collect rubber, and mine gold.
>
> (p. 24)

Slavery *did not end* with legal abolition. The continued exploitation and virtual enslavement were not accidental. The perceived necessity and use of that cheap labor is demonstrated by, for example, the definition of slavery in the Slavery Convention of 1926. Pursuant to the 1926 Convention (Article 5), while states are required "to prevent compulsory or forced labor from developing into conditions analogous to slavery," at the same time "forced labor may only be exacted for public purposes." The definition therefore was expressly circumscribed so as to exclude the forced labor exacted by colonial powers from the natives of their colonial possessions. It was that forced labor that built the roads, public buildings, and other infrastructure of many African colonies. Ironically, if one uses the definition of modern slavery used by these countries and NGOs, all of these past activities were "slavery."

Similarly, the U.S. Civil War, Emancipation Proclamation, and Thirteenth Amendment were followed by the horrors of Jim Crow laws, the Ku Klux Klan, and widespread lynchings and exploitation of the descendants of enslaved African (McKee, 2005; Binder, 1996; Blackmon, 2008).

Effects of the uses of the trans-Atlantic slave trade in anti-trafficking discourse on anti-trafficking efforts

The uses of the analogy to the trans-Atlantic slave trade have focused on affronts to human dignity, the jus cogens violation status of slavery, and the efforts of developed countries to combat this contemporary manifestation of slavery under international law. The integral connection of the modern traffic with the global economic system is substantially unexamined while appearing to be acknowledged in only a token or implicit fashion. An example of this token acknowledgment is provided by Ambassador John Miller (2006):

> I will list a few of the causes of human trafficking. Poverty is a tremendous push factor, and when coupled with the attraction for a more materialistic society, a pull factor, it forms one of the major foundations for human trafficking. Greed is a second cause. We have all heard about organized crime. We now talk about the big sources of revenue for organized crime: the drug trade, the arms trade, the people trade. Greed coupled with the attitude in many cultures towards women imposes a higher toll on sex trade. Greed generates many categories of slavery, such as domestic servitude, child soldiers, factory, and farm labor slavery. There are exotic forms of slavery – such as child camel jockey slavery – in many of these countries. The challenges that these kinds of slavery pose for all nations are threefold. First and foremost, there is the challenge to human rights and dignity. Second, there is the health challenge. When you deal with sex slavery, you are dealing with HIV/AIDS and sexually transmitted diseases. Finally, there is the challenge of national security and stability. This challenge affects the stability of many countries, especially in how the slave trade is connected to organized crime.

Yet, despite this seeming acknowledgment by an anti-human trafficking official, the United States, in its efforts against the traffic in humans, although acknowledging the economic connections of the human trade and the global economy, chooses to focus legislative mechanisms and other anti-trafficking efforts on criminalization and punishment rather than on structural economic solutions. As a result, the U.S. anti-trafficking efforts and the efforts that it encourages from other countries do not focus on the economic forces facilitating human trafficking. The *prevention* element of the four-P anti-human trafficking paradigm (prosecution, protection, prevention, and partnership) centers prevention activities on information dissemination and education about the risks and evils of human trafficking (see U.S. TIP Report, 2010, Update). The efforts do not constitute or evidence an attempt at structural transformation of the economic relationships and connections between vulnerable individuals and groups and their potential (and/or actual) exploiters. The efforts appear to focus on legal prohibitions against exploitation, "rescue" of the exploited, and the imposition of criminal sanction without examination of the economic reasons for and structures of such vulnerabilities. This approach has been adopted by other Western countries. For example, Prime Minister Theresa May refers to "criminal gangs" and "sickening and inhuman crimes" (May, 2018).

The failure to proffer structural solutions does not necessarily denote policymakers' ignorance of the structural causes of human trafficking. For example, in discussing the reasons for the TVPA (2000) on the Senate floor, Senator Paul Wellstone noted that "the trafficking of human beings for forced prostitution and sweatshop labor . . . is one of the greatest aspects of the globalization of the world economy." In the same speech, he further stated that "profit in the trade can be staggering. . . . Trafficking has become a major source of new income for criminal rings." Prime Minister May (2018) referred to "this vile and systematic international business model." However, that seeming understanding of the economic foundations of the trade in human beings has not given rise to a comprehensive or effective solution. Instead, a perhaps subconsciously directed decision to reject uncomfortable reality – a form of willful innocence – may be at play. As a consequence, the discourse and the weapons employed against the targeted exploitation are impoverished by the lack of widespread appreciation of the economic role of trafficking in the globalizing twenty-first century, its integration into the "legitimate" economy, and a failure to confront that role head-on (Bravo, 2014).

A crucial challenge confronting anti-trafficking scholars and activists is to delve deeply enough so as to identify the root structural causes and contributors to modern human trafficking. Many of the examples discussed earlier demonstrate the use of the deeply ingrained image and interpretation of the trans-Atlantic slave trade in the fight against human trafficking: it is a revolting, tragic, and never-to-be-repeated error in human history. However, that depiction ignores the contemporaneous normalcy and mundanity of the exploitation of trans-Atlantic slave trade victims, thus failing to grasp an essential similarity to the mundanity and visibility of the exploitation experienced by victims of human trafficking today.

White slavery in modern anti-trafficking discourse

Domestic and international responses to contemporary human trafficking have evolved from international and domestic U.S. legislative reactions to the white slavery hysteria of the late nineteenth and early twentieth centuries (Chuang, 1998; Farrior, 1997; Rassam, 1999). The trans-Atlantic slave trade analogy is frequently invoked, but the efforts to combat white slavery in the late nineteenth and early twentieth centuries created the blueprint for the dominant conceptual and legal frameworks deployed against modern trafficking (for deeper analysis, refer to Chapter 2, C.deBaca, this volume). According to Andreas and Nadelman (2006),

> Intense media coverage and activism by governmental and nongovernmental organizations have drawn enormous attention to sex trafficking in recent years, leading to *a flurry of new international criminalization initiatives that very much echo the earlier debates and moralizing rhetoric about white slavery.*
>
> *(p. 36, emphasis added)*

What criteria should be used to compare human trafficking and white slavery?

Just as the specter of involuntary sex and despoilment of innocent white maidens seized the Western world's attention in the late 1800s and early 1900s, overtones of that appalled, fascinated, and condemnatory prurience continue to pervade public and institutional perceptions and depictions of human trafficking into the twenty-first century (see U.S. 146th Congress, 2000).[7] The focus on innocent women and children and on the illicit sex inflicted upon them draws the attention of policymakers, scholars, and the public from the systemic reality of the traffic in humans, contributing to the dominant conventional perception of traffickers as aberrant (in)human beings. Further, that focus leads to failure to appreciate that traffickers, like their victims, are cogs in a vast and interconnected economic machine in which we *all* play a role and are beneficiaries.

Thus the modern fight against human trafficking, including commentary, analysis, and would-be legislative solutions, is influenced by the search for the innocent, helpless, and worthy victim who will be rescued by law enforcement or another governmental agency, not on the quotidian and normalized inequalities that create the preconditions for exploitation (Srikantiah, 2007; Haynes, 2006–2007). The economic gains accruing from the enslavement and trafficking of others are spread throughout the society and economy. The economic benefits of trafficking to society as a whole and to individual states were noted by Professor Nora Demleitner in her 1994 article on modern trafficking: "Trafficking in women has become a huge international business that brings immense economic benefits to everyone involved except the women forced to work as prostitutes" (p. 189). Specifically identifying the beneficiaries of the trade, Demleitner notes:

> In addition to the tourist agencies, hotels, and transportation services, the police and the government bureaucracy all benefit directly or indirectly from forced prostitution which has turned into a large industry. In some countries, such as Thailand, government officials and the local elites have come to accept . . . forced prostitution because they view the practice as *the key to regional development* and an important source of foreign currency.
>
> *(p. 189; See also Sassen, 2002 (Describing the increasing role of women and their exploitation in economic development strategies of poorer countries))*

White slavery in historical perspective

The phenomenon of and panic about the enslavement of white women arose in Europe and the United States in the late nineteenth and early twentieth centuries. Beginning in the 1890s, the number of white women engaged in sex work in overseas colonies increased. A universal racial hierarchy took greater hold as women from Western Europe and the United States worked as prostitutes in South America, the Middle East, and Asia (Scully, 2001). Rumors arose of organized networks that procured and sent woman abroad for prostitution, and their existence became a growing affront to the public and legislators in metropolitan centers. The growing visibility of "migratory prostitution" led to increased public perception of an attack on the mother country's very identity and stature (Scully, 2001, pp. 78–79).

Marlene D. Beckman (1984) and Eileen Scully (2001) provided descriptions of public attitudes on both sides of the Atlantic. Beckman (1984) noted:

> The Progressive Era reformers who supported [anti-slavery legislation] had used the words "white slavery" to promote the vision of women held in bondage against their will,

> of mysterious druggings and abductions of helpless young girls, and of unexplained disappearances of innocent and naïve immigrants forced into lives of prostitution and vice.
> *(p. 36)*

Scully (2001) reported:

> By 1910, the image of the white slave trade conjured up by London purity groups had taken full hold of the American imagination. Lurid stories of sullied white womanhood and organized syndicates linking major cities helped bring on board southerners who otherwise would have argued states' rights in the face of a broad expansion of federal police powers. The vision of a vast network of Jewish and French procurers kidnapping and luring white women from Europe and America to service lowly natives and "eastern rich potentates" was captivating, combining as it did racial anxieties, colonial debates, immigration politics, and public morality issues. Similar sensationalism and bourgeois prurience was evident elsewhere, from London to Moscow to Buenos Aires.
> *(p. 86)*

These reported public sentiments are reminiscent of the reactions to the modern traffic in humans. In response, a number of international instruments and domestic statutes were adopted by the United States and European countries. The United States adopted the 1910 White Slave Traffic Act (the Mann Act (U.S., 1910)), which imposed felony liability for the transportation of women across interstate or international borders for "the purpose of prostitution or debauchery or any other immoral purpose." Commentator Marlene D. Beckman (1984) noted:

> The Act was so named because its central purpose was to halt what many believed was a serious and widespread practice: Commercial procurers taking innocent young girls and women by force and holding them captive with threats to their lives, a practice that *resembled black servitude in its exploitative and barbarous nature.*
> *(p. 1112, emphasis added)*

The fear on both sides of the Atlantic that white women were being sold into slavery to non-white males gave rise to the 1904 International Agreement for the Suppression of the White Slave Trade. Pursuant to the provisions of the treaty, victims would be protected, while those who seduced them into prostitution would be punished. Historian Eileen Scully pointed out that the victimization of whites alone was targeted, leaving the exploitation of non-white women normalized and unchallenged. The racialized character of this fight against eighteenth- and early nineteenth-century traffic helped undermine the effectiveness of the international instruments adopted to combat the trade in humans by targeting only the sexual exploitation of a single racial group (Scully, 2001).

After the 1904 Act proved largely ineffective, the International Convention for the Suppression of White Slave Traffic was adopted in 1910. The two international instruments, together with two later treaties addressing the trafficking of women and children of all races (United Nations (1921); United Nations (1933)), were consolidated by the League of Nations in 1949 to produce the Convention for the Suppression of the Traffic in Persons and of the Exploitation of the Prostitution of Others.

References to white slavery: the roles of race and sex

Relatively few overt analogies are made in the anti-trafficking discourse to nineteenth- and early twentieth-century white slavery. Nonetheless, in addition to the role of white slavery in framing the legal architecture of international and domestic laws targeting the coerced sexual servitude of women, white slavery's influence continues to be evident in discussions of modern human trafficking in many venues. The following excerpts reproduced and analyzed from media and legislative sources illustrate the focus on sex and race.

Media reports and commentary

Much like the response to white slavery in the eighteenth and nineteenth centuries, the media's discussion of contemporary human trafficking has been largely framed by race and reveals the perpetuation of a racial hierarchy. For example, a 1998 *New York Times* exposé of modern trafficking reported that:

> The international bazaar for women is hardly new, of course. Asians have been its basic commodity for decades. But economic hopelessness in the Slavic world has opened what experts call the most lucrative market of all to criminal gangs that have flourished since the fall of Communism: *white women* with little to sustain them but their dreams. Pimps, law enforcement officials and relief groups all agree that Ukrainian and Russian women are now the most valuable in the trade.
>
> *(Specter, 1998, emphasis added)*

As reported in the article, an anti-trafficking expert explained:

> It's no secret that the highest prices now go for the white women. . . . They are the novelty item now. It used to be Nigerians and Asians at the top of the market. Now it is the Ukrainians.

A 1997 report by Global Survival Network quotes Vladimir, a Russian trafficker, who explained: "The Japanese will take anything, as long as she has a passport and she is Russian. Whether she is fat or skinny does not concern them" (Caldwell, 1997, p. 5). The authors further explained:

> Russian women are in high demand in many countries because of their "exotic" nature and relative novelty in the sex market. Russia and the Newly Independent States, including Ukraine and Latvia, have become primary "sender" countries, supplementing and sometimes replacing previously significant sources of women from Asia and Latin America.
>
> *(Caldwell, 1997, p. 5)*

These descriptions of the customer demand forces at work in the markets serviced by the international sex trade betray both the objectification and sexualization of the exotic (and perhaps forbidden) and the ongoing impact of the racialized hierarchy of the nineteenth- and early twentieth-century migratory sex trade identified by Eileen Scully (2001). The contemporary public, the traders, and the customers share the same racialized perceptions of the "worth" of white human "merchandise" vis-à-vis non-white "merchandise." Just as the owners of African and African-descended women in the era of the trans-Atlantic slave trade created and exploited a hyper-sexualized erotic image of their slaves, so may the lingering desire to exploit and dominate "otherness" drive the valuation of the traffic's victims (Chuang, 1998, p. 69).

How is white slavery similar to and/or different from human trafficking?

Modern slavery is said not to be based on race, unlike the slavery of yesteryear (Miller, 2006). Yet the racism that arose with and from and that permitted the centuries-long continuation of trans-Atlantic slavery makes today's enslaved white women more valuable vis-à-vis enslaved black or Asian women ("Media under Fire," 2005; "Have You Seen Her," 2005; Robinson, 2005). Moreover, it was the specter of the enslavement of *white* women that most outraged public opinion in the West and spurred to action Western legislators, who had ignored decades-long reports of the enslavement of Asian and African women and children. For example, according to John R. Miller, then director of the U.S. State Department's Office to Monitor and Combat Trafficking in Persons,

> We believe that when we look at victims of the world today – unlike the slavery of preceding centuries where the chief criterion was race – we look at the victims of all races, and sadly as many as 80% are of the female gender, and as many as one-third are children.
> *(Miller, 2006, p. 38)*

Added to the sense of urgency now surrounding the issue was the newly perceived vulnerability of national borders following the fall of the Soviet Union.

Legislative history and "official" positions

Concerns about the enslavement of white women continued to attract the attention of Western legislators as they framed policy and legislative responses to contemporary human trafficking. Despite some acknowledgment of the existence and importance of labor trafficking in public debates leading to the passage of the TVPA, some influential U.S. lawmakers seemed particularly alarmed about the sexual enslavement of white women from Eastern Europe. For example, Senator Sam Brownback (2000), quoting Specter (1998) from the *New York Times* exposé discussed earlier, claimed:

> It happens every single day. Not just in Israel, which has deported nearly 1,500 Russian and Ukrainian women like Irina in the past three years. But throughout the world, where selling naïve and desperate young women into sexual bondage has become one of the fastest-growing criminal enterprises in the robust global economy.

Senator Paul Wellstone expressed similar motivations for supporting the trafficking legislation:

> My wife Sheila urged me to do something about this problem several years ago. Consequently, she and I spent time with women trafficked from the Ukraine to work in brothels in Western Europe and the United States. They told us after the breakup of the Soviet Union and the ascendancy of the mob, trafficking in women and girls became a booming industry that destroyed the lives of the youngest and most vulnerable in their home countries.[8]

Senator Wellstone also noted: "Over a 3-year period, hundreds of women from the Czech Republic who answered advertisements in Czech newspapers for modeling were ensnared in an illegal prostitution ring."

Whose interests are affected by human trafficking (i.e. Who benefits? Who is hurt?, What are those interests?).

The emphasis on sex and sexual exploitation, and a movement toward prohibiting all forms of paid sex work, is exemplified by administration official, Paula Goode, then acting director of the Office to Monitor and Combat Trafficking in Persons, in a 2007 letter responding to a *New York Times* editorial:

> [Your editorial] about sex slavery, leaves the impression that force and rape are somehow separate from prostitution. This impression is wrong. Few activities are as brutal and damaging to people as prostitution. . . . The demand for prostitution creates sex slaves today.
>
> *(Goode, 2007)*

The focus on sex and the conflation of prostitution, forced prostitution, and trafficking for the purposes of sexual exploitation detracts from and weakens the fight against human trafficking. Using the anti-trafficking discourse to attack prostitution in all its forms, even where consensual, diminishes the resources targeted at forced prostitution, trafficking for the purposes of sexual exploitation and labor exploitation. It also creates an image of trafficking as a phenomenon purely exploitative of the sexuality and bodies of women and children, ignoring other systemic exploitation of which human trafficking is a part. This conflation and the focus on sex fail to address the power/subordination dynamic in relationships, the exploitation of labor and the economically vulnerable, as well as the "developing" versus "developed" country imbalances that form the stabilizing matrix facilitating contemporary trafficking. Structural inequalities that may appear to be "natural" because they are historically ingrained or biologically or otherwise "inevitable" all are manifested in modern trafficking: male versus female; rich versus poor; developed versus developing countries; white versus non-white; and the state and corporate interests versus those of the individual.

The effects of white slavery

Who benefits from use of the word "slavery" to describe human trafficking?

White slavery and the efforts against it have had a pervasive effect on the perceptions of and mechanisms used to fight modern trafficking in humans and is present in both explicit and implicit invocations of white slavery in diverse venues. Law professor Elizabeth M. Bruch (2004, p. 3) noted "The early emphasis on protecting white women now seems obviously racist and sexist. Yet that emphasis has continued to pervade the current discussions of, and policy towards, human trafficking." Professor Bruch further noted

> As a result of these biases, the current approaches to human trafficking replicate many of the flaws of earlier approaches – namely, a focus on victimization, a fruitless cycle of debate on the role of prostitution, problematic definitional questions, and a process of decision making that excludes critical voices.

Professor Janie Chuang has also addressed this issue. According to Chuang:

> On one side of the divide are the "abolitionists," who believe that all prostitution is inherently exploitative and degrading to women. Abolitionists recognize no distinction between "forced" and "voluntary" prohibition and believe that the failure of states to prohibit all prostitution violates women's rights to sexual autonomy. On the other side are those who believe that women can choose sex work as a viable livelihood option because

> it is the absence of adequate protections for sex work – not the sex industry itself – that opens the door to trafficking and other abuses. Under this view, state action to penalize adults choosing to engage in prostitution amounts to a denial of individual liberty.
>
> *(Chuang, 2006, citations omitted)*

A 2005 letter to the *New York Times*, reacting to planned regulation of prostitution in Tijuana, Mexico, is also illuminative of this approach. The author, Ambassador John Miller (2005), asserted that:

> In addition to being inherently harmful and dehumanizing, prostitution and related activities fuel the modern-day slavery known as sex trafficking. What other "profession" creates such abuse and devastation? While some attempts to regulate prostitution may be well intentioned, we should not be focusing on regulation of prostitution, but rather on abolition of slavery.
>
> Apologists for the trans-Atlantic slave trade of yesteryear advocated for better ventilation and mattresses on ships for slaves, but all the regulation in the world would not have changed the fact that people used as slaves deserved freedom. The children and women of today deserve freedom too.

Ambassador Miller's letter verges on the conflation of enslavement with sexual exploitation. The "people" enslaved during the trans-Atlantic slave trade "deserved freedom." However, it is women and children – by implication, the sexually exploited – who deserve freedom today. While Ambassador Miller evokes the image of the historic systematic enslavement of Africans and the contemporaneous societal rationalizations in support of the trade, his concern about modern trafficking is focused on the sexual exploitation of innocent and vulnerable women and children, not on the systemic economic, social, political, and other structural forces that make such exploitation possible.

Conclusion

The analogies offer much more

The examples reproduced and analyses conducted in this chapter expose the inherent contradictions of the competing and complementary invocation of analogies to the trans-Atlantic slave trade and white slavery. While the trans-Atlantic slave trade analogy is used to invoke the image of enslaved blacks in order to inspire taking action against modern trafficking, at the same time the subordination of blacks, blackness, and the colored "other" is perceived and treated as more "natural" than the enslavement of whites and whiteness.

The racial hierarchy and subordination that arose with, permitted, and fostered the centuries-long trans-Atlantic slave trade is deeply engrained. Professor Jonathan Todros (2006) discussed the ways in which racial discrimination underlies and facilitates sex tourism, an industry in which many of the victims of human trafficking are exploited:

> While these other forms of discrimination operate to make the poor and minorities more susceptible to trafficking, *such discrimination also serves to fuel the demand for prostitution.* The sex tourism industry in Australia, the United States and Western Europe plays on crude stereotypes of Asian women, by emphasizing the "submissiveness of Asian prostitutes and the [supposed] complicity of their families in their situation." Advertisements for sex tours "build on the patriarchal and racist fantasies of European, Japanese, American, and Australian men by touting the exotic, erotic subservience of Asian women." Racism clearly plays a role when white men from Western countries are

> willing to take advantage of women in Thailand, the Philippines or other developing countries, but would not treat white women in their own countries in the same manner.
> *(Todros, 2006, p. 894)*

It is the exploitation and enslavement of whiteness that, together with the threats to state borders and authority, precipitated coordinated international action by state entities against the modern traffic in humans. But it is the image of enslaved Africans that will arouse and harness visceral public outrage and support for anti-trafficking efforts. Tragically, however, the racism that arose from and sustained the trans-Atlantic slave trade prevents users of the analogy from delving more deeply into the similarities between human trafficking and the trans-Atlantic slave trade, and the role of the legacies of the trans-Atlantic slave trade in contemporary human trafficking.

A layer of irony and contradiction is exposed with the realization that, like the trans-Atlantic slave trade, white slavery was a product of labor imbalances (albeit with greater agency inhering in white women who prostituted themselves during the late nineteenth and early twentieth century) (Bravo, 2007). Yet the leaders of efforts to combat white slavery chose to focus, much as today's anti-trafficking champions, on the sexual enslavement of victimized females rather than on structural economic and social causes of their exploitation.

Re-thinking the lessons offered by these analogies

Both the white slavery and trans-Atlantic slave trade analogies have been ill-used. The analogy to white slavery evokes sexual exploitation of helpless and vulnerable females, while the analogy to trans-Atlantic slavery evokes emotions of horror, rejection, and denial and taps into popular misperceptions of that enslavement – that it was an aberrational practice. The systemic attributes of these two earlier forms of exploitation remain unexamined, despite the production of critical scholarship that offers a deeper understanding of both by situating them within contemporaneous economic, social, and political realities (see Davis, 2006; Kempadoo, 2005; Scully, 2001).

Can better knowledge about and understanding of trans-Atlantic slavery contribute to more effective policies against modern human trafficking? How?

In the legal and conceptual frameworks constructed in response to modern trafficking, the heritage of white slavery is more entrenched than is the heritage of the trans-Atlantic slave trade. The legal weaponry has been broadened so as not to overtly exclude victims of any race, implicitly including both males and females, but the white slavery analogy's evocation of sexual exploitation has a persistent hold on analyses and policy responses. In effect, users of the analogies talk the talk of the trans-Atlantic slave trade but walk the walk of white slavery: they invoke the image and perceptions of trans-Atlantic slavery to evoke visceral reactions and action while employing the largely ineffective tools that are the progeny of the instruments deployed against white slavery. Yet the analogy to the trans-Atlantic slave trade, thoughtfully and substantively explored, may provide a richer understanding of the modern exploitation and illuminate a potentially more effective path to its eradication. Therefore, the focus on abolition and law as the weapons of choice must be widened to address structural economic realities. For example, the rhetoric that invokes the trans-Atlantic slave trade to mobilize action against modern trafficking often inveighs against the greed of the modern trafficker. However, as Willem van Schendel and Itty Abraham (2005) note,

> Many key words are reserved for the bad guys and their organizations. . . . Such language constructs conceptual barriers between illicit bad-guy activities (trafficking,

> smuggling) and state-authorized good-guy activities (trade, migration) that obscure how these are often part of a single spectrum.
>
> *(p. 9)*

Greed may be understood as the desire to make profit, with the desire being an inevitable, necessary, and oft-celebrated component of a market economy. In the context of human trafficking, the word "greed" is employed to characterize as illegitimate a central tenet of economic theory (profit-seeking) that society and economic theorists celebrate when speaking of the industries and activities of which society and the legal system approve. The greed or profit motive of today's owner-participants in human trafficking is no different from the greed or profit motive of the trans-Atlantic slaver and may be no different from that of the modern entrepreneur (Davis, 2006).

Moving away from the neo-abolitionist model

The neo-abolitionist model that arises from *superficial* analysis of the trans-Atlantic slave trade and by white slavery's legislative heritage provides inadequate tools in the efforts against human trafficking. Neo-abolitionist thinking manifests a deep-seated conviction that this vastly complex and intricately networked economic, social, cultural, and political issue will be eradicated or controlled through legal mechanisms that focus almost exclusively on legal prohibition of the exploitation, punishment of the exploiter, and rehabilitation of the violated victims. According to Andreas and Nadelman, "As in the earlier prohibitionist crusade against white slavery, an underlying agenda for some of the most influential state and nonstate actors today is the targeting of prostitution via the transnational angle of targeting trafficking" (Andreas & Nadelman, 2006, p. 37). Neo-abolitionism is also reflected in the efforts to abolish prostitution (see Goode, 2007). Such an approach will fail. As stated by A. Yasmine Rassam,

> Not only does abolition of slavery fail to provide economic measures requisite to remedy the social injustice perpetrated on the enslaved, it fails to create the conditions for agency. The limited utility of abolitionism, which reinforces the victimization of slaves and fails to provide post-emancipatory alternatives, is evidenced in the emancipation movement in the United States.
>
> *(2005, p. 850)*

On its own, abolitionism does not succeed in ending institutionalized exploitation. That is, to the extent that legal instruments are not aimed at structural foundations and incentives for the actors involved in trafficking, mere prohibition and criminalization of the activities will not and *cannot* transform exploitative relationships.

Instead, a structural response to sources of vulnerability and the economic causes and roles of human trafficking will more successfully combat the exploitation. Human trafficking includes many more factors and causes than the greed of "monstrous" traffickers. The trade presents significant economic opportunity to those who may have limited access to legitimate enterprises and for whom human beings are merely a sentient form of capital, and commodification of that capital is the most readily available resource that may be profitably exploited.

A new focus for anti-human trafficking advocates

The challenge confronting anti-trafficking scholars and activists is to identify the root structural causes and contributors to modern trafficking in humans. The analogies to and invocations of the trans-Atlantic slave trade and white slavery offer in-depth insights if further research and analysis is undertaken focusing on all aspects of these forms of exploitation. While references to trans-Atlantic slavery are used to frame the discourse on the subject of modern trafficking, it is the fight against white slavery, rather than the trans-Atlantic slave trade, to which the typical modern trafficking combatant owes her intellectual debts. Even more, the focus of the late nineteenth- and early twentieth-century activists on sex and the protection of women has continued to limit understanding of the fundamental similarities among the trans-Atlantic slave trade, white slavery, and contemporary trafficking in humans.

While studying the applicability of the trans-Atlantic slave trade leads to insight into the economic structure of human trafficking, analysis of white slavery's influence illuminates societal responses to sexual servitude and racial attitudes. The reaction to the reports of white slavery illustrates the virulent visceral reaction to the alleged transgression of racial and sexual boundaries – that is, the transgression of whiteness and its protected womanhood. Does the reaction to human trafficking – the visceral and prurient interest that it arouses regarding the sexual servitude suffered by its victims – lead to insights into society's and the state's analogous reaction to transgression of borders and state sovereignty both by the traffickers in human beings and by their victims? This would explain, for example, the seeming contradiction between sentiments expressed in Ivanka Trump's op-ed and the actions of the administration she omits from the op-ed.

Further, the link between the protection of the nation state's borders and the smuggling and trafficking of humans demands further research and wise policy action. The growth of the nation state and the consequent increase in legislative and other barriers to the mobility of humans has driven and continues to drive humans and their labor underground. Human beings seek to exchange their labor for value – and migrants respond to market forces that promise higher prices for that labor across international borders. For example, it is well-established that the trafficking in humans from Central and Eastern Europe increased in tandem with the tightening of Western European borders and the immigration and refugee laws stimulated by the fall of the Soviet Union. As Willem van Schendel and Itty Abraham have urged,

> We need to approach flows of goods and people as visible manifestations of power configurations that weave in and out of legality, in and out of states, and in and out of individuals' lives, as socially embedded, sometimes long-term processes of production, exchange, consumption and representation.
>
> *(van Schendel & Abraham, p. 9)*

The references to the trans-Atlantic slave trade in the anti-trafficking discourse encapsulate a particular interpretation of the past, seek to project that interpretation onto the present, and extrapolate an inadequate and too-constrained set of lessons. Those who have used the analogy to date have failed to explore it more than superficially, or to adequately map out both the similarities and differences between the two systems of exploitation. As a consequence, the ability to effectively combat the contemporary traffic in human beings has been undermined both internationally and domestically by a failure to recognize and act upon the structural roots of this modern trade. Instead, use of the trans-Atlantic slave trade analogy too often appeals to emotions in order to serve the particular ends of the user. However, the analogy can be relevant if explored more deeply – there are similarities not merely in individual plights but in deeper structures of the world economic system and the factors that caused and fostered the rise of both forms of exploitation.

We should learn from the past, and not merely exploit it for emotional gain. The use made thus far of the trans-Atlantic slave trade in the fight against human trafficking has, in a sense, been self-protective of "contemporary" humanity and the developed world's sense of self and willful innocence. It serves to prevent deep understanding that the world and human-to-human exploitation may not have changed as much as we would have liked to believe since the era of trading enslaved Africans. It serves to protect us from understanding that, like the consumers of the past, we are dependent on the abhorrent exploitation of others. It is easier to characterize traffickers as greedy rather than profit-seeking; as deviant rather than as an integrated piece of the economic structure within which we exist daily. But it is impossible and irresponsible to ignore the cruel irony of anti-trafficking rhetoric that exploits imagery of the trans-Atlantic slave trade alongside willful innocence regarding that trade's continued structural effects in the United States and around the globe, including the universal racial (and gender) hierarchy that continues to subordinate the interests of the non-white and the non-male.

Notes

1 Brazil abolished slavery in 1888, making it the last country in the Western Hemisphere to put a legal end to that form of exploitation.
2 Examples of such commitments include the Universal Declaration of Human Rights, Dec. 10, 1948, G.A. Res. 217(III)(A), U.N Doc. A/810 at 71; the International Covenant on Economic, Social and Cultural Rights, Dec. 16, 1966, 933 U.N.T.S. 3; and the 1966 International Covenant on Civil and Political Rights, Dec. 16, 1966, 999 U.N.T.S. at 171.
3 The use of the word "trade" denotes the buying and selling of human beings. As used herein with respect to human "merchandise," "trade" does not imply the imposition of customs duties or imposts, licenses, or other revenue raising governmental regulation such as those that accompanied the trans-Atlantic trade in Africans in earlier centuries.
4 The UN General Assembly adopted the Convention on November 15, 2000, opening it for member state signature. The TVPA became law in the United States on October 28, 2000. The Council of Europe adopted the European Convention Against Trafficking in Human Beings in 2005; and the ASEAN Declaration Against Trafficking in Persons Particularly Women and Children was adopted in 2014.
5 The traffic of African slaves to Europe and European territories (such as Madeira) preceded the trans-Atlantic trade.
6 According to Article I, Section 9, clause 1 of the U.S. Constitution:

> The Migration or Importation of such Persons as any of the States now existing shall think proper to admit, shall not be prohibited by the Congress prior to the Year one thousand eight hundred and eight, but a tax may be imposed on such Importation, not exceeding ten dollars for each Person.

7 Despite his acknowledgement that some victims were destined for sweatshops and other types of forced labor, Senator Wellstone's proffered examples of trafficking victims centered on women and young girls who had been sexually enslaved.
8 However, the trafficking cases cited by Wellstone included the enslavement of non-white women and children (i.e. Thai, Albanian, Mexican, Russian, Chinese and Czech). Yet despite his focus on sex trafficking during debate on the Senate floor, Senator Wellstone did acknowledge that trafficking victims were exploited in "sweatshops and other types of forced labor" in addition to brothels. And, of the draft of the TVPA, Senator Brownback stated, "this bill challenges the myriad forms of slavery including sex trafficking, temple prostitution, and debt bondage, among other forms."

Supplemental learning materials

Bhabha, J. (2014). *Child migration and human rights in a global age.* Princeton, NJ: Princeton University Press.
Gerdes, L. (2006). *Prostitution and sex trafficking: Opposing viewpoints.* Michigan: Greenhaven Press.
Malarek, V. (2004). *The natashas: Inside the new global sex trade.* New York, NY: Arcade Publishing.
Martin, S. I. (1999). *Britain and the slave trade.* London, UK: Channel 4 Books, an imprint of Macmillan Publishers Ltd.

Musto, J. (2016). *Control and protect: Collaboration, carceral protections, and domestic sex trafficking in the United States*. Oakland: University of California Press.

Shelley, L. (2010). *Human trafficking: A global perspective*. New York, NY: Cambridge University Press.

Sherwood, M. (2007). *After abolition: Britain and the slave trade since 1807*. New York, NY: I. B. Tauris.

Tiano, S., & Murphy-Aguilar, M. (2012). *Borderline slavery: Mexico, United States, and the human trade*. Burlington, VT: Ashgate.

Vijeyarasa, R. (2015). *Sex, slavery and the trafficked woman: Myths and misconceptions about trafficking and its victims*. Burlington, VT: Ashgate.

Zhang, S. X. (2007). *Smuggling and trafficking in human beings: All roads lead to America*. Westport, CT: Praeger.

References

Andreas, P., & Nadelman, E. A. (2006). *Policing the globe: Criminalization and crime control in international relations*. New York, NY: Oxford University Press.

Associated Press. (1999, December 4). Man pleads guilty to enslaving women. *Las Vegas Review*, p. 3A.

Bales, K. (2004). *Disposable people: New slavery in the global economy*. Oakland, CA: University of California Press.

Barry, J. (1998, July 31). Tortured au pair finds a new life. *Miami Herald*, p. 1B.

Batstone, D. (2007, March 15). From sex workers to restaurant workers, the global slave trade is growing. *Third World Traveler*. Retrieved from www.thirdworldtraveler.com/Global_Secrets_Lies/Global_Slave_Trade.html

Beckman, M. D. (1984). The white slave traffic act: The historical impact of a criminal law policy on women. *Georgetown Law Journal, 72*, 1111–1142. Retrieved from https://doi.org/10.1300/J014v04n03_09

Binder, G. (1996). The slavery of emancipation. *Cardozo Law Review, 17*, 2063–2102. Retrieved from https://ssrn.com/abstract=1925130

Blackmon, D. A. (2008). *Slavery by another name: The re-enslavement of black Americans from the Civil War to World War II*. New York, NY: Anchor Books.

Bravo, K. E. (2007). Exploring the analogy between modern trafficking in humans and the trans-Atlantic slave trade. *Boston University International Law Journal, 25*(207), 209–295. Retrieved from https://doi.org/10.2139/ssrn.996455

Bravo, K. E. (2014). Interrogating the state's roles in human trafficking. *Indiana International & Comparative Law Review, 25*(1), 9–31. Retrieved from https://doi.org/10.1800/7909.0002

Bravo, K. E. (2017). Interrogating everyperson's roles in today's slaveries. *Temple International & Comparative Law Journal, 31*(1), 25–43. Retrieved from https://ssrn.com/abstract=2900467

Bruch, E. M. (2004). Models wanted: The search for an effective response to human trafficking. *Stanford Journal of International Law, 40*(1), 1–45. Retrieved from https://scholar.valpo.edu/law_fac_pubs/105/

Burke, G., & Mendoza, M. (2018, November 27). Texas detention camp for teen migrants keeps growing. *U.S. News*. Retrieved from www.usnews.com/news/world/articles/2018-11-27/texas-detention-camp-for-teen-migrants-keeps-growing

Bush, G. W. (2003). *President Bush Addresses United Nations General Assembly* [Transcript]. Retrieved from https://georgewbush-whitehouse.archives.gov/news/releases/2003/09/20030923-4.html

Caldwell, G., Galster, S., & Steinzor, N. (1997). *Crime & servitude: An expose of the traffic in women for prostitution from the newly independent states*. Washington, DC: Global Survivor Network.

Chen, P. (1999, January 5). Australia aims to eradicate Asian sex slave trade. *Central News Agency*. (Taiwan), p. 1B.

Chuang, J. (1998). Redirecting the debate over trafficking in women: Definitions, paradigms, and contexts. *Harvard Human Rights Journal, 11*, 65–107. Retrieved from http://traffickingroundtable.org/wp-content/uploads/2012/08/Redirecting-the-Debate-over-Trafficking-in-Women-Definitions-Paradigms-and-Contexts.pdf

Connolly, K. (1999, January 16). Czechs struggle to curb sex tourism. *The Globe and Mail*. (Toronto), p. A13.

Crecente, B. D. (1999, January 16). Sex-slave ringleader admits role. *Palm Beach Post*, p. 1B.

Davis, D. B. (2006). *Inhuman bondage: The rise and fall of slavery in the new world*. Oxford, England: Oxford University Press.

Demleitner, N. V. (1994). Forced prostitution: Naming an international offense. *Fordham International Law Journal, 18*(1), 163–197. Retrieved from www.justice.gov.il/En/Units/Trafficking/MainDocs/Forced%20Prostitution-%20Naming%20an%20International%20Offense.pdf

Erlanger, S. (1989, March 30). Thriving sex industry in Bangkok is raising fears of an AIDS epidemic. *The New York Times*. Retrieved from www.nytimes.com/1989/03/30/world/thriving-sex-industry-in-bangkok-is-raising-fears-of-an-aids-epidemic.html

Executive Office of the President of the United States. (2000, November 6). Statement on signing the victims of trafficking and violence protection act of 2000. *Weekly Compilation of Presidential Documents, 36*(44), 2662–2665. Retrieved from https://heinonline-org.libproxy.unl.edu/HOL/Page?collection=fedreg&handle=hein.fedreg/wcpd03644&id=14&men_tab=srchresults

Farrior, S. (1997). The international law on trafficking in women and children for prostitution: Making it live up to its potential. *Harvard Human Rights Journal, 10*, 213–237. Retrieved from https://ssrn.com/abstract=886444

Finkelman, P. (2001). *Slavery and the founders: Race and liberty in the age of Jefferson*. London, England: Routledge.

Gallagher, A. (2001). Human rights and the new UN protocols on trafficking and migrant smuggling: A preliminary analysis. *Human Rights Quarterly, 23*, 975–1004. Retrieved from https://doi.org/10.1353/hrq.2001.0049

Goode, P. (2007, March 18). Letter to the editor: Prostitution's brutality. *The New York Times*. Retrieved from www.nytimes.com/2007/03/18/opinion/l18comfort.html

Grenfell Price, A. (1972). *Island continent: Aspects of the historical geography of Australia and its territories*. Sydney, Australia: Angus & Robertson.

Handley, P. (1989, November 2). The lust frontier. *The Far East Economic Review*, p. 44.

Have you seen her? When black women disappear, the silence can be deafening. (2009, December 9). *Essence Magazine*. Retrieved from www.essence.com/news/have-you-seen-her/

Haynes, D. (2007). (Not) found chained in a bed in a brothel: Conceptual, legal, and procedural failures to fulfill the promise of the Trafficking Victims Protection Act. *Georgetown Immigration Law Review Journal, 21*, 337–381. Retrieved from https://ssrn.com/abstract=984927

Hyland, K. E. (2001). The impact of the protocol to prevent, suppress and punish trafficking in persons, especially women and children. *Human Rights Brief, 8*(2), 30–31, 38.

International Organization for Migration. (2017). *Global trafficking trends in focus: IOM victim of trafficking data 2006–2016*. Retrieved from www.iom.int/sites/default/files/our_work/DMM/MAD/A4-Trafficking-External-Brief.pdf

Kapstein, E. B. (2006). The new global slave trade. *Foreign Affairs, 85*(6), 103–115. Retrieved from https://doi.org/10.2307/20032146

Kempadoo, K. (2005). Introduction: From moral panic to global justice: Changing perspectives on trafficking. In K. Kempadoo, J. Sanghera, & B. Pattanaik (Eds.), *Trafficking and prostitution reconsidered: New perspectives on migration, sex work, and human rights* (pp. 3–24). London, England: Routledge.

Kolchin, P. (2003). *American slavery: 1619–1877*. London, England: Macmillan Publishers.

Kristof, N. (Author), & Nathaniel, N. (Producer). (2006, December 18). *Heartbreak and hope: A return to Cambodia* [Motion picture]. Cambodia: The New York Times Video. Retrieved from www.nytimes.com/video/opinion/1194817092163/heartbreak-and-hope.html

May, T. (2016, July 30). My government will lead the way in defeating modern slavery. *The Telegraph*. Retrieved from www.telegraph.co.uk/news/2016/07/30/we-will-lead-the-way-in-defeating-modern-slavery/

McKee, K. A. (2005). Modern-day slavery: Framing effective solutions for an age-old problem. *Catholic University Law Review, 55*(1), 141–192. Retrieved from http://scholarship.law.edu/lawreview/vol55/iss1/6

Media under fire for missing persons coverage: Uneven emphasis on attractive white girls, women criticized. (2005, June 15). *NBC News*. Retrieved from www.nbcnews.com/id/8233195/from#.XED8yxNKjBI

Miers, S. (2003). *Slavery in the twentieth century: The evolution of a global problem*. Lanham, MD: Rowman & Littlefield.

Miller, J. R. (2005, December 20). Letter to the editor: The slavery of prostitution. *The New York Times*. Retrieved from www.nytimes.com/2005/12/20/opinion/the-slavery-of-prostitution-916790.html

Miller, J. R. (2006). The call for a 21st century abolitionist movement. *Intercultural Human Rights Law Review, 1*, 37–42. Retrieved from www.stu.edu/portals/law/docs/human-rights/ihrlr/volumes/1/37-42-johnrmiller-callfora21stcenturyabolitionistmovementthesymposiuminvisiblechainsbreakingthetiesoftraffickinginhumans.pdf

Mintz, S. W. (1985). *Sweetness and power: The place of sugar in modern history*. New York, NY: Viking Press.

Nicholson, K., & Wheeler, S. R. (1998, November 13). 3 held in alleged sex-slave ring. *Denver Post*, p. 2B.

Rassam, A. Y. (1999). Contemporary forms of slavery and the evolution of the prohibition of slavery and the slave trade under customary international law. *Virginia Journal of International Law, 39*, 303–352. Retrieved from https://heinonline.org/HOL/LandingPage?handle=hein.journals/vajint39&div=16&id=&page=

Rassam, A. Y. (2005). International law and contemporary forms of slavery: An economic and social rights-based approach. *Penn State Law Review, 23*(4), 809–855. Retrieved from http://elibrary.law.psu.edu/psilr/vol23/iss4/15

Rawley, J. A., & Behrendt, S. D. (2005). *The transatlantic slave trade: A history*. Lincoln, NE: University of Nebraska Press.

Richard, A. O. (2000). *International trafficking in women to the United States: A contemporary manifestation of slavery and organized crime* (DCI Report). U.S. Department of State.

Robinson, R. (2005, June 10). (White) women we love. *The Washington Post*. Retrieved from www.washingtonpost.com/wp-dyn/content/article/2005/06/09/AR2005060901729.html

Sassen, S. (2002). Women's burden: Counter-geographies of globalization and the feminization of survival. *Nordic Journal of International Law, 71*(2), 255–274. Retrieved from www.jstor.org/stable/24357763

Satre, L. J. (2005). *Chocolate on trial: Slavery, politics, and the ethics of business*. Athens, OH: Ohio University Press.

Scully, E. (2001). Pre-cold war traffic in sexual labor and its foes: Some contemporary lessons. In D. Kyle & R. Koslowski (Eds.), *Global human smuggling* (pp. 74–106). Baltimore, MD: Johns Hopkins University Press.

Sherman, C. (2018, November 25). US agents fire tear gas as some migrants try to breach fence. *The Washington Times*. Retrieved from www.washingtontimes.com/news/2018/nov/25/migrants-march-toward-us-border-in-show-of-force/

Simons, M. (1994, January 16). The littlest prostitutes. *New York Times*. Retrieved from www.nytimes.com/1994/01/16/magazine/the-littlest-prostitutes.html

Specter, M. (1998, January 11). Traffickers' new cargo: Naïve new Slavic women. *The New York Times*. Retrieved from www.nytimes.com/1998/01/11/world/contraband-women-a-special-report-traffickers-new-cargo-naive-slavic-women.html

Srikantiah, J. (2007). Perfect victims and real survivors: The iconic victim in domestic human trafficking law. *Boston University Law Review, 87*, 158–211. Retrieved from www.prostitutionresearch.info/pdfs_all/trafficking%20all/BostonLawReview2007_trafficking.pdf

Tiefenbrun, S. (2002). The saga of Susannah, a U.S. Remedy for sex trafficking in women: The victims of Trafficking and Violence Protection Act of 2000. *Utah Law Review, 107*(1), 107–175. Retrieved from www.tjsl.edu/sites/default/files/susan_tiefenbrun_the_saga_of_susannah_a_u.s._remedy_for_sex_trafficking_in_women_the_victims_of_trafficking_and_violence_protection_act_of_2000_1_utah_l._rev._107_2002.pdf

Todres, J. (2006). The importance of realizing "others rights" to prevent sex trafficking. *Cardozo Journal of Law & Gender, 12*, 885–907. Retrieved from https://lsr.nellco.org/nyu_plltwp/32

Trump, I. (2018, November 30). The Trump administration is taking bold action to combat the evil of human trafficking. *The Washington Post*. Retrieved from www.washingtonpost.com/opinions/the-trump-administration-is-taking-bold-action-to-combat-the-evil-of-human-trafficking/2018/11/29/3e21685c-f411–11e8–80d0-f7e1948d55f4_story.html?utm_term=.db7d79af185f

United Nations. (1904). *International agreement for the suppression of white slave traffic*. Retrieved from https://treaties.un.org/pages/ViewDetails.aspx?src=TREATY&mtdsg_no=VII-8&chapter=7&clang=_en

United Nations. (1910). *International convention for the suppression of the white slave traffic*. Retrieved from https://treaties.un.org/pages/ViewDetails.aspx?src=TREATY&mtdsg_no=VII-9&chapter=7&clang=_en

United Nations. (1921). *International convention on the suppression of the traffic in women and children*. Retrieved from https://treaties.un.org/pages/ViewDetails.aspx?src=TREATY&mtdsg_no=VII-3&chapter=7&clang=_en

United Nations. (1933). *International convention for the suppression of the traffic in women of full age*. Retrieved from https://treaties.un.org/pages/ViewDetails.aspx?src=TREATY&mtdsg_no=VII-5&chapter=7&lang=en

United Nations. (1949). *Convention for the suppression of the traffic in persons and of the exploitation of the prostitution of others*. Retrieved from www.ohchr.org/en/professionalinterest/pages/trafficinpersons.aspx

United Nations. (1966a). *International covenant on civil and political rights*. Retrieved from www.ohchr.org/en/professionalinterest/pages/ccpr.aspx

United Nations. (2001b). *United Nations convention against transnational organized crime and the protocols thereto*. Retrieved from www.unodc.org/unodc/en/organized-crime/intro/UNTOC.html

United States. (1810). *An act to prohibit the importation of slaves into any port or place within the jurisdiction of the United States, from and after the first day of January, in the year of our lord one thousand eight hundred and eight.* Retrieved from www.loc.gov/resource/rbpe.22800200/?st=text

United States. (2000). *Trafficking Victims Protection Act of 2000.* Retrieved from www.state.gov/j/tip/laws/61124.htm

U.S. 146th Congress. (2000). (statement of Sen. Samuel Brownback). *Congressional record no. 125.* Retrieved from www.congress.gov/crec/2000/10/10/CREC-2000-10-10.pdf

U.S. Congress. (1910). *Mann Act,* June 25, 1910 (ch. 395, 36 Stat. 825; codified as amended at 18 U.S.C. §§ 2421–2424).

U.S. Constitution. Art. 1, Sect. 9.

U.S. Department of Justice. (2006). *Attorney general's annual report to congress on U.S. government activities to combat trafficking in persons fiscal year 2005.* Retrieved from www.justice.gov/archive/ag/annualreports/tr2005/agreporthumantrafficing2005.pdf

U.S. Department of State. (2004). *The Trafficking in persons report 2004.* Washington, DC.

U.S. Department of State. (2006). *The trafficking in persons report 2006.* Washington, DC.

U.S. Department of State. (2010). *The trafficking in persons report 2010.* Washington, DC.

U.S. Department of State. (2018). *The trafficking in persons report 2018.* Washington, DC.

U.S. Government Accountability Office. (2006). *Human trafficking: Better data, strategy, and reporting needed to enhance U.S. anti-trafficking efforts abroad.* Retrieved from www.gao.gov/new.items/d06825.pdf

van den Anker, C. (2004). Contemporary slavery, global justice and globalization. In C. van den Anker (Ed.), *The political economy of new slavery* (pp. 15–36). London, England: Palgrave Macmillan.

van Schendel, W., & Abraham, I. (2005). Introduction. In W. van Schendel & I. Abraham (Eds.), *Illicit flows and criminal things* (pp. 1–37). Bloomington, IN: Indiana University Press.

WFMYStaff, Vatican official says human trafficking now is worse than African slave trade. (2006, November 14). *WFMY CBS News 2.* Retrieved from www.wfmynews2.com/article/news/vatican-official-says-human-trafficking-now-worse-than-african-slave-trade/83-403159474

Williams, E. (1984). *From Columbus to Castro: The history of the Caribbean.* New York, NY: Vintage Books.

Women as chattel: The emerging global market in trafficking. Washington, DC: Gender Matters Quarterly.

Wong, D. (2005). The rumor of trafficking: Border controls, illegal migration, and the sovereignty of the nation-state. In W. van Schendel & I. Abraham (Eds.), *Illicit flows and criminal things* (pp. 69–100). Bloomington, IN: Indiana University Press.

2

WHAT WE TALK ABOUT WHEN WE TALK ABOUT TRAFFICKING

A reflection on the first 20 years of the modern anti-slavery fight[1]

Ambassador Luis C.deBaca (Ret.)[2]

Abstract

Almost 20 years since the enactment of the Trafficking Victims Protection Act and promulgation of the United Nations Trafficking Protocol, modern anti-trafficking efforts and U.S. leadership in the global effort to combat modern slavery must be understood in the context of American enforcement efforts dating back to Reconstruction under the labels of peonage, involuntary servitude, and slavery, and now human trafficking. The modern anti-trafficking frame of the 3Ps of prevention, protection, and prosecution was rooted in civil rights and human rights concepts of slavery and freedom rather than concepts of commerce, migration, or regulation of prostitution. That new approach, however, has been limited by unresolved cultural and legal legacies of a competing anti-trafficking framework based on commerce and morality – the "White Slave Trafficking" effort of the early 1900s. At its best, the 3P framework of the modern U.S. and UN instruments and policies drives best practices in critical reporting and implementation standards, criminal and civil enforcement, victim identification, supply chain transparency, and worker-led social responsibility while capturing and incorporating the voices and lived experiences of survivors. Continued implementation of this modern rights-based approach is at risk, however, given the rhetorical and cultural strength of the competing sex trafficking lens.[3]

Learning Objectives

At the end of the chapter, readers will be able to:

1 Understand the development of the issue area currently defined as "human trafficking";
2 Identify the historical uses of the Thirteenth Amendment to the U.S. Constitution, which ended chattel slavery and prohibited subsequent forms of slavery and involuntary servitude but was limited in its efficacy by systemic evasion and lack of resources;
3 Understand how contradictory legal regimes added to confusion in the anti-trafficking space in the twentieth century and left some victims of compelled service unprotected by the law, most notably through the dominance of the "White Slave Trafficking Act" approach in the sex trafficking arena;

4 Identify the conceptual and historical underpinnings of both rights-based anti-trafficking efforts and commerce or morality-based anti-trafficking efforts, as well as the policy approaches that flow from each;
5 Understand the modern history of the U.S. government's involuntary servitude and slavery program and how it became cast as "human trafficking" in the 1990s;
6 Examine how different presidential administrations have approached modern slavery since the promulgation of the United Nations protocol and the Trafficking Victims Protection Act of 2000, both in rhetorical approaches and policy/enforcement actions;
7 Interrogate how and to what extent the rhetoric and implementation of the modern slavery/trafficking movement are correlated; and
8 Identify best practices that deliver on the "3P" paradigm, such as multidisciplinary task forces, victim identification and protection, and worker-led social responsibility (WSR) efforts.

Key Terms: human trafficking; slavery; involuntary servitude, peonage; "The 3Ps"; Civil Rights Division, the Mann Act; worker-led social responsibility; supply chains.

Introduction

At a time in which the American political system appears divided and gridlocked, it sometimes seems that one of the few consensus policy topics of the early twenty-first century has been "human trafficking," or "modern slavery." Statutes are passed unanimously and presidential administrations seize opportunities to highlight bipartisan cooperation, claiming through their titles the mantle of emancipation and historic figures such as William Wilberforce (Trafficking Victims Protection Reauthorization Act, 2008) and Frederick Douglass (Trafficking Victims Prevention and Protection Reauthorization Act, 2018). Local communities, schools, and church groups are starting anti-trafficking groups and even opening shelters and safe houses. Universities are offering courses, convening symposia, and founding journals for a growing body of scholarship. But how has this come to pass? What are the laws and policies that are being built upon by these seemingly consensus-driven statutes? And is everyone actually talking about the same thing?

What do you think about when you hear the word "trafficking?" What mental image do you have? What is your definition of "human trafficking"?

Effectuating and expanding the protection of the Thirteenth Amendment to the U.S. Constitution and Article IV of the Universal Declaration of Rights (both of which guarantee freedom from slavery and servitude), the modern anti-trafficking movement has combined such disparate issues as forced labor, prostitution, economic exploitation of migrants, commercial sexual exploitation of children, child soldiering, supply chains, and border security. But in doing so, did it also inherit the discourses, tropes, legal pitfalls, turf wars, ideological battles, and bureaucratic siloes of its many parts? What is the "value-added" of the slavery/trafficking lens to a world where there were already laws, treaties, and structures tasked with these issues? Is this a slavery problem? A morals issue? Migration policy? Should it be addressed criminally or civilly? Through a reform of capitalism and gender assumptions? By a particular approach to prostitution law or enforcement? Through more open movement or by stricter border controls? This chapter seeks to address some of these questions by tracking the development and implementation of modern anti-trafficking norms in search of a common understanding of this phenomenon. To do so, it is perhaps worthwhile to assess the state of play.

Since 2000, there has been an astonishing level of activity against compelled service, under the umbrella terms "human trafficking" or "modern slavery," which in a nutshell encapsulate all of the activities involved in reducing a person to, or holding them in, a condition of compelled service. Different international instruments (for details on these see Ollus and Joutsen, Chapter 3, this volume) and domestic laws address various types or levels of trafficking activity. One will often see the phenomenon referred to interchangeably as human trafficking, trafficking in persons, involuntary servitude, debt bondage or peonage, slavery, practices similar to slavery, slavery-like practices, modern slavery, or document servitude (this chapter will tend to use the various terms interchangeably unless there is a sharp legal distinction that needs to be made).

Nomenclature

What is your definition of "slavery"? Or involuntary servitude"? How are those different to you?

This issue of nomenclature is not a new problem; the U.S. Department of Justice at various times over the course of 75 years classified these cases under the program titles of "Peonage," "Involuntary Servitude and Slavery (ISS)," or "Human Trafficking," with the dominant label mainly reflecting trends in legislation, case law, and investigative practice as opposed to any real difference in the underlying situation of victims. Despite the plain meaning of the word "trafficking," international treaties and international law norms as well as domestic legislation and enforcement structures in countries around the world that follow the UN "Palermo Protocol," focus not simply on movement but instead on such concepts as the inability of workers to leave their employers' service; the abuse of vulnerabilities and debts; the use of force and coercion (and threats thereof); the use of false or inflated promises of salary or working conditions as a way to induce workers to enter into employment; the taking advantage of immigration status or lack of proper documentation; and the confiscation of immigration or identity documents. There is thus a global policy consensus that compelled service – whether triggered by debt, overt force and threats, psychological manipulation, or document confiscation – is properly criminalized.

The modern anti-trafficking frame combines many different concepts commonly used in legal and non-legal regimes to describe compelled service – concepts that are at times confusing and seemingly contradictory, flow from different instruments and laws, and are accompanied by structures and constituencies that built up over the twentieth century. Before 2000, secure in their siloes and under little pressure for results, often each with an institutional home in competing government offices or UN agencies, actors seemed to define themselves by their mandates, their instruments, or their periodic gatherings rather than by measurable impact on victims' lives.

Under these legacy approaches, international instruments and domestic laws addressing issues of compelled service under such rubrics as slavery, forced labor, child labor, or sex trafficking were steadily promulgated but few people were freed, and few were arrested. Criminal sentences, if obtained at all, were generally low, seeming to reflect an assumption of a victimless crime involving "disreputable" women, or a conception that illegal migrants or marginalized ethnic groups deserved their situation and were lucky to have work, even work enforced through the unholy trinity of debt, threat, and violence. Abuse was not seen as something done to such marginalized people but was a function of "just how they are." While not necessarily officially reflected in statutes or regulations in such stark terms, such attitudes were certainly the dismissive reactions that one could routinely hear working as a prosecutor or diplomat in the early years of the modern anti-trafficking movement.

Responding to institutional lassitude, the need for modern laws, and the vulnerabilities of marginalized populations, the American anti-trafficking policy push of the late 1990s was a conscious attempt to address what in U.S. practice had become a bifurcated regime in which people enslaved for labor were thought of as having suffered a violation of rights (the "ISS approach" sited in concepts of freedom), but those enslaved in commercial sex were relegated to a commerce-based analysis (the "Mann Act approach" sited in concepts of movement and morality) and were treated as criminals rather than as victims worthy of protection. It represented an attempt to move away from regimes that insisted on separating the concepts of moving someone into exploitation from the exploitation itself and to replace regimes in which hortatory language in human rights instruments was not matched by policy or investigative resources. And it grounded itself firmly in international human rights and domestic civil rights approaches while recognizing the overlap with public health, transnational organized crime, and commerce.

The TVPA

In the fall of 2000, the Trafficking Victims Protection Act (TVPA) updated the post–Civil War anti-slavery statutes in the United States under the rubric of "trafficking in persons." Weeks later, the United Nations promulgated the Protocol to Prevent, Suppress, and Punish Trafficking in Persons, especially Women and Children ("Palermo Protocol") (2000), supplementing the UN Convention Against Transnational Organized Crime.

Despite the common usage of the term, the new laws for the first time defined "trafficking" in a manner that was *not limited* to cross-border movement for prostitution. Rather, the heart of the human trafficking concept was recast as the exploitation of a person and addressed all of the activities involved in reducing someone to (or holding them in) compelled service. Effectively, that made liable everyone from the recruiter in the village to the boss who enslaved the worker or the pimp who exploited someone in sexual servitude (Gallagher, 2010). In recent years, this idea of expanded responsibility has extended further, holding accountable those who would profit from trafficking in their supply chain, those who use trafficking victims in commercial sex, and even governments that turn away from their duties of investigation or victim protection.

The new laws didn't just define trafficking but also set out an optimal governmental response. Both the TVPA and Palermo Protocol follow the "Three P" paradigm developed by the Clinton administration, organizing anti-trafficking efforts around a shared goal of "Prevention, Protection, and Prosecution" that sought to place as co-equal with states' criminal justice response the needs of the victims and the structural changes that could prevent the crime in the first place. This construct has been the lodestone of U.S. anti-slavery diplomacy and policy in the post–Cold War era to great effect worldwide. The 3Ps are often supplemented by additional aspects such as "Partnerships" (the "4Ps") or "Rehabilitation" ("3Ps and an R").

This chapter examines the progress in the almost 20 years since the conceptual shift enshrined in the TVPA and Palermo Protocol. It will set out a U.S. policy agenda that has been remarkably consistent across several presidential administrations, including the framework of the 3Ps, the gradual application of the updated servitude statutes and growth of state laws, and the international reporting mechanism and standard-setting of the U.S. Trafficking in Persons Report. It will trace the historical underpinnings of anti-trafficking efforts, including some of the legal and rhetorical inheritances of the legacy approaches, and will highlight some current challenges facing anti-trafficking efforts 20 years on. Hopefully, by reflecting on these last two decades, this chapter will contribute to an understanding of the common themes that run throughout how we talk about trafficking in the modern era, and offer several promising practices for future anti-slavery efforts.

Twenty-first-century U.S. policy: a bipartisan consensus . . . under stress?

One of the things that we talk about when we talk about human trafficking is that it is a crime and a social policy issue as well as a public priority for the U.S. government. It has been signaled as a priority for the Trump administration, as it was for the Obama administration, the George W. Bush administration, and the Clinton administration.

At a White House ceremony commemorating International Women's Day on March 11, 1998, President William J. Clinton tasked his cabinet agencies to undertake a coordinated approach to combating trafficking (then still framed as an issue impacting women and girls). That day, President Clinton directed:

I The Secretary of State, in coordination with the Administrator of the Agency for International Development, to strengthen and expand our efforts to combat violence against women in all its forms around the world. These efforts should be responsive to government and nongovernment requests for partnerships, expert guidance, and technical assistance to address this human rights violation.

II The President's Interagency Council on Women to coordinate the United States Government response on trafficking in women and girls, in consultation with nongovernmental groups.

III The Attorney General to examine current treatment of victims of trafficking including to determine ways to insure: the provision of services for victims and witnesses in settings that secure their safety; precautions for the safe return of victims and witnesses to their originating countries; witness cooperation in criminal trials against traffickers; and consideration of temporary and/or permanent legal status for victims and witnesses of trafficking who lack legal status.

IV The Attorney General to review existing U.S. criminal laws and their current use to determine if they are adequate to prevent and deter trafficking in women and girls, to recommend any appropriate legal changes to ensure that trafficking is criminalized and that the consequences of trafficking are significant, and to review current prosecution efforts against traffickers in order to identify additional intelligence sources, evidentiary needs and resource capabilities.

V The Secretary of State to use our diplomatic presence around the world to work with source, transit, and destination countries to develop strategies for protecting and assisting victims of trafficking and to expand and enhance anti-fraud training to stop the international trafficking of women and girls.

VI The Secretary of State to coordinate an intergovernmental response to the Government of Ukraine's request to jointly develop and implement a comprehensive strategy to combat trafficking in women and girls from and to Ukraine. The U.S.-Ukraine cooperation will serve as a model for a multidisciplinary approach to combat trafficking that can be expanded to other countries.

VII The Secretary of State, in coordination with the Attorney General, to expand and strengthen assistance to the international community in developing and enacting legislation to combat trafficking in women and girls, to provide assistance to victims of trafficking, and to continue to expand efforts to train legal and law enforcement personnel worldwide.

VIII The Secretary of State and the Director of the United States Information Agency to expand public awareness campaigns targeted to warn potential victims of the methods used by traffickers.

IX The President's Interagency Council on Women to convene a gathering of government and nongovernment representatives from source, transit, and destination countries and representatives from international organizations to call attention to the issue of trafficking in women and girls and to develop strategies for combating this fundamental human rights violation.

Within two years, these structures and this priority issue were encapsulated in law by the TVPA, which was intended by Congress "to combat trafficking in persons, a contemporary manifestation of slavery . . . to ensure just and effective punishment of traffickers, and to protect their victims" (Victims of Trafficking and Violence Protection Act, 2000). That statutory imperative, effectuating the "3P approach" developed by the Clinton administration in the spring of 1998, translated into a key global position for the United States in the anti-trafficking arena, driving policy within the United Nations, in regional fora, and bilaterally.

The high profile of the United States has not exempted it from critique, however, whether for having a unilateral reporting and enforcement mechanism as opposed to deferring to the United Nations (Chuang, 2006), for wielding a heavy-hand in bilateral diplomacy, or for seeming to repeat the mistakes of prior crusades against sex trafficking (Desyllas, 2007). Cultural and media attention are often primarily focused on sex trafficking and other emotive aspects of the issue (refer to Bravo, Chapter 1, this volume), and especially in the early years of TVPA implementation, observers of the modern effort – critics and proponents alike – often focused as much on the rhetoric as on the actual policy or enforcement efforts (see Chacon, 2006, who dismissed as "modest" a tripling in open federal investigations, a quadrupling of cases charged, and a doubling of convictions in the four years following the TVPA). This is a valid inquiry, given how human trafficking is often presented in the public sphere with a unidimensional aspect of vice enforcement – a vision that government efforts too often reflect back, rather than holding the line in favor of the human rights basis of the 3Ps.

Rhetoric versus action

Modern anti-trafficking efforts have sometimes taken two divergent paths: the relatively anonymous application of the neutral law and policies of the TVPA and the emotionally charged rhetoric of a morals or anti-vice crusade. Policy makers are not cold-blooded technocrats but react to the same cultural and emotional cues as their constituents. To be blunt, there seems to exist in popular culture – and with some political actors – a market premium for trafficking stories that provide a frisson of danger and sex while not challenging gender or economic norms. This is not limited to movie franchises such as the thriller *Taken*. An analysis of almost 2,500 newspaper articles concluded that victimization stories were favored and root causes of trafficking ignored, while breathlessly presenting the issue as a problem of organized crime and national security (Farrell & Fahy, 2009). As Anthony DeStefano (2007) wrote when assessing his own reporting on the issue in the early years, "Admittedly, we focused on the sex industry because it was a good subject for newspaper treatment."

When he was teaching at Stanford, the late Joel Brinkley of the *New York Times* described "the classic five-paragraph trafficking story," well within a first-year journalism student's capability. Brinkley suggested that the story most likely to get approved by an editor was one that (1) starts by introducing a foreign woman or girl's hopes, (2) moves to her victimization in the destination country at the hands of treacherous cohorts, (3) contextualizes her experience with some easily findable but not critically questioned figures as to the scope of the problem, (4) quotes a local actor who was involved in helping her or prosecuting her trafficker, and (5) concludes with a happy ending, such as a description of the protagonists' new life in the area, free from exploitation.

Such stories are often how people are first introduced to the reality of slavery in the modern era and are not by themselves damaging. However, they do little to challenge economic or social status quos, create a real understanding of the lives of survivors, or make the case as to why the 3P "trafficking frame" would be more valuable than other approaches based on immigration or morals enforcement. The more recent version of the story is similar, but with the shock value coming from the victim being a U.S. citizen child in commercial sex – a frame that flirts with nativism and risks excluding adult victims, migrant populations, and labor trafficking survivors from the protections of the TVPA.

Moreover, as they aggregate, such stories leave a false impression that modern slavery is something that happens somewhere else to people of other classes, races, or national origins. Such a message absolves the reader of any involvement, whether contributing to the problem by their consumption patterns or having a role to play in confronting the problem. Sensationalized media accounts and the policy agendas that flow therefrom often gloss over the many competing motivations and experiences of victims in favor of a unidimensional portrayal of sex trafficking that can be addressed not by ongoing and systemic work but by an overarching legal or normative solution – an often enforcement-based "silver bullet."

Morality-based stories, and the policies behind them, were seen by many observers as driving much of U.S. anti-trafficking policy in the early years of TVPA implementation. Ron Weitzer (2007, 2010) has done an excellent job of setting forth the effect of a coalition that sought to advance an anti-prostitution agenda through the use of anti-trafficking rhetoric. One Bush-era success in turning rhetoric into policy – a ban on international development funding for grantees that did not actively oppose legalized prostitution – was overturned by the U.S. Supreme Court. While that coalition achieved some rhetorical and normative victories, the Bush administration was in its actions more characterized by pragmatic implementation of the TVPA, as it set up immigration relief mechanisms, intensified investigations into labor and sex trafficking, worked with such groups as the Freedom Network to develop best practices in victim care, defended the slavery-based definitions of the TVPA in Congress, and began to stress labor trafficking as a co-equal foreign policy priority by the end of the second term. Pragmatism and the recognition of the value of bipartisan consensus continued into the Obama administration, which (even while dialing back the imbalance pointed out by Weitzer and others) did not exclude from policy conversations faith-based organizations and those who concentrated on sex trafficking, even if they had been favored in the prior administration.

Continuity of counter-trafficking efforts in modern presidential transition periods have been aided by the number of actors who have collaborated with counterparts on legislation and implementation, whether as career employees, legislative staff, grantees, or on task forces convened and funded by the Justice Department, and have also been helped through such collaborative organizations as the Freedom Network and the ATEST Coalition. Such a bipartisan consensus held together in the first two years of the Trump administration, with generally balanced implementation and policy formulation on the part of front-line actors. However, as of this writing, the stressing and conflation of sex trafficking and border security frames by the president himself (see, e.g., Metler, 2019), as well as the use of the 2008 TVPRA's unaccompanied minor provisions to justify family separation and detention, may challenge the issue's pre-political status that has in the modern era prevented it from being used for partisan political purposes or collapsed into immigration policy disputes (refer to Table 2.1 for a summary of U.S. presidential administrations' legacies, rhetoric, and results).

Table 2.1 Administration legacies

Administration	*Characterization*	*Rhetorical Focus*	*Action/Results*
Clinton	Worker Exploitation; Trafficking in Persons	International Women & Children's issue; Sweatshops	Gender- and service-neutral update of slavery statutes; immigrant-focused victim programs; 3P paradigm; Palermo Protocol; DOJ/DOL-led task force
G. W. Bush	Trafficking in Persons	Sex trafficking and prostitution	Local task forces and trainings focused on labor and sex trafficking alike; uptick in prosecutions, both sex/labor; establishment of hotline; victim services programs including U.S. citizens; restrictions on USAID funding for pro-prostitution groups
Obama	Modern Slavery; Human Trafficking	Slavery/servitude; Child sex trafficking	Supply chain and procurement policies; expanded task forces; international forced and child labor reporting; victim services strategy; growth of overlap with CSEC task forces; divergence in civil and criminal sex/labor enforcement patterns; funding neutrality on prostitution issue; survivors advisory council
Trump	Human Trafficking	Border enforcement; Alien smuggling; Child sex trafficking	Family separation and detention instead of use of Unaccompanied Alien Children provisions of TVPRA2008; establishment of forced labor Customs unit and money laundering office; use of trafficking examples as justification for border wall

Prosecution: for the TVPA, slavery was not a metaphor but the starting point

Some have asked whether the use of slavery terms is appropriate in the human trafficking effort (refer to Bravo, Chapter 1, this volume), casting such nomenclature as an appropriation of past suffering or a metaphorical exercise to obtain a moral and political "high ground" for the issue. But for those who negotiated the TVPA, and had been enforcing the Involuntary Servitude and Slavery statutes, these terms were not metaphor but the legal and conceptual underpinning of the entire enterprise as a direct application of the Thirteenth Amendment guarantee of freedom. Accordingly, this chapter examines the development of the U.S. rights-based ISS enforcement effort and how it grew directly into what is now termed "human trafficking."

The Thirteenth Amendment applies to everyone in the United States regardless of race, national origin, or immigration status. It did not just end chattel slavery (the entire American social, economic, and legal system predicated on the multigenerational ownership of African Americans) but did so with language aimed at preventing effective re-enslavement and empowering federal legislation to effectuate its purposes in the future:

> Neither slavery nor involuntary servitude, except as a punishment for crime whereof the party shall have been duly convicted, shall exist within the United States, or any place subject to their jurisdiction.
>
> Congress shall have power to enforce this article by appropriate legislation.
>
> —*U.S. Constitution, Amendment XIII*

Even as it made chattel slavery of African Americans illegal, the Thirteenth Amendment did so without naming them as the only class of people protected from enslavement by its terms. It thus did not simply end slavery on one day, but was a promise of emancipation as an *ongoing process*. In a post-war time of transition with dramatic territorial expansion and the arrival of new immigrant communities, federal legislation enacted pursuant to the enforcement clause made it clear that the protections of the Thirteenth Amendment were for all, regardless of race.

Why were peonage and involuntary servitude cases such a sensitive enforcement matter?

For the same reason that the Department of Justice racial violence or police brutality mandates were also sensitive: because they struck at the heart of economic, cultural, and political arrangements that were predicated on a particular racial hierarchy. As the Civil Rights Division's expertise in investigating and prosecuting cases under the Thirteenth Amendment grew, the focus of the cases continued to be on the denial of a victims' constitutional guarantee of freedom and the need for the government to vindicate that person's rights if they were interfered with. This is the legacy, and the American expertise, that was brought to the issue of "trafficking in persons" as it emerged at the end of the Cold War.

But progress was not universal or ordained, and the amendment's forward-looking aspects were not self-executing. Despite the best efforts of the Grant administration to enforce and expand anti-slavery laws through both civilian and military courts, economic and political structures that had relied on forced labor fought back with both evasion and outright resistance. Hispanic elites in the Southwest claimed that their *peones* were more like loyal family retainers than bonded labor, and waited out territorial law enforcement efforts. In the South, as soon as the post-war military occupation was lifted, African Americans were subjected to domestic terrorism as well as a mounting set of official restrictions on movement, accommodation, employability, and their voting franchise. The reach and enforcement of the Thirteenth Amendment was evaded as southern states seized on legal loopholes for convict labor leasing schemes, debt bondage, and other forms of compelled service. The re-establishment of servitude in the Jim Crow South set a pattern of brutality and exploitation with a thin veneer of legality that would mark southern agriculture and other labor to the modern day[4] and almost a century later inform the development of the TVPA and the Palermo Protocol.

A federal civil rights lens: vulnerable communities deserve access to justice

There is a general bias in the U.S. criminal law regime toward local law enforcement, on the theory that justice administered at the local level has the most credibility and reflects community norms. But state laws have often not aligned with constitutional civil rights guarantees. Attempts to re-enslave freed African American communities were such an economic and social force in the South, and state and local law enforcement was so involved in perpetrating or allowing such practices over the course of almost 100 years, that – just as with racial violence or police brutality – federal efforts were often the only way to address labor abuses and the persistence of involuntary servitude in the South, especially in agriculture, mining, and production of turpentine and pitch (see the "Tapping the Pines" text box) from the pine forests.

"Tapping the Pines"

While we do not think much about turpentine and other wood products in the modern era, the *United States v. Venters* case was not an outlier for the first part of the twentieth century. Many peonage cases were brought in the "naval stores" industry, which produced the turpentine and pitch needed by the U.S. Navy and merchant fleet. Solvents distilled from the sap of pine trees were a multimillion-dollar business, and the remote work camps were the ultimate dirty and dangerous job. Debt bondage, a culture of violence, and outright impunity on the part of the camp operators added to the intrinsic dangers of working with timber and boiling down and distilling the flammable materials. High-profile peonage cases in the woods involved beating and murder of foresters and sexual enslavement of women in shacks and kitchens, creating a multi-tiered exploitation.

Enforcement alone didn't end this era of slavery by another name – as now, trafficking and slavery could not be addressed without addressing the root causes of poverty, racism, and social exclusion. After World War II, new distilling methods allowed solvents to be obtained from ground-up wood, undercutting the need for laborers. Telephones and cars made rural African Americans less isolated and vulnerable to violence and recapture by the operators, and the expansion of cash-and-carry grocery stores broke the back of the "company store" debt bondage system. And hard-fought gains of the Civil Rights Era created alternatives to remaining in debt bondage. In his excellent account of the naval stores industry, Robert Outland (2004) quotes a turpentine operator bemoaning the changes by the late 1950s: "Today's blacks don't want to work in turpentine. They can go to a little town and work at a manufacturing plant and make more money with shorter hours."

Federal anti-slavery efforts seemed to happen in fits and starts historically but were at their most intense in the administrations of Ulysses S. Grant (Reconstruction), Theodore Roosevelt, William Howard Taft (Progressive), and Franklin Delano Roosevelt (New Deal).

In the Progressive Era, the reformist and modernizing spirit of northern urban progressivism – itself a driver of the morals-based war against the "White Slave Traffic" (see footnote below) – was tested strongly by the entrenched economic and social system of the South. Nevertheless, both Roosevelt and Taft repeatedly pushed enforcement agendas under the peonage statute in an attempt to root out debt bondage and the widespread police corruption that fed African Americans into involuntary servitude. In 1903, fresh from making a bold declaration of a "Fair Deal" for the African American community, Roosevelt sent investigators and U.S. attorneys on the path of the most abusive employers, a reformist agenda so strong it included the appointment of the first female federal prosecutor – Mary Grace Quackenbos.

Diversity Matters

As the first woman federal prosecutor at a time when female lawyers were shockingly rare, Mary Grace Quackenbos brought a new perspective to the law, maintaining her own career, using the peonage statute to protect immigrant workers and fighting against domestic violence decades before the women's movement.

A few years later, under President Taft, federal prosecutors around the country received a letter conveying that "The Department is deeply interested in the subject of peonage and the due administration of the statutes in relation thereto." They were tasked with submitting periodic special reports to Department of Justice Headquarters in Washington, delineating cases that were being investigated or prosecuted in their district, and any state laws that could be "used to compel the performance of labor contracts and produce a condition of involuntary servitude," (Wickersham, 1911). Because of the actions of those federal attorneys in the Progressive Era, one advantage that American prosecutors have had in bringing trafficking cases – and that American diplomats and lawyers have had in the international arena (from prosecuting Nazi war crimes to formulating the Universal Declaration of Rights and eventually negotiating the Palermo Protocol) is the depth of U.S. case law available for concepts that are now de rigueur in the modern anti-trafficking approach, such as the traffickers' abuse of a position of vulnerability, the interplay with recruitment or inveiglement, or how to weigh any initial consent to perform the underlying service.

As was often the case in the history of anti-slavery enforcement, the energy brought to these cases by the Roosevelt and Taft administrations fell off with the change in government to the Woodrow Wilson administration. The early 1900s saw the re-establishment of the Ku Klux Klan and a laissez-faire economic approach that left workers at the mercy of their employers. It was not until Franklin Delano Roosevelt's New Deal that the federal anti-slavery enforcement priority returned, but when it did, it came with a vengeance. For the first time, a specialized unit was formed at Department of Justice headquarters to address civil rights violations. In keeping with the radical economic intervention that Roosevelt undertook to address the Great Depression, the Civil Rights Section's work was guided as much through the economic lens of the Thirteenth Amendment as the anti-discrimination approach of the Fourteenth or Fifteenth Amendments (Goluboff, 2007). The growth of the FBI as well as a dramatically expanded federal government began to weaken the power of southern sheriffs and local courts over African American populations.

Many of the current approaches to fighting human trafficking flow out of the use of the Progressive Era case law and its progeny by the highly motivated Civil Rights Section and the prosecutors sent with Justice Jackson – himself one of Roosevelt's attorneys general – to prosecute Nazi slave labor in the Nuremberg trials. But at the same time this anti-slavery practice and case law was being built, another approach to human trafficking had arrived on the scene that was to have dramatic consequences for those who were held not for labor but in sexual servitude. That approach bore what may be the least accurate title of any federal law: the "White Slave Trafficking Act."

A tragic, well-intentioned expansion of values and rhetoric: "white slavery"

In 1909, during the Progressive Era attempts to confront sharecropping and convict labor schemes in the South, Congress amended the federal slavery statutes to consolidate and de-racinate them (protecting "any person" as the class protected by the statute instead of having laws criminalizing the kidnapping or holding of specific groups such as African Americans, Mexicans, or Italian children). The irony should not be lost that only a year after ensuring that these statutes applied to everyone regardless of race or gender, another statute – the "White Slave Trafficking Act" – was passed.

The "White Slavery" statute (also known as the Mann Act after its sponsor) was based not on the Thirteenth Amendment's protections against enslavement but on the state's ability to regulate sexual commerce, or "traffic." This bifurcation, in which women in prostitution were subjected to a wholly separate legal regime based on morals/vice enforcement, was not to be remedied for 90 years.

Anti-trafficking activism seems to ebb and flow. Some presidential administrations are known for their efforts, while enforcement and political attention wanes in others. Why is this? What makes a policy issue capture popular attention? What other issues contribute to anti-trafficking activism?

Following Emancipation, Nineteenth Century reformers in Britain and the United States sought to expand their activism on behalf of other vulnerable communities, often returning to the "slavery" lens which had spurred their efforts. Eventually, following high-profile exposés of forced – or migrant – prostitution, "White Slavery" laws (see Bravo, Chapter 1, this volume) were passed that, despite their name, legally required neither enslavement nor a Caucasian victim but instead euphemistically addressed transporting a woman or girl across a border for prostitution. Just as with related reform agendas against child labor, for temperance, and to obtain women's suffrage, anti-prostitution activism by Progressive Era reformers took place on an international as well as a national scale.

Sadly, periodic anti-slavery or anti-trafficking reforms (whether concentrated on sex or labor) have often been subsumed quickly into competing and more culturally – or politically – entrenched efforts (such as exclusionary immigration policies, race and the use of criminal enforcement to maintain social order, or the regulation of public morals and gender roles and the "White Slavery" activism of the early 1900s was no exception). Despite the best intentions of its initial proponents, the historic "White Slavery" movement's contradictions raise a host of questions:

- Were efforts to address coerced prostitution undercut by their underlying assumptions about poverty, migration, and gender?
- Was the movement actually an attempt to address coerced prostitution, or was the language of slavery and violence simply cover for attempts to criminalize all prostitution, whether or not there was overt abuse or coercion used?
- Was the "White Slavery" effort a "moral panic" that died out because it never existed at all? Because of changes in the economy or culture? Because of "compassion fatigue" or bureaucratic inertia?
- Did forced prostitution die out, or did the movement that claimed to address it?
- What alternative regulatory and migration schemes changed the twentieth-century sex industry?
- Why wasn't this particular class (or perceived class) of victims in the United States simply brought under the protection of the Thirteenth Amendment?
- How did the bifurcation of this victim class out of the slavery lens, and the overlap with general prostitution policy, influence subsequent diplomacy and debate?

> This chapter in many ways argues that *the trafficking lens has been a disruptive one*, challenging many different existing areas of practice or scholarship. One such disruption might be to re-examine that almost universally held modern characterization of the Progressive Era's efforts against sex trafficking as only a "moral panic." From working with sex trafficking victims in the modern era and hearing how they describe what they have been through, one can look at the WSTA-era stories, as floridly written as they may have been for late Victorian and Progressive Era audiences, and get a sense of the lived experience of at least some percentage of the women and girls in prostitution who suffered horrible abuse: beatings, confinement, and rapes. Their memory deserves our attention and our respect.

While notions of whiteness and womanhood and the need to preserve their purity at a time of dramatic social change may have driven the "White Slavery" activists, the U.S. approach was likely also influenced by commerce-based international conventions informed by British and French experience with migrant prostitution; connections between British and American activists were particularly strong around the issue, just as they were around women's suffrage, a policy issue also led in the U.S. Congress by Commerce Committee Chairman James Mann. But there was also a homegrown politics of the moment, as Progressive reformers sought to clean up corruption and vice in urban areas as they were also expanding federal power ("trust-busting") to regulate large conglomerates, as can be seen in Mann's other legacies: the Food & Drug Administration and the Interstate Commerce Commission.

Whatever the reason, by 1910, there were the beginnings of a century-long divide between sex and labor trafficking that would not serve any victims well. The initial title of the Mann Act ("White Slave Trafficking Act") caused great confusion as to whether its "protections" were available to anyone other than Whites. Its focus on interstate transportation created a separate federal statutory scheme for prostitution that – not having to prove enslavement and confronted with the reality that some women in prostitution had not been trapped or kidnapped into it – quickly assumed that the women and girls involved were co-conspirators rather than victims. Rather than liberating enslaved victims from brothels, application of the new law quickly shifted to morality, miscegenation, and non-coerced prostitution, with no conception in the law of the women having been victimized. For much of the twentieth century the Mann Act was typically used as a means to address organized crime (control of prostitution being one of the profit centers for the Mafia), but subsided into an infrequently used statute with low penalties reflecting it being seen as a "victimless crime."

The diminishment of the Mann Act played out even among its opponents, with the entire exercise dismissed as a moral panic intent on regulating female or African American sexuality, based on the all-too-real rhetorical and implementation excesses that followed in its wake. But, just because the public was in a moral or religious panic about a crime issue and policy-making elites responded to heavily gendered or paternalistic arguments with a clumsy or even harmful statute does not mean that crimes were not being committed against real people in the sex industry of the early 1900s. Nevertheless, the term "trafficking" lived on, with the cultural and historic baggage of the Mann Act and the assumption that the harm was not the treatment of the person but the moving of them across borders.[5]

The divide between the slavery statutes and the White Slave Trafficking Act was not a foregone conclusion in its early years, as federal prosecutors who were eagerly investigating and prosecuting cases under the peonage statutes used all of the statutory authorities at their disposal when faced with a situation in which women were held in sexual servitude – even pushing back to headquarters about whether a shift to Mann Act enforcement was distracting from the Thirteenth Amendment work. For instance, Louisiana U.S. Attorney Charlton Beattie, frustrated that his case agents from the nascent Bureau of Investigation (which would, as Jessica Pliley (2014) astutely points out in her book *Policing Sexuality*, soon leverage Mann Act investigations to become the modern FBI), was not shy in complaining to the attorney general that slavery cases should properly take precedence over prostitution investigations or even espionage cases.

In *United States v. Venters*, Beattie used both the peonage statute and the Mann Act to vindicate the rights of African American women held through debt bondage in sex slavery on a turpentine plantation while their male counterparts were similarly held to work in the forests. The novelty of Beattie's use of the new statute on behalf of Black women was pointed out in the press coverage of the case, which was fascinated to see the "White Slave Law Invoked by Negroes" (see New Orleans *Times-Picayune*, 1911). But, with some occasional exceptions, the slavery statutes became the means of prosecuting labor cases, with prostitution situations – even if evidence of slavery and abuse were present – routed into the Mann Act. Through bureaucratic inertia, this divide became hardened into different reporting structures as well as different units and offices and constituencies – structures so hardened that even after the TVPA addressed the conceptual gap, implementation involved trying to establish linkages across siloes rather than de-conflict these two approaches.

Peonage no more: federal criminal civil rights enforcement

While many people think of the 1950s and '60s as the era of the great Civil Rights movement, many of the gains that would transform America had their roots in the 1930s, and much of the initial work was based on the Thirteenth Amendment (Goluboff, 2007). In the face of the Great Depression, the Roosevelt administration dramatically expanded federal power, challenging old political and economic structures and forcing modernization in many of the places where involuntary servitude persisted – everything from rural electricity to close federal oversight of agriculture. Roosevelt's anti-slavery enforcement was in part due to public pressure from civil rights and workers' organizations concerned about the continued practice of peonage in the American South. "Anti-peonage societies" were formed to report cases, assist families in finding their children who had been lured into bondage by labor recruiters, and press for action.

At the Justice Department, that action came in the formation of the Civil Liberties Unit (soon renamed the Civil Rights Section), and just as during the Taft administration a generation earlier, the seriousness of the department was conveyed to U.S. attorneys' offices directly by the attorney general (Biddle, 1941). In the same week that the country was reeling from the attack on Pearl Harbor, Attorney General Francis Biddle instructed federal prosecutors and agents to concentrate on whether the person was being held in compelled service even absent proof of indebtedness (a disturbing number of cases at the time were being declined by southern U.S. attorneys for involving only involuntary servitude rather than peonage).

As evidence of prioritization, prosecutors and the FBI were directed to immediately notify the Civil Rights Section of any new matters, and indictments were only to be sought upon approval by headquarters. To drive the point home that lack of a debt was no longer an excuse not to bring cases, even the name of the enforcement effort was changed. The Roosevelt administration's shift from the "Peonage Program" to the "Involuntary Servitude and Slavery Program" would last until 2001, when another generation launched an intensified anti-slavery effort and the TVPA brought the international term "trafficking" into the mix.

Interestingly, Attorney General Biddle's memo anticipates and addresses many of the concepts that plague countries that must implement the Palermo Protocol without the U.S. history of anti-slavery enforcement – concepts such as the abuse of a position of vulnerability, the irrelevance of initial consent once coercive means have been used, and the difficulty of victim identification. In the memo, Attorney General Biddle instructs staff to look at cases holistically, dictating that open force, threats, or intimidation need not be shown; that it is a crime whether the person was made *either* to enter into or remain in service; and that evidence of occasional kind of treatment is not an absence of involuntary servitude.

The Civil Rights Section's ISS enforcement push, based on involuntary servitude (coerced service) rather than peonage (coerced service to repay a debt), followed almost 40 years in which the typical victim was an African American male in manual labor in a rural area, working under some form of a contract or as a result of a convict leasing or bonding scheme, had an unexpected benefit. Under the new approach, federal prosecutors began to see women workers as an important part of the protected classes, extending the section's work to cases involving domestic servants and, in at least one case (*United States v. Pierce*), using the ISS statutes rather than the Mann Act in a sex trafficking situation. Moreover, the new approach made it clear that the harm was not just against the governmental enforcement interest but also against the interests of the victims: in the pathbreaking 1947 domestic servant case of *United States v. Ingalls*, the court not only articulated a modern definition of "slavery" but for the first time ordered restitution to a survivor.

Slavery in a time of freedom: the transition to immigrant victims

As with the turpentine camps, much of the Southern economy changed dramatically after World War II due to automation, economic expansion, and increased alternatives for the African American community. As peonage became less central, much civil rights activism and enforcement shifted to anti-discrimination cases rather than the Thirteenth Amendment's prohibition of slavery and its legacies. While problems continued with Black migrant agricultural crews (often homeless men held through debt bondage and exploitation of their addiction to alcohol or drugs), by the 1970s cases of involuntary servitude were shifting to other vulnerable communities, especially immigrants.

How did the concepts of "trafficking" and "slavery" develop over the last 150 years? Over the last 25 years?

One of the things that marks the modern anti-trafficking movement is the recognition that migrants are often held in servitude through threats of deportation or by having their immigration documents confiscated. But in 1964 a highly influential case, *United States v. Shackney*, held otherwise. In that case, a Mexican family was kept on a chicken farm in Connecticut through threats of deportation. In effect, the appellate court held that they were not enslaved because the threats of deportation were not threats of putting them in jail but were in effect threats to release them – to give them a free ride home.

Much of the litigation of the next 20 years would be marked with attempts to push back against the *Shackney* decision in light of advances in understanding of power, dependency, and psychology (such as Stockholm syndrome or battered woman syndrome). Civil Rights Division prosecutors worked closely with legal aid lawyers in the South to address the vestiges of the African American debt bondage, brought cases involving religious cults and domestic service, and saw a dramatic increase in allegations involving immigrants. The late 1970s saw the creation of a specific position in the division to coordinate cases and outreach – the Involuntary Servitude and Slavery Coordinator. Momentum within the ISS program continued into the Reagan administration, which adopted provisions for how to deal with immigrant victims as opposed to deporting them.

What were the shortcomings that needed to be addressed in the late 1990s?

- Legal reform to undo the damage of *United States v. Kozminski*;
- Structural reforms such as the creation of task forces to replicate and disseminate the victim-centered multidisciplinary approach;
- Victim-care options that recognized the unique needs of trafficking victims;
- Increased penalties for labor violations to incentivize prosecutors to bring labor inspectors into the mix;
- Short and long-term immigration relief for victims to allow them to stay in the country and to receive services and benefits (undoing the restrictions of the 1996 Immigration Reform Act).

Unfortunately, that forward momentum was not to be long-lived. Restrictions on legal aid funding and pushback from the Farm Bureau and other industry groups began to hamstring efforts to protect agricultural workers. And in the 1988 case *United States v. Kozminski*, the Supreme Court undercut the legal theory that had emerged to challenge *Shackney* over the years in a series of cases – that slavery could be proven by establishing psychological coercion. The Kozminski Court limited the reach of the ISS statues to situations where service was compelled through overt force, threats of force, or threats of legal coercion. While the *Kozminski* decision was understandably seen as a major blow to the modern ISS program, Justice Sandra Day O'Connor provided in her majority opinion a means by which the subjective vulnerabilities of victims could be taken into account when determining if a particular threat was sufficient to overbear their will. Moreover, the opinion as much as invited Congress to revisit the issue should they want to address psychological coercion. Twelve years later, that finally happened, as the TVPA's forced labor and sex trafficking provisions passed overwhelmingly, repudiating *Kozminski* and *Shackney* and adopting the alternative psychological coercion standard almost verbatim while preserving the helpful portions of Justice O'Connor's opinion. Now, with the TVPA and the Palermo Protocol alike, there is a recognition that threats of deportation and other abuses of vulnerability are the types of coercion that can sustain a conviction for trafficking or slavery.

By the time President Clinton stepped into the Rose Garden to announce the 3P approach and Congress responded to the challenge of the *Kozminski* Court, the issue had sharpened greatly, in no small part due to high-profile prosecutions such as *United States v. Manasurangkun* (the "El Monte" garment factory sweatshop), *United States v. Paoletti* (the "deaf Mexican" trinket peddling case), and *United States v. Cadena* (a Florida brothel case). Despite the focus of the president's remarks on women and girls, these cases demonstrated the universality of compelled service and the need to focus on the denial of liberty rather than on international movement across "source, transit, and destination countries." The policies that he announced that day drove both the TVPA and UN Protocol negotiations, and the interagency process tasked by President Clinton provided a mechanism to address the challenges faced in those cases by the agents, prosecutors, and community members who had been working on the front lines of the long-standing ISS program.

While the identification of trafficking as a women's issue brought both political and rhetorical advantages, the TVPA was enacted as gender neutral, as is appropriate for criminal law. It was also neutral as to nationality of the victim and the type of service that victims were forced to perform (covering sex and labor trafficking alike). It addressed not only the needs of prosecutors or victim service providers but also created new structures within the U.S. government, such as the Office to Monitor and Combat Trafficking in Persons and the President's Interagency Task Force. And it created new reporting mechanisms, most notably the annual Trafficking in Persons Report.

Indeed, even before the passage of the TVPA there was a high level of oversight and coordination throughout the interagency process, guided from the White House by the President's Interagency Council on Women, headed by then First Lady Hillary Rodham Clinton, which played a critical function of coordination, support, and policy leadership. Not waiting for passage of legislation, the Justice Department and Labor Department launched an operations-focused interagency group at the sub-cabinet level – the National Worker Exploitation Task Force (WETF), which prioritized cases, produced training materials, convened service providers to workshop victim protection and prevention priorities, and recommended legislative fixes that became the TVPA. From that effort flowed an informal task force system tapping U.S. attorneys' offices in cities with a demonstrated trafficking problem and in-house expertise linking them up with local wage and hour offices and encouraging joint work not only among federal law enforcement (FBI, INS, and Border Patrol) but also the inclusion of local service providers and legal aid attorneys.

The influence of these informal task forces could be seen even a decade later. As their careers progressed, Civil Rights Division alumni replicated these structures as U.S. attorneys, state attorneys general, and district attorneys. During the Bush administration, the WETF task forces were replaced by more formal grant-funded efforts and relabeled as "trafficking" – an effort that was intensified under President Obama as Anti-trafficking Coordination Teams, leveraging localized interagency cooperation with federal funding opportunities, not only for law enforcement activities but also for victim services and legal assistance.

The victim-centered approach and the Thirteenth Amendment

The new techniques, disseminated by the WETF and loosely called the victim-centered, multidisciplinary approach, flowed from the historical cases in the ISS program, but most directly from several high-profile prosecutions of the 1990s: the *Flores*, *Manasurangkun*, and *Cadena* cases.

Miguel Flores was a crew leader who would use any means necessary to get the crops picked in the fields of the Southeastern United States in the early 1990s, and was valued for it by the growers who hired him. In Los Angeles, Auntie Suni Manasurangkun and her henchmen recruited Thai workers and held them behind razor wire in a garment factory in El Monte, California. These complex cases demanded innovative responses resulting in the development of a modern approach that would inform an international movement.

From these cases, federal actors learned to work together and with civil society organizations such as the Coalition of Immokalee Workers (in Southwest Florida) or the Thai Community Development Center (in Los Angeles), realizing that no one agency or entity had enough access, information, or power to operate alone in the dispersed and desperate economies of migrant agriculture and the garment industry. They learned about zones of impunity that were not just physical but also cultural and structural. Flores was able to brutalize his workers because he operated in fields where violence was tolerated like in the old days, where law enforcement's inability to communicate with immigrants silenced their voices, and where the growers would never be brought to justice for profiting from his abuse. Manasurangkun was able to hide in plain sight, maintaining a dummy factory with less exploited American workers for buyers to inspect while keeping her Thai seamstresses chained to their sewing machines in suburban anonymity.

It wasn't immediately apparent, but Miguel Flores even taught federal attorneys that the differences between sex trafficking and labor trafficking were largely an invented difference, as opposed to thinking about the reality of the women who are held in slavery. Redolent of the turpentine cases a century earlier, it was more than just picking fruit and vegetables that women workers were forced to do in the migrant camps.

Critically, these lessons from the *Flores* case were immediately put to the test in the next investigation, *United States v. Cadena*, where the victims were not farmworkers but women held in brothels for farmworker clients. In *Cadena*, which involved about two dozen women and girls from Veracruz held in a series of brothels across Florida and the Southeast and forced to service as many as 40 men a day, the *Flores* team reached not for the Mann Act but for the same Thirteenth Amendment provisions that had protected Flores' farmworker victims. Survivors from *Flores*, working with the nascent Coalition of Immokalee Workers, engaged with the *Cadena* victims, who were able to access attorneys from non-profit groups that handled domestic violence and sexual assault in the immigrant community. By listening to the women and girls, it became clear that the bifurcation between sex and labor trafficking was a false construct that ignored the lived experience of women in the workplace as well as in the sex industry. This did not have just a theoretical impact: only when federal investigators recast the case as Involuntary Servitude and Slavery as opposed to the Mann Act were the victims able to get out of immigration detention, where they had been jailed as alien prostitutes under immigration laws that dated back to the "White Slave Trafficking" years.

As discussed earlier, with only a few rare exceptions before the *Cadena* case, sex trafficking was dealt with throughout the twentieth century via the Mann Act, which only required proof that someone was taken across a state line or international border for prostitution, while labor trafficking was dealt with under the involuntary servitude statutes. Indeed, before *Cadena*, federal "sex trafficking" investigations had become a minor crime that focused on movement across state lines, assumed that the people who were involved were complicit in what was happening, and resulted in at best a slap on the wrist for the pimps, even if they had used force or threats.

The *Cadena* case changed all that, influencing not only U.S. enforcement strategies but also the development of the 3Ps, the Palermo Protocol, and the Trafficking Victims Protection Act. Indeed, the testimony of *Cadena* survivor "Inez" was seen by observers as having been the most important part of the TVPA debates, not only making senators concentrate more seriously on victim protection as opposed to just raising criminal penalties, but standing as an honest first-person account rather than the rehashing of "White Slavery" tropes and morality appeals that the committee was hearing from witnesses from the advocacy community (DeStefano, 2007).

So what does the new approach bring to the table?

Prevention: reporting and diplomatic engagement

In the wake of the new laws and international instruments of the year 2000, a foreign policy priority for the United States has been to establish the 3Ps and resulting policies and structures as the global anti-trafficking standard. The "3P approach" is no more self-executing in the modern era than were the Thirteenth Amendment and its implementing statutes in the 1800s. It takes implementation and institutionalization, which means government action. To accomplish institutionalization, the United States has used bilateral and multilateral diplomacy to drive toward "universal ratification" of the Palermo Protocol. Countries that accede to and ratify the Palermo Protocol agree to abide by its ethos and terms and make changes as necessary in domestic law or policy to carry out its mandates. Countries that are parties to the protocol typically therefore arrange their anti-trafficking regimes around the 3P structure, criminalize the acts of trafficking in a manner consistent with the new approach that focuses on exploitation of the victim, and establish victim identification and victim care standards in keeping with its provisions. The effort to achieve universal ratification of the protocol continues apace, with only 18 countries not yet being parties as of June 2019. As necessary as it was, even the Palermo Protocol is not a magic bullet. It is simply a guide to the laws and structures that need to be in place to address modern slavery.

What are some of the underlying drivers of modern slavery? Are they the same as in the early 1900s? What policy solutions would best address those root causes? What challenges would a policymaker face in focusing on the systemic underpinnings of human trafficking?

As with many international treaties, especially in the human rights field, states might ratify and participate in international fora but not incorporate the treaty obligations into domestic legislation, whether through lack of capacity, corruption, gridlock, or purposeful evasion. So each year, the United States publicly assesses what every country is doing to fight human trafficking as a way to not only capture the data but also to push active implementation and ongoing improvement. An annual report is mandated by the TVPA ("TIP Report") to assess countries' activities against minimum standards – themselves set forth in the TVPA – that flow from the 3Ps and are aligned to the Palermo Protocol. Carrying out in practice the obligations under that instrument should bring a country into full compliance with the TVPA minimum standards and vice versa. To compile this report, undertake diplomatic and development efforts in support of ongoing progress, and coordinate U.S. efforts against modern slavery, the TVPA created a dedicated unit at the State Department: the Office to Monitor and Combat Trafficking in Persons (the "TIP Office" or "J/TIP").

Section 108 of the TVPA sets forth a series of "Minimum Standards for the Elimination of Trafficking" against which countries' efforts are to be assessed. These minimum standards and their underlying criteria are made public each year in the TIP Report and on the TIP Office's website, including in-depth country narratives and an explanatory aid included in the report in recent years on "how to read a country narrative," delineating how the standards and criteria are applied in each analysis.

There are four minimum standards under the TVPA. The first three deal with prohibiting and adequately punishing the offense. The fourth minimum standard contains 12 sub-parts. These criteria are the heart of the analysis and roughly conform to the Palermo Protocol's "3P approach" of prevention, protection, and prosecution. Greater weight is given to protection and prosecution, since those are activities that have a real-world impact in rescuing victims and bringing their captors to justice, as opposed to incentivizing governments to undertake relatively low-cost and low-impact public awareness campaigns.

The TIP Report sets forth in detail the situation in each country, what the country is (or is not) doing to address human trafficking, and recommendations for how the country can come into compliance with the standards (refer to Table 2.2). The reports over time tell the story of the ebb and flow of policy development, political will, changes in migration patterns, and corruption. In

Table 2.2 Tier placement, criteria and examples

Tier Placement	*Criteria*	*Examples*[6]
Tier One	Countries whose governments fully meet the Minimum Standards.	Australia Denmark Israel Taiwan
Tier Two	Countries whose governments do not fully meet the Minimum Standards but are making significant efforts to meet them.	Albania Brunei Cambodia Turkey Uganda
Tier Two Watch List	Countries who fulfill the Tier Two criteria but: (a) the number of victims is very significant or is significantly increasing; (b) there is a failure to provide evidence of increasing efforts from the prior year; or (c) the finding that the country was making significant efforts was made on the basis of "commitments by the country to take additional future steps over the next year."	Algeria Bangladesh Hong Kong Malaysia Niger Saudi Arabia Togo Uzbekistan
Tier Three	Countries whose governments do not fully meet the Minimum Standards and are not making significant efforts to do so. Tier Three status can bear with it reputational harm and may also be subject to restrictions on U.S. foreign assistance funding.	Belize Eritrea Iran North Korea Russia Syria Venezuela

addition to the granular factual information in the country narratives, the report each year places each country into a "tier," based on its efforts within their national context and capabilities to address human trafficking through prevention, protection, and prosecution. While the statutory mandate of the report could have been met by simply posting a list of countries ranked in tiers, the need for transparency, recommendations for further action, and policy insights have instead resulted in a highly researched annual publication that provides an in-depth snapshot not only of the situation in each country but also trends and best practices in the trafficking arena as a whole.

The trafficking approach is not just a set of laws or policies that might conform to the U.S. minimum standards or the requirements of the Palermo Protocol, but it has also become a set of structural best practices, the success of which has been demonstrated in countries of varying capacity, legal system, and state of development. Tier One countries will often have both policy-level *interministerial task forces* and operations driving local-level multisectoral task forces through which police and prosecutors (hopefully in specialized units) can work with service providers and other local advocates. A transparent *national referral mechanism* and victim care scheme can be relied upon by service providers, survivors, and government anti-trafficking staff alike. The idea of a national referral mechanism works best when it is part of a *national plan of action* that is public, that everybody can buy into, and against which the state can be held accountable. And finally, there is *self-critical public reporting* analyzing the government's efforts with input from civil society and other actors. These structures, when not just announced but committed to and followed, continue to produce results.

Protection: the effect of the modern approach on victim identification

As set forth earlier, much of the last 40 years in the United States has been spent trying to solidify the legal recognition that coercion can be as much psychological as physical. By the early 1980s, it had become a generally accepted principle in U.S. law that once a person's will has been overborne and a climate of fear established, continued service, opportunity to escape, or even payment by the defendants did not excuse liability. The Palermo Protocol addresses this concept as well:

> The consent of a victim of trafficking in persons to the intended exploitation set forth in paragraph (a) or this article shall be irrelevant where any of the means set forth [e.g. coercion, fraud, deception, abuse or power or of a position of vulnerability] have been used.

These legal norms are not just instrumental insights to make enforcement easier, but are the underpinning of why victim protection is seen as co-equal to prosecution or prevention in the modern paradigm. In the modern anti-trafficking approach, creation and exploitation of a climate of fear through observable coercion (an objective fact) and the resulting overbearing of the victims' will (a subjective fact, as Justice O'Connor recognized in *Kozminski*) can be demonstrated not only by victims' retrospective accounts of their then existing physical or mental condition but also through objective manifestations of the victims' subjective mental state.

Protection – The Logics of the Competing Frames

A *slavery lens* focuses on the denial of a person's rights, so an inherent part of the solution is restoration and care.

A *commerce lens* focuses on movement of a person for prostitution (a form of contraband); as with all forms of contraband, the solution is to get rid of the offending item, in this case by punishing or deporting the "immoral" person.

What do the TVPA's victim protection provisions reveal about the 3P approach?

This is why trauma-informed responses are critical (see Williamson and Roe-Sepowitz, Chapter 14, this volume), not just for triers of fact in a courtroom but also for medical and social service providers and state actors whose analysis can make the difference between services and safety on the one hand and punishment and deportation on the other. The creation or exploitation of a climate of fear can result in actions that seem to contradict how a layperson might assume a victim should respond, such as by running to authorities for help and relaying the details of their ordeal. Those who labor under a climate of fear are likely to tell authorities the story that their bosses coached them to tell. Law enforcement or social service workers are seen not as rescuers or resources but as threats to one's daily existence, to keeping one's children, or being able to continue to work in an underground economy on their own terms if they could just get away from their exploiter. Moreover, people who have been held in sexual servitude (or suffered demeaning abuse in any slavery situation) often self-marginalize by anticipating that potential allies or rescuers will reject them, and pre-empting that response by simply staying silent about any abuse.

Police or other government officials are often present in work sites, but the workers are not in any position to tell their story without the supervisors knowing. Even officials who are in a factory to provide civil or administrative remedies (such as payment of back wages) are not trusted, especially because managers typically come up with ways to claw back any such payments. Especially when workers are from authoritarian countries, visits by officials from their home country (especially high-ranking officials) are often seen as attempts to suppress workers' demands in collusion with the factory owners instead of sincere attempts to uncover abuse and protect their nationals. Those who are under a climate of fear are unlikely to try to escape or seek help from authorities unless an opportunity to escape suddenly presents itself or the situation reaches a breaking point for the individual victim, in which they feel that to stay is to die or to see a loved one be ravaged. People under a climate of fear are much more likely to confide in or seek help from co-nationals or other workers than they are from authorities. And the time frame on which people under a climate of fear will get word out about their situation is not necessarily the time frame that an outside observer or government official would assume, prefer, or demand. Accordingly, in attempting to identify someone as a trafficking victim, a subjective test should be used, seeking to consider the individual workers' unique circumstances and vulnerabilities as well as objective manifestations of coercion.

The UNODC PEACE model for interviewing potential trafficking victims involves:

1. *Planning* and preparing for the interview;
2. *Engaging* with the victim/witness and explaining the process and content so that they are informed and empowered;
3. Obtaining the *account* of the victim-witness;
4. *Closing* an interview appropriately and respectfully; and
5. Carefully *evaluating* the content of the interview.

The tendencies of victims not to confide in authorities, and the ineffective techniques for addressing allegations of abuse are not only recognized in the United States but have also been highlighted in publications by the United Nations, the World Health Organization, and others. Indeed, the UN Office for Drugs and Crime sets forth a model for interviewing trafficking victims that represents an international standard for effective investigations, under a model that it terms "PEACE" (UNODC, 2009). In a nutshell, this approach requires a carefully thought-out, well-recorded inquiry in which care is taken to incorporate known effects of human trafficking into an investigative or diagnostic plan, including but not limited to fear of authorities, tendency for accounts to change over time, psychological impacts on victims, and problems with interpretation.

Prosecution: criminal law tools and techniques

The criminal provisions of the U.S. Trafficking Victims Protection Act share important aspects with the Palermo Protocol. All focus on the holistic experience of the victim, including reaching actors who are involved in each stage of the victim's journey into servitude. Whether recruiting or transporting someone, obtaining or maintaining their labor while harboring and employing them, or benefiting from the resulting revenue, one is liable for a trafficking offense whether the forms of coercion used to effectuate the exploitation are dramatic and overt (e.g. beatings, rapes, locks) or are more subtle (e.g. psychological coercion, manipulation of particular vulnerabilities, holding of documents).

The TVPA supplemented the pre-existing slavery and involuntary servitude statutes set forth in Chapter 77 of Title 18 of the U.S. Code, building on the cases that had successfully expanded the landscape of coercion beyond the initially appearing limitations of the *Kozminski* case. Despite the best efforts of the Civil Rights Division to continue bringing cases after *Kozminski*, by the late 1990s it was clear that for U.S. anti-slavery law to fully incorporate the lived reality of victims in the modern era, it would take congressional action. The TVPA thus updated the federal anti-slavery statutes to include victims who were enslaved through broader forms of coercion. It made it clear that psychological coercion, in the form of threats of serious harm and taking into consideration the victim's background, was sufficient to support a criminal conviction for these updated servitude statutes.

United States v. Bradley (2004)

Several groups of Jamaican men were held in forced labor as lumberjacks in New Hampshire through threats of serious harm and document confiscation. The Court of Appeals held that important concepts set forth in the pre-TVPA involuntary servitude cases continued to apply, even in cases brought under the new statutes. The court understood that the physically imposing young men could be held in servitude through threats of deportation, the creation of a climate of fear, and through the secondary effects of observed or rumored victimization, and held that once that climate of fear had been established the men had no affirmative duty to attempt an escape.

The two primary criminal statutes of the TVPA focus on sex trafficking and labor trafficking, respectively. While the sex trafficking statute does not require a showing of coercion when the victim is a child (in effect, a "statutory rape" approach), their definition of coercion is otherwise a shared one. The new statutes made it unlawful to provide or obtain the labor or services of a person by placing them in fear of serious harm, and a companion crime in the TVPA, the "document servitude" statute, sought to introduce an option for cases in which the coercion was more structural (that is, through seizure or holding of documents) than overtly physical. In rulings such as *United States v. Bradley* that maintain the hard-fought gains of prior litigation, post-TVPA courts have held that concepts set forth in cases brought under the pre-existing slavery statutes can be applied in modern cases as well.

Following the TVPA, corresponding anti-trafficking statutes have been passed across the United States, supplementing, but largely following the federal standards. Since the bulk of law enforcement in the United States is done at the state and local level, it was critical to put a state-level anti-trafficking legal structure in place, lest the field continue to be seen as a niche or specialized issue restricted to the much smaller federal criminal justice system that is better suited to complex, multidistrict, or international cases. Perhaps because of pre-existing familiarity with child prostitution enforcement techniques, as of this writing labor trafficking cases are only starting to be brought, with cases in California (farmworkers), Texas (Chinese buffets), and Minnesota (construction). It is a welcome development that state and local task forces that initially focused exclusively on child sex trafficking are now recognizing and responding to a broader set of exploitations while continuing to confront the needs of children in prostitution.

Prosecution: civil law remedies

Enforcement of the anti-trafficking statutes is not left to federal or even state and local law enforcement. Innovative plaintiffs and attorneys in the United States and other countries are increasingly taking on both individual cases and broad impact litigation. Federal civil and administrative enforcement offices such as the Equal Employment Opportunity Commission and the Department of Labor have created a well-rounded approach that cuts off avenues through which unscrupulous employers might evade responsibility.

The federal criminal anti-trafficking statutes became available for use by civil litigants through the Trafficking Victims Protection Reauthorization Act of 2003. Congress later clarified the breadth of the civil remedy, which is available against whomever "knowingly benefits, financially or by receiving anything of value from participation in a venture which that person knew or should have known has engaged in [trafficking]."

> The term "serious harm" means any harm, whether physical or nonphysical, including psychological, financial, or reputational harm, which is sufficiently serious, under all the surrounding circumstances, to compel a reasonable person of the same background and in the same circumstances to perform or to continue performing labor or services in order to avoid incurring that harm.

As with the criminal provisions of the TVPA, it took a few years for civil efforts to hit their stride, but by 2018 (the fifteenth anniversary of the statute) 299 federal civil cases had been brought under the TVPA. Unlike human trafficking in the criminal justice system, the civil cases to date have been overwhelmingly (92%) those involving labor trafficking, with domestic servants making up almost a third of all plaintiffs. Almost two thirds of the defendants have been corporate entities or organizations, and almost $108 million has awarded in public settlements and judgments (Vandenberg et al., 2018).

This trend toward civil litigation necessarily means that exploitative employers, abusive pimps, and those who benefit from their actions are now at risk of consequences from non-government actors – as well as exposure not just for the traffickers, but for those who do business with them. This then creates a duty of care up corporate supply chains and beyond the cut-outs of contractor relationships. Civil remedies, therefore, are not just avenues for justice and alternative forms of prosecution but will in coming years play an important role in prevention.

"3Ps and an R" (but in this chapter, that stands for rhetoric)

As mentioned earlier, the 3P concept has become so dominant that anti-trafficking actors often try to supplement it, whether by adding extra "Ps" such as partnership, or most commonly by adding the "R" of restoration/rehabilitation rather than subordinating such concepts into protection. This chapter, however, addresses another "R" – rhetoric. It is sometimes a distraction, sometimes a tool with which to obtain policy outcomes, and always a risk. This section examines some of the current rhetorical state of play and concludes that rhetorical echoes around morality, childhood, and nationalism pose perhaps the biggest threat to the continued implementation of the modern anti-trafficking regime.

How important should recruitment or movement be to the ideas of human trafficking? What impact does a movement or commerce-based lens have on policies?

First, the flip side to assumptions that trafficking involves kidnapping is a corresponding trope of recruitment. The recruitment trope is a very powerful one, especially in sex trafficking cases involving children who are U.S. citizens. Recruitment is often a key stage of a trafficking event, but it is not the heart of the issue. Think about the images in books from the early 1900s about the horrors of "White Slave Trafficking" – images of a dapper man claiming to be a talent agent wooing a woman from Eastern Europe about how glamorous it was going to be as a model or actress in America. Over a century later, almost the exact same idea of an untrustworthy Prince Charming appears in the "Blue Campaign," the Department of Homeland Security's public awareness effort against human trafficking. Whether long ago or today, it is perhaps more comfortable to think that people are only in the sex industry because they were kidnapped – or at least wooed and deceived into it.

> How do we respond to a victim in need who might also profess to love her trafficker, or who runs back to him despite the help we offer? How do we credit the initial decisions that people make, whether it is to trust a recruiter's tales or to do what it takes to survive once they are in the trafficking situation? How do we compete with recruiters who use the same methods of love and opportunity and glamour as did their predecessors of the early 1900s, for the exact same reason – because they work?

Thinking of those old images is important, not only to interrogate the recruitment trope but also because in order to effectuate the human rights ethos of the 3Ps and the Thirteenth Amendment, we need to actually think about what the women in those images may have wanted. Rather than focusing on what the man may have been promising or how reformers in America saw them, to instead think about the women that the illustrations represent – not as victims *but as empowered people who can and do make rational decisions about their lives.*

People who end up in servitude make rational decisions to emigrate for work, for opportunity, to escape abuse or poverty, or even simply boredom. They make decisions that might be noble, such as paying for a sibling's schooling. And they make decisions that might be seen as selfish or even immoral.

Some common (and wildly contradictory) myths about trafficking

Trafficking is a moral panic
Trafficking approach wasn't needed because of legacy laws/structures
Trafficking fits in everywhere and nowhere
Trafficking was/is a threat to pre-existing structures
Trafficking is too interdisciplinary a concept so it doesn't "fit"
Trafficking is too specialized a concept so it doesn't "fit"
Trafficking is about prostitution
Trafficking is about migrant prostitution
Trafficking is a migration issue
Trafficking is not a migration issue but about citizen children in prostitution
Trafficking is bad because it is backdoor criminalization of sex workers
Trafficking is bad because it is backdoor de-criminalization of prostitution
Trafficking is good because is a way to achieve an anti-prostitution victory
Trafficking is just about migrant workers
Trafficking as a frame ignores labor standards or need for unions
Trafficking gets too much funding and attention
Trafficking gets too little funding and attention
Trafficking is the same as chattel slavery
Trafficking isn't slavery or servitude at all
Trafficking is people smuggling
Trafficking is kidnapping
Trafficking happens "somewhere else"
Trafficking only happens to people who don't look like me
Trafficking is someone else's responsibility to confront, not mine.

They might not be the virginal and innocent victims that policymakers and the reformers would like to encounter instead of having more complex histories of drug abuse, promiscuity, crime, illegal migration, or prostitution. Rather than punishing survivors for failing to conform to pre-conceived notions of morality and worthiness that date back to the "White Slave Trafficking" years, perhaps we can strive to see them as empowered people making decisions about their lives that need to be understood and honored, even if they are not the decisions we would have wished for them.

Trafficking victims are first and foremost people, and they are as complex as that entails. To address their needs and bring traffickers to justice will typically bring us up against our own assumptions about race, sex, national origin, immigration, gender, capitalism, addiction, and social class (you know, all of the "easy topics"). One of the most pressing challenges of the trafficking movement in the United States, born as it was from the melding of the two closely related approaches (emerging perhaps in this chapter as freedom on the one hand and commerce/morality on the other) is to not drift into the comfortable policy space of the most sympathetic or consensus cases, but to instead consciously focus on the underlying harm: *violating a person's right of freedom by holding them in compelled service.*

Case Study: The "Deaf Mexicans"

In the late 1990s, dozens of deaf and hearing impaired young men and women from Mexico were discovered in New York City where they were being forced to beg on the streets and subways, not only through their disability and vulnerability as undocumented immigrants but also by a poisonous mix of threats and flattery, incentives and violence. During the months-long debriefing process that followed, investigators and social support team members learned almost as much about Deaf culture as they did about the traffickers' scheme. Because of trauma effects and the differences between American Sign Language and Mexican Sign Language, witness interviews that should have taken only hours took days. Notable throughout the process was that when the workers did not want to answer a thorny or emotional question, or did not want to be asked it in the first place, they turned their heads away from the questioner. Unlike in the hearing world, the deaf Mexicans could, merely by averting their gaze, end the interaction and delay or avoid the offending interaction. Investigators had to work hard to earn the witnesses' trust, enough to have them rejoin the conversation even as they had to recount assaults, rapes, and the shattering of the American dream by their traffickers. Turning away is a protective mechanism, releasing stress and providing at least a moment in a place of comfort.

Discussion Questions

1. What are the ways in which we ourselves turn away from trafficking victims, whether directly, rhetorically, or in policy choices?
2. Do we favor one type of trafficking because it conforms to our expectations or is easier to confront?
3. Do we turn away from victims who disappoint us or do not conform to our expectations of how they "should" react?

If reminding the reader of the primacy of the underlying right to freedom (whether guaranteed in the United States by the Thirteenth Amendment or globally by Article IV of the Universal Declaration of Rights) sounds like a note of caution, there's a reason. The types of servitude that are being addressed and that receive the most rhetorical and political attention seem to have become imbalanced in recent years in the United States. For instance, in fiscal year 2017, sex trafficking prosecutions made up 471 (94%) of the 499 federal convictions obtained in trafficking cases, and calls to the national hotline were running at about 71% sex trafficking. This is in dramatic contrast to the civil lawsuits that have been filed in the United States, where 92% involved labor trafficking, or in the United Kingdom, a country with similar legal system and economy, where 72% of the calls to their hotline concerned labor trafficking. Instead of long-term civil rights or organized crime investigations, enforcement efforts are often undertaken by local law enforcement or federal task forces using anti-prostitution "sting" operations, with officers posing online as prostituted children or pimps. Such approaches might result in arrests and prosecutions but often do not free any victims from servitude.

It may seem strange to have to stress the centrality of involuntary servitude in a movement that so often uses (and has even been criticized for using) the language of slavery. But the price of admission for claiming to stand in the shoes of the antebellum abolitionists or to dare to equate modern slavery to the chattel slavery of the trans-Atlantic trade has to be to actually then live up to that frame rather than cavalierly use the words as rhetoric only to ignore many of the forms of modern slavery, to ignore the underlying causes of human trafficking, or to favor only one victim class when it comes time for services or funding.

To engage in comfortable enforcement patterns, political wins, or familiar fights is to turn away from the foreign victim, the adult in prostitution (perhaps initially as a matter of non-coerced choice), or the immigrant worker. It is to avoid uncomfortable conversations about the devolution of child care to women who themselves have left their families, about how foreign construction workers have become critical to wealthy economies, and about business and consumer responsibility for abuses in supply chains. But to turn away in that manner does not make those inconvenient or uncomfortable truths go away: such a shifting of externalities has just as pernicious an effect as does corruption or outright evasion.

Prevention: transparency and worker-led social responsibility (WSR)

One way to shift those externalities back to those who benefit from modern slavery is transparency. Transparency efforts expose abuses in supply chains or business models that might be a conscious choice or may have simply become accepted practice over the years. Transparency can have a "soft" effect (allowing consumers to weigh their buying preference) or "hard" effect (providing a roadmap for criminal investigators, civil litigants, and regulators). The United States has been quite active in this aspect of the anti-trafficking fight with the passage of the California Supply Chain Transparency Act, the promulgation of federal procurement standards for government contractors, and the closing of loopholes in the Tariff Act to prevent the importation of goods tainted by forced labor. Building on the American experience, the United Kingdom's 2015 Modern Slavery Act (MSA) not only re-focused its criminal law lens on servitude rather than transportation but also included robust transparency legislation that puts an even greater responsibility on corporations.

The California law is a pure "sunlight' law, requiring companies of a certain size to publicly post whether they have anti-slavery policies, and if so, what they are. The UK law is more directive. It doesn't give companies the option to not have such procedures in place but requires CEOs and company directors to personally sign a submission setting forth their anti-slavery activities and file it with regulators. That document can be looked at by regulators and police, and the initial years' submissions are already being analyzed by nonprofits and academics. Rather than being attacked as a restraint on free enterprise, the MSA is being lauded by scrupulous businesses because it levels their ethical playing fields. Companies that are examining their inputs for sexual assault, sexual harassment, and forced labor – whether through a sense of morality or in response to scandals – fear being put at a disadvantage against unscrupulous competitors. In early 2018, Australia adopted similar requirements both at the national level and in the major population and economic hub of New South Wales.

Under the sunlight of the MSA filings, companies cannot for long outsource their social auditing to firms or organizations focused on environmental sustainability rather than worker protection (LaBaron, 2018), and it will be harder to shunt off trafficking and child labor into corporate social responsibility (CSR) departments as opposed to including them in the work of business operations, procurement, or risk management professionals.

These laws could be transformative: by including companies and consumers, responsibility for this issue is no longer confined to small, underfunded enforcement agencies alone. Going forward, it will take sustained oversight by both government and civil society to prevent the new transparency laws from being undercut by the all-too-common problem of good-hearted CSR specialists being ignored within their companies, or marketing departments spinning sustainability into a false picture of happy workers, grateful communities, and an improved environment by "greenwashing" through toothless certification schemes.

How best to prevent greenwashing? The other side of the transparency coin is worker-led social responsibility (WSR), which flows from the combination of the victim-centered anti-trafficking approach and the traditional ethos of the labor movement. Unlike CSR, which responds to businesses' needs to be seen as virtuous and sustainable and is thus susceptible to corporate pressure, WSR is grounded in the centrality of the workers and their experiences. Under WSR, a product cannot be seen as sustainable if the hands that made it were unfree or suffering from abuse, no matter how environmentally sound or organic it might appear.

> How will the Immokalee approach work in other industries?
>
> How can we see an impact on workers' rights more broadly, as well as in slavery, sexual harassment, and sexual abuse?
>
> How can the modern anti-trafficking movement incorporate the Fair Food ethos of workers as auditors and the CIW ethos of survivors as leaders?

One of the leading examples of WSR is that of the Coalition of Immokalee Workers (CIW) and the Fair Food Program. Following *United States v. Flores*, so many trafficking cases were uncovered in Southwest Florida that it became known as "Ground Zero for modern slavery." But the survivors of those cases were not just passive participants in criminal prosecutions. As members of the CIW, they have transformed the very fields in which they were abused. Years of pressure – including boycotts, marches, shareholder activism, and street theatre – resulted in close alliances with major tomato buyers such as Walmart and McDonalds in order to pressure the growers who had profited from the abuses of Flores and other crew leaders. After fierce resistance, the growers agreed to oversight by the Fair Food Standards Council, a rigorous mechanism that monitors conditions in the fields, effectively harnessing over 30,000 educated and empowered workers as auditors. Knowing that they will not be retaliated against for reporting abuse, workers are not just preventing beatings and enslavement but also improving health and safety. Moreover, the effort has had a dramatic effect on the lives of women workers, as once rampant sexual harassment and gender discrimination are becoming a thing of the past. Growers and retailers who had resisted inclusion of workers' voices in the process are now proud of the model that they have built together.

The Immokalee model, arising from survivors and bringing buyers and growers to the table, is the future. As its lessons are brought to scale, it will honor the survivors of almost 200 years of abuse in Southwest Florida – not just the victims in the *Flores* case and other modern prosecutions but also the unacknowledged people who labored in those same fields in antebellum slavery or Jim Crow debt peonage, with no one hearing their cries or crediting their experiences. Incorporating survivors into all aspects of the modern slavery fight as part of a worker-led social responsibility movement will truly deserve to be called a "best practice."

Prevention: survivor inclusion and empowerment

The idea of worker-led social responsibility, as embodied by the CIW and Fair Food Program, is not only a model for labor relations; it is also living proof of the power of survivors as actors and full partners in the fight against trafficking. As with supply-chain transparency, the idea of survivor input is coming into vogue, with the U.S. Advisory Council and the awarding of the Nobel Peace Prize to Yazidi survivor Nadia Murad for her activism against ISIS' enslavement of young women in Syria and Iraq (see Murad, 2017).

The U.S. Advisory Council advises the president and the interagency bodies on anti-trafficking policy. Created by Congress in 2015, it is a blend of U.S. citizens and immigrants of all races, of men and women, of those who have suffered sex trafficking and labor trafficking. It has made recommendations on issues such as the rule of law, public awareness, victim services, labor laws, and grantmaking. And what is inspiring and interesting is that this blend, this community, is a coming together driven by the survivors' understanding of each other.

This solidarity among survivors is happening even as various advocacy or policy groups that address different aspects of trafficking have drifted apart or taken oppositional stances, often around whether to concentrate on labor or sex trafficking, or whether all prostitution should be considered trafficking per se. And yet, when survivors come together, those things drop away because they recognize in each other what happened to themselves. Particularly interesting, given the different camps in the advocacy community on the sex/labor continuum, has been the Survivor Advisory Committee's call for increased participation by the Department of Labor in the anti-trafficking fight (a restoration in some ways of the Clinton-era Worker Exploitation Task Force) in recognition that labor standards and enforcement might just prevent exploitation in the first place (U.S. Advisory Council on Human Trafficking, 2016).

Incorporation of survivors' experience and expertise perhaps is the most important best practice of all, and perhaps the most challenging for a movement that has for 200 years been driven by compassionate allies as much by as survivors themselves. If the anti-trafficking movement (whether in civil society or government) is serious about being modern abolitionists rather than simply using metaphors of slavery and freedom to advance other policy goals, the conversation has to be one which talks about people – that meets them on *their* turf, in their own lived and perceived reality.

But to do so will mean to finally focus on what people went through rather than what we think about what they did, to listen to their opinion about effective interventions rather than impose what we think is the answer, and to accept them as multi-faceted and multi-motivated independent actors rather than simply assigning them to the most convenient bureaucratic or conceptual silo that already exists.

Best practices and next steps

Having set forth the development of the various legacy approaches that combined into the modern anti-trafficking effort, U.S. diplomatic and enforcement activities, some important rhetorical and conceptual aspects, and some causes for hope by harnessing workers' and survivors' voices, this chapter concludes with a couple of quick thoughts on best practices and where the modern anti-slavery movement might be headed.

By some measures, the U.S. response continues to be in the lead. Across the country, one sees integrated task force models, where partnerships have been established in which participants understand each other's perspectives and missions and are able to cede control to each other when necessary. That means law enforcement is willing to listen to and trust nonprofit and service provider partners, and service providers are willing to listen to and trust law enforcement partners.

We are currently seeing an uptick in shelter options. The energy around shelter has exploded in the United States, often because of compassionate local responses from people whose hearts go out to child sex trafficking victims. State child protective services departments are much less likely than in the past to view the anti-trafficking movement as a threat to budgets or authority, and are working to respond to child victims. Now will come the challenge of making sure that there are also shelter operation standards, thought-out methods for therapy and response, and professionalization within this part of the movement (see Meshelemiah, Chapter 12 and Torres, Nsonwu, Cook Heffron, and Busch-Armendariz, Chapter 13, this volume).

In recognition that the trafficking offense negates voluntariness and therefore culpability, both U.S. and international regimes are examining how to deal with crimes committed in the course of being trafficked. In the United States, high-profile cases of clemency for sex trafficking victims who have been convicted for fighting back against their abusers or clients have periodically captured public attention. State and local governments have passed "safe harbor" laws to shield sex trafficking victims from prosecution, and some jurisdictions are experimenting with ways to expunge past criminal convictions. In the United Kingdom, cases involving children held in cannabis cultivation and processing have sharpened that country's approach to trafficking for forced criminality. Hopefully, these developments will not simply have limited legal effect in particular cases, but will chip away at the old Mann Act way of thinking that a disreputable or delinquent child is less entitled to have their tormenters brought to justice.[7]

Anti-trafficking efforts are ranging from old-fashioned detective work and relationships to high-tech frontiers. Technology is being harnessed to better understand pimps' business models, labor recruiters' schemes, and best practices in victim care across regions. Online platforms used by traffickers have been identified and legislated against. Artificial intelligence such as textual analysis and facial recognition are helping not just to identify victims but also to contextualize their narratives. Even satellites are being brought to bear to track slave vessels in the fishing fleet and to chart the effect of climate change on at-risk communities.

Less promising, however, are some of the cracks in the system. In the United States, service providers and even law enforcement are reporting that stricter application of the T-visa and continued presence rules by U.S. Citizenship and Immigration Services (CIS) are making an application for immigration relief a chancy proposition, and CIS has announced that applicants who are rejected will be put in removal proceedings rather than allowing them to revert to their prior informal situations, as was past practice. Victim care seems at risk, with challenges to legal representation of victims (or potential victims) as well as an attempt by the Trump administration to use the Unaccompanied Alien Minors provision of the 2008 TVPRA to separate families in an ill-conceived border control push.

So too, efforts to bring the issue of commercial sexual exploitation of children into the trafficking lens so that prostituted children are not seen as delinquent but instead dependent have been successful in lowering the arrest rate for child prostitution, but they seem to have created a favored class for many policymakers and police agencies – so much so that many new anti-trafficking efforts in the United States see trafficking only as an issue of prostituted U.S. citizen children (a worthy cause itself) and make little provision for investigating cases involving other situations or caring for other types of victims. Against those challenges, however, remains a well-conceived anti-trafficking regime, based on freedom and the 3Ps, staffed by committed and innovative public servants and citizens, with an ever-growing research base and community of interest.

In 2010, at the rollout of the Trafficking in Persons Report, Secretary of State Hillary Rodham Clinton characterized 2000–2010 as a decade of development in which the first laws and structures came online and a global understanding of trafficking took place. That day she called for 2010–2020 to be a "decade of delivery," and in many ways that has happened. As of this writing, the Palermo Protocol is nearing universal ratification, traffickers are being arrested, and victims are being assisted worldwide. International best practices in governance structures are now well-known and have been adopted widely: interministerial policy groups and dedicated police units; national referral mechanisms that chart the path of victim identification and care (at least on paper); national plans of action that track policy development and practice; and public reporting schemes that serve not only as a periodic public release of facts but also as a signal of political will.

These structures are valuable and are the result of the years of hard policy work. But the test of these structures now needs to be to what use they are put and what resources and actions flow from them. It will take a dramatic increase in enforcement, identification, and victim care to narrow the yawning gap between the number of victims governments report having identified (100,408 in the 2018 TIP Report) and the number of estimated victims in the world (24.9 million in the 2018 report from Walk Free and the International Labour Organization reports). It is going to be a challenge. There will be successes and there will be failures. Perhaps the biggest challenge is to channel the rhetorical and emotional energy around the issue to change justice systems – not only to bring some modicum of justice but to do so in a manner that minimizes the hurt that individual survivors go through in the process.

Conclusion

This chapter has interrogated the language of the anti-trafficking movement, the history of anti-slavery enforcement, and some of the responses that the modern approach has made possible. So what is next?

In this coming third decade of the modern anti-slavery movement, perhaps talking about trafficking honestly and in a manner that honors the lived experience of survivors will require a shift beyond the plain language of the legal instruments. There will always be a need for discussion about important and persistent topics, such as the heartbreak of child slavery, the impact on women of the sex industry and the domestic service economy, or the globalization of marginalized labor and the need for better data. But perhaps in this next decade those conversations, and the research that drives them, could demand responses that are *service-neutral, universal, victim-centered, justice-seeking*, and *responsible.*

A service-neutral approach is one in which governments identify victims and address their needs no matter what the underlying service is: whether they suffered in a brothel or a garment factory; whether they were in prostitution, domestic service, or on a farm. Universality focuses not on the origin or citizenship, sex, or age of the victim but on one's status as a person with an inalienable right to freedom, irrespective of gender, age, nationality, or present with authorization or illegally.

Can better knowledge about and understanding of the development of modern anti-slavery efforts contribute to more effective policies against human trafficking? How?

Service neutrality and universality flow naturally from a rights-based approach and demand that policy and practice focus on the lived experiences and needs of the victim. A rights-based approach (which focuses on the protection of an individuals' human or civil rights, vindication of those rights if denied, and restoration of the victim following a breach) demands in turn a victim-centered approach in which the needs of the victim are paramount rather than the security imperative of the state, the processes and procedures of the justice system, or the bureaucratic mandates of governments or international agencies. Such an approach, which should be an aspiration for all involved in human trafficking, brings the focus on slavery and freedom, so that one class of victim is not favored over another.

Justice-seeking may sound naïve in a world where much of law enforcement is tasked with maintaining social order rather than vindicating the rights of the individual or making them whole, but so much of trafficking operates in the zones of impunity caused by the inability of vulnerable people and communities to access justice. A justice-seeking approach therefore combines criminal law outcomes with real penalties for traffickers, restitution and other forms of compensation, civil remedies, and even restorative justice where appropriate (see Bussey-Garza, Dempsey, Martin, and Rhodes, Chapter 5, this volume).

Finally, systems must factor in responsibility, not simply shunting off legal responsibility to low-level employers or recruiters – who may be in precarious positions themselves or may even have been victims at one point; certainly not by blaming victims for being immoral, criminal, illegal migrants, or simply credulous; and certainly not by failing to recognize systemic underpinnings such as global capital, unexamined supply chains, and the failure to look for slavery hidden in plain sight. Responsibility, and even criminal culpability, needs not to be an externality in the modern economy shifted off onto convenient villains or vulnerable victims but instead recognized by consumers, companies, bankers, and governments.

So what *are* we talking about when we talk about trafficking? From a U.S. civil rights perspective, this modern movement was called human trafficking largely because the government simultaneously negotiated the international treaty and rewrote domestic legislation. In the late 1990s, the attention of the world was largely on a resurgent trade in Eastern European women as a result of the end of the Cold War and the conflict in the former Yugoslavia. At the Justice Department, the first one-paragraph draft that grew into the Trafficking Victim Protection Act was simply to achieve a much-needed update to the post–Civil War involuntary servitude and slavery statutes – a "*Kozminski* fix" that would respond to the lessons of *Flores, Manasurangkun*, and *Cadena*. The cost of admission was the importation of this term "trafficking" from the international discourse.

And what that naming decision did, of course, is confuse everyone, because then people thought that it was a crime of movement or of prostitution, which returns us to concepts embodied in U.S. law by the Mann Act as opposed to the Thirteenth Amendment, rather than having a crisp anti-slavery lens with a clear focus on the rights-based approach that drove the 3Ps, the TVPA's attempt to bridge and combine the legacy of the "White Slave Trafficking" approach may have in some ways brought with it that effort's controversies, shortcomings, and moral and gender assumptions, leading to 20 years of misunderstandings and false starts.

Perhaps therefore the title of this chapter should instead have been "Twenty Years of Confusion." But hopefully, as the modern movement enters its next phase, the voices and experiences of practitioners, investigators, service providers, and especially survivors will bring clarity and drive rights-based responses that in deeds as well as words bring to life the 3Ps and the promises contained in the Thirteenth Amendment, the Palermo Protocol, and the TVPA. Hopefully, we will not avert our gaze but will confront their lived experiences, so that when we talk about trafficking, everyone who hears us will know that we are talking about that quixotic and quintessentially American notion – that we are talking about freedom.

Notes

1 This chapter expands on the symposium keynote for the conference "Evolving Promising Practices in the U.S. Anti-trafficking Field," Florida State University Center for the Advancement of Human Rights, February 1, 2018 (commemorating the 20th Anniversary of *United States v. Cadena*). Apologies to Raymond Carver.

2 Robina Fellow in Modern Slavery, Gilder Lehrman Center for the Study of Slavery, Resistance, and Abolition of the MacMillan Center for International and Area Studies, Yale University. Formerly

Ambassador-at-Large to Monitor and Combat Trafficking in Persons (U.S. Department of State), and Involuntary Servitude and Slavery Coordinator (U.S. Department of Justice, Civil Rights Division). Research for this chapter was supported in part by the Open Society Foundations. The opinions expressed herein are the author's own and do not necessarily express the view of the Open Society Foundations.

3 The United States' version of the "White Slave Trafficking Act" of the early 20th Century is also referred to as the "Mann Act," having been introduced by Congressman James Mann.

4 Maps and other materials on display in the Coalition of Immokalee Workers' Modern Slavery museum demonstrate the continuity of forced labor in the same fields from which their members have been liberated in recent years. See Katrina vanden Heuvel, "Florida's modern slavery . . . the museum." *The Nation*, March 29, 2010. Retrieved from www.npr.org/templates/story/story.php?storyId=125296794.

5 Doezema (1999) places the Mann Act in the context of the white slavery campaigns and notes the re-emergence of the concept as "trafficking in women" starting in the 1980s.

6 U.S. Department of State. (2018). Retrieved from www.state.gov/j/tip/rls/tiprpt/2018/282584.htm.

7 See, e.g., *In re Lamb*, DJ#50–20–38, Investigative Report of Special Agent Malcom Carr, Classified Subject Files of the Department of Justice, National Archives, Washington DC, Record Group 50 (1945) (recommending no prosecution of allegations by 16-year-old that she had been held against her will and forced into prostitution because of secondhand information provided by local law enforcement that the teenager "was considered undesirable generally because of her drinking of intoxicants and because of her running with men and boys").

Supplemental learning materials

Books

Blackmon, D. (2008) *Slavery by another name: The re-enslavement of black people in America from the Civil War to World War II.* New York, NY: Anchor.

Busch-Armendariz, N. B., Nsonwu, M., & Heffron, L. C. (2018). *Human trafficking: Applying research, theory, and case studies.* Los Angeles, CA: SAGE Publications, Inc.

Carver, R. (1981). *What we talk about when we talk about love: Stories.* New York, NY: Knopf.

Daniel, P. (1973). The *shadow of slavery: Peonage in the South, 1901–1969.* Urbana: University Illinois Press.

Gallagher, A. (2010). *The international law of human trafficking.* Cambridge: Cambridge University Press.

Goluboff, R. (2007). *The lost promise of civil rights.* Cambridge: Harvard University Press.

Hall, S. (2014). *Hidden girl: A true story of a modern day child slave.* New York, NY: Simon & Schuster.

Institute of Medicine and National Research Council. (2014). *Confronting commercial sexual exploitation and sex trafficking of minors in the United States: A guide for providers of victim and support services.* Washington, DC: National Academies Press.

Marquis, S. L. (2017). *I am not a tractor: How Florida farmworkers took on the fast food giants and* won. Ithaca, NY: Cornell University Press.

Pliley, J. (2014). *Policing sexuality.* Cambridge: Harvard University Press.

Quirk, J. (2011). *The anti-slavery project: From the slave trade to human trafficking.* Philadelphia, PA: University Pennsylvania Press.

Smith, H. (2014). Walking *prey: How America's youth are vulnerable to sex slavery.* New York, NY: Palgrave Macmillan.

Articles and reports

Besant, A. (1888, June 23). White slavery in London. *The Link: A Journal for the Servants of Man.* Retrieved from www.mernick.org.uk/thhol/thelink.html

Bowe, J. (2003, April 21). Nobodies. *The New Yorker.* Retrieved from www.newyorker.com/magazine/2003/04/21/nobodies

Brunvskis, A., & Surtees, R. (2015). *Reframing trafficking prevention: Lessons from a "Positive Deviance" approach.* Nexus Institute Allkopi, AS: Norway.

Chase, R. T. (2015). We are not slaves: Rethinking the rise of carceral states through the lens of the prisoners' rights movement. *Journal of American History, 102,* 73. Retrieved from https://academic.oup.com/jah/article/102/1/73/686880

Fair Food Program. (2018, April). *Annual report 2017.* Retrieved from www.fairfoodstandards.org/reports/

Gleason, K. A., & Cockayne, J. (2018). *Official development assistance and target 8.7: Measuring aid to address forced labor, modern slavery, human trafficking and child labor.* United Nations University.
Government of the United Kingdom. (2018). *Slavery and human trafficking in supply chains: guidance for businesses.* Retrieved from www.gov.uk/government/publications/transparency-in-supply-chains-a-practical-guide
International Bar Association (September 2016). Presidential Task Force on Human Trafficking, Human Trafficking and Public Corruption. London.
Laite, J. (2017). Traffickers and pimps in the era of white slavery 237. *Past & Present*, 237–269. Retrieved from https://academic.oup.com/past/article/237/1/237/4627928
Levy, A. (2018). *Fact sheet: Human trafficking & forced labor in for-profit detention facilities*, Washington, D.C. The Human Trafficking Legal Center.
Lui, M.T.Y. (2009). Saving young girls from Chinatown: White slavery and woman suffrage. *Journal of the History of Sexuality, 18*, 393. Retrieved from www.jstor.org/stable/20542730?seq=1#metadata_info_tab_contents
McCarthy, J., & Moloney, K. (2018, February). *Sydney archdiocesan Anti-slavery task force.* Report to the Archbishop of Sydney.
McKeown, M., & Ryo, E. (2008). The lost sanctuary: Examining sex trafficking through the lens of United States v. Ah Sou. *Cornell International Law Journal, 41*, 739.
Smith, S. L. (2015). Emancipating peons, excluding coolies: Reconstructing coercion in the American West. In G. Downs & K. Masur (Eds.), *The world the Civil War made* (pp. 46–74). Chapel Hill: University of North Carolina Press.
(1917, May). The scope of the white slave trafficking act. *Virginia Law Review, 4*, 653.
United States Customs & Border Protection. *Forced labor.* Retrieved from www.cbp.gov/trade/programs-administration/forced-labor
U.S. Department of State. (2001). *Trafficking in persons reports* (annual reports since 2001) ("TIP Report")

References

Chacon, J. M. (2006). Misery and myopia: The failures of U.S. efforts to stop trafficking. *Fordham Law Review*, 74(6), 2977–3040.
Chuang, J. (2006). The United States as global sheriff: Using unilateral sanctions to combat human trafficking. *Michigan Journal of International Law*, 27(2), 437–494.
Clinton, W. J. (1998, March 11). Memorandum on steps to combat violence against women and trafficking in women and girls. *U.S. Government Publishing Office.* Retrieved from www.govinfo.gov/content/pkg/WCPD-1998-03-16/pdf/WCPD-1998-03-16-Pg412.pdf
DeStefano, A. (2007). *The war on human trafficking: U.S. policy assessed.* New Brunswick, NJ: Rutgers University Press.
Desyllas, M. C. (2007). A critique of the global trafficking discourse and U.S. policy. *Journal of Sociology & Social Welfare, 34*, 4, Article 4.
Doezema, J. (1999). Loose women or lost women? The re-emergence of the myth of white slavery in contemporary discourse of trafficking in women. *Gender Issues, 18*(1), 23–50.
Farrell, A., & Fahy, S. (2009). The problem of human trafficking in the U.S: Public frames and policy responses. *Journal of Criminal Justice, 37*(6), 617–626.
Gallagher, A. (2010). *The international law of human trafficking.* Cambridge, NY: Cambridge University Press.
LaBaron, G. (2018). The global business of forced labour. *Sheffield political economy research institute.* Retrieved from http://globalbusinessofforcedlabour.ac.uk/wp-content/uploads/2018/05/Report-of-Findings-Global-Business-of-Forced-Labour.pdf
Levy, Alexandria and Vandenberg, Martina, (December 2018). *Federal Human Trafficking Civil Litigation: 15 Years of the Private Right of Action.* The Human Trafficking Legal Center. Washington DC.
Metler, K. (2019, January 17). Trump keeps mentioning taped-up women at the border. Experts don't know what he is talking about. *The Washington Post.* Retrieved from www.washingtonpost.com/politics/2019/01/17/trumps-stories-taped-up-women-smuggled-into-us-are-divorced-reality-experts-say/?noredirect=on&utm_term=.75501b7684c6
Murad, N. (2017). *The last girl: My story of captivity, and my fight against the Islamic State.* New York, NY: Time Duggan Books.
Outland, R. B. (2004). *Tapping the Pines: The Naval Stores Industry in the American South.* Baton Rouge, Louisiana State University Press.
Rawls, W. Jr. (1981, November 19). Migrant slavery persists on Southeast's farms. *The New York Times*, p. A1.
(1911, August 18). The white slave law invoked by negroes. *New Orleans Times-Picayune.*

Trafficking Victims Prevention and Protection Reauthorization Act of 2018, Pub. L. No. 115–393, as codified at 22 U.S.C. § 3903.

Trafficking Victims Protection Reauthorization Act of 2008, Pub. L. No. 110–457, 122 Stat. 5044, as codified at 22 U.S.C. § 7101.

United Nations. (2001). *Protocol to prevent, suppress and punish trafficking in persons, especially women and children, supplementing the United Nations convention against transnational organized crime.* Retrieved from www.ohchr.org/en/professionalinterest/pages/protocoltraffickinginpersons.aspx

United Nations Office on Drugs and Crime. (2009). *Anti-human trafficking manual for criminal justice practitioners.* Retrieved from www.unodc.org/documents/human-trafficking/TIP_module8_Ebook.pdf

U.S. Advisory Council on Human Trafficking. (2016). *Annual report.* Retrieved from www.state.gov/documents/organization/263434.pdf

U.S. Congress. (2017). The Frederick Douglass Trafficking Victims Protection and Reauthorization Act of 2018, P.L. 115–425 (January 8, 2019).

Victims of Trafficking and Violence Protection Act of 2000, Pub. L. No. 106–386, 144 Stat. 1464, as codified at 22 U.S.C. § 7101.

Weitzer, R. (2007). The social construction of sex trafficking: Ideology and institutionalization of a moral crusade. *Politics & Society, 35*(3), 447–475.

Weitzer, R. (2010). The movement to criminalize sex work in the United States. *Journal of Law and Society, 37*(1), 61–84.

Wickersham, G. (1911, August 10). Department of Justice letter # 150153–50. *The Peonage Files of the U.S. Department of Justice*, p. B18325. In National Records and Archives Administration (1901–1945) [microfilm]. (Reel 9, microfilm 0640).

3

INTERNATIONAL POLICIES TO COMBAT HUMAN TRAFFICKING

Natalia Ollus and Matti Joutsen

Abstract

Trafficking in human beings has received increased attention internationally, regionally and nationally, and a variety of policy approaches have been adopted. This chapter examines the evolution of international policy to prevent and respond to human trafficking. Examples of local and national policies from different parts of the globe are provided, and their impact is assessed.

Learning Objectives

At the end of the chapter, readers will be able to:

1. Understand the key factors that have guided the emergence of international concern in responding to human trafficking;
2. Identify the most important international frameworks for and key actors involved in responding to human trafficking, and their main elements; and
3. Understand the main motivations of the different actors involved in responding to human trafficking, and in particular, the difficult balance between ensuring the rights of the victims of trafficking versus the interests of the state.

Key Terms: push factors; pull factors; hard law; soft law; UN Trafficking Protocol to Prevent, Suppress and Punish Trafficking in Persons.

Introduction

The framework of this chapter is provided by what are called the "four Ps of policy" in responding to trafficking in persons: prevention, protection, prosecution and partnership. These four P's form the cornerstones for the development of anti-trafficking policies worldwide.

Trafficking in persons takes different forms, with sexual exploitation and forms of labour exploitation being the most common globally (UNODC, 2016). Other forms include trafficking for the purpose of begging, benefit fraud and criminal activities, the use of child soldiers and "wives" of soldiers, forced and sham marriages, illegal adoptions and the extracting of human organs or tissues (Aronowitz, 2009; UNODC, 2016; Viuhko, Lietonen, Jokinen, and Joutsen, 2016; see Meriläinen, Chapter 4, this volume).

In view of the push and pull factors affecting trafficking, how can trafficking be prevented? What roles can individuals play? What responsibilities do states and corporations have in preventing trafficking?

Despite many efforts to eradicate trafficking, the phenomenon continues to be fed by strong push and pull factors. Push factors and the "supply" side of trafficking refer to negative conditions that cause the persons trafficked to leave their homes or countries of origin. These include economic inequality, poverty (especially the feminization of poverty), lack of education and employment opportunities, disappearance of traditional livelihoods, ethnic or gender discrimination, political and ethnic conflicts, and war (see, e.g., UNODC, 2008). Pull factors and the "demand" side of trafficking refer to factors that create trafficking of persons to certain destinations and include the demand for the services that trafficked persons provide, for instance in the labour market and the sex industry in countries of destination. Unmet labour demands in destination countries, combined with the prospect of finding a job, creates a strong "pull" factor for certain migrants (Chuang, 2014, pp. 144–145). It is therefore not only consumers or clients who create demand but also employers and businesses who seek (cheap) labour as well as migrants themselves, who seek work and better opportunities elsewhere (see Ollus & Jokinen, 2017).

Global and regional legal frameworks

International conventions

Trafficking in persons is to a large extent a transnational activity, and a corresponding international will and international action is needed to prevent it and respond to it. The framework for this international cooperation is provided by a mixture of "hard law" (instruments that are legally binding) and "soft law" (declarations, resolutions and other statements of policy that carry some political weight and may guide practical action but are not legally binding). These different instruments have been drafted to respond to a variety of concerns and at different times over the past century. Among these concerns are slavery and forced labour, human rights, prostitution, migration, the rights of children and transnational organized crime (see Table 3.1). The contents of these instruments vary considerably, depending on the concern and the time that they were drafted.

The first conventions: the prohibition of slavery

During the second half of the 1700s, slavery began to be seen as incompatible with the inalienable rights of human beings and perhaps not so incidentally also as less profitable than wage Laboure (Quirk, 2011; Miers, 2003). Abolition gradually spread around the world, and in 1926 the League of Nations adopted the first international treaty against slavery and the slave trade, the Slavery, Servitude, Forced Labour and Similar Institutions and Practices Convention (see Bravo, Chapter 1, this volume). A supplementary convention entered into force in 1957.

Forced labour conventions

Despite the Slavery Convention, colonial powers continued to exploit so-called native peoples as forced labour in the colonies (Ollus, 2015). Forced labour differs from slavery in that while slaves are the property of their owners, persons in forced labour live under the threat of some form of punishment, such as violence, if they refuse to work. In today's world, forced labour may occur in domestic

Table 3.1 International conventions on trafficking

Primary Concern	*International Conventions*
Slavery	• Slavery, Servitude, Forced Labour and Similar Institutions and Practices Convention 1926; supplementary convention 1957
Labour	• ILO Forced Labour Convention No. 29 1930; supplementary convention 1957, Protocol 2014
Migration	• ILO Convention No. 97 concerning Migration for Employment • ILO Convention No. 143 concerning Migration in Abusive Conditions and the Promotion of Equality of Opportunity and Treatment of Migrant Workers • International Convention on the Protection of the Rights of All Migrant Workers and Members of Their Families 2003 (art, 11)
Prostitution	• International Agreement for the Suppression of the White Slave Traffic 1904 • International Convention for the Suppression of the White Slave Traffic 1910 • International Convention for the Suppression of the Traffic in Women and Children 1921 • International Convention for the Suppression of the Traffic in Women of Full Age 1933 • Convention for the Suppression of the Traffic in Persons and of the Exploitation of the Prostitution of Others 1949 • Convention on the Elimination of All Forms of Discrimination against Women 1979 (art. 6) • South Asian Association for Regional Cooperation Convention on Preventing and Combating Trafficking in Women and Children for Prostitution 2011
Human rights	• Universal Declaration of Human Rights of 1948 • International Covenant on Civil and Political Rights of 1966 • International Convention on the Elimination of All Forms of Racial Discrimination • Council of Europe Convention for the Protection of Human Rights and Fundamental Freedoms • 2000 Charter of Fundamental Rights in the European Union
Child exploitation	• Convention on the Rights of the Child 1989 • Optional protocol to the Convention on the Rights of the Child, on the sale of children, child prostitution and child pornography 2000 • Council of Europe Convention on the Protection of Children against Sexual Exploitation and Sexual Abuse 2007 • EU Directive 2011/92/EU of the European Parliament and of the Council of 13 December 2011 on combating the sexual abuse and sexual exploitation of children and child pornography • Hague Convention on Protection of Children and Co-operation in Respect of Intercountry Adoption • ILO Minimum Age Convention 1973 • ILO Convention No. 182 Concerning the Worst Forms of Child Labour 1999
Criminal justice	• Protocol to Prevent, Suppress and Punish Trafficking in Persons, Especially Women and Children 2000 • Council of Europe Convention on Action against Trafficking in Human Beings 2005 • European Union Framework Decision 2002/629/JHA 2002, updated by Directive 2011/36/EU on preventing and combating trafficking in human beings and protecting its victims 2011

work, the primary industries (agriculture, fishing, mining and forestry), unskilled labour (for example in manufacturing and in the accommodation, catering or other service industries) and in begging.

Forced labour has been dealt with in a number of conventions prepared within the framework of the International Labour Organization (ILO). The most important such convention is the ILO Forced Labour Convention No. 29 of 1930, which has been supplemented by the ILO Abolition of Forced Labour Convention of 1957. More recent ILO conventions deal with a closely related issue, the rights of migrant workers: ILO Convention No. 97 concerning Migration for Employment, and ILO Convention No. 143 concerning Migration in Abusive Conditions and the Promotion of Equality of Opportunity and Treatment of Migrant Workers. The International Convention on the Protection of the Rights of All Migrant Workers and Members of Their Families entered into force in 2003. Among its provisions, it prohibits holding migrant workers in slavery or forced labour (art. 11). Most recently, the ILO Protocol of 2014 to the Forced Labour Convention contains provisions on prevention, protection, remedies and sanctions.

"White slavery" and prostitution conventions

Around the same time as work was under way on the first conventions on slavery and forced labour, a moral panic arose over concerns that Western women and girls were being forced into prostitution abroad. This was shaded with xenophobic, racial and gendered undertones, seeing "innocent white women" as victims of sexual exploitation in particular by "dark men" (Leppänen, 2006; Bruch, 2004). The term "white slavery" was used to refer to forcible or fraudulent recruitment into prostitution or as a euphemism for forced prostitution (for more on "White Slavery" see Bravo, Chapter 1, this volume). The two earliest international treaties, the 1904 International Agreement for the Suppression of the White Slave Traffic, followed in 1910 by the similar-sounding International Convention for the Suppression of the White Slave Traffic, focused on preventing the recruitment and criminal traffic of women and girls for immoral purposes and on the repatriation (return to their countries) of victims (Gallagher, 2010; Bruch, 2004). These were followed by the International Convention for the Suppression of the Traffic in Women and Children in 1921 and the International Convention for the Suppression of the Traffic in Women of Full Age in 1933.

Following the Second World War and the establishment of the United Nations, the United Nations Convention for the Suppression of the Traffic in Persons and of the Exploitation of the Prostitution of Others was adopted in 1949. This Convention requires that States Parties criminalize benefiting from and exploiting the prostitution of another person, even when that person consented to prostitution.

Conventions on human rights

Following the Second World War, a number of conventions were adopted on human rights. Several of them contained specific provisions prohibiting slavery. Examples are Article 4 of the Universal Declaration of Human Rights of 1948, Article 8 of the International Covenant on Civil and Political Rights of 1966, Article 4 of the Council of Europe Convention for the Protection of Human Rights and Fundamental Freedoms and Article 5 of the Charter of Fundamental Rights in the European Union.

Conventions on child protection and the rights of the child

The basic convention on child protection is the 1989 Convention on the Rights of the Child. Article 34 of the convention states that "States Parties undertake to protect the child from all forms of sexual exploitation and sexual abuse." An optional protocol to this Convention was adopted in 2000 on the sale of children, child prostitution and child pornography.

Two important regional instruments deal with the same issue, the Council of Europe Convention on the Protection of Children against Sexual Exploitation and Sexual Abuse, 2007, and EU Directive 2011/92/EU of 2011 on combating the sexual abuse and sexual exploitation of children and child pornography.

A subset of the forced labour conventions concern child labour. The 1973 ILO Minimum Age Convention requires that states that are parties to the Convention specify a minimum age for labour – at least 15 years. ILO Convention No. 182 of 1999 Concerning the Worst Forms of Child Labour, in turn, specifically requires that States Parties take action against the sale and trafficking of children, as well as forced or compulsory child labour.

Criminal justice conventions

It was not until the end of the 1900s that trafficking moved from the anti-slavery and human rights framework into the framework of criminal justice (Gallagher, 2010; Haynes, 2009; Howard & Lalani, 2008). The first comprehensive international instrument on trafficking is the Protocol to Prevent, Suppress and Punish Trafficking in Persons, Especially Women and Children, supplementing the United Nations Convention against Transnational Organized Crime of 2000. The UN Trafficking Protocol seeks to ensure the prosecution of traffickers through enhanced law enforcement and cross-border cooperation (Roth, 2010, p. 114) (for more on this see C.deBaca, Chapter 2, this volume).

The UN Trafficking Protocol provides, for the first time, a comprehensive and internationally agreed definition of trafficking in humans (art. 3(a); see below). It was soon followed by the Council of Europe Convention on Action against Trafficking in Human Beings (2005) and a European Union instrument (Council Framework Decision 2002/629/JHA), which was updated in 2011 (Directive 2011/36/EU on preventing and combating trafficking in human beings and protecting its victims). Both of these international instruments follow the lead of the definition of trafficking in human beings on the UN Trafficking Protocol. One minor difference is that the EU Directive also includes begging and the exploitation of criminal activities as specific forms of exploitation (see Table 3.2).

In comparison with the UN Trafficking Protocol, both the Council of Europe Convention and the EU instruments place a greater focus on the protection of victims of trafficking and the safeguarding of their rights. Roth (2010), for example, considers the Council of Europe Convention to be a human rights instrument with strong victim assistance and protection obligations. She notes that assistance to victims of human trafficking is obligatory under the Council of Europe Convention but discretionary under the UN Protocol. Protection of victims, in turn, is obligatory under both. The EU Directive goes further than the Council of Europe Convention in obliging member states to provide *unconditional* assistance and protection.[1]

The Council of Europe Convention and the EU instruments also contain, in comparison to the UN Trafficking Protocol, more developed provisions on prevention. In addition, the Council of Europe Convention provides for the setting up of an effective and independent monitoring mechanism capable of overseeing the implementation of the Convention, the Group of Experts on Action against Trafficking in Human Beings (GRETA). GRETA has produced a compendium of good practices in the implementation of the Convention (see https://rm.coe.int/16806af624).

The UN Convention applies to trafficking in persons in connection with transnational organized crime, while the Council of Europe and the EU instruments apply regardless of whether the trafficking is transnational or involves organized crime. From the point of view of the definition

Table 3.2 Comparison of main international hard-law instruments on trafficking in persons

Issue	*UN Trafficking Protocol 2000*	*Council of Europe Convention 2005*	*European Union Directive 2011*
Coverage	Global; over 170 parties	Council of Europe member states (46 parties)	European Union member states (28) (in addition, five "candidate countries" are integrating the Directive into their legislation)
Mandatory Nature	Legally binding, but many individual provisions are not mandatory, allowing discretion in application	Legally binding. Many provisions are mandatory and set a minimum standard	Legally binding. Many provisions are mandatory and set a minimum standard
Definition of Trafficking	Art. 3(a)	Based on the UN Trafficking Protocol definition (Art. 4(a))	Based on the UN Trafficking Protocol definition; includes begging and the exploitation of criminal activities as specific forms (Art. 2)
Prevention	Art. 9–13 (and art. 31 of UNTOC)	Art. 5–9	Art. 18
Protection	Art. 6–8 (and art. 25 of UNTOC)	Extensive provisions, many of which are mandatory (Art. 10–17)	Extensive provisions, many of which are mandatory (Art. 11–17)
Prosecution	Art. 5 (and art. 10–24 of UNTOC)	Art. 18–31	Art. 2–10
Partnership	Art. 9(3)	Art. 35–36	National mechanisms (Art. 19) Anti-trafficking coordinator (Art. 20)

of trafficking in persons in national law, however, this distinction is not important. The practical relevance applies to international cooperation: states may use the Council of Europe and the EU instruments as a basis for law enforcement and judicial cooperation even if no organized crime is involved, while UNTOC would not apply in such cases.

These three international conventions have considerably influenced law and practice. In addition, three other regional conventions should be mentioned:

- The Commonwealth of Independent States Agreement on Cooperation in Combating Trafficking in Persons, Human Organs and Tissues, 2005, in comparison with the Council of Europe and European Union instruments;
- The Framework Act on Combating Trafficking in Persons of the League of Arab States, 2008;
- The South Asian Association for Regional Cooperation Convention on Preventing and Combating Trafficking in Women and Children for Prostitution, 2002.

While the focus originally in responding to trafficking was on protecting women and children from sexual exploitation, most of these international instruments make it clear that men and women, boys and girls can all be trafficked, and that the exploitation may include labour exploitation and trafficking of persons for the removal of body parts. Trafficking can also take place within a country without crossing international borders. It can even take place without the victim moving from one place to another; it is enough that the person is placed into, or maintained in, an exploitative situation. When exploitation takes place, the consent of the victim is no longer legally relevant. A victim cannot "consent" to being trafficked, and such consent cannot be used as a legal defence by the exploiters (see in particular UNODC, 2014a).

International soft instruments

International conventions are "hard law" instruments which are binding on countries that decide to join them as parties. Policy, however, can also be guided by "soft law" (non-binding) instruments, such as political declarations, action plans and recommendations. In the same way as international conventions have approached trafficking in persons from different perspectives, various international bodies have issued non-binding instruments on trafficking, from the point of view of their own specific mandates (see Meriläinen, Chapter 4, this volume). Among the most important of these are the United Nations, the United Nations International Children's Emergency Fund (UNICEF), the Office of the United Nations High Commissioner on Refugees (UNHCR), and the United Nations Commission on Human Rights.

For example, in 2002, soon after the UN Trafficking Protocol was adopted, UNICEF issued the Recommended Principles and Guidelines on Human Rights and Human Trafficking (E/2002/68/Add.1). These strengthened the prevention, protection, prosecution and partnership measures called for in the UN Trafficking Protocol. UNICEF has also issued guidelines[2] on the protection of child victims of trafficking, as well as a set of textbooks dealing with the combating of trafficking in children.

The main global soft law framework is the United Nations Global Plan of Action to Combat Trafficking in Persons (A/RES/64/293, annex), which was adopted by the General Assembly in 2010, and which builds on several earlier General Assembly resolutions.[3] The Global Plan is constructed using the "Four P" format, with separate sections on prevention, protection, prosecution and partnership.

Regional soft law

Largely since the entry into force of the UN Trafficking Protocol, virtually every region around the world has developed action plans designed to enhance the prevention of trafficking, improve the protection of and assistance to victims, increase the efficiency of prosecution (including identification and interdiction of trafficking and bringing the offenders to justice) and strengthen partnerships. The following are examples of such regional soft law:

- African Union: the Ouagadougou Action Plan to Combat Trafficking in Human Beings, Especially Women and Children (2006);
- The Southern African Development Community (SADC): the 2009–2019 SADC Strategic Plan of Action on Combating Trafficking in Persons, Especially Women and Children;
- The Economic Community of Western African States: the 2001 Declaration of the Economic Community of Western African States on the Fight against Trafficking in Persons (ECOWAS);

- Middle East and North Africa: the UN Regional Action Plan for MENA against Trafficking in Persons and the Smuggling of Migrants (2006);
- The Council of Arab Ministers of Justice: the Comprehensive Arab Strategy for Combating Trafficking in Human Beings (2012);
- The Arab Initiative for Building National Capacities to Combat Human Trafficking (2010);
- The Association of South East Asian Nations: Declaration Against Trafficking in Persons, Particularly Women and Children (2004). In 2010, ASEAN published the ASEAN Trafficking in Persons Handbook on International Cooperation (ASEAN, 2010);
- The Organization of American States: the resolution of the Organization of American States on "Fighting the Crime of Trafficking in Persons, especially Women, Adolescents, and Children" (OAS, 2004). Subsequently the OAS has established an OAS Anti-Trafficking Section and coordinator;
- The Organization for Security and Co-operation in Europe: in 2003, the OSCE set up the Office and post of Special Representative and Co-ordinator for Combating Trafficking in Human Beings

Separate reference should also be made to the 2014 Declaration by the major leaders of many different religions (Buddhist, Anglican, Catholic, Orthodox Christian, Hindu, Jewish, and Muslim), which calls for the elimination of slavery and human trafficking by the year 2020 (2014 Declaration).

Prevention measures

Prevention of trafficking in persons is included in the three main international hard-law instruments (refer to Table 3.2). This section deals with prevention efforts that address the push and pull factors of trafficking. Security, migration or border measures are therefore not discussed.

Awareness-raising and campaigns

Awareness-raising against human trafficking can broadly be divided into overall mass-media campaigns that target the general public or specific groups of professionals, and campaigns focusing on specific communities and groups of people that are considered vulnerable and at risk of becoming victims of trafficking or re-victimized.

General mass media campaigns or public service announcements can be broadcast as newspaper ads, on TV, on social media or in public places such as airports or bus stops. Such campaigns often attempt to depict trafficking through portrayals of victims, drawing on emotions to stir a reaction among the viewer. The campaigns may for instance depict women or girls as commodities that have a price tag, or focus on urging viewers to "open their eyes to trafficking." By searching online (e.g. for "trafficking campaign"), several examples of mass media campaigns can be found. Campaigns often emphasize either sexual exploitation or labour exploitation. Other forms of exploitation are less often the focus of overall awareness-raising campaigns.

UNODC has run a public service announcement (PSA) campaign entitled "Work Abroad" (see Image 3.1), which used short videos with "powerful images to reveal the harsh realities behind attractive job offers abroad, and seeks to educate potential victims of the dangers involved in human trafficking."[4]

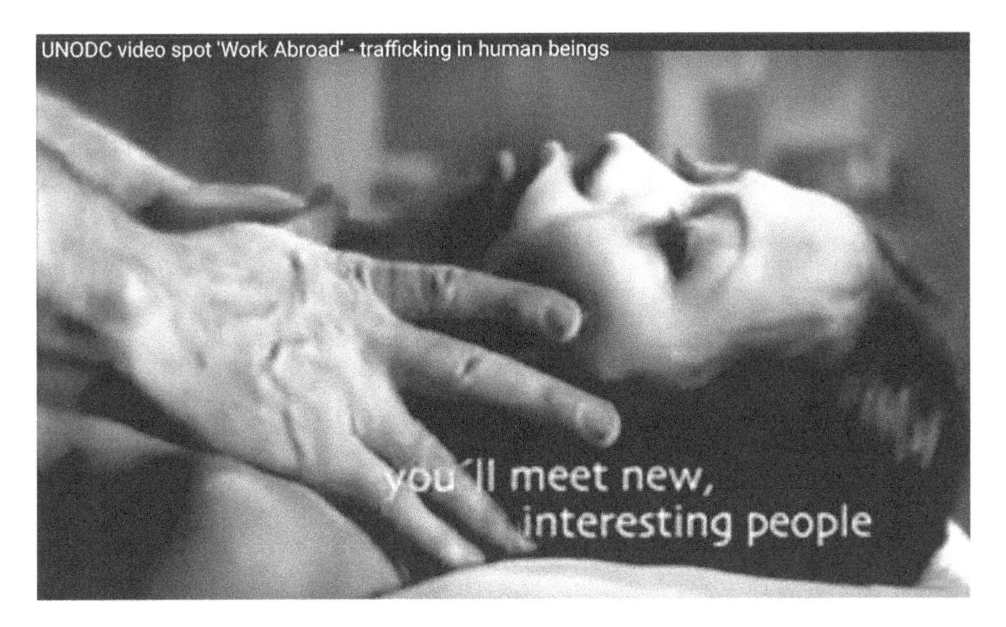

Image 3.1 Screenshot of the UNODC PSA "Work Abroad" campaign

The Office on Trafficking in Persons (TIP) within the Administration for Children and Families at the U.S. Department of Health and Human Services has a campaign to increase awareness of different forms of trafficking.[5] The labour trafficking poster (see Image 3.2) emphasizes the fact that much of labour trafficking actually looks like regular work.

The International Organisation for Migration (IOM) in Jamaica ran a campaign in 2013 to promote safe migration aimed at vulnerable Jamaicans likely to migrate, especially children. The campaign included sensitization sessions (e.g. for school guidance counsellors) (see Image 3.3) on the "dangers of irregular migration, human trafficking and the vulnerability of children."[6]

Campaigns and capacity building for key actors at the local level are also a form of awareness-raising. One example of such a campaign is the U.S. Department of Homeland Security's Blue Campaign for first responders, law enforcement officers and federal employees (www.dhs.gov/blue-campaign) (see Box 3.1). The campaign offers training to law enforcement to increase detection and investigation of human trafficking and to protect victims and bring suspected traffickers to justice.

Addressing vulnerabilities and strengthening empowerment

Many of the root causes of human trafficking are related to a lack of equal economic opportunities and economic inequalities in different parts of the world. Many preventive efforts therefore focus on addressing poverty and inequality among groups of people considered particularly vulnerable to trafficking. Such efforts may take place through national projects or through bilateral or multilateral cooperation.

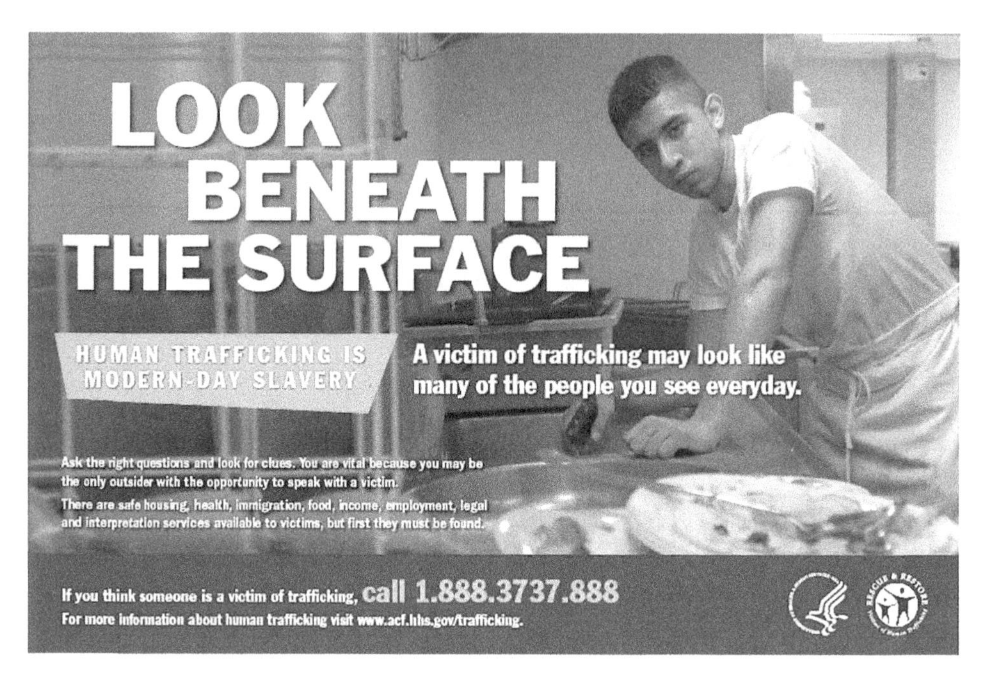

Image 3.2 Poster on labour trafficking from the TIP Office of the U.S. DHHS

Image 3.3 Poster for the IOM Jamaica campaign for safe migration

Box 3.1 Awareness-raising campaigns

While prevention of trafficking through awareness-raising is an international obligation for countries, there is a difficult balance in how to portray trafficking without resorting to simplistic notions of trafficking while at the same time conveying an effective message. The challenge with anti-trafficking campaigns, in particular those that target the general public, is that they by default have to simplify the phenomenon of trafficking. This often leads to the use of images of "typical" or "ideal" victims of trafficking, images that therefore misrepresent the nature of trafficking (e.g. O'Brien, 2013). These anti-trafficking campaigns have been criticized on the grounds that such campaigns do not intend to prevent trafficking per se, but rather aim to prevent migration of women in general, and prevent women from entering prostitution in particular (Nieuwenhuys & Pécoud, 2007; Andrijasevic & Anderson, 2009; Andrijasevic & Mai, 2016).

Since a lack of education and employment alternatives may be one of the main reasons why a person falls victim to trafficking, one of the most efficient ways of preventing trafficking is to ensure that potential victims have sufficient alternatives. Such alternatives may include *education* and *vocational or professional training* for persons who have few other employment or livelihood opportunities. In some societies, girls in particular are discouraged from obtaining an education or do not receive education due to a lack of economic means. Vocational training may help women at risk find safer jobs where they have a lower risk of falling victim to traffickers. Reintegration and rehabilitation of victims is an important form of prevention. Rehabilitation and reintegration may help break the cycle of re-victimization. In order for such programmes to be successful, they should not stigmatise those who participate in them or label them. The programmes should also offer real, realistic and meaningful training and employment alternatives (see UNODC, 2008, p. 379). In reality, however, reintegration efforts, including training of victims, may be hampered by the lack of possibilities and alternatives in their home community. An assessment of reintegration programmes in the Greater Mekong Sub-region shows that vocational training courses often do not respond to the needs of labour markets in those areas into which victims are (re)integrated, and victims may not be able to use their newly acquired skills, for example due to patriarchal family structures (Surtees, 2013). This means that in order to be able to utilize and market their skills, victims may choose – or be forced due to the circumstances – to move to larger cities. The living costs in urban areas tend to be much higher than in remote areas, which again may increase the risk of re-victimization. Victims therefore might need assistance not only in being trained for new skills, but also in how to obtain – and keep – a job.

Box 3.2 Case study (Maiti Nepal)

Maiti Nepal was founded in Nepal in 1993 by a group of teachers, journalists and social workers who shared a vision of protecting Nepali girls and women from domestic violence, trafficking, child prostitution, child labour and exploitation. Their work focuses on prevention of trafficking for sexual exploitation, rescuing victims, rehabilitating them, and seeking justice for the victims. In order to prevent re-victimization, Maiti Nepal aims to provide women with training and skills development in their chosen area of interest, such as tailoring crafts or cooking, to a level where they can become fully functioning members of society and be financially self-sufficient.

Source: www.maitinepal.org/program/training-and-job-placement/#sthash-tGwP1d8Idpuf

One alternative to paid employment – which may be difficult to acquire – is income-generating activities, such as micro-loans to establish small businesses. In some parts of the world, cooperatives are formed to prevent trafficking and re-victimization. Through these income-generating means, the risk of trafficking and re-victimization can be reduced (refer to Box 3.2). Often such measures also include capacity building on broader issues, such as basic knowledge on healthcare and sanitation, rights and responsibilities, and marketing and management, for instance. Driscoll (2011), however, argues that microcredits may in fact perpetuate poverty and increase women's susceptibility to trafficking because they do not reach the women most vulnerable to trafficking, because of the high interest rates and quick repayment plans, and because of the cultural and gender limitations of microcredit plans. She therefore calls for more efforts to reach the poorest women, more flexibility in repayment plans, the creation of savings plans instead of solely credit plans, business skills training for women, more attention to cultural and gender barriers, and better cooperation with local governments to eradicate poverty.

Addressing demand

One means of preventing human trafficking is to address the pull factors for trafficking, most notably the demand for the labour and services of trafficked persons. Numerous international treaties as well as national laws now incorporate "demand-reduction" among their counter-trafficking efforts. The United Nations Trafficking Protocol (article 9(5)) requires States to "adopt or strengthen legislative or other measures, such as educational, social or cultural measures . . . to *discourage the demand that fosters all forms of exploitation of persons, especially women and children, that leads to trafficking*" (emphasis here). The Protocol focuses on the exploitation that leads to trafficking and the need to tackle the demand that enables such exploitation. The Protocol does not offer guidance on what should be considered as demand or what legislative and other measures are the most appropriate to discourage demand. This has led countries to take different approaches to understanding what constitutes demand and in implementing measures to address it (Rogoz et al., 2016).

The idea of preventing trafficking through addressing demand is not new. The abolitionists during the early 1800s made moral appeals to consumers as a strategy for eliminating slavery (O'Connell Davidson, 2012), as did the abolitionists against prostitution during the early 1900s (Leppänen, 2006). In the negotiations on the UN Trafficking Protocol, the issue of demand generated significant controversy. Some negotiators argued that demand is an ambiguous term, is harmful against women in prostitution and is judgmental towards men (Ditmore & Wijers, 2003). Although demand can be seen in broader terms, at the time, the issue of demand was largely seen as targeting particular men as clients of sexual services (Cyrus & Vogel, 2015).

It is difficult to provide an exact definition of demand. In economic terms, demand can be understood as "the willingness and ability to buy a particular commodity" (Cyrus & Vogel, 2015). Demand, however, includes elements other than the mere buying of services or commodities. What is considered demand depends on the time, place and context in which it occurs (O'Connell Davidson, 2012). Instead of aiming at an exact definition of demand, it is more useful to think of *demand as a comprehensive approach to the prevention of trafficking* (Ollus & Jokinen, 2017). Such a comprehensive approach acknowledges that those benefiting from transactions that affect victims of trafficking should be addressed in all preventive efforts, including the roles and responsibilities of the private sector as well as consumers or buyers of services. In the context of sexual exploitation *demand is largely understood as the demand of clients for sexual services.* In 1999, prior to the adoption of the UN Trafficking Protocol, Sweden introduced a law that criminalized the buying of sexual services (see Box 3.3).

Box 3.3 The Swedish model

The "Swedish model" emphasizes that prostitution should be seen as a form of male violence against women and that prostitution should be addressed by focusing on those, men in particular, who buy the sexual services of women. The Swedish model has been both praised and criticized. Those in favour of the law argue that it provides a strong message of principle that persons are not commodities that can be bought and sold, and that criminalization reduces prostitution and trafficking overall (e.g. Niemi, 2010; Monasky, 2010–2011). Those critical of the law argue that it has forced prostitution underground and has made women more vulnerable to violence by customers and to the control of pimps, and that it disregards the agency of women who choose prostitution (e.g. Kilvington, Day, & Ward, 2001; Levy & Jakobsson, 2014). Despite the criticism, many other countries (e.g. France, Iceland, Northern Ireland and Norway) have adopted similar laws.

In the context of trafficking for labour exploitation, demand can be understood as constructed through three levels: the consumer's demand for certain goods or services, the recruiter's or employer's demand for labour, and the migrant worker's demand for work (Ollus & Jokinen, 2017). While consumers do have responsibilities and indirect roles in preventing exploitation and trafficking, the responsibility for preventing trafficking cannot be left to consumers alone.

Box 3.4 The ten principles of the UN Global Compact

Human Rights

Principle 1: Businesses should support and respect the protection of internationally proclaimed human rights; and
Principle 2: make sure that they are not complicit in human rights abuses.

Labour

Principle 3: Businesses should uphold the freedom of association and the effective recognition of the right to collective bargaining;
Principle 4: the elimination of all forms of forced and compulsory labour;
Principle 5: the effective abolition of child labour; and
Principle 6: the elimination of discrimination in respect of employment and occupation.

Environment

Principle 7: Businesses should support a precautionary approach to environmental challenges;
Principle 8: undertake initiatives to promote greater environmental responsibility; and
Principle 9: encourage the development and diffusion of environmentally friendly technologies.

Anti-corruption

Principle 10: Businesses should work against corruption in all its forms, including extortion and bribery.

The role of the private sector

Within the private sector, companies and corporations have an important role in addressing trafficking. In recent years there has been an increased commitment by the private sector in this regard. The UN Global Compact was launched in 2000, and is a voluntary initiative for companies committed to including human rights, labour standards, the environment and anti-corruption within their business endeavours. Trafficking is not explicitly referred to in the Compact, but is implicit in the commitment to uphold human rights (refer to Box 3.4).

In the early 2000s, the UN Secretary-General appointed a Special Representative with the task of examining business and human rights, and developing guidance in this regard. The UN Guiding Principles on Business and Human Rights (see Box 3.5) that were endorsed in 2011 require businesses to exercise due diligence in identifying, preventing, mitigating and accounting for how they address their impacts on human rights (principle 15).

The UN Guiding Principles do not specifically address trafficking, but trafficking can be seen to be included within the human rights violations that the principles seek to prevent and address. One trafficking-specific voluntary framework for businesses has been adopted: the Athens Ethical Principles against Human Trafficking of 2006, which focus in particular on trafficking for sexual exploitation. The Athens Principles are accompanied by implementation guidelines (the so-called Luxor Protocol), which give companies tools to implement concrete actions against human trafficking. More recently, the 2014 ILO Protocol on Forced Labour requires states to promote due diligence in both the public and private sector in order to prevent and respond to risks of forced or compulsory labour (Article 2e).

Box 3.5 The UN Guiding Principles on Business and Human Rights

The UN Guiding Principles consist of 31 principles, which give guidance to states and businesses on how to address businesses' negative impact on human rights. The Principles are built around three core pillars.

Protect: By international law, states have been vested with the duty to protect human rights through policies, regulation, legislation and effective enforcement. States should ensure that businesses do not breach human rights, but should also support companies in adopting human rights policies. States should advise businesses, for example on how to ensure that the rights of indigenous peoples, women, national or ethnic minorities, religious and linguistic minorities, children, persons with disabilities, and migrant workers and their families are secured (OHCHR, 2011, pp. 5–6).

Respect: Businesses have a responsibility to respect human rights and to ensure that their business conduct does not jeopardize human rights, and to act upon any harm that may be done. Businesses need to assess the human rights risks in their business and create means of addressing these risks, and commit to following human rights policies.

Remedy: "Remedies" refer to mechanisms for effective redress for those who may have been harmed. The Guiding Principles call for state-based judicial remedies in courts of law, and state-based non-judicial remedies such as through national human rights institutions. The Principles also provide guidance on non-state-based grievance mechanisms, such as how to ensure that dialogue between affected communities and businesses is predictable, equitable, transparent and accessible (OHCHR, 2011, pp. 33–34).

Many states have introduced national legislation and regulation with the aim of preventing exploitation and trafficking in business enterprises, in local or global supply chains and in public procurement (as an example, see Box 3.6). These include the UK Modern Slavery Act, which obliges businesses with an annual turnover of more than £36 million to audit and report on modern slavery in their business and supply chains. The introduction of a similar law is currently being discussed in Australia. The California Transparency in Supply Chains Act of 2010 requires companies with worldwide annual revenues of $100 million or more to report on their specific actions to eradicate slavery and human trafficking in their supply chains. The U.S. Executive Order on Strengthening Protection Against Trafficking in Persons in Federal Contracts of 2012 prohibits federal contractors, subcontractors and their employees from engaging in trafficking-related practices.

Box 3.6 Trafficking in local public procurement in Denmark

In 2012 a case of severe exploitation and trafficking of migrant cleaning workers was uncovered in Denmark. The victims worked for a company subcontracted by one of the largest Danish cleaning companies. The subcontractor recruited workers from Romania, and upon arrival in Denmark, took their bank accounts and ID cards. The subcontractor paid them a poor salary for very long working hours, threatened the workers and accommodated them in a garage and a basement. The exploited migrant workers cleaned municipal schools and other public institutions. As a result of this case, the Danish Centre against Human Trafficking, in collaboration with representatives of the large cleaning company and other business representatives, developed guidelines for counteracting exploitation and trafficking in local subcontracting chains.

Source: www.gla.gov.uk/media/1578/guidelines-riskmanagement-eng-version-1-0.pdf

Because all of the aforementioned standards, codes and principles are soft law, they are voluntary, and compliance with and adherence to the codes are difficult to ensure. There is currently a discussion regarding the need for an international instrument to regulate the activities of transnational corporations and other business enterprises.[7]

Protection measures

The second of the "Four P's," following prevention, is protection. There are fundamental and strategic reasons that the protection of the victims of trafficking in persons is mentioned before the third "P," prosecution. The life and health of the victim are often in danger, and the priority should be to rescue victims from exploitative situations, protect them from retaliation by the traffickers and help them reintegrate into the community. Furthermore, often prosecution of the traffickers depends on the willingness of the victims to provide evidence. If the victims have concerns about their safety and well-being, there is little incentive to cooperate with the criminal justice system. And finally, protecting a person against trafficking is fundamentally an issue of human rights.

Defining a person as a victim of trafficking has consequences. Being defined as a victim may create rights but also pressures. In the international treaties and in domestic legislation, victims of trafficking are awarded special rights, assistance and protection, often in exchange for cooperation with the criminal justice system. On the other hand, being labelled as a victim may invoke stereotypes that the trafficked person is a passive victim with no agency of his or her own, and this may affect how the individual is perceived and treated by the criminal justice system and more widely by society (O'Connell Davidson, 2010; Bravo, 2009).

Many victims of trafficking do not define themselves as victims. Few (actively) seek help, and few want to cooperate with authorities. If persons who are the victims of trafficking do not regard themselves as victims, investigation is difficult because the victims often do not want to cooperate (Brunovskis & Surtees, 2012). Both smuggled persons and trafficked persons are hoping for a better life, and fear (in many cases, correctly) that if they turn to the authorities they would be prosecuted for illegal entry into the country, or at the very least they would be deported. They may fear retaliation from the smugglers/traffickers if they cooperate with the authorities; the threats may be against themselves, but also against family members still living in the country of origin. Also, many victims come from countries where law enforcement is regarded as corrupt and violent, and so they may not trust the police. Cooperation with criminal justice, in general, brings few if any benefits to victims, and understandably victims may decide not to cooperate and assume the risks, if the criminal justice system cannot promise adequate protection, assistance and support for a period sufficiently long for the victims to recover and organize their life (see, e.g., Lee, 2011; Farrel et al., 2012).

Early identification of potential victims

The UN Trafficking Protocol does not contain special provisions on the early identification of potential victims. Article 10(1) of the Council of Europe convention calls for training in the prevention and combating of trafficking in human beings, and in identifying and helping victims, and for collaboration between the different authorities as well as with relevant support organizations, so that victims can be identified. Article 11(3) of the EU Directive, in turn, requires that states "establish appropriate mechanisms aimed at the early identification of, assistance to and support for victims, in cooperation with relevant support organisations."

The primary responsibility for identifying potential victims of trafficking lies with the front-line authorities, in particular law enforcement authorities, border control and immigration authorities, labour inspectors, and medical and social welfare authorities. Some jurisdictions have created specialized units for detecting and investigating trafficking, whether for sexual or labour exploitation.

Training can also be given to persons in other sectors who may come into contact with victims in the line of work, such as in the transportation and hotel industries. In particular ECPAT International, which is a global network of organizations and individuals seeking to eliminate trafficking of children for sexual exploitation, has been active in this regard (www.ecpat.org). Various hotlines have been established around the world to allow members of the public to provide information on potential cases of trafficking.

Emergency treatment and physical safety

Victims of trafficking often need a wide range of emergency services, such as emergency medical and psychological treatment, appropriate accommodation (including protective homes or shelters for rehabilitation), and security against the traffickers (refer to Torres, Nsonwu, Cook Heffron, and Busch-Armendariz, Chapter 13, this volume). The UN Trafficking Protocol requires that states consider the provision of a range of social services to enable recovery from trauma caused by trafficking experiences. Similarly, Article 12(2) of the Council of Europe Convention requires that each party shall take due account of the victim's safety and protection needs. Although this issue is not referred to in the EU Directive, it is noted in a separate binding EU instrument, the EU Victims Directive of 2012 (2012/29/EU).

The IOM Handbook on Direct Assistance for Victims of Trafficking (IOM, 2007) provides detailed guidance on the arrangement of victim assistance. Assistance is often provided by selected service providers, such as non-governmental organizations (NGOs). In most countries, the government buys such services from NGOs, while in other countries, the government may organize the assistance itself through government entities.

Possibility of obtaining compensation

Article 6(6) of the UN Trafficking Protocol and Article 15 of the Council of Europe Convention and the EU Victims Directive requires that States Parties provide victims the legal possibility of obtaining compensation.

There are different ways to arrange for compensation, including requiring that the offender pay the victim compensation. Since few offenders are brought to justice, this is rarely a real option. Many countries around the world have established victim compensation programmes. However, entitlements under these programmes are generally restricted to victims of violent offences. If the trafficking did not involve serious assault or rape against the victim, the state compensation programme would therefore not apply. Consequently, the Council of Europe Convention suggests that states establish a fund for victim compensation or measures or programmes aimed at social assistance and social integration of victims, which could be funded by assets confiscated from traffickers. The COMP.ACT project (see Box 3.7) is aimed at improving victims' access to justice and compensation.

Box 3.7 COMP.ACT project

In 2010, La Strada International, a network of anti-trafficking NGOs operating in Europe, launched the COMP.ACT (European Action Pact for Compensation for Trafficked Persons) project – in cooperation with Anti-slavery International – to improve access to justice and to guarantee compensation for trafficked victims. The project has formed a European coalition that consists of the legal community, service providers, labour unions, migrant workers' rights organizations and academics. The coalition has conducted research at the national level to create a practical system to enable trafficked persons to access compensation. The COMP.ACT project works to create a sustainable compensation system by assisting countries to develop specific working plans as they conduct case studies that identify reform needs. The project also entails the preparation of national handbooks about compensation for NGOs, lawyers and prosecutors.

Article 17 of the EU Directive goes much further, and requires that states ensure that victims of trafficking have access to existing schemes of compensation to victims of violent crimes. Furthermore, the European Union Victims Directive referred to above applies also to victims of trafficking. According to Article 16 of the Victims Directive, EU states are to ensure that victims are entitled to obtain compensation in criminal proceedings within a reasonable time, "except where national law provides for such a decision to be made in other legal proceedings." In addition, EU states are required to "promote measures to encourage offenders to provide adequate compensation to victims."

Counselling and information on rights

Victims are often in an unfamiliar environment, lacking even basic information on legal options. Article 6(2)(a) of the UN Trafficking Protocol requires that states ensure that their "legal or administrative system contains measures that provide victims of trafficking, in appropriate cases, information on relevant court and administrative proceedings," and Art 6(3)(b) of the UN Trafficking Protocol calls on states to consider, in particular, the "provision of counselling and information, in particular as regards their legal rights, in a language that the victims of trafficking in persons can understand." Articles 12(1) and 15 of the Council of Europe Convention are broadly similar in scope. Although the EU Directive does not contain a corresponding provision on providing victims with information, Articles 3–7 of the separate EU Victims Directive grants extensive rights to victims, including victims of trafficking.

Protection of the privacy of the victim

Article 6(1) of the UN Trafficking Protocol requires that "in appropriate cases and to the extent possible under its domestic law," states are to protect the privacy and identity of victims of trafficking, including by making legal proceedings relating to such trafficking confidential. Articles 11 and 12 of the Council of Europe Convention goes into somewhat greater detail, for example in referring to data protection, and in requiring that states ensure "in particular" that the identity of child victims of trafficking are not made publicly known, whether through the media or by any other means "except, in exceptional circumstances, in order to facilitate the tracing of family members or otherwise secure the well-being and protection of the child."

Where should the balance lie between protecting the rights of victims (for example providing them with assistance, not threatening them with punishment) and the rights of the state (in particular, the need to get victims to assist in the identification and prosecution of offenders)?

One decision that the victim is often called upon to make is whether or not to cooperate in the investigation of the case and in the prosecution of the offender. The police and the prosecutor may place pressure on the victim to cooperate, as the victim's information and evidence is often the only practical way to build the case. Indeed, many jurisdictions may require that the victim file a complaint against the offender (i.e. report the crime), as a condition for starting the investigation. However, as noted earlier, the victim may be reluctant and even fearful to do so.

The UN Trafficking Protocol does not address this issue directly. The Council of Europe Convention (art. 27) and the EU Directive (art. 9), both provide that states are to ensure that the investigation or prosecution are not dependent on the report or accusation of the victim.

In many jurisdictions, government assistance to victims is made *conditional* on a victim's willingness to act as a witness or otherwise participate in the investigation, prosecution or trial. Article 12 of the Council of Europe Convention specifically stipulates that states should ensure that assistance to victims is not made conditional on their willingness to act as a witness, and that the services "are provided on a consensual and informed basis, taking due account of the special needs of persons in a vulnerable position and the rights of children in terms of accommodation, education and appropriate health care." Article 11(3) and (4) of the EU Directive use much the same language.

Involvement in the legal system

Article 6(2) of the UN Trafficking Protocol requires that states should provide victims "in appropriate cases" assistance to enable their views and concerns to be presented and considered at appropriate stages of criminal proceedings against offenders, in a manner not prejudicial to the rights of the defence. Also Article 12 of the Council of Europe requires that states provide assistance to victims "to enable their rights and interests to be presented and considered at appropriate stages of criminal proceedings against offenders." In this respect, victims have very different rights and possibilities in the different criminal justice systems around the world. Phrases such as "in appropriate cases," "at appropriate stages" and the passive wording "enable their views and concerns to be presented and considered" allow states extensive leeway in deciding what measures to take. In addition, Article 27(3) of the Council of Europe Convention calls on states to ensure to any group, foundation, association or non-governmental organizations which aim at fighting trafficking in human beings or protection of human rights the possibility to assist and/or support the victim with his or her consent during criminal proceedings concerning trafficking in persons.

The EU Victim Directive goes much farther than the UN Trafficking Protocol in granting victims various rights in criminal proceedings. Article 10 grants victims the right to be heard and to give evidence in criminal proceedings; this is thus an active right of the victim, which cannot be satisfied for example by the prosecutor presenting the concerns and views of the victim. If the prosecutor decides not to prosecute the case, the victim should have the right to have this decision reviewed (art. 11). Victim safeguards in restorative justice services is covered in Article 12. Article 13 deals with the victim's right to legal aid, Article 14 refers to the right to compensation for legal costs, and Article 15 to the return of property.

Reintegrating the victim into the community

All three of the major crime control conventions on trafficking in persons contain provisions on measures that are to be taken in order to reintegrate the victim into the community. Article 6(3) of the UN Trafficking Protocol is short, and requires that states "consider" in particular the provision of appropriate housing; medical, psychological, and material assistance; and employment, educational and training opportunities. Article 12(1) of the Council of Europe Convention and Articles 11 and 12 of the EU Directive provide much more substance, as shown in Table 3.3.

Demographic considerations and needs of victims

Article 6(4) of the UN Trafficking Protocol requires that each state party takes into account, in applying the provisions of this article, the age, gender and special needs of victims of trafficking in persons, in particular the special needs of children, including appropriate housing, education and care.

Child victims are dealt with in somewhat greater detail in Article 10 of the Council of Europe Convention, which requires for example that they receive representation acting in their best interests, that necessary steps be taken to establish their identity and nationality, and that every effort is made to locate their family when this is in their best interests.

Article 11(7) of the EU Directive obliges states to "attend to victims with special needs, where those needs derive, in particular, from whether they are pregnant, their health, a disability, a mental or psychological disorder they have, or a serious form of psychological, physical or sexual violence they have suffered." Further substance on assistance, support and protection to child victims is provided in Articles 13–16.

Do countries have a legal or moral obligation to provide permanent residence status to trafficking victims?

Table 3.3 Comparisons of victim assistance by the three main international conventions

Topic	*UN Trafficking Protocol*	*Council of Europe Convention*	*EU Directive*
Early identification of victims	No provisions	Art. 11	Art. 11(3)
Emergency treatment and physical safety	Art. 6(3)	Art. 12(2)	(EU Victims Directive)
Compensation	Art. 6(6)	Art. 15(3) and 15(4)	Art. 17, backed up by the EU Victims Directive
Counselling and information on rights	Art. 6(2)(a) and 6(3)(b)	Art 12(1) and 15(1)–(2)	EU Victims Directive, Arts. 3–7
Protection of privacy	Art. 6(1)	Arts. 11–12	(EU Victims Directive)
Dependence of the investigation on the cooperation of the victim	No provisions	No – Art. 27	No – Art. 9
Involvement in the legal system	Art. 6(2): views and concerns to be considered "in appropriate cases"	Art. 12: views and concerns to be considered "in appropriate cases"	Arts. 10–15 – e.g. the right to be heard and to give evidence
Reintegration of the victim into the community	Art. 6(3): states are to "consider" providing various reintegrative services: housing medical, psychological and material assistance employment, educational and training opportunities	Art. 12(1): appropriate and secure housing; psychological and material assistance; access to emergency medical treatment; access to the labour market for legally resident victims; access to education for children; access to education and vocational training for legally resident victims	Arts. 11–12: appropriate and safe accommodation material assistance, as well as necessary medical treatment, including psychological assistance (also: EU Victims Directive)
Child victims	Art. 6(4)	Art. 10	Arts. 11(7) and 13–16
Recovery and reflection period	Art. 7 – states are to "consider" providing a reflection period	Arts. 13–14: mandatory reflection period	
Repatriation	Arts. 7 and 8	Art. 16	

Recovery and reflection period; residence permit

Victims who are rescued from trafficking are often in an unfamiliar environment and are unsure about their rights and status. They may also have conflicting views regarding whether or not to cooperate in the investigation of the traffickers. For this reason, many countries provide for the possibility of a recovery and reflection period, generally a few months, during which the victim is allowed to remain in the country and reflect on whether he or she wants to return to his or her place of origin, or seek a residence permit (if possible). During the period, the victim is generally (but not always) entitled to government assistance in finding housing, training or employment.

In addition, for example the United States and European Union countries provide a residence permit, allowing the victim to remain in the country and work.

Article 7 of the UN Trafficking Protocol requires that States Parties consider allowing victims to remain in their territory, whether permanently or temporarily "in appropriate cases" and in doing so "give appropriate consideration to humanitarian and compassionate factors." The provisions in Articles 13 and 14 of the Council of Europe Convention are more explicit and mandatory. For example, instead of calling for "consideration" of a recovery and reflection period "in appropriate cases," Article 13 of the Council of Europe Convention *requires* a recovery and reflection period of at least 30 days, when there are reasonable grounds to believe that the person concerned is a victim. Article 14, in turn, requires that each state issues a renewable residence permit to victims of trafficking if their stay is deemed necessary owing to their personal situation, and/or their stay is necessary for the purpose of their co-operation in investigation or criminal proceedings. In the case of child victims, such a residence permit is to be issued in accordance with the best interests of the child.

The way in which reflection periods have been implemented has been criticized. In particular, they have often been so brief that many victims feel pressured to cooperate with authorities (UNODC, 2008). Beyond the scope of the states that are parties to the Council of Europe Convention, jurisdictions often explicitly tie the granting of a temporary residence (non-immigrant status) to the readiness of the victim to cooperate in the investigation and prosecution of the traffickers. In the United States, this is the case with the so-called T-visa. Almost invariably, the suspected trafficking offence will be reported to the police regardless of the victim's decision on whether or not to cooperate, thus placing pressure on the victim to cooperate or risk the possibility of deportation on the grounds of illegal entry into the country.

A study of reflection periods in the Nordic countries, Belgium, and Italy shows that the length of the reflection period and the extent to which the victim must cooperate with police in order to be granted temporary residence after the reflection period varies between countries (Brunovskis, 2012). The study concludes that shorter reflection periods often cater to the needs of police investigations, while longer reflection periods better accommodate the needs of victims, but only if the process is clear and predictable.

Voluntary return/repatriation

Articles 7 and 8 of the UN Trafficking Protocol deal with the return of the victim to the state of origin. States of origin are required to accept the return of any victims of trafficking who are their nationals or who had permanent residence in their territory at the time of entry to the receiving state. Due regard should be taken of the safety of the victims, with the return preferably being voluntary.

Article 16 of the Council of Europe Convention is broadly along the same lines, although with somewhat more detail. In addition, it requires that states establish repatriation programmes, working together with relevant national or international institutions and non-governmental organizations. These programmes should be designed to avoid re-victimization and to promote reintegration of victims. The Convention also specifies that child victims shall not be repatriated if there is indication that this would not be in the best interests of the child.

Prosecution measures

The third "P" in the four Ps for responding to human trafficking is "prosecution," which should be understood to refer broadly to measures designed to identify, apprehend and bring to justice the traffickers. Worldwide, the majority of offenders involved in trafficking in persons are not detected by the authorities, much less prosecuted or punished.

If victims of trafficking are prepared to testify or otherwise participate in criminal proceeding, they often need protection and assistance. In line with the United Nations Declaration of Basic Principles for Victims of Crime and Abuse of Power (A/RES/40/34), victims should be assisted in order to enable their views and concerns to be presented and considered at appropriate stages of criminal proceedings against offenders in a manner not prejudicial to the rights of the defence. The privacy and identity of victims should be protected, inter alia, by holding the legal proceedings relating to such trafficking in camera, and victims should be protected, as appropriate, from intimidation.

Criminal law

The three main international conventions on trafficking in persons (with some minor differences) require that the States Parties criminalize

- The recruitment, transportation, transfer, harbouring or receipt of persons;
- By means of the threat or use of force or other forms of coercion, of abduction, of fraud, of deception, of the abuse of power or of a position of vulnerability or of the giving or receiving of payments or benefits to achieve the consent of a person having control over another person;
- For the purpose of exploitation. (In this context, exploitation is understood to mean, at a minimum, the exploitation of the prostitution of others or other forms of sexual exploitation, forced labour or services, slavery or practices similar to slavery, servitude or the removal of organs.)

In line with this definition, trafficking in persons consists of three elements (for more on these, refer to Bussey-Garza, Dempsey, Martin, andRhodes, Chapter 5, this volume):

- The act (recruitment, transportation and so on)
- The means (threat, the use of force, etc.)
- The purpose (exploitation).

In the case of trafficking in children (i.e. persons under 18 years of age), the "means" element need not be present in order for the conduct to constitute trafficking. It is thus not necessary to prove that threats or force were used against the child. It is necessary to show only the "action" (such as recruitment, buying and selling) and that this action was for the specific purpose of exploitation. For adults, the "means" element has proven contentious in particular in the case of sexual exploitation. The argument here is not whether or not an adult may voluntarily engage in sex work (leaving aside the issue of whether prostitution is legal in the country in question), but whether or not he or she may consent to someone else organizing (and profiting from) his or her prostitution. For example, in the United Kingdom, the Sexual Offences Act 2003 deals with trafficking for sexual exploitation but does not require that those committing the offence use coercion, deception or force. As a result, any person who enters the United Kingdom in order to engage in sex work with consent is considered to have been "trafficked."

Sanctions

Article 11 of UNTOC, which is the "mother convention" that applies alongside of the UN Trafficking Protocol, requires that states make the commission of the offences in question "liable to sanctions that take into account the gravity of that offence." This general formulation leaves states with considerable flexibility in establishing the appropriate level of punishment.

Article 23 of the Council of Europe Convention calls for "effective, proportionate and dissuasive sanctions." The provision further requires that the sanctions include "penalties involving deprivation of liberty which can give rise to extradition." Legal persons, in turn, should be subject to "effective, proportionate and dissuasive criminal or non-criminal sanctions or measures, including monetary sanctions," and that establishments used in the trafficking can be temporarily or permanently closed.

Article 4 of the EU Directive provides a greater level of detail, in requiring that states ensure that trafficking is subject to at a maximum sentence of at least five years of imprisonment, and in serious cases at least ten years of imprisonment.

Non-application of the sanctions to the victim

Some trafficked persons begin their journey as smuggled migrants and have contracted with other persons or organizations to facilitate their travel. They may thus be guilty of offences such as illegal entry into a country, use of forged documents, and giving false information to authorities. At the destination, they may further engage in work without a valid work permit or engage in illegal work (such as prostitution in jurisdictions where this is illegal). However, once they become exploited – which can be very early in the journey – they become victims and should be treated as such.

In many cases, moreover, trafficked persons are forced to commit these offences. For example, while smuggled migrants are prepared to enter the destination country illegally, the degree to which they voluntarily consent to use forged documents or give false information to authorities may be questioned. The smugglers may use different means to secure the consent of the smuggled migrants to these actions, including implicit or explicit threats or even violence. These points should be combined with the human rights–based approach to trafficking in persons. The human rights of trafficked persons should be at the centre of all efforts to prevent and combat trafficking and to protect, assist and provide redress to victims (International Framework for Action 2009). Building on these points, both Article 26 of the Council of Europe Convention and Article 8 of the EU Directive explicitly call on states to provide for the possibility of not punishing trafficking victims for such offences, if the victims had been compelled to commit these offences. A special situation arises when the trafficking victim has reasonable grounds to fear persecution in his or her country of origin, for example on the grounds of race, religion, nationality, membership in a particular social group, or political opinion. Such a person has a right to request asylum. If this status is granted, he or she would not be prosecuted or punished for offences that were reasonably committed in order to secure asylum.

Investigative measures

Trafficking cases tend to be complex and difficult to detect (refer to Bryant, Joudo, Larsen, and Gordon, Chapter 6, this volume). Traditional investigative measures such as collection of physical evidence and the questioning of witnesses are of limited utility if, for example, victims are not identified by others as being victims of trafficking, or if witnesses (including the victims) do not want to cooperate in the investigation.

One particular tactic – the use of raids to detect trafficking, break up the criminal organizations and rescue the victims – has been questioned. Whether the raids are on suspected brothels, factories, farms or other places, the persons caught up are generally not identified as victims of trafficking, but for example as persons engaged in illegal activity (prostitution) or as undocumented aliens. For this reason, victims of trafficking can be intimidated and would presumably not cooperate with law enforcement. Law enforcement raids may have the secondary effect of forcing sex trafficking and trafficking for labour exploitation underground, thereby increasing the risks for the victims and decreasing the possibility that they will seek help. It is for these reasons that jurisdictions are increasingly turning to modern investigative means and to increasing the risk of detection of the offence. This trend is encouraged by Article 20 of the UN Convention on Transnational Organized Crime (which underlies the UN Trafficking Protocol), which calls upon states to allow for the appropriate use of controlled delivery, electronic surveillance, other surveillance, and undercover operations. Article 9(4) of the EU Directive goes along the same lines.

Because of the difficulties in investigation of trafficking, it requires appropriately staffed, trained, organized and funded agency structures, and ideally also specialized anti-trafficking units and specialized prosecutors. A recent trend has been to broaden the investigation of trafficking (as well as of organized crime in general) to include investigations into the flow of the profits that the traffickers obtain through the offence. Since financial profit is the major goal of traffickers, particular efforts should be made to freeze, seize and confiscate the proceeds of crime, thus reducing the profit incentive. The illegal profits can be large, and the pattern of financial transfers that the traffickers use domestically and in particular internationally in order to launder these proceeds can raise indicators of ongoing criminal activity.

Protection of victims in the course of investigations and prosecution

As noted earlier, the UN Trafficking Protocol (alongside other instruments) calls upon states to ensure the protection of the victims of trafficking. The Council of Europe Convention contains extensive provisions (art. 28) on protecting victims and others who are cooperating with the authorities in investigation and prosecution. This protection should also be extended, when necessary, to members of their family. The protection may include physical protection, relocation, change in identity, and assistance in obtaining jobs.

International police and judicial cooperation

Trafficking in persons is often a transnational crime, in that the victim and/or the offenders cross international borders or the proceeds of crime are taken across borders. For this reason, international police and judicial cooperation is required in order to protect the victims, bring the offenders to justice and recover the proceeds of crime.

UNTOC provides the framework for extradition and for the following types of mutual legal assistance: the taking of evidence, effecting service of documents, execution of searches, identification of the proceeds of crime, and production of information and documentation (such as criminal records). In addition, the UN Trafficking Protocol requires that States Parties strengthen cooperation with other states in the exchange of information (e.g. the means and methods employed by traffickers). States Parties are also required to provide or strengthen training for officials in the recognition and prevention of trafficking, including human rights awareness training.

Partnerships

National coordination and oversight mechanisms

Technically, national coordination mechanisms are considered part of prevention of trafficking, but for the purposes of this chapter they are treated as a form of partnerships. The UN Trafficking Protocol does not provide any explicit guidance on national coordination structures, apart from Article 9(1), which urges states to establish "comprehensive policies, programmes and other measures (a) To prevent and combat trafficking in persons; and (b) To protect victims of trafficking in persons, especially women and children, from re-victimization." Article 9(3), in turn, notes that such policies, programmes and other measures shall, as appropriate, include cooperation with non-governmental organizations, other relevant organizations and other elements of civil society.

How should activities against trafficking best be organized at the national and international levels?

The Council of Europe Convention states that "Each Party shall take measures to establish or strengthen national co-ordination between the various bodies responsible for preventing and combating trafficking in human beings" (art. 5(1)). The EU Directive requires that "national monitoring systems such as national rapporteurs or equivalent mechanisms should be established by Member States" and that they should carry out assessments of trends in trafficking in human beings, gather statistics, measure the results of anti-trafficking actions, and regularly report on the findings (art. 27). The OSCE recommends that states consider establishing the position of National Rapporteur or other mechanisms for monitoring the anti-trafficking activities of state institutions and the implementation of national legislation requirements, as well as consider establishing Anti-trafficking Commissions (task forces) or similar bodies responsible for co-ordinating activities (OSCE, 2008).

Many countries have followed these recommendations and have established national coordination mechanisms, national action plans and/or national rapporteurs (see OSCE, 2008):

- National coordination mechanisms may include an appointed National Coordinator, who oversees the work against human trafficking at the national level and acts as a coordinator between different ministries and departments. Many countries have also established a specific task force, working group or commission, which incorporates representatives from different sectors. Many countries include NGOs in these groups; in the OSCE region, civil society representatives were included in 62% of national coordination mechanisms (OSCE, 2008).
- In order to ensure effective action against human trafficking, many countries have developed *national action plans* to provide a structure and purpose for the anti-trafficking efforts. These plans should be as specific as possible, and list concrete activities, for example in respect of legislative reform, prevention, victim protection and assistance, law enforcement and prosecution, international cooperation and the roles of different stakeholders (OSCE, 2008). The plans should also include clear timelines and a budget and indicate which entity or organization is responsible for implementing which activity.
- Some European countries have established so-called National Rapporteurs to oversee the anti-trafficking work at the national level (see Box 3.8 for an example in Finland). In some countries, the National Rapporteur has the mandate to report on national anti-trafficking efforts to the government or parliament.

Box 3.8 An independent national rapporteur

In Finland, the Non-discrimination Ombudsman is the National Rapporteur on Trafficking in Human Beings. The National Rapporteur is an independent body functioning under the auspices of the Ministry of Justice and monitors action against human trafficking in Finland, human trafficking at large, compliance with international obligations and the effectiveness of national legislation. The

National Rapporteur issues suggestions, recommendations, statements and advice and follows the realization of the rights of victims. The National Rapporteur may also provide legal counselling and, in exceptional cases, assist victims in court cases. The National Rapporteur submits an annual report to the government and an extensive report with recommendations to Parliament every four years.

Source: www.syrjinta.fi/web/en/rapporteur-on-trafficking.

One of the main problems in the national work against human trafficking is the lack of dedicated financial and human resources (OSCE, 2008). The OSCE (2004) recommends that any action plan on trafficking be developed with an associated funding plan (refer to Box 3.9).

Box 3.9 Ten guiding principles in developing action plans and strategies against trafficking in persons

1 Protecting the rights of trafficked persons should be the first priority of all anti- trafficking measures;
2 An infrastructure to combat human trafficking should work on the basis of a broad definition of trafficking in order to have the ability to respond rapidly to different forms of trafficking;
3 Support and protection services should be accessible for all categories of trafficked persons;
4 A protection mechanism should include a wide range of different specialized services, addressing the specific needs of each individual;
5 Victim-protection mechanisms based on human rights can help secure successful prosecution;
6 Combating trafficking in human beings requires a multidisciplinary and cross- sector approach, involving all relevant actors from government and civil society;
7 A structure to combat trafficking in human beings should assess and build on existing national capacity in order to foster ownership and sustainability;
8 The guiding principles of an action plan or strategy should include transparency and assignment of clear responsibilities and competencies according to the different mandates of all actors involved;
9 Action plans and strategies are building blocks of effective regional and international cooperation to combat trafficking and assist its victims;
10 The process of implementing an action plan or strategy should be embedded in an overall democratization process to ensure accountability and legitimacy.

Multiagency cooperation mechanisms: the National Referral Mechanism

Any comprehensive anti-trafficking policy relies on cooperation between all relevant actors, both nationally and internationally. This means cooperation not only between states and NGOs to protect victims, but also between states and the private sector, between states and labour unions/confederations of employers as well as among various government actors (police, prosecutors, social welfare, health, education, employment, etc.).

One form of multiagency cooperation that has proven to be quite effective is known as a National Referral Mechanism (NRM). The NRM is a "co-operative framework through which state actors fulfil their obligations to protect and promote the human rights of trafficked persons, co-ordinating their efforts in a strategic partnership with civil society" and also with other actors working to counteract trafficking (OSCE, 2004, p. 15). The NRM is a form of formalized

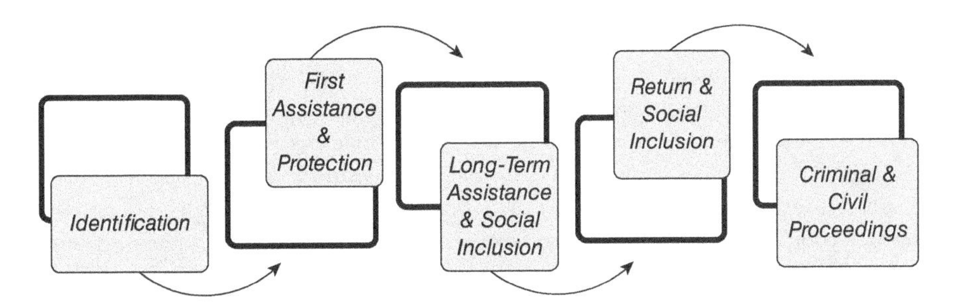

Figure 3.1 The steps of the National Referral Mechanism
Source: www.ravot-eur.eu/en/transnational-referral-mechanism.

co-operation among government agencies and non-governmental groups dealing with trafficked persons (OSCE, 2004). The NRM should include an official agreement on how victim assistance and the criminal justice process are harmonized, and should also be tied to the national anti-trafficking structures so as to ensure broad participation, monitoring and evaluation (OSCE, 2004). The NRM consists of several stages and phases, but should include:

- Guidance on victim identification and treatment: who identifies victims, what are the signs/indicators and how to ensure a human-rights based treatment of victims; and
- Guidance on where and how to refer victims of trafficking: lists of specialized service providers that can give the victim medical, social and psychological support, legal aid, immigration assistance and help with a possible voluntary return or resettlement.

The NRM can be seen as a process that starts with victim identification, followed by victim assistance and rehabilitation (both immediate and longer term), and finally by (re)integration and/or return of the victim to his/her home community. In many cases, criminal proceedings follow along with the assistance process (refer to Figure 3.1). If the victim is from a country other than the one where the victimization takes place, the NRM becomes intertwined with a transnational referral mechanism.

NRMs have been implemented in different parts of the world, most notably in Europe. The United Kingdom has a comprehensive NRM that underwent a review in 2014. The conclusions found, for instance, that support to victims should be provided based on an assessment of the individual needs of the victim, and that additional awareness-raising is needed among professionals and the general public alike to increase identification of victims (Home Office, 2014). An assessment of the situation in Vietnam, in turn, shows that there is a standardized referral mechanism in place to identify victims and refer them to care services, but this system is inconsistent (UNODC, 2013). The creation of an NRM requires the establishment of a National Competent Authority (NCA) to be in charge of victim identification and to streamline data collection so as to more accurately illustrate the scope and nature of the crime in Vietnam (UNODC, 2013). Also, for example, Swaziland in Southern Africa has established a referral mechanism, providing guidance on identification, support, reintegration and repatriation as well as criminal investigations.[8]

International coordination mechanisms

In March 2007, a number of international organizations, including the UNODC, UNICEF, UNHRC, the International Organization for Migration, and the Organization for Security and

Cooperation in Europe, established UN.GIFT (United Nations Global Initiative to Fight Human Trafficking), which is designed to strengthen a global, multi-stakeholder strategy to prevent and respond to trafficking, bringing together governments, UN agencies, intergovernmental and non-governmental organizations, the private sector, academia, civil society, the media and other stakeholders. As another example, the Inter-Agency Coordination Group against Trafficking in Persons was established in 2007 by United Nations General Assembly Resolution 61/180 to improve coordination among UN agencies and other relevant international organizations to facilitate a holistic and comprehensive approach to preventing and combating trafficking in persons, including protection and support for victims of trafficking.[9]

How do we improve the collection of data on trafficking, and what elements must be considered to guarantee that the data are relatively accurate?

Data collection and research

There has in the past been criticism of the "sketchy" data on human trafficking (Goodey, 2008), resulting at least partly from the hidden nature of the crime and the difficulties in obtaining data (Laczko, 2007). The lack of data makes the planning of policy responses difficult. The collection of data on cases of trafficking is called for by the main international conventions on trafficking and is an integral part of a well-functioning National Referral Mechanism. In recent years, there have been major efforts at the international level to collect data on human trafficking. The most notable effort is that of the UNODC, which has so far published four Global Reports on human trafficking (UNODC, 2009, 2012, 2014b, 2016). The data is collected through a questionnaire distributed to governments and by the collection of publicly available official information (e.g. national police reports, Ministry of Justice reports, and national trafficking in persons reports) (UNODC, 2016). The data therefore represent cases that have come to the attention of authorities (i.e. known or identified cases of trafficking) and therefore does not reflect the "real" extent of human trafficking at the global level. In a recent attempt to uncover the "dark figure" of trafficking, UNODC together with the office of the Dutch National Rapporteur on Trafficking used the so-called multiple systems estimate model to estimate the total presumed yearly number of trafficking victims in the Netherlands. The estimate gives an amount of 6,250–6,500 victims per year, which is four to five times higher than the number of victims recorded by authorities and NGOs (UNODC, 2017).

There are several databases on trafficking in human beings. For more than ten years, IOM has collected information on victims of trafficking in human beings. At the end of 2016 the database included details on almost 50,000 victims from countries around the world (IOM, 2017). In addition, ILO together with the Walk Free Foundation and IOM have developed an estimate of modern slavery: according to a recent study, 40.3 million people were victims of modern slavery in 2016 (ILO, 2017). The data was collected through surveys in 48 countries in Africa, the Arab states, Asia and the Pacific, the Americas, Europe and Central Asia assessing people's first-hand experiences of becoming victims of forced labour. The estimate has been criticized for having a weak empirical foundation, for the definitions used, the aggregation of data, and the combination of different forms of exploitation into single figures.[10]

Conclusions and discussion

Trafficking is a complex crime. Its process-like nature makes it difficult to address. It has also been approached from a number of perspectives, such as those of slavery and forced labour, human rights, prostitution, migration, the rights of children, and criminal justice. Addressing global inequality, poverty, and demand – the push and pull factors underlying trafficking in persons – may well offer the only lasting solutions.

The four P's of prevention, protection, prosecution and partnership provide a comprehensive framework, but require that trafficking is identified, acknowledged, and addressed appropriately. Regrettably, only a small proportion of victims are identified and provided assistance, and in even fewer cases are the traffickers identified and brought to justice.

Various international instruments, both binding and non-binding, have been formulated and have guided national and local action. The three instruments that have arguably been the most influential are the UN Trafficking Protocol (2000), the Council of Europe Convention on Action against Trafficking in Human Beings (2005) and the European Union Directive 2011/36/EU.

Finding a proper balance between the four P's, and in particular between the protection of victims and the prosecution of traffickers, is difficult. Many trafficked persons do not regard themselves as victims and for a variety of reasons may not want to be in contact with – much less cooperate with – the authorities. The prosecution of traffickers, in turn, often depends on the cooperation of and evidence given by the victims. Greater use of recovery periods and more generous provisions on residence permits may facilitate cooperation. Given the different concerns of the victims and the various stakeholders, an effective response to trafficking in persons requires strong partnerships where everyone is heard and their concerns taken into consideration. Partnerships are also needed to identify and remedy gaps in the implementation of the various instruments on trafficking in persons.

Notes

1 Although conventions and other hard law instruments are binding on the states that have ratified or acceded to them, attention should be paid to whether the individual provisions are indeed mandatory (typically, "states *shall*" undertake certain measures) or non-mandatory (for example, "states *shall consider*" undertaking certain measures).
2 www.unicef.org/eca/0610-Unicef_Victims_Guidelines_en.pdf.
3 General Assembly resolutions 58/137, 61/180, 61/144, 63/194 and 64/178.
4 www.unodc.org/unodc/en/human-trafficking/video-and-audio-on-human-trafficking-and-migrant-smuggling.html.
5 www.acf.hhs.gov/otip/resource/labor-trafficking-poster.
6 www.iom.int/news/public-awareness-campaign-launched-jamaica-protect-vulnerable-migrants.
7 www.ohchr.org/EN/HRBodies/HRC/WGTransCorp/Pages/IGWGOnTNC.aspx.
8 www.unodc.org/southernafrica/en/stories/swaziland-launches-victim-identification-guidelines-and-referral-mechanism-for-assisting-victims-of-human-trafficking.html.
9 http://icat.network.
10 www.opendemocracy.net/beyondslavery/daniel-m-gge/403-million-slaves-four-reasons-to-question-new-global-estimates-of-moder.

Supplemental learning materials

HEUNI has prepared an online course on human trafficking. This is very informative and provides basic information on what human trafficking is. Retrieved from http://heuni.education/page3139001.html

Since our article mostly deals with international policies, I think our course on the UN Crime programme, in particular the section on the history of the UN Trafficking Protocol, is relevant. Retrieved from http://heuni.education/un_crime_programme_course#rec66273020

As for general websites, the EU and Council of Europe anti-trafficking websites should be included. Retrieved from https://ec.europa.eu/anti-trafficking/ www.coe.int/en/web/anti-human-trafficking

The IOM website on trafficking also contains a lot of information on policies and practices. Retrieved from www.iom.int/counter-trafficking

The UNODC Online Toolkit to Combat Trafficking in Persons is also very useful. Retrieved from www.unodc.org/unodc/en/human-trafficking/2008/electronic-toolkit/electronic-toolkit-to-combat-trafficking-in-persons – index.html

This study on the integration of victims of trafficking who are also asylum-seekers; this report is rather recent and includes international comparison of policies. Retrieved from www.icmpd.org/fileadmin/1_2018/Bridging_the_Gap_between_Migration__Asylum_and_Anti-Trafficking.pdf www.cbss.org/wp-content/uploads/2018/12/Integration-Rad-Map.pdf

References

Andrijasevic, R., & Anderson, B. (2009). Anti-trafficking campaigns: Decent? Honest? Truthful? *Feminist Review*, *92*, 151–155.

Andrijasevic, R., & Mai, N. (2016). Editorial: Trafficking (in) representations: Understanding the recurring appeal of victimhood and slavery in neoliberal times. *Anti-Trafficking Review*, 7, 1–10.

Aronowitz, A. (2009). *Human trafficking, human misery: The global trade in human beings*. Westport, CT: Praeger Publishers.

ASEAN (2010). ASEAN Handbook on International Legal Cooperation in Trafficking in Persons Cases, Jakarta: ASEAN. Retrieved from https://www.unodc.org/documents/human-trafficking/ASEAN_Handbook_on_International_Legal_Cooperation_in_TIP_Cases.pdf

Bravo, K. E. (2009). Free labor! A labor liberalization solution to modern trafficking in humans. *Transnational Law and Contemporary Problems*, *18*(3), 545–616.

Bruch, E. M. (2004). Models wanted: The search for an effective response to human trafficking. *Stanford Journal of International Law*, *40*(1), 1–45.

Brunovskis, A. (2012). *Balancing protection and prosecution in anti-trafficking policies. A comparative analysis of reflection periods and related temporary residence permits for victims of trafficking in the Nordic countries, Belgium and Italy*. TemaNord 2012:556. Copenhagen: Nordic Council of Ministers.

Brunovskis, A., & Surtees, R. (2012). *Leaving the past behind? When victims of trafficking decline assistance*. Fafo-report 2012:31. Oslo & Washington: FAFO and Nexus Institute.

Chuang, J. A. (2014). Exploitation creep and the unmaking of human trafficking law. *The American Journal of International Law*, *108*(4), 609–649.

Cyrus, N., & Vogel, D. (2015). *Demand arguments in debates on trafficking in human beings: Using an historical and economic approach to achieve conceptual clarification*. DemandAT Working Paper No. 1. Retrieved from www.demandat.eu/sites/default/files/DemandAT%20WP1%20Cyrus%20Vogel%20June%202015a.pdf

Ditmore, M., & Wijers, M. (2003). The negotiations on the UN protocol on trafficking in persons: Moving the focus from morality to actual conditions. *NEMESIS*, *4*, 73–88.

Driscoll, K. (2011). Microcredit: Not yet a panacea to end trafficking in women. *University of Pennsylvania Journal of Business Law*, *13*(1), 275–300.

Farrell, A., McDevitt, J., Pfeffer, R., Fahy, S., Owens, C., Dank, M., & Adams, W. (2012). *Identifying challenges to improve the investigation and prosecution of state and local human trafficking cases: Executive summary*. Northeastern University and Urban Institute. Submitted for NIJ. Retrieved from www.in.gov/icw/files/412592-State-and-Local-Human-Trafficking-Cases.pdf

Gallagher, A. T. (2010). *The international law of human trafficking*. New York, NY: Cambridge University Press.

Goodey, J. (2008). Human trafficking: Sketchy data and policy responses. *Criminology and Criminal Justice*, *8*(4), 421–442.

Haynes, D. F. (2009). Exploitation nation: The thin and grey legal lines between trafficked persons and abused migrant laborers. *Notre Dame Journal of Legal Ethics and Public Policy*, *23*(1), 1–71.

Home Office. (2014). *Review of the national referral mechanism for victims of human trafficking*. Home Office. Retrieved from https://assets.publishing.service.gov.uk/government/uploads/system/uploads/attachment_data/file/467434/Review_of_the_National_Referral_Mechanism_for_victims_of_human_trafficking.pdf

Howard, N., & Lalani, M. (2008). Editorial introduction: The politics of human trafficking. *STAIR (St Anthony's International Review)*, *4*(1), 5–15.

ILO. (2017). *Global estimates of modern slavery: Forced labour and forced marriage*. Geneva: ILO.

IOM. (2007). *IOM handbook on direct assistance for victims of trafficking*. Geneva: IOM.
IOM. (2017, August). *Global trafficking trends in focus: IOM victim of trafficking data 2006–2016*. Retrieved from www.iom.int/sites/default/files/our_work/DMM/MAD/A4-Trafficking-External-Brief.pdf
Kilvington, J., Day, S., & Ward, H. (2001). *Prostitution policy in Europe: A time of change? Feminist Review, 47*, 78–93.
Laczko, F. (2007). Enhancing data collection and research on trafficking in persons. In E. U. Savona & S. Stefanizzi (Eds.), *Measuring human trafficking. Complexities and pitfalls* (pp. 37–44). New York, NY: Springer.
Lee, M. (2011). *Trafficking and global crime control*. London: SAGE.
Leppänen, K. (2006). International reorganisation and traffic in women: Venues of vulnerability and resistance. *Lychnos – rsbok för idé- och lärdomshistoria, 2006*, 110–128.
Levy, J., & Jakobsson, P. (2014). Sweden's abolitionist discourse and law: Effects on the dynamics of Swedish sex work and on the lives of Sweden's sex workers. *Criminology and Criminal Justice, 14*(5), 593–607.
Miers, S. (2003). *Slavery in the twentieth century: The evolution of a global problem*. Walnut Creek, CA: Altamira Press.
Monasky, H. (2010–2011). Note: On comprehensive prostitution reform: Criminalizing the trafficker and the trick, but not the victim. Sweden's sexköpslagen in America. *William Mitchell Law Reform, 37*, 1989–2045.
Niemi, J. (2010). What we talk about when we talk about buying sex. *Violence Against Women, 16*(2), 159–172.
Nieuwenhuys, C., & Pécoud, A. (2007). Human trafficking, information campaigns, and strategies of migration control. *American Behavioral Scientist, 50*(12), 1674–1695.
OAS (2004). Fighting the Crime of Trafficking in Persons, Especially Women, Adolescents, and Children, resolution 2019 (XXXIV-O/04 adopted by the General Assembly of the Organization of American States, Washington, D.C.: OAS. Retrieved from http://www.oas.org/juridico/english/ga03/agres_1948.htm.
O'Brien, E. (2013). Ideal victims in trafficking awareness campaigns. In K. Carrington, M. Ball, E. O'Brien, & J. Tauri (Eds.), *Crime, justice and social democracy: International perspectives* (pp. 315–325). Basingstoke: Palgrave Macmillan.
O'Connell Davidson, J. (2010). New slavery, old binaries: Human trafficking and the borders of "freedom." *Global Networks: A Journal of Transnational Affairs, 10*(2), 244–261.
O'Connell Davidson, J. (2012). Absolving the State: The trafficking-slavery metaphor. *Global Dialogue, 14*(2), 31–41.
OHCHR. (2011). *Guiding principles on business and human rights: Implementing the United Nations "Protect, Respect and Remedy" framework*. New York, NY and Geneva: United Nations.
Ollus, N. (2015). Regulating forced labour and combating human trafficking: The relevance of historical definitions in a contemporary perspective. *Crime, Law and Social Change, 63*(5), 221–246.
Ollus, N., & Jokinen, A. (2017). Exploitation of migrant workers and trafficking in human beings: A nexus of the demand by employers, workers and consumers. In R. Piotrowicz, C. Rijken, & B. Uhl (Eds.), *Routledge handbook of human trafficking* (pp. 473–486). Abingdon and New York, NY: Routledge.
OSCE. (2004). *National referral mechanisms: Joining efforts to protect the rights of trafficked persons*. Warsaw: OSCE ODIHR.
OSCE. (2008). *Efforts to combat trafficking in human beings in the OSCE area: Co-ordination and reporting mechanisms*. Vienna: OSCE Office of the Special Representative and Co-ordinator for Combating Trafficking in Human Beings
Quirk, J. (2011). *The anti-slavery project: From the slave trade to human trafficking*. Philadelphia, PA: University of Pennsylvania Press.
Rogoz, M., Deegan, L., Healy, C., Hendow, M., Hronková, M., Huddleston, W., . . . Zampagni, F. (2016). *Responses to demand in the context of trafficking in human beings: Regulatory measures from twelve national contexts*. DemandAT Working Paper No. 6. Retrieved from www.demandat.eu/sites/default/files/DemandAT_WP6_Rogoz_April2016_FINAL.pdf
Roth, V. (2010). *Defining human trafficking, identifying its victims. A study on the impact and future challenges of the international, European and Finnish legal responses to prostitution-related trafficking in human beings* (Doctoral dissertation), Turun yliopisto, Turku.
Surtees, R. (2013). *After trafficking: Experiences and challenges in the (re)integration of trafficked persons in the greater Mekong sub-region*. Bangkok: UNIAP/NEXUS Institute.
UNODC. (2008). *Toolkit to combat trafficking in persons*. Global programme against trafficking in human beings. New York, NY: United Nations.

UNODC. (2009). *Global report on trafficking in persons.* New York, NY: United Nations.
UNODC. (2012). *Global report on trafficking in persons 2012.* New York, NY: United Nations.
UNODC. (2013). *Needs assessment for establishing a national referral mechanism in Vietnam.* Bangkok: UNODC.
UNODC. (2014a). *Issue paper: The role of "consent" in the trafficking in persons protocol.* New York, NY: United Nations.
UNODC. (2014b). *Global report on trafficking in persons 2014.* New York, NY: United Nations.
UNODC. (2016). *Global report on trafficking in persons 2016.* New York, NY: United Nations.
UNODC. (2017). *Monitoring target 16.2 of the United Nations sustainable development goals: A multiple systems estimation of the numbers of presumed human trafficking victims in the Netherlands in 2010–2015 by year, age, gender, form of exploitation and nationality.* UNODC Research brief. UNODC and the National Rapporteur on Trafficking in Human Beings and Sexual Violence against Children.
Viuhko, M., Lietonen, A., Jokinen, A., & Joutsen, M. (Eds.). (2016). *Exploitative sham marriages: Exploring the links between human trafficking and sham marriages in Estonia, Ireland, Latvia, Lithuania and Slovakia.* HEUNI Report series No. 82. Helsinki: HEUNI.

4

NARRATIVES OF HUMAN TRAFFICKING IN INTERNATIONAL ISSUE ARENAS WITH IMPLICATIONS FOR POLICY FORMATION

Niina Meriläinen

Abstract

The purpose of this multidisciplinary research was to explore the various narratives of human trafficking by three gatekeeper actors including Amnesty International (Amnesty), Human Rights Watch (HRW) and the European Parliament (EP). The research questions addressed were the following: (1) What narratives are found regarding human trafficking? and (2) How do the actors frame human trafficking in their narratives? To answer these questions, a systematic content analysis was completed of documents that included official statements and research reports of NGOs as well as resolutions and recommendations of the EP. Altogether 298 documents were analyzed in detail. The findings indicate that Amnesty, HRW and EP create multiple narratives when addressing human trafficking. Each actor has a different method of correlating human trafficking with other social issues, thereby emphasizing different causes and effects in their narratives, while at the core sharing the same narratives relating to the causes and effects of human trafficking. The findings suggest that the formation of various human rights policies in the international arenas are deeply affected by selective narratives that include the dynamic interrelatedness between various human rights violations and other political and social issues, actors and events.

Learning Objectives

At the end of the chapter, readers will be able to:

1 Understand how narratives create understanding on complex social issues;
2 Understand the causes and effects of human trafficking;
3 Understand how narrative studies can be utilized to create better policy solutions; and
4 Understand why there are no one-size-fits-all policy solutions in relation to human trafficking.

Key Terms: human trafficking; human rights; narratives; bandwagoning; issue arenas; framing; policy formation.

Introduction

Human trafficking is a challenging social problem to overcome. There is overwhelming scientific evidence of the linkages between inequality and human trafficking (Barner, Okech, & Camp, 2014). The causes and effects are interwoven, and there are no easy solutions that are readily available that could be used to prevent and/or tackle human trafficking. According to Pettigrew (1973), in order to find a solution, the "demands have to be communicated" (p. 233). Communication is about sharing one's narrative(s). Narratives are each actors' communication and agendas, which are used to create understandings of issues, actors and events and the causal relations they create. Narratives are created by using selective framing. Given that understanding of issues (such as human trafficking) are created via narratives, narratives function as a basis of policy formulation, thus narratives regarding human trafficking should be studied in order to formulate policy suggestions. This underlines the importance of multidisciplinary qualitative research of the narratives that various actors have formulated in order to create understanding of complex issues such as human trafficking. Also, a previous study shows that various types of framing and narratives are found in the human rights literature (Meriläinen & Vos, 2013).

For there to be effective real-world policies and solutions regarding human trafficking, there first should be a shared understanding of the narratives that political decisions are consequently based upon. Policy formation based on narratives and consensus in its various forms is a mandatory condition. However, as Pallas and Urpelainen (2013) argue, "in the absence of consensus, power becomes a key issue" (p. 405). Yet, consensus is not the main goal in policy formation regarding human rights violations (Bob, 2012; Meriläinen, 2014), and thus there should not be the assumption that each actor shares the same understandings or narrative(s). The central gatekeepers control the debates and policy formation and use agenda setting to push their narratives to the centre to function as a base for policy formation (Meriläinen, 2014). The debates and policy formation processes regarding human trafficking are selective by nature (see C.deBaca, Chapter 2, this volume). This research begins from the premise that each actor has their own narratives, which they create by using framing to create understanding of human trafficking with the aim of securing their narrative(s) as a basis in the policy formation processes. This observation has special relevance for this research, as the purpose is to better understand how human trafficking is addressed in the public discourse in order to create better understanding of the complex issue of human trafficking within the policy formation process. In particular, the focus of this research is on well-established political actors' non-governmental organizations (NGOs, including Amnesty International [Amnesty] and Human Rights Watch [HRW]) and the European Parliament (EP) and how they utilize framing in creating narratives about human trafficking.

Analyses of narratives based on documents of the three gatekeepers (between 2011–2012 and from January 1, 2016 to August 31, 2017) reveals the determination of how the social and political debate surrounding human trafficking was structured and framed by each. Subsequently, comparisons can be made in the presentations of the actors, thereby allowing similarities and differences to be highlighted. By revealing possible different narratives from three gatekeepers, profound policy suggestions can be made on the basis of the understanding of the narratives that may hinder (or facilitate) development of solutions for human trafficking. Moreover, a better understanding of the context wherein human trafficking is debated and how the issue is framed offers insight into actors' beliefs about causal factors; such insight is necessary for policy formulation. However, analyses are based on the narratives of three gatekeeper actors only. Various other narratives may exist at local and global levels and should be included in future research.

This chapter is structured as follows: first, a multidisciplinary view of human rights issues is presented; second, the topic of human trafficking and power relations is briefly discussed; third, the research methodology is described followed with a presentation of the results and policy suggestions.

Multidisciplinary views on human rights narratives

Human rights are political and never absolute (Meriläinen, 2014). The forming of policies regarding human rights are preceded by the debate and power plays of various actors such as individuals, NGOs (who are newer forms of political actors), and traditional political actors including parliaments, the European Union (EU) and the U.S. Congress. Every actor who debates and works with human rights topics such as human trafficking is a political actor, because they aim for political effectiveness – thus NGOs and parliaments are both political actors (Meriläinen, 2014). Although traditionally, treaties and policies appear to be made by a few established political actors, various actors such as groups and organizations, which are members of civil society as well as private actors involved in agenda setting (Meriläinen & Vos, 2011), contribute to the process of debating and shaping narratives of human rights issues and policies. NGOs have been involved in developing international policies and formulating and implementing public norms for decades. They therefore act in a manner similar to political parties (Martens, 2002). Joachim (2003) in turn argues that "NGOs engage in strategic framing processes to set the agenda in three stages: the definition of problems, the development of solutions or policies, and politicization" (p. 268). NGOs have become key political powers that set the agenda and frame, and promote various power strategies (Steinberg, 2011). Murdie (2009) found that human rights NGOs have a political impact on the policy-making process, and this can have a moderate impact on human rights performance. Human rights issues, narratives and subsequent decisions are influenced by selectiveness and power relations. Dahre (2010) argues that human rights are political instruments and the discourse about human rights is about influence, force and political power. This discourse is political by nature, thus calling for both social and political solutions. Indeed, if the understanding of human rights issues that comes through shared narratives is not collectively seen as legitimate and accepted, human rights policies will not be respected on the grassroots level. The disconnect between narratives of the human law versus the narratives of human rights realities can be vast. Human rights legislators and researchers must realize that having human rights treaties and implementing them on national and international legislation does not equal *respect for the rights* that the legislation addresses. Legal realities and grassroots realities comprise two different narratives.

What narratives can you think of regarding human rights issues? Which actor(s) have formulated them, and why were those particular narratives formulated?

Given that human rights are never absolute (Meriläinen, 2014), the changes in human rights situations (whether through activism, NGO work or legislation) is always based on narratives that each actor or group of actors formulate together via framing. Human rights narratives do not appear and disappear by themselves. As Ibhawoh (2010, p. 80) states, "the language of human rights has become a principal means of legitimizing political and social agendas," and human rights framing can be used to include or exclude certain norms and policies (DeBono, 2013). Moreover, human rights narratives are not static; some issues that had long been accepted as part of a given culture have now become known as human rights violations (Schott, 2011). Because perceptions of human rights issues are closely connected to particular cultural environments, they are consequently highly sensitive topics affecting the formation of public policy and law in the human rights domain (Alidadi & Foblets, 2012). According to Nash (2009), human rights are cultural and their meaning essentially contestable. Thus, due to different sets of cultural beliefs, values and experiences, actors have different understandings of what human rights are (Keck & Sikkink, 1998; Okin, 1998; Marsh & Payne, 2007), which means there are various narratives about human rights. This can lead to lack of consensus on the so-called right narratives, which in turn directly influences whose rights should be protected (Miller, 2013). Dahre (2010) argues that human rights are used to justify particular cultural, moral and political views internationally, and can be said to be a form of cultural imperialism. Guttenplan and Margaronis (2010) wonder if the distrust between actors will continue and if human rights agendas can be developed. Donnelly (1982) states that there are different views on human rights and that while we are debating which view (or narrative) is correct, the practice of monitoring human rights may be lost. Hence, it is essential to research the narratives of various actors regarding human trafficking to identify shared understanding and narratives (if such exist) as well as competing understandings and realities of how human trafficking is understood. Indeed, governments can draw up treaties and agree to human rights norms, but if citizens are not ready to accept them as legitimate, the support to sustain them will not exist (Marsh & Payne, 2007). Human rights treaties and agendas may even be used as a tool by competing states. Hafner-Burton, Tsutsui, and Meyer (2008) argue that repressive states, especially those with greater autonomy, may ratify human rights treaties because no sanctions will be implemented, and ratification legitimizes their policies at a low cost while human rights violations will continue as usual.

Framing

Various actors participate (or try to participate) in the debate and policy formation concerning social problems by agenda setting. Actors use framing (defined as "to select some aspects of a perceived reality and make them more salient in a communicating text, in such a way as to promote a particular problem definition, causal interpretation, moral evaluation, and/or treatment recommendation") (Entman, 1993, p. 52) as part of their agenda setting processes to add salience to their narratives. Framing is a selective process, as it stresses certain aspects over others (Lecheler & de Vreese, 2010). In reality, various human rights concerns are constantly pitted against each other in public discourse (Bob, 2009). Different narratives compete for attention in issue arenas that have limited carrying capacities, and only the narratives that are in some way attractive – for example, have drama attached to them – are rewarded with attention and consequently become salient concerns. Thus, the frameworks of various narratives actually compete for attention (Hilgartner & Bosk, 1988). Moreover, real-world events and other social concerns act as rivals and possibly influence the attention and thus the narratives that will be paid to a social issue in various arenas.

Bandwagoning and value framing

In addition to emphasizing certain salient aspects of a social problem, the process of framing can also be used in a narrative to connect one issue, actor or event with another. Nicholson and Chong (2011) call the process of linking topics together "bandwagoning." Linking social concerns to one another in a narrative can have a positive effect, especially when a non-salient problem is linked with a more salient one. For example, linking human rights issues with women's rights has proven to be a powerful framework that has mobilized international support (Joachim, 2003). Actors assess the social issue by considering possible linkages between the topic of concern and established human rights concerns (Carpenter, 2011). For example, Amnesty generally introduces a new topic by establishing a link with an already established human rights theme (Rodio & Schmitz, 2010). Framing is a strategic process that may also be used to connect one social issue with certain values. Values are essential motivational beliefs about outcomes of favorable modes of individual behavior (Kilburn, 2009). If frames do not resonate with the pre-existing system of values and beliefs, then an issue or a policy solution may be disregarded by the public (Meriläinen & Vos, 2013; Meriläinen, 2014). A value frame thus connects a certain social issue with established values that support one view on the issue (Brewer & Gross, 2005). Busby (2007) states that to persuade policy actors to become involved in the decision-making process, advocacy frameworks should include values that have wide societal appeal and personal relevance. Repeated framing of a political problem in a particular manner can eventually influence public opinion (Shen & Edwards, 2005), thus for example influencing how victims of human trafficking are viewed and treated in the society and how victim services are provided.

Human trafficking

In your view, which actors are the current gatekeepers in the human rights issue arenas?

Human trafficking can be described as the cross-border global trading of people in which there is, on the one hand, a low risk of being apprehended by state officials and, on the other hand, a high profit margin compared to other illegal activities for the traffickers. Human trafficking usually involves victimizing people through the use of extreme violence and various forms of social, economic and political discrimination (Aston & Paranjape, 2012; Hughes, 2000; Agbu, 2003). As Barner et al. (2014) state, "with an established relationship to poverty and violence, and its exploitative, profiteering nature, human trafficking has become the most prevalent manifestation of contemporary slavery in the world today" (p. 151). Victimization is indeed common in human rights violations and usage of power. Victimization goes hand in hand with "othering" used to create and reaffirm power relationships between actors, thereby creating outsiders (Kamler, 2013; Jensen, 2011; Schoff, 2011; Petros, Airhihenbuwa, Simbayi, Ramlagan, & Brown, 2006). There are various shapes and forms of othering which are connected to social and political power relations. Through framing, narratives are created that shape the understanding of issue owners and gatekeepers, whereas some others (actors) are framed in the narratives as "victims," "problematic," "wrong," "disgusting" and "unworthy" by character and values. This is done to cement power relations between actors and to name so-called good and bad actors, legitimate and non-legitimate actors and to gain legitimacy for one's own actions.

International concern put the topic of human trafficking on the international agenda in the 1980s and 1990s, initially through the feminist violence against women movement that combined issues such as rape, domestic violence, pornography and prostitution at a time when international law did not envision trafficking outside the parameters of prostitution (Sullivan, 2010). Political and economic factors and lucrative job opportunities push people from one country, often in the Global South, pulling them to other countries, often Western countries in the Global North (Hughes, 2000; Hankivsky, 2011). Human trafficking is a very complex issue and therefore difficult to effectively mitigate (Van den Anker & van Liempt, 2012; Agbu, 2003). Scholars and political advisors suggest that, in order to target this problem, the broader socioeconomic context needs to be taken into account (Chuang, 2006). Agbu (2003), for example, explains that the volume of trafficking that takes place within a state is connected to the level of corruption in immigration organizations and the number of organized crime networks that are active within a society. Human trafficking networks have often operated in conjunction with other illegal trade prior to involvement in trafficking in persons, where the aim has been to get money and fulfil their "American dream" (Nikolić-Ristanović, 2012). Maedl (2011) addresses the development of these hierarchical systems in sexual crime, where trafficked women form a "second wave" of criminal activity when they return to their home country and recruit more victims, thus contributing to further human rights violations. Similarly, victims once trafficked often continue to be trafficked, also demonstrating that human trafficking is part of a cycle of oppression that connects various actors, events and violations to one another (Shelley, 2012; Eurostat, 2013). Clearly, multiple narratives exist on various issues, actors and events in human rights literature (Kamler, 2013), and cultural aspects and various forms of social inequality may be forgotten when (Western) actors debate human trafficking and possible solutions. Culturally, scholars describe human trafficking as having deep roots (DeBono, 2013). The interrelatedness of specific social problems, and the context in which these problems take place, is not fully understood or agreed upon. Subsequently, understanding what human trafficking is, and how actors and events are interrelated, may be due to culturally bound definitions (Dembour & Kelly, 2011). Thus, it is important to research human trafficking narratives used by human rights and political actors, paying particular attention to the social and cultural contexts and power relations between actors.

Power politics

Actors operate in issue arenas and form various networks. Studies on NGOs by Keck and Sikkink (1998) clarify that:

> Networks are forms of organization characterized by voluntary, reciprocal, and horizontal patterns on communication exchange. . . . The network concept travels well because it stresses fluid and open relations among committed and knowledgeable actors working in specialized issue areas.
>
> *(p. 8)*

However, power represents a more prominent role in the networks than Dahl's (1957) definition. Information is not shared freely; power games are played and narratives created accordingly by using framing in the human rights networks (Meriläinen, 2014). Power can be gained by focusing on certain issues, actors and events (and not others) through selective framing and agenda setting (Meriläinen, 2014). Many different political actors, including various NGOs, are active in the human rights debate (Bob, 2009) and have different interests and narratives to promote (Meriläinen & Vos, 2012; Meriläinen, 2014). They battle for power positions armed with their own frames and agendas relating what are currently the most salient human rights issues and violations. The causes and effects of these problems are not always shared or agreed upon, which further illustrates the importance of power during the debates and policy formation processes. Bachrach and Baratz (1962) argue there are two faces of power: decision-making and non-decision-making. During the process of decision-making (policy-making), powerful actors participate and make other actors do something they did not originally want to do, for example making them accept certain narratives and further legitimating them, whereas during non-decision-making (non-policy-making) situations, certain political issues, narratives or conflicts are intentionally left out of the debates (Anton, 2007). Lukes (1974) added that there is a third form of power: ideological power. This takes place when one actor has the ability to manipulate and/or influence the values and points of view, or narratives, of another actor or group of actors. Once an actor has acquired a certain level of power, that actor can then begin to act as a gatekeeper with the ability to influence the course of the debate and, subsequently, the actual policy formation process.

Gatekeeping

When multiple actors take or try to take part in the debate, differences of opinion can create blockages between the actors during the debates and policy formation processes, turning the debates into a political power play of negotiations. Gatekeeping is a successful form of power politics. Barzilai-Nahon (2008) defines it as a process of information control, which can include the selection, addition and channeling of information; it can also include withholding, shaping and the manipulation of information, as well as the repetition, localization, integration, disregarding and even the deletion of information. Lewin (1947) is credited with developing the notion of gatekeeping, which has since been adopted by various disciplines. He argues that coalition forces in and outside of the gated region decide who is "in power" during the policy formation process and who is "not in power" (p. 145). Bob (2009) states that most gatekeepers are organizations with a good staff, a good budget, and a high level of credibility. These powerful actors have the ability and the means to give a certain level of visibility to their favorite human rights issues, and "when gatekeepers adopt the claim as a rights issue, the right becomes a recognizable issue on the international scene" (Bob, 2009, p. 8).

Which actors in your view are the current gatekeepers in the human rights issue arenas?

The distribution of power, and the position of the actors and their resources, thus permit some to become gatekeepers, while others must continue to follow their lead in order to continue receiving support for their own agendas (Bennett, Foot, & Xenos, 2011). Gated actors can, via content production, control agendas and frames, relationship building and producing alternative narratives, and can thereby change the course of a debate and influence power relations in different issue arenas. Moreover, to gain issue ownership and power, "issue handling competence is the key" (Petrocik, 1996, p. 847), which entails the intelligent case-by-case use of power. With the clever use of information and other means, gated actors may be able to break existing power structures in issue arenas. Moreover, the fragmentation of coalitions and tension within groups, as well as the forced reality in which the gated actors must comply with the gatekeeper's narratives, can lead some actors to form competing networks and alliances (Bennett et al., 2011), subsequently challenging the central hub and its power relations. Similarly, if a debate takes place in one issue arena, such as in a national or in the EU parliament, then a counter-debate can occur in online media. For example, victim narrative videos have proven that the social media can create opportunities to disseminate information on important social issues that rarely get attention in the traditional mainstream media (Gregory, 2006; DeLuca, Lawson, & Sun, 2012). Therefore, the innovative use of communication tools and arenas can also lead to changes in the distribution of information. For example, NGOs' use of social media to inform the general public about human trafficking may lead to the transfer of the debate about this problem to a parliamentary context. It is important to understand how different actors debate human trafficking and to what extent they emphasize certain criteria while they frame the issue, as it is clear that shared opinions about this problem may facilitate the development of global norms and solutions.

Research methods

This research was aimed at discovering narratives of human trafficking by studying the documents of two human rights organizations, Amnesty International (Amnesty) and Human Rights Watch (HRW) as well as the European Parliament (EP). Amnesty and HRW were chosen because they are well-known international NGOs that participate in the development of public policy and law formation. The EP was selected as it is actively engaged in debating the topic of human trafficking and finding solutions to this international problem. The research questions included: (1) What narratives are found regarding human trafficking? (2) How do the actors frame human trafficking in their narratives?

Procedures

To answer the research questions, a selection of documents was completed and further analyzed. The time frame for the research was twofold: a two-year period from January 1, 2011, through December 31, 2012, and then revised research from January 1, 2016, through August 31, 2017. Initially, this research yielded 3,623 documents and research reports from Amnesty and the HRW and 212 decision-making documents from the EP. Using a thematic analysis, the narratives in which human trafficking was discussed and debated were identified. A total of 298 documents were selected and further analyzed to identify how human trafficking was addressed by the actors. All the English language research data was available online on Amnesty's and HRW's websites as well as on the European Parliament's Legal Observatory website. The structured search was done by using the keywords "human trafficking" and "trafficking of/in [humans]." The material for our analysis was selected using three main criteria:

1 The document had to be created during the time periods of January 2011–December 2012 and January 2016–August 2017.
2 The selected materials had to include either the term "human trafficking" or "trafficking of/in humans."
3 The selected documents had to include at least one sentence about human trafficking; a simple two-word mention of human trafficking was not deemed as providing real data for answering the research question. Documents that only mentioned the words "trafficking" or "human" were excluded, since they did not cover *human trafficking* as an action or social phenomenon, but discussed other matters such as drug trafficking or weapon treaties.
4 For EP's materials, an additional criterion was added in that for each English-language PDF document, the labels "Procedure completed" and "Text adopted by Parliament, 1st reading/single reading" were required (meaning the document was a final product of a political discussion and the subsequent decision-making process).

Analyses

After studying all of the documents for each actor, narratives of human trafficking were compiled. During the studying phase of all 298 documents, direct citations about human trafficking were underlined in order to return to them later during the analytical stage of the research process. Direct citations about human trafficking were then copied into the data-extraction table. Next, direct citations were placed into the data-extraction table to create an overview of the narratives addressing human trafficking, and the various framings and bandwagoned issues, actors and events were noted. In the analysis, narratives regarding human trafficking were examined.

This was done to gain a multidisciplinary understanding of the possible various narratives regarding human trafficking, how trafficking is framed, and to discover cause-and-effect narratives that focused on bandwagoning issues.

Results: 2011–2012

The findings for the 2011–2012 period are briefly summarized here and discussed in detail in the original report (see Meriläinen & Vos, 2015).

Amnesty International and Human Rights Watch

Amnesty and HRW have both extensively reported on human trafficking. In their narratives, human trafficking is typically bandwagoned with multiple issues (e.g. rape, labour violations, sexual exploitation, blackmail, government corruption and murder), actors and events. In their narratives, the NGOs use a strategy called *framing of responsibility*, which is briefly noted in the seven narratives used by the NGOs. Alphabetically, these include:

- *Corrupt officials narrative.* Here, corrupt officials are framed as responsible for trafficking as they take part and benefit financially from human trafficking. Recruiters and employment agencies are part of trafficking networks that cooperate or have ties to state and security officials that allow, facilitate and profit from human trafficking. According to many of the HRW and Amnesty documents, human trafficking is controlled by competing drug cartels receiving protection from political proxies that have expanded their criminal activities in drug trafficking to include human trafficking.
- *Exploitation of women narrative.* In the exploitation of women narrative, trafficking, domestic violence, dowry-related violence, rape and sexual assault are serious problems not addressed effectively by police. According to the two NGOs, women and children were the most commonly reported victims of trafficking networks. This narrative includes forced sex work in the commercial sex industry, street prostitution and work in massage parlors and brothels. Other forms of exploitation and slavery (e.g, domestic service work, agricultural labor, construction work, hotel services, manufacturing and healthcare jobs) were also frequently noted such that the topic of human trafficking was noted as part of a wider context of human rights violations.
- *Organ markets narrative.* Amnesty uses an organ markets narrative to illustrate how traffickers forcibly remove organs to sell on the black market; victims most commonly die, either during or after the surgery. By using this narrative, Amnesty draws attention in their agenda setting to another context of human trafficking by bandwagoning it to the organ transplant tourism industry. Moreover, Amnesty states that organ trafficking with transplant tourism violates the principles of equity, justice, and respect for human dignity. "Because transplant commercialism targets impoverished and otherwise vulnerable donors, it leads inexorably to inequity and injustice and should be prohibited" (Codes of Ethics, 2011). Amnesty calls for states to prevent organ trafficking, emphasizing states' responsibility by framing once again.
- *Poverty and migration narrative.* According to the NGOs' poverty and migration narrative, people who become trafficking victims are individuals who usually have lived in poverty and may have experienced a violent home life that generated distress. The documents suggest the idea of obtaining lucrative work abroad gives hope to people living in poverty that their quality of life will improve. Instead they are sold as slaves who work in horrendous conditions with little or no pay, with any profit from their work taken by the traffickers.

In the narrative, both Amnesty and HRW bandwagon various forms of exploitation faced by domestic migrant workers worldwide, including excessive working hours, forced labor, non-payment of wages and forced debts, involuntary confinement, physical and sexual abuse and trafficking: "Migrant workers faced exploitation by recruiters who exposed them to human trafficking and forced labour" (see Amnesty, 2012). According to narratives of both NGOs, poverty clearly plays an important role in the exploitation and trafficking of humans globally, and children in particular. Further, the two NGOs argue that local and regional officials often disregard the abuses and allow exploitation of workers to continue, which bandwagons with the earlier mentioned corrupt officials narrative. Human trafficking is thus described as a chain of interlinked events that includes brokers, agencies and state officials.

- *The refugee narrative.* In this narrative, both NGOs describe how human trafficking is a widespread problem in the Mediterranean region. HRW reported that in 2011 the UN Special Rapporteur called the conditions of Greece's immigration detention facilities inhumane and degrading. Since joining the EU, Cyprus has become a destination for migrant laborers and for the trafficking of women for sexual exploitation. Moreover, the "desire of some European countries to prevent 'irregular migration' is undermining safe and timely rescues at sea" (see Egypt, 2011). HRW's narrative shows that the Mediterranean region is a heavily trafficked area and that some Mediterranean countries, such as Italy and Greece, do not have adequate systems to screen and aid victims of trafficking.
- *Sub-Saharan narrative.* Ineffective or corrupt governmental officials, gender-based violence, and extreme poverty are root causes of human trafficking which comes across in the NGOs' sub-Saharan narrative. This narrative illustrates how these issues are exacerbated by a lack of border security and power struggles between vying elites or militias. In the narrative, the NGOs focused on the human rights situation and widespread trafficking of mostly sub-Saharan migrant workers and asylum seekers in the Sahel and Sinai areas. Amnesty claims "there is an extensive network of people-traffickers throughout Eritrea, Ethiopia, Sudan, Egypt and Israel. The traffickers are both well-equipped and well-armed," and further "foreign nationals have reportedly been held, tortured(including raped), and murdered by people-traffickers, while the authorities have done little to protect them" (see Egypt: Broken Promises, 2011). Similarly, HRW states that due to an absence of law enforcement, "thousands of sub-Saharan asylum seekers and migrants attempting to cross the Sinai have fallen victim to abusive traffickers and other criminals" (see Egypt: End Sinai, 2012). Traffickers imprison victims and then demand a ransom from their families; according to HRW, those who cannot pay for their ransom are forced to pay the debt by working. HRW estimates traffickers' demands have risen from $2,500 to $30,000 per person between the years 2009 and 2012.
- *Victim support services narrative.* NGOs also present a narrative whereby well-meaning governmental authorities often use ineffective methods of support for trafficking victims. To illustrate, HRW mentions that victims were unaware of hotlines set up by a labor ministry, that the hotlines rarely worked or that there were no qualified interpreters available to help them understand their rights. Both HRW and Amnesty report that a police crackdown on human trafficking usually consists of closing down brothels and randomly detaining sex workers instead of actually prosecuting perpetrators. Moreover, for government officials, the line between lawfully employed migrant laborers and trafficked people is not always clear. One of Amnesty's narratives shows that victims of trafficking and torture have been detained in Denmark and the Netherlands, as they are considered illegal immigrants. Both Amnesty and HRW emphasize that trafficked people often are not recognized as victims.

Which of these narratives do you see or recognize in NGOs in which you work?

Summary

The NGO narratives illustrate how deeply rooted social practices and prejudices can contribute or even lead to human trafficking. Narratives illustrate the cause and effect realities where human trafficking must be understood within a broader global context as human rights and various bandwagoned issues that are interwoven into the NGOs' documents. Both Amnesty's and HRW's narratives illustrate that global poverty, gendered violence, insecure borders and the poor functioning of juridical systems exacerbate human rights violations. Thus, to tackle the problem of human trafficking, the root causes of why people are seeking work and better life has to be addressed within the context of the various political, social, economic, legal and cultural environments in which they live.

European Parliament

The EP addressed human trafficking less frequently than the two NGOs. The EP's main narrative frames human trafficking within the context of several other social issues and human rights violations. The EP's main human trafficking narrative is strongly connected to gender equality and women's rights, gender equality, fundamental rights and freedoms, and general concepts about democracy. Moreover, economic and trade relations, humanitarian and aid issues and the enlargement of the EU were described as connected to social problems that facilitate the development of human trafficking rings. Narratives produced by the EP appear alphabetically and include:

- *Devastation of societies narrative.* Looking at human trafficking in a broader context, the EP's devastation of societies narrative shows how human trafficking, in connection with various other crimes, can contribute to the widespread devastation of societies, especially in the Sahel-Saharan and Sinai regions. Bandwagoning is done between, for example, terrorist groups in the Sahel-Saharan region and traffickers in drugs, arms, cigarettes and human beings. They report:

  > State fragility, poor governance and corruption in the Sahel countries, accompanied by economic underdevelopment resulting in chronic poverty, provide a perfect environment for terrorist groups, drug and human traffickers, and groups engaged in piracy, arms trade, money laundering, illegal immigration and organized crime networks, which combine to destabilize the region, with a negative impact also on neighbouring regions.
  >
  > *(Resolution, 2012)*

  In this way, the issue is placed in the context of various other crimes and a narrative similarly created by the two NGOs.
- *Gender-based violence narrative.* Within this narrative, human trafficking is framed as an issue that affects the world community in relation to gender-based violence and the global economic and labor markets. Gender-based violence is defined by the EP as

  > a form of discrimination and a violation of the fundamental freedoms of the victim and includes violence in close relationships, sexual violence (including rape, sexual

> assault and harassment), trafficking in human beings, slavery, and different forms of harmful practices, such as forced marriages, female genital mutilation and so-called "honour crimes."
>
> *(Rights, 2011)*

With respect to the economic or labor market situation, the EP uses the narrative to argue "male violence against women shapes women's place in society: their health, access to employment and education, integration into social and cultural activities, economic independence, participation in public and political life and decision-making, and relations with men" (Priorities, 2010). Based on this narrative, human trafficking is a lucrative business run by organized crime syndicates with international networks, along with other forms of trafficking (e.g. arms and drug trafficking).

- *European Union narrative.* In the European context narrative, the EP notes "local" EU related issues that are connected to trafficking (e.g. asylum seekers from Serbia are trafficked to EU member states). The EP therefore calls for the EU to cooperate in combating the links between false asylum seekers and human trafficking and to fight against organized criminal groups involved in human trafficking. The EP and both NGOs urge Kosovar and Albanian authorities to cooperate with neighboring countries and to give their full support to the EULEX Special Investigative Task Force that investigates the inhumane treatment of people and the illegal trafficking in human organs.
- *Fishing narrative.* The EP also has a narrative linking fishing to human trafficking, as does HRW. Illegal, unreported and unregulated (IUU) fishing attracts many illegal activities. The EP

> is alarmed at the use of such criminal activities as human exploitation and trafficking, money laundering, corruption, handling of stolen goods, tax evasion and customs fraud by those engaged in IUU fishing, which should be viewed as a form of organized transnational crime.
>
> *(see Combatting illegal fishing, 2010)*

Consequently, the EP asked for more attention at the EU and Interpol levels to fight IUU fishing.

- *Missing support systems narrative.* Similar to the two NGOs' narratives, the EP's missing support systems narrative underlines that victims of human trafficking should not be treated as criminals or refused support. The EP mentions its deep concern regarding media reports about victims of human trafficking being treated as criminals, consequently calling for the EU Commission to investigate the treatment of victims of trafficking, sexual slavery and forced prostitution in EU states. In many documents, the EP mentions looking forward to the results of systems put in place for monitoring transparency and financial fair play in combating corruption and human trafficking.
- *Natural disasters narrative.* In the natural disasters narrative, the EP notes how natural disasters may also lead to the devastation of societies and exploitation of vulnerable populations. Thus, the narrative shows how an unexpected occurrence creates a possibility to exploit people and thus worsen the human rights situation.
- *Surrogacy and adoption narrative.* The EP uses a surrogacy and adoption narrative that requests that EU states "acknowledge the serious problem of surrogacy which constitutes an exploitation of the female body and her reproductive organs" (Priorities, 2010). Besides reproductive markets, the EP uses this narrative to focus on the problem of illegal adoption in the EU

by stating that children are trafficked for adoption, begging, forced marriages, illegal labor, prostitution and other purposes.

- *Trafficking in sports narrative.* The EP also framed human trafficking in the context of sports in one narrative (see European dimension, 2011). The EP argues that any kind of discrimination should be excluded from sport, as should political, religious or racist propaganda at sporting events, and that women should not be excluded from sports due to political pressure. Further, match fixing and the use of illegal prostitution take place at sporting events, thus bandwagoning these with human trafficking and abuses of women.

Summary

The data show that various forms of gender-based violence, social inequality and serious human rights violations are bandwagoned in the EP's political discussions. Human trafficking is part of a large and complex conglomerate of social justice issues. The traditional way of thinking about human rights issues as occurring singly and in isolation no longer applies. Addressing the problem of human trafficking and finding a solution must take into consideration that social issues are intertwined and framed together. Thus, discussing human rights violations as separate issues in the absence of any broader social-political dimensions seems vastly outdated. According to the EP, grassroots participation by NGOs is essential for solving issues such as human trafficking and gender-based violence, as is utilizing the skills of women in problem-solving and conflict resolution. The EP urges EU authorities to put all forms of human rights at the censer of EU foreign policies and take into consideration the broader geopolitical context.

Comparison of NGO and EP narratives

Comparing the NGO narratives with those of the EP, it is evident that each gatekeeper actors focuses on the causal effects that are found by formulating and analyzing the narratives. The three gatekeeper actors have similar narratives, as seen in Table 4.1. This illustrates that the actors have created a similar understanding of the cause and effect realities that involve human trafficking as part of the lager chain that includes multiple events, actors and issues. The key findings are that all three actors are aware of how the global gender-based violence, refugee crises, corrupt officials and the role of poverty plays in creating possibilities for human trafficking to turn people in to commodities and to profit off selling and exploiting especially women and children. The

Table 4.1 Comparison of NGO and EP narratives: 2011–2012

Comparative Narratives 2011–2012	
Amnesty and HRW	*European Parliament*
Slavery (sexual and other) and women's exploitation	Gender-based violence
Poverty: migration and child labor	Missing support systems
Corrupt official	Surrogacy and adoption
Victim support services	Devastation of societies
Refugees	European Union
Sub-Saharan	Fishing
Organ markets	Trafficking in sports

narratives show a clear cause and effect. All three actors bandwagon various issues but especially for EP, no clear political solutions were presented to tackle human trafficking, especially the root causes of it.

Results: 2016–2017

NGO's narratives

Compared to earlier analyses (2011–2012) with seven narratives, recent analyses revealed the two NGOs had instead six primary narratives. Amnesty's narratives focused on sex work and the refugee crises, whereas HRW narratives focused on food industry, forced labor and corrupt officials, education and assistance and detention centres.

- *Detention centres narratives.* Here, HRW illustrates how unsafe detention centres provide a space for continued human rights violations. "Smugglers could be seen openly operating at the site, and officials of nongovernmental groups expressed concern about the security of the people stranded there and their potential exposure to extortion, violence, sexual abuse, and human trafficking networks" (see Greece/Macedonia, 2016). HRW clarifies the need for training, noting in one of their case studies: "All the other police officers we interviewed also said they were unaware of any victims of trafficking or gender-based violence among the unaccompanied children whose detention they had overseen" (Why are you keeping me here, 2016). HRW notes the need to create alternatives for detention centres where vulnerable groups such as children, migrants with disabilities and victims of trafficking or gender-based violence are placed. Here we see how HRW bandwagons victims of trafficking with other groups and simultaneously creates an understanding of larger groups of vulnerable victims which should be taken into account.
- *Education and assistance narrative.* Education emerged in HRW's narrative in relation to locals, refugees and officials, for instance, including the need for better identification services to detect victims of trafficking in order to provide services as well as the importance of children, and other victims, to be given the opportunity to speak with officials with the help of an interpreter. In this narrative HRW drew a causal connection between education and human trafficking, noting:

  > Education is also a powerful protection factor: children who are in school are less likely to come into conflict with the law and much less vulnerable to rampant forms of child exploitation, including child labour, trafficking, and recruitment into armed groups and forces.
  >
  > *(Education deficit, 2016)*

  HRW strengthens the narrative by calling for increased funding "for and support to structures and organizations providing legal assistance to *talibé* children who are victims of abuse, exploitation, and trafficking" (Senegal, 2016). Here we see how HRW calls for a direct policy suggestion: increased funding.
- *Food industry, forced labour and corrupt officials narrative.* In one of its central narratives, HRW bandwagoned human trafficking with the food industry, forced labour and corrupt officials. In one instance, HRW illustrated how corrupt Thai officials were involved in human trafficking and described the link between trafficking and the food industry, stating

> Trafficked men . . . are deceived or simply forced to work on the fishing boats, where they endure 20 hours or more workdays, physical abuse by captains and boatswains, dirty and dangerous working conditions that result in injuries or sickness for which they get no time off, inadequate nutritious food and potable water, and little or no pay.
>
> *(Australia, 2017)*

The trafficking was organized and upheld by underground brokers, traffickers themselves and corrupt Thai police who, according to HRW, had done little to tackle the serious problem of human trafficking and to prosecute those responsible.

- *The refugee crises narrative.* The refugee crises was another central narrative for Amnesty, a narrative that was also previously utilized in the 2011–2012 analysis period. In each refugee crisis-narrative example, Amnesty bandwagons the refugee crises and human trafficking with other human rights violations while it frames the issue of refugee crisis as important by stressing how

> Refugees and migrants in transit are at high risk of abuse, including violence and human trafficking. Women, girls and LGBTI individuals face specific threats such as sexual harassment, rape and other forms of gender-based violence, underscoring the urgent need for safe and legal routes.
>
> *(see Refugees in need, 2016)*

Amnesty noted speaking to "least 90 refugees . . . who were abused by people smugglers, traffickers, organized criminal gangs and armed groups" (see Refugees and migrants fleeing, 2016). Here it is again evident how human trafficking continues to be bandwagoned with people smuggling, organized crime and violence of various forms, as it was in the previous analysis period. Amnesty strengthened the refugee-crises narrative by showcasing the reality where travelling refugee women are prepared for human rights abuses *beforehand*, stating

> sexual abuse is endemic for refugees travelling through Libya, so much so that women have told us they take contraceptives before travelling, because they expect to be raped and want to avoid becoming pregnant as a result of it. Women are constantly at risk of sexual violence at the hands of smugglers, traffickers, armed groups or in immigration detention centres and all the women Amnesty International spoke to had experienced it themselves or knew other women who had.
>
> *(see Through their eyes, 2016)*

Amnesty's narrative highlights the crude reality of victims by illustrating how the European decision-makers are not taking any real-world policy measures to tackle trafficking.

- *Sex worker narrative.* Different from the 2011–2012 narratives was Amnesty's agenda setting highlighting the role of volunteer sex workers and their treatment in relation to human trafficking policies and victim services. In Amnesty's narrative, there are distinctions made between human trafficking victims and sex workers. Amnesty calls for separation of these two groups because sometimes sex workers "can be categorized as trafficking victims, even if they claim otherwise, whether they are working autonomously or with others (or "third parties")" (see Argentina, 2016). In the narrative a reality where the police still go after the sex workers, not traffickers or pimps, comes alive. In this narrative the sex worker is the criminal, not the traffickers or pimps who can continue their abusive work, thus shifting the responsibility of events from pimps and traffickers to the sex worker. The reality which comes across in this narrative is problematic since the responsibility of the human rights violation is placed on the sex worker, whereas those who are in actuality responsible for the violations – the traffickers and pimps – are not held responsible. In Amnesty's narrative, the othering practice in policies can be seen: sex workers are denied of self-agency and othered to the role of a victim, in a situation where they perhaps are not actual victims but legitimately working in a profession of their own choosing. Additionally, those who do not feel violated volunteer sex workers, are othered and treated as victims without defining themselves as such. Amnesty's aim is to set the agenda where the awareness and discussion of the work and rights of sex workers would gain more attention; although there is in many cases a real causal relation between human trafficking and sex work, not all sex workers are trafficking victims.

- *Vulnerable people narrative.* In its various documents HRW uses case examples to illustrate the mistreatment of vulnerable people or treatment of people which places them in vulnerable situations. This cycle comes across as a reality in the refugee crisis narrative. HRW illustrates how refugees become and remain vulnerable when protection is denied to

> asylum seekers who have been beaten for being gay, who have suffered horrific domestic abuse, who have been treated as property by virtue of their status as women, or who have been sex trafficked by gangs, to name but a few examples.
> *(see Joint Letter, 2017)*

To add to this narrative of how refugees are treated, HRW highlights that children are often registered as adults in refugee centers, leaving them "vulnerable to exploitation, trafficking, and other abuse" (see Greece, 2017). In its narrative HRW covers the issue of identification of victims of human trafficking. As HRW states, "The inadequacy of identification procedures means that there is a serious risk that trafficked children are not recognized as such." Similar to Amnesty, HRW frames attention to the Libyan immigration crisis in relation to human trafficking, which it bandwagoned together. Noteworthy is that "Libyan immigration law does not distinguish between migrants, refugees, asylum seekers, victims of trafficking, or other particularly vulnerable groups" (see EU shifting, 2017). This underlines again the problems in policy formation; the same policies are applied to multiple groups that have various special needs which cannot be met with a single policy alone.

In the current analyses, HRW notes news articles that report of women being trafficked and sexually abused by ISIS – an issue not addressed at all previously. Additionally, HRW raises an important but often overlooked issue of female hygiene in refugee centres (which also house victims of trafficking). An issue that can seem irrelevant in the setting of human trafficking and in victims' lives becomes a major factor that sustains the cycle of human rights violations, making it central for HRW to frame the issue as important.

> Women should have the means necessary to manage their menstrual hygiene with dignity, including access to safe and private sanitation facilities and menstrual hygiene products. Authorities should provide suitable accommodation and assistance for particularly vulnerable asylum seekers, including children, people with disabilities, torture survivors, and trafficking victims.
> *(see Greece humanitarian, 2016)*

Summary of NGO narratives and comparison with 2010–2011 analyses

The time frame of 2011–2017 illustrates that there is a common understanding between the two NGOs regarding human trafficking. All that is needed is the political will to tackle the serious issue of trafficking. As can be seen in Table 4.2, the overlapping narratives between 2011–2012 and 2016–2017 are exploitation of women, corrupt officials and the worsening international refugee crisis situation, which intertwine with various other human rights abuses and methods of continued causal exploitation. What the various narratives of the two gatekeeper NGOs tells us is that indeed human trafficking is just one knot in the spiderweb of multiple cause-and-effect realities that involve failing of states, actions of corrupt officials, climate change and forced migration, illegal selling of various goods and multiple forms of exploitation of people, especially women and children. Human trafficking does not occur alone, there are deep-rooted reasons for it, and to tackle these reasons a longer political action must be taken internationally, and funding must be given to victim support services. What the longer narrative analysis shows that the patters of human trafficking have not changed much due to corruption, the supply and demand of trafficked persons, lack and unwillingness of protection and victim support services by states, and corruption on national and international scales.

The European Parliament

Similar to narratives identified in 2011–2012 analyses, the analyses of more recent documents (2016–2017 August) revealed four narratives in which human trafficking continued to be closely bandwagoned with honour crimes, gender-based violence and violence against women, girls and children as well as with the technological development.

- *The criminal networks narrative.* When addressing human trafficking, EP frames focus on the criminal networks as well as border management issues, thus creating a criminal networks narrative inciting the prosecution of human traffickers and those who facilitate trafficking. In this narrative, EP calls attention to the criminal networks who take advantage of the migration crisis and also mention unsafe migration channels and the vulnerable migrants and refugees (especially women, girls and children) who are subjected to "smuggling, trafficking in human beings, slavery and sexual exploitation by the criminal networks" (see European Parliament, 2016).

Table 4.2 NGO narrative comparisons 2011–2012 and 2016–2017

NGO Narratives 2011–2012	*NGO Narratives 2016–2017*	
	Amnesty	*HRW*
Corrupt officials narrative	Sex worker narrative	Detention centres narratives
Exploitation of women narrative	The refugee crises narrative	Education and assistance narrative
Organ markets narrative		Food industry, forced labour and corrupt officials narrative
Poverty and migration narrative		Vulnerable people narrative
The refugee narrative		
Sub-Saharan narrative		
Victim support services narrative		

- *Gender-based violence and children narrative.* In one of its central narratives, the EP framed human trafficking with the field of violence against women, girls and children as well as with forced marriages (including child marriages), honour killings and female genital mutilation. Specifically, EP framed the victims of human trafficking as mainly unaccompanied minors, women and girls. Consequently, EP bandwagons trafficking to children's rights and as one of the threats that children regularly face in conflict and warzones. To this end EP especially mentions in its narrative that vulnerability makes children a preferred target for traffickers and identifying victims remains a growing problem and challenge.
- *Identification and victim services narrative.* Connected to gender-based violence and children narrative is the identification processes and victim services narrative. Here, EP stresses efforts to identify possible victims of all forms of exploitation and "considers that the severely traumatised survivors should be recognised as victims of a form of prosecutable human trafficking and receive protection, care and support" (see Situation, 2016). This narrative emphasizes how identification protocols continue to be inefficient, underused or missing from the member states and conveys a reality that victim services cannot be offered and provided if identification services do not exist, which in turn calls for social-political interests (i.e. decision-makers) to fund and set up protocols for victim services. Certainly, victim services cannot be provided if victims remain unknown. However, as the literature and the narrative analysis shows, there are multiple factors such as fear, shame, cultural traditions, othering practices, power relations that can prevent women, and other victims from reporting sexual violence and exploitation such as human trafficking.

  In this narrative, the EP continues to create a caring narrative by expressing "its solidarity with the refugees and migrants who suffer grave human rights violations in high numbers, as victims of conflicts, governance failure and trafficking networks" (see Annual Report, 2016). However, this begs the question: are there real-world policies aimed at tackling this particular issue of human trafficking, or is this lip service from the standpoint of the EP, especially when it comes to the issue of missing victim services and protocols?
- *Technology narrative.* What was largely missing from previous content analysis was the role of IT and technologies and which part, if any, they play in human trafficking. In the analysis of the documents from 2016–2017, the EP did frame technologies having a growing role in human trafficking in terms of managing and organizing the "goods" (i.e. people). In its narrative, EP states: "Technologies enable organised crime groups to access a large pool of potential victims on a much larger scale than ever before, as many victims of trafficking, especially for sexual, and labour exploitation, are recruited online" (see Situation, 2016).

Summary and comparative analyses of EP narratives: 2011–2012 and 2016–2017

As evident in Table 4.3, the overlapping narratives on EP between 2011–2012 and 2016–2017 include gender-based violence, the devastation of societies and lack of victim support services, with a new narrative of the role of technologies in the context of human trafficking. What the EP does mostly is to urge the member states to put victim identification services and subsequent support services in place while acknowledging the root causes of human trafficking: poverty, the refugee crisis, the poor treatment of women and the overlapping large theme of the collapsing of societies, the missing rule of law and juridical procedures which creates room for willing and forced migration, which turns eventually into human trafficking that allows the traffickers to exploit and traffic vulnerable people. The EP shows concern regarding the treatment of trafficking people and solidarity towards refugees, victims of trafficking and stands with vulnerable

Table 4.3 EP narrative comparisons 2011–2012 and 2016–2017

EP Narratives 2011–2012	*EP Narratives 2016–2017*
Devastation of societies narratives	The criminal networks narrative
Gender-based violence narrative	Gender-based violence and children narrative
European Union narrative	Identification and victim services narrative
Fishing narratives	Technology narrative
Missing support systems narrative	
Natural disasters narrative	
Surrogacy and adoption narrative	
Trafficking in sports narrative.	

groups – EP calls for political solutions on the member state levels, but has much been done on the member state levels? Thus, the EP continues to pay lip service to the victims of human trafficking.

Summary and comparative analysis of NGOs and EP: 2016–2017

Referring to Table 4.4, the main narratives of the two NGOs and EP are similar throught 2016–2017: exploitation of women and children, gender-based abuses, collapsing of societies, the refugee crisis and victim support services.

A main narrative for all three actors focused on gender-based violence. This goes beyond human trafficking research by speaking of the structures of the society that enables policies, practices and actions that focus on various means of exploiting women and girls. The results of this study show a clear pattern of exploitation and how corrupt officials and traffickers continue to exploit women, to the extent that women are willing to endure it (e.g. by taking contraception in advance of anticipated abuse). The exploitation of women will not end with one policy suggestion, but is the topic of entire change processes of global, societal and grassroots ways of thinking with regard to the treatment of women and girls. If nothing is done, gender-based violence will continue to enable and sustain human trafficking.

What was completely new during the 2016–2017 analysis was the sex workers narrative by Amnesty and the role of technology in human trafficking and exploitation in EP's narrative. Amnesty framed a distinction to be made between volunteer sex workers and victims of trafficking while the EP argued that organized crime groups access a large pool of potential victims on a much larger scale by contacting and recruiting them online, issues which were not addressed during the 2011–2012 narratives. This shows how new narratives are developed by actors and how they re-frame existing narratives with new(er) current frames that have better relevance to the current realities. These narratives illustrate, first, how one-size-fits-all policies do not work on the grassroots level; the role and rights of sex workers should be addressed on a much larger scale despite the stigma that sex workers face daily. Second, the technology narrative illustrates the darker side of technological progress which, on the one hand, has given various people the possibility to engage in society, to empower themselves, and to take ownership of their rights globally, while at the same time enabling traffickers and corrupt officials to use the same tools to find, abuse and exploit future victims. The policy implication here goes to the large and complex issue arena of the digital human rights sphere, which should be a topic of much larger discussion and future research.

Table 4.4 Comparison of NGOs and EP narratives: 2016–2017

NGO Narratives (2016–2017)		*EP Narratives (2016–2017)*
Amnesty	*HRW*	
Sex work	Food industry, forced labour and corrupt officials	Gender-based violence and children
Refugee crises	Refugee and women's hygiene	Identification and victim services
	Education and assistance	Criminal networks
	Detention centres	Technology

As the results show, both NGOs and EP called for various training and education activities. This narrative was not visible during the 2011–2012 analysis. In the 2016–2017 analysis the theme of education emerged, especially in the HRW's narrative in relation to locals, refugees and officials. This narratives frames education as the central tool for tackling trafficking as well as in the processes of identifying and aiding victims. It highlights the need for children to have access to education globally as a way of mitigating the risk of trafficking victimization. This narrative also calls for locals of all ages to be educated about their rights and the legal procedures to address human rights violations. Naturally this is seemingly impossible to be done when societies are failing and no school systems or state structures are in place, such as is evident in Libya and various African nations. However, the training and education narrative also speaks to local communities to be educated in knowing how to proceed when trafficking is suspected (e.g. what to do, who to contact, how to act as first responders if official aid takes too long). Additionally this narrative speaks of how to train officials to identify the victims of trafficking globally, including in Europe and the United States. This narrative connects to policy formation by calling for real-world protocols to identify and aid possible victims and how to assist victims according to their individual needs. HRW strengthens the narrative by calling for increased funding for education and victim support services, which should be a central focus in the policy formulations nationally and internationally. NGOs, researchers and victims and other social actors can aid in formulating the educational materials and procedures, but success is incumbent upon political will and funding to execute the education and training. Training and education of all levels of society and administration is highly central in EP's 2016–2017 narrative in regards to human trafficking. This issue was not framed as a priority during the 2011–2012 analysis period – which is not to say that it was not relevant at the time for EP. Perhaps the training and education has grown more salient in the previous years as the refugee crisis and the vast reality of human trafficking has become more well-known in the member states.

Discussion

This comparative study looked at the narratives of three gatekeeper actors between the time period of 2011–2012 (calendar year) and January 2016 – August 2017. Altogether 298 documents from Amnesty International, Human Rights Watch and the European Parliament were analyzed in detail with qualitative methods.

First, based on theoretical framework, all actors form narratives, which are based on agenda setting and framing. Subsequently, narratives function as a base of policy formation, and due to power relations between actors, the gatekeepers' narratives function as a base in policy formation and also in human rights policy formation (Meriläinen, 2014). As illustrated in Figure 4.1, the process of policy formation has no start or finish due to continual agenda setting, framing and re-framing during negotiations with the subsequent narrative formation, and power relations with subsequent policy formation. This process is not linear; agendas, frames and narratives change continuously, power relations shift and new policies are formulated. This is due to the dynamic nature of policy formation (Meriläinen, 2014), which is why the study of policy formation should not focus on the end product (a policy) but rather the process itself, which is influenced by selective agenda setting and framing and the usage of narratives as part of the actors' power relations, where indeed the endgame may not be a final outcome (e.g. better human rights policies) but rather to sustain or change power relations between actors, as Meriläinen (2014) has illustrated previously.

The research questions for this study were: (1) What narratives are found regarding human trafficking? (2) How do the actors frame human trafficking in their narratives?

Based on results of the data analysis, the three gatekeeper actors share similar understanding of the cause-and-effect realities relating to human trafficking while addressing human trafficking in multiple ways by framing it differently in their narratives. In their narratives, human trafficking is interwoven with multiple other human rights violations. Based on the narratives, human trafficking does not occur by itself, it is not an isolated issue and it should not be addressed as such in the policy formulation processes. The three gatekeepers use multiple framing strategies in their various narratives that draw attention to the root causes of trafficking: global poverty, gender inequality, the refugee crisis and the lack of political will to resolve various human rights violations which form a web of human rights abuses bandwagoned together. The three actors frame human trafficking as a global trade of people that allows criminal networks to exploit and profit from others in sexual, labour and other illegal manners while the states lack proper identification and victim support services. Based on the narratives, various societal and political events, actors and issues contribute to human trafficking. The three gatekeeper actors name the responsible

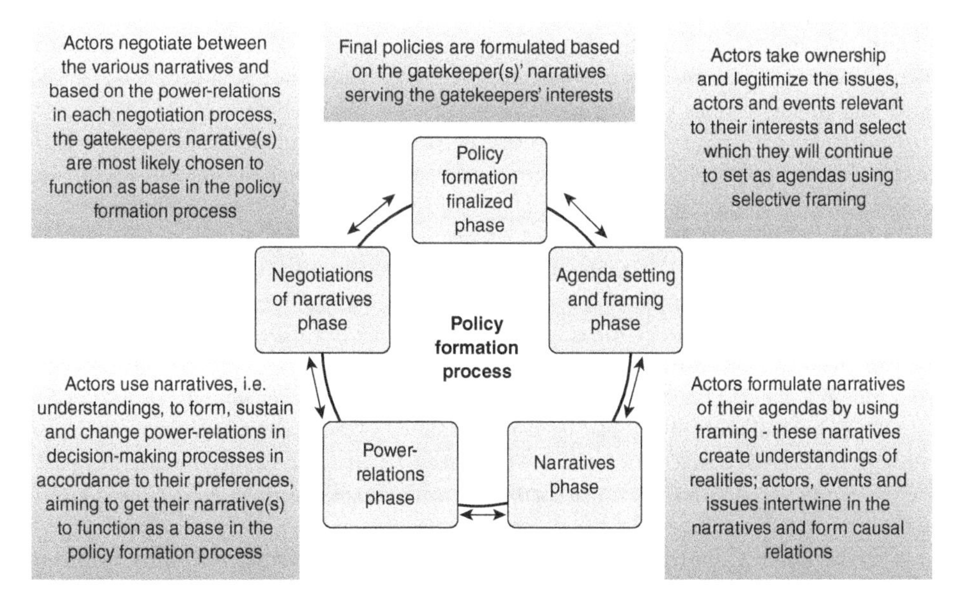

Figure 4.1 Policy formation process

parties for trafficking: people smugglers, traffickers and corrupt officials, who continue to enable and profit from trafficking.

Amnesty, HRW and EP also agree, based on their narratives inclusive of 2011–2017, that humans and other commodities are trafficked by organized crime groups using the same routes and, further, that human trafficking is enabled by corrupt officials involved in the arms trade and the illegal possession of weapons, drugs and various pirated goods. The research results illustrate a cycle of human rights abuses and other violations which continue to occur in a similar manner. Based on the narratives between 2011–2017, various events, such as the refugee crisis, natural disasters, the emergence of new technologies and the continued collapsing of societies create opportunities for traffickers, which international policies have not been able to touch, while the victims remain exploited by traffickers and corrupt officials who gain more money from trafficking.

During the period of 2011–2012 and 2016–2017 the criminal network narrative was central. However, during the later period, similar to the two NGOs, the EP started to frame the need for legal immigration routes as central to tackling trafficking. In the narrative, EP emphasizes cooperation agreements with effective border management as well as cooperation with non-EU countries to focus on creating legal and safe routes for asylum seekers and vulnerable migrants, which would in turn rightfully undermine the business model of trafficking networks and smugglers. Here a clear political solution narrative is presented. People immigrate to other countries; this cannot be stopped and thus EP is calling for safer routes, much like the two NGOs during the entire analysis period. However, again there needs to be the political will to implement this agenda into an actual legal reality. Due to the political realities of EU and various other countries, the question remains: can legal routes be implemented in the policy?

Based on the results, all the narratives incorporated vulnerable people. Amnesty's main narrative during 2016–2017 highlighted the plight of various vulnerable groups, such as women and children. This narrative was also mentioned in the earlier analysis of 2011–2012. In connection to this narrative, the NGOs continued to address the unsafe and dangerous living realities of refugee centres, especially for vulnerable groups. This narrative carried through the entire analysis period, with no change evident. Based on the narrative, vulnerable groups are often violated multiple times before reaching the detention or refugee centres in Europe or the United States. The detention or refugee centres provide safe spaces not for the trafficked people but for continued human rights violations, while officers seem oblivious to victims of trafficking as well as the presence of human rights violations that occur on site. In addition, according to HRW's narrative, female hygiene and sexual rights are violated continuously in the detention centres (e.g. menstrual hygiene products are unavailable), which further violates women's dignity and basic human rights. Further, in the detention and refugee centres children are left alone without protection. This accordingly makes them vulnerable to exploitation including trafficking, begging and sexual abuses. How can policy aid when various human rights violations are combined in causal relation webs and officials, such as the police, seem not to be aware, do not care or perhaps even participate and profit from the violations?

Throughout the 2011–2012 narratives, policy suggestions were presented, but based on the 2016–2017 narratives, not many had been implemented. The results of the narrative research illustrate that bandwagoning of issues is used to increase salience, such as bandwagoning being an issue with already recognized issues (e.g. trafficking with organized crime, gender-based violence and poverty), but above all, causal relations are explicated even if these, while contributing to public understanding of a complex issue, may not always be favorable for issue salience. Some issues were only mentioned by one actor (e.g. child labor in the mines of Mali, sex workers' rights, or the role of technology in human trafficking), showing the selectiveness of framing of narratives by actors, as it is also evident that EP's trafficking in sports narrative from 2011–2012 was not found in the 2016–2017 analysis, showcasing also the continuing process of re-framing of narratives by actors. Yet, there seems to be a consensus among the gatekeepers that human trafficking is both a national and an international problem. The actors share the notion that human trafficking must be seen within a larger context of issues, actors and events, as it is intertwined with multiple other issues, mainly various social injustices and violations that result from and feed off poverty and the poor functioning of juridical and state systems.

Additionally the fishing narrative continued to be mentioned throughout 2011–2012 and 2016–2017. The narrative combines corrupt officials, the food industry and trafficking with forced male labour. It is important to state that not only women and children are in danger of being trafficked, as the food and fishing narrative illustrates. Men are trafficked specifically to work in fishing boats. What is similar with the food industry and sex worker narratives is the difficulty in engaging in policy formation as corrupt officials partake in or benefit from trafficking or have their own values according to which they carry out the policies at the grassroots level.

In various narratives, all three actors described situations related to human trafficking as very worrying, demanding a more results-oriented approach from the various parties involved. The EP showed solidarity towards refugees and victims of trafficking but also called for decision makers to make the prevention of gender-based violations a priority in their economic strategies. Amnesty, HRW and the EP used framing to underline causality between poverty, gender-based violence and gender inequality along with disruptive natural disasters, the collapse of states and corruption in various forms of governance and policing. All three actors called for international cooperation and treaties to be drawn up, and for the implementation of already existing policies at the national legislative level.

This research contributes to a better understanding of how human trafficking is addressed in the narratives of three gatekeeper actors and how the narratives can work as a basis for policy formation. It has clarified how the actors used framing to increase issue salience and how they have emphasized the chain of causality between the root causes and effects on various other issues, events and actors. Framing was used as method of placing responsibility on traffickers and corrupt officials but also on decision-makers. Moreover, the EP called for NGOs and civil society to participate in the process of preventing trafficking and helping victims, whilst the NGOs asked traditional political actors to take responsibility for state corruption and called for funding for education. The targets of human rights violations, in this case mostly women and children, do not yet have a direct voice in the social and political debate, which is why the EP proposed including them in finding sustainable solutions. In Amnesty's, HRW's and EP's narratives from 2011–2012 and 2016–2017, it is striking that the victims' self-agency has been taken away to some extent, although victim narratives were used. To reference Dalla, Xia and Kennedy (2003), individuals who operate in crime-infested contexts are in vulnerable positions and in danger of victimization, which in turn influences persons' well-being and self-agency, especially if support systems are not available. Thus, in the policy formation side, experienced experts – victims of human trafficking – should be heard in their own voices or via trusted interpreters to formulate better victim services that address victims' needs.

What can be said is that maintaining issue salience for human trafficking poses a challenge. Possibly, an issue of this magnitude and severity can only be kept at bay because of its deeply rooted and multifaceted challenges. Human trafficking is merely one of numerous serious social issues that demand urgent attention. Serious human rights violations occur daily across the world. Human rights are universal in theory but often violated. The UN Declaration of Human

Rights promotes the protection of human rights of all people, and this should not be culturally bound or selective. Not all people enjoy universal rights, and human rights violations warrant attention in public and political issue arenas. Moreover, not all actors deem the same human rights as salient. Different belief systems and cultural, political, and moral systems influence othering practices and thus how social issues such as human trafficking are seen and how these are tackled or not tackled at the grassroots level and in policy formation processes. The problem in issue arena discussions and subsequent policy formation processes concerning human trafficking may be that the issue is known but has not yet gained enough salience in the policy level or perhaps it seems to be simply too much of a challenge, and is thus pushed from the centre of the debate by policy makers. It is also likely that the interrelatedness of social issues, actors and events as well as the contexts in which these issues take place are not yet fully understood. However, a shared understanding of the social context and the cause and blame with respect to human trafficking seem to be evident between the three actors studied here. Human trafficking was seen in the early 1990s as a women's rights issue that was the concern of feminist groups and NGOs. Based on the results of this updated research, currently, human trafficking is as complex yet salient global political issue demanding attention. In the documents of Amnesty, HRW and the EP, the gatekeepers called for collaboration in finding political solutions. Paying attention to the multiple and complex causal relations and how these are addressed in the narratives about human trafficking may support this goal.

Policy suggestions

Training

People who work in fields relating to human trafficking, whether it be on the ground or at the policy levels, should be trained to understand the complex realities of human trafficking. People should be educated of the various root causes of trafficking as well as the multitude of ways victims are exploited during the trafficking process. Education such as this is necessary for effectively aiding severely traumatized victims. Additionally, training and education should include narratives from various victims as further insight into their experiences, which would subsequently give those working at the grassroots or at the policy level a deeper knowledge on human trafficking and the realities of it. Those who are being trained should become aware of the multiple issues, actors and events that connect in human trafficking, in order to understand the complex reality of this phenomenon. Finally, training should address various cultural, political, social and economic contexts in which trafficking occurs, as well as how these influence trafficking actors, including victims and perpetrators.

Victim support services and protocols

Identification services must be included in the local and state level budgets to ensure that critical services are available and can be implemented. Victim identification protocols should be mandatory; lacking identification, direct care services cannot be rendered. Further, services must exist to train service providers; trafficking victims' needs vary tremendously (see Williamson & Roe-Sepowitz, Chapter 14, this volume). Identifying needs and providing sensitive care requires a unique set of knowledge and skills. Victim support services should be designed taken into account cultural differences and allow the victims dignity and autonomy in determining their own living conditions and healing processes without fear of prosecution or further exploitation.

Service providers must share a common respect and understanding of victims' lived experiences and services must never aggravate prior abuses and exploitation. Trusted interpreters must be made available and victims should be allowed to seek legal and other forms of help according to their own personal needs.

Policy-making versus realities

It is important to acknowledge that having human rights sanctioned within polices and treaties does not equate to implementation of those rights on national legislative levels, nor does it equate to respect for those rights at the grassroots level. Legal realities and grassroots realities comprise two different narratives. For real change, human rights policies must be accepted by legitimate parties in all levels of society and if needed, societal teaching and discussion of those must occur with the help of NGOs, victim groups and various societal actors. Policy makers should be aware of how to differentiate and design victim support services to various groups, since the law may not distinguish between migrants, refugees, asylum seekers, victims of trafficking, paperless migrants or other particularly vulnerable groups. The same policies should not be applied to multiple groups who often have different and special needs, which perhaps cannot be met with one policy alone.

Limitations

This research focused on three gatekeeper actors only during the specific timescale. A longer study of multiple actors and their narratives could shed more light and provide more insight into human trafficking and how it is addressed or not addressed by various actors on grassroots actions and policy formation processes. Additional research is needed to investigate the various cultural interpretations of what human trafficking is and how it is connected with other critical social justice issues.

Author contributions

This research was funded by Strategic Research Council at the Academy of Finland, decision no 312689, 326604. A previous version of this chapter was published in *Societies* (2015), *5*(1), 14–42. The research of the earlier version was designed together by the first author, Niina Meriläinen, PhD, with the second author being Professor Emerita Marita Vos. Regarding the original article, Meriläinen gathered the data and wrote the manuscript together with Vos. This second version was designed and authored by Meriläinen alone. Meriläinen gives warmest thank-you to Professor Emerita Vos for her encouragement during the updating and writing process.

Supplemental learning materials

Agenda Setting and Framing. Retrieved from www.coursera.org/learn/communicationtheory-academia-practice/lecture/QSWZm/agenda-setting-and-framing

Hunjan, R., & Pettit, J. (2011). *Power: A practical guide for facilitating social change*. Carnegie, UK and Trust: Fife. Retrieved from www.participatorymethods.org/sites/-participatorymethods.org/files/Power-A-Practical-Guide-for-Facilitating-Social-Change_0.pdf

Murphy, H. (2010). *The making of international trade policy: NGOs, agenda-setting and the WTO*. Cheltenham, UK: Edward Elgar Publishing, Inc.

Vojak, C. (2009). Choosing language: Social service framing and social justice. *The British Journal of Social Work, 39*(5), 936–949.

Zahariadis, N. (2016). *Handbook on public policy agenda setting.* Cheltenham, UK: Edward Elgar Publishing, Inc.

References

Agbu, O. (2003). Corruption and human trafficking: The Nigerian case. *West Africa Review, 4*, 1–13.

Alidadi, K., & Foblets, M. (2012). Framing multicultural challenges in freedom of religion terms: Limitations of minimal human rights for managing religious diversity in Europe. *Netherlands Quarterly of Human Rights, 30*, 460–488.

Amnesty International Report. (2012). *Facts and figures.* Retrieved December 18, 2014 from www.amnesty.org/en/library/info/POL10/003/2012/en

Amnesty International (2016). Through their eyes: Refugees' own accounts of abuses in Libya. Retrieved August 15, 2016, from www.amnesty.org/en/latest/campaigns/2016/08/through-their-eyes-refugees-own-accounts-of-abuses-in-libya/

Annual Report on Human Rights and Democracy in the world and the European Union's policy on the matter 2015 (December 14, 2016) – Strasbourg. Retrieved May 29, 2018, from www.europarl.europa.eu/sides/getDoc.do?type=TA&language=EN&reference=P8-TA-2016-0502

Anton, A. (2007). Socialist voices. In R. Schmitt & A. Anton (Eds.), *Toward a new socialism* (pp. 21–52). Plymouth, UK: Lexington Books.

Argentina: "What I'm doing is not a crime," Index number: AMR 13/4042/2016. Retrieved August 15, 2016, from www.amnesty.org/en/documents/amr13/4042/2016/en/

Aston, J. N., & Paranjape, V. N. (2012). *Abolishment of human trafficking: A distant dream.* Retrieved September 12, 2013, from http://papers.ssrn.com/sol3/papers.cfm?abstract_id=2112455

Australia: Submission to the Joint Standing Committee on Foreign Affairs, Defence and Trade Inquiry into Establishing a Modern Slavery Act in Australia. Retrieved May 29, 2018, from www.hrw.org/news/2017/05/19/australia-submission-joint-standing-committee-foreign-affairs-defence-and-trade

Bachrach, P., & Baratz, M.S. (1962). Two faces of power. *American Political Science Review, 56*, 947–952.

Barner, J.R., Okech, D., & Camp, M.A. (2014). Socio-economic inequality, human trafficking, and the global slave trade. *Societies, 4*, 148–160.

Barzilai-Nahon, K. (2008). Toward a theory of network gatekeeping: A framework for exploring information control. *Journal of the Association for Information Science and Technology, 59*, 1493–1512.

Bennett, W.L., Foot, K., & Xenos, M. (2011). Narratives and network organization: A comparison of fair trade systems in two nations. *Journal of Communication, 61*, 219–245.

Bob, C. (2009). *The international struggle for new human rights.* Philadelphia, PA: University of Pennsylvania Press and USA.

Bob, C. (2012). *The Right Wing and the Clash of World Politics.* New York: Cambridge University Press.

Brewer, P.R., & Gross, K. (2005). Values, framing, and citizens' thoughts about policy issues: Effects on content and quantity. *Political Psychology, 26*, 929–948.

Busby, J. W. (2007). Bono made Jesse helms cry: Jubilee 2000, debt relief, and moral action in international politics. *International Studies Quarterly, 51*, 247–275.

Carpenter, R. C. (2011). Vetting the advocacy agenda: Network centrality and the paradox of weapons norms. *The Review of International Organizations, 65*, 69–102.

Chuang, J. (2006). Beyond a snapshot: Preventing human trafficking in the global economy. *Indiana Journal of Global Legal Studies, 13*, 137–163.

Codes of ethics and declarations relevant to the health professions. Fifth Edition: 2011 Update. Retrieved December 18, 2014, from www.amnesty.org/en/library/info/ACT75/002/2011/en

Combating illegal fishing at the global level – The role of the EU. (2010/2210). Retrieved December 18, 2014, from www.europarl.europa.eu/oeil/popups/ficheprocedure-.do?reference=2010/2210%28INI%29&l=en

Dahl, R. (1957). The concept of power. *Behavioral Science, 2*, 201–215.

Dahre, J. (2010). There are no such things as universal human rights – On the predicament of indigenous peoples, for example. *International Journal of Human Rights, 14*, 641–657.

Dalla, R.L., Xia, Y., & Kennedy, H. (2003). "You just give them what they want and pray they don't kill you": Street-level sex workers' reports of victimization, personal resources and coping strategies. *Violence Against Women, 9(11)*, 1367–1394.

DeBono, D. (2013). "Less than human": The detention of irregular immigrants in Malta. *Race & Class, 55,* 60–81.

DeLuca, K. M., Lawson, S., & Sun, Y. (2012). Occupy wall street on the public screens of social media: The many framings of the birth of a protest movement. *Communication and Critical Cultural Studies, 5,* 483–509.

Dembour, M. B., & Kelly, T. (2011). Introduction. In M. B. Dembour & T. Kelly (Eds.), *Are human rights for migrants? Critical reflections on the status of irregular migrants in Europe and the United States* (pp. 1–16). New York, NY: Routledge.

Donnelly, J. (1982). Human rights and human dignity: An analytic critique of non-Western conceptions of human rights. *American Political Science Review, 76,* 303–316.

The Education Deficit Failures to Protect and Fulfill the Right to Education through Global Development Agendas. Retrieved May 29, 2018, from www.hrw.org/report/2016/06/09/education-deficit/failures-protect-and-fulfill-right-education-through-global

Egypt: Broken promises: Egypt's military rulers erode human rights. Retrieved December 18, 2014, from www.amnesty.org/en/library/info/MDE12/053/2011/en

Egypt: End Sinai Nightmare for Migrants. Retrieved December 18, 2014, from www.hrw.org/news/2012/09/05/Egypt-end-sinai-nightmare-migrants

Entman, R. M. (1993). Framing: Toward clarification of a fractured paradigm. *Journal of Communication, 43,* 51–58.

EP (European Parliament), Situation of fundamental rights in the European Union in 2015 European Parliament resolution of 13 December 2016 on the situation of fundamental rights in the European Union in 2015 (2016/2009(INI)). Retrieved from www.europarl.europa.eu/sides/-getDoc.do?type=TA&reference=P8-TA-2016-0485&language=EN

Equality between Women and men in the European Union – 2010. (2010/2138). Retrieved December 18, 2014, from www.europarl.europa.eu/oeil/popups/ficheprocedure.do?-reference=2010/2138%28INI%29&l=en

Equality between Women and men in the European Union – 2011. (2011/2244). Retrieved December 18, 2014, from www.europarl.europa.eu/oeil/popups/ficheprocedure.do?reference-=2011/2244%28INI%29&l=en

European Parliament Resolution on the Annual Report on Human Rights and Democracy in the World and the European Union's Policy on the Matter 2015. Retrieved December 14, 2016, from www.europarl.europa.eu/sides/getDoc.do?type=TA&language=EN&reference=P8-TA-2016-0502

EU: Shifting Rescue to Libya Risks Lives Italy Should Direct Safe Rescues. Retrieved May 29, 2018, from www.hrw.org/news/2017/06/19/eu-shifting-rescue-libya-risks-lives

European Dimension in Sport. (2011/2087). Retrieved December 18, 2014, from www.europarl.europ.eu oeil/popups/ficheprocedure.do?reference2011/2087%28INI%29&I=en

Eurostat. Trafficking in human beings – 2013 edition. Retrieved September 23, 2014 from http://epp.eurostat.ec.europa.eu/portal/page/portal/product_details/publication?p_product_code=KS-RA-13-005

Gregory, S. (2006). Transnational storytelling: Human rights, WITNESS, and Video advocacy. *American Anthropologist, 108,* 195–204.

Guttenplan, D. D., & Margaronis, M. (2010). *Who speaks for human rights? A clash between a feminist activist and a former Guantánamo detainee divides the left.* Retrieved September 2013, from www.thenation.com/article/who-speaks-human-rights#axzz2-ef45u610

Hafner-Burton, E. M., Tsutsui, K., & Meyer, J. M. (2008). International human rights law and the politics of legitimation repressive states and human rights treaties. *International Sociology, 23,* 115–141.

Hankivsky, O. (2011). The dark side on care: The push factors of human trafficking. In R. Mahon & F. Robison (Eds.), *Feminist ethics and social policy – Towards a new global political economy of care* (pp. 145–161). Vancouver, BC, Canada: UBC Press.

Hilgartner, S., & Bosk, C. L. (1988). The rise and fall of social problems: A public arenas model. *American Journal of Sociology, 94,* 53–78.

Hughes, D. M. (2000). The "Natasha" trade: The transnational shadow market of trafficking in women. *Journal of International Affairs, 53,* 625–651.

Human Rights Watch, Refugees are in urgent need of protection from sexual and gender-based violence news. Retrieved November 24, 2016, from www.amnesty.ca/news/refugees-are-urgent-need-protection-sexual-and-gender-based-violence-0

Human Rights Watch, Senegal: New Steps to Protect Talibés, Street Children Sustain Momentum with Investigations, Prosecutions. Retrieved May 29, 2018, from www.hrw.org/news/2016/07/28/senegal-new-steps-protect-talibes-street-children

Human Rights Watch (2016). Greece: Humanitarian Crisis at Athens Port EU, Greek Authorities Should Urgently Address Needs. Retrieved May 29, 2018, from www.hrw.org/news/2016/03/24/greece-humanitarian-crisis-athens-port

Human Rights Watch (2016). Greece: Lone Migrant Children Left Unprotected Flawed Procedures Leave Those on Lesbos at Risk of Abuse. Retrieved May 29, 2018, from www.hrw.org/news/2017/07/19/greece-lone-migrant-children-left-unprotected

Human Rights Watch (2016). Greece/Macedonia: Asylum Seekers Trapped at Border, Blocked Access to Asylum; Beatings by Soldiers; Poor Conditions. Retrieved February 11, 2016, from www.hrw.org/news/2016/02/11/-greece/macedonia-asylum-seekers-trapped-border

Human Rights Watch (2017). Joint Letter to the House Committee on the Judiciary on the "Asylum Reform and Border Protection Act" (H.R. 391). Retrieved May 29, 2018, from www.hrw.org/news/2017/07/26/joint-letter-house-committee-judiciary-asylum-reform-and-border-protection-act-hr

Ibhawoh, B. (2010). The right to development: The politics and polemics of power and resistance. *Human Rights Quarterly*, *33*, 76–104.

Jensen, S. Q. (2011). Othering, identity formation and agency. *Qualitative studies*, 2(2), 63–78.

Joachim, J. (2003). Framing issues and seizing opportunities: The UN, NGOs, and women's rights. *International Studies Quarterly*, *47*, 247–274.

Kamler, E. M. (2013). Negotiating narratives of human trafficking: NGOs, communication and the power of culture. *Journal of Intercultural Communication Research*, *42*(1), 73–90.

Keck, M., & Sikkink, K. (1998). *Activists beyond Borders: Advocacy networks in international politics*. Ithaca, NY: Cornell University Press.

Kilburn, H. W. (2009). Personal values and public opinion. *Social Science Quarterly*, *90*, 868–885.

Lecheler, S., & de Vreese, C. H. (2010). Framing Serbia: The effects of news framing on public support for EU enlargement. *European Political Science Review*, *2*, 73–93.

Lewin, K. (1947). Frontiers in group dynamics II: Channels of group life social planning and action research. *Human Relations*, *1*, 143–153.

Lukes, S. (1974). *Power: A radical view*. London, UK: Palgrave Macmillan.

Maedl, A. (2011). Rape as weapon of war in the Eastern DRC? The victims' perspective. *Human Rights Quarterly*, *33*, 128–147.

Marsh, C., & Payne, D. P. (2007). The globalization of human rights and the socialization of human rights norms. *Brigham Young University Law Review*, *3*, 65–688.

Martens, K. (2002). Mission impossible? Defining nongovernmental organizations. *VOLUNTAS: International Journal of Voluntary and Nonprofit Organizations*, *13*, 271–285.

Meriläinen, N. (2014). Understanding the framing of issues in multi-actor arenas: Power relations in the human rights debate. *Jyväskylä Studies in Humanities 1459–4331, 238.*

Meriläinen, N., & Vos, M. (2011). Human rights organizations and online agenda setting. *Corporate Communication*, *16*, 293–310.

Meriläinen, N., & Vos, M. (2013). Framing issues in the public debate: The case of human rights. *Corporate Communication*, *18*, 119–134.

Meriläinen, N., & Vos, M. (2014). Framing by actors in the human rights debate: The Kony 2012 Campaign. *Nordic Journal of Human Rights*, *32*, 238–257.

Meriläinen, N., & Vos, M. (2015). Public discourse on human trafficking in international issue arenas. *Societies*, *5(1)*, 14–42.

Miller, L. F. (2013). Rights of Self-delimiting peoples: Protecting those who want no part of U.S. *Human Rights Review*, *14*, 31–51.

Murdie, A. (2009). The impact of human rights NGOs activity on human right practices. *International NGO Journal*, *4*, 421–440.

Nash, K. (2009). *The cultural politics of human rights: Comparing the US and UK*. Cambridge: Cambridge University Press.

Nicholson, S., & Chong, D. (2011). Jumping on the human rights bandwagon: How Rights based linkages can refocus climate politics. *Global Environmental Politics*, *11*, 121–136.

Nikolić-Ristanović, V. (2012). Human trafficking between profit and survival. In A. elih & A. Zavr nik (Eds.), *Crime and transition in central and Eastern Europe* (pp. 205–227). New York, NY: Springer.

Okin, S. M. (1998). Feminism, women's human rights, and cultural differences. *Hypatia*, *13*, 32–52.

Pallas, C. L., & Urpelainen, J. (2013). Mission and interests: The strategic formation and function of north-south NGO campaigns. *Global Governance*, 401–423.
Petrocik, J. R. (1996). Issue ownership in presidential elections, with a 1980 case study. *American Journal of Political Science, 40*, 825–850.
Petros, G., Airhihenbuwa, C. O., Simbayi, L., Ramlagan, S., & Brown, B. (2006). HIV/AIDS and 'othering' in South Africa: The blame goes on. *Culture, health & sexuality*, 8(1), 67–77.
Pettigrew, A. M. (1973). *The politics of organizational decision-making*. London, UK: Tavistock.
Priorities and outline of a new EU policy framework to fight violence against women. (2010/2209). Retrieved December 18, 2014, from www.europarl.europa.eu/oeil/popups/-ficheprocedure.do?reference=2010/ 2209%28INI%29&l=en
Refugees and migrants fleeing sexual violence, abuse and exploitation in Libya. Retrieved from July 1, 2016, from www.amnesty.org/en/latest/news/2016/07/refugees-and-migrants-fleeing-sexual-violence-abuse-and-exploitation-in-libya/
Resolution on the European integration process of Kosovo. (2011/2885). Retrieved December 18, 2014, from www.europarl.europa.eu/oeil/popups/ficheprocedure.do?reference=2011/2885%28RSP%2&l=en
Resolution on human rights and the security situation in the Sahel region (2012/2680). Retrieved December 18, 2014, from www.europarl.europa.eu/oeil/popups/ficheprocedure-. do?reference= 2012/2680%RSP%29&I
Resolution on the human rights situation in the United Arab Emirates. (2012/2842). Retrieved December 18, 2014, from www.europarl.europa.eu/oeil/popups/ficheprocedure.do reference=2012/2842%28RSP% 29&1=en
Resolution on the use of sexual violence in conflicts in North Africa and the Rights, support and protection of victims of crime: Minimum standards (2011/0129). Retrieved December 18, 2014, from www. europarl.europa.eu/oeil/popups/ ficheproceure.do reference=2011/0129%28COD%29&l=en
Rodio, E. B., & Schmitz, H. P. (2010). Beyond norms and interests: Understanding the evolution of transnational human rights activism. *International Journal of Human Rights, 14*, 442–459.
Schott, R. M. (2011). War rape, natality and genocide. *Journal of Genocide Research, 13*, 5–21.
Shelley, L. (2012). The relationship of drug and human trafficking: A global perspective. *European Journal of Criminal Policy Research, 18*, 241–253.
Shen, F., & Edwards, H. H. (2005). Economic individualism, humanitarianism, and welfare reform: A value-based account of framing effects. *Journal of Communication, 55*, 795–809.
Steinberg, G. M. (2011). The politics of NGOs, human rights and the Arab-Israel conflict. *Israel Studies, 16*, 24–54.
Sullivan, B. (2010). Trafficking in human beings. In L. J. Shepherd (Ed.), *Gender matters in global politics: A feminist introduction to international relations* (pp. 89–102). London: Routledge.
Van den Anker, C., & van Liempt, I. (2012). *Human rights and migration: Trafficking for forced labour*. New York, NY: Palgrave Macmillan.
"Why Are You Keeping Me Here?" Unaccompanied Children Detained in Greece." Retrieved September 8, 2016, from www.hrw.org/report/2016/09/08/why-are-you-keeping-me-here/unaccompanied-children-detained-greece

SECTION II

Criminal justice

5

WHERE IS THE JUSTICE IN CRIMINAL JUSTICE?

Marie Bussey-Garza, Michelle M. Dempsey, Christian Martin, and Shea M. Rhodes

Abstract

The objective of this chapter is to answer the question, "Where is the justice in criminal justice?" – specifically in the context of the criminal justice system's response to sex trafficking. This goal is advanced through an in-depth discussion of the ways in which the criminal legal system achieves, or more often fails to achieve, procedural, retributive, corrective, therapeutic, transformative, and conceptual justice. This chapter evaluates the criminal law's response to trafficking against each of these six conceptions of justice and concludes that the criminal legal system typically fails to secure justice in any sense. While the chapter focuses primarily on the U.S. criminal justice system's attempts to secure justice in the context of sex trafficking, brief consideration is given to alternative approaches adopted in other countries (e.g. legalization/regulation and the Nordic Model), and to the international definition of trafficking (see Siller, Chapter 7, this volume).

Learning Objectives

At the end of the chapter, readers will be able to:

1. Identify six conceptions of criminal justice;
2. Explain how each of the six conceptions of justice applies in the context of sex trafficking;
3. Understand how each of the six conceptions of justice fails in the context of sex trafficking;
4. Articulate solutions for improving the effectiveness of each of the six conceptions of justice in the context of sex trafficking; and
5. Think critically about the societal and criminal justice system responses to commercial sexual exploitation.

Key Terms: sex trafficking; criminal law; justice; procedural justice; retributive justice; corrective justice; therapeutic justice; transformative justice; conceptual justice; Nordic Model; Palermo Protocol.

Introduction: where is the justice in criminal justice?

Under ideal circumstances, the criminal justice system delivers what its name promises: *justice*. Citizens and suspects alike are treated fairly, the guilty are punished, the victimized are made whole, communities are healed, social norms are improved, and the scope of criminal offenses accurately reflect what *should* be criminalized. Unfortunately, the criminal justice system is oftentimes guilty of false advertising – failing to deliver justice and instead creating, sustaining, perpetuating, and exacerbating various forms of *injustice*, especially with respect to gender and race (Crenshaw, 1991; Alexander, 2010) (see Bryant, Joudo Larsen and Gordon, Chapter 6, this volume). Indeed, attempts to use the criminal justice system to dismantle injustices along lines of gender, sexuality, race, class, age, ability, and other forms of intersecting structural inequalities have failed to achieve measurable success, all while exacerbating many of these injustices, and leading many to conclude that prison abolition is a more promising path to securing true justice (Ritchie, 2012, 2015; McLeod, 2015).

The criminal justice system's response to human trafficking illustrates both the potential for the criminal law to secure justice and its frequent failure to do so. In this chapter, we unpack this claim by analyzing the criminal justice system's response to human trafficking according to six distinct conceptions of justice. Each conception will be explained in detail, but for now, a short introduction will suffice:

- *Procedural justice*: law enforcement treating the public (including criminal suspects) with fairness and respect;
- *Retributive justice*: punishing wrongdoers;
- *Corrective justice*: making victims of crime "whole" through restitution;
- *Therapeutic justice*: rehabilitating those who have committed criminal acts;
- *Transformative justice*: changing social norms;
- *Conceptual justice*: labeling and defining criminal offenses (here, sex trafficking) to accurately and fully reflect the scope of the wrongdoing.

Each conception of justice will be discussed in turn, with further explanation of its meaning and illustrations of how the criminal justice system has either secured justice according to the particular conception under consideration or, more often, has failed to do so. The primary focus throughout the chapter will be on sex trafficking (trafficking for the purpose of sexual exploitation) within the various criminal justice systems in the United States.[1] At times, our discussion will refer more generally to "prostitution" or "prostituted persons." Although it is beyond the scope of this chapter to thoroughly discuss whether truly voluntary, consensual commercial sex can ever exist, our analysis in this chapter is based on the premise that, as Sigma Huda (2006) explains, "prostitution as actually practiced in the world usually *does* satisfy the elements of trafficking" (p. 9). With respect to our discussion of transformative justice, the chapter will present a comparative analysis of criminal justice responses to sex trafficking, as illustrated in the approaches adopted in other countries. Finally, in our discussion of conceptual justice, we will comment on the internationally recognized definition of trafficking (Palermo, 2000).

Procedural justice

The concept of procedural justice, as we use it here, refers to law enforcement officers "treating people with dignity and respect, giving citizens 'voice' during encounters, being neutral in decision making, and conveying trustworthy motives" (NIBCTJ, n.d.). In its initial articulation, procedural justice in the criminal law context was valued as a means to promote compliance with police directives and increase obedience to the law (Tyler, 2003). Yet, more fundamentally, we can recognize a basic value in police officers treating people with dignity and respect during their law enforcement encounters. This basic value informs the meaning of procedural justice employed below. In particular, our examination of procedural justice focuses on police interactions with victims of sex trafficking.

Historically, police officers' interactions with victims of sex trafficking have often failed to secure procedural justice, in large part because sex trafficking has for so long been widely regarded as simply a matter of "prostitution" – and its victims have been treated with an appalling lack of dignity and respect, as nothing more than "whores" (Curtis, 2012; Farley, 2006; Saar, 2011). Recent efforts throughout the United States have sought to address and remediate this problem by training law enforcement on the realities of sex trafficking and the force, fraud, and coercion that are typically employed to keep people trapped in "the life" of prostitution. For example, in response to a 2012 ballot initiative passed by California voters, police officers assigned to field or investigative duty are required to receive at least two hours of training on human trafficking within their first six months on assignment (California Commission on Peace Officer Standards and Training [POST], 2014, pp. 5–6). Also in 2012, the state of Michigan held a two-day training program aimed at teaching "law enforcement to communicate effectively with victims and detect potential perpetrators" in order to "fight modern-day slavery in [the] state" ("Law Enforcement Resources," n.d.). More recently, the Pennsylvania Municipal Police Officers Education and Training Commission, which is the state regulatory authority tasked with certifying all police officers in Pennsylvania, mandated a three-hour curriculum on human trafficking, covering the state and federal laws, how victims are identified, and interview techniques (Allen, 2014; Municipal Police Officers' Education and Training Commission, n.d.).

Despite these positive efforts, procedural injustice often remains the hallmark of police interactions with victims of sex trafficking. Indeed, in some jurisdictions, shockingly disrespectful behavior by police during investigations of prostitution is authorized according to statutory laws. In Hawaii, for example, "any member of a police department, a sheriff, or a law enforcement officer acting in the course and scope of duties" is specifically authorized by law to engage in sexual acts with a prostituted person (Haw. Rev. Stat. Ann. § 712–1200). Likewise, Michigan law expressly allows a law enforcement officer to purchase sex acts "in the performance of his duties as a law enforcement officer" (Mich. Comp. Laws Ann. § 750.451a). Notably, neither state's law differentiates between the purchase of sex from a minor or an adult when a law officer buys sex in the course of his official duties (Haw. Rev. Stat. Ann. § 712–1200; Mich. Comp. Laws Ann. § 750.451a).

While the remaining states and the District of Columbia do not give police officers express immunity from prosecution for engaging in sexual conduct with prostituted persons, the reality is that police officers across the country engage in such activity without any consequences, criminal or otherwise. For example, one Arkansas police officer conducting a prostitution sting arrested a woman only after he stripped naked and had the woman perform a sex act on him (Bergan, 2015). As evidence to support the prostitution charge, the officer described the interaction in an affidavit of arrest, noting "she began rubbing lotion on my penis and masturbating me" (Eifling, 2015). Another officer who read the affidavit believed the arresting officer had violated a department policy and complained to his supervisor. The complaining officer was fired. The arresting officer was not. Rather, the police chief "concluded the [arresting] officer did not violate that rule because he was engaging in sexual conduct only to obtain evidence as part of an arrest" (Bergan, 2015).

While most jurisdictions officially recognize that police officers should not be allowed to engage in sex acts with women in order to effect prostitution arrests, the issue provokes debate in others. For example, a 2017 bill considered by Alaska lawmakers would have closed a supposed loophole in Alaska's criminal code that some argue provides officer immunity from sexual touching when investigating a prostituted person prior to arrest (Bernish, 2017; Boots, 2017; Raines, 2017). The bill met stark opposition from law enforcement officials who argued that they *need* the ability to make sexual contact with the women they investigate in order to effect arrests. This argument seems disingenuous, given that Alaska's law – like typical state laws prohibiting prostitution – requires only an *offer* of a sex act in exchange for money before the crime is complete (Alaska Stat. Ann. § 11.66.100).

While having sex with a woman for the specific purpose of arresting her for that very act does not comport with the procedural justice ideal of "treating people with dignity and respect, . . . and conveying trustworthy motives" (NIBCTJ, n.d.), police conduct often goes beyond sex-for-arrest and becomes sexual violence. One study on the link between police practices and the HIV risk in populations of prostituted persons observed, "The normalisation of sexual violence as a tool of law enforcement has been documented worldwide" (Footer, Silberzahn, Tormohlen, & Sherman, 2016, p. 2). This sexual violence comes in the form of "forced unprotected sex," "coercive sex (e.g. sex in exchange for no arrest)," and "financial extortion to avoid arrest" (Footer et al., 2016, p. 2).

As another group of researchers who conducted a three-year ethnographic study of persons prostituted on the streets of Denver, Colorado, explain, "Criminalization and stigma actively discourage women from reporting instances of criminal victimization in any form, but particularly from police" (Dewey & Germain, 2014, p. 268). Knowing that their acts will go unreported makes it especially easy for police officers to take advantage of prostituted persons. In one blatant example of exploiting this power differential, New York police officer Michael Golden allegedly had sexual intercourse and engaged in other sex acts with at least six different women, all illegal immigrants, during several Manhattan prostitution stings conducted in 2014 (Dimon, Parascandola, & Rayman, 2017). "The alleged victims came from China, Eastern Europe[,] . . . the Dominican Republic and other Spanish-speaking countries" (Dimon et al., 2017). Although in June of 2017 Golden faced an internal trial by the New York Police Department over these allegations, the Manhattan District Attorney declined to bring criminal charges against Golden, in part due to lack of witnesses because all but one of the alleged victims were no longer in the United States (Dimon et al., 2017).

While Golden's case offers a clear example of procedural injustice suffered by victims of sex trafficking at the hands of police officers, one case arising out of Oakland, California, illustrates to chilling effect that this phenomenon literally occurs from coast to coast. In June of 2017 – ironically the same month in which Golden faced his internal police trial – the city of Oakland settled a lawsuit with a 19-year-old woman who claimed she was sexually abused by more than a dozen city police officers. These officers allegedly abused their power by tipping her off to prostitution stings in exchange for sex. While civil cases were still pending against law enforcement officers in San Francisco, Livermore, Richmond, Alameda County, and Contra Costa County, Oakland settled with this young woman for just under $1 million. Desley Brooks, the lone city council member who voted against the settlement, said the city should have paid more (Wamsley, 2017). Brooks emphasized the nature of the wrongdoing against this survivor, noting she was repeatedly victimized by law enforcement officials acting "under the color of law" (Wamsley, 2017).

Should the way in which laws are enforced be viewed as important as the laws themselves? Or does the end goal of upholding the law justify any procedural means that might be used to enforce those laws? To what extent?

This story first received attention in 2015 when one of the victim's officer-abusers left a suicide note in which he confessed to having engaged in sexual relations with her. Notably, she would have been only 17 at that time, and in fact, many of the alleged sex acts occurred while she was a minor. In addition to the civil settlement, four officers have been indicted on criminal charges for their involvement (Seldon, 2017). Yet, despite the potential for some modicum of retributive or corrective justice (see below), given these criminal charges and her civil settlement, this young woman's experience provides a glaring example of procedural injustice. Rather than being treated with dignity and respect, she was manipulated, exploited, and subjected to repeated sexual abuse at the hands of government officials who are sworn to serve and protect.

While the stories of this young woman and the six unnamed victims in New York represent examples of extreme injustice, it is important to note that they are not outliers. Rather, they mirror stories told by prostituted women across the country and around the globe – stories that too often go unreported and ignored (Gafni & Debolt, 2016). But with an increased focus on training police officers, there may be hope for improvement. In fact, Michigan lawmakers are considering a bill that would eliminate police officer immunity for sex acts with a prostituted person while on duty. Yet, as noted earlier, Alaska's police force fought to block the Alaska bill that would have prevented officers from sexual touching in the course of investigation (Bernish, 2017; Boots, 2017; Raines, 2017). Thus, despite some steps towards positive improvement, effective procedural justice for victims of prostitution and sex trafficking remains elusive, at least for now.

Retributive justice

Retributive justice – the justice found in wrongdoers receiving their "just deserts" – demands a punishment that is proportionate to the wrongdoing ("an eye for an eye") (Exodus 21:24, New International Version). From its ancient roots as articulated in the Code of Hammurabi (Harper, 1904) to modern accounts that give retributive justice a central role in theories regarding the justification of criminal law (Moore, 1997), the two key pillars of retributive justice are, first, that wrongdoers should be punished, and second, that *only* wrongdoers should be punished. That is to say, if someone has committed a blameworthy criminal act, then he or she should be punished accordingly. But, equally important, if someone has *not* committed a blameworthy act, then he or she should *not* be subjected to punishment.

Retributive justice can be, and sometimes is, secured through the criminal justice response to sex trafficking. For example, in 2014, four members of a Los Angeles street gang were sentenced to 30 years' imprisonment after pleading guilty to charges of sex trafficking of a minor and conspiracy to engage in sex trafficking after preying on teenage girls at local schools, housing them in hotels, and forcing them to engage in commercial sex (U.S. Attorney's Office, Central District of California, 2014). While this case illustrates retributive justice against members of an organized crime ring, sex trafficking is often perpetrated by individuals acting alone or in small groups. For example, in a recent case out of Pennsylvania, a man was sentenced to life in prison for sex trafficking three individuals, including a 16-year-old girl he met in Atlantic City. After taking her to a local hotel where he verbally and physically abused her, the trafficker forced the girl into commercial sex. He then took the young victim to a house where she was threatened at gunpoint and gang-raped by 15 men (Logue, 2014). In another case out of Missouri, a man was sentenced to 20 years in prison without parole for trafficking his son's girlfriend. Using various methods of force, fraud, and coercion – including supplying the victim with controlled substances, locking her in a cage, and physically torturing her – the trafficker recorded and distributed videos of himself and others performing sexual and torturous acts on the young girl over a six-year period. (U.S. Attorney's Office, Western District of Missouri, 2013).

Yet another example of the criminal justice system securing retributive justice against a sex trafficker is illustrated by the case of Paul Sewell, a Pennsylvania man who went by the nickname "God" (Weaver, 2015). Sewell trafficked numerous girls aged 14 to 17 years and branded them with tattoos on the back of their necks. The tattoos included the word "God's" followed by a nickname he gave each girl that was considered her "working name" ("God's Diva," "God's Golden One," "God's Secret," "God's Blessing," "God's Toy," etc.) (Wood, 2015). In exchange for his guilty plea, Sewell was sentenced to 23 years' imprisonment (Weaver, 2015).

While these cases provide examples of properly administered retributive justice, too often the criminal justice system fails in this respect by violating one or both of the key pillars of retributive justice. To review, the first pillar of retributive justice is that wrongdoers should be punished. While, as described above, this pillar of retributive justice is occasionally realized, too often traffickers escape punishment. The primary reason traffickers are not punished in the criminal justice system is that they simply are not targeted by law enforcement in the first place, leaving many pimps and traffickers feeling untouchable (Dank et al., 2014). Moreover, even in cases where police pursue criminal investigations and prosecutors file criminal charges, alleged traffickers often avoid conviction due to a lack of evidence or a reluctance by jurors to convict. For example, when alleged trafficking kingpin Calvin Freeman was arrested in Philadelphia in 2012, the evidence against him quickly disappeared. Freeman was arrested "for allegedly beating and strangling a woman, then forcing her at gunpoint to go back out and work the street" ("Officials Discuss Why Philly's 'Poised to Become Major Hub of Human Trafficking,'" 2012). Not recognizing the woman as a victim of human trafficking, investigators sent her home, and she quickly disappeared. Without her testimony, prosecutors were unable to make a case against Freeman, and all charges were withdrawn ("Officials Discuss Why Philly's 'Poised to Become Major Hub of Human Trafficking,'" 2012).

While Freeman was able to escape trial altogether, other traffickers face trial but escape conviction. The prosecution of the father-and-son team of Vincent George Sr. and Vincent George Jr. in New York State offers an example of jurors' reluctance to convict in cases of sex trafficking that present as cases of domestic violence. The Georges were acquitted of sex trafficking charges, despite evidence that they used coercion, intimidation, and threats of beatings to keep several women in prostitution (Buettner, 2013a). The jury acquitted the defendants of the most serious charges (sex trafficking), opting instead to convict them of lesser included offenses of promoting prostitution and money laundering, based on testimony from three of the women that the trafficking ring operated as a "family" (Buettner, 2013a, 2013b). Yet, as Assistant District Attorney Kim Han explained to the jury, "While these women were not chained up, they did not have real options" (Buettner, 2013a).

While these failed prosecutions represent failures of the criminal justice system to comport with the first pillar of retributive justice, the system more often fails to secure retributive justice by violating its second pillar (i.e. that *only* wrongdoers should be punished), so if someone has *not* committed a blameworthy act, that person should *not* be subjected to punishment. The long history of law enforcement's response to policing and prosecuting prostitution illustrates the grave injustices committed by the criminal justice system's targeting victims of sex trafficking. There are three primary – and interconnected – reasons why the criminal justice system continues to impose unjust punishment on victims of sex trafficking: (1) investigative practices that target prostituted persons, rather than focusing on traffickers and those who purchase sex; (2) the effect of cash bail on prostituted persons, who are typically unable to "bail out" of jail while awaiting trial; and (3) recidivist sentencing statutes that impose disparate penalties on prostituted persons.

Can you think of ways for the criminal justice system to police and prosecute sex trafficking so as to uphold both pillars of retributive justice?

As Lieutenant Steve Marcin (2013) of the Anaheim Police Department in California describes it: the [traditional] response to street prostitution has been to arrest hookers. This approach was narrow in scope and usually did not involve the pimp. The standard procedure was for undercover officers to pose as customers, obtain a solicitation, and arrest the prostitute. They repeated the process often *to incarcerate as many women as possible*. This approach is premised on the underlying beliefs that prostitutes are merely whores – "boys will be boys" – and communities do not want to *see* prostitution (i.e. cops attempt to move the "problem" out of sight by arresting prostituted persons). Not surprisingly, these tactics result in women being arrested for selling sex with far greater frequency than men are arrested for buying sex (Johnson, 2014, pp. 725–729). In fact, despite recent national efforts to target the demand for commercial sex (i.e. the sex buyers), the arrest rate of women continues to far outpace that of men. According to the Federal Bureau of Investigation, an estimated 67% of all people arrested nationwide for "prostitution and commercialized vice" in 2012 were female (Bureau of Justice, n.d.). In many states, this problem may be even more pronounced. For example, despite statewide initiatives to target demand in Pennsylvania, approximately 80% of all prostitution arrests in 2016 were for selling sex (CSE Institute, 2017, p. 12). Given that sellers tend to be almost exclusively female, these data suggest a significant imbalance in the female-to-male arrest ratio.

Not only is this disparate enforcement inherently unjust, but it also perpetuates a cycle in which women are subjected to further injustice. Typically unable to afford bail to secure her own release, a woman arrested for prostitution is often dependent on the whim of a pimp to secure her "freedom." As Kathleen Barry (1995) describes, "Depending on his mood and circumstances, a pimp may choose to leave his woman in jail, ignoring her call to be bailed out, or he may get her out immediately if he wants her back on the street working" (p. 212). If he chooses to post bail, it is not done gratuitously. Consequently, the woman finds herself in deeper debt to the pimp and is forced to return to the very act that got her arrested as her sole option to repay the debt. Thus, the mere arrest of a prostituted person – which itself violates the second pillar of retributive justice – subjects the woman to the risk of subsequent arrest for the same offense, thereby sustaining a cycle of injustice.

This cycle, in turn, contributes to further unjust punishment of victims of sex trafficking because women arrested for subsequent prostitution offenses often face draconian recidivist penalties. Under the recidivist provisions of many prostitution laws, a woman faces a harsher penalty each time she is arrested (CSE Institute, 2015). The purpose of these increasingly harsh punishments is to deter women from committing the crime of prostitution. Not surprisingly, such deterrence is ineffective because "the reality is that most women do not sell sex by choice, but rather as a means of survival" (CSE Institute, 2015) and many women involved in "the life" are, in fact, victims of sex trafficking.[2] Instead, these recidivist penalties simply subject victims of commercial sexual exploitation to further unjust treatment by the criminal justice system.

How should the law treat those who are both victims and perpetrators of trafficking? Many states allow those charged with trafficking to assert an affirmative defense that they themselves are victims of trafficking. Does this approach satisfy the two pillars of retributive justice?

In sum, the American criminal justice system is, at times, successful in upholding the first pillar of retributive justice – that wrongdoers should be punished – by prosecuting and securing convictions against human traffickers. More often, however, retributive justice remains elusive. The first pillar goes unachieved as traffickers escape conviction and sex buyers are simply disregarded. Moreover, the second pillar – that *only* wrongdoers should be punished – is repeatedly violated as victims of commercial sexual exploitation are arrested, forced back into prostitution to pay debts to their pimps, rearrested, and subjected to increasingly harsh penalties in a perpetual cycle of injustice.

Corrective justice

The central tenet of corrective justice is that wrongdoers have a duty to make their victims whole, through monetary compensation or other corrective measures, so as to repair the wrongs they have committed (Coleman, 1992; Weinrib, 2002). Like retributive justice, corrective justice has ancient roots, as illustrated in Aristotle's discussion in book V of the *Nicomachean Ethics* (Aristotle, 2012/349 BC). While modern legal theory invokes conceptions of corrective justice primarily in the context of private law, especially tort, theorists from Aristotle onward have envisioned a role for corrective justice in the context of criminal law as well.[3]

The principal example of the criminal justice system's ability to secure corrective justice in the context of trafficking cases can be found in the practice of criminal courts ordering restitution for trafficking victims as part of the criminal sentence handed down upon conviction. Since 2000, the federal Trafficking Victims Protection Act (TVPA) has mandated that every person convicted of trafficking be ordered to pay restitution to his (or her) victims in "the full amount of the victim's losses" (18 U.S.C. § 1593). In one example of facially effective corrective justice, a federal judge in Washington, DC, ordered a convicted sex trafficker to pay $3,892,055 to his four minor victims (*United States v. Lewis*, 2011; see also Levy, Vandenberg, & Chen, 2014). In a methodical opinion, the judge provided detailed loss calculations for each victim, which included an amount for the trafficker's "ill-gotten gains" from prostituting each young girl and an amount for "costs of future psychological treatment and tutoring" (*United States v. Lewis*, 2011, pp. 92–94). This order, and the judge's approach to issuing it, stands as a model of corrective justice.

Yet, while the *Lewis* case reflects the *ideal* of corrective justice, the criminal justice system is all too often unable to achieve the *reality* of making victims whole through corrective justice. Three reasons underlie this disconnect between ideal and reality. First, even if we limit our focus to financial compensation for victims of trafficking, traffickers rarely have the financial resources to provide anything close to adequate restitution. For example, in the *Lewis* case, the trafficker's reported gross income in the three years prior to sentencing "was $7,343, $12,002, and $9,835" (*United States v. Lewis*, 2011, p. 95). Given the trafficker's financial situation and his 20-year term of incarceration, the court determined "that [the] defendant [did] not have the financial ability to pay any amount of restitution other than nominal periodic payments" (*United States v. Lewis*, 2011, p. 95). Moreover, Lewis's case is not unique. Despite earning as much as $33,000 per week, pimps tend to spend money as fast as they make it (Dockterman, 2014), meaning restitution awards against them are often little more than symbolic.

Second, as is often the case, there is an enormous disparity between the law on the books and the law in action. In fact, after examining all federal labor and sex trafficking cases filed between 2009 and 2012, the Human Trafficking Pro Bono Legal Center concluded, "The TVPA's mandatory restitution provision is frequently overlooked, leaving trafficking victims empty-handed, deprived of the resources that would enable them to rebuild their lives" (Levy et al., 2014, p. 3). According to Levy and colleagues (2014), despite the mandatory nature of the law, restitution was ordered in only 31% of the sex trafficking cases they reviewed (p. 3). By contrast, 94% of labor trafficking convictions were accompanied by an order of restitution (Levy et al., 2014, p. 3). This disparity stems from the stigma that persists even as victims of sex trafficking assist the government as witnesses against their traffickers. Although prosecutors requested restitution in 87% of the labor cases that Levy and colleagues examined, the government asked for restitution in sex trafficking cases only 61% of the time (Levy et al., 2014, p. 3). Even when prosecutors requested restitution, some defense attorneys successfully argued against it, claiming that any restitution would amount to government-sponsored prostitution (Levy et al., 2014, pp. 16–17). One judge who ignored the statutory mandate simply stated, "Restitution is not ordered because *there is no victim other than society at large*" (*United States v. Gadley*, 2013, p. 3).

Aside from financial compensation, what else might courts order a convicted trafficker to do to better achieve corrective justice for victims? Would these or other measures be effective in contributing to the corrective justice owed the victim?

Third, and finally, corrective justice is elusive for victims of sex trafficking because truly making victims whole after the experience of being trafficked requires a set of remedies that extend well beyond financial compensation through restitution orders. Rather, truly making victims whole – helping victims become survivors – requires a trauma-informed approach that involves helping each woman gain access to services tailored to her own unique and complex needs. Such needs may, and often do, include drug and alcohol treatment, counseling, legal services, job training, and housing assistance, to name a few. While corrective justice is insufficient to address these needs and truly make victims of sex trafficking whole, therapeutic justice, to which we turn next, seeks to do just that.

Therapeutic justice

A more recent conceptualization of justice to feature in criminal law practice and academic literature is referred to as therapeutic justice. The key focus on therapeutic justice is to design and implement "legal rule(s) [and] practice[s] [that] promote the psychological and physical well-being of the people [they] affect" (Carns, Hotchkin, & Andrews, 2002; citing Hora, Schma, & Rosenthal, 1999; citing Slobogin, 1995). Primarily, this goal is pursued in the context of what have come to be known as "problem-solving courts," in which the main focus of law enforcement intervention is to promote rehabilitation and healing through the provision of "trauma-informed" social services. While the conception of therapeutic justice continues to develop and crystallize as a distinctive set of goals and methods for implementing the criminal justice responses (Winick & Wexler, 2003), these problem-solving courts have not gone without legitimate criticism by those who fear that such courts may "sustain the view that commercial sex is primarily a criminal problem that merits, at a minimum, a penal welfare, if not a law-and-order solution" (Gruber, Cohen, & Mogulescu, 2016, p. 1395).

Do you agree that problem-solving courts are ineffective tools for therapeutic justice because they are court mandated ("therapy at gunpoint")? Why or why not?

One example of the criminal justice system pursuing therapeutic justice through a problem-solving court is Philadelphia's Project Dawn Court. Project Dawn Court "seeks to connect non-violent repeat prostitution offenders with therapeutic and reentry services, while attempting to reduce recidivism of prostitution and related crimes" (Philadelphia District Attorney's Office, n.d.). At the discretion of the district attorney, women with prior arrests for prostitution may plead no contest to a current prostitution charge and be granted admittance to the program. Once admitted, each woman receives "drug treatment as well as trauma counseling for abuse (physical, sexual and emotional) that often dates back to adolescence" (Philadelphia District Attorney's Office, n.d.).

The program proceeds in four phases, which can be completed within one year. In phase one, the participant must remain drug-free for 30 consecutive days. Phase two requires that she must attend 90 days of outpatient treatment. Phase three requires 120 days of "intensive treatment for sexual trauma," and phase four concludes with "120 of days of reintegration preparation" (Philadelphia District Attorney's Office, n.d.). Throughout the program, all participants check in at least monthly with the judge who oversees their progress. Upon successful completion of the program, the participant's current prostitution charge is dismissed, and if the individual has no additional arrests within a year, the charge can be expunged. The program's supporters praise it for "offering hope and healing to women seeking to change their lives after being repeatedly charged with prostitution offenses" (Harris, 2013).

One woman who credits Project Dawn Court with changing her life is Anne Marie Jones. Like so many women who fall into "the life" of prostitution, Anne Marie was molested as a teenager by a member of her own family and turned to drugs as a coping mechanism (Rybak, 2014). Years later, Anne Marie saw the cycle of abuse continue when her younger brother molested her own daughter. When Anne Marie reported her brother to law enforcement officials, her entire family turned against her. Unable to cope with the stress, Anne Marie turned to crack cocaine and eventually began selling sex to pay for her drug addiction. Recognizing her vulnerability, a pimp wooed her with promises of a better life. Instead, he "turned her life into a living hell," often beating her so badly she would spend weeks in the hospital (Rybak, 2014). For Anne Marie, Project Dawn Court was instrumental in helping her pull herself out of that hell. She graduated from the program in 2011 and "now serves as an advocate, peer specialist, and mentor at Dawn's Place," a safe house that provides support services to victims of sex trafficking (Roncinske, 2014).

While Anne Marie's story illustrates the potential benefits of therapeutic justice, these innovative therapeutic courts face, at a minimum, two substantial problems. First, many of the defendants involved in the courts are unable to successfully complete the court-ordered treatment and, therefore, fail to benefit from the potential therapeutic value offered in these settings. For example, about 30% of the women who enter Project Dawn Court do not complete the program (Roncinske, 2014). Even worse, nearly 70% of the women who enter Chicago's "intensive two-year" diversion program fail to graduate (Weigel, 2014). Given the duration and intensity of these programs – not to mention the iron grip of drug addiction that tends to accompany prostitution – it is not surprising that so many women fall short of completion.

In addition to problem-solving courts, what other approaches might the legal system take to assist victims in achieving therapeutic justice in a manner that feels less like "therapy at gunpoint" (e.g. mentorship programs)?

Second, and more fundamentally, the prostituted people (including sex trafficking victims) who are involved in these courts are involved as criminal defendants – and their participation in the therapeutic treatments made available through these courts is done pursuant to a court order. One commentator, who questions the appropriateness of treatment courts, succinctly described the programs as "therapy at gunpoint" (Blumgart, 2015). Perhaps more eloquently, Gruber et al. (2016) observe,

> Ultimately, [trafficking courts] maintain the illusion that criminal management of individuals, including prostitution defendants, is the answer to social dysfunction. As such, [these courts,] like criminal court interventions generally, insufficiently advance the social restructuring necessary to address the root causes of prostitution crimes.
>
> (*p. 1402*)

Such social restructuring, however, may arise from transformative justice, as discussed in the next section.

Transformative justice

Transformative justice seeks to change social norms. Some advantageous effects that may follow from such transformation include benefits such as reducing harmful conduct and protecting victims from further harm. Yet, these potential positive effects are not the driving force behind transformative justice. Rather, at its core, the idea of transformative justice borrows from "educational theories" or "communicative theories," which seek either to describe the function of criminal law, or to contribute to its justification, simply in virtue of its expressive function (Duff, 2001; Feinberg, 1970; Hampton, 1984). These theories view the criminal justice process as not merely an occasion to punish wrongdoers or to protect potential victims; rather, they view the criminal justice process as an elaborate process of communication, within which "criminal indictment . . . is an institutional analogue to a moral accusation" (Duff, 1986, p. 116), and the process of determining guilt and administering punishment is, in Duff's (2001) influential phrasing, a form of "penitential communication."[4]

Examples of this elaborate process of penitential communication are difficult to identify in the U.S. criminal justice system, which tends to favor retributive justice (Whitman, 2011), but so-called john's schools offer perhaps the best example of transformative justice in the realm of domestic commercial sexual exploitation. A john's school is "an education or treatment program for men arrested for soliciting illegal commercial sex" (Shively, Kliorys, Wheeler, & Hunt, 2013, p. 1). Although these programs exist in varied formats, the basic goal is the same: to reduce the demand for commercial sex by increasing knowledge and effecting "attitude change," that is, by *transforming* sex-buyer behavior (Shively et al., 2013, pp. 3, 10; see also "First Offender Prostitution Program," n.d.). San Francisco's First Offender Program (FOPP) is typical. The FOPP employs a one-day, eight-hour course that covers a range of issues, including the legal consequences of future arrests, health risks such as HIV and sexually transmitted infections, and the exploitative nature of prostitution (Shively et al., 2008, p. 14).

Can the criminal justice system change societal predispositions related to commercial sex (e.g. prostitution is the world's oldest profession) that perpetuate illegal commercial sex?

Proponents of john's schools laud low recidivism rates and positive post-participation comments as concrete evidence of the positive societal impact and transformative nature of these programs. Most programs, for example, report re-arrest rates ranging from 0 to 3% (Jungels, 2007, pp. 23–24). One study, which compared overall recidivism rates in San Francisco before and after the implementation of the FOPP, found that "there was a sharp drop in recidivism rates in the year of implementation (1995), and these lower levels were sustained over the subsequent 10 years" (Shively et al., 2008, p. iv). In fact, Shively and colleagues (2008) "estimate[d] that the San Francisco john's school program cuts the one-year re-arrest rate by roughly half" (p. 78).

Additionally, surveys administered to participants both before and after completion of a john's school program offer insight into changed attitudes. Based on surveys completed at one large john's school, researcher Amanda Jungels (2007) concluded that the program *may* have been "successful in creating sympathy for the female prostitutes, and portraying them as victims of their circumstance and of abusive men, rather than calculating, money-hungry women who chose street prostitution as a career" (p. 48). Jungels (2007) further concluded that the "program *is* effective in challenging the myths that prostitutes enjoy their work" and "in challenging the idea of prostitution as a career choice" (pp. 48–49).

Jungels (2007) also evaluated freeform comments provided after the program and reported that the course may have helped some participants realize how prostitution impacts communities "and the dangerous nature of prostitution for the women involved in it" (p. 51). For example, one program participant indicated that he would teach his son "that prostitution is evil and is bondage, slavery and against the law!" (as reported in Jungels, 2007, p. 54). Another commented that "prostitution victimizes the women" (as reported in Jungels, 2007, p. 54). Yet another reported learning that prostitution "is a lot more than the 'myths' (Hollywood image) and it is not glamorous by any means" (as reported in Jungels, 2007, p. 54). Such comments, coupled with the reportedly low recidivism rates, suggest that john's schools may be an efficient and effective means of achieving transformative justice through the criminal justice system.

Even so, john's schools have their critics, and many argue they may not be effective at all. As some suggest, not being re-arrested does not necessarily equate with not buying sex. Rather, buyers may simply avoid re-arrest because law enforcement fails to target demand, or buyers may learn from their arrests and turn to less risky avenues, such as the internet or massage parlors, to purchase sex (Levine, 2017). Thus, recidivism rates may be a poor marker of the rate at which program participants subsequently purchase sex.

Even if recidivism rates actually do reflect the rate of subsequent sex buying, other critics argue that researchers have failed to show a causal link between john's schools and this changed behavior, reasoning the arrest itself or other factors may be the true source of deterrence. For example, Rachel Lovell and Ann Jordan (2012) concluded that the aforementioned study by Shively and colleagues "offers *no* reliable evidence that the john school classes reduce the rate of re-arrests" (p. 1). They further stressed that "no study to date has documented a causal connection between a john school program and a decline in recidivism (re-arrest) rates among male purchasers of commercial sex or a reduction in the incidence of prostitution or human trafficking" (Lovell & Jordan, 2012, p. 2). According to Lovell and Jordan (2012), the FOPP study is unreliable because, among other factors, the researchers failed to acknowledge a steep decline in San Francisco's recidivism rate *in the two years before the FOPP was implemented*, and the researchers failed to account for the impact of the arrest itself or the promise of a cleared record upon completion of the program (pp. 3–5, 9). In fact, Shively and colleagues (2008) reported that 73% of program participants indicated *prior to participation in the FOPP* that they would not solicit a prostitute in the future (p. 66). "In other words, before the men even started the classes, they had already decided not to re-offend" (Lovell & Jordan, 2012, p. 10).

As Lovell and Jordan contend, their conclusions are consistent with the findings of prior studies on the effectiveness of john's schools. In one study comparing the re-arrest rates in Portland, Oregon, of offenders who participated in a john's school with those who did not, the researchers "found no statistically significant differences in recidivism between the offenders who attended the [john's school] and the offenders who did not attend" (Montco & Garcia, 2002). In another study that evaluated a john's school in Toronto, Canada, the researchers concluded "that – besides the possible deterrent effects of being arrested – participation in the John School educational program has relatively little impact on the Johns' anticipated future use of prostitutes" (Wortley, Fischer, & Webster, 2002, p. 389). Yet another study conducted in Colorado Springs, Colorado, found "that arrest reduces the likelihood of a future patronizing arrest by about 70%" (Brewer, Potterat, Muth, & Roberts, 2006, p. 5). Brewer and colleagues (2006) concluded that, "given the large specific deterrent effect of arrest for patronizing, any special post-arrest intervention or extra penalty for patronizing" (such as a john's school) "may not have a noticeable impact, as there may be little additional deterrence that could be achieved" (p. 5).

While some critics focus on the lack of evidence regarding program efficacy, others argue that john's schools actually do more harm than good. For example, Eleanor Levine (2017) contends that john's schools "not only . . . reinforce double standards for buyers and prostitutes within the criminal justice system and society, they [also] do not address the broader issues that cause sex trafficking." Specifically, Levine (2017) asserts that john's schools "perpetuate the centuries-old pattern in which prostitutes are treated worse and stigmatized more than buyers by the criminal justice system," which "provide[s] an avenue that continues to allow buyers off the hook for their crimes while those who sell sex continue to be arrested, fined, and hold felony or misdemeanor records that negatively impact their lives and choices." Levine (2017) further contends that john's schools "perpetuate the societal stigmas about prostitutes" and reject "incorporating feminist values into their curriculums." Even the cliché argument against soliciting a prostitute – often presented in a john's school curriculum – that the woman is "someone's daughter, mother or sister disregards the fact that this [woman] is someone of value regardless of her relationship to a man" (Levine, 2017).

This inherent gender bias of prostitution[5] that Levine discusses – and the unequal criminal justice response to it – is perhaps best illustrated by a 2001 Nevada Supreme Court case: *Salaiscooper v. Eighth Judicial District Court ex rel. County of Clark. Salaiscooper* (2001) was a test case representative of 56 then pending cases in Las Vegas, Nevada (p. 513). The defendant, a woman charged with prostitution, argued that the district attorney's (DA's) policy for plea agreements in prostitution cases "violated the Equal Protection Clauses of the U.S. and Nevada Constitutions because it resulted in impermissible gender discrimination" (*Salaiscooper*, 2001, p. 512).

Specifically, attorneys in the DA's office were expressly prohibited from negotiating plea agreements in prostitution cases "for any reason," "except in cases of first time *male* offenders who opt[ed] for the diversion program" (*Salaiscooper*, 2001, p. 512). Under the policy's single exception, a *man* arrested for a first offense of solicitation of a prostitute could pay $400 to attend "a one-day counseling session on the dangers of prostitution," upon completion of which, the offender's record of arrest would be expunged ("State's High Court," 2001). Women, by contrast, were to be prosecuted to the full extent of the law and denied any opportunity for alternative dispute resolution.

Despite acknowledging that "the plain language of the policy . . . excepted first time male defendants" only and that the program was called the "First Offender Program for Men," the Nevada Court found no equal protection violation (*Salaiscooper*, 2001, pp. 512–513, 518–519). Furthermore, despite expert testimony "that the vast majority of sellers of sex are females," while "buyers of sex . . . are statistically almost always male," the court rejected the argument "that the policy's distinction between buyers and sellers of sex [was] 'nothing more than a facade' concealing 'conscious, intentional discrimination' against women" (*Salaiscooper*, 2001, pp. 513, 516). Rather, the court concluded, "the district attorney had a valid, gender-neutral motivation for creating the policy classification – to draw a distinction between buyers and sellers of sex in order to deter acts of prostitution" (*Salaiscooper*, 2001, p. 517).

Notably, despite the court's analysis that the state reasonably distinguished between buyers and sellers in their efforts to deter prostitution, the Nevada state legislature itself does not distinguish between the crimes of selling and buying sex (Nev. Rev. Stat. § 201.354). As such, analyzing data on prostitution arrests in Nevada proves difficult. Nevertheless, in 2001, the year the Nevada Court issued its opinion in *Salaiscooper*, 82% of adults arrested in Las Vegas for prostitution and commercialized vice were female (Bureau of Justice, n.d.). Additionally, despite the state's reliance on "deterrent effect" to further its policy of discriminating against sellers – who are typically female – Las Vegas has not had any appreciable decline in the number of prostitution arrests since 2001 (Bureau of Justice, n.d.). Moreover, during the time period spanning 2001–2012, 84% of all individuals arrested for prostitution were female, while virtually all participants in the Las Vegas "John's School" have been, and continue to be, exclusively male (Bureau of Justice, n.d.; "State's High Court," 2001; Goldman, 2008; Smith, 2001). Thus, while john's schools offer transformative justice to men – although their effectiveness is debatable – the criminal justice response to prostituted women, as illuminated by the *Salaiscooper* case, is one of inherent gender bias and raw *injustice.*

Does the curriculum taught at john's schools come too late for a person's viewpoint to change? If so, how can the information from john's schools be communicated to the general population in order to affect societal change?

While john's schools have fallen short of achieving transformative justice, various jurisdictions have adopted different approaches to transforming social norms relating to commercial sex in hopes of changing the norms and behaviors that result in sex trafficking. The two most prominent approaches are (1) legalization and (2) regulation of the commercial sex industry, or an approach referred to as the "Nordic Model" (or "Swedish Model"), which provides a comprehensive method for shifting social norms by communicating the idea that "prostitution [is] a form of sex inequality related to gender-based violence, exploiting and harming the prostituted person" (Waltman, 2011, p. 451).

Those who advocate full legalization view as outdated and paternalistic any criminal law prohibiting commercial sexual transactions between consenting adults (Mudde, 2016; Wallace, 2011). One such advocate is Bob Wallace, the Principal Policy Officer of the Prostitution Licensing Authority of Queensland Australia, where prostitution is fully legal. According to Wallace (2011), "At the core of [the legalization] approach is agency and freedom of choice and a view that sexual relations between freely consenting adults should not be subject to interference or regulation by the state" (p. 5). Wallace (2011) describes legalization as "a pragmatic response to centuries of human behaviour, based on the impossibility of stamping out the sex industry," which "puts aside moralistic concerns, and in acknowledging the harms that can be associated with sex work, is focused squarely on harm minimisation" (p. 9).

This "harm minimisation" model "acknowledges that violence is an occupational hazard of sex work" but insists that legalizing prostitution will "reduce the risk of harm to sex workers, their clients, and thereby the entire community" (Wallace, 2011, pp. 6, 9). As Wallace (2011) puts it,

> Violence, rape, and coercion are separate to prostitution. They are not part of the contract between the sex worker and the client. For it to be prostitution, the sex worker must have freely consented without the application of duress or coercion and the activities in which they engage should be the result of negotiation and agreement between the sex worker and client.
>
> *(p. 6)*

Thus, legalization advocates envision a system in which a woman, fully empowered to exercise her "right to choose what she does with her body, who she wants to have sex with, and the form that sex will take," acts as a "free agent" who can, under whatever terms she defines, "enter into a contract with a client for the supply of a sexual service" (Wallace, 2011, pp. 5–6). Under this model, legalization theoretically achieves transformative justice by creating a society in which a woman can be an agent of her body, using it as a means of gainful employment without risk of physical violence, criminal recourse, moral judgment, or societal stigma.

Such justice, however, has not been the reality of legalized prostitution. In fact, all states that have legalized prostitution have failed to achieve any of the purported goals or benefits of legalization. On the contrary, the reality of legalized prostitution is that women who sell sex remain stigmatized in society, but in an environment where prostitution is legal, these women are often forced to work in brothels that take as much as 80% of their earnings while failing to protect them from violent buyers who often refuse to wear condoms and feel completely entitled to do anything they wish with the women they purchase (Bingham, 1998; Forrey, 2014; Meyer, Neumann, Schmid, Truckendanner, & Winter, 2013; Sullivan, 2005; Waltman, 2011). Thus in practice, legalization has not created a system in which a woman has the freedom – as Bob Wallace (2011) described – "to choose what she does with her body, who she wants to have sex with, and the form that sex will take" (p. 5). Rather, where prostitution has been legalized, "prostitutes have little or no say in choosing their customers or the numbers of hours they work" (Bingham, 1998, p. 94). In Germany's legalized brothels, for example, that lack of choice often means providing sexual services to one man after another who has paid a flat rate for as many sex acts as he wishes (Meyer et al., 2013). One such German brothel advertised its services as follows: "Sex with all women as long as you want, as often as you want and the way you want. Sex. Anal sex. Oral sex without a condom. Three-ways. Group sex. Gang bangs" (Meyer et al., 2013).

Furthermore, in addition to actually increasing harm to women, legalizing prostitution has had the detrimental knock-on effect of increasing sex trafficking. Researchers Seo-Young Cho, Axel Dreher, and Eric Neumayer (2013) conducted a comprehensive global study on the impact of legalized prostitution on human trafficking and concluded that, "[o]n average, countries with legalized prostitution experience a larger degree of reported human trafficking inflows" (pp. 75–76). Specifically, Cho and colleagues (2013) compared the "substitution effect" of prostitution, whereby illegal trafficking is replaced with legalized prostitution, with the "scale effect," whereby legalization increases demand beyond voluntary supply such that trafficking increases to fill the excess demand, and concluded, "the scale effects . . . dominate the substitution effects" (pp. 68, 74). In short, rather than securing positive transformative justice, legalizing prostitution tends to increase both harm to women and the incidence of sex trafficking.

By contrast, the "Nordic Model" of decriminalization, discussed briefly above, provides a blueprint for positive transformative justice. Under the Nordic Model, (1) the act of buying sex is illegal, and the buyer can be punished by the criminal justice system; (2) selling sex is not illegal, and the seller cannot be punished criminally (i.e, prostitution is "decriminalized"); and (3) support services are provided by the government to assist prostituted persons, including support to exit prostitution if desired (Equality Now, n.d.). Consistent with the notion of transformative justice as an elaborate process of penitential communication, Swedish lawmakers sought to communicate the idea "that it is shameful and unacceptable that, in a gender equal society, men obtain casual sexual relations with women in return for payment" (Government Offices of Sweden, 2010, p. 29).

Is full legalization or the Nordic Model preferable? Why?

The Nordic Model has proven to be incredibly successful in Sweden since its adoption in 1999. Street prostitution has been reduced by half, and although some argue that prostitution in Sweden has merely moved indoors or online, the evidence suggests that total prostitution has declined as well (Government Offices of Sweden, 2010; Waltman, 2011). As of 2008, Sweden's population of prostituted persons was just one-tenth the size of Denmark's, although Sweden's total population is twice as big (Waltman, 2011, p. 459). Additionally, this decline in prostitution has been accompanied by a reduction in sex trafficking as pimps and traffickers, disappointed with the Swedish market, have moved out of the area or reduced their operations (Waltman, 2011, p. 459).

The law also seems to have changed attitudes towards prostitution. As of 2008, approximately 80% of Swedes surveyed were in favor of Sweden's decriminalization model (Waltman, 2011, p. 459). Additionally, survey data suggest the percent of men who report having ever purchased sex dropped from 12.7% before Sweden implemented the Nordic Model to 7.6% approximately ten years after the law took effect (Waltman, 2011, p. 460). Indeed, the influence of criminal laws in shifting norms around commercial sex extend beyond Sweden. A recent study of eight European jurisdictions concluded that "citizens living in countries where the purchase of sex is criminalized are less tolerant toward the buying of sex compared to citizens living in countries where the purchase of sex is legalized" (Jonsson & Jakobsson, 2017). As Pierrette Pape, spokeswoman for the European Women's Lobby, put it,

> Nowadays, a little boy in Sweden grows up with the fact that buying sex is a crime. A little boy in the Netherlands grows up with the knowledge that women sit in display windows and can be ordered like mass-produced goods.
>
> *(as reported in Meyer et al., 2013)*

This difference has mattered in shaping both societies over the past two decades, and the result has been positive transformative justice for many women in Sweden.

Could the Nordic Model be implemented in the United States? How would concerns raised by "sex worker" advocates who favor full legalization be addressed?

Despite the Nordic Model's enormous success, however, the law's implementation has been imperfect. According to Max Waltman (2011), the law has not been implemented as effectively as possible, in part, due to early court decisions that recognized prostitution as an offense against the public order, rather than an offense against a person (p. 463). Waltman (2011) argues these decisions are contrary to the legislative intent to acknowledge prostitution, not as a victimless crime but rather as "a form of sex inequality related to gender-based violence" (pp. 463–464). According to Waltman (2011), the law will not achieve its full potential until Sweden corrects these problems in application and cures "serious deficiencies" in providing appropriate support services and exit strategies for prostituted women (pp. 463–464). Even so, Sweden is leading the way in achieving transformative justice for victims of prostitution and sex trafficking.

Conceptual justice

The final conception of justice considered in this chapter is what we refer to as "conceptual justice" – the sense in which justice is done when the criminal law properly labels and defines different kinds of criminal wrongdoing. Achieving conceptual justice with respect to sex trafficking has proven difficult in respect to both labels and definitions. In this section, we examine these difficulties and explain that, in some jurisdictions at least, conceptual justice is now being realized.

From the time when sex trafficking was first recognized as a legal wrong in the early 1900s, in documents such as the *International Agreement for the Suppression of the "White Slave Traffic"* (1904), there was an utter failure of conceptual justice in labelling the nature of the wrong. The label, "'white slavery' . . . had immediate appeal to racists who could and did conclude that the antitrafficking efforts were directed against an international traffic in *white* women," and thus "embodied all of the sexist, classist, and racist bigotry that was ultimately incorporated within the movement dominated by religious morality" (Barry, 1995, p. 115). As Doezema (1999, p. 30) explains, "Only white women were considered 'victims'; for example, campaigners against the 'white slave trade' from Britain to Argentina were not concerned about the situation of native born prostitutes nor were American reformers concerned about non-Anglo Saxon prostitutes."

While the label "white slavery" has largely been abandoned and replaced in law and popular culture with the labels "sex trafficking" or "trafficking for the purpose of sexual exploitation,"[6] Doezema (1999) argues that conceptualizing the wrong at issue as "sex trafficking" perpetuates the racism, sexism, and classism embodied in the fight against "white slavery." As such, she concludes that we should abandon the label of "sex trafficking" and related "narratives of innocent, virginal victims purveyed in the 'trafficking in women' discourse," which, she claims, "are a modern version of the myth of 'white slavery'" (Doezema, 1999, p. 23). In place of labeling the wrongdoing as "sex trafficking," Doezema urges us to reconceptualize conduct such as "debt-bondage and other slavery-like practices [in the commercial sex industry]" as "abuses of sex workers' rights" (p. 47).

Despite widespread agreement that the practices Doezema cites are indeed abuses of *human* rights, many object to Doezema's suggestion to use the phrase "sex worker" in labelling the problem. As Janice Raymond argues, the label "sex worker" is problematic because it "gives buyers, pimps, recruiters, and other key perpetrators of sexual exploitation more legitimacy than they could otherwise obtain" (Raymond, 2013, p. xlii), and incorrectly suggests that "sex work" is no more harmful than jobs outside of the commercial sex industry, despite evidence to the contrary (Potterat et al., 2004). Debates continue as to whether the criminal wrong at issue is best labeled as "sex trafficking" or "abuses of sex workers' rights" (Kristof, 2015).[7] Meanwhile, some advocates have adopted an alternative label, "commercial sexual exploitation," either as an alternative or in combination with the label "sex trafficking," so as to avoid the problematic features of the term, "sex work" (DiBacco, 2016). However, in the context of the criminal justice system, the labels "sex trafficking" and "trafficking for sexual exploitation" continue to be widely used in many jurisdictions.

When it comes to achieving conceptual justice through properly *defining* a criminal wrong, criminal justice systems throughout the world were given a tremendous opportunity to achieve uniformity and relative clarity when the United Nations adopted its Protocol to Prevent, Suppress, and Punish Trafficking in Persons, commonly referred to as the Palermo Protocol, in 2000 (Palermo, 2000). Prior to this time, there was no internationally recognized definition of human trafficking of any kind – neither labor trafficking nor sex trafficking. Rather, there were simply international legal conventions that purported to prohibit trafficking, without offering any definition of what was actually being prohibited. In this definitional vacuum, very different conceptions of what counted as sex trafficking arose. Some advocates sought to define trafficking narrowly, so that its conceptual scope would cover only the most serious, egregious, clear-cut cases – such as those involving abduction, debt bondage, and extreme physical violence. Others advocated for a broad definition that recognized that the central feature of sex trafficking is *exploitation*, not force (Raymond, 2013, pp. 22–23). After years of debate and negotiation, an internationally recognized definition of "trafficking in persons" was finally adopted, in Article 3 of the Palermo Protocol:

> (a) "Trafficking in persons" shall mean the recruitment, transportation, transfer, harbouring or receipt of persons, by means of the threat or use of force or other forms of coercion, of abduction, of fraud, of deception, of the abuse of power or of a position of vulnerability or of the giving or receiving of payments or benefits to achieve the consent of a person having control over another person, for the purpose of exploitation.
>
> Exploitation shall include, at a minimum, the exploitation of the prostitution of others or other forms of sexual exploitation, forced labour or services, slavery or practices similar to slavery, servitude or the removal of organs;

(b) The consent of a victim of trafficking in persons to the intended exploitation set forth in subparagraph (a) of this article shall be irrelevant where any of the means set forth in subparagraph (a) have been used;
(c) The recruitment, transportation, transfer, harbouring or receipt of a child for the purpose of exploitation shall be considered "trafficking in persons" even if this does not involve any of the means set forth in subparagraph (a) of this article;
(d) "Child" shall mean any person under eighteen years of age.

There are four key points to note about this definition. First, no travel or transportation is required for a case to count as trafficking. Rather, trafficking can occur through any one of five different acts: recruitment, transportation, transfer, harbouring, or receipt. Second, all child prostitution is trafficking, even if the child was not forced, threatened, coerced, defrauded, subjected to an abuse of his or her vulnerability, or an abuse of another's power, or any other means delineated in the Palermo definition. Third, this definition covers a broad scope of conduct – with 12 mutually independent means, from "the threat or use of force" all the way to "the abuse of power or of a position of vulnerability," satisfying the definition of trafficking. Thus, even if someone has never been forced or threatened with force, has never once been subjected to any kind of coercion, fraud, or deception, the case can still count as a case of trafficking under the Palermo definition. Finally, the victim's consent is entirely irrelevant to whether someone has been trafficked (Palermo, 2000, Art. 3(b)), consistent with the view that trafficking is primarily about *exploitation*, not consent.

The Palermo definition has gained widespread acceptance, with 170 States Parties having ratified, making it one of the most universally recognized legal instruments in the history of humanity. Indeed, as the former United Nations Special Rapporteur on Trafficking in Persons observed, "The Protocol definition of trafficking stands today as the accepted international definition of trafficking. . . . [It] establishes clear criteria for understanding what counts as trafficking, and makes it possible to frame anti-trafficking initiatives with consistency and clarity" (Huda, 2006, p. 32).

Despite its wide recognition as the internationally accepted definition of trafficking and the fact that States Parties are obligated under Article 5 to criminalize trafficking in persons as the offense is defined in Article 3 of the Palermo Protocol, many of the States Parties' criminal justice systems have failed to define sex trafficking consistently with the Palermo Protocol. Indeed, in a survey of States Parties' criminal laws conducted in 2011, Dempsey, Hoyle, and Bosworth (2012) identified numerous domestic criminal laws that fail to conform to the international definition by eliminating the possibility of trafficking being committed by means of an abuse of power or position of vulnerability, by requiring border crossing, by making non-consent a required element, by requiring proof of force, and so forth in cases involving minors, and other differences that, in effect, mean these states parties criminalize only part of what the Palermo Protocol defines as trafficking.

If you were a lawmaker, how would you advocate defining this crime? Would you expand or narrow the Palermo definition? How would you label it (e.g. "trafficking," "slavery," "commercial sexual exploitation")? Would you require force or lack of consent? Why or why not?

In order to achieve conceptual justice with respect to sex trafficking, criminal justice systems must appropriately label and define this wrong. Whether the proper label is "sex trafficking," "abuses of sex worker rights," or "commercial sexual exploitation," it remains clear that doing conceptual justice requires criminal laws and policies that clearly reject the racism, sexism, and classism embodied in the historic label "white slavery." So, too, achieving conceptual justice with respect to properly defining the wrong requires criminal laws to track closely the internationally recognized definition of trafficking adopted in Article 3 of the Palermo Protocol. For, by adopting a narrower definition of trafficking, these criminal laws not only violate their States Parties' obligations under Article 5 of the Palermo Protocol, but they fail to recognize the broad scope of trafficking, properly understood as a wrong involving not only force and non-consent, but also a wide range of coercion and exploitation.

Conclusion

This chapter has addressed the question, "where is the justice in criminal justice?" when it comes to human trafficking by examining six distinct ways in which criminal laws, policies, and actors seek to achieve justice when addressing sex trafficking. This examination has been, in many respects, disheartening, because it has demonstrated the many ways in which the criminal justice system has failed to achieve its stated aims of doing justice. The discriminatory and abusive treatment of victims by law enforcement officers demonstrates a failure of *procedural justice*. The persistent targeting of prostituted persons for arrest and prosecution, rather than focusing on the punishment of traffickers, pimps, and buyers, illustrates the still too common failures of *retributive justice*. The limited tools and lack of political will to make victims "whole" after their trafficking experience reveals that the criminal justice system is largely inept in delivering *corrective justice*. The inappropriateness of using the coercive mechanisms of the state to heal and restore victims illustrates the failure of criminal justice systems to deliver *therapeutic justice*. The persistence of myths that depict prostitution as a "victimless crime" and the concomitant failure to provide appropriate support services and exit strategies for prostituted women demonstrates the difficulties in using the criminal law to achieve *transformative justice*. The lingering impact of racist, sexist, and classist ideologies in the labels we use to refer to human trafficking, and the failure of many criminal justice systems to adopt an appropriately broad definition of trafficking, reflect the continuing challenges for criminal justice systems in securing *conceptual justice*. In each of these six ways, this chapter supports the conclusion that the criminal legal system typically fails to secure justice when it comes to sex trafficking.

Still, the examination in this chapter was not without glimmers of hope when it comes to achieving justice through the criminal legal system's response to trafficking. In some jurisdictions, at some times, some police officers are receiving training to respond more compassionately to victims, some traffickers are being sentenced to deserved punishments, some victims are receiving restitution from those who have harmed them, and experiencing positive interventions from criminal "problem solving courts," some social norms are beginning to shift away from traditional views that sustain and perpetuate trafficking, and some jurisdictions are conceptualizing trafficking in a way that fully reflects the broad scope of the problem. The task that now lies ahead for criminal justice systems is to ensure that not merely *some*, but *all* of these forms of justice are pursued and attained in responding to human trafficking. Thus, perhaps the fitting conclusion to reach from this chapter's examination is that criminal justice systems must continue to change and adapt their responses to human trafficking, so as to better achieve justice in every sense of the word.

Notes

1 Our working definition of sex trafficking borrows from the U.S. Trafficking Victims Protection Act of 2000, as amended by the Justice for Victims of Trafficking Act of 2015. Under this federal definition, "severe forms of trafficking in persons" includes sex trafficking by force, fraud, or coercion (22 U.S.C.

§ 7102(9)). Sex trafficking, as we use the term here, occurs when a person, through force, fraud, or coercion, "recruits, entices, harbors, transports, provides, obtains, advertises, maintains, patronizes, or solicits" another person for the purpose of a commercial sex act (18 U.S.C. § 1591). In the section regarding conceptual justice, we will consider alternative frameworks for defining trafficking.

2 A "bottom" is a prostituted person who has been trafficked and victimized by the trafficker for the longest period of time and who has been tasked with assisting the trafficker in operating the business and recruiting new trafficking victims.

3 Aristotle conceptualized corrective justice as consisting of two sub-divisions, corresponding to both modern tort and contract disputes (what he called "voluntary transactions"), and to criminal acts ("involuntary transactions") such as "theft . . . assault, imprisonment, murder, robbery with violence, maiming, abusive language," and so forth (Aristotle, 2012/349 BC).

4 The literature on expressive theories of law go beyond a focus on criminal justice, with notable contributions by Anderson and Pildes (2000), and Sunstein's (1996) discussion of "norm entrepreneurs."

5 For an in-depth analysis of the inherent gender bias of prostitution and sex trafficking, see Catharine A. MacKinnon's *Trafficking, Prostitution, and Inequality* (2011).

6 Although, see *United States v. Young*, 590 F.3d 467 (7th Cir. 2009), where the term was used without irony or critique as a synonym for sex trafficking by the U.S. Seventh Circuit Court of Appeal in 2009.

7 From a legal perspective, if the wrongs at issue are properly criminalized, then labelling them as merely "abuses of . . . workers' rights" (whether "sex workers" or not), risks confusion as to whether the remedy to these wrongs is a responsibility that rests solely in the victims' hands – or is a matter that calls for a state response. On why only the state may inflict criminal sanctions, see Harel (2008).

Supplemental learning material

Dempsey, M. M. (2010). Sex trafficking and criminalization: In defense of feminist abolitionism. *University of Pennsylvania Law Review, 158*, 1729–1778.

MacKinnon, C. A. (2011). Trafficking, prostitution, and inequality. *Harvard Civil Rights-Civil Liberties Law Review, 46*, 271–309.

Mary Mazzio's film, *I Am Jane Doe*, available on Netflix, iTunes, Vimeo, Google Play, Amazon, and DVD. Mazzio, M. (Director). (2017). *I Am Jane Doe* [Motion picture]. United States: 50 Eggs.

The website of Demand Abolition. Retrieved from www.demandabolition.org

The website of the Villanova Law Institute to Address Commercial Sexual Exploitation. Retrieved from http://cseinstitute.org

References

18 U.S.C. §§ 1591–1593.

22 U.S.C. § 7102(9)

Alaska Stat. Ann. § 11.66.100.

Alexander, M. (2010). *The new Jim Crow: Mass incarceration in the age of colorblindness*. New York, NY: The New Press.

Allen, B. (2014, May 21). Human trafficking course added to police training for next year. Retrieved from www.witf.org/news/2014/05/human-trafficking-course-added-to-police-training-for-next-year.php

Anderson, E., & Pildes, R. (2000). Expressive theories of law: A general restatement. *University of Pennsylvania Law Review, 148*, 1503-****.

Aristotle. (2012). *Nicomachean ethics*. (R. C. Bartlett & S. D. Collins, Trans.). Chicago, IL: University of Chicago Press. (Original work published 349 BC).

Barry, K. (1995). *The prostitution of sexuality*. New York, NY: New York University Press.

Bergan, S. (2015, January 20). *Officer appeals firing after undercover cop's sex act in prostitution bust*. Retrieved from http://5newsonline.com/2015/01/14/fired-officer-who-released-report-on-undercover-cops-sex-act-with-prostitute-sues-police

Bernish, C. (2017, June 17). *Police pushing 2 bills to allow cops to have sex with prostitutes they arrest*. Retrieved from www.thefringenews.com/police-pushing-2-bills-to-allow-cops-to-have-sex-with-prostitutes-they-arrest

Bingham, M. (1998). Nevada sex trade: A gamble for the workers. *Yale Journal of Law & Feminism, 10*(1), 69–100. Retrieved from http://digitalcommons.law.yale.edu/cgi/viewcontent.cgi?article=1137&context=yjlf

Blumgart, J. (2015, February 24). *Therapy at gunpoint: Can this controversial Philly program put an end to sex work?* Retrieved from http://talkingpointsmemo.com/theslice/can-dawn-court-solve-a-problem-like-prostitution

Boots, M. T. (2017, May 8). *Bills to ban police sexual contact with prostitutes they investigate met with opposition.* Retrieved from www.adn.com/alaska-news/crime-courts/2017/05/07/bills-to-ban-police-sexual-contact-with-prostitutes-they-investigate-met-with-opposition

Brewer, D. D., Potterat, J. J., Muth, S. Q., & Roberts, J. M., Jr. (2006). A large specific deterrent effect of arrest for patronizing a prostitute. *PLoS ONE, 1*(1). Retrieved from https://doi.org/10.1371/journal.pone.0000060.

Buettner, R. (2013a, May 28). Prostitutes testify in defense of pimps at sex trafficking trial. *New York Times.* Retrieved from www.nytimes.com/2013/05/29/nyregion/prostitutes-testify-in-defense-of-pimps-at-sex-trafficking-trial.html

Buettner, R. (2013b, June 19). Father and son acquitted of sex trafficking charges. *New York Times.* Retrieved from www.nytimes.com/2013/06/20/nyregion/sex-trafficking-prosecution-fails-in-case-of-pimps-defended-by-prostitutes.html

Bureau of Justice Statistics Home page. (n.d.). Retrieved from www.bjs.gov/index.cfm?ty=datool&surl=%2Farrests%2Findex.cfm

California Commission on Peace Officer Standards and Training (POST). (2014). POST guidelines on law enforcement response to human trafficking. Retrieved from http://lib.post.ca.gov/Publications/human_trafficking.pdf

Carns, T. W., Hotchkin, M. G., & Andrews, E. M. (2002). Therapeutic justice in Alaska's courts. *Alaska Law Review, 19*(1), 1–55.

Cho, S.Y., Dreher, A., Neumayer, E. (2013). Does Legalized Prostitution Increase Human Trafficking? World Development, 41(1), 67–82. Retrieved from https://www.sciencedirect.com/science/article/pii/S0305750X12001453

Coleman, J. (1992). *Risks and wrongs.* Cambridge: Cambridge University Press.

Crenshaw, K. (1991). Mapping the margins: Intersectionality, identity politics, and violence against women of color. *Stanford Law Review, 43*, 1241–1299.

Curtis, R. R. (2012). *Sex trafficking: How the media portrays victims and reflects legislation* (Unpublished master's thesis). Iowa State University. Retrieved from http://lib.dr.iastate.edu/cgi/viewcontent.cgi?article=3312&context=etd

Dank, M., Khan, B., Downey, P. M., Kotonias, C., Mayer, D., Owens, C., . . . Yu, L. (2014). *Estimating the size and structure of the underground commercial sex economy in eight major US cities.* Washington, DC: Urban Institute.

Dempsey, M. M. (2010). Sex trafficking and criminalization: In defense of feminist abolitionism. *University of Pennsylvania Law Review, 158*, 1729–1778.

Dempsey, M.M., Hoyle, C., Bosworth, M. (2012). Defining Sex Trafficking in International and Domestic Law: Mind the Gaps. *Emory International Law Review*, 26(1).

Dewey, S., & Germain, T. S. (2014). "It depends on the cop:" Street-based sex workers' perspectives on police patrol officers. *Sexuality Research and Social Policy, 11*(3), 256–270. Retrieved from https://doi.org/10.1007/s13178-014-0163-8.

DiBacco, J. (2016). "Sex worker": Empowering or exploitative? Retrieved from https://cseinstitute.org/mini-series-essay-3-sex-worker-empowering-exploitative

Dimon, L., Parascandola, R., & Rayman, G. (2017, June 26). *NYPD cop allegedly paid for sex acts during prostitution stings.* Retrieved from www.nydailynews.com/new-york/nypd-allegedly-paid-sex-acts-prostitution-stings-article-1.3279082

Dockterman, E. (2014, March 12). *Economics of prostitution study shows pimping isn't that profitable.* Retrieved from http://time.com/21351/prostitution-isnt-as-profitable-as-you-think.

Doezema, J. (1999). Loose women or lost women? The re-emergence of the myth of white slavery in contemporary discourses of trafficking in women. *Gender Issues, 18*(1), 23–50.

Duff, R. A. (1986). *Trials and punishment.* Cambridge: Cambridge University Press.

Duff, R. A. (2001). *Punishment, communication, and community.* Oxford: Oxford University Press.

Eifling, S. (2015, January 28). Above the law, under the sheets. *The New Republic.* Retrieved from https://newrepublic.com/article/120879/can-police-legally-have-sex-prostitutes-only-michigan

Equality Now. (n.d.). What is the Nordic model? Retrieved from www.equalitynow.org/sites/default/files/Nordic%20Model%20Fact%20Sheet_0.pdf

Farley, M. (2006). Prostitution, trafficking, and cultural amnesia: What we must not know in order to keep the business of sexual exploitation running smoothly. *Yale Journal of Law & Feminism, 18*(1), 109–144. Retrieved from http://digitalcommons.law.yale.edu/cgi/viewcontent.cgi?article=1243&context=yjlf

Feinberg, J. (1970). The expressive function of punishment. In *Doing and deserving: Essays in the theory of responsibility* (pp. 95–118). Princeton, NJ: Princeton University Press.

First offender prostitution program: John school diversion classes. (n.d.). Retrieved from www.logan institute.com/index.php

Footer, K. H., Silberzahn, B. E., Tormohlen, K. N., & Sherman, S. G. (2016). Policing practices as a structural determinant for HIV among sex workers: A systematic review of empirical findings. *Journal of the International AIDS Society, 19*(4, Suppl 3). Retrieved from https://doi.org/10.7448/ias.19.4.20883.

Forrey, C. (2014). America's "Disneyland of sex": Exploring the problem of sex trafficking in Las Vegas and Nevada's response. *Nevada Law Journal, 14*(3), 970–999. Retrieved from http://scholars.law.unlv.edu/nlj/vol14/iss3/17

Gafni, M. and Debolt, D. (2016). *Oakland police scandal: How often are cops having sex with prostitutes?* Retrieved from www.mercurynews.com/2016/07/02/oakland-police-scandal-how-often-are-cops-having-sex-with-prostitutes

Goldman, A. (2008, January 6). *"John School" teaches men the uglier facts of life.* Retrieved from https://lasvegassun.com/news/2008/jan/06/john-school-teaches-menthe-uglier-facts-life

Government Offices of Sweden. (2010). *English Summary of the report prohibition of the purchase of sexual services. An evaluation 1999–2008* (Rep. No. SOU 2010:49). Retrieved from www.government.se/4a4908/contentassets/8f0c2ccaa84e455f8bd2b7e9c557ff3e/english-summary-of-sou-2010-49.pdf

Gruber, A., Cohen, A., & Mogulescu, K. (2016). Penal welfare and the new human trafficking intervention courts. *Florida Law Review, 68*, 1333–1402.

Hampton, J. (1984). The moral education theory of punishment. *Philosophy & Public Affairs, 13*(3), 208–238.

Harel, A. (2008). Why only the state may inflict criminal sanctions: The case against privately inflicted sanctions. *Legal Theory, 14*(2), 113–133.

Harper, R. (1904). *The code of Hammurabi, King of Babylon, about 2250 B.C.* Chicago, IL: University of Chicago Press.

Harris, E. (2013, July 9). *Women with prostitution charges find compassion, new start.* Retrieved from www.catholicnewsagency.com/news/women-with-prostitution-charges-find-compassion-new-start

Haw. Rev. Stat. Ann. § 712–1200.

Hora, P. F., Schma, W. G., & Rosenthal, J. T. A. (1999). Therapeutic jurisprudence and the drug treatment court movement: Revolutionizing the criminal justice system's response to drug abuse and crime in America. *Notre Dame Law Review, 74*(2), 439–538.

Huda, S. (2006, February 20). *Integration of the human rights of women and a gender perspective: Report of the Special Rapporteur on the human rights aspects of the victims of trafficking in persons, especially women and children* (U.N. Doc. E/CN.4/2006/62). Commission on Human Rights.

International Agreement for the Suppression of the "White Slave Traffic." (1904). League of Nations Treaty Series (Vol. I, p. 83).

Johnson, E. (2014). Buyers without remorse: Ending the discriminatory enforcement of prostitution laws. *Texas Law Review, 92*, 717–748. Retrieved from www.texaslrev.com/wp-content/uploads/2015/08/Johnson.pdf

Jonsson, S., & Jakobsson, N. (2017). Is buying sex morally wrong? Comparing attitudes toward prostitution using individual-level data across eight Western European countries. *Women's Studies International Forum, 61*, 58–69. Retrieved from https://doi.org/10.1016/j.wsif.2016.12.007

Jungels, A. M. (2007). *"Just say no": A process evaluation of a johns' school* (Unpublished doctoral dissertation). Georgia State University. Retrieved from http://scholarworks.gsu.edu/sociology_theses/18

Kristof, N. (August 6, 2015). Making life harder for pimps. The New York Times. Retrieved from https://www.nytimes.com/2015/08/06/opinion/nicholaskristof-making-lifeharder-for-pimps.html

Law enforcement resources. (n.d). Retrieved from www.michigan.gov/ag/0,4534,7-164-60857_60863 –,00.html

Levine, E. (2017). The impact of john schools on demand for prostitution. In E. C. Heil & A. J. Nichols (Eds.), *Broadening the scope of human trafficking research* (online). Durham, NC: Carolina Academic Press. Retrieved from www.cap-press.com/books/isbn/9781611637656/Broadening-the-Scope-of-Human-Trafficking-Research

Levy, A., Vandenberg, M., & Chen, L. (2014, September). *When "mandatory" does not mean mandatory: Failure to obtain criminal restitution in federal prosecution of human trafficking cases in the United States.* Retrieved from The Human Trafficking Pro Bono Legal Center website www.htprobono.org/htprobono-mandatory-restitution-report-9-2014

Logue, T. (2014, December 20). *Chester man gets life in jail for sex trafficking*. Retrieved from www.delcotimes.com/article/DC/20141219/NEWS/141219570

Lovell, R., & Jordan, A. (2012, July). *Do john schools really decrease recidivism?: A methodological critique of an evaluation of the San Francisco First Offender Prostitution Program*. Retrieved from Begun Center for Violence Prevention Research and Education, Case Western Reserve University website http://begun.case.edu/wp-content/uploads/2016/06/JohnSchoolsAndRecidivism.pdf

MacKinnon, C. A. (2011). Trafficking, prostitution, and inequality. *Harvard Civil Rights-Civil Liberties Law Review, 46*, 271–309.

Marcin, S. (2013, January 22). *Prostitution and human trafficking: A paradigm shift*. Retrieved from https://leb.fbi.gov/2013/march/prostitution-and-human-trafficking-a-paradigm-shift

McLeod, A. M. (2015). Prison abolition and grounded justice. *UCLA Law Review, 62*, 1156–1239.

Meyer, C., Neumann, C., Schmid, F., Truckendanner, P., & Winter, S. (2013). *Unprotected: How legalizing prostitution has failed*. Retrieved from www.spiegel.de/international/germany/human-trafficking-persists-despite-legality-of-prostitution-in-germany-a-902533.html

Mich. Comp. Laws Ann. § 750.451a.

Monto, M. A., & Garcia, S. (2002). Recidivism among the customers of female street prostitutes: Do intervention programs help? *Western Criminology Review, 3*(2). Retrieved from www.westerncriminology.org/documents/WCR/v03n2/monto/monto.html

Moore, M. S. (1997). *Placing blame: A theory of criminal law*. Oxford: Oxford University Press.

Mudde, C. (2016). The paternalistic fallacy of the "Nordic Model" of prostitution. *HuffPost*. Retrieved from www.huffingtonpost.com/cas-mudde/the-paternalistic-fallacy_b_9644972.html

Municipal Police Officers' Education and Training Commission. (n.d.). *2015 mandatory in-service training program*. Retrieved from www.psp.pa.gov/MPOETC/training/Documents/2015%20Mandatory%20In-Service%20Training%20Topics.pdf

National Initiative for Building Community Trust and Justice (NIBCTJ). (n.d.). *Procedural justice*. Retrieved from https://trustandjustice.org/resources/intervention/procedural-justice.

Nev. Rev. Stat. § 201.354.

Officials discuss why Philly's "poised to become major hub of human trafficking." (2012, December 11). *Metro*. Retrieved from www.metro.us/local/officials-discuss-why-philly-s-poised-to-become-major-hub-of-human-trafficking/tmWllk – 8bpXAgwtXr8p

Palermo. (2000). United Nations protocol to prevent, suppress, and punish trafficking in persons, especially women and children, supplementing the United Nations Convention Against Transnational Organized Crime. U.N. Doc. A/55/383.

Philadelphia District Attorney's Office. (n.d.). *Pre-trial diversion programs*. Retrieved from http://phlcouncil.com/wp-content/uploads/2016/04/Pre-Trial-Diversion.Philadelphia.pdf

Potterat, J. J., Brewer, D. D., Muth, S. Q., Rothenberg, R. B., Woodhouse, D. E., Muth, J. B., . . . Brody, S. (2004). Mortality in a long-term open cohort of prostitute women. *American Journal of Epidemiology, 159*(8), 778–785.

Raines, L. (2017, January 31). *Legal loophole lets undercover officers have sex with prostitutes, group alleges*. Retrieved from www.ktva.com/legal-loophole-lets-undercover-officers-sex-prostitutes-group-alleges-365

Raymond, J. (2013). *Not a choice, not a job: Exposing the myths about prostitution and the global sex trade*. Dulles, VA: Potomac Books.

Ritchie, B. (2012). *Arrested justice: Black women, violence, and America's prison nation*. New York, NY: New York University Press.

Ritchie, B. (2015). Keynote: Reimagining the movement to end gender violence: Anti-racism, prison abolition, women of color feminisms, and other radical visions of justice. *University of Miami Race & Social Justice Law Review, 5*(2), 257–273.

Roncinske, J. (2014, February 26). *Women's history month to kick off with a keynote address on 3/5*. Retrieved from https://fas.camden.rutgers.edu/2014/02/26/womens-history-month-to-kick-off-with-a-keynote-address-on-35

Rybak, S. A. (2014, September 4). *Dawn's place: Safe haven for sexually exploited women*. Retrieved from www.chestnuthilllocal.com/2014/09/04/dawns-place-safe-haven-sexually-exploited-women

Saar, M. S. (2011, February 7). *U.S. should stop criminalizing sex trafficking victims*. Retrieved from www.cnn.com/2011/OPINION/02/05/saar.ending.girl.slavery

Salaiscooper v. Eighth Judicial Dist. Court ex rel. Cty. of Clark, 34 P. 3d 509 (Nev. 2001).

Seldon, K. A. (2017, June 1). *Oakland reaches settlement with woman at center of police sex scandal*. Retrieved from http://kron4.com/2017/05/31/settlement-approved-in-oakland-police-sex-scandal

Shively, M., Jalbert, S. K., Kling, R., Rhodes, W., Finn, P., Flygare, C., . . . Wheeler, K. (2008). *Final report on the evaluation of the First Offender Prostitution Program* (Rep. No. 221894). Cambridge, MA: Abt Associates Inc.

Shively, M., Kliorys, K., Wheeler, K., & Hunt, D. (2013). *An overview of john schools in the United States.* Retrieved from www.demandforum.net/wp-content/uploads/2012/01/john-school-overview-from-national-assessment.pdf

Slobogin, C. (1995). Therapeutic jurisprudence: Five dilemmas to ponder. *Psychology, Public Policy & Law, 1*(1), 193–219.

State's High Court Upholds Policy on Hookers. (November 16, 2001). Las Vegas Sun. Retrieved from https://lasvegassun.com/news/2001/nov/16/states-high-court-upholds-policyon-hookers/

Sullivan, M. (2005). *What happens when prostitution becomes work?: An update on legalisation of prostitution in Australia.* North Amherst, MA: Coalition Against Trafficking in Women. Retrieved from http://catwinternational.org/Content/Images/Article/93/attachment.pdf

Sunstein, C. (1996). Social norms and social roles. *Columbia Law Review, 96*, 903–968.

Tyler, T. R. (2003). Procedural justice, legitimacy, and the effective rule of law. *Crime and Justice, 30*, 283–357.

United States v. Gadley (United States District Court, Northern District of Texas, Fort Worth Division June 4, 2013).

United States v. Lewis, 791 F. Supp. 2d 81 (United States District Court, District of Columbia June 13, 2011).

U.S. Attorney's Office, Central District of California. (2014b, March 31). *Los Angeles-area gang member who trafficked teens as prostitutes sentenced to 30 years in federal prison* [Press release]. Retrieved from www.justice.gov/usao-cdca/pr/los-angeles-area-gang-member-who-trafficked-teens-prostitutes-sentenced-30-years

U.S. Attorney's Office, Western District of Missouri (2013, September 12). *Three more defendants sentenced in sadomasochistic sex trafficking conspiracy* [Press release]. Retrieved from www.justice.gov/usao-wdmo/pr/human-trafficking-rescue-project-2

The Villanova Law Institute to Address Commercial Sexual Exploitation (CSE Institute). (2015, September 28). *Open letter critiquing PA's recidivism penalties for prostitution.* Retrieved from https://cseinstitute.org/open-letter-critiquing-pas-recidivism-penalties-for-prostitution

The Villanova Law Institute to Address Commercial Sexual Exploitation (CSE Institute). (2017, Spring). *Report on commercial sexual exploitation in Pennsylvania.* Retrieved from http://cseinstitute.org/wp-content/uploads/2016/12/CSE-Report-Spring-2017.pdf

Wallace, B. (2011). *The ban on purchasing sex in Sweden: The so-called "Swedish model."* Queensland, Australia: Prostitution Licensing Authority. Retrieved from www.pla.qld.gov.au/Resources/PLA/reportsPublications/documents/THE%20BAN%20ON%20PURCHASING%20SEX%20IN%20SWEDEN%20-%20THE%20SWEDISH%20MODEL.pdf

Waltman, M. (2011). Sweden's prohibition of purchase of sex: The law's reasons, impact, and potential. *Women's Studies International Forum, 34*(5), 449–474.

Wamsley, L. (2017, June 1). *Oakland to pay 19-year-old nearly $1 million in police scandal settlement.* Retrieved from www.npr.org/sections/thetwo-way/2017/06/01/531056653/oakland-to-pay-19-year-old-nearly-1-million-in-police-scandal-settlement

Weaver, J. (2015, June 19). Man who led sex-trafficking ring based in Reading gets 23 years in federal prison. *Reading Eagle.* Retrieved from www.readingeagle.com/news/article/man-who-led-sex-trafficking-ring-based-in-reading-gets-23-years-in-federal-prison

Weigel, J. (2014, August 15). Rosemary Grant Higgins, Cook County associate judge. Retrieved from www.chicagotribune.com/lifestyles/ct-remarkable-rosemary-grant-higgins-20140817-story.html

Weinrib, E. J. (2002). Corrective justice in a nutshell. *The University of Toronto Law Journal, 52*(4), 349–356.

Whitman, J. Q. (2011, January 21). When the focus is retribution. *The New York Times.* Retrieved from www.nytimes.com/roomfordebate/2011/01/20/who-qualifies-for-the-insanity-defense/when-the-focus-is-retribution

Winick, B., & Wexler, D. (2003). *Judging in a therapeutic key: Therapeutic jurisprudence and the courts.* Durham, NC: Carolina University Press.

Wood, S. (2015, June 18). *Ex-school counselor who calls himself "God" sentenced in sex trafficking.* Retrieved from www.philly.com/philly/news/Ex-school_counselor_who_calls_himself_God_sentenced_in_sex_trafficking.html?c=r

Wortley, S., Fischer, B., & Webster, C. (2002). Vice lessons: A survey of prostitution offenders enrolled in the Toronto John School Diversion Program. *Canadian Journal of Criminology, 44*(4), 369–402. Retrieved from www.proquest.com

6

COMBATING HUMAN TRAFFICKING

Challenges to the criminal justice system and what practitioners need to know

Katharine Bryant, Jacqueline Joudo Larsen and Elise Gordon

Abstract

This chapter provides students and practitioners with an introduction to the challenges that combating human trafficking presents to the criminal justice system. It outlines some of the key features of a criminal justice response to human trafficking at the international, regional and national levels. The challenges that human trafficking presents to this system are then presented, including overlapping definitions, the complexity of the crime, including transnational and organized crime elements, limited data, the forms of coercion that are used to control victims, the specific needs of children and the challenges inherent in addressing contextual factors. This chapter includes descriptions of current efforts to combat these challenges and concludes with some emerging opportunities to tackle these crimes going forward. Throughout, case studies and real-life examples allow readers to critically engage with the challenges that human trafficking presents to the criminal justice system.

Learning Objectives

At the end of the chapter, readers will be able to:

1. Understand key elements of the criminal justice system used to tackle human trafficking;
2. Understand and critically engage with the specific challenges that human trafficking presents to the criminal justice system;
3. Understand current efforts to combat human trafficking; and
4. Understand potential opportunities to tackle human trafficking in the future.

Key Terms: convention; human rights-based approach; member states; proactive investigative techniques; protocol; reactive investigative techniques; Situational Crime Prevention theory; treaty.

Introduction

Human trafficking is a complex crime and a grave human rights abuse. Every year men, women and children are exploited at the hands of traffickers and experience forced sexual exploitation, forced labor, forced marriage, servitude, slavery, debt bondage and the removal of organs. Human trafficking affects most countries around the world and continues to pose a threat to the development of nations, the respect for human rights and the abilities of governments, international organizations, civil society and the private sector to respond.

There exist at the international, regional and national level many instruments and guidelines to tackle human trafficking. These include international conventions, guidelines developed by UN bodies and national good practice. Despite the existence of these normative frameworks and tools, human trafficking presents many challenges to the criminal justice system. These challenges are inherent in the complexity of the crime and the overlapping definitions between human trafficking and related phenomena such as slavery, forced labor and slavery-like practices. Human trafficking is not a single event but a process that often occurs across borders and involves organized criminal networks. As a human rights abuse, the forms of control and coercion used by traffickers further complicates the criminal justice response by making victims of trafficking unwilling to cooperate with law enforcement. Understanding the importance of gender, that children represent a particularly vulnerable group, and contextual factors such as corruption and increasingly restrictive migration policies helps to inform specific responses to human trafficking. Current efforts are attempting to tackle these challenges by encouraging international and national cooperation, providing more and more data and establishing specialist responses. Looking forward, recent developments, such as the increasing focus on this issue by business, the use of evidence-based policy and the promising role of technology, point the way to more innovative responses to these challenges.

What are the key elements of a criminal justice response to human trafficking?

There are multiple frameworks that can be used to describe a criminal justice response to human trafficking. One theoretical framework for understanding human trafficking is situational crime prevention theory (Homel & Clarke, 1997; Ekblom & Tilley, 2000; Lampe, 2011). This is based on the understanding that for the crime of human trafficking to occur, there needs to be a vulnerable victim, a motivated offender and the absence of a capable guardian as illustrated in Figure 6.1. It recognizes that crime does not happen in a vacuum and that broad contextual factors like state instability, discrimination and disregard of human rights can hinder any criminal justice response.

Therefore, to reduce the prevalence of crime, a criminal justice response should:

- Reduce the opportunity for offenders to commit the crime;
- Increase the risks for offenders;
- Decrease the vulnerability of potential victims;
- Increase the capacity of law enforcement and other guardians; and
- Address the people or factors that stimulate or facilitate slavery (Walk Free Foundation, 2018a).

Gallagher and Holmes (2008) propose that there are eight essential components to a criminal justice response to human trafficking. These include the following:

1 Legislative frameworks
2 Specialist police response
3 Front-line law enforcement response
4 Prosecutorial and judicial response

5 Accurate identification of victims and the provision of protection and support once they have been identified
6 Support to victims as witnesses
7 International cooperation
8 Coordinating support to the criminal justice response to trafficking.

Human trafficking is a complex crime and a violation of human rights (Gallagher & Holmes, 2008). The criminal justice response should therefore ensure that the rights of the victims are upheld by employing a victim-centred and human rights–based approach to seeking justice (Gallagher & Holmes, 2008). A victim-centred criminal justice response to human trafficking is one that considers the rights and well-being of the victim at any and all stages of the criminal justice process. Not only does this have the clear benefit to the victim by supporting their recovery, but it supports the desired outcome for criminal proceedings (UNODC, 2008a).

For the purposes of this chapter, Gallagher and Holmes' (2008) eight components are incorporated into the five pillars for action proposed by the United Nations Office on Drugs and Crime (UNODC) Framework for Action on Trafficking in Persons (UNODC, 2009b) and the United Nations Global Plan of Action to Combat Trafficking in Persons (UN General Assembly, 2010) to summarize the key elements of a criminal justice response. These five pillars are prosecution, protection, prevention, national coordination and cooperation, and international cooperation and coordination (UNODC, 2009b). A human rights–based lens is applied throughout.

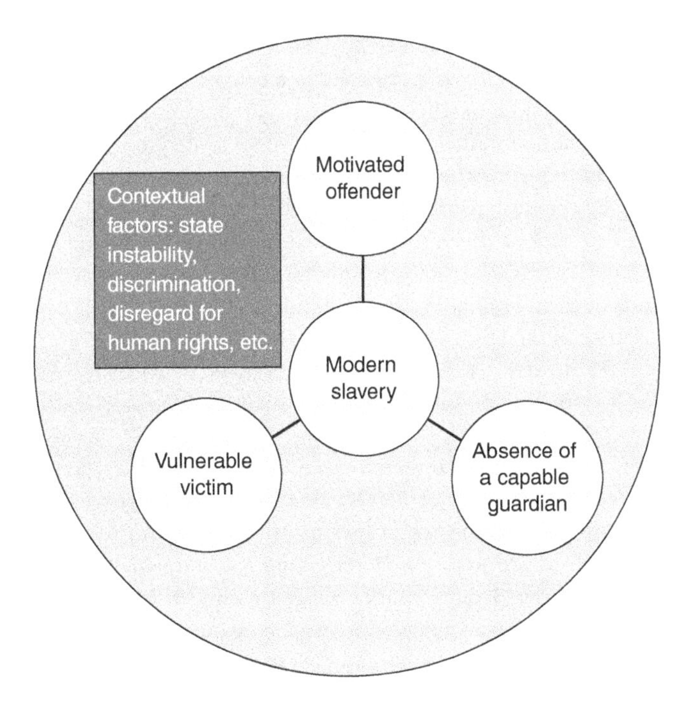

Figure 6.1 Modern slavery through the lens of Situational Crime Prevention theory

Source: Walk Free Foundation, 2018a.

Prosecution

Legislative frameworks

The most relevant international instrument for a criminal justice response to human trafficking is the 2000 United Nations Convention against Transnational Organized Crime (CTOC) and its related protocols: the United Nations Protocol to Prevent, Suppress, and Punish Trafficking in Persons, Especially Women and Children (the Trafficking Protocol) and the United Nations Protocol against the Smuggling of Migrants by Land, Sea, and Air ("United Nations Convention against Transnational Organized Crime and the Protocols Thereto (CTOC)," 2004). CTOC and the Trafficking Protocol provide the normative framework for addressing human trafficking.

The Trafficking Protocol provides a definition of human trafficking, an outline for the development of a national response for Member States, and describes steps to facilitate international cooperation in prosecuting trafficking cases and protecting victims. It introduces the concept of the "3P" model of prevention, protection and prosecution. This model includes criminalizing trafficking and providing appropriate penalties; diligently investigating and prosecuting traffickers; actively identifying, assisting and protecting victims; providing adequate and appropriate remedies to victims of trafficking; working towards preventing trafficking; and cooperating across borders (as cited in David, 2007). To date, 189 countries have ratified CTOC (United Nations, 2019), and according to the 2018 Global Slavery Index, at least 122 have translated it into domestic legislation[1] (Walk Free Foundation, 2018b).

Punishment of offenders and securing justice for victims cannot be achieved without comprehensive and effective domestic human trafficking legislation (Gallagher & Karlebach, 2011). An effective legal framework includes laws that provide a solid legal basis for the investigation and prosecution of offences, including forced labor and forced sexual exploitation, among others (Smith, 2010). Also required are laws, treaties and agreements that allow international cooperation among governments, close loopholes or prevent safe havens for traffickers or their assets and safeguard the protection of trafficking victims. Crimes related to human trafficking, such as corruption, money laundering, obstruction of justice and participation in an organized criminal network, should also be criminalized (UNODC, 2009b).

The Trafficking Protocol has been supplemented by regional legal and policy instruments that, in some cases, impose even higher standards on States. These include the Recommended Principles and Guidelines on Human Rights and Human Trafficking developed by the United Nations in 2002 (Office of the High Commissioner for Human Rights, 2002) and the Council of Europe Convention on Action against Trafficking adopted in 2005 (also known as the Warsaw Convention) ("Council of Europe Convention on Action against Trafficking in Human Beings," 2005).

Various monitoring bodies exist to review states' obligations set out in these international and regional instruments. Article 32 of CTOC establishes a Conference of the Parties to the Convention, which aims to improve the capacity of States Parties to combat transnational organized crime as well as promoting and reviewing the implementation of CTOC. One of the Conference's Working Groups focuses on Trafficking in Persons (UNODC, n.d.). In Europe, the independent Group of Experts on Action against Trafficking in Human Beings (GRETA) monitors the implementation of the Warsaw Convention (Council of Europe, 2018). Globally, the U.S. Department of State's annual Trafficking in Persons Report utilizes the "3P" framework, as described by Section 108 of the 2000 U.S. Trafficking Victims Protection Act (TVPA) and its subsequent reauthorizations, to track government action on human trafficking (U.S. Department of State, 2018). Since 2014, the Walk Free Foundation has included an assessment of 161 government responses as part of the Global Slavery Index (Walk Free Foundation, 2018a). The Special Rapporteur on trafficking in persons, especially in women and children, also plays a monitoring role, namely to ensure that the rights of victims are upheld (King, n.d.).

Specialist law enforcement

A specialist law enforcement response to human trafficking has significant benefits to the efficacy of investigations, with human trafficking law enforcement units in operation in a number of countries (Gallagher & Holmes, 2008). Specialist law enforcement should be trained in specialist reactive and proactive investigative techniques. Reactive investigation requires an effective and efficient response to requests for help from potential victims or other individuals or groups (Gallagher & Holmes, 2008). On the other hand, proactive, intelligence-led investigative techniques reduce reliance on victim testimony. Proactive techniques include undercover operations, human and financial surveillance and intelligence gathering (UNODC, 2009b). The Warsaw Convention establishes that investigation or prosecution of human trafficking cases must not be contingent on the reports of victims (Council of Europe, 2016); however, the reality is that victim testimony is often critical to securing convictions for serious trafficking-related offences. Specialist law enforcement must therefore be aware of the importance of protecting victims' rights.

Where sufficiently resourced, specialist law enforcement have greater capacity to be proactive in their investigation of human trafficking cases as well as to develop, test and refine effective standard operating procedures and training (Gallagher & Holmes, 2008). Specialist law enforcement may also help to combat corruption in trafficking.

Front-line law enforcement

Front-line law enforcement officials (which can include general duties police, border guards, and immigration and customs officials) are most likely to come into contact with victims and perpetrators of trafficking or to receive the initial information or complaint. It is therefore essential that front-line officials have the knowledge, skills and ability to provide an effective first response when confronted with a human trafficking case (Smith, 2010) and that they are facilitated to collaborate effectively with specialist law enforcement units.

Prosecutorial and judicial response

Prosecutors, judges and magistrates play a critical role in ensuring that perpetrators are prosecuted and that victims are protected. All prosecutors, for example, should maintain their professionalism, independence and impartiality and play an active role in criminal proceedings (UNODC, 2008c). Human trafficking is a high-profit, low-risk crime, therefore in handing down sentences to offenders, judges must ensure that the penalties take account of and be proportionate to the gravity of the offence and culpability of the offender.

Victims' rights should be upheld before, during and after the prosecution of the crime. A victim-centred prosecutorial and judicial response should include the protection of victims from harm and intimidation (ICMPD, 2006). Training in victim-centred prosecutorial and judicial responses and the establishment of specialist prosecutors and judges is necessary for an effective criminal justice response.

Protection

In 2016, there were an estimated 40.3 million people in modern slavery (International Labour Organization & Walk Free Foundation, 2017). However, the most recent UNODC report stated that in the same year only 24,000 people were identified (UNODC, 2018). Critical to a criminal justice response is the identification and protection of victims. A number of general principles guide the treatment of victims of all forms of human trafficking. These include the following:

- Victims of trafficking should be identified as victims of crime.
- Victims should not be treated as criminals.
- Victims should not be treated only as a source of evidence (UNODC, 2009a).

Accurate identification of victims and the provision of protection and support once they have been identified

The identification of a trafficking victim is vital to ensure access to protection and justice, while positive identification as a victim facilitates access to support services in many countries. Inability to access services may hamper the victim's recovery and the criminal investigation, where victims may not feel sufficiently confident or secure to participate in proceedings (UNODC, 2008a). There exist many tools to support victim protection and assistance, including domestic legislation, administrative guidelines on enforcement of relevant legislation, comprehensive guidelines on victim identification procedures and a national referral mechanism to coordinate all relevant stakeholders (UNODC, 2008a).

Victim support services should be provided irrespective of the victim's role as a witness or their cooperation with law enforcement. Where the victim is a child, these services should be tailored in a way that meets the specific needs of children. Legislation should ensure the following services are available to all identified victims:

- Legal advice on their available options, including their rights as a witness (Gallagher & Holmes, 2008);
- A reflection or recovery period to provide time to consider whether they would like to be part of criminal proceedings and to receive services (Gallagher & Holmes, 2008);
- Legal redress and compensation for damages incurred as a result of exploitation including from physical injuries, severe mental stress, and psychological problems (ICMPD, 2006); and
- Voluntary repatriation after a risk assessment to ensure the victim's safety (UNODC, 2009b). Where repatriation of the victim is deemed to be unsafe, options to remain in the country where they were identified should be provided (Walk Free Foundation, 2018b).

Support to victims as witnesses

Given the central role victim and witness testimony often plays in prosecuting traffickers, it is essential that justice system officials, including law enforcement, prosecutors and judges, treat victims with sensitivity, taking care to prevent re-traumatization and support recovery (Gallagher & Karlebach, 2011; UNODC, 2009a). The Warsaw Convention makes special provisions for child victims of human trafficking. In addition to those rights specified generally for victims of trafficking, children and those who are believed to be under 18 years old are entitled to benefit from special protection measures during investigations and court proceedings (Council of Europe, 2014).

Ensuring victims are not treated as criminals is a guiding principle in the treatment of trafficking victims (UNODC, 2009a), and this should remain regardless of immigration status or their role as a witness (Foundation Against Trafficking in Women, International Human Rights Law Group, and Global Alliance Against Traffic in Women, 1999). Victim-witnesses have the right to protection from intimidation or reprisals and, as such, police, prosecutors and the court should ensure the safety of victims is maintained both inside and outside the court (ICMPD, 2006). This may include witness protection programs for victim-witnesses and their families, or by allowing victim-witnesses to give testimony via video-link, among other means of protection (Council of Europe, 2016).

Prevention

An effective criminal justice response to human trafficking requires not just that offenders are punished and victims are able to secure justice but also that actions are taken to prevent new cases of human trafficking. Government action should be underpinned by a comprehensive understanding of the risk factors, drivers and patterns of human trafficking and ensure that interventions are tailored to known risks. Legislation, policies and programs should include measures to:

- Promote and support lawful migration for decent work;
- Tackle official corruption and complicity;
- Establish effective national child protection systems;
- Ensure coherence among public policies related to trafficking in persons, including migration, education, employment, health, security, non-discrimination, economic development, protection of human rights and gender equality, among others;
- Provide vulnerable populations with pathways out of poverty;
- Conduct needs assessments and impact evaluations of prevention strategies and programs; and
- Promote cooperation and joint programming among international and regional organizations (UNODC, 2009b).

National coordination and cooperation

Tackling human trafficking requires the involvement of a wide array of national institutions. This can potentially lead to duplication of efforts, inefficient use of resources and incoherent or contradictory interventions. A coordinated, multidisciplinary approach, involving effective and regular communication, is essential to combat this crime.

At the national level, states should establish inter-agency coordination and cooperation mechanisms that allow for information exchange, strategic planning, division of responsibilities and sustainability of results (UNODC, 2009b). For example, a national referral mechanism, involving law enforcement agencies, non-governmental organizations, victim service providers, health institutions, child protection institutions, workers' and employers' organizations and the private sector, among others, is one way in which victim referrals and assistance can be coordinated (UN Working Group on Trafficking in Persons, 2009; UNODC, 2009a, 2009b). Likewise, a national coordinating body with government and non-government representatives can facilitate the coordination of government policy at the national level.

International coordination and cooperation

Given that human trafficking is often committed across multiple countries, it cannot be addressed without international cooperation and joint programming (David, 2007; UNODC, 2008c, 2009b) (see Siller, Chapter 7, this volume). Article 1 of the Organized Crime Convention states that "the purpose of this Convention is to promote cooperation to prevent and combat transnational organized crime more effectively" ("CTOC," 2004). Coordination between countries can be strengthened through formal or informal agreements, which cover communication procedures to ensure efficient and effective data and information exchange, and procedures related to voluntary repatriation of victims, extradition and joint investigations (Gallagher & Karlebach, 2011; UNODC, 2009b). International cooperation can be enhanced through technical assistance provided by international and regional organizations.

The challenges of human trafficking to the criminal justice system and current efforts to respond

As a complex and multifaceted crime, human trafficking provides a set of unique challenges to the criminal justice system. This section outlines some of the key challenges and current efforts to respond to these. These challenges are by no means exhaustive but were selected based on prominent themes in the current literature.

Definitions

Definitions of human trafficking and related phenomena, such as modern slavery, forced labor, slavery and slavery-like practices, have complicated attempts to tackle this crime. While a lengthy discussion of the development of definitions is beyond the scope of this chapter,[2] any understanding of the current challenges human trafficking represents to the criminal justice system would be remiss without an understanding of current definitions.

Is human trafficking a crime or human rights issue? Can it be both?

Until the Trafficking Protocol was adopted in 2000, there was no internationally agreed upon definition of human trafficking. Prior to this time, trafficking had been primarily associated with the trafficking of women and girls across borders for the purpose of sexual exploitation ("Convention for the Suppression of the Traffic in Persons and of the Exploitation of the Prostitution of Others," 1949; "International Convention for the Suppression of the Traffic in Women of Full Age," 1933). Debates throughout the 1980s and 1990s included, among other areas, whether trafficking should move beyond sexual exploitation of women and girls to include a range of end "purposes" and men and boys, as well as concerns regarding the links between trafficking and movement between states. This latter concern reflected reports of increased cross-border exploitation of women and girls and the link to organized criminal trends, and the movement of people across borders for profit (Gallagher, 2010).

That trafficking became part of CTOC is not without controversy. Some argue its inclusion reflected a statist concern that trafficking is a criminal activity that violates the state's right to control its borders (O'Connell Donaldson, 2013). As Gallagher notes, she was among those international human rights lawyers who "decried the removal of trafficking from the sacred chambers of the international human rights system to the area of the United Nations that dealt with drugs and crime" (Gallagher, 2010). However, the final definition was necessarily broad enough to cover most forms of exploitation, and while there were rightful criticisms regarding the weak provisions for victim protection in the Protocol, international law provides a variety of conventions and guidance to plug these gaps.[3]

The final definition of trafficking in the Protocol stated:

> (a) "Trafficking in persons" shall mean the recruitment, transportation, transfer, harbouring or receipt of persons, by means of the threat or use of force or other forms of coercion, of abduction, of fraud, of deception, of the abuse of power or of a position of vulnerability or of the giving or receiving of payments or benefits to achieve the consent of a person having control over another person, for the purpose of exploitation. Exploitation shall include, at a minimum, the exploitation of the prostitution of others or other forms of sexual exploitation, forced labour or services, slavery or practices similar to slavery, servitude or the removal of organs;
> (b) The consent of a victim of trafficking in persons to the intended exploitation set forth in subparagraph (a) of this article shall be irrelevant where any of the means set forth in subparagraph (a) have been used;
> (c) The recruitment, transportation, transfer, harbouring or receipt of a child for the purpose of exploitation shall be considered "trafficking in persons" even if this does not involve any of the means set forth in subparagraph (a) of this article;
> (d) "Child" shall mean any person under eighteen years of age.
>
> *("CTOC," 2004)*

The "purposes" of the human trafficking definition are broad and encompass forms of exploitation defined by other international conventions. These forms of exploitation are not defined in the Trafficking Protocol, and it can be difficult to distinguish what is a trafficking crime and what is covered by other international conventions. To take forced labor as an example: forced labor is defined by the International Labour Organization (ILO) Convention No. 29 as "all work or service which is exacted from any person under the menace of any penalty and for which the said person has not offered himself voluntarily" ("C029 – Forced Labour Convention, 1930 (No. 29)," 1930). The 2014 Protocol to the Forced Labour Convention reaffirms this definition and states that "therefore measures referred to in this Protocol shall include specific action against trafficking in persons for the purposes of forced or compulsory labour" ("P029 – Protocol of 2014 to the Forced Labour Convention, 1930," 2014). Looking at the activity, means and purpose of the trafficking definition it may be hard to determine when a forced labor crime is a trafficking for forced labor crime and vice versa. There are, however, some exceptions to this; for example, where a person intends to traffic someone for the purpose of forced labor, but this exploitation does not occur. This would be a trafficking crime, but not a forced labor crime as the exploitation has not yet happened. In the UK, for example, it is a trafficking crime to facilitate the travel of an individual with the intent of exploiting them soon after (National Crime Agency, n.d.).

While international agreement on the definition of human trafficking occurred in 2000, there has been a shift in recent years to refer to human trafficking as "modern-day slavery." Some organizations and governments use "modern slavery" as an umbrella term that encompasses many different forms of exploitation, including slavery, human trafficking, forced labor, debt bondage, forced or servile marriage and the sale and exploitation of children as shown in Figure 6.2. "Essentially, it refers to situations of exploitation that a person cannot refuse or leave because of threats, violence, coercion, abuse of power, or deception" (Walk Free Foundation, 2018a).

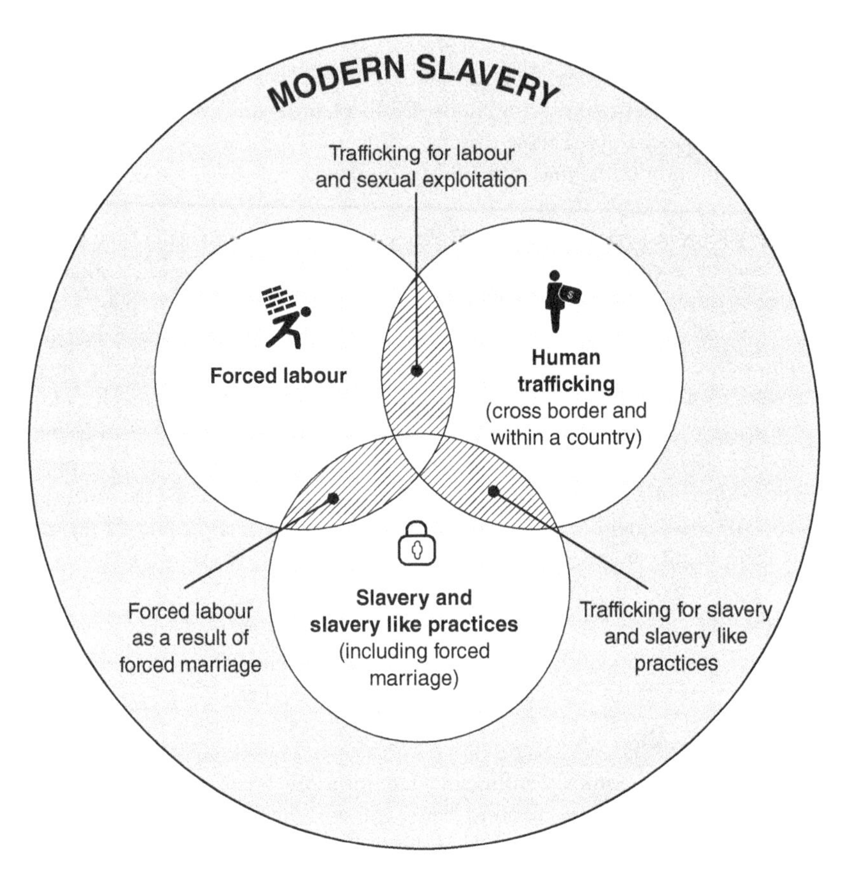

Figure 6.2 Modern slavery as an umbrella term
Source: Walk Free Foundation, 2018a.

This shift is not without controversy. Slavery is defined by the 1926 Slavery Convention as the "status or condition of a person over whom any or all of the powers attaching to the right of ownership are exercised" ("Slavery Convention," 1926). The Harvard-Bellagio Guidelines broadened "powers attaching to the right of ownership" to constitute "control over a person in such a way as to significantly deprive that person of his or her individual liberty, with the intent of exploitation through the use, management, profit, transfer or disposal of that person" (Research Network on the Legal Parameters of Slavery, 2011). Modern slavery, however, is without an international definition, and therefore it could be applied to multiple forms of exploitation, blurring the distinction between these forms and causing difficulties in quantifying (Gallagher, 2017) or hindering any response. Another concern is that as "historical" slavery is primarily associated with the trans-Atlantic slave trade, using "modern slavery" to describe conditions that are not tantamount to the 1926 legal definition of slavery belittles the experience of those affected by the trans-Atlantic slave trade and removes responsibility from those countries that benefited from it (Dottridge, 2017). The use of modern slavery could hide a "civilizing mission" that has little to do with human rights, but rather seeks to "civilize" cultures that do not adhere to the expectations of the West (Faulkner, 2017).

What is the difference between human trafficking, forced labor and modern slavery? Do definitions matter? Why/why not?

Despite these concerns, the use of the term modern slavery to describe human trafficking and related forms of exploitation has increased, including as part of the 2030 Sustainable Development Agenda. Sustainable Development Goal (SDG) 8.7 calls on all nations to *take immediate and effective measures to end forced labour, modern slavery, and human trafficking, as well as child labour in all its forms* (Sustainable Development Solutions Network (SDSN), 2019).

The UK government is a champion in the fight against modern slavery, as shown by amalgamation of its trafficking and related legislation under the UK Modern Slavery Act ("Modern Slavery Act 2015," 2015), which also includes provisions relating to transparency in supply chains. Australia recently followed suit with the passage of a Modern Slavery Act, which provides for mandatory reporting for business on their efforts to combat modern slavery in their supply chains ("Modern Slavery Act 2018," 2018). The UK also launched a Call to Action at the 2017 United Nations General Assembly, which calls on states to "End Forced Labour, Modern Slavery, and Human Trafficking" as defined by the Sustainable Development Goal 8.7 (*A Call to Action to End Forced Labour, Modern Slavery, and Human Trafficking*, 2017). Any criminal justice response must take these issues around definitions into account by ensuring that there is clarity and understanding among all stakeholders regarding the specificities of the types of crime associated with human trafficking. Definitions of key components, such as exploitation and coercion, must be included in legislation, and training provided for law enforcement, service providers and judicial and prosecutorial authorities. Resources should also be given to specialist police units to build their capacity to respond to these complex crime types.

Different forms of exploitation: a spotlight on forced marriage

Under the Trafficking Protocol, exploitation can include at minimum "the exploitation of the prostitution of others or other forms of sexual exploitation forced labour or services slavery or practices similar to slavery servitude or the removal of organs." Forced marriage is increasingly included in the definition of exploitation,[4] although this has been criticized (Božić, 2017; Faulkner, 2017; MYRIA Federal Migration Centre, 2015; Warria, 2017).

These forms of exploitation require different approaches and highlight the difficulties in establishing a one-size-fits-all approach to human trafficking. While there are commonalities between these forms, the reality remains for a criminal justice practitioner that each form of exploitation requires a very different response and expertise. A woman leaving a forced marriage, for example, will have a different set of needs and priorities to a man leaving forced labor in the agriculture industry.

Specifically, a response to forced marriage requires a specialized response. Often the person or people facilitating the marriage are family or have a close relationship to the victim. This can prevent the individual from reporting the crime (Vidal, 2016). Criminalization in forced marriage cases should therefore be but one tool that may be able to prevent and respond to forced marriage (F. Simmons & Burn, 2011). In the UK, for example, forced marriage is a crime ("Anti-social Behaviour, Crime and Policing Act," 2014) and there is a Forced Marriage Unit which leads on the government's related policy, outreach and casework (Government of the United Kingdom, 2018). The UK also uses Forced Marriage Protection Orders (FMPOs), which are an alternative civil protection mechanism to entering the criminal justice system. They prevent victims from being married or harmed, but do not lead to the prosecution of their parents

(Vidal, 2016). Recognizing this issue, the Australian government has allowed victims of forced marriage to access support without having to participate in a criminal justice process on a trial basis (Department of Social Services, 2018). Responding to human trafficking crimes, such as forced marriage, therefore requires a more nuanced understanding of the factors at play and the multiple pressures that victims may face.

Gender

Gender is central to human trafficking cases. The Global Estimates of Modern Slavery (GEMS) provided estimates that some 25 million people were in forced labor and 15.4 million people in forced marriage in 2016 (International Labour Organization & Walk Free Foundation, 2017). They found that women and girls accounted for 71% of the victims, but that this varied according to type. For example, women and girls were disproportionately affected by forced labor in the private economy, including in the sex industry and in domestic work, and in forced marriage. Men were disproportionately subject to state-imposed forms of forced labor and forced labor in sectors such as construction, manufacturing, and agriculture or fishing. The GEMS concluded that preventative efforts should reflect this profile, and that national laws and responses to victimization should protect women and girls, but also make allowance for male victims (International Labour Organization & Walk Free Foundation, 2017).

Complexity

The complexity of human trafficking may lead to gaps, confusion or lack of clarity in legislation, which will have a flow-on effect throughout the criminal justice system (David, 2007). For example, trafficking is a process that occurs over a period of time, not a singular event. It often involves a range of perpetrators from one single perpetrator to large international organizations and organized criminal networks (van der Watt & van der Westhuizen, 2017) and multiple crime sites (David, 2007). Any criminal justice response should recognize this complexity and that, as a result, human trafficking "requires an equally multifaceted and integrated response to effectively address the fluid and systematic nature of organised crime involved in its perpetration" (van der Watt & van der Westhuizen, 2017).

One of the areas where the complexity of the crime plays out is in the identification of victims. In order to prove that an adult individual is a trafficking victim, one must prove that they have experienced all three elements of activities, means and purpose. However, there is a subtlety to many trafficking cases that makes this determination difficult. Sometimes, a victim may have rightful grievances regarding their treatment by their employer, but this is not tantamount to human trafficking.

Case study: human trafficking or labor dispute?

A 35-year-old Burmese man working on a fishing boat swims to shore while the vessel is moored off the coast of Timor-Leste and is picked up by the local police. He complains that he was approached in Myanmar approximately ten months ago with an offer to work as a fisher for two years. The fishing vessel was docked in Bangkok. He agrees to go with the recruiter to Bangkok and sets sail to fish in Indonesian and Timor-Leste waters. The conditions onboard are hard, with long hours and physical violence, although the man himself is not abused. The fishers are fed and able to get some rest each day, but payment is sporadic and not the same amount the man was promised in Myanmar. There are others on the vessel who speak of not going to shore in many years and who felt they had been deceived regarding the nature of the work on their recruitment in Myanmar. After six months on board, the vessel moors off Timor-Leste and the man and five of his colleagues decide to swim to shore to see if they can return to Myanmar.

Case study discussion questions

1 Is this a case of human trafficking? Why/why not?
2 What questions would you ask the man to help in your determination?

Fundamental to any criminal justice response is therefore clear legislation, training, and guidance for all front-line workers and first responders who may come into contact with trafficking victims in order to identify and refer individuals to relevant services.

Counting the hidden

Accurate data are essential to informing criminal justice responses. Until recently, there existed multiple global estimates of human trafficking or modern slavery, drawn primarily from identified cases and expert input or techniques such as capture-recapture (Datta & Bales, 2013, 2014; International Labour Organization, 2012; Walk Free Foundation, 2013). In 2017, the first global estimates of modern slavery were released, with an estimated 40.3 million people in modern slavery on any given day in 2016, defined as forced labor and forced marriage (International Labour Organization & Walk Free Foundation, 2017).

Despite these efforts, challenges remain. Civil society is vocal about the fact that the current estimates are not able to fully capture human trafficking. The estimates are derived from nationally representative surveys, which are not designed to capture all stages of trafficking but instead capture the end point, that is the point of exploitation. One alternative technique to measure human trafficking is the use of multiple systems estimation (MSE) – a form of capture-recapture which uses multiple administrative datasets to calculate the size of the overlap between them and thus estimate the total population of human trafficking victims based on the likelihood of appearing on one or more lists within a certain time period.

Given that these lists are often lists of human trafficking victims, in theory this technique could be used to estimate the number of people in human trafficking (van Dijk & van der Heijden, n.d.). However, as a relatively new methodology to the human trafficking space, there remain reasons to be cautious. MSE, for example, is reliant on clear definitions of human trafficking, independence of the lists, and a precise application of the mechanisms for identifying victims (van Dijk & van der Heijden, n.d.). A better approach to global estimations might be a mixed method combining survey research and analysis of collected statistics.

How might incomplete or inaccurate data affect the criminal justice system? Can we ever know the true scale of crime?

While it might not be possible to ever truly know the number of people who are trafficked, data remain essential to understanding crime phenomena, including trends, nature and scale. Data also helps to understand where to put resources and where to target police time. Data from identified victims has helped, for example, to establish a typology of modern slavery crimes in the UK in order improve "understanding of the different ways that modern slavery manifests in the UK and to inform tailored policy and operational responses" (Cooper, Hesketh, Ellis, & Fair, 2017). The collection of national data and use of this data in policy-making are essential to combating human trafficking.

Transnational elements

Human trafficking is intrinsically linked with the economic and political liberalization of the 1990s and globalization of the 2000s, which allowed for an expansive flow of people and goods (Simmons, Lloyd, & Stewart, 2018). The decline in nation states and border controls led to an increase in transnational crime, including the cross-border trade in drugs, arms and people (Shelley, 2011). Recent years have seen the growth in human trafficking and human smuggling due to the low costs of entry, the large demand for smuggled and trafficked people and the increased risk for narcotics traffickers (Shelley, 2011). Whether involving men being trafficked across borders for forced labor, or women being trafficked for sexual exploitation, one of the commonalities of human trafficking cases is that it can entail crossing an international border.

Case study: trafficking of Nigerian women

In 2016, 27,289 Nigerian migrants arrived in Italy, making them the largest group of migrants. Around 7,500 of these migrants were women (Group of Experts on Action against Trafficking in Human Beings (GRETA), 2017b; Ministerio dell'Interno, 2016). The International Organization for Migration (IOM) estimates that about 80% of Nigerian women and girls who arrived in Italy by sea in 2016 are likely to have been trafficked for the purpose of sexual exploitation in Italy or other European Union (EU) countries (International Organization for Migration, 2017b). In many cases, Nigerian women come from a specific part of the country, the Edo region, and are controlled by "madams" who force them to work in the sex industry in order to repay debts incurred in transit (International Organization for Migration, 2015; Nwaubani & Guilbert, 2016; Taub, 2017). There have been reports of trafficked Nigerian women in the UK (National Crime Agency, 2018), the Netherlands (Olabisi Oluwatoyin & Akinyoade, 2015) and France (Andrews, 2018), among other countries.

Case study discussion questions

1. Which countries and organizations would need to be involved in any response to the trafficking of Nigerian women?
2. What are some of the challenges that this transnational case presents for a criminal justice response?
3. What are some of the solutions to these challenges?

Transnational crime provides many challenges to the criminal justice system. Criminal justice responses tend to operate within state jurisdictions with international law placing the obligation and responsibility to respond primarily with states. It is national police forces or other front-line bodies that identify victims and investigate cases. However, while many investigations will be conducted in the country of destination where the exploitation occurred and the victim was identified, important evidence will exist in the country of origin and transit, such as evidence of deceptive recruitment practices or the coercion of a trafficked person (David, 2007). Investigating trafficking cases requires the sharing of information and evidence between different jurisdictions as well as potentially extraditing offenders.

There is evidence of regional cooperation – a plethora of memoranda of understandings and agreements exist to cooperate on trafficking issues at both the bilateral and multilateral level. Indeed, every country in the world is part of a regional response that takes some action to respond to human trafficking (Walk Free Foundation, 2018a). A total of 117 countries of the 161 contained in the 2018 Global Slavery Index have agreed to participate regarding human trafficking issues, be it from sharing information, joint investigations, mutual legal assistance or activities relating to prevention (Walk Free Foundation, 2018b). Effective implementation of these agreements is essential to a criminal justice response.

Evolving criminal networks

Related to the transnational nature of human trafficking is the involvement of organized crime groups (Lampe, 2012). There is some controversy over how "transnational" and "organized" transnational organized crime is and the extent to which it is responsible for human trafficking. Mittelman and Johnston in 1999 wrote of the growth of organized crime since the 1970s, responding to the eradication of state boundaries, the growth of globalization and the patchiness of international law. In this respect, the gaps of national and international law led to the expansion of organized crime (Mittelman & Johnston, 1999), which are "highly mobile, vertically integrated criminal enterprises with offenders systematically crossing borders in the execution of crimes and in eluding law enforcement" (Lampe, 2012). Hobbs (1998) instead argues for the local context of organized crime, which is better characterized by ever-mutating interlocking networks of locally based serious criminality (Hobbs, 1998). More recently, scholars speak of "criminal networks" that evolve and respond to the legal and financial risks associated with the transnational illegal activities (Bruinsma & Bernasco, 2004). What emerges is that most forms of organized criminal networks appear to be opportunistic partnerships and small enterprises, which respond to short-term gain from market-based transactions (Lampe, 2012).

Whether the result of global established organized criminal networks, what is apparent is that the evolving nature of criminal networks behind human trafficking continues to present a real challenge to law enforcement. The numbers of identified victims and convictions have increased in recent years (UNODC, 2018); however, the quality of these convictions remains low. Most prosecutions are of "low-level" criminals within these networks, which prevents the dismantling of these groups or the law from acting as a preventative measure. Many countries, particularly in Africa and Asia, have low numbers of convictions, allowing traffickers to operate with impunity (UNODC, 2018).

One way in which the criminal justice system can respond is by anticipating the actions of organized crime by using data and information on existing human trafficking cases to develop key models of organized crime. By shifting from a reactive response to a more proactive approach, law enforcement might be better placed to anticipate future developments and to develop warnings about how criminal organizations might evolve and behave in the future (Williams & Godson, 2002).

Forms of coercion

The preceding case study on Nigerian women trafficked to Europe also highlights the forms of coercion used by traffickers. In this instance, *juju* is used as a control mechanism over victims.

Juju covers a range of traditional practices that are locally based and are, to some extent, religious practices (van der Watt & Kruger, 2017). The *juju* ceremony involves a supernatural event where a victim may be undressed, cut and rubbed with soot, and where samples of human tissue are taken and given to a "madam" who operates as the trafficker or female pimp in the destination country. As part of this ceremony, the victim participates in an oath-taking contract where they will swear to pay back the debt associated with travel and never disclose the identity of those performing the ceremony (Baarda, 2015; van der Watt & Kruger, 2017; van Dijk, 2001). The oaths play an important role in the trafficking process; the person swearing the oath tells the *juju* to punish him or her if she lies or breaks the oath (Oba, 2008). The role of *juju* in trafficking leads to multiple layers of control, where the victim will not run away, even if travelling on their own, for fear of harm coming to themselves or their family (Baarda, 2015; Meiler, 2017; Sanderson, 2017).

How do forms of coercion in trafficking cases hinder the criminal justice system?

The role of *juju* complicates a criminal justice response to human trafficking, as victims will often not disclose the exploitation or denounce their exploiters for fear of harm or death. Limited understanding of the complexities of these forms of coercion on the part of law enforcement can lead to insensitivity when dealing with victims and re-traumatization or a loss of agency for those who have been trafficked (van Dijk, 2001).

While an interesting example of coercion in trafficking cases, *juju* is by no means unique in terms of the level of control that traffickers can exert on their victims, and the challenges this presents. Victims, for example, may not identify as victims. A 2003 study of trafficked women in Europe found that in most cases women came into contact with authorities through NGOs, or through police or immigration actions, not by presenting themselves to authorities as a victim of a crime (Zimmerman et al., 2003). Trauma can prevent cooperation with law enforcement (Zimmerman et al., 2003). A study of men, women and children trafficked for forced labor and sexual exploitation in Southeast Asia revealed severe mental and physical health problems; almost half of participants had been physically or sexually abused, two-thirds reported symptoms of depression, and two-fifths reported symptoms of anxiety (Kiss et al., 2015). While undoubtedly critical to the well-being of the victim, trauma can manifest itself in a number of ways including the recall and perception of the events relevant to criminal proceedings. Victim evidence may be difficult to corroborate, and there can be institutional resistance to providing the time and support that is necessary to build trust between criminal justice officials and victim-witnesses (Gallagher & Karlebach, 2011).

Why are victims of trafficking sometimes criminalized or deported without accessing support?

Other deterrents to reporting trafficking crimes include fear of reprisals from traffickers, fear of deportation for being "undocumented," an ever-increasing "debt" that must be repaid, fear of law enforcement working in collusion with traffickers, and social pressures that work against sex workers reporting abuse (David, 2007). Fear of deportation is not irrational; there is evidence in multiple countries of destination that victims have been detained or deported without investigation into their potential exploitation. In 62 countries of the 161 contained in the 2018 Global Slavery Index, there was evidence that foreign victims had been detained or deported without access to support or the opportunity to seek justice (Walk Free Foundation, 2018b).

Victims may fear criminalization for crimes committed while trafficked. The principle of non-punishment of victims of human trafficking is included in Article 26 of the Warsaw

Convention and is central to any human rights response to human trafficking (Jovanovic, 2007). Globally, there have been reports of victims being treated as criminals, which denies their protection (Jovanovic, 2007), with instances of criminalization of adults and children for prostitution offences in the United States,[5] drug production in the UK (Group of Experts on Action against Trafficking in Human Beings (GRETA), 2016), and reports by civil society in France of numerous examples where trafficking victims, including children, were imprisoned for offences committed under the influence of traffickers (Group of Experts on Action against Trafficking in Human Beings (GRETA), 2017a).

An unwillingness to cooperate means that law enforcement must play an important role in ensuring that victims are sufficiently informed, supported and protected to participate in the criminal justice process. This requires close and effective working relationships between general law enforcement, law enforcement in other jurisdictions and government and non-government victim support services (David, 2007; Gallagher & Holmes, 2008).

Specific needs of children

Although all victims of trafficking often have complex needs and require specialist support, the needs of children require special consideration (see Bloom and Brotherton, Chapter 8, and Titchen and Stoklosa, Chapter 9, this volume). Children who have been exploited in the sex industry, for example, may have acute physical and sexual trauma and adverse health effects, including mental illness, substance abuse, sexually transmitted diseases, pregnancy and abortion-related complications (Fong & Berger Cardoso, 2010). Children who have been trafficked may have experienced pre-trafficking trauma such as marginalization due to poverty and war, and familial trauma, such as child abuse and separation from family. While trafficked, the child may be subject to repeated psychological torture, manipulation and forced sexual exploitation. Child victims of trafficking suffer several inter- and intra-personal injuries that may lead to future victimization and relapse in the trafficking cycle (Abu-Ali & Al-Bahar, 2011).

The specific needs and vulnerabilities of children are recognized in the definition of trafficking in the Trafficking Protocol. A child victim of trafficking cannot consent to their exploitation; the use of "means," that is "force, coercion, abduction, fraud, deception, the abuse of power or of a position of vulnerability, or the giving or receiving of payments of benefits to achieve consent" (UNCTOC, 2004), are irrelevant in determining if a child has been trafficked (UNICEF, 2006). The specificities of a child-friendly response to human trafficking is included under the Protocol's sections on protection, prevention and protection. For example, Article 6(4) of the Protocol provides that each State Party shall consider the "special needs of children, including appropriate housing, education and care" (UNCTOC, 2004).

Responses to trafficked children are guided by human rights and the rights defined by the United Nations Convention on the Rights of the Child ("Convention on the Rights of the Child (CRC)," 1990), the Optional Protocol to the CRC on the sale of children, child prostitution and child pornography, 2000 (United Nations Human Rights Office of the High Commissioner, 2000b), the Optional Protocol to the CRC on the involvement of children in armed conflict (United Nations Human Rights Office of the High Commissioner, 2000a) and the ILO Convention 182 on the Worst Forms of Child Labour (International Labour Organization, 1999), among others. The CRC identifies general principles that apply to all children, including child victims of trafficking, regardless of their nationality, migration status or statelessness (ICRC, IRC, Save the Children, UNHCR, & UNICEF, 2004; UNICEF, 2006; UNICEF & CEE/CIS Regional office, 2003). These include respect for the rights of the child, the best interests of the child, the right to non-discrimination, respect for the views of the child, right to information, right to confidentiality and right to be protected (UNICEF,

2006). Good practice in terms of responding to child trafficking includes measures related to identification such as presumption of age, the appointment of a guardian to support the child, support to regularize migration status and provide registration and documentation, and measures for interim care and protection including family tracing (UNICEF, 2006). More specific to the criminal justice system, those interviewing or questioning children, such as law enforcement and judges, should be trained in child-friendly questioning techniques. Court processes should be modified to take into account the specific trauma that children face, including the use of video testimony and scheduling court appearances at a time suitable to a child's age (UNICEF, 2006).

Coordination between the criminal justice system and child services, such as a national child protection system, is critical to providing support to child victims of trafficking. This coordination can both help to provide support to victims in the criminal justice system and support the identification of victims. There have been reports in the United Kingdom and the United States, for example, that children in protective services are highly vulnerable to exploitation. Coordination between these groups will therefore protect the rights and best interests of child victims, but also raise awareness of the issue in order to protect and identify those that are vulnerable. NGOs that work with children, such as End Child Prostitution, Child Pornography, and Trafficking for Sexual Purposes (ECPAT), also provide a series of guidance and training for those engaging with children who have been trafficked (ECPAT UK, 2016).

Combating corruption

What role should the criminal justice system play in tackling corruption?

Tackling corruption is a challenge to any criminal justice system but creates a unique set of challenges to any response to human trafficking. Corruption is one of the most significant factors in explaining human trafficking (Cho, Dreher, & Neumayer, 2014; Zhang & Pineda, 2008), and it can be both an underlying root cause and a facilitating tool (UNODC, 2008b). Corruption takes many forms. The Council of Europe noted three areas where opportunities for corruption may thrive related to trafficking: in the trafficking chain; in the criminal justice chain; and in the protection of and support provided to victims (Council of Europe, 2002). Throughout each of these areas, officials can be passive, for example ignoring the exploitation of workers or the use of forged documents to enter a country; or more active, such as obstructing investigations or revealing or selling information on victims to traffickers (Council of Europe, 2002). There have also been reports of law enforcement and prosecutors requesting sexual services or payments from victims in order to pursue their case (UNODC, 2008b).

The link between a reduction in corruption and the empowerment of women provides an opportunity for an interesting approach to tackling corruption. Women and girls are disproportionately affected by human trafficking (International Labour Organization & Walk Free Foundation, 2017). Human trafficking can be seen as gender-based violence, or at the very least, applying a gender lens has the potential to offer some solutions. Studies in the early 2000s determined that women were less prone to corruption than men, and there was less corruption in countries where women are represented more strongly in parliaments and local administrations and more generally in the workforce (Swamy, Knack, Lee, & Azfar, 2001). These factors led to attempts to "feminize" notoriously corrupt public institutions or to raise women's quotas for senior government positions (Schimmel & Pech, 2004). While the increase in quotas may have not led to a "quick fix" for corruption, what it instead reveals is the importance of women's empowerment to combating trafficking and corruption. Therefore, combining the joint concerns of anti-corruption and gender equality could reduce discrimination against women and corruption by strengthening transparency and accountability (Schimmel & Pech, 2004).

How can women's empowerment more generally tackle human trafficking?

Beyond a gender lens to tackle corruption in human trafficking, UNODC draws on the CTOC and highlights the importance of streamlining approaches between anti-trafficking and anti-corruption measures, providing training and awareness raising for relevant officials, establishing clear procedures including disciplinary and judicial responses and providing protection for victims and whistle-blowers who wish to come forward. The importance of data and collaboration with government, civil society and the private sector is also emphasized (UNODC, 2011).

Addressing risk factors

Criminalization of human trafficking is front and centre to a criminal justice response. The goal should be the successful prosecution and conviction of offenders both as a punishment and a deterrent of the crime. However, with potentially millions of people affected by human trafficking, any attempt to "prosecute our way out of the problem" could be ineffective. The approach instead must address the structural and contextual factors that place individuals at risk of human trafficking and strengthen respect for human rights.

Addressing risk factors is a challenge to any criminal justice response. There is little agreement on what these factors are and how they interact to create scenarios of human trafficking. In the production of the most recent Global Slavery Index, Joudo Larsen and Diego-Rosell identified individual level risk factors – demographic factors, such as age, gender and employment status; and socioeconomic and psychographic factors, such as feelings about household income, life evaluation scores and negative experienced affect – as predictors of risk when combined with country-level vulnerability factors (Joudo Larsen & Diego-Rosell, 2018). A literature review of vulnerability to human trafficking and migration identified age, gender, lack of documentation, marginalization and discrimination, poverty, social and cultural norms, globalization and restrictive immigration policies as factors that increased vulnerability to exploitation (David, Bryant, Latham, & Joudo Larsen, 2019 (forthcoming)). Risk factors can include "push" factors (such as poverty, oppression, lack of human rights, lack of economic or social opportunity, dangers from conflict or instability) and "pull" factors (such as desire to escape extreme poverty to move to conditions of less-extreme poverty, advertised by telecommunications and the internet) (UNODC, 2008c). Corruption must also be added to these lists (Zhang & Pineda, 2008).

Many of these risk factors are specific to a particular country or trafficking pattern. A criminal justice response must therefore determine the specific contextual factors that play a role in causing human trafficking, either by conducting research or analysis of criminal justice statistics. From this, states should determine how best to prevent trafficking in coordination with NGOs and other states.

Case study: restrictive immigration policies

Restrictive immigration policies increase vulnerability to human trafficking by reducing the opportunities for safe migration options, especially when combined with strong economic incentives and aspirations for improved quality of life.

One migration pathway that has received much attention is the migration from sub-Saharan Africa through Northern Africa (van Reisen & Estefanos, 2017) and into Europe. While sometimes portrayed as an onslaught on Europe (Kern, 2017; Tingle, 2017), the reality is that these migrants have multiple reasons for migrating, ranging from seeking economic opportunities to reuniting with families or for escaping conflict and human rights abuses (MEDMIG, 2018). A desire to migrate and increasing frustration at the slow European bureaucracy leads these individuals to make risky migration decisions, which in turn leaves them vulnerable to exploitation. A survey conducted by IOM in 2017 interviewed migrants entering Europe through Eastern and Central Europe. Of those entering via Central Europe, 75% answered "yes" to at least one indicator of trafficking and exploitative practices (International Organization for Migration, 2017a).

In the face of the so-called migration crisis, European governments and the EU increased restrictions on migration (van Setten, Scheepers, & Lubbers, 2017), which in turn left migrants vulnerable to exploitation in Europe (Digidiki & Bhabha, 2018), death on the high seas or enslavement in Libya. Since 2015, there has been a reduction in the number of EU state-led search and rescue operations. The burden shifted to NGOs and large merchant ships which are often ill-fitted to conduct search and rescue operations (Heller & Pezzani, 2016). Since 2017, the EU has "outsourced responsibility" (Human Rights Watch, 2017) for migration control to Libya and Niger, pledging €90 million ($107 million) in April 2018 to Libya for "improved migration management," despite warnings by the UN that Libya does not have the infrastructure or training to abide by international law (Ayoub, 2017).

There are reports that those intercepted by the Libyan Coast Guard end up in detention centres where they are used as slaves (Gouliamaki, 2018) or sold as slaves in open markets in Libya (Euronews, 2017). The prioritization of immigration control over anti-trafficking initiatives may reduce state ability to tackle human trafficking. Beyond the example of "Fortress Europe," examples include the introduction of "pink cards" to identify migrant workers in Thailand, which are kept by employers or ship captains and used as a method of control (Human Rights Watch, 2018); the revocation of labor protections for UK overseas domestic workers due to fears of increases in low-skilled migration (Moss, 2015); and Israel's refusal to accept Eritrean refugees, which led to them to being tortured and ransomed by traffickers in the Sinai (Lijnders & Robinson, 2013).

Questions for discussion

1. What are some of the positive and negative impacts of restrictive immigration policies?
2. How could criminal justice actors respond to these new policies to ensure that victims of trafficking are protected and offenders prosecuted?

Conflict and natural disasters

One final challenge to the criminal justice system is the nexus between conflict or natural disasters and human trafficking. Various UN security resolutions and reports (United Nations Security Council, 2018) have highlighted how cycles of violence and disruption to state institutions have caused exploitation and crime to thrive, including forced marriage, forced sexual exploitation and the use of children in armed conflict (United Nations Security Council, 2018). Similar patterns of exploitation occur after natural disasters. After the 2015 earthquake in Nepal, there were a number of reports of women and girls trafficked into India with promises of a better life (de Pablo & Zurita, 2019).

While the absence of functioning state institutions may hinder the criminal justice system, there are steps that civil society and UN agencies can take to respond to human trafficking. Gathering data and sharing information with future functioning criminal justice systems, for example, may help to prosecute human trafficking crimes during times of conflict and natural disaster (United Nations University, 2016).

Opportunities to respond to these challenges

While human trafficking presents many challenges to the criminal justice system, there are developments in the anti-trafficking space that may offer real opportunity to respond to human trafficking. Three of these trends are summarized below.

Role of business

Business has an increasingly important role to play in combating human trafficking, based primarily on the (albeit voluntary) UN Guiding Principles on Business and Human Rights (Office of the High Commissioner for Human Rights, 2011). Many international organizations, such as UNODC, ILO and the Organization for Security and Cooperation in Europe (OSCE) recognize the opportunity that the role of business represents to tackle human trafficking, particularly for forced labor exploitation.

This role can take many forms. In recent years, there has been an increase in regulation of business and business practices by governments. Legislation such as the California Transparency in Supply Chains Act ("California Transparency in Supply Chains Act of 2010," 2010), the UK Modern Slavery Act ("Modern Slavery Act 2015," 2015), the French Duty of Vigilance Law ("Loi no. 2017–399 du mars 2017 relative au devoir de vigilance des sociétés mères et des entreprises donneuses d'ordre," 2017), the Australian Modern Slavery Act ("Modern Slavery Act 2018," 2018), and the EU non-financial reporting directive ("Directive 2014/95/EU," 2014) requires businesses of a certain size or in a certain sector to provide a statement on, or a plan for, the steps they are taking to tackle human trafficking or forced labor in their supply chains. These requirements increasingly also apply to government supply chains, as shown by the Australian Modern Slavery Act and recent announcements to extend the UK reporting requirements from businesses to include modern slavery statements by public procurement (Guilbert, 2018).

The private sector is also being proactive in tackling forced labor in supply chains by supporting the identification of victims through whistle-blower mechanisms and training for employees as well as instituting policies that prevent forced labor in their supply chains, such as ethical recruitment policies, training for suppliers, establishing due diligence processes and implementing mechanisms by which exploited workers can access redress. Some multilateral corporations have gone further and taken steps to investigate beyond tier one suppliers to potentially identify and address instances of human trafficking.

This raises an interesting question regarding criminal liability of businesses for forced labor that occurs in their supply chains. A recent case may test this. In December 2018, a criminal complaint was brought against a Dutch Shipbuilding Company by a North Korean worker who was exploited at a shipbuilding yard in Poland which supplied the Dutch company. The complainant alleged that the shipbuilding company profited from the abuse of workers in its supply chains in Poland and was aware of the "slave-like conditions" (Guilbert & Mis, 2018). If successful, this would be an interesting case in terms of corporate liability and sends a strong message to multinational corporations that "profiting from forced labor entails serious legal risk" (Geraoid O Cuinn as cited in Guilbert & Mis, 2018).

Role of technology

The use of technology by traffickers has in tandem led to an increase in the use of technology to combat it. Technology plays a role in trafficking crimes, including the use of the internet to lure trafficking victims and the use of social networking sites and online classified ads to facilitate trafficking (Latonero, 2012). In response, many in the tech space have taken steps to combat trafficking networks that use tech to perpetrate trafficking crimes. Thorn, a U.S.-based non-profit, brings together experts in tech, NGOs, government and law enforcement to tackle child sex trafficking (Thorn, 2019). Spotlight, produced by Thorn, Digital Reasoning, the McCain Institute and Google, is a web application that provides law enforcement with information on suspected human trafficking networks to identify and assist victims (Thorn, n.d.). It uses elements of machine learning to analyze millions of ads to proactively identify suspicious ads. Technology therefore presents a real opportunity for the criminal justice system to potentially stay one step ahead of organized criminal networks.

Case study: regulating the internet to prevent sex trafficking

Criminal justice responses to forms of online exploitation have included legislation such as Proposition 34 – the Californians Against Sexual Exploitation Act, and Fight Online Sex Trafficking Act (FOSTA) ("H.R. 1865 – Allow States and Victims to Fight Online Sex Trafficking Act," 2017) and Stop Enabling Sex Traffickers Act (SESTA). These pieces of legislation allow those who own, manage or operate a web page or website that promotes or facilitates the prostitution of another person to be prosecuted. Once enacted, websites such as Craigslist were forced to shut down their personal ads amid fears that they could be seen as sex-related. The impact of the legislation was fairly immediate, with estimates that 80% of the online marketplace was eviscerated within a week (Valiant Richard, as cited in Green, 2019). These laws are not without their controversy, with critics questioning their efficacy – Backpage.com was shut down in the lead up to, and not as a result of, the passing of FOSTA-SESTA. Others state that the Acts threaten free speech, have led to the pushing underground of sex work and can take down tools that sex workers use to screen clients and share health and safety concerns (Electronic Frontier Foundation, 2018). Arguably, closing the websites has made human trafficking harder to monitor and has cut the access of law enforcement to identifying potential trafficking victims – many of the online forums and sites that were shut down had been previously used by law enforcement to identify victims, or these forums were proactively sharing information on any troubling cases (Green, 2019).

Questions for discussion

1. What were some of the unintended consequences of FOSTA-SESTA?
2. What is the solution for preventing the advertising of sexual services online of those who may have been trafficked?

Evidence-based policy

While there is a recognized gap in data to understand the phenomenon of human trafficking, there has been an increased appreciation of the importance of evidence-based policy to combat it. Post the announcement of the 2030 Sustainable Development Agenda, there has been an increase in calls for robust data and evidence to track progress and to hold governments to account for their actions to achieve the Sustainable Development Goals (SDGs), including SDG 8.7, which calls on governments to eradicate modern slavery, human trafficking and forced labor by 2030 (SDSN, 2019).

One such initiative includes Alliance 8.7 and the policy platform Delta 8.7. Alliance 8.7 is a global partnership committed to achieving Target 8.7 of the 2030 SDGs by increasing collaborative action, driving innovation and providing a platform to engage in dialogue and to share knowledge and information (Alliance 8.7, n.d.). The Alliance has established a series of working groups to tackle key issues, such as migration, conflict and the role of the supply chains. Linked to this, and partly in recognition of the growing amount of data available, is the development of Delta 8.7, a global knowledge platform exploring what works to eradicate forced labor, modern slavery, human trafficking and child labor (Delta 8.7, n.d.).

Since its launch in September 2019, the platform has hosted a variety of symposiums, blogs and data from researchers, civil society and academics in the anti-trafficking and anti-modern slavery field. In December 2018, it launched "country dashboards," which allow policy makers to critically engage with the data available and use it in the development of their own policy. This is crucial to increase the use of data in the fight against human trafficking and responds to the need for data to be shared in an actionable format.

Conclusion

Human trafficking presents many challenges to the criminal justice system. As a complex and multifaceted crime as well as a severe human rights abuse, criminal justice practitioners must be aware of the nuances and subtleties of any human trafficking case, including its transnational nature, links to organized crime and the difficulties that victims may face in coming forward and talking about their exploitation. While criminalizing human trafficking and its related crimes are important to any criminal justice system, equally fundamental is the protection of victims, as well as tailoring responses to address the nature, patterns and trends of human trafficking cases, which may be specific to a particular country or trafficking pattern. Aggravating circumstances, such as if the victim is a child, or if trafficking takes place in a conflict or as a result of natural disasters also present a challenge to the criminal justice system. Opportunities do exist, as shown by the role of business, technology and evidence-based policy.

A variety of international instruments, guidelines and regional and national good practice exist to support the development of the criminal justice system. Central to many of these is the importance of coordination at the national, regional and international level and involving a variety of stakeholders, including civil society and the private sector. Equally essential is the sharing of information and lessons learnt so that others might draw upon existing standards and experiences. Finally, critical to any criminal justice system is the central role of human rights, and the protection of victims in particular, in order to combat human trafficking.

Notes

1 Of the 161 countries assessed as part of the 2018 Global Slavery Index. See www.globalslaveryindex.org.
2 See Gallagher (2010) for a detailed description of the development of the human trafficking definition.
3 See for example ICRC, IRC, Save the Children, World Vision, UNHCR, and UNICEF. (2004). Inter-Agency Guiding Principles on Unaccompanied and Separated Children. Retrieved from www.unicef.org/protection/IAG_UASCs.pdf, and C182 – Worst Forms of Child Labour Convention, 1999, among others.
4 For example, Preamble 11 of European Directive 2011/36/EU states that "The definition also covers . . . other behaviour such as illegal adoption or forced marriage in so far as they fulfil the constitutive elements

of trafficking in human beings." ("Directive 2011/36/EU of the European Parliament and of the Council of 5 April 2011 on preventing and combating trafficking in human beings and protecting its victims, and replacing Council Framework Decision 2002/629/JHA," 2011).

5 In 2014, 714 children were arrested on prostitution charges in the United States. See Bureau of Justice Statistics (2014). *Arrests by Age in the US, 2014.* Arrest Data Analysis Tool. Retrieved from: www.bjs.gov/index.cfm?ty=datool&surl=/arrests/index.cfm#. [5 July 2018].

Supplemental learning materials

Gallagher, A. T. (2010). *The international law of human trafficking.* Cambridge: Cambridge University Press.

International Labour Organization. (2017, September 19). *Global estimates for modern slavery and child labour* [video file]. Retrieved from www.youtube.com/watch?v=bJ5kNDAI0ZE

International Labour Organization & Walk Free Foundation. (2017). *Global estimates of modern slavery: Forced labour and forced marriage.* Retrieved from www.alliance87.org/global_estimates_of_modern_slavery-forced_labour_and_forced_marriage.pdf

United Nations Office on Drugs and Crime. (2008). *Toolkit to combat trafficking in persons: Global programme against trafficking in human beings.* Retrieved from https://sherloc.unodc.org/res/cld/bibliography/toolkit-to-combat-trafficking-in-persons_html/07-89375_Ebook1.pdf

United Nations Office on Drugs and Crime. (2009). *International framework for action to implement the trafficking in persons protocol.* Retrieved from www.unodc.org/documents/human-trafficking/Framework_for_Action_TIP.pdf

References

Abu-Ali, A., & Al-Bahar, M. (2011). Understanding child survivors of human trafficking: A micro and macro level analysis. *Procedia – Social and Behavioral Sciences, 30*, 791–796. Retrieved from https://doi.org/10.1016/j.sbspro.2011.10.154

Alliance 8.7. (n.d.). *Alliance 8.7 – Terms of reference.* Retrieved from www.alliance87.org/wp-content/uploads/2019/01/Terms20of20Reference20-20final.pdf

Andrews, F. (2018). The Paris park where Nigerian women are forced into prostitution. *CNN.* Retrieved from https://edition.cnn.com/2018/10/04/africa/paris-nigerian-women-trafficking/index.html

Anti-social Behaviour, Crime and Policing Act, § Part 10 (2014).

Ayoub, J. (2017). How the EU is responsible for slavery in Libya. *Al Jazeera.* Retrieved from www.aljazeera.com/indepth/opinion/slavery-walls-fortress-europe-171128094218944.html

Baarda, C.S. (2015). Human trafficking for sexual exploitation from Nigeria into Western Europe: The role of voodoo rituals in the functioning of a criminal network. *European Journal of Criminology, 13*(2), 257–273.

Bo ić, V., PhD. (2017). Forced marriages of children as a form of exploitation of human trafficking victims. *EU and Comparative Law Issues and Challenges Series*, 48–66.

Bruinsma, G., & Bernasco, W. (2004). Criminal groups and transnational illegal markets: A more detailed examination on the basis of social network theory. *Crime, Law & Social Change, 41*, 79–94.

C029 – Forced Labour Convention, 1930 (No. 29), (1930).

C182 – Worst Forms of Child Labour Convention, 1999 (No. 182). Convention concerning the Prohibition and Immediate Action for the Elimination of the Worst Forms of Child Labour (Entry into force: 19 November 2000). (1999).

California Transparency in Supply Chains Act of 2010, (2010).

Call to Action to End Forced Labour, Modern Slavery, and Human Trafficking. (2017). Retrieved from https://assets.publishing.service.gov.uk/government/uploads/system/uploads/attachment_data/file/759332/End-Forced-Labour-Modern-Slavery1.pdf

Cho, S-Y., Dreher, A., & Neumayer, E. (2014). Determinants of anti-trafficking policies: Evidence from a new index. *Scandinavian Journal of Economics, 116*(2), 429–454.

Convention for the Suppression of the Traffic in Persons and of the Exploitation of the Prostitution of Others. (1949). Lake Success, New York, 21 March 1950.

Convention on the Rights of the Child (CRC). (1990).

Cooper, C., Hesketh, O., Ellis, N., & Fair, A. (2017). *A typology of modern slavery offences in the UK.* Retrieved from https://assets.publishing.service.gov.uk/government/uploads/system/uploads/attachment_data/file/652652/typology-modern-slavery-offences-horr93.pdf

Council of Europe. (2002). *Trafficking in human beings and corruption: Report on the regional seminar, Portoroz, Slovenia, 22 June 2002.* Retrieved from http://lastradainternational.org/lsidocs/297%20Trafficking%20 and%20Corruption%20(PACO).pdf
Council of Europe. (2014). *Council of Europe convention on action against trafficking in human beings: Victims' rights.* Retrieved from https://edoc.coe.int/en/trafficking-in-human-beings/5880-council-of-europe-convention-on-action-against-trafficking-in-human-beings-victims-rights.html
Council of Europe. (2016). *Compendium of good practices on the implementation of the council of Europe convention on action against trafficking in human beings.* Retrieved from https://edoc.coe.int/en/trafficking-in-human-beings/7203-compendium-of-good-practices-on-the-implementation-of-the-council-of-europe-convention-on-action-against-trafficking-in-human-beings.html
Council of Europe. (2018). *Action against trafficking in human beings: Monitoring mechanism.* Retrieved from www.coe.int/en/web/anti-human-trafficking/monitoring-mechanism
Council of Europe Convention on Action against Trafficking in Human Beings. (2005). May 6, 2005, CETS 197.
Datta, M. N., & Bales, K. (2013). Slavery in Europe: Part 1, estimating the dark figure. *Human Rights Quarterly, 35*(4), 817–829. Retrieved from https://doi.org/10.1353/hrq.2013.0051
Datta, M. N., & Bales, K. (2014). Slavery in Europe: Part 2, testing a predictive model. *Human Rights Quarterly, 36*(2), 277–295. Retrieved from https://doi.org/10.1353/hrq.2014.0025
David, F. (2007). *Law enforcement responses to trafficking in persons: Challenges and emerging good practice.* Retrieved from https://aic.gov.au/publications/tandi/tandi347
David, F., Bryant, K., Latham, J., & Joudo Larsen, J. (2019 forthcoming). *Migrants and their vulnerability to human trafficking, modern slavery, and forced labour.* Retrieved from
de Pablo, O., & Zurita, J. (2019). "My boyfriend sold one of my kidneys- then he sold me": Trafficking in Nepal. *The Guardian.* Retrieved from www.theguardian.com/global-development/2019/feb/08/the-girl-sold-at-11-helps-police-save-nepal-trafficking-victims
Delta 8.7. (n.d.). *Welcome to Delta 8.7.* Retrieved from https://delta87.org/
Department of Social Services. (2018). *Increased support for forced marriage victims.* Retrieved from www.dss.gov.au/sites/default/files/documents/05_2018/d18_479015-forced-marriage-stream-trial.pdf
Digidiki, V., & Bhabha, J. (2018). Sexual abuse and exploitation of unaccompanied migrant children in Greece: Identifying risk factors and gaps in services during the European migration crisis. *Children and Youth Services Review, 92*(C), 114–121. Retrieved from https://doi.org/10.1016/j.childyouth.2018
Directive 2011/36/EU of the European Parliament and of the Council of 5 April 2011 on preventing and combating trafficking in human beings and protecting its victims, and replacing Council Framework Decision 2002/629/JHA, (2011).
Directive 2014/95/EU, (2014).
Dottridge, M. (2017). *Eight reasons why we shouldn't use the term "modern slavery".* Retrieved from www.opendemocracy.net/beyondslavery/michael-dottridge/eight-reasons-why-we-shouldn-t-use-term-modern-slavery
ECPAT UK. (2016). *What we do: Training.* Retrieved from www.ecpat.org.uk/Pages/Events/Category/training
Ekblom, P., & Tilley, N. (2000). GOING EQUIPPED: Criminology, situational crime prevention and the resourceful offender. *The British Journal of Criminology, 40*(3), 376–398.
Electronic Frontier Foundation. (2018). *Stop SESTA and FOSTA.* Retrieved from https://stopsesta.org/
Euronews. (2017). Italy's code of conduct for NGOs involved in migrant rescue: Text. *Euronews.* Retrieved from www.euronews.com/2017/08/03/text-of-italys-code-of-conduct-for-ngos-involved-in-migrant-rescue
Faulkner, E. A. (2017). *40.3 million slaves: Challenging the hypocrisy of modern slavery statistics.* Retrieved from www.opendemocracy.net/elizabeth-faulkner/403-million-slaves-challenging-hypocrisy-of-modern-slavery-statistics
Fong, R., & Berger Cardoso, J. (2010). Child human trafficking victims: Challenges for the child welfare system. *Evaluation and Program Planning, 33*(3), 311–316. Retrieved from https://doi.org/10.1016/j.evalprogplan.2009.06.018
Foundation Against Trafficking in Women, International Human Rights Law Group, & Global Alliance Against Traffic in Women. (1999). *Human rights standards for the treatment of trafficked persons.* Retrieved from www.gaatw.org/resources/publications/902-human-rights-standards-for-the-treatment-of-trafficked-persons
Gallagher, A. T. (2010). *The international law of human trafficking.* Cambridge: Cambridge University Press.

Gallagher, A. T. (2017). What's wrong with the Global Slavery Index? *Anti-Trafficking Review, 8*, 90–112.

Gallagher, A. T., & Holmes, P. (2008). Developing an effective criminal justice response to human trafficking: Lessons from the front line. *International Criminal Justice Review, 18*(3), 318–343. Retrieved from https://doi.org/10.1177/1057567708320746

Gallagher, A. T., & Karlebach, N. (2011). *Prosecution of trafficking in persons cases: Integrating a human rights-based approach in the administration of criminal justice.* Retrieved from https://works.bepress.com/anne_gallagher/18/

Gouliamaki, L. (2018). Migrant slavery in Libya: Nigerians tell of being used as slaves. *BBC.* Retrieved from www.bbc.co.uk/news/world-africa-4249268

Government of the United Kingdom. (2018). *Forced marriage.* Retrieved from www.gov.uk/guidance/forced-marriage

Green, R. (2019). *US anti-trafficking law continues to court controversy.* Retrieved from. www.ibanet.org/Article/NewDetail.aspx?ArticleUid=34bb1ebc-782e-4bdc-a5e4-13b738d98831

Group of Experts on Action against Trafficking in Human Beings (GRETA). (2016). *Report concerning the implementation of the council of Europe convention on action against trafficking in human beings by the United Kingdom, second evaluation round.* Retrieved from https://rm.coe.int/CoERMPublicCommonSearchServices/DisplayDCTMContent?documentId=09000016806abcdc

Group of Experts on Action against Trafficking in Human Beings (GRETA). (2017a). *Report concerning the implementation of the council of Europe convention on action against trafficking in human beings by France, second evaluation round.* Retrieved from https://rm.coe.int/greta-2017-17-fgr-fra-en/16807454bf

Group of Experts on Action against Trafficking in Human Beings (GRETA). (2017b). *Report on Italy under rule 7 of the rules of procedure for evaluating implementation of the council of Europe convention on action against trafficking in human beings.* Retrieved from https://rm.coe.int/16806edf35

Guilbert, K. (2018). UK faces tough task to ensure government supply chains are slave-free: Experts. *Thomson Reuters Foundation.* Retrieved from www.reuters.com/article/us-britain-slavery-government/uk-faces-tough-task-to-ensure-government-supply-chains-are-slave-free-experts-idUSKBN1O327N

Guilbert, K., & Mis, M. (2018). Exclusive: North Korean worker seeks Dutch shipbuilder's prosecution over labor abuses. *Thomason Reuters Foundation.* Retrieved from www.reuters.com/article/us-netherlands-lawsuit-trafficking-exclu/exclusive-north-korean-worker-seeks-dutch-shipbuilders-prosecution-over-labor-abuses-idUSKCN1ND1BR

H.R. 1865 – Allow States and Victims to Fight Online Sex Trafficking Act. (2017).

Heller, C., & Pezzani, L. (2016). Death by (Failure to) rescue. *Forensic Oceanography.* Retrieved from https://deathbyrescue.org/foreword/

Hobbs, D. (1998). Going down the global: The local context of organized Crime. *The Howard Journal, 37*(4), 407–422.

Homel, R., & Clarke, R. (1997). A Revised Classification of Situational Crime Prevention Techniques. *In Crime Prevention at a Crossroads* (pp. 17–27). Cincinnati, OH: Anderson.

Human Rights Watch. (2017). *EU: Shifting rescue to Libya Risks lives.* Retrieved from www.hrw.org/news/2017/06/19/eu-shifting-rescue-libya-risks-lives

Human Rights Watch. (2018). *Hidden chains: Rights abuses and forced labour in Thailand's fishing industry.* Retrieved from www.hrw.org/sites/default/files/report_pdf/thailand0118_report_web.pdf

ICMPD. (2006). *Guidelines for the development and implementation of a comprehensive national anti-trafficking response.* Retrieved from https://ec.europa.eu/anti-trafficking/sites/antitrafficking/files/icmpd_national_response_2006_en_1.pdf

ICRC, IRC, Save the Children, UNHCR, & UNICEF. (2004). *Inter-agency guiding principles on unaccompanied and separated children.* Retrieved from www.unicef.org/protection/IAG_UASCs.pdf

International Convention for the Suppression of the Traffic in Women of Full Age. (1933).

International Labour Organization. (2012). *ILO global estimate of forced labour: Results and methodology.* Retrieved from www.ilo.org/wcmsp5/groups/public/ – ed_norm/ – declaration/documents/publication/wcms_182004.pdf

International Labour Organization & Walk Free Foundation. (2017). *Global estimates of modern slavery: Forced labour and forced marriage.* Retrieved from www.alliance87.org/global_estimates_of_modern_slavery-forced_labour_and_forced_marriage.pdf

International Organization for Migration. (2015). *Rapporto sulle vittime di tratta nell'ambito dei flussi migratori misti in arrive via mare, aprile 2014-ottobre 2015.* Retrieved from www.italy.iom.int/sites/default/files/news-documents/RapportoAntitratta.pdf

International Organization for Migration. (2017a). *Flow monitoring surveys: The human trafficking and other exploitative practices indication survey analysis on adult and children on the Mediterranean routes compared*

September 2017. Retrieved from www.iom.int/sites/default/files/dtm/Analysis_Flow_Monitoring_and_Human_Trafficking_Surveys_in_the_Mediterranean_and_Beyond_adults_children.pdf

International Organization for Migration. (2017b). *Human trafficking through the central Mediterranean route: Data, stories and information collected by the international organization for migration*. Retrieved from www.italy.iom.int/sites/default/files/news-documents/IOMReport_Trafficking.pdf

Joudo Larsen, J., & Diego-Rosell, P. (2018). *Symposium: An introduction to modelling the risk of modern slavery*. Retrieved from https://delta87.org/2018/12/modelling-risk-modern-slavery-introduction/

Jovanovic, M. (2007). The principle of non-punishment of victims of trafficking in human beings: A quest for rationale and practical guidance. *Journal of Trafficking and Human Exploitation, 1*, 41–76.

Kern, S. (2017). *Europe's migrant crisis: Millions still to come'*. Retrieved from www.gatestoneinstitute.org/11480/europe-migrant-crisis-exodus

King, L. (n.d.). *International law and human trafficking*. Retrieved from www.du.edu/korbel/hrhw/researchdigest/trafficking/InternationalLaw.pdf

Kiss, L., Pocock, N., Naisanguansri, V., Suos, S., Dickson, B., Thuy, D., . . . Zimmerman, C. (2015). Health of men, women, and children in post-trafficking services in Cambodia, Thailand, and Vietnam: An observational cross-sectional study. *The Lancet* 3: e154–61.

Lampe, K. (2011). The application of the framework of situational crime prevention to "organized crime." *Criminology and Criminal Justice, 11*, 145–163.

Lampe, K. (2012). Transnational organized crime challenges for future research. *Crime, Law and Social Change, 58*(2), 179–194. Retrieved from https://doi.org/10.1007/s10611–012–9377-y

Latonero, M. (2012). Human trafficking online: The role of social networking sites and online classifieds. *SSRN*. Retrieved from: http://dx.doi.org/10.2139/ssrn.2045851

Lijnders, L., & Robinson, S. (2013). From the horn of Africa to the middle East: Human trafficking of Eritrean asylum seekers across borders. *Anti-Trafficking Review, 2*, 137–154. Retrieved from https://doi.org/10.14197/atr.20121329

Loi no. 2017–399 du mars 2017 relative au devoir de vigilance des sociétés mères et des entreprises donneuses d'ordre, (2017).

MEDMIG. (2018). *Unravelling the Mediterranean migration crisis*. Retrieved from www.medmig.info/

Meiler, O. (2017). Wie nigerianische Frauen in Italien zur Prostitution gezwungen werden. *Süddeutsche Zeitung*. Retrieved from www.sueddeutsche.de/panorama/italien-ciao-sumpf-1.3808654

Ministerio dell'Interno. (2016). *Dati Asilo 2015–2016*. Retrieved from www.libertaciviliimmigrazione.dlci.interno.gov.it/sites/default/files/allegati/riepilogo_dati_2015_2016_0.pdf

Mittelman, J. H., & Johnston, R. (1999). The globalization of organized crime, the courtesan state, and the corruption of civil society. *Global Governance, 5*, 103–126.

Modern Slavery Act 2015. (2015).

Modern Slavery Act 2018. (2018).

Moss, J. (2015). Migrant domestic workers, the national minimum wage, and the "Family Worker" concept. In R. Cox (Ed.), *Au Pairs' lives in global context: Sisters or servants?* United Kingdom: Palgrave Macmillan.

MYRIA Federal Migration Centre. (2015). *Annual Report: Trafficking and smuggling of human beings: Tightening the links*. Retrieved from https://ec.europa.eu/anti-trafficking/sites/antitrafficking/files/annual-report-2015-trafficking-and-smuggling-full.pdf

National Crime Agency. (2018). *National referral mechanism statistics quarter 3 2018 – July to September*. Retrieved from www.nationalcrimeagency.gov.uk/publications/national-referral-mechanism-statistics/2018-nrm-statistics/973-modern-slavery-and-human-trafficking-national-referral-mechanism-statistics-july-to-september-2018/file

National Crime Agency. (n.d.). *Modern slavery and human trafficking*. Retrieved from www.nationalcrimeagency.gov.uk/crime-threats/human-trafficking

Nwaubani, A. T., & Guilbert, K. (2016). Migrant crisis fuels sex trafficking of Nigerian girls to Europe. *Reuters Africa*. Retrieved from https://af.reuters.com/article/topNews/idAFKCN0YM156?pageNumber=3&virtualBrandChannel=0

O'Connell Donaldson, J. (2013). *Viewpoint: What's wrong with modern slavery? Why Theresa May in Wilberforce's clothing won't appeal to all*. Retrieved from https://discoversociety.org/2013/11/05/586/

Oba, A. A. (2008). Juju Oaths in customary law arbitration and their legal validity in Nigerian courts. *Journal of African Law, 52*(1), 139–158.

Office of the High Commissioner for Human Rights. (2002). *Recommended principles and guidelines on human rights and human trafficking*. Retrieved from www.ohchr.org/Documents/Publications/Traffickingen.pdf

Office of the High Commissioner for Human Rights. (2011). *Guiding principles on business and human rights: Implementing the United Nations "Protect, Respect and Remedy" framework*. Retrieved from New York and Geneva: www.ohchr.org/Documents/Publications/GuidingPrinciplesBusinessHR_EN.pdf

Oluwatoyin, T. O, & Akinyoade, A. (2015). Coercion or volition: making sense of the experiences of female victims of trafficking from Nigeria in the Netherlands. In *African Roads to Prosperity: People en Route to Socio-Cultural and Economic Transformations* (pp. 170–194). doi:10.1163/9789004306059_012

Optional Protocol to the Convention on the Rights of the Child on the involvement of children in armed conflict, A/RES/54/263 of 25 May 2000 C.F.R. (2000a).

Optional Protocol to the Convention on the Rights of the Child on the sale of children, child prostitution and child pornography, A/RES/54/263 of 25 May 2000 C.F.R. (2000b).

P029 – Protocol of 2014 to the Forced Labour Convention, 1930, (2014).

Research Network on the Legal Parameters of Slavery. (2011). *Bellagio-Harvard guidelines on the legal parameters of slavery*. Retrieved from www.law.qub.ac.uk/schools/SchoolofLaw/FileStore/Filetoupload,651854,en.pdf

Sanderson, P. (2017). On the road. *The Guardian*. Retrieved from www.theguardian.com/world/ng-interactive/2017/nov/24/on-the-road-living-and-working-on-the-italian-road-of-love

Schimmel, B., & Pech, B. (2004). *Corruption and gender: Approaches and recommendations for TA. Focal theme: Corruption and trafficking in women*. Retrieved from www.dgf.ug/sites/default/files/dgf_publications/en-corruption-and-gender%20%281%29.pdf

Shelley, L. (2011). Human trafficking as a form of transnational crime. In M. Lee (Ed.), *Human trafficking*. London: Willan.

Simmons, B. A., Lloyd, P., & Stewart, B. M. (2018). The global diffusion of law: Transnational crime and the case of human trafficking. *International Organization*, *72*(2), 249–281. Retrieved from https://doi.org/10.1017/S0020818318000036

Simmons, F., & Burn, J. (2011). *Without consent: Forced marriage in Australia*. Retrieved from

Slavery Convention, (1926).

Smith, G. (2010). *The criminal justice response to human trafficking: Recent developments in the greater Mekong sub-region*. Retrieved from http://un-act.org/publication/view/siren-gms-08-crimimal-justice-response-human-trafficking/

Sustainable Development Solutions Network (SDSN). (2019). *Indicators and a monitoring framework: SDG 8.7*. Retrieved from http://indicators.report/targets/8-7/

Swamy, A., Knack, S., Lee, Y., & Azfar, O. (2001). Gender and corruption. *Journal of Development Economics*, *64*(1), 25–55. Retrieved from https://doi.org/10.1016/S0304-3878(00)00123-1

Taub, B. (2017). The desperate journey of a trafficked girl. *The New Yorker*. Retrieved from www.newyorker.com/magazine/2017/04/10/the-desperate-journey-of-a-trafficked-girl

Thorn. (2019). *About us*. Retrieved from www.thorn.org/about-our-fight-against-sexual-exploitation-of-children/

Thorn. (n.d.). *Spotlight: Human trafficking intelligence and insight*. Retrieved from http://assets.htspotlight.com/portal/Spotlight-Handout.pdf

Tingle, R. (2017). Europe is "underestimating" scale of migrant crisis and could be flooded by millions of Africans in "biblical exodus" unless urgent action is taken says top official. *Daily Mail*. Retrieved from www.dailymail.co.uk/news/article-4676640/Europe-underestimating-scale-migrant-crisis.html

UN General Assembly. (2010). *Resolution 64/293 United Nations global plan of action to combat trafficking in persons*. Retrieved from www.unodc.org/documents/human-trafficking/United_Nations_Global_Plan_of_Action_to_Combat_Trafficking_in_Persons.pdf

UN Working Group on Trafficking in Persons. (2009). *Non-punishment and non-prosecution of victims of trafficking in persons: Administrative and judicial approaches to offences committed in the process of such trafficking: Background paper prepared by the Secretariat*. Retrieved from www.unodc.org/documents/treaties/organized_crime/2010_CTOC_COP_WG4/WG4_2010_4_E.pdf

UNICEF. (2006). *Guidelines on the protection of child victims of trafficking*. Retrieved from www.unicef.org/protection/Unicef_Victims_Guidelines_en.pdf

UNICEF, & CEE/CIS Regional office. (2003). *Guidelines for the protection of the rights of child victims of trafficking in South Eastern Europe*. Retrieved from http://www1.umn.edu/humanrts/instree/Unicef-Guidelines2004.doc

United Nations. (2019). *Status/ratification of the Protocol*. Retrieved from https://treaties.un.org/pages/ViewDetails.aspx?src=TREATY&mtdsg_no=XVIII-12&chapter=18&clang=_en

United Nations Convention against Transnational Organized Crime and the Protocols Thereto (CTOC). (2004).

United Nations Security Council. (2018). *Report of the secretary general on trafficking in persons in armed conflict pursuant to security council resolution 2388 (2017)*. Retrieved from www.un.org/sc/ctc/wp-content/uploads/2018/11/N1833923_EN.pdf

United Nations University. (2016). *Fighting human trafficking in conflict: 10 ideas for action by the United Nations security council*. Retrieved from http://collections.unu.edu/eserv/unu:5780/UNUReport_Pages.pdf

UNODC. (2008a). *006 Workshop: Criminal justice responses to human trafficking, the Vienna forum to fight human trafficking 13–15 February 2008, Austria Center Vienna background paper*. Retrieved from www.unodc.org/documents/human-trafficking/2008/BP006CriminalJusticeResponses.pdf

UNODC. (2008b). *020 Workshop: Corruption and human trafficking: The grease that facilitates the crime: The Vienna forum to fight human trafficking 13–15 February 2008, Austria Center Vienna background*. Retrieved from www.unodc.org/documents/human-trafficking/2008/BP020CorruptionandHumanTrafficking.pdf

UNODC. (2008c). *Toolkit to combat trafficking in persons: Global Programme against trafficking in human beings*. Retrieved from https://sherloc.unodc.org/res/cld/bibliography/toolkit-to-combat-trafficking-in-persons_html/07-89375_Ebook1.pdf

UNODC. (2009a). *Anti-human trafficking manual for criminal justice practitioners, Module 11: Victims' needs in criminal justice proceedings in trafficking in persons cases*. Retrieved from www.unodc.org/documents/human-trafficking/TIP_module11_Ebook.pdf

UNODC. (2009b). *International framework for action to Implement the trafficking in persons protocol*. Retrieved from www.unodc.org/documents/human-trafficking/Framework_for_Action_TIP.pdf

UNODC. (2011). *Issue paper: The role of corruption in trafficking in persons*. Retrieved from Vienna: www.unodc.org/documents/human-trafficking/2011/Issue_Paper_-_The_Role_of_Corruption_in_Trafficking_in_Persons.pdf

UNODC. (2018). *Global report on trafficking in persons 2018*. Retrieved from www.unodc.org/documents/data-and-analysis/glotip/2018/GLOTiP_2018_BOOK_web_small.pdf

UNODC. (n.d.). *Working group on trafficking in persons*. Retrieved from www.unodc.org/unodc/en/treaties/CTOC/working-group-on-trafficking-2018.html

U.S. Department of State. (2018). *Trafficking in persons report 2018*. Retrieved from www.state.gov/documents/organization/282799.pdf

van der Watt, M., & Kruger, B. (2017). Exploring "juju" and human trafficking: Towards a demystified perspective and response. *South African Review of Sociology*, *48*(2), 70–86.

van der Watt, M., & van der Westhuizen, A. (2017). (Re)configuring the criminal justice response to human trafficking: A complex-systems perspective. *Police Practice and Research*, *18*(3), 218–229. Retrieved from https://doi.org/10.1080/15614263.2017.1291560

van Dijk, J., & van der Heijden, P.G.M. (n.d.). *Research brief: Multiple systems estimation for estimating the number of victims of human trafficking across the world*. Retrieved from www.unodc.org/documents/data-and-analysis/tip/TiPMSE.pdf

van Dijk, R. (2001). "Voodoo" on the doorstep young Nigerian prostitutes and magic policing in the Netherlands. *Africa (pre-2011)*, *71*(4), 558–586.

van Reisen, M., & Estefanos, M. (2017). Human trafficking connecting to terrorism and Organ trafficking: Libya and Egypt. In M. van Reisen & M. Mawere (Eds.), *Human trafficking and trauma in the digital era: The ongoing tragedy of the trade in refugees from Eritrea*. Mankon, Bamenda: Laanga Research & Publishing CIG.

van Setten, M., Scheepers, P., & Lubbers, M. (2017). Support for restrictive immigration policies in the European Union 2002–2013: The impact of economic strain and ethnic threat for vulnerable economic groups. *European Societies*, *19*(4), 440–465. Retrieved from https://doi.org/10.1080/14616696.2016.1268705

Vidal, L. (2016). *Developing innovative, best practice solutions to address forced marriage in Australia*. Retrieved from www.churchilltrust.com.au/media/fellows/Vidal_L_2016_Solutions_to_addressing_forced_marriage_in_Australia.pdf

Walk Free Foundation. (2013). *The global slavery index 2013*. Retrieved from www.walkfreefoundation.org/news/resource/the-global-slavery-index-2013/

Walk Free Foundation. (2018a). *The global slavery index 2018*. Retrieved from www.globalslaveryindex.org

Walk Free Foundation. (2018b). *The global slavery index 2018: Government responses data*. Retrieved from www.globalslaveryindex.org/

Warria, A. (2017). Forced child marriages as a form of child trafficking. *Children and Youth Services Review*, *79*, 274–279. Retrieved from https://doi.org/10.1016/j.childyouth.2017.06.024

Williams, P., & Godson, R. (2002). Anticipating organized and transnational crime. *Crime, Law & Social Change*, *37*(4), 311–355.

Zhang S. X., Pineda S. L. (2008). Corruption as a Causal Factor in Human Trafficking. In: Siegel D., Nelen H. (eds) *Organized Crime: Culture, Markets and Policies*. Studies in Organized Crime, vol 7. Springer, New York, NY.

Zimmerman, C., Yun, K., Shvab, I., Watts, C., Trappolin, L., Treppete, M., . . . Regan, L. (2003). *The health risks and consequences of trafficking in women and adolescents: Findings from European study*. Retrieved from London: https://childhub.org/en/system/tdf/library/attachments/zimmermann_2003_health_risks_consequences_trafficking_1.pdf?file=1&type=node&id=16989

7

THE LAW OF HUMAN TRAFFICKING

From international law to domestic codification in the U.S. and abroad

Nicole J. Siller

Abstract

The crime of human trafficking is perpetrated all over the world and has been for a long time. The creation of law criminalizing trafficking, however, is a relatively new phenomenon. Do you know what the definition of human trafficking is? Do you know that the crime of human trafficking changes depending where you are in the world? This chapter will introduce you to the international law concerning human trafficking as well as the criminalization of this crime under U.S. federal law. Then these codifications will be compared with codifications from other parts of the world in an attempt to understand the legal confines of this offense (see Bussey-Garza, Dempsey, Martin and Rhodes, Chapter 5, this volume).

Learning Objectives

At the end of the chapter, readers will be able to:

1. Identify and understand the primary source of international law addressing trafficking in persons and the duty placed on States Parties with respect to domestic criminalization of this offense;
2. Understand the elements of the crime of "trafficking in persons" as defined under international law;
3. Understand the elements of the crime of "trafficking in persons" as defined under U.S. federal law; and
4. Compare and analyze the similarities and differences between the international definition of "trafficking in persons" and various national codifications of this offense.

Key Terms: trafficking in persons; exploitation; act; means; consent; duty to criminalize.

Legal Glossary

- Common law, also known as "case law" or "judge-made law": Common law is law developed by judicial entities through the issuing of judicial decisions. A common law jurisdiction will look to statutory law if it exists as well as judicial precedent when deciding the merits of a case.
- Defendant: A person charged with a criminal offense.
- Judicial precedent: Past judicial decisions from relevant courts. Judges from a common law system will give considerable weight to precedent (past judicial decisions) and are usually bound to follow a previous court's reasoning where applicable.
- Primary source of law: A statement of the law. The law will most often come from the relevant governmental body including legislature, a court or executive order.
- Prosecution: The governmental entity typically responsible for attempting to holding defendant accountable under criminal law.
- Secondary source of law: Various materials created before, during or after the primary source of law was created which explain or interpret the primary source of law. Examples can include books, journal articles and legal reports.
- Statutory law, codification or legislation: Terms used when referencing the enactment of laws. Codification is the arrangement of statutory provisions that govern a subject of law. For example, each state in the United States has its own criminal code which identifies the crimes within its jurisdiction. Statutory law is a law created by a governing or legislative body.
- *Travaux préparatoires*/Preparatory works: The official record of negotiations that transpired between state delegates and various representatives that participated in the drafting of international instruments (e.g. the Palermo Protocol).

Introduction

The primary legal mechanism used to hold perpetrators accountable for human trafficking is criminal prosecution. The first component of any criminal justice system includes the identification of conduct that a particular society seeks to criminalize. This body of law is typically referred to as substantive criminal law and encompasses the defining of criminal offenses (typically via the enumeration of their elements), the outlining of the crime's scope of application and identification of relevant defenses to the conduct. Some defenses can mitigate a defendant's criminal liability, while others (affirmative defenses) completely negate criminal responsibility.

In general, only persons engaging in conduct meeting the definition and scope of a criminal offense can be held criminally responsible under the law. The only exception is the applicability of an affirmative defense. For example, murder is a codified criminal offense and is specifically defined in law. If the prosecution proves that the defendant's conduct satisfies the elements of murder beyond a reasonable doubt, then the defendant should be convicted of the crime. However, if the defendant successfully puts forth a claim of self-defense that the prosecution cannot rebut, it will serve as a complete defense to the crime of murder and the defendant should be found not guilty at trial.

It is not enough to merely state that a particular type of conduct (e.g. human trafficking) is a crime. It is likely that if you asked several people to define "human trafficking," they would give you various interpretations. The law must operate with more precision. It requires the identification of particular elements constituting the given criminal offense. This method attempts to guarantee a sense of certainty to the law so that people know what specific conduct can incur criminal liability and what will not.

Governments across the world typically identify and define the crimes prohibited within their jurisdiction by way of creating laws through statute. While criminal conduct is often defined in these laws, sometimes terms within the definitions are left open to interpretation. Ambiguous provisions can cause significant issues in legal practice. For example, crimes that include an element of non-consent (e.g. rape) have historically faced interpretational issues. Among others, these issues have included determining whether the consent must be vocalized or whether consent obtained by deception or force is enough to negate criminal responsibility.

In common law jurisdictions (like the United States), laws can also be created through the courts in their judicial decisions. Additionally, judges can interpret or clarify statutory terms or concepts that are vague. Because each jurisdiction can determine its own law, laws addressing the same criminal conduct may differ between jurisdictions in their actual codification or how courts have interpreted those provisions.

This chapter will discuss and compare the codification of anti-human trafficking laws from an international and national law perspective. The underpinning of most domestic laws on human trafficking originate from international law. Accordingly, this chapter will begin with a discussion of the most current international law addressing human trafficking: the Protocol to Prevent, Suppress and Punish Trafficking in Persons, Especially Women and Children, supplementing the United Nations Convention against Transnational Organized Crime (Palermo Protocol, 2000).

Even though the Palermo Protocol defines "trafficking in persons," most countries have elected to institute their own domestic definitions of this crime. This chapter will review and compare the U.S. federal anti-trafficking codification against the Palermo Protocol and contrast aspects of anti-trafficking laws with other domestic jurisdictions around the globe.

The international law of trafficking in persons

In 1998, the United Nations General Assembly put forth Resolution 53/111, initiating the start of work to draft a "comprehensive international convention against transnational organized crime," which included addressing "illegal trafficking" (McClean, 2007). This movement was largely motivated by the idea that international law could facilitate national criminal justice responses to organized criminal activities via domestic criminalization of conduct. The United Nations Office on Drugs and Crime (UNODC) assumed the task of coordinating this international legislative effort.

In 2000, the Convention Against Transnational Organized Crime (CTNOC) was opened for signature. It entered into force on September 29, 2003. The CTNOC is supplemented by three protocols: the Palermo Protocol; the protocol against the Smuggling of Migrants by Land, Sea and Air; and the protocol against the Illicit Manufacturing of and Trafficking in Firearms, their Parts and Components and Ammunition. As of May 9, 2017, the Palermo Protocol has 117 signatories and 170 parties, making it one of the most internationally accepted instruments (Palermo Protocol Ratification Status, 2017).

As explained within its Preamble, the Palermo Protocol's purpose is to provide a comprehensive approach to trafficking. This international instrument's method of addressing trafficking essentially adopted the Clinton administration's "3P" anti-trafficking policy framework: prevention, prosecution and protection (see C.deBaca, Chapter 2, this volume; Chuang, 2014). "Prevention" pertains to the enactment of domestic legislature (which should be erected to target all types of traffickers and cover all types of potential victims), specialized training of law enforcement personnel and an increase of public awareness efforts on this subject matter (UNODC

Trafficking Website, 2017). "Prosecution" is the accountability mechanism states engage with in their respective system to enact justice (UNODC Trafficking Website, 2017). "Protection" is the victim-centered prong of this framework, concerning itself with victim identification and assistance through various efforts including "rescue, rehabilitation, and reintegration" (UNODC Trafficking Website, 2017).

As it pertains to the prosecution limb of the Palermo Protocol's (2000) 3P response, Article 5 requires that States Parties engage in domestic criminalization of trafficking. Article 5(1) states: "Each State Party shall adopt such legislative and other measures as may be necessary to establish as criminal offenses the conduct set forth in article 3 of this Protocol, when committed intentionally" (Palermo Protocol, 2000). Under Article 5(1), the duty to criminalize also extends to conduct of those attempting to engage in the commission of trafficking, participating as an accomplice to the crime of trafficking and organizing or directing other persons to commit human trafficking (Palermo Protocol, 2000).

Do you think it is important for countries all over the world to standardize the concept of human trafficking? Why or why not?

Of utmost importance to the success of the Palermo Protocol was reaching a consensus on *how* the crime of trafficking would be defined (McClean, 2007). Representatives from over 100 different nations, many intergovernmental agents and non-governmental organization delegations participated in the instrument's drafting process (Scarpa, 2008). It was very important that countries all over the world agree on a definition in order to globally standardize the concept, thus affording the opportunity to harmonize substantive and procedural issues in laws on human trafficking among international jurisdictions.

In an effort to standardize substantive laws in countries around the globe, the Palermo Protocol (2000) defined the term "trafficking in persons." Article 3 states:

(a) "Trafficking in persons" (Raymond, 2002) shall mean the recruitment, transportation, transfer, harbouring or receipt of persons, by means of the threat or use of force or other forms of coercion, of abduction, of fraud, of deception, of the abuse of power or of a position of vulnerability or of the giving or receiving of payments or benefits to achieve the consent of a person having control over another person, for the purpose of exploitation. Exploitation shall include, at a minimum, the exploitation of the prostitution of others or other forms of sexual exploitation, forced labour or services, slavery or practices similar to slavery, servitude or the removal of organs;
(b) The consent of a victim of trafficking in persons to the intended exploitation set forth in subparagraph (a) of this article shall be irrelevant where any of the means set forth in subparagraph (a) have been used;
(c) The recruitment, transportation, transfer, harbouring or receipt of a child for the purpose of exploitation shall be considered "trafficking in persons" even if this does not involve any of the means set forth in subparagraph (a) of this article;
(d) "Child" shall mean any person under eighteen years of age.

Article 3(a) identifies the three elements which constitute trafficking: (1) an act (recruitment, transportation, transfer, harboring or receipt of persons); (2) a means (the threat or use of force or other forms of coercion, of abduction, of fraud, of deception, of the abuse of power or of a position of vulnerability or of the giving or receiving of payments or benefits to achieve the consent of a person having control over another person); with both committed (3) for the purpose of exploitation. Article 3(b) solidifies that consent to trafficking is an invalid defense so long as the "means" element is satisfied. Article 3(c) and (d) qualify the definitional confines of this offense as it relates to the trafficking of children (Palermo Protocol, 2000).

While Article 3(a) identifies numerous qualifying actions, means and types of exploitation for each element, all terms are left undefined. Under international law, if the specific source of law does not contain definitions for its own terms, one often looks at the instrument's *travaux préparatoires* (preparatory works). Unfortunately, these documents do not define or comment on the vast majority of these terms. The UNODC is the self-proclaimed guardian of the Palermo Protocol and has published several explanatory documents (Catalogue of Materials, 2017). While shedding some light on the issue of statutory interpretation, these publications generally fail to individually define many of the terms incorporated in the Palermo Protocol's definition of "trafficking in persons."

The decision to leave these terms undefined was likely a strategic one on the part of the Palermo Protocol's drafters. In leaving the terms free from definitional constraints, States Parties to the instrument would have more autonomy in crafting their own anti-trafficking offense by their domestic legislators. National governments would thus be more inclined to commit to this international agreement. Consequently, this definitional ambiguity has left some uncertainty in interpreting the legal contours of the international definition of "trafficking in persons."

Before turning to the national codifications discussed in this chapter, it is important to unpack trafficking terminology. When left undefined in statute or unaddressed in jurisprudence, a term's plain meaning assists to garner further understanding of what it encompasses. In this respect, dictionaries can be a great interpretive tool. It is also one of the first tools legislators and judges use to attach meaning to terms. When a definition cannot clear up one's legal query, additional secondary sources of law are often used to provide further insight.

Moreover, discussing the purpose of each trafficking element individually provides for a deeper understanding of the international codification. The following sub-sections will therefore endeavour to discuss the purpose of each element separately and then attempt to pinpoint definitions of the terms within each element. This exercise brings greater clarity to the criminal offense which could be used to ensure a better workability of the codification in domestic practice.

The "action" element

The first element of trafficking in persons is the "action" element which essentially references the crime's "main conduct" (Obokata, 2015). Article 3(a) enumerates a finite list of qualifying acts. These include recruitment, transportation, transfer, harboring or receipt of persons (Palermo Protocol, 2000). It is important to understand that the act does not have to be criminal in and of itself as long as the other elements are also satisfied (Wijers, 2005). For example, the action element could be satisfied by the physical transportation of a person from point A to point B by automobile. This conduct would rarely be understood as criminal. The rationale behind this premise recognizes that human trafficking is a multi-step process of which the exploitative intentions of the trafficker may not be apparent to his or her victims during their recruitment or physical movement in to exploitative conditions.

The significance of this element is that it can attach criminal liability to each person intentionally working in the "trafficking chain" (Jordan, 2010). As such, Gallagher (2010) explains that criminal liability can be attributed to persons involved with trafficking at its various stages including: recruiters, brokers, transporters, owners, managers, supervisors or controllers, for example, brothel, farm, boat, factory, medical facility, or household.

Table 7.1 Defining the "acts" in trafficking in persons

Type of Act	*Definition or Understanding of the term*
Recruitment	The act or process of finding new people to join a company, an organization, the armed forces, etc.
Transportation	The action of transporting someone or something or the process of being transported.
Transfer	A conveyance of property to another or to make over the possession of (property, a right or a responsibility) to another.
Harboring	Providing a place of refuge or to shelter or hide.
Receipt of Persons	A common definition of "receipt" is understood as the action of receiving or to take delivery of.

Table 7.1 lists each of the element's codified acts and provides the common dictionary (Oxford English Dictionary, 2015) definition of the term. These definitions provide insight into this element's included conduct.

In reviewing the action element definitions, it is relatively easy to distinguish many of the terms from one another. There are however a few important points of clarification concerning the definitions of "transfer," "transportation" and "receipt of persons."

Common definitions of "transfer" denote two different meanings. The first could lead one to read it synonymously with the concept of "transportation," signifying a focus on the physical movement of another.[1] The second definition of "transfer" which was included in Table 7.1 defines the term as "a conveyance of property . . . to another" or to "make over the possession of (property, a right, or a responsibility) to another" (Oxford English Dictionary, 2015). The latter definition is preferred considering the contextual references of "transfer" found in other secondary sources of law. For example, in the early stages of the drafting process, representatives from Argentina proposed a section which listed the "purposes" of creating the Palermo Protocol. Among others, one of the drafted "purposes" was "to abolish progressively those practices which allow a husband, family or clan to order the *transfer* of a woman to another person for payment or otherwise for the benefit of an international criminal organization" (CTNOC and its Protocols' *Travaux Préparatoires*, 2006, p. 336).[2] A reading of this text noticeably evokes a meaning of "transfer" more akin to the concept of a reallocation of custody, possession, or perceived (de facto) ownership.

Do you think that the crime of trafficking should require the movement of persons from one place to another?

Whereas "transfer" focuses on the one relinquishing their interest to another, "receipt of persons" could encompass the one accepting the above described transfer. McClean (2007, p. 323) explains that "'receipt' is the correlative of 'transfer' in this context." However, this term also appears to cover anyone receiving persons in a more general sense. In the context of Article 3, the "receipt of persons" has been described as "not limited to receiving them at the place where the exploitation takes place either, but also means meeting victims at agreed places on their journey to give them further information on where to go or what to do" (CoE/UN Joint Study, 2009, pp. 78–79). These offenders are typically understood as those intermediaries working within the trafficking chain.

Based on a common understanding of the term in the context of trafficking, "receipt of persons" therefore requires the acquirement of a person. This can be in the conveyance sense as the correlative of transfer, but also in the physical sense for offenders at various stages of the trafficking process.

An understanding of the "action" element is important. Perpetration of the action element is required in all cases of trafficking. In a case of child trafficking, the means element is inapplicable, so a large portion of the criminal case will rest on proving this element. Moreover, the commission of this element often produces the best sources of evidence in a criminal case since perpetration of the "act" often compels the use of commercial enterprises (travel companies, newspapers, etc.) and various forms of technology which can be obtained by investigators (Evidential Issues, 2017). Even though the Palermo Protocol does not specifically define the action element terms, identifying and associating meaning to each of the enumerated acts as well as the element itself is an achievable task (Bales, 2005).

The "means" element

The second element of trafficking is concerned with identifying the trafficker's distortion or manipulation of their target's personal choice. As Elliott (2014) explains, this element "follows on from the 'action' element, and refers to the manner in which the action is executed" (p. 85). Qualified "means" listed in the definition of "trafficking in persons" include

> threat or use of force or other forms of coercion, of abduction, of fraud, of deception, of the abuse of power or of a position of vulnerability or of the giving or receiving of payments or benefits to achieve the consent of a person having control over another person.
>
> *(Palermo Protocol, 2000)*

It is important to note that in an instance where the trafficked person is a child (anyone younger than 18 years of age), this element is inapplicable.

Trafficking scholars have described this element as having "varying degrees . . . which can be viewed on a continuum" from direct to less direct methods of placing persons in a state to be exploited (Aronowitz, 2001, p. 166; Gallagher, 2010, p. 31). "Means" employed, such as the use or threat of force, abduction and the giving of payments or benefits, are characterized as direct means. These types of "means" will typically manifest either through physical contact against the body of the trafficked person, through words which are used to instill fear of bodily harm or via transactional acquisitions. Indirect "means" include fraud, deception and the abuse of power or of a position of vulnerability, and are often disguised when executed using mental as opposed to physical control tactics.

Providing individual definitions to these terms is more problematic as several of them enjoy overlapping definitions. Table 7.2 attempts to provide for interpretational insight of these concepts in law using the term's common dictionary definition (Oxford English Dictionary, 2015).

The most difficult terms to synthesize in Table 7.2 are the "abuse of power or of a position of vulnerability" and "the giving or receiving of payments or benefits to achieve the consent of a person having control over another person," requiring additional discussion.

Abuse of a position of power was described in earlier drafts of the Palermo Protocol as an abuse of a position of authority. The Interpretative Note to the Palermo Protocol (2000) reports that the intended meaning of the word "authority" expanded beyond public officials and "should be understood to include the power that male family members might have over female family members in some legal systems and the power that parents might have over their children" (p. 343, note 20).

Table 7.2 Defining the "means" in trafficking in persons

Type of means	*Definition or Understanding of the term*
Threat or use of force or other forms of coercion	"Coercion" is the "action or practice of persuading someone to do something by using force or threats." Note that coercion includes the use or threat of force but is understood as "broader term than force" (*Travaux Préparatoires*, 2006).
Abduction	Physically taking someone away (movement) via the use or threat of the use of force.
Fraud	The wrongful or criminal deception intended to result in financial or personal gain.
Deception	To deliberately cause (someone) to believe something that is not true, especially for personal gain.
Abuse of power or of a position of vulnerability	Abuse of power encompasses two elements: (1) power; (2) misuse of that power. "Power" is the capacity or ability to direct or influence the behavior of others or the course of events. Abuse of a position of vulnerability requires (1) the identification of a "vulnerable person" (2) followed by identifying the abuse of that vulnerability. Being vulnerable includes exposed to the possibility of being attacked or harmed, either physically or emotionally.
The giving or receiving of payments or benefits to achieve the consent of a person having control over another person	No specific definition exists. Note this type of means includes situations of legal control and de facto control over another.

This type of "means" is said to be "especially relevant in cases where an individual has the power to take decisions over other people" (CoE/UN Joint Study, 2009, p. 79). Rijken (2003) has described an "abuse of power" or dominant position to "range from confiscating personal documents in order to place another person in a dependent position, to abusing one's dominant social position or natural parental authority or abusing the vulnerable position of persons without legal status" (p. 63). Accordingly, "power" can be understood as originating from any source which a person can wield.

The abuse of a position of vulnerability (APOV) is one of the most discussed "means" and is considered a central part of trafficking's definition (APOV Issue Paper, 2013; APOV Guidance Note, 2012). Unlike other types of means, the Palermo Protocol's preparatory works (2006, p. 347) did discuss this concept, describing APOV to encompass "any situation in which the person involved has no real and acceptable alternative but to submit to the abuse involved." The preparatory works refrain from clarifying "real and acceptable alternative." This description is reminiscent of the definition of coercion, confirming its link, yet failing to distinguish it from APOV.

The UNODC Model Law (2009) provides a list of conditions which could qualify a person as being "vulnerable" under the law, including:

- Having entered the country illegally or without proper documentation;
- Pregnancy or any physical or mental disease or disability of the person, including addiction to the use of any substance;

- Reduced capacity to form judgments by virtue of being a child, illness, infirmity or a physical or mental disability;
- Promises or giving sums of money or other advantages to those having authority over a person; and
- Being in a precarious situation from the standpoint of social survival;
- Other relevant factors (pp. 9–10).[3]

The UNODC's vulnerability characteristics have been included in several national criminal codes including those of Belgium, the Republic of Moldova, Italy (which also requires profiting of the abuser and permits a "situation of necessity" as one way to qualify someone as vulnerable), Zambia, Liberia, Sierra Leone and the U.S. State Department Model Law to Combat Trafficking in Persons (UNODC Model Law, 2009).

Identification of the existence of one of these characteristics is not enough to substantiate a prosecution using the Palermo Protocol's definition of trafficking. As the UNODC explains in its Guidance Note (2012):

> The mere existence of proven vulnerability is not sufficient to support a prosecution that alleges APOV as the means by which a specific "act" was undertaken. In such cases both the *existence* of vulnerability and the *abuse* of that vulnerability must be established by credible evidence.
>
> *(p. 1)*

Establishing the first component of this "means" element will include a fact-specific and qualitative analysis of the personal characteristics of the alleged trafficked person, as well as the external forces which may lead a fact-finder to classify the person as vulnerable or not. The second component examines whether the identified position of vulnerability was abused.

The final enumerated type of "means" is "the giving or receiving of payments or benefits to achieve the consent of a person having control over another person". Several of the Palermo Protocol's drafting delegates believed that this type of "means" was already "covered by the other qualifiers, that is, force, fraud, deception, coercion and inducement" (CTNOC and its Protocols' *Travaux Préparatoires*, 2006, p. 343, note 21).[4] Nevertheless, it was included in Article 3(a) without further justification.

There is some discrepancy among those working in this field as to whether this type of "means" refers to situations of factual control, legal control or both. For example, in the Commentary to the Palermo Protocol, McClean (2007) writes:

> The notion of "having control over another person" is a factual rather than a legal one: there is, for example, no reference to ideas of legal custody. In many trafficking situations, the persons trafficked are de facto under the control of others, and their position of vulnerability creates an overlap with [APOV].
>
> *(p. 325)*

Other experts including Gallagher (2010) and Rijken (2003), however, assert that this type of "means" is generally and primarily understood to cover situations of "legal control" (as in a parent over a child or the legal guardianship of another) and have questioned whether an omission in defining this conduct also enables its applicability in "de facto control (such as that which may be exercised by an employer over an employee)."[5]

If exclusively economic forms of "means" are applicable under the Palermo Protocol, it should be necessary to distinguish between deviant economic methods and economic hardship in order to preserve the integrity of this criminalized offense. Smith and Kangaspunta (2012) aver that this distinction should be made in that wherein the alleged victim is free to leave, regardless of how difficult the decision is, their economic hardship would not satisfy the coercive nature of the "means" element of trafficking.

While briefly described, the second element reveals a general lack of drafting precision as practically all of the Palermo Protocol's enumerated "means" have overlapping characteristics and qualities. While the individual terms are not as clearly definable or delineable as in the "action" element, an understanding of this element's objective, namely the deprivation of liberty or personal choice is unmistakably evident.

The "purpose" element

The Palermo Protocol does not define exploitation outright. Instead, Article 3(a) states that "exploitation shall include, at a minimum, the exploitation of the prostitution of others or other forms of sexual exploitation, forced labour or services, slavery or practices similar to slavery, servitude or the removal of organs" (Palermo Protocol, 2000). Whereas the first two elements of trafficking enumerate a finite list of "acts" and "means," the third element provides a non-exhaustive list of forms of exploitation.

The third element of trafficking is constructed differently. A common understanding of "exploitation" is the practice by which someone is treated in such a way that would at the very least be considered as taking unfair advantage of another or subjecting another to unfair treatment (Wertheimer, 1999). The Palermo Protocol's enumerated forms of exploitation can clearly be considered more severe than subjection to "unfair treatment." There is also an aspect of harm (Gallagher, 2010).

Whether some type of severely bright line must be crossed in order for a practice to be included as a form of exploitation within the Palermo Protocol's concept of trafficking in persons – its location on this continuum is unclear. A review of the preparatory works does clarify that the personal gain of another is not a requirement to satisfy this element.

While no definition of "exploitation" exists under international law, the same cannot be said for several of the named exploitative practices. Using the international instruments which define the exploitative practices listed in Article 3(a) of the Palermo Protocol (2000) can assist one in understanding how many of these types of exploitation can be understood in a case of trafficking.

Table 7.3 lists the identified forms of exploitation, their definition and definitional origin under international law, should they exist. "Exploitation of the prostitution of others or other forms of sexual exploitation" and the "removal of organs" are not currently defined under international law. Their interpretation will be discussed below.

The most heavily contested and debated forms of exploitation during the Palermo Protocol's drafting process occurred when discussing the terms "exploitation of the prostitution of others" and "sexual exploitation" (Allain, 2013). Discussing these concepts involved plunging into over a century's worth of international political and legislative baggage on the ideologies and positions surrounding prostitution and sex work (Chuang, 2010). Government representatives strove to reach a legislative consensus on this issue (Ditmore & Wijers, 2003). Their central inquiries were (1) whether women actually elect to work in the sex industry and (2) whether the definition of trafficking should be dominated by the nature of the work performed *or* by the "means" used to engage another in the type of work performed (Ditmore & Wijers, 2003).

Table 7.3 Defining the types of exploitation in trafficking in persons' "purpose" element

Type of Exploitation	*Definition*	*Source of International Law*
Exploitation of the prostitution of others or other forms of sexual exploitation	Codified definitions do not exist under international law for these terms.	The legal term "exploitation of the prostitution of others" first appeared in the Convention for the Suppression of the Traffic in Persons and of the Exploitation of the Prostitution of Others (1949 Convention).
Forced labour or services	Forced or compulsory labor is defined as: "all work or service which is exacted from any person under the menace of penalty and for which the said person has not offered himself voluntarily."[6]	Forced Labour Convention 1930.
Slavery	The status or condition of a person over whom any or all of the powers attaching to the right of ownership are exercised.	1926 Convention to Suppress the Slave Trade and Slavery (Slavery Convention, 1957).
Practices similar to slavery and servitude	No codified definition of "servitude" exists. "Institutions and practices similar to slavery" include: 1. Debt bondage: the status or condition arising from a pledge by a debtor of his personal services or of those of a person under his control as security for a debt, if the value of those services as reasonably assessed is not applied towards the liquidation of the debt or the length and nature of those services are not respectively limited and defined. 2. Serfdom: the condition or status of a tenant who is by law, custom or agreement bound to live and labour on land belonging to another person and to render some determinate service to such other person, whether for reward or not, and is not free to change his status. 3. Servile marriage: Any institution or practice whereby: (i) A woman, without the right to refuse, is promised or given in marriage on payment of a consideration in money or in kind to her parents, guardian, family or any other person or group; or (ii) The husband of a woman, his family, or his clan, has the right to transfer her to another person for value received or otherwise; or (iii) A woman on the death of her husband is liable to be inherited by another person. 4. Child exploitation: Any institution or practice whereby a child or young person under the age of 18 years, is delivered by either or both of his natural parents or by his guardian to another person, whether for reward or not, with a view to the exploitation of the child or young person or of his labour.	Supplementary Convention on the Abolition of Slavery, the Slave Trade, and Institutions and Practices Similar to Slavery (Supplementary Slavery Convention).
Removal of organs	No definition exists under international law.	

The result of these inquiries eventually led to the inclusion of "the exploitation of the prostitution of others or other forms of sexual exploitation" within trafficking's list of forms of exploitation. This construction favored the more liberal perspective that sex work could be voluntarily entered into considering that the phrasing "exploitation of the prostitution of others" presupposes that prostitution is an activity that can be engaged into without exploitation. It would seem that the ultimate category here is "sexual exploitation" with the "exploitation of the prostitution of others" being a subdivision thereof.

Describe each of the three elements of trafficking under international law. How do these elements differ from one another?

Because the term "sexual exploitation" does not have any corresponding international definitional reference, it was heavily criticized as being too "imprecise and emotive" and fated to cause friction amongst states with differing positions on prostitution. The term "exploitation of the prostitution of others" did come with an international interpretative contextual reference: the 1949 Convention (Ditmore & Wijers, 2003; Gallagher, 2010).[7] However, this instrument does not provide for a precise definition of the concept. In fact, the 1949 Convention is the precursory international instrument to the Palermo Protocol.

These undefined concepts lead one to question what conduct is encompassed within this type of exploitation under international law? At the second drafting session of the Palermo Protocol, some delegates requested a definition for "sexual exploitation." During the sixth drafting session, a definition was proposed, which read:

> "Sexual exploitation" shall mean:
>
> (i) Of an adult [forced] prostitution, sexual servitude or participation in the production of pornographic materials for which the person does not offer himself or herself with free and informed consent;
> (ii) Of a child, prostitution, sexual servitude or the use of a child in pornography.
>
> *(Ad Hoc Committee on TIP, 2000)*

Ultimately the term was left undefined in the Palermo Protocol and various "proposed alternatives such as forced prostitution or the subsuming of sexual exploitation under broader headings such as servitude, slavery and forced labour were discussed but not accepted" (Exploitation Issue Paper, 2015, p. 29). The *Travaux Préparatoires* (2006) highlights the diverging state perspectives on this topic which is worth reproducing in full:

> The Protocol addresses the exploitation of the prostitution of others and other forms of sexual exploitation only in the context of trafficking in persons. The terms "exploitation of the prostitution of others" or "other forms of sexual exploitation" are not defined in the protocol, which is therefore without prejudice to how States Parties address prostitution in their respective domestic laws.
>
> *(p. 347)*

As previously, mentioned, the more specific type of sexual exploitation enumerated in the Palermo Protocol (2000) is the "exploitation of the prostitution of others." While left undefined in the 1949 Convention, pinpointing an understanding of this concept is a little easier than the concept of "sexual exploitation." The chairperson to the Palermo Protocol's drafting committee reasoned that this "phrase distinguished between individuals who might derive some benefit from their own prostitution and those who derived some benefit from the prostitution of others" (CTNOC and its Protocols' *Travaux Préparatoires*, 2006, p. 344). Similarly, on this point McClean (2007) concludes that "the debate on prostitution which formed the background to so much of the negotiations was unresolved; only pimping is covered by the express language of the Protocol" (p. 326).

The other form of exploitation without any international legal definition is the "removal of organs" (see Manzano, Chapter 11, this volume). This late inclusion into the Palermo Protocol's list of forms of human exploitation was inconsistently accepted among delegates. Many drafters of the Palermo Protocol wanted the focus of trafficking to remain on the person as opposed to their parts (CTNOC and its Protocols' *Travaux Préparatoires*, 2006).

The preparatory works are fairly silent on this form of exploitation. However, they do state that "the removal of organs from children with the consent of a parent or guardian for legitimate medical or therapeutic reasons should not be considered exploitation" (CTNOC and its Protocols' *Travaux Préparatoires*, 2006).

The UNODC articulates that "'organ removal' as an end purpose of trafficking can occur for reasons of culture and religious ritual, as well as for the commercial trade in organs for transplantation" (Exploitation Issue Paper, 2015, pp. 37–38). As opposed to the other enumerated forms of exploitation in the Palermo Protocol, the UNODC's Exploitation Issue Paper (2015) explains that

> it is only "removal of organs" that does not necessarily constitute an inherent wrong – or indeed a crime in its own right in national law. In other words, unlike sexual exploitation, forced labour or services, slavery, practices similar to slavery and servitude, which are "wrong" irrespective of whether or not they take place in the context of trafficking, the removal of organs may be lawful or unlawful depending on the purpose and circumstances of that removal.
>
> *(p. 37)*

Determining whether the removal of organs will fall under exploitation as envisaged by the Palermo Protocol will therefore hinge on those additional considerations.

What can be done to ensure anti-trafficking laws are better understood by criminal investigators, legal practitioners and judges?

Having a legal definition of a form of exploitation is however only the first step. The definition itself must be accurately understood by those using it. Let us take for example, the definition of "forced or compulsory labor" from the 1930 Forced Labour Convention. This concept is defined in international law as "all work or service which is exacted from any person under the menace of penalty and for which the said person has not offered himself voluntarily." What does this definition mean? When dissected, this offense comprises three elements: (1) any work or service (2) performed under "menace of penalty" and (3) performed involuntarily. Each of these elements must then be understood and correctly applied to operate successfully in attributing criminal liability to offenders (ILO, 1930).

The first element concerns the performance of "work or service." It has been interpreted to encompass "all types of work, service and employment, regardless of the industry, sector or occupation within which it is found, and encompasses legal and formal employment as well as illegal and informal employment" (ILO Handbook, p. 8) (ILO, 2008). Although the rationale for adding "services" into the text of the Palermo Protocol ("forced labor or services") was not specifically explained by drafters, "it is reasonable to speculate that this addition reflected general compromises made during the drafting process in relation to the issue of prostitution" (Exploitation Issue Paper, p. 31). Moreover, it is understood that the work or service provider can include the state, private persons and corporations (Forced Labour Convention, Art. 4(1).

The second element, "under menace of penalty," is understood as encompassing a range of deviant approaches used by the exploiter to exact continued work or services which can include threats (in various forms and degrees to the laborer or their next of kin), physical coercion, sexual violence, violence of a psychological nature, physical violence, retention of identity documents, harassment, intimidation isolation, loss of rights or privileges, confinement and instillment of fear (regardless if it was reasonable) (ILO Handbook, p. 8).

The term "penalty" can be interpreted a couple of ways. During the Forced Labor Convention's drafting process, it was confirmed that such a meaning was not "'in a strict sense to mean punishment inflicted by a court of justice,' but instead that it was to mean 'any penalty or punishment, inflicted by persons or body whatever'" (Allain, 2013, p. 219).

The third element of forced labor focuses on the issue of consent and the inalienable "right of workers to free choice of employment" (Report III (1B) para. 271). The International Labour Organization has determined that work performed against a person's free will or an inability to terminate one's own employment within "a reasonable period of notice, and without forgoing payment or other entitlements" signifies involuntariness (ILO Handbook, p. 8). Although there can be an overlap between the second and third elements of forced labor, a concrete way to differentiate them is that "menace of penalty" corresponds to the freedom to leave the abusive employer, whereas the involuntariness element relates to the freedom of choice (in work) of the employee.

While trafficking's final element requires an understanding of the concept of "exploitation," its primary function serves as the mental component of the offense. The act and means elements must be perpetrated. One should not lose sight of the fact those two elements must be committed *with the intent to exploit* which will in turn satisfy trafficking's third element. For that reason, actual exploitation need not occur to substantiate the offense as defined under international law.

As such, the classification of this element as a *dolus specialis* offense is commonly agreed upon by the international community. On this point the UNODC explains that:

> The "purpose of exploitation" is a *dolus specialis* mental element: *Dolus specialis* can be defined as the purpose aimed at by the perpetrator when committing the material acts of the offence. It is the purpose that matters, not the practical result attained by the perpetrator. Thus, the fulfilment of the *dolus specialis* element does not require that the aim be actually achieved. In other words, the "acts" and "means" of the perpetrator must *aim* to exploit the victim. It is not therefore necessary that the perpetrator actually exploits the victim.
>
> *(Module 1, 2009, p. 5, note 1)*

It is important to understand that even though there is an international law addressing human trafficking, a human trafficker will not be brought before an international court for committing the crime defined in Article 3 of the Palermo Protocol (2000). No such courtroom or judiciary exists. The Palermo Protocol is an instrument that requires its State Parties to criminalize the offense in their own country. Accountability of traffickers is the responsibility of national prosecutorial entities. With the Palermo Protocol's construct of "trafficking in persons" clarified in law, the following subsection shifts focus to review anti-trafficking laws within domestic criminal justice systems.

Case study

Jodi is a 26-year-old foreign national living in a small town in the state of Utah and seeking employment. Jodi is not legally allowed to reside or work in the United States. During a job search on the internet, Jodi sees that a local clothing retailer has posted a job advertisement. The business is looking to hire a part-time sales person for $17 per hour. Jodi applies for the position online and is offered the job without a formal interview. She is told that further information will be provided to her on the first day of work. On her first day of work, Jodi's employer asks to see her passport and any documents granting her the right to reside or work in the United States. Jodi only gives her employer her foreign passport. The employer keeps Jodi's passport and escorts her to a room in the back of the business filled with many sewing machines and people. The employer tells Jodi that she will not be selling clothing, but will be making clothing. Jodi's employer states that she must report to work at 5:00 a.m. every day of the week and that she will be allowed to leave work each day at 9:00 p.m. The employer tells Jodi she will be permitted two 15-minute breaks during the workday and that she will be paid at the end of each week. Even though this is not the job advertised, Jodi works for one week. At the end of the week, Jodi's employer gives her $100. Jodi tells her employer that the amount she received is not the payment that was advertised. Jodi's employer tells her that is all she will be paid and states that if Jodi stops working for the retailer, she will report her to immigration and see to her immediate deportation out of the United States.

Case study discussion questions

1. Considering what you already know about or believe human trafficking to be, do you think Jodi is a victim of human trafficking?
2. What is your basis for this belief after reading the case study fact pattern?
3. In Jodi's situation, was there a perpetration of the action element of trafficking in persons? If so, which act(s) from the Palermo Protocol's list apply and what facts lead you to conclude this?
4. In this situation, was there a perpetration of the means element? If so, which one(s) from the Palermo Protocol's list and what facts lead you to conclude this?
5. Was there a perpetration of the purpose element? If so, which form(s) of human exploitation from the Palermo Protocol's list and what facts lead you to conclude this?
6. Would your answer change if Jodi would have never performed any work for the employer?
7. Would your answer change if Jodi's employer refused to pay Jodi any wages?

From international law to domestic codification

The Palermo Protocol's definition of "trafficking in persons" is universally recognized and its statutory construction of trafficking has been the source of legislative inspiration for countless regional and domestic codifications all over the globe (Allain, 2014). Delegates from the United States actively participated in the Palermo Protocol's drafting process (Chuang, 2015). Presently, human trafficking is considered a criminal offense at the state and federal level. Federal U.S. anti-trafficking law emerged shortly before the Palermo Protocol opened for signature and will be the focus of the rest of this chapter as well as other national anti-trafficking laws in the following subsections.

Federal law on human trafficking in the United States

How have domestic codifications of human trafficking manifested?

In 2000, the Trafficking Victims Protection Act (TVPA) codified U.S. federal law on the matter introducing anti-trafficking measures via federal investigations and the criminalization of particular conduct. These statutory provisions can be found in Title 22, chapter 78 of the U.S. Code. The TVPA has been reauthorized and amended several times since its legislative debut (TVPRA, 2003, 2005, 2008, 2013). This subsequent legislation adds to the previous legislation and covers a wide range of issues, including but not limited to the introduction of grant programs to assist state investigators and prosecutors in local prosecutions, the introduction of prevention strategies, the introduction of more severe penalties for traffickers and the strengthening of programs which identify commercial products made by victims of trafficking.

Pursuant to section 7106, the TVPA also enables the United States to impose economic sanctions on countries who fail to comply with the U.S.-created anti-trafficking "minimum standards." Since 2001, the U.S. Department of State has published an annual Trafficking in Persons Report which details how compliant the United States deems each country to be with these anti-trafficking standards.

As it concerns criminalization, the TVPA codifies a trafficking offense and introduces definitions of key terms in the fight against human trafficking. The legal definition of trafficking in the United States is different from international law on the matter. U.S. federal law divides trafficking into two categories: "severe forms of trafficking in persons" and "sex trafficking." The TVPA (2000) defines these terms as follows under section 7102(9):

> "Severe forms of trafficking in persons" means:
>
> (A) sex trafficking in which a commercial sex act is induced by force, fraud, or coercion, or in which the person induced to perform such act has not attained 18 years of age; or
> (B) the recruitment, harboring, transportation, provision, or obtaining of a person for labor or services, through the use of force, fraud, or coercion for the purpose of subjection to involuntary servitude, peonage, debt bondage, or slavery.
>
> The term "sex trafficking" means the recruitment, harboring, transportation, provision, obtaining, patronizing, or soliciting of a person for the purpose of a commercial sex act.

In comparing these definitions, there are similarities and differences between U.S. and international law defining trafficking. "Severe forms of trafficking" includes sex trafficking of minors as well as a portion of the acts, means and purpose configuration of trafficking seen in the Palermo Protocol's definition of trafficking in persons. "Sex trafficking" is separately defined and appears to require the acts element of trafficking for the purpose of a commercial sex act. The term "commercial sex act" has been defined in the TVPA (2000) to include "any sex act on account of which anything of value is given to or received by any person."

It appears that the U.S. trafficking law changes depending on the type of exploitation in question. If the exploitation is a commercial sex act of a person over the age of 18, then no form of inducement is required. This is an interesting contrast to the Palermo Protocol considering that no form of inducement (e.g. perpetration of the "means" element) is ever required for a person under the age of 18 to qualify as trafficking in persons under international law.

Unlike the Palermo Protocol, section 103(2) of the TVPA (2000) defines some of its law's key terms. "Coercion" has been defined as including:

(A) threats of serious harm to or physical restraint against any person;
(B) any scheme, plan, or pattern intended to cause a person to believe that failure to perform an act would result in serious harm to or physical restraint against any person; or
(C) the abuse or threatened abuse of the legal process.

This piece of legislation also defines two of its recognized forms of exploitation. "Involuntary servitude" is defined in the TVPA (2000) which includes a condition of servitude induced by means of:

(A) any scheme, plan, or pattern intended to cause a person to believe that, if the person did not enter into or continue in such condition, that person or another person would suffer serious harm or physical restraint; or
(B) the abuse or threatened abuse of the legal process.

This definition is reminiscent of the common understanding of this term discussed earlier. The concept of "the abuse or threatened abuse of process" is however not in the Palermo Protocol. The concept is defined under U.S. law as follows:

> The term "abuse or threatened abuse of law or legal process" means the use or threatened use of a law or legal process, whether administrative, civil, or criminal, in any manner or for any purpose for which the law was not designed, in order to exert pressure on another person to cause that person to take some action or refrain from taking some action.
>
> *(22 U.S.C. §7102(1))*

It seems that though some similarities exist between this concept and the Palermo Protocol's concept of APOV in the context of legal process, the TVPA (2000) defines "debt bondage" as:

> The status or condition of a debtor arising from a pledge by the debtor of his or her personal services or of those of a person under his or her control as a security for debt, if the value of those services as reasonably assessed is not applied toward the liquidation of the debt or the length and nature of those services are not respectively limited and defined.

This definition is identical to the one used under international law in the Supplementary Slavery Convention.

With the international and U.S. trafficking definitions in mind, the chapter will now look at provisions of anti-trafficking laws found in other domestic criminal justice systems around the world.

Other national codifications of human trafficking

Ratification of the Palermo Protocol instigated the creation of anti-trafficking legislation around the globe. This push in national codification of anti-trafficking laws was further induced by U.S. political pressure and the threat of economic sanctions (Allain, 2014; Chuang, 2015). As such, the widespread codification of national anti-trafficking laws ensued in a relatively short period of time.

What are the differences in statutory construction between the international definition of "trafficking in persons" and the definitions for trafficking under U.S. federal law?

A minority of countries elected to adopt legislation identical or almost identical to the Palermo Protocol's construction of "trafficking in persons." This list of nations includes the Bahamas, Liberia and the Philippines (Allain, 2014). The Council of Europe Convention on Action against Trafficking in Human Beings (2005) has also adopted the Palermo Protocol's definition verbatim in its regional instrument. Nevertheless, each European member state has also adopted its own definition of trafficking within its domestic system.

In fact, the majority of States Parties to the Palermo Protocol have decided to use the Palermo Protocol's definitional construction as a source of inspiration for their own legislation. Most states have used some form of the "acts, means, purpose" configuration. For example, Afghanistan's domestic law has defined "trafficking in persons" as follows:

> Trafficking in Persons: Is transferring, transiting, employment, keeping of a person for the purpose of exploitation by taking advantage of poor economic and desperate condition of the victim through paying and receiving money, interest or using other deceiving means in order to obtain the consent of the victim or his/her guardian.
>
> *(Art. 3(2))*

As you can see, the structure of the offense appears to comply with the Palermo Protocol. However, Afghanistan's law has opted for differing terminology. States also vary on their adoption of this model. Some states have eliminated the means or exploitation element altogether, while some have required exploitation actually occur as opposed to requiring that the perpetrator intended to exploit.

However, the largest differences in domestic codification tend to involve the recognition of various other types of human exploitation, separating the crime of sex trafficking from labor trafficking and the requirement of movement (whether international or domestic) to substantiate the national offence.

Some states have tried to clarify what exploitation means by defining the concept. For example, Thailand defines exploitation as follows:

> means seeking benefits from the prostitution, production or distribution of pornographic materials, other forms of sexual exploitation, slavery, causing another person to be a beggar, forced labour or service, coerced removal of organs for the purpose of trade, or any other similar practices resulting in forced extortion, regardless of such person's consent.
>
> *(The Anti-Trafficking in Persons Act B.E 2551 (2008) § 0004)*

As it concerns the identification of forms of exploitation in domestic law, Allain's study (2014) found a variety of types not itemized in the Palermo Protocol. These include the exploitation of criminal activities, begging, servile or forced marriage, pornography, sex tourism and removal of one or more of the following: blood, cells, organs, tissues, or body parts; bio-medical research on a person; or assault (Allain, 2014).

The Council of Europe is one of the entities that recognizes "forced begging" as a form of exploitation fitting within its construction of this crime even though its Trafficking Convention uses the Palermo Protocol's definition of trafficking. It reasoned that

> forced begging should be understood as a form of forced labour or services as defined in the 1930 ILO Convention No 29 concerning Forced or Compulsory Labour. Therefore, the exploitation of begging, including the use of a trafficked dependent person for begging, falls within the scope of the definition of trafficking in human beings only when all the elements of forced labour or services occur.
>
> *(Council Directive 2011/36/EU, 2011, para. 11)*

There are also a wide variety of countries that include various aspects of insemination, reproduction and sale of children as designated forms of human exploitation recognized under their respective anti-trafficking laws. Among others, these have included illegal adoption (Costa Rica), surrogacy (Azerbaijan), forced fertilization (Macedonia), forced pregnancy (Ukraine) and forced impregnations for the purpose of selling the child when it is born (South Africa) (Allain, 2014).

Pakistan has included the "purpose of exploitative entertainment" into its anti-trafficking legislation (Prevention and Control of Human Trafficking Ordinance (2002), art. 2–3 (Pak.)). It defines this concept to mean "all activities in connection with human sports or sexual practices or sex and related abusive practices."

As discussed above, neither the Palermo Protocol nor its *Travaux Préparatoires* do much to aid in interpreting the terms within this offense. Regardless of the domestic customization of anti-trafficking laws, it appears that an inadequate understanding of trafficking's legal definition and its scope of practical application has in effect trickled down to domestic practice in a variety of countries. In the United States, a failure to understand this law in practice is frequently cited as contributing to offender impunity (Farrell et al., 2012). This problem is reported in other countries as well. For example, McCarthy (2014) reports that

> Definitional confusion is also an issue in trafficking trials, as judges struggle to apply the laws on the books to actual situations. Research on court cases in jurisdictions as diverse as Norway, Ukraine, and Russia have shown how judges have struggled to apply abstract concepts such as exploitation and vulnerability to real-life situations.
>
> *(p. 234)*

Some states have attempted to remedy these definitional omissions by defining most of these terms in their own legislation. Sierra Leone's national trafficking law is an example of this. For the majority of other countries, however, the precise confines of their domestic codifications will only manifest in the form of jurisprudence or legislative review.

Conclusion

The aim of this chapter was threefold: first, to introduce the international definition of "trafficking in persons"; second, to introduce criminal codification of human trafficking under U.S. law; and finally, to contrast the international and U.S. codifications with various domestic criminal justice regimes. As discussed, international law on this matter has instigated the widespread domestic criminalization of this crime. It is evident that the Palermo Protocol's construction of "trafficking in persons" has also been instrumental in shaping domestic codifications of this offense.

Trafficking can be understood as a criminal offense encompassing three elements. The first element is the "action" element. This element relates to the central physical conduct of the accused which is responsible for bringing someone into a state of exploitation. The second element is the "means" element. This element is what is used that facilitates the "action" element. Traffickers can use direct means like force or indirect means like deception to acquire the consent of the person they aim to exploit. Both the "action" and "means" element must be perpetrated by the accused with the intent to exploit to satisfy trafficking's third and final element under international law. While "exploitation" is not defined, the Palermo Protocol includes a list of forms of exploitation.

Explanatory omissions of legal terminology can result in uncertainty in legal practice. This consequence is an understandable by-product of international law-making considering that the Palermo Protocol is first and foremost intended as an instrument triggering the obligation to criminalize trafficking within domestic criminal justice systems. In order to garner as many ratifications as possible, terms and definitions were left open to accommodate for individual domestic interpretation and codification.

Holding traffickers accountable before domestic criminal institutions will prove to be a difficult task for local prosecutors if the crime itself if not accurately understood. The need for interpretational clarity of the terms contained within a given legal framework is vital to its success. A failure to comprehensively understand the elements of an offense can result in its misuse, in the prosecutorial disuse of the offense or in the unnecessary acquittal of defendants (Wade, 2012). As such, an objective of this chapter centered on defining the terms contained within each element of the definition of "trafficking in persons" as codified in Article 3(a) of the Palermo Protocol and encouraging you to determine how an understanding of the international definition can be applied to a given case study. Understanding the international law can in turn serve to clarify domestic interpretational issues of domestic anti-trafficking legislation as well.

Notes

1 As a verb, "transfer" can be defined as "to move from one place to another." As a noun, it is defined as the "act of moving something or someone to another place, organization, team, etc." (Oxford English Dictionary, 2015).

2 Emphasis added.

3 See also Gallagher (2010, pp. 32–33) who explains that additional indicators of APOV include "the abuse of an individual's precarious financial, psychological, and social situation, as well as on linguistic, physical and social isolation."

4 The term "inducement" was debated at length, however, and eventually removed from the final definition of trafficking.

5 See also, CoE/UN Joint Study (2009). The report states that "the giving or receiving of payments or benefits to achieve the consent of a person having control over another person in particular refers to the misuse of a person's authority over another individual, especially with regard to children and persons who are not capable of giving full and valid consent" (p. 79). Again, another example of the overlap of these terms and concepts.

6 Under Article 2(2), this convention specifically excludes the following types of labor from this definition:

(a) any work or service exacted in virtue of compulsory military service laws for work of a purely military character;

(b) any work or service which forms part of the normal civic obligations of the citizens of a fully self-governing country;

(c) any work or service exacted from any person as a consequence of a conviction in a court of law, provided that the said work or service is carried out under the supervision and control of a public authority and that the said person is not hired to or placed at the disposal of private individuals, companies or associations;
(d) any work or service exacted in cases of emergency, that is to say, in the event of war or of a calamity or threatened calamity, such as fire, flood, famine, earthquake, violent epidemic or epizootic diseases, invasion by animal, insect or vegetable pests, and in general any circumstance that would endanger the existence or the well-being of the whole or part of the population;
(e) minor communal services of a kind which, being performed by the members of the community in the direct interest of the said community, can therefore be considered as normal civic obligations incumbent upon the members of the community, provided that the members of the community or their direct representatives shall have the right to be consulted in regard to the need for such services.

7 This phrase is also included in the Convention on the Elimination of All Forms of Discrimination Against Women (CEDAW, 1979) in Art. 6 which reads: "States Parties shall take all appropriate measures, including legislation, to suppress all forms of traffic in women and exploitation of prostitution of women."

Supplemental learning materials

Allain, J. (2013). *Slavery in international law: Of human exploitation and trafficking*. Leiden, the Netherlands: Martinus Nijhoff Publishers.
Chuang, J. (2014). Exploitation creep and the unmaking of human trafficking law. *The American Journal of International Law, 108*(4), 609.
Gallagher, A. T. (2010). *The international law of human trafficking*. New York, NY: Cambridge University Press.
UNODC. (2017, May). *Catalogue of materials: Global programme against trafficking in persons & global programme against smuggling of migrants*. Retrieved from www.unodc.org/documents/human-trafficking/2017/UNODC_Catalogue_of_Materials.pdf
Winterdyk, J., Perrin, B., & Reichel, P. (Eds.). (2012). *Human trafficking: Exploring the international nature, concerns, and complexities*. Boca Raton, FL: CRC Press.

References

U.S.C. §7102 Afghanistan, Law on the Campaign against Abduction and Human Trafficking. Retrieved from www.unodc.org/cld/legislation/afg/law_on_the_campaign_against_abduction_and_human_trafficking/chapter_1/article_1-5/chapter_1.html?lng=en
Allain, J. (2013). *Slavery in international law: Of human exploitation and trafficking*. Leiden, the Netherlands: Martinus Nijhoff Publishers.
Allain, J. (2014). No effective trafficking definition exists: Domestic implementation of the Palermo Protocol. *Albany Government Law Review, 7*, 111–142.
Aronowitz, A. A. (2001). Smuggling and trafficking in human beings: The phenomenon, the markets that drive it and the organisations that promote it. *European Journal on Criminal Policy and Research, 9*, 163.
Bales, K., & Lize, S. (2005). *Trafficking in Persons in the United States: A report to the National Institute of Justice*. Croft Institute for International Studies, University of Mississippi (original May 2004, revised August 2005).
Chuang, J. A. (2010). Rescuing trafficking from ideological capture: Prostitution reform and anti-trafficking law and policy. *University of Pennsylvania Law Review*, 158, 1655–1728.
Chuang, J. (2014). Exploitation creep and the unmaking of human trafficking law. *The American Journal of International Law, 108*(4), 609.
Chuang, J. (2015). The Challenges and Perils of Reframing Trafficking as "Modern-Day Slavery" *Anti-Trafficking Review, 5*, 146.
CoE & UN. (2009). *Trafficking in organs, tissues and cells and trafficking in persons for the purpose of the removal of organs*. Retrieved from www.edqm.eu/medias/fichiers/Joint_Council_of_EuropeUnited_Nations_Study_on_tra1.pdf (CoE/UN Joint Study).
Convention on the Elimination of All Forms of Discrimination Against Women (entered into force 18 December 1979) 1249 UNTS 13 (CEDAW).
Convention for the Suppression of the Traffic in Persons and of the Exploitation of the Prostitution of Others (adopted 2 December 1949, entered into force 25 July 1951) 96 UNTS 271 (1949 Convention).

Ditmore, M., & Wijers, M. (2003). The negotiations on the UN Protocol on Trafficking in Persons. *NEMESIS*, *4*, 79.
Elliott, J. (2014). *The Role of Consent in Human Trafficking*. Routledge. New York, NY.
Farrell, A., et al. (2012). *Identifying challenges to improve the investigation and prosecution of state and local human trafficking cases*. Retrieved from www.ncjrs.gov/pdffiles1/nij/grants/238795.pdf
Gallagher, A. T. (2010). *The international law of human trafficking*. New York, NY: Cambridge University Press.
ILO, Forced Labour Convention (adopted 28 June 1930, entered into force 1 May 1932) C29.
ILO. (2008). *Combatting forced labour: A handbook for employers and businesses, Booklet 1*. Retrieved from www.ilo.org/global/topics/forced-labour/news/WCMS_099621/lang – en/index.htm
Jordan, J. (2010). UN trafficking protocol: An imperfect approach. *Issue Paper 1, Center for Human Rights and Humanitarian Law at American University Washington College of Law*. Retrieved from http://salvos.org.au/scribe/sites/justiceunit/files/Trafficking%20outreach%20materials/Research/UN%20Protocol_ImperfectApproach.pdf
McCarthy, L. A. (2014). Human trafficking and the new slavery. *Annual Review of Law and Social Science*, *10*, 221.
McClean, D. (2007). *Transnational organized crime: A commentary on the UN conventions on its protocols*. Oxford, UK: Oxford University Press.
Obokata, T. (2015). Human trafficking. In N. Boister & R. J. Currie (Eds.), *Routledge handbook of transnational criminal law*. Abingdon Oxford, UK: Routledge.
Oxford English Dictionary, 2015. Oxford University Press: Oxford, England, UK.
Palermo Protocol Ratification Status. (2017, June). Retrieved from https://treaties.un.org/Pages/ViewDetails.aspx?src=TREATY&mtdsg_no=XVIII-12-a&chapter=18&lang=en
Prevention and Control of Human Trafficking Ordinance. (2002). Retrieved from http://qub.ac.uk/slavery/?page=countries&category=1& country=128
Raymond, J. G. (2002). The new UN trafficking protocol. *Women's Studies International Forum*, *25*, 491.
Rijken, C. (2003). *Trafficking in persons: Prosecution from a European perspective*. The Hague, the Netherlands: TMC Asser Press.
Scarpa, S. (2008). *Trafficking in human beings: Modern slavery*. Oxford, UK: Oxford University Press.
Sierra Leone. (2005). *The anti-Human Trafficking Act*. Retrieved from www.unodc.org/cld/legislation/sle/the_anti-human_trafficking_act_2005/part_i-ii/article_1-8/part_i-ii.html?lng=en
Smith, C. J., & Kangaspunta, K. (2012). Defining human trafficking and its nuances in a cultural context. In J. Winterdyk et al. (Eds.), *Human trafficking: Exploring the international nature, concerns, and complexities*. Boca Raton, FL: CRC Press.
Supplementary Convention on the Abolition of Slavery, the Slave Trade, and Institutions and Practices Similar to Slavery (entered into force 30 April 1957) 226 UNTS 3 (Supplementary Slavery Convention).

The Anti-trafficking in Persons Act B.E 2551 (2008)

United Nations General Assembly. (2000). UN Convention against Transnational Organized Crime (adopted by GA Res A/RES/55/25 on 8 January 2001, entered into force 29 September 2003). UN Doc A/55/383 (CTNOC).
United Nations General Assembly. (2000, April 4). "Ad Hoc Committee on the Elaboration of a Convention against Transnational Organized Crime, Consideration of the additional international legal instrument against trafficking in persons, especially women and children." UN Doc A/AC.254/4/Add.3/Rev.6, 3 (Ad Hoc Committee on TIP, 2000).
United Nations General Assembly. Protocol to Prevent, Suppress and Punish Trafficking in Persons, Especially Women and Children, Supplementing the United Nations Convention against Transnational Organized Crime (adopted 15 November 2000, entered into force 25 December 2003) (2000) UN Doc A/53/383 (Palermo Protocol).
UNODC. (2004). Legislative Guides for the Implementation of the United Nations Convention Against Transnational Organized Crime and the Protocols Thereto.
UNODC. (2006). Travaux Préparatoires of the negotiations for the elaboration of the United Nations Convention against Transnational Organized Crime and the Protocols thereto (CTNOC and Protocols' *Travaux Préparatoires)*.
UNODC. (2009a). Anti-human trafficking manual for criminal justice practitioners, Module 1: Definitions of trafficking in persons and smuggling of migrants.

UNODC. (2009b). Model Law against Trafficking in Persons. V.09–81990 (E).
UNODC. (2012a). Guidance Note on "abuse of a position of vulnerability" as a means of trafficking in persons in Article 3 of the Protocol to Prevent, Suppress and Punish Trafficking in Persons, Especially Women and Children, supplementing the United Nations Convention against Transnational Organized Crime. Retrieved from www.unodc.org/documents/human-trafficking/2012/UNODC_2012_Guidance_Note_-_Abuse_of_a_Position_of_Vulnerability_E.pdf (Guidance Note).
UNODC. (2012b). Issue Paper: Abuse of a position of vulnerability and other "means" within the definition of trafficking in persons. Retrieved from www.unodc.org/documents/human-trafficking/2012/UNODC_2012_Issue_Paper_-_Abuse_of_a_Position_of_Vulnerability.pdf (APOV Issue Paper)
UNODC. (2015). Issue paper: The concept of "exploitation" in the trafficking in persons protocol. Retrieved from www.unodc.org/documents/human-trafficking/2015/UNODC_IP_Exploitation_2015.pdf (Exploitation Issue Paper).
Wade, M. (2012). Prosecution of trafficking in human beings cases. In J. Winterdyk et al. (Eds.), *Human trafficking: Exploring the international nature, concerns, and complexities*. Boca Raton, FL: CRC Press.
Wertheimer, A. (1999). *Exploitation*. Princeton University Press: Princeton, New Jersey.
Wijers, M. (2005). Analysis of the definition of trafficking in human beings in the Palermo protocol. Report upon request of UNDP Belarus. Retrieved from http://lastradainternational.org/doc-center/1354/analysis-of-the-definition-of-trafficking-in-human-beings-in-the-palermo-protocol

SECTION III

Healthcare

8

THE COMPLEX MENTAL HEALTH CONSEQUENCES OF HUMAN TRAFFICKING

What every provider needs to know

Sandra L. Bloom and Susan Brotherton

Abstract

To fully grasp the traumatic effects of trafficking, one must appreciate the impact of childhood adversity and repeated victimization. More often than not victims of human trafficking have experienced sexual and physical abuse from those on whom they were reliant for basic needs. Years of abuse creates a vulnerability to traffickers who, under the guise of love and protection, manipulate young victims into a life of sexual servitude and abuse. Victims endure traumatization prior to being trafficked, as well as while "in the life," and are often coerced to commit violent acts toward others. Leaving "the life" seems impossible to victims due to fear, shame and the biological impact of the trauma they have survived. Yet, victims are freed from their traffickers often with the assistance of law enforcement. This is a crucial time, as rarely do victims identify as such. They enter treatment, often by mandate, with incomplete histories and challenging symptoms. Victims are often misdiagnosed and struggle for understanding in treatment. Accurate diagnosis via understanding of the many facets of complex trauma is critical for one's successful transformation from victim to survivor.

Learning Objectives

At the end of the chapter, readers will be able to:

1 Understand risk factors that play a role in individuals becoming victims of trafficking;
2 Define trauma bonding and explain how it impacts a victim's ability to leave "the life" and his/her trafficker;
3 Define complex PTSD (CPTSD) and articulate why this is such an appropriate diagnosis for victims of trafficking;
4 Explain traumatic reenactment and how this phenomenon impacts trafficking victims, and why this so important for clinicians to understand; and
5 Articulate the three phases of the Sequenced Approach and explain why this method is so efficacious in work with victims/survivors.

Key Terms: complex trauma, complex PTSD (CPTSD), hyperarousal; dissociation; state-dependent learning; fear conditioning; learned helplessness; traumatic memory; emotional numbing; alexithymia; traumatic reenactment; trauma bonding; stages of change; Sequenced Approach.

Introduction

The intention of this chapter is to provide a summary of what any health, mental health, child welfare, or other social service worker needs to know if they are to become an effective force in addressing what is arguably the most heinous aspect of our modern world. We begin by examining what is known about situations that put people at risk for becoming victims of trafficking and briefly discuss how the process unfolds for the victims. Using case examples from a Salvation Army anti-trafficking program, we will illustrate the importance behind the ability to assess and evaluate a client from the point of view of trauma theory and, based on that theory, what may be involved in efforts to intervene in the life of a victim in a way that supports healing and recovery. Because of our shared experiences, our focus in the chapter will be on sexual trafficking and less on labor trafficking or state-sponsored trafficking.

Risk factors for human trafficking

There is no question that there are a number of factors that play a role in individuals becoming victims of human trafficking, be it labor or sex trafficking. Table 8.1 lists a number of known risk factors for sex trafficking (see Titchen and Stoklosa, Chapter 9, this volume).

A history of childhood adversity – characterized by maltreatment, parental mental illness, exposure to family violence, and abandonment – is associated with high-risk behaviors and criminal activity in both adolescents and adults (Anda et al., 2006; Dube et al., 2003; Edwards et al., 2005; Maxia, Robert, Shanta, Wayne, & Vincent, 2003). Furthermore, individuals with histories of child maltreatment are at higher risk for engaging in risky sexual behavior, experiencing re-victimization, and in some cases, becoming sexual offenders (see Ravi, Chapter 10, this volume).

Table 8.1 Risk factors for sex trafficking

Risk Factors for Sex Trafficking	
• History of sexual/physical abuse	• Age out of foster care
• Youth that are orphaned	• Runaways
• Children between the ages of 12 and 16	• Domestic violence
• Homelessness	• Isolation
	• Poverty
• Living in high crime neighborhoods	• Ethnic minorities
• Socially marginalized groups	• Family dysfunction
• Substance abuse	• Mental illness
• Learning disabilities	• Developmental delay
• Friends as traffickers	• Lack of social support
• Parents/caregivers as traffickers	• Poor academic performance
• Lack of work opportunities	• Subculture of gendered exploitation
• Deficiency in social skills	• Involvement in gangs
• Ineffective public systems	• Corrupt systems of justice

Source: Adapted from Hardy, Compton, & McPhatter, 2013a; Hartinger-Saunders, 2017; Rafferty, 2008.

Table 8.2 Indicators of human trafficking

- Does the person appear disconnected from family, friends, community organizations, or houses of worship?
- Has a child stopped attending school?
- Has the person had a sudden or dramatic change in behavior?
- Is a juvenile engaged in commercial sex acts?
- Is the person disoriented or confused, or showing signs of mental or physical abuse?
- Does the person have bruises in various stages of healing?
- Is the person fearful, timid, or submissive?
- Does the person show signs of having been denied food, water, sleep, or medical care?
- Is the person often in the company of someone to whom he or she defers? Or someone who seems to be in control of the situation (e.g. where they go or who they talk to)?
- Does the person appear to be coached on what to say?
- Is the person living in unsuitable conditions?
- Does the person lack personal possessions and appear not to have a stable living situation?
- Does the person have freedom of movement? Can the person freely leave where they live?
- Are there unreasonable security measures?

Source: See www.dhs.gov/blue-campaign/indicators-human-trafficking.

How the trafficking process unfolds

To describe how the process of victimization occurs – in this case sex trafficking – we will use the life stories of several women (Louisa, Shonte, and Benita) to make real the impact of trafficking on actual human beings. Table 8.2 describes some indicators of human trafficking.

Ensnaring, grooming, recruitment

The seasoning, or grooming, process refers to the progression of power used by traffickers to control their victims and, in some cases, forge a trauma bond. Similar to "Stockholm syndrome," in which hostages relate to and defend their captors, trauma bonding is a form of coercive control in which traffickers instill a sense of fear in their victims as well as gratitude for being allowed to live (Smith, Vardaman, & Snow, 2009).

Case Study: Louisa

Louisa was the fifth child and only girl born to a single, impoverished, and uneducated mother. By the time Louisa was born, her mother was deeply involved in substance abuse, and other than her aunts who tried to care for her, Louisa's early childhood experiences with safe attachment were quite limited. She was sexually abused by her older brothers beginning when she was six or seven, and when she was 12, she was sold to a pimp by her mother who needed money for her own drug habit. Her mother was acquainted with Paul, the man who became Louisa's pimp, because he hung out in the neighborhood and was involved in drug dealing. In the beginning, he bought Louisa some pretty clothes and

Louisa was happy that he had chosen her. As soon as she could, Louisa moved in with Paul. She had little contact with her family after that.

Louisa had no frame of reference for recognizing that the things Paul was asking her to do were unsafe or wrong in any way. He kept several other girls and they all became Louisa's substitute family – all supported by the girls' sex work. That Paul would sometimes beat the girls, or require them to participate in the rape of new girls, sometimes by gangs of men, did not seem abnormal to Louisa, although at times she felt guilty for some of the things she did. She didn't like it when Paul allowed her johns to hit her, but he would always take her to the hospital afterward. He was good about keeping her supplied with drugs, at least in the early days. But as time went on, he expected her to work increasingly hard to get drugs, food, and even shelter.

Poverty, familial abuse, and impoverished attachment relationships are all factors in Louisa's vulnerability, easily spotted by a trafficker who lost no opportunity in befriending her. As noted earlier, the typical victim of trafficking has been exposed to a variety of adverse childhood conditions, including sexual and physical abuse, before they become recruited into trafficking. Victims are often recruited and controlled through a grooming process and therefore do not recognize the trafficker as someone who has captured them. For the mental health worker, being actually sold by a family member may be incomprehensible and difficult to even contemplate, much less suspect (Litam, 2017).

Knowing the risk factors for human trafficking, what kinds of community-based early intervention activities could be developed to address sex trafficking in a proactive manner?

The repetitive exposure to violence comes with a significant cost beyond the obvious physical injuries. The human stress response is typically known as fight-flight-freeze and is normal when we are startled or scared. But for people who have been severely or repeatedly traumatized, the capacity to modulate their level of physiological arousal is lost, so that they stay hyperaroused and guarded and are unable to calm themselves down even when they see that there is no danger. They feel embarrassed by their response, while at the same time they are irritable, angry, and frightened for no apparent reason. They are prepared to fight or flee, even though there is no danger. They may also become flooded with memories, images, and sensations that are overwhelming. As a result, they are likely to feel they are "going crazy." This reaction can be triggered by almost anything.

In Louisa's case, fighting back was not an option. Paul was far too dangerous and Louisa knew it. So she did the only two things she could do: used drugs to manage overwhelming distress and taught herself how to "go away." The formal term for "going away" is dissociation, defined as the "temporary breakdown in continuous, interrelated processes of perception, memory, or identity" (Brewin, 2011, p. 211). Dissociation has much in common with the freeze component of stress. The brain is overloaded and cannot do its usual integrating work of creating a biographical narrative. Instead, fragments of the experience may become locked into that dissociative state unavailable to full biographical narrative formation, and instead they become the substrate for flashbacks and behavioral reenactments.

Children who experience sexual trafficking confront all the dangers associated with sexual abuse (see Bryant, Joudo Larsen and Gordon, Chapter 6, this volume). They are also subjected to routine beatings and abuse by traffickers, employers, pimps, madams, and customers. It is the extent and persistence of the psychological and physical abuse and the coercive, deceitful, and exploitative relationship with the traffickers that distinguishes trafficking from other forms of maltreatment and that are the same methods employed by torturers. Reported methods include physical, sexual, and psychological violence; isolation; deployment in areas unknown to them; dependence on alcohol or drugs; controlled access to food and water; and monitoring through the use of weapons, cameras, and dogs; and threats to harm loved ones (National Research Council & Medicine, 2014; Zimmerman & Pocock, 2013).

The taking control stage, or "in the life"

The taking control stage of trafficking is characterized by a shift in the traffickers' behavior from caring and supportive to controlling and possessive (O'Connor & Healy, 2006). Threats, violence and testing of the victim's commitment to the relationship begin along with demands that she start selling sex to prove her love (Litam, 2017).

Case study: Benita

Benita, 16 years old, was one of five siblings raised by her mother and stepfather in a crowded urban home. She never knew her biological father, who died the year she was born. Her siblings were the natural children of her stepfather, and Benita never felt that she was a part of the family in the same way.

She met Mark when she was a junior in high school. He was older, looked like he was rich, and he had his own car. He charmed Benita and took her on dates to expensive nightclubs, buying her dresses to wear and paying for her to get her hair and nails done. He told her she was beautiful and suggested she could have a career as a model. Her self-esteem, which had been low, soared at his words and she believed him when he said he would take her to New York to get some pictures done so that she could start her modeling career. At Mark's request, Benita had started lying to her family and friends about where she was going at times when she was meeting Mark, how she was able to afford to keep up her hair and nails, and why she was missing school. She felt special for the first time and loved every minute she spent with her secret boyfriend. Without telling her parents, she set off to New York with him.

Mark took Benita directly to his friend's apartment in Queens. Lights and a camera were set up in the living room. She brought dresses that Mark had purchased for her for the shoot and changed into one right away. After a few pictures were taken, Mark and his friend asked Benita to remove her clothes. Benita was uncomfortable, but Mark convinced her. Trusting Mark, Benita complied. When they finished with the photo shoot, Mark said he could not afford to pay the photographer and he asked Benita to have sex with his friend as payment for the photo session. When she emerged from the bedroom, Mark beat her with his fists. He took her identification, her phone and money, and told her she was his property and that she was going to work for him just like she had the night before. That night Mark posted photographs of Benita on a well-known internet site and arranged for several "dates" to come to the hotel. Mark held Benita down while the men raped her. Benita watched Mark collecting cash from each man but was offered only a fast food meal at the end of the night. These events were repeated night after night until Benita complied with what was asked of her. She even worked hard to please Mark, earning as much as she could to make him happy and love her again. Heartbroken and feeling ashamed, Benita found herself reliant on Mark for her every need.

Benita was then Mark's captive. Even if she could have theoretically escaped, she was likely not to even try. She had experienced the trauma bonding process of alternating abuse with relief from that abuse. Traffickers have made a science out of centuries of torture experience and know exactly how to manipulate a victim in fulfilling their desires. Their methods inevitably involve fraud, coercion, and force. She has also developed "learned helplessness" – a phenomenon that has been verified in animals and humans. With repeated punishment and captivity, she has learned that there is no escape, so that even when she can, she will not leave (Maier & Seligman, 1976).

The promises used throughout the grooming process are fraudulent. The traffickers make any promise that will work to induce the victim to comply. For some it is food and shelter; for others it is the promise of a highly sought out job or marriage in another country. Force typically includes beatings and/or gang rape to break down the spirit of the victim. Traffickers use the same methods as seasoned interrogators: beatings, near starvation, isolation and confinement, ice baths, cigarette burns, forced drug use, and repeated rape as punishment, witnessing violence, threatening violence against loved ones, witnessing murder and then alternating with relief (Litam, 2017; Zimmerman & Pocock, 2013).

It is not unusual for traffickers to create "debt bondage" by withholding wages to pay off an escalating debt of so-called expenses to the trafficker supposedly incurred by "helping" the victim. Employers of forced laborers will charge for every consumable to create a never-ending cycle of debt. Persons in forced labor scenarios then become trapped as traffickers enforce high interest rates, withhold payment, and charge for miscellaneous expenses such as the cost for food, transportation, condoms, and other supplies (Litam, 2017).

Post-trafficking

Often, human trafficking victims may have a hard time adapting to life in a residential treatment program they are placed in. Human trafficking victims "in the life" are granted little choice about anything. Basic things like eating, sleeping, and bathing may be up to the discretion of the pimp. Structured residential programs may also mandate specific times for meals, bedtime, and bathing. It is not uncommon for victims to be unable to sleep at night as they have been living their lives awake all night and sleeping all day. Victims' resistance to following basic rules can lead to disagreements with staff, often resulting in punitive consequences. Residential treatment programs need to rely on structures to safely manage the youth they serve; however, they would better serve victims if they could provide flexibility, opportunities to individualize care, and create opportunities to maximize choice.

There are many post-trafficking problems. Running away from treatment programs and group homes is common for juvenile victims. While the risk is high that victims will return to traffickers, the consequences for running are often punitive and restrictive, again mirroring the process of the trafficker. The question then is how we provide safe places for victims to heal, achieve, and recover from the cumulative trauma they have endured. Victims may not be recognized as victims by law enforcement and the courts, who are likely to attribute much more free will than actually exists. Many bridges may have been burnt with family, friends, and community by the victim as the trafficker's manipulation began. It is important to remember that the trafficking occurs within the context of highly organized criminal networks, so it is typical for victims to fear retribution, especially if they have participated in criminal proceedings against the trafficker. Nonetheless, a common aim of post-trafficking assistance organizations is to repatriate individuals to their families even when the families have been complicit in facilitating the trafficking in the first place (Zimmerman & Pocock, 2013). Shonte's story is a good example of these complicating factors.

Case study: Shonte

Shonte, 15 years old, was brought to juvenile court for delinquency. She had a history of running away from home, and as her story emerged it became clear that she had been trafficked by a boyfriend of her mother's, but no one was able to get a clear picture of how this had all happened. Shonte was sent to a secure facility for girls and adjusted quickly to institutional life. In months, she was back at grade level, attended and participated in groups, and shared a positive outlook with her counselors. She was released into the custody of her mother and expected to return to school and complete her senior year of high school. Mental health services were put in place along with case management. Within two weeks post-discharge she was using PCP and looking for the girls she knew from the hotel where she had been prostituted. Shonte tested positive for drug use at her next court visit and was remanded to another residential program for girls. Shonte again quickly acclimated to the program. While in placement she graduated from high school and was returned home to the custody of her mother. It was not long before Shonte was again using drugs and finding her way back to "the life." Again, Shonte was remanded to treatment, this time a drug and alcohol program. Shonte was 20 years old and had been known to the system since she was 12. Each time Shonte was released, she relapsed. With each relapse, she was mandated to treatment. But no one in her treatment environments knew enough about trafficking to discover that her mother was her original trafficker and had encouraged her to make money off of her body whenever she was around her.

The process of "leaving the life" has been compared to other forms of recovery. How is this process similar to traditional forms of recovery? How does it differ?

Recovery from being trafficked is akin to other forms of recovery. Recovery is not only about staying clean, or out of "the life." It is about managing relapse. It is about making choices minute by minute, hour by hour, day by day. Recovery is a process where mistakes are made, examined, perhaps repeated, and again examined, until strategies are learned to navigate a different path. But as in Shonte's case, the history prior to involvement in trafficking by the pimp and then the subsequent course of her experience was not connected to what was happening in treatment. No one had taken the time or knew enough to obtain the information that may have put her on an entirely different course. Court-mandated recovery usually does not allow for mistakes and subsequent learning. Youth who relapse and test positive for drugs or alcohol may find themselves, like Shonte, placed in secure facilities or suffer other consequences. Victims thus follow the path of least consequence until their time is served. We would not teach a child to ride a bike if we were not willing to let go and allow the child to find her/his balance.

The stressors put upon trafficking victims after getting out of the life are continuous and usually overwhelming. Concerns over housing, employment, immigration, training, benefits, children, and retribution from the traffickers are prevalent (Zimmerman & Pocock, 2013). Traffickers will not allow victims access to mental health services and only rarely for health services, so victims may have serious health problems that have long been ignored. They are likely to have serious challenges in trusting anyone enough to allow them to get the help they need. They have learned not to trust anyone, so establishing rapport is critical and requires a non-judgmental attitude, time, and willingness to listen to painful stories without pointing out how the person could have responded differently (Chesnay, 2013).

Diagnosing post-trafficking mental health–related symptoms

Given the complex, cumulative, and long-standing nature of sexual trafficking, especially when it begins in childhood, the panoply of possible symptoms can be quite challenging to put into any specific diagnostic category, as Table 8.3 illustrates (Zimmerman et al., 2006).

The end result of this diagnostic complexity is that the victim frequently ends up with many different diagnoses, a situation that can easily overwhelm the helper's grasp of what exactly they are to do. Someone with panic attacks and difficulty being in confined spaces, nervousness and sleep problems, suicidal thoughts and difficulties getting along with others may easily end up diagnosed with a number of comorbid conditions such as panic disorder with agoraphobia, generalized anxiety disorder, major depressive disorder or bipolar disorder, accompanied by a personality disorder such as borderline personality disorder or antisocial personality disorder. Each one of these may result in a different medication and a different set of treatment protocols, while none of the treatment providers may have any idea how to integrate all of this together in a meaningful way. They are also not likely to recognize that the problems the person has are essential elements of complicated post-traumatic adaptations. This is especially the case when a victim of trafficking has not even been identified as a victim. The victim, now survivor, is in a better position if they are diagnosed with PTSD or a dissociative disorder, which is only likely to happen if the traumatic past is recognized, but at least it is more likely to lead to more consistent, staged treatment. Some resources for more specific assessment of trauma include Armstrong, 2017; Dalenberg & Briere, 2017; Ford, Grasso, Elhai, & Courtois, 2015; and Pole, 2017.

There is a better diagnostic way to view the survivors of trafficking. It is called "complex PTSD" (CPTSD). Complex trauma refers to a type of trauma that occurs repeatedly and cumulatively, usually over a period of time and within specific relationships and contexts. The term emerged over the past several decades as clinicians and researchers found that some forms of trauma were much more pervasive and complicated than others. These were people who had survived wide ranges of exposure to human cruelty who were extremely difficult to treat. The level and the extent of their trauma varied according to the age and stage at which the trauma occurred; the relationship

Table 8.3 Signs and symptoms of trafficking

Depression	Loss of interest in things	No concentration
Hostility	Hopelessness about future	Insomnia
Anxiety, tense, keyed up	Feelings of worthlessness	On guard
Fearful	Loneliness	Paranoid
Out of it, confused	Sadness	Avoiding everything
Terror, panic	Suicidal thoughts, actions	Self-mutilation
Restlessness	Urges to beat, injure, hurt	Binging, purging
Sudden fear	Urges to smash things	No appetite
Nervousness, shaky	Frequent arguments	Sadism
Irritability	Temper outbursts	Masochism
Recurrent thoughts	Recurrent memories	Flashbacks
Nightmares	Withdrawal, detachment	Unable to feel
Compulsive sex	Splitting	Deceitful
Lack of empathy	Cruel to others	Memory problems
Guilt	Shame	Lack of self-worth

to the perpetrator of the trauma; the complexity of the trauma itself and the victim's role and role grooming (if any); the duration and objective seriousness of the trauma; and the support received at the time at the point of disclosure and discovery, and later. A new diagnostic conceptualization of CPTSD/ DESNOS (disorders of extreme stress, not otherwise specified) was defined for the field trial of an earlier version of the *Diagnostic and Statistical Manual* (DSM) (Roth, Newman, Pelcovitz, Kolk, & Mandel, 1997). Complex PTSD consists of seven different problem areas shown by research to be associated with early repetitive, interpersonal and cumulative trauma (Courtois, 2008; Courtois & Ford, 2009; Herman, 1992a). These include:

1. Alterations in the regulation of affective impulses, including difficulty with modulation of anger and self-destructiveness;
2. Alterations in attention and consciousness leading to amnesias and dissociative episodes and depersonalization;
3. Alterations in self-perception, such as a chronic sense of guilt and responsibility, and ongoing feelings of intense shame;
4. Alterations in perception of the perpetrator, including incorporation of his or her belief system;
5. Alterations in relationship to others, such as not being able to trust and not being able to feel intimate with others;
6. Somatization and/or medical problems; and
7. Alterations in systems of meaning. Chronically abused individuals often feel hopeless about finding anyone to understand them or their suffering.

It is easy to see how a victim of human trafficking could fall much more easily into this more understandable explanation for multiple symptoms while at the same time making clear linkages between cause and effect. It is less about what is wrong with the person and much more about what happened to them (Bloom, 1994).

Understanding through a trauma-informed lens

Children who become victims of trafficking are likely to already have significant problems that are a result of previous physical or sexual abuse, or inadequate and neglectful parenting experiences. Adults who have been abused as children do not just outgrow these difficulties. Understanding the impact of repetitive and cumulative trauma can help give a new perspective on the attitudes and behaviors that then unfold in the trafficking situation. When we understand how mind, body, and spirit have been impacted by cumulative trauma, then we can develop better intervention strategies.

The physical response to danger referred to earlier is best known as the "fight-flight-freeze" response, the basic mammalian survival response. Our senses perceive danger and set off a response in a structure called the amygdala, our internal alarm bell. The amygdala triggers release of critical impulses that activate the sympathetic nervous system, preparing us to fight, run, or take any defensive position that will keep us safe. The result is increased blood pressure, heart rate, and breathing, accelerated delivery of nutrients to muscles, blunted pain perception, increased blood clotting, activation of the immune system, and a brain that is on alert. At the same time, long-term digestion, growth, tissue repair, and reproduction are all turned off. If and when the danger passes, the opposite system – the parasympathetic system – will be activated so that you will calm down, relax, be able to sleep, and resume normal activities.

Chronic stress can come about from living in chronically dangerous situations – war zones, domestic violence, torture, refugee status, child abuse, and of course, trafficking. Chronic stress for humans can occur under conditions that are not actually physically dangerous but that are psychologically threatening, even events that are not currently happening but which we *anticipate* might happen. It is the generalization of the stress response that sets us apart from other animals – that we can elicit a fight-flight-freeze response about situations that are not physically threatening and that have not even happened yet and may never happen. Therefore, the systematic coercion and threats the traffickers use can be very effective in controlling their victim.

Under conditions of chronic stress, something goes wrong as the body repeatedly attempts to cope with this massive overload of physiological responses. The effectiveness of the response diminishes and the body becomes desensitized to some of the effects of the neurohormones and hypersensitive to others. The entire system can become dysregulated in many different ways. This results in a set of highly dysfunctional and maladaptive brain activities (Perry & Pate, 1994). The person experiences this as a state of chronic hyperarousal, one of the hallmark characteristics of PTSD. Essentially, the baseline level of arousal for the person has changed and they cannot control their own responses to stimuli.

Once people who have been severely or repeatedly traumatized lose the capacity to modulate their level of arousal they stay hyperaroused and guarded and are unable to calm themselves down even when they see that there is no danger. They feel embarrassed by their response, while at the same time they are irritable, angry, and frightened for no apparent reason. They are prepared to fight or flee, even though there is no danger. They may also become flooded with memories, images, and sensations that are extremely distressing. This reaction can be triggered by almost anything that serves as a post-traumatic reminder. If a trafficker induces an escalation in this overwhelming state of distress and then offers the child or adult a drug that alters that state, the situation is easily set up for addiction and all the manipulation that goes into maintaining it.

The "freeze" component of the stress response is mirrored in the dissociative component of the trauma response. Dissociation is the loss of integrated function of consciousness, identity, memory, or perception of the environment and is a typical accompaniment of post-traumatic stress disorder. When trauma exposure is chronic, an individual will rely more upon dissociation to manage the distress; however, reliance on dissociation as a coping strategy in the response to chronic stress contributes to behavior problems, affect dysregulation, and poor self-concept (Cole, Sprang, Lee, & Cohen, 2016).

Victims of trafficking rarely identify as victims. Why do you think this is the case?

These effects are compounded by the immature brain. The ability to process information and think rationally and clearly may not be matured at all, and deficits are most likely to emerge under stress. The adult brain does not complete its initial "wiring" until the mid-twenties, so adolescents are very susceptible to making bad judgments and poor decisions. People who are abused as children often lack good decision-making skills, and judgment can become very impaired at any age because of these deficits. Under such circumstances, people's thinking is likely to become overly simplistic and less complex. They may find it difficult to think about anything except the immediate present, which impairs the ability to consider the long-range consequences of an action. In such a state, people tend to make decisions based on impulse and the need to self-protect (Janis, 1982). Many victims have long-term problems with various aspects of thinking that impede decision-making and the exercise of good judgment.

Traffickers take advantage of another biological vulnerability that affects abused children – state-dependent learning. Learning is dependent on the ability to categorize incoming material, but that can only happen properly when we are in a state of calm attentiveness. Learning is dependent on the state we are in when the learning occurs, and fear creates a very special state of consciousness. Children raised in abusive, violent homes have become "fear conditioned." Fear conditioning happens very rapidly in animals and humans – a single pairing is sufficient and once established, the fearful reaction is relatively permanent. People can overcome their fear response but they really do not "unlearn." Instead, higher brain centers inhibit and control the fear response, but the "emotional memory" remains (LeDoux, 1994).

Once fear is learned, it is likely that it can never be unlearned at a basic physiological level. Then later, when people are triggered by reminders of past trauma, they become hyperaroused and only the learning gained during past experiences with hyperarousal and danger will be available to them. Because of this, state-dependent learning can interfere with the efforts of others to help the victim. Strategies designed in the calm surroundings of a therapist's office may bear little relationship to the level of arousal the same person is in when confronted by a perceived danger. Trafficking victims may intend to take action to protect themselves and get away from the trafficker, but when back in the situation again, they find themselves unable to make the promised change. State-dependent learning combined with the learned helplessness and experienced lack of control over one's own physiological states associated with a traumatic experience or a series of traumatic experiences leads then to a diminished sense of self-efficacy, so that even when the person could take constructive action to prevent further harm, they seem unable to do so.

For the past century, many observers have noticed that the imprint of traumatic experiences is very different from the memories of normal events. Traumatic memory often poses the greatest problems for people who have suffered repeated or severe traumatic experience. The intrusive symptoms of post-traumatic stress disorder – the nightmares, the sensory, emotional, and physical flashbacks, and the behavioral reenactments – all appear to be a result of disordered memory functioning. The alternation between flashbacks and amnesia is one of the most problematic aspects of stress disorders. On the one hand, the traumatic memories are vivid and intrusive. These memories do not fade, nor do they seem to be altered by ordinary experiences. They are state-dependent, meaning they tend to intrude into consciousness when they are triggered by a state that resembles the state experienced at the time of the original traumatic event. Flashbacks are likely to occur when people are upset, stressed, frightened, or aroused, or when triggered by any association to the traumatic event (Van der Kolk, 1996b). This can be experienced by the person as a total or partial reliving of the traumatic experience.

The trafficker is well aware that when he beats an adult victim, he is putting her in a state that replicates when she was helpless, little and could not resist, and he takes full advantage of that to further empower himself in her eyes. It can be a sensory fragment of the trauma or the entire traumatic sequence running like a virtual reality movie. In such a state, the traumatized person has difficulties distinguishing reality from flashback. The sensory experience is often quite vivid, feeding a vicious cycle of autonomic arousal that increases the sense of reality of the flashback even more. When people experience intrusive flashbacks as visual, olfactory, affective, auditory, or kinesthetic sensations, although we term this "traumatic memory" it bears little if any relationship to the normal process of remembering.

With an understanding of sex traffickers and trauma, can you think of a situation where someone you encountered may have been a victim of trafficking? What were the indicators? What might you have done differently?

Victims of trauma will do anything they need to do to prevent the evocation of these horrible memories and the toxic feelings that accompany them. Traffickers intuitively know this. In their methods of systematic betrayal and abuse, alternating with relief of abuse, they know that choosing girls or women who have already suffered childhood abuse will make them much easier to manipulate and to hold captive.

Because of the physiological changes that occur when frightened, the ability of the brain to verbally categorize incoming information can be shut down. The result is a partial or complete loss of the ability to assign words to incoming experience, the biological equivalent of "speechless terror" (Van der Kolk, 1994, 1996b; Van der Kolk & Fisler, 1995). Dependent upon words, our capacity to logically think through a problem is diminished or entirely shut down and a person's mind shifts to a mode of consciousness that is characterized by visual, auditory, kinesthetic images, and physical sensations as well as strong feelings.

Under normal conditions, emotions serve as "sensitive mental radar" alerting us to the significance of things around us (Harber & Pennebaker, 1992). When people have been traumatized, they no longer can predictably count on their emotions to provide the proper evaluative information (Van der Kolk, 1996a). When this has occurred, survivors can no longer use their emotional states as directional signals. The psychological function of emotions is to alert people to pay attention to what is happening so that they can take adaptive action. The emotions of people with PTSD do not seem to serve their usual alerting function – namely as warning signals to take adaptive action (Krystal, 1978). In these situations, emotional arousal and goal-directed action are often disconnected from each other.

These changes are particularly problematic when the traumatic exposure begins in childhood. Gradually, over the course of development and with the responsive and protective care of adults, the child's brain develops the ability to modulate the level of emotional arousal based on the importance or relevance of the stimulus. This is part of the reason why the capacity of adults to soothe frightened children is so essential to their development. They cannot soothe themselves until they have been soothed by adults. In the child development literature, as many as 80% of abused infants and children develop disorganized/disoriented attachment patterns. These patterns are associated with an inability to utilize caregivers for soothing and with pathological self-regulatory behaviors. A substantial body of research has shown that early and prolonged trauma in childhood affects the capacity to regulate the intensity of emotional responses, problems that continue into adolescence and adulthood (Shonkoff et al., 2012).

Trafficking victims either have far too much emotional arousal, inappropriate to the circumstances they are in, or they develop a sense of emotional numbness, an under-reactivity that leaves them feeling depressed, empty, unable to relate to other people and even to life. They respond to reminders of a previous traumatic event as if it were happening in the present, not the past, with increases in heart rate, skin conductance, and blood pressure (Van der Kolk, 1996a). People who have been traumatized lose the capacity to "modulate arousal." They tend to stay irritable, jumpy, and on edge. This loss of the ability to modulate internal emotional states means that people become very labile, with rapidly shifting, easily triggered, and powerful negative emotions that are beyond their control. This picture will be obvious to anyone who has worked with victims of trafficking.

The intrusive memories and flashbacks are likely to disrupt the emotional numbing and dissociative defenses that have become protective. Under such circumstances, people frequently turn to substances, like drugs or alcohol, or behaviors like sex or eating or even engagement in violence, all of which help them to calm down, at least temporarily, as do many different forms of self-injurious behavior. It is well established that children who are sexually abused often engage in very inappropriate and sexualized behavior. This is a significant advantage for the trafficker, who can use this for his own benefit. The victim, however, having recognized this in herself might hold only herself accountable for the acts of prostitution that have occurred and define herself as a willing sexual partner in all her acts and resist any other interpretation. Understanding the relationship between current sexual exploitation and early childhood sexual abuse would mean that she would need to process the earlier abuse – a challenge that often takes years in a trustworthy therapeutic relationship to accomplish. As a result, chronic PTSD and chronic substance abuse as well as personality distortions often appear simultaneously in the same individual, and diagnosis may depend entirely on the level of expertise of the diagnostician or the system to which they present.

Alexithymia, meaning the inability or loss of the ability to identify specific emotions and put those emotions into words that can be shared, was first described in concentration camp survivors but is a common accompaniment of any captivity and abuse situation (Krystal, 1988). Concepts of post-traumatic stress disorder (PTSD) propose that incomplete, disrupted emotional processing of the traumatic event underlies the symptoms of PTSD. Engaging the emotions has been shown to be a vital ingredient in the successful emotional processing of traumatic experiences while emotional numbing and alexithymia may interfere with the success of treatment (Harber & Pennebaker, 1992; LeDoux, 1996). The person who demonstrates alexithymia often unconsciously finds other forms of expression through behavior and through psychosomatic symptoms (Lumley & Norman, 1996). There are also connections between alexithymia and the development of substance abuse (Handelsman et al., 2000). Teaching trafficking victims how to tune into their feelings, develop words for their emotions, and inhibit the destructive adaptations they may have made to contain toxic emotions becomes a vital part of therapy.

One of the most puzzling aspects of trauma is the tendency to repeat it in either a very obvious way or in a more cloaked and symbolized way known as "traumatic reenactment." Why do we repeat the past, particularly when the patterns of behavior that we are repeating are at best, unfulfilling and often traumatic? The philosopher Santayana observed that "those who cannot remember the past are condemned to repeat it," and this is as true in the lives of individual trauma survivors as it is for societies. Both Pierre Janet and Sigmund Freud – seminal figures in the history of psychology – understood much about the dynamics of trauma and both claimed that the crucial factor that determines the repetition of trauma is the presence of mute, unsymbolized, and unintegrated experiences (van der Kolk & Ducey, 1989). Freud termed this the "repetition compulsion" and wrote that for feelings to be experienced and become conscious, words had to be linked to them. It was the linkage with word representations that allowed the affect to cross the repression barrier and become conscious (Sashin, 1993).

We must assume that as human beings, we are meant to function at our maximum level of integration and that any barrier to this integration will produce some innate compensatory mechanism that allows us to overcome it. Splitting traumatic memories and feelings off into nonverbal images and sensations by the mechanism of dissociation is lifesaving in the short term but is a barrier to full integration in the long term. The memories of the traumatic experience are dissociated, nonverbal, and unintegrated, possibly lodged in the right brain. Over and over, people find themselves in situations that recapitulate earlier trauma and lack any awareness of how it happened, much less how to prevent it from happening the next time. The lack of conscious awareness may be secondary to the dissociative blockade between left and right hemisphere integration that places the behavior out of the context of the left hemisphere's verbal, linear, and conscious control. Since words are not available to sufficiently explain the experience, thinking cannot really occur.

Under these circumstances, people will usually come up with explanations for their strange and mysterious behavior, because the rational part of their mind is struggling to make sense of the situation. Even after it becomes obvious to the trafficking victim that she can leave and stop the abuse, she may feel powerfully drawn to return, influenced by trauma bonding and the indescribable but unconscious compulsion to repeat the past. Without access to the dissociated material, the rational mind flounders helplessly, interpreting behavior in a simplistic, often stupid and punitive way, while the person helplessly re-exposes himself or herself to further trauma. The reenactment behavior can be seen as the "cries for help" as the trafficked victim fails to see a way out of the situation she is in.

Self-harming behaviors are other symptoms of trauma that are often difficult for helpers to understand. People who self-mutilate have learned that if they hurt the body, they will experience a temporary relief from a state that is described by some as one of hyperarousal and acute distress and by others as a state of numbed emptiness, probably mediated chemically by the opiate our own bodies make. Clinical reports consistently show that self-mutilators have childhood histories of physical or sexual abuse or other kinds of trauma and that the earlier and more extensive the abuse or neglect, the more likely it was that their aggression would be turned toward self-harming behavior. Sexual abuse victims may be even more likely to self-mutilate than people exposed to other forms of early trauma. Significant neglect in childhood is also known to be a strong predictor of self-mutilation. Self-harming behavior is thought to be related to childhood abuse and then reinforced by a lack of secure attachments (Van der Kolk, 1996c). Betrayal trauma, those circumstances when people we are dependent upon for survival violate us, is for many a major barrier to recovery and is at the very heart of the trafficking experience (Freyd, 1996).

Usually, people who hurt themselves feel little or no pain. It has been suggested that this response is due to an endorphin response and that the repeated use of self-mutilation as a coping skill may alter the endorphin response and thus become an addictive behavior that is reinforced every time it works. The cutting does not make the person feel good – it simply makes life bearable for another hour or day. But the self-mutilation is also a form of traumatic reenactment and leads to addiction to trauma. The victims frequently wound themselves at the same real or symbolic place that their perpetrator hurt them. The visible gashes, burns, and scars are bodily expressions of a much deeper inward pain that is visible only to the victims. In their desperate and largely unconscious attempt to communicate their distress to the world that lies beyond the boundary of their skin, they reenact the trauma by inflicting more traumas upon themselves. For the trafficking victim, especially if the person has been a victim of childhood sexual abuse, the self-harming behavior may focus on mutilation of the breast or genital area including inserting weapons or corrosive substances into their orifices or eating inappropriate objects or noxious agents.

Self-destructive eating behavior, another form of self-harm, may occur alone or with self-mutilation and can be understood as the nonverbal narration for what people cannot remember or their words cannot say. Binge-purge behavior and self-mutilating behaviors have also been found to be associated with a history of childhood physical and sexual abuse with disturbances of mood, body image, and gender identity all consistent with the traumatized right brain's function (Farber, 1997).

Similarly, individuals exposed to stress are more likely to abuse alcohol and other drugs and to undergo relapse. This is supported by research with animals showing that stress increases the tendency of animals to self-administer drugs that are defined as illicit substances for humans. Research has shown that there is an overlap between the neurocircuitry that responds to drugs and those that respond to stress, and that it is these same neurocircuits that are involved in the development of post-traumatic stress disorder and related syndromes (NIDA, 2002).

The two key survival strategies common to the human species are caretaking and attachment (Valent, 2007). When the people to whom one has become attached are the same people who are the source of the danger, the result is increased attachment to the abusing person. As pointed out earlier, this is called "trauma bonding" and is part of the complicated picture for trafficking victims, battered spouses, abused children, prisoners, cults, victims of torture, and any other situation in which the abuse is prolonged and repeated (Herman, 1992b). A vital part of the recovery process will be to help survivors break the "trauma bond" they feel with their captors. The result of trauma bonding is likely to be a dysfunctional attachment with the trafficker that occurs in the presence of danger, shame, exploitation, seduction, deception, or betrayal (Hardy et al., 2013b; Strenz, 1982).

As a result, highly untrustworthy and destructive relationships come to be considered normative (Dutton & Painter, 1981; Herman, 1992b; James, 1994; Van der Kolk, 1989). The natural, innate protective mechanism of turning to people to whom you are attached for safety is turned on its head. Your persecutors become the same ones you turn to for relief. If these same persecutors also provide intermittent nurturance in the form of food, shelter, relief from pain, or even affection, then the situation is even more confused, both cognitively and at a basic biological adaptive level. It has become clear that the victim's pre-existing personality is not a major factor of what has become known as the "Stockholm syndrome" (Bloom, 2009; LaViolette & Barnett, 2000). It is instead a result of the experience of helpless captivity and helps us to understand why so many trafficking victims return to their traffickers and defend and protect them.

Many trafficking victims when seen in clinical settings will be diagnosed with a personality disorder of one type or another. It is difficult to imagine how anyone could be subjected to the kinds of treatment we have been describing and *not* end up with what is called a personality disorder. To early workers such as Freud and Janet, it became obvious that traumatic experience had the effect of halting development.

> Unable to integrate the traumatic memories, they seem to have lost their capacity to assimilate new experiences as well. It is . . . as if their personality which definitely stopped at a certain point and cannot enlarge any more by the addition or assimilation of new elements.
>
> *(Van der Kolk & Van der Hart, 1989, p. 1533).*

The survivor's personality does not really stop, but it can certainly become distorted, thrown off of its trajectory and onto a new and often destructive course. This change in life trajectory can occur to virtually anyone if the circumstances are sufficiently injurious. But when the traumatic experience occurs in childhood or adolescence, before the personality has fully developed, the person may develop severe personality problems, such as multiple personality disorder or any of the defined personality disorders (Herman, 1992b; Herman, Perry, & Van der Kolk, 1989; Perry, Herman, Van der Kolk, & Hoke, 1990).

When caregivers first encounter a trafficking victim, their unwillingness to be rescued is often quite puzzling. But people who suffer profound trauma may no longer feel that they are alive or deserving of anything other than what they are. Instead, they feel like zombies, the walking dead wandering in the wilderness. Trauma sets people outside the bounds of the normal human community. The assumptions that allow most of us to feel relatively safe in the world are shattered (Janoff-Bulman, 1992). A victim of trafficking will be hard-pressed to recognize that there is benevolence in the world or justice, meaning, or comfort. If this shattering happens when you are a child, it may sabotage the development of moral intelligence, the central intelligence for all human beings that binds us to our social group, culture, and moral system, defining how to use our other forms of intelligence to give our lives purpose and meaning (Lennick & Kiel, 2005). The term "moral injury" was first used by Dr. Jonathan Shay as a descriptor for some of the profound experiences of combat veterans who experience a betrayal of what is right in a high-stakes situation by someone who holds power (Shay, 2003). But all people who have been intentionally hurt by others upon whom they must depend, contend with the abuse of power that inevitably is a part of the sense of fundamental betrayal. Moral injury when it occurs in childhood may influence moral preferences away from altruism and mutual self-interest and toward self-protection and self-interest (Bloom, 2017).

The experience of trauma shatters – often irrevocably – some very basic assumptions about our world, our relationship to others, and our basic sense of identity and place in the world.

A sense of meaning and purpose for being alive are shaken (Janoff-Bulman, 1992). This being such a normative experience of trauma, what is inspiring about the human species is how survivors struggle to make sense out of violence, transcending its effects, and transforming the energy of violence into something powerfully good for themselves and their communities. This describes what Dr. Judith Herman has called "a survivor mission" (Herman, 1992b). It is often a mission that encompasses the remainder of one's life.

Intervention

Assessment

Assessment in situations of trafficking will be an ongoing process within the context of building trust in relationship. Guidelines for screening for human trafficking are available through the Vera Institute of Justice (Vera Institute of Justice, 2014). The consideration of complex PTSD when conducting a comprehensive evaluation is an important component. This factor can be compounded by the presence of alcohol and substance use disorders. One of the greatest challenges of working with trafficked individuals is that victims rarely identify themselves as victims. Adult and juvenile victims often enter the behavioral health system following involvement with law enforcement. Placed in programs against their will, having no voice, or choice, victims rarely trust the process. While some simply do not see themselves as victims, others experience shame, guilt, and fear of being exposed. Some victims feel they are unworthy of help. Or they fear their trafficker will retaliate with violence targeted them or their families. Lastly, intense attachment to their traffickers in the form of trauma bonding intensifies the victim's loyalty and unwillingness to disclose. The fact that victims rarely identify as such is not surprising considering the polyvictimization of trauma experienced by victims. Table 8.4 suggests some assessment questions for the clinician to consider and that can be useful in establishing an initial relationship and finding out more about what has happened to the person.

Victim identification, then, falls into the hands of service providers. Yet without training, providers do not know the questions to ask or how to identify signs of trafficking. We have described

Table 8.4 Assessment of trauma: key questions

- Was the traumatic event interpersonal – more severe and wide-ranging effects?
- If the trauma was interpersonal, was the perpetrator a trusted other, such as a family member or intimate partner?
- Was the trauma sexual?
- Is culture of socioeconomic status a factor?
- Does the victim/survivor blame himself/herself for the event, or blame an unjust or hostile world – attributional sets often associated with more negative outcomes?
- Are there physical, emotional, cognitive, and practical aftermaths of the trauma that complicate the client's current presentation?
- Did the victim/survivor have physical or psychological difficulties prior to the traumatic event that complicate his/her current post-traumatic functioning?
- Does the client's culture affect his or her symptoms presentation?
- Are the client's presenting symptoms the cause of the trauma, the result of it, or both?
- Is the index trauma the only adverse event the client has experienced? Or is it cumulative?

Source: Adapted from Dalenberg & Briere, 2017.

Louisa and her introduction to trafficking above; now let's look at how she was introduced to the system that was supposed to help her.

Case study: Louisa (continued)

Louisa, 17 years old, had been in "the life" since she was 12. Initially trafficked by her mother she was sold to her current pimp at 14. Louisa was in love with her trafficker. Regardless of what he asked of her, she complied. Soon they had a child. The police arrested everyone during a sting at the hotel. Louisa's child was taken into custody by child welfare. Louisa was taken into police custody and locked in a cell. Louisa, angry, frightened, and worried about her child, threatened to hurt herself. The police facilitated her admission to an emergency psychiatric facility. Over the next few weeks Louisa was diagnosed with borderline personality disorder, bipolar disorder, and an eating disorder. A variety of medications were prescribed, but the side effects made Louisa refuse to continue them.

If you were to create an assessment tool to assess whether a client may be a victim of trafficking, what would you assess for and why?

Louisa never identified herself as a victim. Her treatment team focused on her symptoms at admission, not on her life history. Not only do Louisa's admitting diagnoses inform her treatment but also impact her next placement as her diagnoses travel with her. Choice and self-determination are critical aspects of providing services to trafficked individuals because of the learned helplessness that they have already experienced. When juvenile victims do come to the attention of those in a position to help, interventions often involve law enforcement. Subsequently, youth become part of the legal system and are mandated for therapy and services. Compliance with treatment is not a choice but an obligation, mirroring the obligation to one's trafficker, to avoid a consequence for not doing what one is told to do. The victim's motivation moves from engaging in services to heal from trauma to a focus on compliance to avoid consequence. Healing cannot occur when the parallel process of victim/perpetrator remains uninterrupted. Whether in or out of "the life," in addiction or recovery, or somewhere in between, it is important that staff offer support and services, meeting participants where they are both literally and figuratively. Great emphasis needs to be placed on relationship development. Victims are initially mistrustful. Even when staff are non-judgmental, honest, and treat clients with dignity, trust takes a long time to develop. Services without rigid time frames would benefit victims. Victims are often authorized for three months of individual therapy, when in three months they may only begin to share their stories. Additionally, services need to continue regardless of the life choices made by clients. For example, clients who relapse, or return to the life, still require support services. A large part of case management is assessing and processing a client's readiness for change in a nonjudgmental way.

Stages of change

For clients that are currently trafficked, the stages of change may be a helpful tool for examining clients' willingness to engage in treatment and the best strategies to employ based on the stage of change they are currently in. Table 8.5 lists the stages (Norcross, Krebs, & Prochaska, 2011; Prochaska, Norcross, & Diclemente, 1994).

Table 8.5 Stages of change

Stage	*Presentation*	*Strategy*
Precontemplation	• Not thinking about change • May be resigned • Feeling of no control • Denial: does not believe it applies to self • Believes consequences are not serious	• Education • Point out discrepancy • Use of leverage • Don't push
Contemplation	• "Yes, but . . ." • Highly ambivalent • Weighing benefits and costs of behavior, proposed change	• Explore ambivalence • Neutral stance • Decisional balance
Preparation	• Intend to make a change • Beginning to establish criteria • Experimenting with small changes	• Change becomes priority • Encourage movement • Realistic plans • Consultant role
Action	• Person commits time and effort deciding on details • Taking a definitive action to change	• "Right-sized" steps • Plan for high-risk situations
Maintenance	• Extended stage • New behaviors and coping strategies	• Support system – personally and culturally relevant • Therapy
Relapse	• The rule rather than exception • Experiencing normal part of process of change • Particularly likely when trauma bonding a factor • Individual will revert back to earlier stage • Usually feels demoralized • Can come out of it more experienced, wiser	• Learning opportunity • Focus on gains made instead of failure

Source: Norcross et al., 2011; Prochaska et al., 1994.

When assessing victims, the recommendation is to conduct a complete psychiatric evaluation to determine a client's psychological needs, to determine which issues were present before the trafficking experience, and to check for comorbid disorders. This will also ascertain the client's functioning and the availability of basic resources. When conducting the evaluation, providers should be sensitive but not shy away from screening for sexual abuse, and should do so by shifting the responsibility to perpetrators by holding them, not the victim, accountable for the abuse. It is also important to assess for sexually transmitted diseases and to understand various aspects of the trafficking experience. The attending clinician should venture to explore areas concerning initial vulnerability, the manner of recruitment or capture, the primary trafficking process, and the exploitation as experienced by victims. Factors that should be noted are vulnerabilities and risks, exploitation and abuse, as well as strengths and resources (Pascual-Leone, Kim, & Morrison, 2017).

Intervention strategies

When planning an intervention, it is useful to keep in mind the "common factors" research that emphasizes how important therapeutic relationship factors are to client improvement including the demonstration of accurate empathy, positive regard, non-possessive warmth, and genuineness (Armstrong, 2017; Hubble, Duncan, & Miller, 1999). Empathy for what trafficking victims have gone through requires a thorough education in what early sexual abuse does to people and what the added dimensions of trafficking evoke.

Be wary of the now universal strategy of insisting on "evidence-based" methods alone. Use of cognitive-behavioral therapy (CBT) interventions, including prolonged exposure (PE) and cognitive restructuring (CR) techniques, for which empirical support exists, may be retraumatizing for trafficking victims. Successful alleviation of intrusive symptoms will ultimately be necessary but if imposed too soon may be completely unsuccessful, harmful, and even precipitate flight from treatment (Courtois, 2008).

Court-mandated recovery does not allow for mistakes and subsequent learning. Youth who relapse and test positive for drugs or alcohol may find themselves placed in secure facilities or suffer other consequences. Victims thus follow the path of least consequence until their time is served. We can teach recovery skills but are aware that self-determination leads to self-control.

Youth who are identified as victims of trafficking are often sent to secure facilities for safety and treatment. Can treatment be mandated? When and how does safety outweigh client self-determination?

Sensitivity to the effect of complex trauma on youth, in particular the role of disorganized memories, inability to self-soothe, attachment problems, difficulties with appropriate interpersonal boundaries, and understanding how to implement evidence-based treatments for youth with complex trauma will greatly improve professionals' ability to engage with and respond effectively to youth exploited in commercial sex (Cohen, Mannarino, Kliethermes, & Murray, 2012; Smith et al., 2009). Treatment goals must target these issues of trust, intimacy, and safety, and service environments must offer refuge from exploitive, unsafe conditions if recovery is to occur (Cole et al., 2016).

An expert survey was conducted by the International Society for Traumatic Stress Studies (ISTSS) to develop some consensus among clinicians experienced with treating clients who have the complex problems associated with cumulative trauma exposure. Experts agreed on several aspects of treatment, with 84% endorsing a phase-based or sequenced therapy as the most appropriate treatment approach with interventions tailored to specific symptom sets (Cloitre et al., 2011).

Sequenced approach

The three phases that Judith Herman first outlined in 1992 have stood the test of time (Herman, 1998). In the first phase of safety, the beginning focus is on attending to basic needs, the regulation of basic physical functions, the management of intrusive thoughts and memories and control over self-destructive behaviors. Trafficking victims may need clothing, housing, and food. Like victims of domestic violence, they will need a protective place that ensures safety against pursuit by the traffickers and other victims who are also trafficked and have been sent to find them and retrieve them (Yakushko & Oksana, 2009). Safety may require the coordination of many different services that are required to achieve any kind of successful stabilization: language interpreters, transportation to treatment locations, phones, money, child welfare assistance, legal assistance, employment, healthcare (Pascual-Leone et al., 2017). When the immediate needs are addressed, only then can the survivor begin to focus on the psychological impacts of their experiences.

The achievement of safety and stability can take a long time. Getting control over self-destructive behaviors such as substance abuse, compulsive sexuality, eating disorders, and the compulsion to reenact by returning to the trafficker are all exceedingly difficult in part due to difficulties in trusting that helpers can help. And yet change is only likely to occur within the context of a trusting relationship. The earlier the abuse started, the more it is important for the therapist to be able to identify whatever developmental gaps may stand in the way of growth and development. If left unidentified and unaddressed, dissociative symptoms will sabotage treatment and precipitate more unsafe behaviors that are not within the individual's conscious control. The survivor may need to be in a highly structured, safe, and stable environment to do this work. Development cannot be hurried, nor can changing the trajectory of disrupted development.

Psychoeducation is an important component throughout the course of recovery but is most vital in the first phase. The combined forces of terror, learned helplessness, addiction, trauma bonding, and traumatic reenactment will be pulling powerfully on the victim to return to the trafficker. It is likely that she will return, perhaps several times, before she successfully can leave her abuser. This is why it is so important to respect the stages of change literature and apply strategies that are consistent with where she is in the change process. Educating people about the psychobiological effects of trauma can help to mobilize cognitive resources that will support the change process within the person so that finally she is able to manage and control her own emotions and emotional responses. She can be taught many skills that will help her in her journey to become free of her captivity and keep herself safe, including simple things that she can do that help move her into a different stage of change (Bloom, Foderaro, & Ryan, 2006).

The second phase of recovery was described by Herman as "Remembrance, Integration and Mourning," a time for paced, in-depth exploration of trauma; the integration of memories, feelings, and thoughts; and intense grieving over all that has been lost. In order to do this trauma-specific exposure work, the survivor will have to maintain a safe therapeutic relationship and have developed sufficient emotional regulatory skills that this critical work will not precipitate more self-harming behavior and relapse. It is during this second phase that interventions such as exposure therapy, eye movement desensitization reprocessing (EMDR), and many kinds of creative approaches can be best utilized (Chesnay, 2013; Litam, 2017; Yakushko & Oksana, 2009).

In the third phase of recovery, reconnection, the emphasis is on rebuilding a life or building one for the first time. This phase may last for a lifetime, as the survivor creates meaning and purpose out of the disastrous events of her earlier life.

Barriers to service

Despite great strides in our understanding of trauma, victims of human trafficking challenge our legal, law enforcement, behavioral health, public health, and social service communities. These systems, unaccustomed to working so closely together, are suddenly expected to coalesce to address the pervasive service needs of this population. The reality is that our systems are not currently prepared to deal with the results of human trafficking. They are just beginning to understand what it is much less have appropriate services available. Victims emerging from trafficking situations often have numerous needs not easily met – lack of housing, lack of money, lack of organizational funding, lack of financial support to the victim, lack of funding for a sufficient length of time that treatment will take, and lack of appropriate treatment resources.

At the heart of our current political discourse is the issue of responsibility. We are failing to prevent and stop organized criminal behavior and the profiteering that comes from exploiting other people's labor that lies at the very core of our economic system. As long as that is the case, then the culture gives permission for the atrocities that are committed in the name of profit. A paradigm shift will be essential if we are to provide victims with adequate social, emotional and spiritual support for healing and preventing victimization from happening in the first place.

Conclusion

Considering all that may have happened in a young victim's life, how might you engage with a young victim and start to develop trust? How would you prioritize service delivery?

Unfortunately, more often than not victims of human trafficking have experienced sexual and physical abuse from those on whom they were reliant for basic needs. Young victims, often raised in poverty, easily fall for the promises and affections of their would-be traffickers. Various styles of recruitment and grooming are used by traffickers including fraud, rape, beatings, forced drug dependency, and threat of exposure, to create total isolation and dependency of victims. The intentional use of violence and kindness on behalf of the trafficker renders the victim helpless and tightly connected to the trafficker. Over time, victims essentially experience learned helplessness, believing there is no escape. Even if there is a way out, the victim will stay. The relationship between trafficker and victim is known as trauma bonding. The trauma bond is very powerful and impacts a victim's ability to leave the life and engage in treatment.

We know that victims who are able to exit their situation can have many needs including medical, housing, food, legal, financial, emotional, and substance abuse support. Often court-ordered to treatment and required to follow program mandates, victims have little choice about their future. In some cases the system actually replicates the process of the trafficker, forcing compliance for potential freedom. Victims may have a hard time adjusting to life in a residential setting. In fact, many run away and return to their traffickers. Residential treatment programs need to rely on structures to safely manage the youth they serve; however, they would better serve victims if they could provide flexibility, opportunities to individualize care, and create opportunities to maximize choice.

As stated above, diagnosing victims can be difficult owing to the numerous symptoms they present with. A better diagnostic way to view the survivors of trafficking is with the diagnosis of "complex PTSD" (CPTSD) which refers to a type of trauma that occurs repeatedly and cumulatively, usually over a period of time and within specific relationships and contexts. Understanding the impact of repetitive and cumulative trauma can help give a new perspective on the attitudes and behaviors that then unfold in the trafficking situation. When we understand how mind, body, and spirit have been impacted by cumulative trauma, then we can develop better intervention strategies.

Traffickers operate by taking advantage of a biological vulnerability that affects abused children: state-dependent learning. State-dependent learning combined with the learned helplessness and experienced lack of control over one's own physiological states associated with a traumatic experience or a series of traumatic experiences leads to a diminished sense of self-efficacy. The result is that even when the person could take action to prevent further harm, they seem unable to do so.

Traumatic memory often poses the greatest problems for people who have suffered repeated or severe traumatic experience as it places victims in a state that replicates when they were helpless, little and could not resist. Traffickers take full advantage of that to further empower themselves in victims' eyes.

Among the symptoms of trauma are self-harming behaviors that are often difficult for helpers to understand. Aside from self-mutilation, self-destructive eating behavior, another form of self-harm, may occur alone or with self-mutilation and can be understood as the nonverbal narration for what people cannot remember or their words cannot say.

When caregivers first encounter a trafficking victim, their unwillingness to be rescued is often quite puzzling. But we need to understand that people who suffer profound trauma may no longer feel that they are alive or that they deserve help or support, or that they have worth. It can take a trafficking victim a long time to recognize that there is benevolence, justice, meaning, or comfort in the world.

The mental health consequences of being trafficked are numerous and complex. Hopefully, this chapter has provided readers with information about mental health issues related to human trafficking and how to better help, understand and support trafficking victims' recovery. Being aware of and understanding risk factors, trauma bonding, Complex PTSD, traumatic reenactment and the Sequence Approach is essential information for those working with victims to have.

Despite great strides in our understanding of trauma, victims of human trafficking challenge our legal, law enforcement, behavioral health, public health, and social service communities. The reality is that our systems are not currently prepared to deal with the results of human trafficking. We are failing to prevent and stop organized criminal behavior and the profiteering that comes from exploiting other people's labor that lies at the very core of our economic system. As long as that is the case, then the culture gives permission for the atrocities that are committed in the name of profit. A paradigm shift will be essential if we are to provide victims with adequate social, emotional and spiritual support for healing and prevent victimization from happening in the first place.

Supplemental learning materials

Films/videos

Buckley, J. (Producer). (2013) *The making of a girl* [Video file]. Retrieved from https://youtu.be/ZvnRYte3PAk

Cruz, P. (Producer), & Pablos, D. (Director). (2015). *Las elegiadas [The Chosen Ones]* [Motion Picture] Mexico: Canana.

ECPAT International. (2011, October 28) *What I've been through is not who I am* [Video file]. Retrieved from https://youtu.be/BmmRTjoL3R0

Schisgall, D. (Co Director), & Alvarez, N. (Co-Director). (2007). *Very young girls* [Motion Picture] USA.

Books

Lloyd, R. (2011). *Girls like us: Fighting for a world where girls are not for sale, an activist finds her calling and heals herself.* New York, NY: HarperCollins.

References

Anda, R. F., Felitta, V. J., Bermner, J. D., Walker, J. D., Whitfield, C., Perry, B., & Dube, S. R. (2006). The enduring effects of abuse and related adverse experiences in childhood: A convergence of evidence from neurobiology and epidemiology. *Archives of Psychiatry and Clinical Neuroscience, 256*(3), 174–186.

Armstrong, J. (2017). Incorporating trauma into an assessment interview. In S. N. Gold (Ed.), *APA handbook of trauma psychology* (Volume 2: Trauma Practice, pp. 31–40). Washington, DC: American Psychological Association.

Bloom, S. L. (1994). The sanctuary model: Developing generic inpatient programs for the treatment of psychological trauma. In M. B. Williams & J. F. Sommer (Eds.), *Handbook of post-traumatic therapy, a practical guide to intervention, treatment, and research* (pp. 474–491) Westport, CT: Greenwood Publishing.

Bloom, S. L. (2009). Domestic violence. In P. O'Brien (Ed.), *Encyclopedia of gender and violence* (pp. 216–221). Thousand Oaks, CA: Sage

Bloom, S. L. (2017). The sanctuary model: Through the lens of moral safety. In J. Cook, C. J. Dalenberg, & S. Gold (Eds.), *Handbook of trauma psychology* (pp. 499–513). Washington, DC: American Psychological Association.

Bloom, S. L., Foderaro, J. F., & Ryan, R. A. (2006). *S.E.L.F.: A trauma-informed, psychoeducational group curriculum*: Retrieved from www.sanctuaryweb.com

Brewin, C. R. (2011). The nature and significance of memory disturbance in posttraumatic stress disorder. *Annual Review of Clinical Psychology*, 7(1), 203–227.

Chesnay, M. de. (2013). Psychiatric-mental health nurses and the sex trafficking pandemic. *Issues in Mental Health Nursing*, *34*(12), 901–907.

Cloitre, M., Courtois, C. A., Charuvastra, A., Carapezza, R., Stolbach, B. C., & Green, B. L. (2011). Treatment of complex PTSD: Results of the ISTSS expert clinician survey on best practices. *Journal of Traumatic Stress*, *24*(6), 615–627.

Cohen, J. A., et al. (2012). "Trauma-focused CBT for youth with complex trauma." *Child abuse & neglect* 36(6): 528–541.

Cole, J., Sprang, G., Lee, R., & Cohen, J. (2016). The trauma of commercial sexual exploitation of youth. *Journal of Interpersonal Violence*, *31*(1), 122–146.

Courtois, C. A. (2008). Complex trauma, complex reactions: Assessment and treatment. *Psychological Trauma: Theory, Research, Practice, & Policy*, *S*(1), 86–100.

Courtois, C. A., & Ford, J. D. (Eds.). (2009). *Treating complex traumatic stress disorders: An evidence-based guide.* New York, NY: Guilford Press.

Dalenberg, C. J., & Briere, J. (2017). Psychometric assessment of trauma. In S. N. Gold (Ed.), *APA handbook of trauma psychology* (pp. 41–63). Washington, DC: American Psychological Association.

Dube, S., Felitti, V., Dong, M., Chapman, D., Giles, W., & Anda, R. (2003). Childhood abuse, neglect, and household dysfunction and the risk of illicit drug use: The adverse childhood experiences study. *Pediatrics*, *111*(3), 564–572.

Dutton, D., & Painter, S. L. (1981). Traumatic bonding: The development of emotional attachments in battered women and other relationships of intermittent abuse. *Victimology: An International Journal*, *6*(1–4), 139–155.

Edwards, V., Anda, R., Dube, S., Dong, M., Chapman, D., & Felitti, V. (2005). The wide-ranging health consequences of adverse childhood experiences In K. Kendall-Tackett & S. Giacomoni (Eds.), *Victimization of children and youth: Patterns of abuse, response strategies.* Kingston, NJ: Civic Research Institute.

Farber, S. K. (1997). Self-medication, traumatic reenactment and somatic expression in bulimic and self-mutilating behavior. *Clinical Social Work Journal*, *25*(1), 87–106.

Ford, J. D., Grasso, D. J., Elhai, J. D., & Courtois, C. A. (2015). *Posttraumatic stress disorder: Scientific and professional dimensions* (2nd ed.). San Diego, CA: Elsevier.

Freyd, J. J. (1996). *Betrayal trauma: The logic of forgetting childhood abuse.* Cambridge, MA: Harvard University Press.

Handelsman, L., Stein, J. A., Bernstein, D. P., Oppenheim, S. E., Rosenblum, A., & Magura, S. (2000). A latent variable analysis of coexisting emotional deficits in substance abusers: Alexithymia, hostility, and PTSD. *Addictive Behaviors*, *25*(3), 423–428.

Harber, K. D., & Pennebaker, J. W. (1992). Overcoming traumatic memories. In S. A. Christianson (Ed.), *The handbook of emotion and memory: Research and theory* (pp. 359–387). Hillsdale, NJ: Lawrence Erlbaum.

Hardy, V. L., Compton, K. D., & McPhatter, V. S. (2013a). Domestic minor sex Trafficking. *Affilia*, *28*(1), 8–18.

Hardy, V. L., Compton, K. D., & McPhatter, V. S. (2013b). Domestic minor sex trafficking: Practice implications for mental health professionals. *Affilia*, *28*(1), 8–18.

Hartinger-Saunders, R. M. (2017). Mandated reporters' perceptions of and encounters with domestic minor sex trafficking of adolescent females in the United States. *American Journal of Orthopsychiatry*, *87*(3), 195–205.

Herman, J. L. (1992a). Complex PTSD: A syndrome in survivors of prolonged and repeated trauma. *Journal of Traumatic Stress*, *5*, 377–391.

Herman, J. L. (1992b). *Trauma and recovery.* New York, NY: Basic Books.

Herman, J. L. (1998). *Trauma and recovery: The aftermath of violence – From domestic abuse to political terror* (14th ed.). New York, NY: Basic Books.

Herman, J. L., Perry, J. C., & van der Kolk, B. A. (1989). Childhood trauma in borderline personality disorder. *American Journal of Psychiatry*, *146*(4), 490–495.

Hubble, M. A., Duncan, B. L., & Miller, S. D. (Eds.). (1999). *The heart and soul of change: What works in therapy.* Washington, DC: American Psychological Press.

James, B. (1994). *Handbook for treatment of attachment trauma problems in children.* New York, NY: Lexington Books.

Janis, I. L. (1982). Decision making under stress. In L. Goldberger & S. Breznitz (Eds.), *Handbook of stress: Theoretical and clinical aspects* (pp. 69–87). New York, NY: Free Press.

Janoff-Bulman, R. (1992). *Shattered assumptions: Towards a new psychology of trauma*. New York, NY: Free Press.

Krystal, H. (1978). Trauma and affects. *Psychoanalytic Study of the Child, 33*, 81–116.

Krystal, H. (1988). *Integration and self healing: Affect, trauma, alexithymia*. Hillsdale, NJ: Analytic Press.

LaViolette, A. D., & Barnett, O. W. (2000). *It could happen to anyone: Why battered women stay* (2nd ed.). Thousand Oaks, CA: Sage Publications.

LeDoux, J. (1994). Emotion, memory, and the brain. *Scientific American, 270*, 50–57.

LeDoux, J. (1996). *The emotional brain: The mysterious underpinnings of emotional life*. New York, NY: Simon and Schuster.

Lennick, D., & Kiel, F. (2005). *Moral intelligence: Enhancing business performance and leadership success*. Upper Saddle River, NJ: Wharton School Publishing.

Litam, S.D.A. (2017). Human sex trafficking in America: What counselors need to know. *The Professional Counselor*, 7(1), 45–61.

Lumley, M. A., & Norman, S. (1996). Alexithymia and health care utilization. *Psychosomatic Medicine, 58*(3), 197–202.

Maier, S. F., & Seligman, M. P. (1976). Learned helplessness: Theory and evidence. *Journal of Experimental Psychology, 105*, 3–46.

Maxia, D., Robert, F. A., Shanta, R. D., Wayne, H. G., & Vincent, J. F. (2003). The relationship of exposure to childhood sexual abuse to other forms of abuse, neglect, and household dysfunction during childhood. *Child Abuse and Neglect*, 27, 625.

National Research Council, & Institute of Medicine. (2014). *Confronting commercial sexual exploitation and sex trafficking of minors in the United States: A guide for providers of victim and support services*. Washington, DC: National Academies Press.

NIDA. (2002). *Stress and substance abuse: Community drug alert bulletin*. Rockville, MD. Retrieved from www.drugabuse.gov/StressAlert/StressAlert.html

Norcross, J. C., Krebs, P. M., & Prochaska, J. O. (2011). Stages of change. *Journal of Clinical Psychology, 67*(2), 143–154.

O'Connor, M. and G. Healy (2006). The Links between Prostitution and Sex Trafficking: A Briefing Handbook. http://www.catwinternational.org/Home/Article/175-the-links-between-prostitution-and-sex-trafficking-a-briefing-handbook, European Women's Lobby and Coalition Against Trafficking Women.

Pascual-Leone, A., Kim, J., & Morrison, O.-P. (2017). Working with victims of human trafficking. *Journal of Contemporary Psychotherapy, 47*(1), 51–59.

Perry, B. D., & Pate, J. E. (1994). Neurodevelopment and the psychobiological roots of post-traumatic stress disorder. In L. Koziol & C. Stout (Eds.), *In the neuropsychology of mental disorders: A practical guide* (pp. 81–98). Springfield: Charles C. Thomas.

Perry, J. C., Herman, J. L., Van der Kolk, B. A., & Hoke, L. A. (1990). Psychotherapy and psychological trauma in borderline personality disorder. *Psychiatric Annals, 20*, 33–43.

Pole, N. (2017). Behavioral and psychophysiological assessment of trauma. In S. N. Gold (Ed.), *APA handbook of trauma psychology* (Vol. 2: Trauma Practice, pp. 65–88). Washington, DC: American Psychological Association.

Prochaska, J. O., Norcross, J. C., & Diclemente, C. C. (1994). *Changing for good: A revolutionary six-stage program for overcoming bad habits and moving your life positively forward*. New York, NY: HarperCollins.

Rafferty, Y. (2008). The impact of trafficking on children: Psychological and social policy perspectives. *Child Development Perspectives, 2*(1), 13–18.

Roth, S., Newman, E., Pelcovitz, D., Kolk, B. v. d., & Mandel, F. S. (1997). Complex PTSD in victims exposed to sexual and physical abuse: Results from the DSM-IV field trial for posttraumatic stress disorder. *Journal of Traumatic Stress, 10*(4), 539–555.

Sashin, J. (1993). Duke Ellington: The creative process and the ability to experience and tolerate affect. In S. L. Ablon, D. Brown, E. J. Khantzian, & J. E. Mack (Eds.), *Human feelings: Explorations in affect development and meaning*. Hillsdale, NJ: The Analytic Press.

Shay, J. (2003). *Odysseus in America: Combat trauma and the trials of homecoming*. New York, NY: Scribner.

Shonkoff, J. P., Garner, A. S., Siegel, B. S., Dobbins, M. I., Earls, M. F., McGuinn, L., Pascoe, J., & Wood, D. L. (2012). The lifelong effects of early childhood adversity and toxic stress. *Pediatrics, 129*(1), e232–e246.

Smith, L. A., Vardaman, S. H., & Snow, M. A. (2009). *The national report on domestic minor sex trafficking*: Shared Hope International. Retrieved August 14, 2017, from https://sharedhope.org/wp-content/uploads/2012/09/SHI_National_Report_on_DMST_2009.pdf

Strenz, T. (1982). The Stockholm syndrome. In F. Ochberg & D. Soskis (Eds.), *Victims of terrorism* (pp. 149–164). Boulder, CO: Westview.

Valent, P. (2007). Eight survival strategies in traumatic stress. *Traumatology (Tallahassee, Fla.), 13*(2), 4–14.

Van der Kolk, B. A. (1989). The compulsion to repeat the trauma: Reenactment, revictimization, and masochism. *Psychiatric Clinics of North America, 12*, 389–411.

Van der Kolk, B. A. (1994). The body keeps the score: Memory and the evolving psychobiology of posttraumatic stress. *Harvard Review of Psychiatry, 1*, 253–265.

Van der Kolk, B. A. (1996a). The body keeps the score: Approaches to the psychobiology of posttraumatic stress disorder. In B. A. van der Kolk, A. C. McFarlane, & L. Weisaeth (Eds.), *Traumatic stress: The effects of overwhelming experience on mind, body and society* (pp. 214–241). New York, NY: Guilford Press.

Van der Kolk, B. A. (1996b). Trauma and memory. In B. Van der Kolk, A. McFarlane, & L. Weisaeth (Eds.), *Traumatic stress: The effects of overwhelming experience on mind, body and society* (pp. 279–302). New York, NY: Guilford Press.

Van der Kolk, B. A. (1996c). The complexity of adaptation to trauma self-regulation, stimulus discrimination, and characterological development. In B. A. van der Kolk, A. C. McFarlane, & L. Weisaeth (Eds.), *Traumatic stress: The effects of overwhelming experience on mind, body and society* (pp. 182–213). New York, NY: Guilford Press.

Van der Kolk, B. A., & Ducey, C. P. (1989). The psychological processing of traumatic experience: Rorschach patterns in PTSD. *Journal of Traumatic Stress, 2*, 259–274.

Van der Kolk, B. A., & Fisler, R. (1995). Dissociation and the fragmentary nature of traumatic memories: An exploratory study. *Journal of Traumatic Stress, 8*(4), 505–525.

Van der Kolk, B. A., & Van der Hart, O. (1989). Pierre Janet and the breakdown of adaptation in psychological trauma. *American Journal of Psychiatry, 146*, 1530–1540.

Vera Institute of Justice. (2014). *Out of the shadows: Screening for human trafficking and guidelines for administering the trafficking victim identification tool (TVIT)*. Brooklyn and New York, NY: Vera Institute of Justice. Retrieved August 16, 2017, from www.vera.org/publications/out-of-the-shadows-identification-of-victims-of-human-trafficking.

Yakushko, O., & Oksana, Y. (2009). Human trafficking: A review for mental health professionals. *International Journal for the Advancement of Counselling, 31*(3), 158–167.

Zimmerman, C., Hossain, M., Yun, K., Roche, B., Morison, L., & Watts, C. (2006). *Stolen smiles: A summary report on the physical and psychological health consequences of women and adolescents trafficked in Europe*. London: The London School of Hygiene & Tropical Medicine.

Zimmerman, C., & Pocock, N. (2013). Human trafficking and mental health: "My wounds are inside; they are not visible." *The Brown Journal of World Affairs, 19*(2), 265.

9

SYNCOPE AND MALNUTRITION IN AN ADOLESCENT GIRL

Kanani E. Titchen and Hanni M. Stoklosa

Abstract

A 17-year-old girl from Venezuela with no significant medical history presents to a New York City emergency department after a recent episode of syncope. She is disoriented and withdrawn, and her father speaks on her behalf. On physical exam, she is underweight with tachycardia, exhibits diffuse abdominal tenderness, and displays poor eye contact. Labs are significant for mild microcytic anemia and electrolyte abnormalities, and there is concern for anorexia nervosa and malnourishment. After hospitalization and subsequent follow-up visits, a history of abuse is brought to light, and concern for both labor trafficking and sexual exploitation emerge. Because patients who are victims of human trafficking rarely self-disclose, it is important for healthcare professionals to receive training to recognize the signs of human trafficking, to establish a relationship built on trust, to utilize a trauma-informed and victim-centered approach to care, to provide close clinical follow up, and to be familiar with nationwide and local resources for victims of human trafficking.

Learning Objectives

At the end of the chapter, readers will be able to:

1. Articulate one push factor and one pull factor for human trafficking;
2. Describe 3 distinct phases of human trafficking;
3. Identify at least 3 key steps to a trauma-informed approach when working with victims and survivors of human trafficking; and
4. Give examples of at least 2 resources available to victims of human trafficking.

Key Terms: human trafficking; modern-day slavery; child sexual abuse; commercial sexual exploitation; labor trafficking; forced labor.

Case study: FM

FM is a 17-year-old girl with no significant medical history who presents to a New York City emergency department after a recent episode of syncope. Her father accompanies her. The patient states that she was in her usual state of health when all of a sudden she "didn't feel well." At around 8:00 p.m. she was doing the dishes when she began to feel short of breath, "weak," and dizzy. She denies any chest pain or palpitations, nausea, or sweating. Her father heard a "thud," found FM on the floor of the kitchen, and called 911. She does not remember falling and does not know how long she "blacked out." There was no shaking or eye rolling per report. By the time emergency medical service personnel arrived, FM had regained consciousness but appeared confused and gave her location to the emergency medical technician as "Miami, Florida."[a] She states that she started feeling a little better in the ambulance after emergency medical technicians gave her oxygen.

FM denies drug ingestion or recent trauma. She takes no medications. An emergency medicine nurse notes that FM's last food intake was at 6:00 a.m. that morning.[b] FM does not know if she hit her head, but she reports no scalp bruising, pain, or laceration. She denies tingling in her extremities or feeling anxious or depressed, but she does experience sleep disturbance with late sleep onset and early awakening. She has no known psychiatric history, and there is no primary medical doctor involved in her care.[c] She complains of "months" of epigastric pain and pelvic pain. Her father states that she has never complained to him of pain, sleeps quite well in his estimation, and speculates that FM is "just quite shaken up."[d]

The patient's father says that his English is better than FM's, so he answers most of the questions.[e] He reports no known allergies, no prior surgeries, and that FM is up to date on vaccines but that the immunization record is in their native country of Venezuela. Family history is significant for no early heart disease or seizure disorders.

In terms of social history, her father says that FM lives with him and her three younger brothers (16, 15, and 14 years old) but often spends time at her stepmother's house "down the street" with her stepmother's mother (Ms. D) and her three younger stepsiblings (9 months, 20 months, and 4 years old). FM, her father, and her brothers are from Venezuela and immigrated to the United States separately over the past ten years, with FM's father immigrating first, followed by FM's brothers, and then followed by FM approximately one year ago. FM's father states that FM "doesn't do anything" – she does not work or attend school.[f] He states that her stepmother's mother Ms. D gives her three meals per day, but FM "doesn't eat." FM looks at the floor and mumbles that she "isn't hungry."[g] When asked about activities and friends, FM states that she likes to spend time with her family, prefers to stay at home all day, and has no friends.[h] On confidential history taking, FM endorses history of sexual activity, no drug use, and no suicidal ideation. She denies sexual abuse or trauma.

In the emergency department, vital signs are as follows: temperature 97.9°F, heart rate 106 beats per minute, respiratory rate 18 breaths per minute, blood pressure 96/54, 100% oxygen saturation in room air. Weight is 40 kg, and body mass index is 15.1 kg/m .[i]

The physical exam is significant for a thin girl wincing in pain but with otherwise flat and withdrawn affect. She displays poor eye contact, is reticent to answer questions, and appears mildly drowsy but is otherwise alert and oriented.[g] She demonstrates diffuse abdominal pain to palpation but no focal findings. Extremities are cool, and there is a 3/6 systolic ejection murmur on cardiac auscultation. There is no thyromegaly. She has Tanner 5 breasts and Tanner 4 pubic hair, and pelvic exam demonstrates no lesions or abnormal vaginal discharge, and no cervical motion, adnexal, or uterine tenderness.

Labs are significant for white blood cells 3.0 K/uL, hemoglobin 10.8 g/dL with MCV 72 fL, lactic acid 6.8 mmol/L, serum potassium 3.0 mEq/L, phosphorus 2.3 mg/dL, magnesium 1.5 mg/dL, and calcium 8.4 mg/dL, negative acetaminophen, salicylate, and alcohol levels.[i] Head CT is normal. EKG is significant for prolonged QTc of 500 ms. HIV antigen and antibody test is negative. FM receives a normal saline bolus and a dose of famotidine and is admitted for further management. The hospital floor nurse comments that FM's father and stepmother remain at the bedside during the entirety of her admission.[j] (See Table 9.1.)

Table 9.1 Salient points from the case study indicate possible human trafficking

	FM: Anatomy of a Human Trafficking Case
a	She is disoriented and does not know what city or state she is in.
b	She has not eaten recently.
c	Despite recent immigration status, she has no primary physician.
d	Her "father" minimizes her illness.
e	An older man answers questions for her and speaks on her behalf.
f	Despite one year in the United States, she has no job and is not in school.
g	Her body language indicates extreme discomfort and unease.
h	Despite one year in the United States with an extended "family," she has no friends.
i	She is malnourished.
j	She is never left alone.

Clinical Questions to Consider for the Physician

1 What is human trafficking?
2 What causes human trafficking?
3 Who is at risk for human trafficking?
4 What are some of the common physical and psychological health sequelae of human trafficking?
5 Something just feels "off." What are the factors in FM's history and physical exam that should raise my clinical suspicion for FM's being a victim of labor trafficking?
6 The physician approach: How do I approach a patient who I think is a victim of human trafficking? What do I ask?
7 Do I have an obligation to report? If the patient is a minor, what are my obligations as a mandated reporter if I suspect labor trafficking? Do these differ from my obligations if I suspect sex trafficking?
8 What are some of the resources available to me and to my patient?

Introduction: what is human trafficking?

Several details of FM's history and findings on physical exam are concerning for human trafficking, defined by the U.S. Trafficking Victims Protection Act (TVPA) as "acts involved in recruiting, harboring, transporting, providing, or obtaining a person for compelled service or commercial sex acts through the use of force, fraud, or coercion" (U.S. Department of State, 2010). Thus, in the United States, a crucial component to proving human trafficking is proving *lack* of consent *and* the presence of force, fraud, or coercion. One of the most common forms of coercion is "debt bondage," an illegal practice where the victim is isolated from the community and then forced to provide services to pay off some fabricated debt for immigration, housing, or other living expenses (Hodge, 2008; Sabella, 2011).

Given the clandestine nature of human trafficking, estimates of prevalence are difficult to calculate. However, the International Labour Organization (ILO), using 54 surveys involving 71,000 interviews with respondents across 48 countries, found that worldwide, modern-day slavery, including human trafficking for labor, sex, and organs as well as forced marriage, is a major public health problem and a violation of human rights that involves an estimated 40.3 million people each year (ILO, 2017). Labor trafficking comprises 24.9 million people and includes exploitation in a variety of sectors including domestic servitude, farm labor, and construction. Sex trafficking includes exploitation for commercial sexual acts including child pornography. In 2016, children represented 21% of victims of commercial sexual exploitation (ILO, 2017). A third major type of human trafficking, organ trafficking, involves the removal of vital organs (e.g. kidneys, liver), eggs, and uteri from victims for a small sum of money or to pay off a debt (whether real or fabricated) for the purposes of black market transplantation. In fact, in 2017, the Polaris Project identified up to 35 types of human trafficking in data collected through Polaris-operated hotlines (Anthony, Penrose, & Jakiel, 2017).

What is human trafficking?

U.S. law delineates that for the two most common forms of human trafficking, labor and for sex, force, fraud, or coercion must be proved unless the victim is under the age of 18 years *and* is being trafficked for commercial sex (Justice for Victims of Trafficking Act, 2015; U.S. TVPA, 2000). Therefore, for a 17-year-old such as FM in the case study, force, fraud, or coercion must be proved even though FM is a minor. If, on the other hand, it is discovered that FM is the victim of sex trafficking, no coercion would need to be proved. Even if FM had consented to commercial sex, it is reasoned that minors do not have the capacity to consent to sexual acts for pay.

Importantly, 22% of victims of labor trafficking also are sexually exploited. The majority of transnational sex and labor trafficking victims are female (ILO, 2017), and roughly half of these are recruited while under the age of 18 (U.S. Trafficking In Persons Report, 2007). However, *adult* females are exploited more than any other group, and migrant and domestic workers (e.g. house cleaners, cooks, and home servants) are considered to be quite vulnerable (ILO, 2017). Domestic workers, in fact, are not protected under federal laws such as the National Labor Relations Act, the Fair Labor Standards Act, or the Occupational Safety and Health Act that ensure a maximum number of hours, minimum wage, safe working conditions, and overtime pay. Further, these workers are not protected under civil rights laws against discrimination based on age, race, religion, sexual orientation, or nationality (Domestic Worker Under Labor Law, n.d.; U.S. Department of Labor Fact Sheet, 2013). Often, these workers are subject not only to poor working conditions and labor exploitation but also to sexual abuse and exploitation.

In contrast to the TVPA cited above, the United Nations Protocol to Prevent, Suppress and Punish Trafficking in Persons defines human trafficking in similar language but stipulates that *even if a victim offers consent*, if her consent was obtained while she was under duress or vulnerable to a person of greater control or power, she is nonetheless a victim of human trafficking. In short, the consent of the victim is not a factor (United Nations, 2001).

While both sex trafficking and labor trafficking are under-reported, the disparity is striking in the United States between sex trafficking prosecutions (98 arrests and 52 convictions in fiscal year 2014) and labor trafficking prosecutions (one arrest and one conviction in fiscal year 2014) when we recall that labor trafficking constitutes over 60% of all human trafficking. Furthermore, only 8.7% of all U.S. federal prosecutions for human trafficking in 2014 in the United States involved forced labor (OSCE, 2016).

What leads to human trafficking?

Human trafficking thrives because of a variety of push factors and pull factors (see Bloom and Brotherton, Chapter 8, this volume). It is impossible to discuss human trafficking without mentioning push factors that are largely grounded in socioeconomics: poverty; discrimination based on race and ethnicity, gender, and sexual orientation; lack of access to free and quality education; social, family, and political violence; natural disasters; lack of affordable housing; and lack of employment opportunities. Therefore, a person who finds herself marginalized and/or without the means to support herself in her home community may seek opportunity elsewhere, even if that opportunity involves considerable risk. Social protections such as access to housing, medical care, education, and job training are critical to minimizing these push factor vulnerabilities.

What causes human trafficking?

Pull factors surround and impact almost all of us. They include a demand for affordable or cheap food, products, and labor, maximizing profit; male sexual demand; and the need for healthy vital organs for transplantation. A significant pull factor is profit, and trafficking in humans is highly profitable. According to the International Labour Office of the ILO, human trafficking is a $150 billion industry, with approximately $50 billion derived from labor trafficking in such industries as construction, mining, manufacturing, agriculture, fishing, forestry, and domestic work, and almost $100 billion stemming from commercial sexual exploitation (ILO, 2014). Each woman or girl who is a victim of sex trafficking may generate profits of approximately $100,000 for her trafficker, and studies show that sexual exploitation may yield a return on investment of up to 1,000%, largely due to the fact that a victim can be sold over and over again night after night (ILO, 2014).

Technological methods facilitate the sale and resale of humans, and especially minors for sex trafficking. These methods include social media commonly used by children such as Facebook, Instagram, Twitter, and Snapchat, as well as well-established online publications with "personals" sections (Dawson, 2017). Traffickers, in fact, have embraced the vocabulary of emojis in order to advertise their underage victims without being detected by law enforcement (Van Grove, 2017). As of this writing, little empirical research exists regarding the extent to which online technologies are used in sex and labor trafficking (Latonero, 2011).

Who is at risk for human trafficking?

Who is at risk for human trafficking?

As discussed earlier, people who experience poverty or who are otherwise marginalized are at increased risk for human trafficking, but human trafficking affects people of any race, ethnicity, nationality, sex, sexual orientation, and class. Particularly at risk in the United States are children in foster care or in the child welfare and juvenile justice systems; runaway and homeless youth; migrant laborers (including children); foreign domestic workers (Domestic Workers united, n.d); American Indians and Alaska Natives; those with limited English proficiency; and lesbian, gay, bisexual, and transgender individuals. Because foster care services and protections do not extend past the age of 18 years, transitional youth aged 18–24 years are especially targeted by traffickers (Domestic Abuse Intervention Project, n.d.). On the other hand, traffickers also target younger children because they are easier to manipulate and control due to limited life experiences and vulnerable social standing, and because they can be exploited longer (Executive Board of ACOG, 2017). Sex traffickers easily form bonds with their victims through promises of housing, financial security, love, and even marriage (Stolpe, 2014).

Physical and psychological sequelae of human trafficking: three stages

Whether for labor or for sexual exploitation, we can think about human trafficking–related health issues as occurring within three distinct phases: (1) pre-trafficking or prior to victimization, (2) during the transportation or harboring phase, and (3) during the destination phase or the point of exploitation.

Persons trafficked for labor in the pre-trafficking phase may suffer chronic health conditions such as diabetes, asthma, or hypertension. Depending on their pre-trafficking exposures, they may be chronically exposed to infectious diseases that are prevalent in their communities such as cholera, typhoid, malaria, hepatitis, or tuberculosis (Human Smuggling and Trafficking Center, 2008). Persons trafficked for sex overwhelmingly have been sexually and/or physically abused in the past and may also have a history of substance use disorders (ILO, 2000).

In cases of labor trafficking, an "employer" may offer a promise of work in such desirable industries as massage, fashion, and television, or highly lucrative work in fishing, agriculture, and mining. This "employer" may be known to the victim as a friend or even a family member.

Perpetrators of trafficking, especially sex trafficking, may use a process of "grooming" to gain their victims' trust, draw their victims away from any potentially stable relationship or environment such as a parent or sibling or home or school, and create a relationship of dependency. In cases of sex trafficking, a "Romeo" or "boyfriend" approach may be used, whereby the victim is showered with attention and material gifts such as food, drugs, jewelry, clothing, and money, and enticed to initiate a sexual relationship with her "boyfriend." She will be encouraged to stay away from home for increasing lengths of time. Soon after, the victim is invited to live with her "boyfriend" or take a short trip or "vacation" with him, and it is typically at this time that the victim will be asked to reimburse her boyfriend or to contribute to the "family" income by having sex with other men for money. If she refuses to cooperate, she frequently will be reminded that no one loves her as much as her "boyfriend," that she is "damaged goods" and nobody wants her, and that she has nowhere else to go. The victim and/or her family may be subjected to threats and violence. In some cases, a victim of trafficking will be encouraged to recruit other children from schools, malls, bus stops, or other areas in order to improve her own status with her trafficker (Human Smuggling and Trafficking Center, 2008).

During the transportation or harboring phase, victims of labor and sex trafficking both may be exposed to crowded and unsanitary living conditions such as confinement to a shipping container or a van or a room lacking toilets and plumbing, thus increasing the risk of exposure to communicable diseases, starvation, suffocation, sleep deprivation, and physical and sexual violence.

What are some of the common physical and psychological health sequelae of human trafficking?

Finally, at the point of exploitation (destination phase), victims of labor and sex trafficking both may experience unsanitary living conditions, lack of clean water and adequate food, unsafe working conditions, long work hours, sleep deprivation, exposure to toxic chemicals and/or addictive substances, lack of safety training, and lack of healthcare. In many cases, traffickers control their victims through the use of psychological manipulation, confiscation of immigration and identification documents, physical and/or sexual abuse, threats of harm to the victim or the victim's family, and threats of deportation (Turner-Moss, Zimmerman, Howard, & Oram, 2014; Zimmerman et al., 2008). "House rules" may be established to dictate how victims are to interact with authorities, customers, and other victims, and to clarify expected daily or nightly quotas for income. House rules may be enforced with public displays of violence as a warning to other victims (Human Smuggling and Trafficking Center, Department of State, 2008).

The "Power and Control" wheel (see Figure 9.1) originally was created to describe the actions that a batterer uses to dominate his intimate partner in cases of domestic violence and intimate partner violence, and this visual aid has since been adapted to represent the pattern of actions that traffickers may use to intentionally control or dominate victims of human trafficking (Domestic Abuse Intervention Project, n.d.). A trafficker systematically uses threats, intimidation, and coercion to instill fear in the victim: these behaviors are the spokes of the wheel. Physical and sexual violence (or the ever-present threat of these) bind the victim to the trafficker. This violence or constant threat of violence is the rim of the wheel (Domestic Abuse Intervention Project, n.d.).

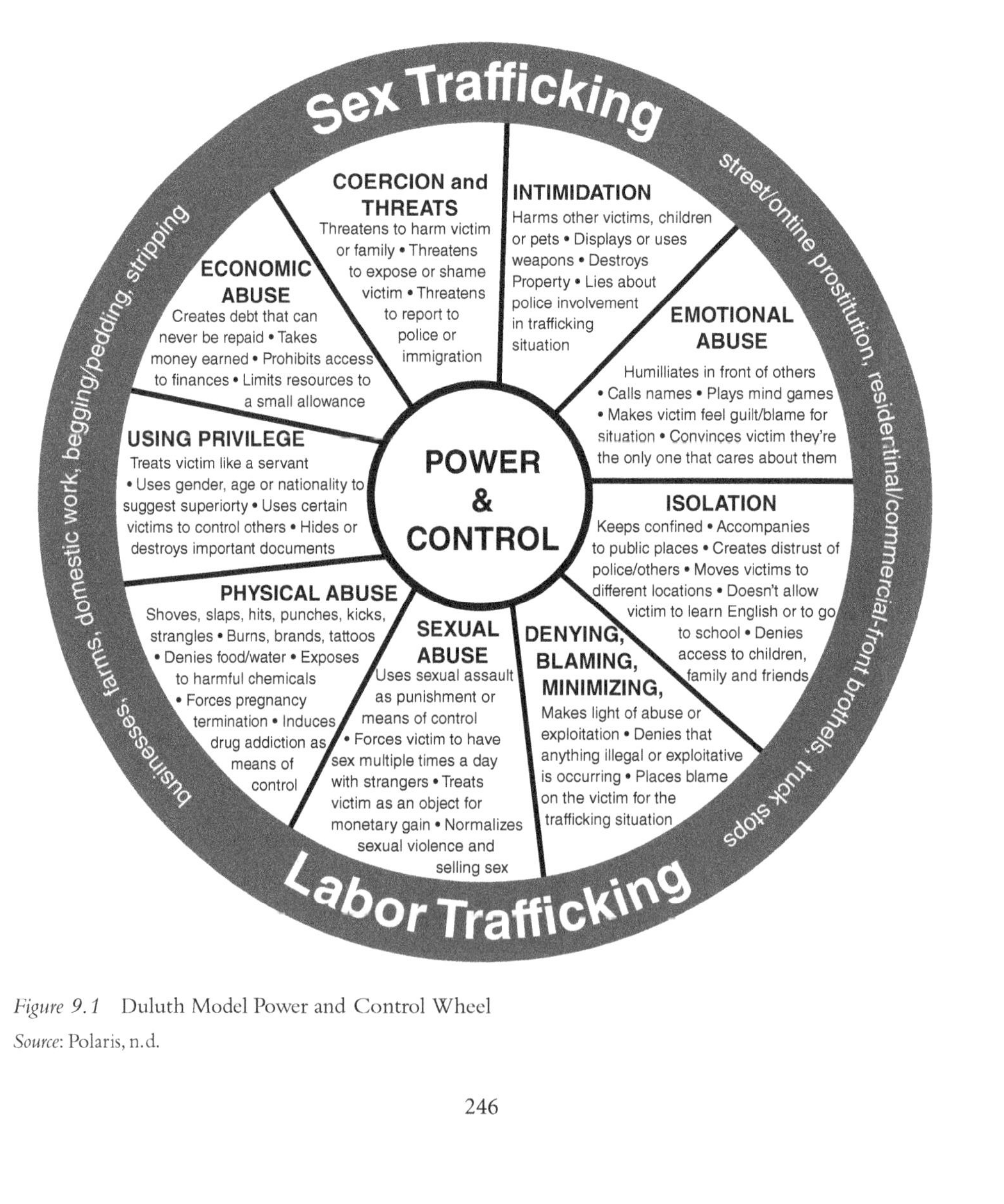

Figure 9.1 Duluth Model Power and Control Wheel

Source: Polaris, n.d.

Physical and psychological sequelae of human trafficking as related to the case of FM

In considering the diagnosis of human trafficking, it is important to maintain a wide differential diagnosis and address accompanying illnesses. In FM's case, the significant weight loss could be attributable to an autoimmune or immune-mediated condition such as inflammatory bowel disease (IBD), a restrictive eating disorder such as anorexia nervosa, a mental health issue such as severe anxiety, an infectious disease such as HIV-related malnutrition, or a socioeconomic issue such as poverty and related inadequate nutrition. Severe malnourishment raises concern for electrolyte abnormalities and potential for prolonged QTc with risk of cardiac arrhythmia and failure (Swenne & Larsson, 1999); in FM's case, these electrolyte abnormalities were addressed both acutely and in the long term. Laboratory studies ruled out IBD. Upon further questioning and examination, FM did not endorse any body dysmorphism, making typical anorexia nervosa unlikely. Anxiety seemed to play a significant role, but the etiology of FM's anxiety remained in question; perhaps her unease was related to her immigrant status, but further history-taking would be required to clarify FM's background. The patient's history was not consistent with increased risk of HIV, and indeed HIV testing was negative. Abdominal pain was attributed largely to hunger, although FM seemed to have lost any sense of feeling hungry and did not experience normal hunger cues, even after psychiatric counseling and intervention for low weight. By report, the family was not impoverished, and an abundance of food was seemingly available. It became clear that FM's chronic abdominopelvic pain likely was caused by hunger and possibly also to sexual abuse, although the latter would require careful history-taking in a confidential, trauma-informed manner. Female victims of human trafficking may present with chronic pelvic pain as a result of sexual abuse, sexually transmitted infections, late presentation for reproductive pathology such as masses or torsion or endometriosis, and/or pregnancy (Powell, 2014; Titchen, Katz, Martinez, & White, 2016).

In the emergency department, the physician examiner noted poor eye contact and a flat and withdrawn affect – signs that are consistent with depression. While mood disorders may be associated with malnourishment and anorexia nervosa (Kaye et al., 1987), the psychological impacts of human trafficking also are profound, and history-taking may be complicated by mental health issues such as post-traumatic stress disorder, depression, anxiety, disorientation, and traumatic bonding or Stockholm syndrome, a condition whereby some victims form an emotional bond with their abusers (McClain & Garrity, 2011; Office of Refugee Resettlement, 2017; Oram, Khondoker, Abas, Broadbent, & Howard, 2015; Zimmerman et al., 2008). Stockholm syndrome was first described after a 1973 bank heist in Sweden, where hostages developed sympathies for their captor (Westcott, 2013). Similarly, victims of human trafficking may develop sympathy and "love" for their trafficker and for being allowed to live. During FM's hospitalization, a social worker noted the variations in FM's narrative with each subsequent interview, as well as her "sense of isolation, her flat affect, and some anxiety." The complex family dynamic was not fully explored, and FM herself was withdrawn and appeared to be uncomfortable speaking without her father present.

Something just feels "off"

The history for FM and her illness raised several red flags. Many patients who have been victims of human trafficking present to healthcare settings while still being exploited (Baldwin, Eisenman, Sayles, Ryan, & Chuang, 2011; Lederer & Wetzel, 2014). They may be accompanied by an adult posing as a family member who is actually the trafficker, or it may be a family member who is exploiting them (Macy & Graham, 2012) (see Table 9.1).

Despite living in the United States for over one year, FM had no job, had no friends, did not attend school, had no primary care physician on record, and had very little medical history available. FM presented with severe malnourishment, nutritional anemia, and evidence of hemodynamic instability (status post-syncope). FM was consistently interviewed with her father present in the emergency department, and her father or stepmother was present and at the bedside while she was hospitalized. She was rarely alone. Further, FM requested that her father be present for interviews, perhaps because she was uncomfortable as a fairly recent immigrant but also possibly because she was coached to request this. Multiple studies show that adolescents more willingly engage with healthcare professionals when seeking sexual and reproductive services when confidentiality is structurally guaranteed (Bender & Fulbright, 2013). One way to ensure confidentiality for patients is through enforcement of "policy" that all patients aged 12 and over are afforded private time with their physicians.

What are the factors in FM's history and physical exam that should raise clinical suspicion for FM's being a victim of labor trafficking?

In many cases, victims may be unaware that they are victims of a crime, or they may be unaware of their rights and instead may fear that the health professional will report them (Office of Refugee Resettlement, 2017). Because they may fear being reported to U.S. Immigration and Customs Enforcement and subsequent deportation, patients may not divulge private aspects of their histories or even seek medical care if they believe that their privacy will be compromised – whether to family members or to state officials. Health professionals must establish trust by first stating explicitly their ability and willingness to protect their patients' privacy and confidentiality according to physician-patient privilege. In this vein, physicians also must explain explicitly any state-imposed limits to confidentiality for patients who are minors and for patients who are deemed a harm to themselves or others.

In FM's case, it was not until an adolescent medicine physician conducted a lengthy confidential adolescent interview with the patient alone that FM was able to tell her story in private.

Case study: FM (continued)

At an emergency medicine follow-up visit in the adolescent medicine clinic three days later, FM reported that she did all of the cooking and cleaning for her father and brothers and then did the same at her "stepmother's" house while also being responsible for the three younger children; she did this without pay and without freedom to leave the home. Hours for sleep were designated from 11:00 p.m. until 5:00 a.m., and FM was afforded no day off. Meals were given twice daily and consisted of one egg, a slice of bread, and either fruit juice or milk.

At her second follow-up visit to the adolescent medicine clinic two weeks later for a weight check, FM was accompanied by her "stepmother" – discovered at this visit to be a "friend of the family" and not actually romantically or legally involved with the patient's father at all. Therefore, the stepmother's home – where the patient spent much of her time – was not really the patient's home, and the "stepmother" and "stepsiblings" were not the patient's family at all.

At her third follow-up visit to adolescent medicine another two weeks later, the patient disclosed a history of sexual abuse in her native Venezuela at the hands of her biological mother's boyfriend when FM was nine years old. FM was left in charge of her three brothers and was forced to stop going to school. Her mother and the boyfriend disappeared, and (as their father had already emigrated to the United States) FM and her brothers were sent to live with a paternal aunt. The paternal aunt's husband began molesting FM at age 13 years, and this continued for over a year with a threat of rape if FM told anyone. FM was also beaten by her uncle with a "belt or whatever he could find" if the house was untidy or for other minor infractions. Her brothers were sent to the United States to be with the father. Finally, FM was sent to the United States to care for her brothers and father and to work for another family.

The medical professional approach

Although victims of human trafficking may face barriers in accessing medical care, studies show that trafficked persons do access health services while being trafficked (Baldwin et al., 2011; Chisolm-Straker et al., 2017; Lederer & Wetzel, 2014). In fact, in a 2018 survey of human trafficking survivors, over half of respondents received treatment for an illness or injury directly related to their exploitation *while being exploited* (Polaris Project, 2017). Survivors reported accessing services ranging from emergency medicine to primary care to medical subspecialties and even school nurse services (Polaris Project, 2017). Furthermore, cases of human trafficking *within the healthcare industry itself* have been reported (Polaris Project, 2017).

Physicians, nurses, and other medical personnel may play a crucial role in identifying victims of human trafficking in the medical setting by seeing the victim-survivor patient regularly in clinic and eliciting a more complete narrative; by providing a confidential and safe setting for victim-survivors to reveal sensitive details of their complex histories; and by connecting victim-survivors to much needed resources. Physicians at all levels of training believe that knowing about human trafficking is important, but many find themselves ill-equipped to help patients who are victims of human trafficking (Beck et al., 2015; Titchen et al., 2015). To this end, medical groups have developed protocols, mostly for use in emergency departments, where a majority of human trafficking victims have been identified so far (Baldwin, Barrows, & Stoklosa, 2017; HT Assessment, 2016; Schwarz et al., 2016; Stoklosa, Dawson, Williams-Oni, & Rothman, 2016). An underlying tenet of all of these protocols is the expectation that at some point during the medical intake, the patient will be interviewed alone, using appropriate, certified medical foreign language interpreters if needed instead of using the patient's family or friends to interpret.

Equally important is for the medical professional to utilize a patient-centered, trauma-informed approach, with the goal of providing medically necessary care in a compassionate manner and restoring a sense of personhood and humanity to the patient rather than forcing a disclosure (Stoklosa, Grace, & Littenberg, 2015).

In FM's case, the medical professional should try to find a plausible excuse to separate FM from her father, and then identify the least noisy and most private area in the emergency department and ensure that FM is comfortable, providing a blanket, water, and food if possible. The medical professional should disclose any mandated reporting obligations in simple, clear language. Only then should the healthcare provider use open-ended questions to inquire about FM's safety and immediate needs, asking only for information on a need-to-know basis and receiving any answers (including refusal to answer) without judgment (see Table 9.2).

Careful attention to body language and acknowledgment of body language and facial expression is important. For example, if FM continued to avoid eye contact and was reticent to answer even the simplest questions, a statement such as "I notice that you keep looking at the floor and are not answering my questions" is perfectly acceptable if conveyed with compassion and

Table 9.2 Important questions to ask the potentially trafficked patient

Important Questions

- Do you have a place to stay? Where are you living?
- Do you feel safe?
- Do you work, live, and sleep all in the same place?
- Tell me about this tattoo. . . . Did you choose to get your tattoo(s)?
- Do you have any scars on your body due to someone harming you? (Or on physical exam: How did you get this scar?)
- Has anyone hit you or hurt you?
- Has anyone forced you to do anything you didn't want to do?
- Have you ever traded anything for sex? Food, money, shelter?
- Did you have any problems with persons working for the government, military, police, or any other group?

If an Immigrant:

- What made you leave your home country?
- In your home country, did you ever have problems because of religion, political beliefs, culture, or any other reason?
- Were you ever a victim of violence in your home country?

Source: Adapted from Chow Ahrenholz, Haider, & Niyogi, 2015.

patience. A follow-up question or statement such as "Do you feel up to telling me what happened?" or "I am concerned about you, and it would be helpful to us if you are willing to tell me what has happened, but it is up to you, and I understand if is too difficult to talk about it" can be helpful (Rothman, Bazzi, & Bair-Merritt, 2015).

Although a patient may disclose a history of trafficking on first presentation in an acute setting (Hauksson, 2003), it is possible and even likely that the patient will only disclose abuse and trafficking over several medical visits once a physician-patient relationship of trust is established (Titchen et al., 2016). For this reason, close follow-up with these patients is recommended, and it may be necessary to "prescribe" a follow-up visit so that the patient-victim has permission from her trafficker to return to medical care (Lloyd & Orman, 2009). The medical professional should collect follow-up information such as FM's cell phone number and the phone number of a close friend or family member of the patient. (Frequently, the cell phone numbers for victims of human trafficking change rapidly, and it may be advisable to call the phone number from the clinic in order to verify that it is a working number.) The goal in FM's case is to maintain continuity of care and provide an avenue for building the physician-patient relationship (see Table 9.3).

How should medical personnel approach a patients whom s/he thinks is a victim of human trafficking? What questions should be asked?

Notably, it should not be the goal of the physician or medical team to "rescue" the patient. If the medical professional continues to suspect human trafficking, she should verbally provide to FM the easily memorized phone number for the National Human Trafficking hotline, 888-3737-888. Similar to victims of intimate partner violence, victims of human trafficking may be at

Table 9.3 A 12-step approach to human trafficking in the healthcare setting

12-Step Patient-Centered Trauma-Informed Approach to the Potential Victim of Human Trafficking	
1	Get the patient alone and comfortable
2	Disclose mandated reporting obligations
3	Inquire re: immediate needs and safety
4	Ask only for need-to-know info without judgment
5	Listen to body language, especially during the exam
6	Ask the patient if s/he feels safe
7	Ask direct questions sensitively
8	Provide verbally, 888–3737–888*
9	Involve social work
10	Obtain follow-up info
11	**Prescribe** follow-up appointment
12	Preferred method of disclosure? Restore control.

*National Human Trafficking Hotline

greatest risk in the hours before and after they leave their abuser, so a carefully planned approach is recommended, and information about resources should always be given verbally or in a coded fashion, lest it be found by a potentially violent trafficker (Lloyd & Orman, 2009; Wilson & Daly, 1993). It is important to avoid giving fliers or cards with advertisements of human trafficking resources, as these can endanger the victim if found by his or her trafficker.

At this point, it would be advisable to engage a social worker to discuss briefly with FM supportive resources available to FM. Frequently, patients are unaware of the resources available to them, and sometimes the disclosure of these resources can provide a sense of safety for the patient and encourage disclosure. It is important to have healthcare protocols in place, so that there is a structured, systematic approach to delivering high-quality care to potential trafficking victims. This systematic approach may involve not only medical professionals and social workers but non-governmental agencies (NGOs), social service agencies, and law enforcement officers who have been trained in human trafficking to address the victim's needs for "housing, food, clothing, access to health and mental health care and legal consultation" (Burke et al., 2015).

The medical professional should coordinate, and then *write a prescription* for a follow-up appointment instead of simply telling FM to schedule a follow-up appointment: a written prescription for follow-up may legitimize the request for continued medical care in the eyes of the trafficker, since traffickers have a financial interest in keeping their victims healthy.

Medical professional education

As of this writing, the majority of medical professional education has focused on sex trafficking and has not addressed labor trafficking to the same degree. In part, this may be due to (1) the perceived greater vulnerability of children to sex trafficking versus labor trafficking and (2) the belief that children are unwitting victims of trafficking while adults "choose" a life of commercial sex. In addition, certain medical specialties such as obstetrics and gynecology and adolescent medicine are already trained and equipped to screen for intimate partner violence and sexual abuse and to treat health sequelae related to sex trafficking and abuse, such as sexually transmitted infections, vaginal trauma, and unplanned pregnancy. As in the case of FM, signs of labor trafficking may be quite general, subtler, harder to detect, and more easily explained away.

In 2013, the National Academy of Medicine (NAM, formerly the Institute of Medicine) advised that, in relation to sex trafficking, ongoing training programs should be evidence-based and should ensure that knowledge and training are sustained among mental health professionals, social workers, child welfare professionals, and physicians and other healthcare professionals.

With regard to research, NAM prioritized research in several areas including the prevalence of sex trafficking crimes among certain vulnerable populations and the associated needs of these populations; development of evidence-based prevention and intervention strategies; and the risk and protective factors associated with sex trafficking. Further, NAM called on the Office of Juvenile Justice and Delinquency Prevention to build a technological platform for digital information-sharing of resources for preventing, identifying, and responding to sex trafficking of minors in the United States (IOM, 2013).

The American Public Health Association (APHA) in 2015 called for the integration of education related to human trafficking (in all of its forms including labor trafficking) into the existing health professional curricula on domestic violence, elder abuse, mandated reporting, and intimate partner violence. APHA also called on the federal and state governments, as well as private foundations and NGOs, to fund research on the mental and physical health effects of all forms of human trafficking and on the diverse population of people victimized by various forms of trafficking.

Professional medical societies also have called for change and issued position statements about human trafficking and the need for physician education, including the American College of Obstetrics and Gynecologists (2011), the American Medical Women's Association (2014), the American Academy of Pediatrics, the American Public Health Association (2015), and the American College of Emergency Physicians (2016). And in fact, as of this writing, 14 states had enacted laws related to human trafficking education for professionals who carry a mandate to report child abuse and neglect, including healthcare professionals, educators, clergy, and social workers. In most of these states, human trafficking education is not mandatory, but the legislation stipulates that educational resources must be developed and available, and they call for an oversight committee or position to be established (Atkinson, Curnin, & Hanson, 2016). Increasingly, medical professionals who work with victims of human trafficking and who specialize in human trafficking research and policy development are sharing their knowledge and resources through medical textbooks like this one, training manuals, medical literature and case studies, and instructional videos (Chisolm-Straker & Stoklosa, 2017; Gibbons & Stoklosa, 2016; Scott-Tilley & Crites, 2016; Stoklosa, MacGibbon, & Stoklosa, 2017; Titchen et al., 2016; Titchen & Talib, 2017).

Mandated reporting: ethical and legal obligations

In the case of FM, the Administration for Child Services (ACS) was contacted. They investigated, and made their recommendations. The Justice for Victims of Trafficking Act of 2015 amended the Child Abuse Prevention and Treatment Act (CAPTA) 42 U.S.C. § 5106, making it a requirement for states who receive federal funding for child welfare programs to amend their current definitions of child abuse and neglect to include victims of labor and sex trafficking of minors. As a result, increasingly, state-specific mandated reporting laws for child abuse are incorporating language to require reporting of human trafficking of minors (Atkinson et al., 2016; Justice for Victims of Trafficking Act, 2015). As of 2016 only 21 states – for example California, Colorado, Florida, Illinois, Maryland, Massachusetts, and North Carolina – included human trafficking as abuse under child abuse and neglect laws (Child Welfare Information Gateway, 2016). Some of these states – including California, Colorado, and Maryland – only require reporting of sex trafficking of minors and do not include labor trafficking under these child abuse and neglect laws (Atkinson et al., 2016). However, while other states may not formally mandate trafficking reporting, the forms of exploitation involved in trafficking may fall under the scope of their existing child abuse mandated reporting statutes.

Who has an obligation to report? Do obligations for reporting differ if a mandatory reporter suspects labor versus sex trafficking victimization?

However, in seeking to "first do no harm," physicians must consider both the potential benefits and the risks of mandatory reporting of human trafficking (Todres, 2011). While identifying and reporting human trafficking victims has the potential to connect these individuals with legal and social services, if such services are overburdened, inadequate, or too difficult to access, more harm than good may be done; victims understandably may grow wary of physicians' empty promises and cease seeking medical care altogether (Children's Advocacy Institute of the University of San Diego School of Law and First Star, 2015; English, 2017). In some cases, the overburdened child protective services system may not prioritize cases of human trafficking if there is no evidence of immediate risk or harm. In other cases, mandatory reporting will necessitate transfer of custody of the patient from parents to child welfare, which may place the patient at greater risk for human trafficking and sexual exploitation (IOM, 2013).

Therefore, a well-planned, patient-centered, trauma-informed approach involving legal advocates and social workers experienced in the care of victims of human trafficking is paramount. As stated earlier, medical professionals can best advocate for their patients by forming medical legal partnerships and by fostering working relationships with community stakeholders, such as shelters and job placement services (Burke et al., 2015).

Opportunities for future patient interactions like FM

With regard to FM, there were a number of points for possible intervention during her presentation to medical care. Prior to arrival at the New York City emergency department, FM told the emergency technician (EMT) that she was in Miami, Florida, and this could have prompted suspicion and further questioning by the EMT.

An observant nurse in the emergency department noted that FM last ate at 6:00 a.m. that morning, even though she presented to medical attention sometime after 8:00 p.m. that night. Further questioning at that time might have elicited a more complete picture of FM's poor nutritional status and apparent food deprivation.

Most important is that an older man representing himself as FM's father minimized her medical condition and continued to answer all questions for her. It appears that no attempt was made to (1) verify that this man really was FM's father, or to (2) separate FM from this man to facilitate confidential questioning and a more complete history. Traffickers can make it difficult for medical personnel to question the victim alone and may use technology such as implanted GPS tracking chips or cell phones to track the patient's movements, distribute images without their consent, and even eavesdrop on their conversations, emails, phone calls, and other communications through use of smartphone malware applications in order to keep victims under their control and observation (Gibbons & Stoklosa, 2016; Olsen & Street, 2017). These applications allow the trafficker to control the camera, microphone, and/or web access of the victim's smartphone. However, medical professionals such as nurses, radiology technicians, orderlies, and physicians can devise reasons to get the patient alone. For example, the nurse involved in FM's care could have advised FM's father that FM required radiologic imaging in a location of the hospital where even family would not be permitted. Or a female medical professional could have suggested that she would accompany FM to the bathroom for a urine test, where a private conversation would be possible. In these cases, creativity is warranted.

A floor nurse in the hospital had also noted the constant presence of FM's father and stepmother. Again, if there is suspicion for abuse or human trafficking, creative methods are needed and justified for isolating the patient to allow for the privacy that might be needed for a disclosure.

Importantly, disclosure may not necessarily be the goal. FM, in fact, saw adolescent medicine physicians for follow-up three times before she felt comfortable disclosing the details of her history of abuse. This is not unusual, and a danger for any medical professional trained to recognize human trafficking is the desire to "rescue" the patient. Again, a victim of human trafficking likely will need to plan for escape carefully. Social workers and legal advocates may need to assist the victim in gathering needed legal documents, putting in place provisions for emergency shelter in an undisclosed location, securing food stamps and health insurance, and arranging legal services. This is difficult to accomplish in one medical clinic visit. Therefore, a single interaction with a patient who is a victim of human trafficking may be just the first step in a long process toward freedom and recovery. But this first step of establishing trust and restoring a sense of humanness and power to the patient is paramount.

Resources for medical professionals

A growing number of resources are available to medical professionals who encounter victims and survivors of human trafficking in their workplace. Although a relatively nascent field as of this writing, human trafficking intervention and rehabilitation increasingly rely upon knowledge gleaned from the fields of dating violence, sexual assault, and intimate partner violence (Leidholdt, 2013; Rothman et al., 2015). In addition, professional medical associations nationwide have begun to address the problem of human trafficking and to recognize it as a public health problem (APHA, 2015; Executive Board of the American College of Obstetricians and Gynecologists, 2012; Greenbaum & Crawford-Jakubiak, 2015; Gurney et al., 2015; Harrison et al., 2013; Todres, 2011). As a result, working groups among physicians, nurses, and social workers have sprung up to grapple with issues surrounding screening and intervention techniques, to develop standardized screening tools, to introduce patient-centered trauma-informed care practices, and to advocate for mandatory physician education through legislative efforts (see Table 9.4). In addition, several groups have created or embraced medical legal partnerships in an effort to better provide coordinated care for the patient-client who is a victim of human trafficking.

Resources for patients

Victims of trafficking have myriad needs including housing, vocational trading, substance use disorder treatment, and legal services. Resources for victims of human trafficking vary widely depending on the country of origin (U.S.-born or foreign), the age of the victim, the sex of the victim, and the type of trafficking (labor versus sex) (U.S. Citizenship and Immigration Services, 2017).

Two types of visas are available to non-citizen victims of human trafficking: (1) The T-visa is available to victims of trafficking as defined by law in the United States, American Samoa, or the Commonwealth of the Northern Mariana Islands if the victim complies with "any reasonable request" by law enforcement in an investigation or prosecution of human trafficking unless the victim is under the age of 18 or is unable to cooperate due to physical or psychological trauma. In addition, it must be demonstrated that the victim would suffer extreme hardship such as the threat of violence or war were she deported to her country of origin. Recipients of the T-visa may remain in the United States during this investigation, may apply for a green card in three years,

Table 9.4 Resources

Description	*Organization Resources*	*Website*
"Polaris is a leader in the global fight to eradicate modern day slavery."	• Typology of modern slavery • Advocacy initiatives • Policy and legislative updates • Survivor narratives	https://polarisproject.org
"The National Human Trafficking Hotline is a national anti-trafficking hotline serving victims and survivors of human trafficking and the anti-trafficking community in the United States. The toll-free hotline is available to answer calls from anywhere in the country, 24 hours a day, 7 days a week, every day of the year in more than 200 languages."	• Call the hotline: 888–3737–888 • Text the hotline: "BeFree" • Access hotline statistics • Access state and national resources • Download free fliers and posters • Report suspected human trafficking	https://humantraffickinghotline.org
"We are a united group of multidisciplinary professionals dedicated to ending human trafficking and supporting its survivors, from a public health perspective."	• Speakers' bureau for trainings • Updated online repository of various publications • Listing of nationally recognized educational programs • Advocacy articles and videos • Protocol Toolkit • TEDMED talk on HT intervention through healthcare • Committees for Research, Advocacy, Media and Technology and more • Linkages to federal agencies, NGOs, health societies, and academic centers	https://healtrafficking.org
"In 2014, the American Medical Women's Association founded Physicians Against the Trafficking of Humans (PATH) to help educate physicians, residents, and medical students about issues surrounding human sex trafficking."	• Four-part CME video series to teach medical professionals about sex trafficking • TEDx talk about one physician's experience with HT patients • Video of a survivor's perspective • Human Trafficking Summits • Monthly newsletter updates • Nationwide training seminars • Network of women across all fields of medicine	www.amwa-doc.org/our-work/initiatives/human-trafficking/ www.doc-path.org/path
"Via Christi Health is training physicians, nurses and other clinicians to recognize warning signs that a patient may be a victim of human trafficking and then to provide help to the victims."	• Pocket-sized human trafficking assessment tool with an action flowchart for the medical professional • Video of grand rounds to train healthcare professionals about HT	www.viachristi.org/sites/default/files/pdf/about_us/HT/2017-0802%20Human%20Trafficking%20Card%20Generl%20Co-Branded.pdf

(Continued)

Table 9.4 (Continued)

Description	*Organization Resources*	*Website*
"For more than 30 years, FUTURES has been providing groundbreaking programs, policies, and campaigns that empower individuals and organizations working to end violence against women and children around the world."	• Policy and legislation updates • Education and awareness • Coalition building	www.futureswithoutviolence.org
"The Human Trafficking Pro Bono Legal Center empowers trafficked women, men, and children to seek justice. HT Pro Bono leads national efforts to hold human traffickers accountable for their crimes and to raise awareness of victims' rights."	• Technical assistance with trafficking cases for pro bono lawyers • Free CLE training for law centers with pro bono programs • Free training for law students interested in HT • Referrals for lawyers who will assist victims of HT and NGOs that provide services to trafficking survivors	www.htprobono.org

and may sponsor their families to the United States. (2) The U-visa is available to non-citizens who are crime victims who have "suffered substantial mental or physical abuse as a result of the crime." Individuals may be awarded a U-visa if they have information about the criminal activity or are likely to be helpful to law enforcement in the investigation or prosecution of the crime. When a U-visa is granted, it is valid for four years with opportunity for extension. Similar to the recipients of the T-visa, recipients of a U-visa may apply for permanent resident status through a green card in three years (U.S. Citizenship and Immigration Services, 2017).

The cap on the number of T-visas and U-visas, the complex application process, and the necessity of cooperating with law enforcement all serve as barriers to victims in obtaining these visas. A medical professional can facilitate this process for victims in several ways: by engaging appropriate language interpreters if needed, by connecting the victim to a legal advocate trained in human trafficking, and by supplying the legal advocate with necessary documentation regarding findings from history-taking, physical exams, and laboratory tests and imaging that may support the history of abuse or trafficking (U.S. Citizenship and Immigration Services, 2017).

Importantly, resources connected with these visas, including food stamps, continuing education, job training, employment services, housing, and healthcare are not as readily available to the victims of human trafficking who are U.S. citizens. However, a number of non-profit organizations and non-governmental organizations throughout the United States are equipped to provide U.S. citizen victims with these resources. Several dedicated physicians and lawyers have used grant money or dedicated pro bono hours to create gynecology clinics and legal advocacy centers for victims of human trafficking. Other Good Samaritans have extended housing to homeless youth, many of whom are vulnerable to or involved in human trafficking. The need continues to outstrip existing resources, and one of the key roles healthcare professionals can play is to advocate for these patients.

Case study: FM (resolution)

In FM's case, adolescent medicine clinicians worked with clinic social workers to contact the Administration for Children's Services (ACS) to report suspicion of child neglect and labor trafficking. Unfortunately, after investigation, ACS closed FM's case due to "low risk" – there was too little evidence to justify separation of FM from her father. This likely reflected the overburdened ACS system and a lack of evidence of immediate danger. However, FM continued to follow up with physicians at the adolescent medicine clinic; a local non-governmental organization (NGO) was engaged, and a local legal advocate was contacted through the National Human Trafficking Resource Center. Emergency housing was identified through the NGO, and the patient was connected with continuing education resources. The legal advocate agreed to provide pro bono counseling for the patient and facilitate FM's attainment of a T-visa in return for her cooperation with law enforcement.

Advocate!

- Learn about policy and legislation related to human trafficking at the Polaris Project Action Center, www.polarisproject.org/action.
- Initiate postcard campaigns to local, state, and federal representatives to support funding for social services and to hold lawmakers responsible for securing funds for additional research, housing, legal, and job training services for non-citizen *and citizen* victims of human trafficking.
- Read and learn more about human trafficking, and organize a lecture or discussion at your home institution, hospital, or clinic.
- Write letters to the editor to call attention to socioeconomic disparities in your neighborhood that could promote human trafficking.
- Buy Fair Trade products whenever possible.
- Engage in research on trafficking to advance the knowledge of our field in caring for trafficking victims.

Conclusion

For a variety of reasons, patients who are victims of human trafficking rarely self-disclose their trafficking status. They may not recognize themselves as victims; they may encounter barriers to accessing help and services because of language, culture, immigration and/or socioeconomic status, or societal stigma; or they may fear for their lives or the lives and well-being of their loved ones. Therefore, health care professionals must be equipped to recognize signs of human trafficking; must be trained to offer trauma-informed care and to foster a physician-patient relationship built on trust; must learn to use a victim-centered approach when offering clinical care; should provide close clinical follow-up; and finally need to be familiar with nationwide and local resources for victims of human trafficking. Resources for these patients continue to expand, and opportunities for advocacy abound.

Supplemental learning materials

Videos

"Faces of Human Trafficking" Video Series by Office of Victims of Crime. Retrieved from https://ovc.ncjrs.gov/humantrafficking/publicawareness.html

How to Spot Human Trafficking, TEDx talk by Dr. Kanani Titchen. Retrieved from https://youtu.be/hrxhptvEOTs

Intervention in Human Trafficking Through Health Care, TEDMED talk by Dr. Susie Baldwin. Retrieved from http://tedmed.com/talks/show?id=627336

Physicians Against the Trafficking of Humans, 4-part CME-accredited video curriculum. Retrieved from www.doc-path.org/path

Lay press

The CNN Freedom Project: Ending Modern-Day Slavery. "Why human trafficking is a public health problem," by Margeaux Gray. Retrieved from www.cnn.com/2016/07/11/opinions/human-trafficking-health-margeaux-gray/

Huffington Post. "Healthcare: Are your staff educated to recognize human trafficking?" by Holly Austin Smith. Retrieved from www.huffingtonpost.com/holly-austin-smith/healthcare-are-your-staff_b_9767778.html

Marketplace. Identifying trafficking victims is just the start of health care's challenge. Retrieved from www.marketplace.org/2016/03/04/health-care/identifying-trafficking-victims-just-start-health-cares-challenge

Q&A: America's "Invisible" Child Labor Problem. Retrieved from www.pbs.org/wgbh/frontline/article/qa-americas-invisible-child-labor-problem/

Books

Chisolm-Straker, M., & Stoklosa, H. (Eds.). (2017). *Human trafficking is a public health issue: A paradigm expansion in the United States.* Cham, Switzerland: Springer. Print.

Kara, S. (2009). *Sex Trafficking: Inside the business of modern slavery.* New York, NY: Columbia University Press. Print.

Peer-reviewed literature

In addition to the references listed above and below, for a list of peer-reviewed literature related to human trafficking, go to www.healtrafficking.org.

Kaufka Walts, K. (2017). Child labor trafficking in the United States: A hidden crime. *Social Inclusion, 5*(2), 59–68. Retrieved from www.luc.edu/media/lucedu/chrc/pdfs/Child%20Labor%20Trafficking%20in%20the%20U.S.pdf

Murphy, L. T. (2016). Labor and sex trafficking among homeless youth. A Ten City Study (Executive Summary). Retrieved from https://nspn.memberclicks.net/assets/docs/NSPN/labor%20and%20sex%20trafficking%20among%20homeless%20youth.pdf

References

Ahrenholz, N. C., Haider, M., & Niyogi, A. (2015). Caring for refugee and asylee torture survivors in primary care. *Society of General Internal Medicine Forum, 38*(10), 12–13. Retrieved from www.sgim.org/File%20Library/SGIM/Resource%20Library/Forum/2015/SGIMOct2015_04.pdf

The American College of Obstetricians and Gynecologists. (2012). *Global women's health and rights.* Retrieved from www.acog.org/Clinical-Guidance-and-Publications/Statements-of-Policy/Global-Womens-Health-and-Rights

American Public Health Association. (2015). *Expanding and coordinating human trafficking-related public health research, evaluation, education, and prevention.* Retrieved from www.apha.org/policies-and-advocacy/public-health-policy-statements/policy-database/2016/01/26/14/28/expanding-and-coordinating-human-trafficking-related-public-health-activities

Anthony, B., Penrose, J. K., & Jakiel, S. (2017). The typology of modern slavery. *Polaris Project.* Retrieved from https://polarisproject.org/sites/default/files/Polaris-Typology-of-Modern-Slavery.pdf

Ascension Via Christi. (2016). *Human trafficking assessment.* Retrieved from www.viachristi.org/sites/default/files/pdf/about_us/HT/2017-0802%20Human%20Trafficking%20Card%20Generl%20Co-Branded.pdf

Atkinson, H. G., Curnin, K. J., & Hanson, N. C. (2016). U.S. state laws addressing human trafficking: Education of and mandatory reporting by health care providers and other professionals. *Journal of Human Trafficking, 2*(2), 111–138. Retrieved from https://doi.org/10.1080/23322705.2016.1175885

Baldwin, S. B., Barrows, J., & Stoklosa, H. (2017). Protocol toolkit for developing a response to victims of human trafficking. *HEAL Trafficking and Hope for Justice.* Retrieved from https://healtrafficking.org/protocol-toolkit-technical-assistance/

Baldwin, S. B., Eisenman, D. P., Sayles, J. N., Ryan, G., & Chuang, K. S. (2011). Identification of human trafficking victims in health care settings. *Health and Human Rights, 13*(1), 36–49. Retrieved from www.hhrjournal.org/2013/08/identification-of-human-trafficking-victims-in-health-care-setting/

Beck, M. E., Lineer, M. M., & Melzer-Lange, M., Simpson, P., Nugent, M., & Rabbitt, A. (2015). Medical providers' understanding of sex trafficking and their experience with at-risk patients. *Pediatrics, 135*(4), 895–902. Retrieved from https://doi.org/10.1542/peds.2014-2814

Bender, S. S., & Fulbright, Y. K. (2013). Content analysis: A review of perceived barriers to sexual and reproductive health services by young people. The *European Journal of Contraception & Reproductive Health Care, 18*(3), 159–167. Retrieved from https://doi.org/10.3109/13625187.2013.776672

Burke, M., McCauley, H. L., Rackow, A., Orsini, B., Simunovic, B., & Miller, E. (2015). Implementing a coordinated care model for sex trafficked minors in smaller cities. *Journal of Applied Research on Children: Informing Policy for Children at Risk, 6*(1), 1–13. Retrieved from https://digitalcommons.library.tmc.edu/childrenatrisk/vol6/iss1/7

Child Welfare Information Gateway. (2016). *Definitions of child abuse and neglect.* Retrieved from www.childwelfare.gov/pubpdfs/define.pdf

Children's Advocacy Institute of the University of San Diego School of Law. (2015). *Shame on U.S.: Failings by all three branches of our federal government leave abused and neglected children vulnerable to further harm.* San Diego, CA: Author.

Chisolm-Straker, M., & Stoklosa, H. (Eds.). (2017). *Human trafficking is a public health issue: A paradigm expansion in the United States.* Cham, Switzerland: Springer International Publishing.

Dawson, R. S. (2017). Talking to adolescents about social media. *Pediatric Annals, 46*(8), e274–e276. Retrieved from https://doi.org/10.3928/19382359-20170718-01

Domestic Abuse Intervention Programs. (n.d.). *Duluth model power and Ccontrol wheel.* Retrieved from www.theduluthmodel.org/wheels/

Domestic Workers United. (n.d.). *Domestic workers under labor law.* Retrieved from www.domesticworkersunited.org/index.php/en/pressroom/press-releases/item/download/1_cb7fdb965d9b9d2c4965d2a8726bafca

English, A. (2017). Mandatory reporting of human trafficking: Potential benefits and risks of harm. *AMA Journal of Ethics, 19*(1), 54–62. Retrieved from https://doi.org/10.1001.journalofethics.2016.19.1.pfor1-1701

Gibbons, P., & Stoklosa, H. (2016). Identification and treatment of human trafficking victims in the emergency department: A case report. *Journal of Emergency Medicine, 50*(5), 715–719. Retrieved from https://doi.org/10.1016/j.jemermed.2016.01.004

Greenbaum, J., & Crawford-Jakubiak, J. E. (2015). Child sex trafficking and commercial sexual exploitation: Health care needs of victims. *Pediatrics, 135*(3), 566–574. Retrieved from https://doi.org/10.1542/peds.2014-4138

Gurney, D., Bush, K., Gillespie, G., Walsh, R., Wilson, M. E., Chance, K., . . . Wallerich, D. (2015). Human trafficking patient awareness in the emergency setting. *Journal of Emergency Nursing, 42*(2), 150–152. Retrieved from https://doi.org/10.1016/S0099-1767(16)00108-2

Harrison, S. L., Atkinson, H. G., Newman, C. B., Leavell, Y., Miller, D., Brown, C. M., . . . Titchen, K. (2014). Position paper on the sex trafficking of women and girls in the United States. *American Medical Women's Association.* Retrieved from www.amwa-doc.org/wp-content/uploads/2013/12/AMWA-Position-Paper-on-Human-Sex-Trafficking_May-20141.pdf

Hauksson, P. (2003). Psychological evidence of torture: How to conduct an interview with a detainee to document mental health consequences of torture or ill-treatment. *Council of Europe: Committee for the Prevention of Torture.* Retrieved from https://rm.coe.int/16806987f8

Hodge, D. R. (2008). Sexual trafficking in the United States: A domestic problem with transnational dimensions. *Social Work, 53*(2), 143–152. Retrieved from https://doi.org/10.1093/sw/53.2.143

Human Smuggling and Trafficking Center. (2008). *Domestic human trafficking: An internal issue.* Retrieved from www.hsdl.org/?abstract&did=21721

Institute of Medicine; National Research Council. Confronting Commercial Sexual Exploitation and Sex Trafficking of Minors in the United States. Washington, D.C.: National Academies Press; 2013.

International Labour Organization. (2014). *Profits and poverty: The economics of forced labour.* Retrieved from www.ilo.org/wcmsp5/groups/public/ – ed_norm/ – declaration/documents/publication/wcms_243391.pdf

International Labour Organization. (2017). *Global estimates of modern slavery: Forced labour and forced marriage.* Retrieved from www.ilo.org/wcmsp5/groups/public/ – dgreports/ – dcomm/documents/publication/wcms_575479.pdf

International Organization for Migration. (2000). Trafficking of migrants – Hidden health concerns. IOM Migration and Health Newsletter.

Justice for Victims of Trafficking Act of 2015, Pub. L. No. 114–22, 129 Stat. 227, as codified at 18 U.S.C. § 3014.

Kaye, W. F., Gwirtsman, H. E., George, D. T., Ebert, M. H., Jimerson, D. C., Tomai, T. P., . . . Gold, P. W. (1987). Elevated cerebrospinal fluid levels of immunoreactive corticotropin-releasing hormone in anorexia nervosa: Relation to state of nutrition, adrenal function, and intensity of depression. *The Journal of Clinical Endocrinology & Metabolism, 64*(2), 203–208. Retrieved from https://doi.org/10.1210/jcem-64-2-203

Latonero, M. (2011). Human trafficking online: The role of social networking sites and online classifieds. Retrieved from https://technologyandtrafficking.usc.edu/files/2011/09/HumanTrafficking_FINAL.pdf

Lederer, L., & Wetzel, C. A. (2014). The health consequences of sex trafficking and their implications for identifying victims in healthcare facilities. *Annals of Health Law, 23*(1), 61–91.

Leidholdt, D. (2013). Human trafficking and domestic violence: A primer for judges. *Judges' Journal, 52*(1), 16–21. Retrieved from www.americanbar.org/publications/judges_journal/2013/winter/human_trafficking_and_domestic_violence_a_primer_for_judges.html

Lloyd, R., & Orman, A. (2009). *Training manual on the commercial sexual exploitation of children (CSEC).* New York, NY: Girls Educational Mentoring Services – GEMS.

Macy, R. J., & Graham, L. M. (2012). Identifying domestic and international sex-trafficking victims during human service provision. *Trauma, Violence, & Abuse, 13*(2), 59–76. Retrieved from https://doi.org/10.1177/1524838012440340

McClain, N. M., & Garrity, S. E. (2011). Sex trafficking and the exploitation of adolescents. *Journal of Obstetric, Gynecologic, and Neonatal Nursing, 40*(2), 243–252. Retrieved from https://doi.org/10.1111/j.1552-6909.2011.01221.x

Office of Refugee Resettlement, Administration for Children and Families, U.S. Department of Health and Human Services. Fact Sheet: Labor Trafficking. Accessed May 29, 2017: https://www.acf.hhs.gov/sites/default/files/orr/fact_sheet_labor_trafficking_english.pdf.

Olsen, E., & Street, C. (2017). Intimate partner violence in a digital age. In *Proceedings from the Conference on Crimes Against Women*, Dallax, TX.

Oram, S., Khondoker, M., Abas, M., Broadbent, M., & Howard, L. M. (2015). Characteristics of trafficked adults and children with severe mental illness: A historical cohort study. *Lancet Psychiatry, 2*(12), 1084–1091. Retrieved from https://doi.org/10.1016/S2215-0366(15)00290-4

Organization for Security and Co-operation in Europe. (2016). *Report by special representative and co-ordinator for combating trafficking in human beings, Madina Jarbussynova, following her official visit to the United States of America.* Retrieved from www.osce.org/secretariat/289446?download=true

Polaris Project. (2018). *On-ramps, intersections, and exit routes: A roadmap for systems and industries to prevent and disrupt human trafficking.* Retrieved from https://polarisproject.org/sites/default/files/A%20Roadmap%20for%20Systems%20and%20Industries%20to%20Prevent%20and%20Disrupt%20Human%20Trafficking.pdf

Powell, J. (2014). The approach to chronic pelvic pain in the adolescent. *Obstetrics and Gynecology Clinics of North America, 41*(3), 343–355. Retrieved from https://doi.org/10.1016/j.ogc.2014.06.001

Reddy, D. M., Fleming, R., & Swain, C. (2002). Effect of mandatory parental notification on adolescent girls' use of sexual health care services. *Journal of the American Medical Association, 288*, 710–714. Retrieved from https://doi.org/10.1001.jama.288.6.710

Rothman, E. F., Bazzi, A. R., & Bair-Merritt, M. (2015). "I'll do whatever as long as you keep telling me that I'm important": A case study illustrating the link between adolescent dating violence and sex trafficking victimization. *Journal of Applied Research on Children: Informing Policy for Children at Risk, 6*(1), 1–21. Retrieved from http://digitalcommons.library.tmc.edu/childrenatrisk/vol6/iss1/8

Sabella, D. (2011). The role of the nurse in combating human trafficking. *American Journal of Nursing, 111*(2), 28–37. Retrieved from https://doi.org/10.1097.01.NAJ.0000394289.55577.b6

Schwarz, C., Unruh, E., Cronin, K., Evans-Simpson, S., Britton, H., & Ramaswamy, M. (2016). Human trafficking identification and service provision in the medical and social service sectors.

Health and Human Rights Journal, *18*(1), 181–192. Retrieved from www.hhrjournal.org/2016/04/human-trafficking-identification-and-service-provision-in-the-medical-and-social-service-sectors/

Scott-Tilley, D., & Crites, H. (2016). Human trafficking, sexual assault, or something else? A complicated case with an unexpected outcome. *Journal of Forensic Nursing*, *12*(4), 198–202. Retrieved from http://doi.org/10.1097/JFN.0000000000000125

Stoklosa, H., Dawson, M. B., Williams-Oni, F., & Rothman, E. (2016). A review of U.S. health care institution protocols for the identification and treatment of victims of human trafficking. *Journal of Human Trafficking*, *3*(2), 116–124. Retrieved from https://doi.org/10.1080.2332705.2016.1187965

Stoklosa, H., Grace, A. M., & Littenberg, N. (2015). Medical education on human trafficking. *AMA Journal of Ethics*, *17*(10), 914–921. Retrieved from https://doi.org/10.1001/journalofethics.2015.17.10.medu1-1510

Stoklosa, H., MacGibbon, M., & Stoklosa, J. (2017). Human trafficking, mental illness, and addiction: Avoiding diagnostic overshadowing. *AMA Journal of Ethics*, *19*(1), 23–34. Retrieved from https://nrs.harvard.edu/urn-3:HUL.InstRepos:34638828

Stolpe, K. E. (2014). MS-13 and domestic juvenile sex trafficking: Causes, correlates, and solutions. *Virginia Journal of Social Policy & the Law*, *21*(2), 341–372.

Swenne, I., & Larsson, P. (1999). Heart risk associated with weight loss in anorexia nervosa and eating disorders: Risk factors for QTc interval prolongation and dispersion. *Acta Paediatrica*, *88*(3), 304–309. Retrieved from https://doi.org/10.1111.j.1651-2227.1999.tb01101.x

Titchen, K. E., Katz, D., Martinez, K., & White, K. (2016). Ovarian cystadenoma in a trafficked patient. *Pediatrics*, *137*(5), e1–e5. Retrieved from https://doi.org/10.1542/peds.2015-2201

Titchen, K. E., Loo, D., Berdan, L., Rysavy, M. B., Ng, J. J., & Sharif, I. (2015). Domestic sex trafficking of minors: Medical student and physician awareness. *Journal of Pediatric and Adolescent Gynecology*, *30*(1), 102–108. Retrieved from https://doi.org/10.1016/j-jpag.2015.05.006

Titchen, K. E., & Talib, H. J. (2017). Case of a girl with chronic abdominal pain, frequent emergency room visits, and opioid abuse. In H. J. Talib (Ed.) *Adolescent gynecology: A clinical casebook* (pp. 251–265). New York, NY: Springer.

Todres, J. (2011). Moving upstream: The merits of a public health law approach to human trafficking. *North Carolina Law Review*, *89*(2), 447–506. Retrieved from https://scholarship.law.unc.edu/nclr/vol89/iss2/3

Turner-Moss, E., Zimmerman, C., Howard, L. M., & Oram, S. (2014). Labour exploitation and health: A case series of men and women seeking post-trafficking services. *Journal of Immigrant and Minority Health*, *16*(3), 473–480. Retrieved from https://doi.org/10.1007/s10903-013-9832-6

United Nations. (2001). *Protocol to prevent, suppress and punish trafficking in persons, especially women and children, supplementing the United Nations convention against transnational organized crime*. Retrieved from www.ohchr.org/en/professional interest/pages/protocoltraffickinginpersons.aspx

United States Department of Labor. (2013). *Fact sheet #79B: Live-in domestic service workers under the Fair Labor Standards Act (FLSA)*. Retrieved from www.dol.gov/whd/regs/compliance/whdfs79b.htm

U.S. Citizenship and Immigration Services. (2017). *Victims of Human Trafficking and Other Crimes*. Available at: https://www.uscis.gov/humanitarian/victims-human-trafficking-other-crimes. Accessed September 24, 2017.

U.S. Department of Health & Human Services. (2012). *Fact sheet: Labor trafficking*. Retrieved from www.acf.hhs.gov/archive/otip/resource/fact-sheet-labor-trafficking-english

U.S. Department of State. (2000). *Trafficking Victims Protection Act of 2000*. Retrieved from www.state.gov/j/tip/laws/61124.htm

U.S. Department of State. (2007). *The trafficking in persons report 2007*. Washington, DC: Author.

U.S. Department of State. (2010). *What is modern slavery?* Retrieved from www.state.gov/j/tip/what/index.htm

Van Grove, J. (2017, May 26). Emojis and sex trafficking: SDSU researchers crack the code. *The San Diego Union-Tribune*. Retrieved from www.sandiegouniontribune.com/business/technology/sd-fi-emojis-trafficking-20170526-story.html

Westcott, K. (2013, August 22). What is Stockholm syndrome? *BBC News Magazine*. Retrieved from www.bbc.com/news/magazine-22447726

Wilson, M., & Daly, M. (1993). Spousal homicide risk and estrangement. *Violence and Victims*, *8*(1), 3–16.

Zimmerman, C., Hossain, M., Yun, K., Gajdadziev, V., Guzun, N., Tchomarova, M., . . . Mofus, M. N. (2008). The health of trafficked women: A survey of women entering posttrafficking services in Europe. *American Journal of Public Health*, *98*(1), 55–59. Retrieved from https://doi.org/10.2105/AJPH.2006.108357

10

HUMAN TRAFFICKING AND PUBLIC HEALTH

Anita Ravi

Abstract

The socioecological framework of public health is a potent approach to understanding, addressing, and preventing human trafficking. This chapter reviews ways in which six areas important to human trafficking can be understood through a public health approach: infectious disease, substance use, incarceration, environmental health, technology, and media. Applying a public health lens to issues of social determinants of health and trauma, including adverse childhood experiences, further links human trafficking-related issues to these six areas and related sectors.

Learning Objectives

At the end of the chapter, readers will be able to:

1. Understand the way that the socioecological model can be used to conceptualize human trafficking as a public health issue;
2. Recognize the links between human trafficking and social determinants of health, adverse childhood experiences, and trauma-informed care;
3. Determine the ways that infectious disease, substance use, and the criminal justice system intersect with human trafficking and health;
4. Recognize the ways in which environmental issues impact health and human trafficking; and
5. Understand the role of the media and technology in perpetuating and preventing human trafficking.

Key Terms: Socioecological model; upstream/midstream/downstream interventions; social determinants of health; adverse childhood experiences; trauma-informed care; reproductive justice; environmental migrants.

Introduction

The framing of human trafficking as a public health issue is essential in its prevention. The World Health Organization's "Violence Prevention Alliance" describes a public health approach as having four essential components: (1) Surveillance: what is the problem; (2) Identifying risk and protective factors: what are the causes; (3) Develop and evaluate interventions: what works and for whom; and (4) Implementation: expanding effective policy and programs to additional settings (World Health Organization, 2017b). A public health approach necessarily highlights the interconnectedness between the multiple sectors that perpetuate human trafficking (e.g. education, immigration, law, medicine, housing, employment, social services), as the issue of health influences and is influenced by all of these sectors. Furthermore, a public health approach identifies areas for prevention and intervention strategies.

On a broad scale, a public health approach allows for the nesting of human trafficking within the spectrum of other, similar multi-sector issues such as gender-based or interpersonal violence. Doing so allows us to learn and build from other movements to identify best policies and practices for affected populations. One example is the "Power and Control Wheel" (see Figure 10.1), which was initially designed to depict the multiple methods by which domestic violence perpetrators exert control over victims (Domestic Abuse Intervention Programs, n.d: Home of the Duluth Model, 2017). Given the commonalities in techniques exhibited by traffickers, a similar

Figure 10.1 Power and Control Wheel

wheel of power and control has been adapted for sex and labor trafficking (National Human Trafficking Resource Center, 2010), which among other utilities can also provide insight when designing prevention and intervention programs.

Review the Power and Control Wheel. Identify three public health policies perpetuating exploitation. Why did you select these policies, and what changes would you make to improve them?

This chapter will lead you through two main sections. The first addresses key public health frameworks to consider when reviewing human trafficking–related practice, policy, and programming, and the second will discuss the intersection between six key public health related areas and human trafficking: infectious diseases, substance use, mass incarceration, climate change, technology, and media. Throughout each of the following sections, you will see overlap among sectors and themes of social determinants of health and trauma, further emphasizing the importance of a public health approach to trafficking.

Public health frameworks and human trafficking

Because the concept of health is a shared tenet across humanity, it offers a potent approach to understand, address, and prevent human trafficking. Trafficked people experience a wide array of acute and chronic physical and mental health conditions, and thus approaching human trafficking through the lens of health allows for a comprehensive identification of trafficking-related risk and protective factors, while simultaneously informing interventions and prevention efforts across relevant sectors and populations. In the following section we will examine the ways in which conceptualizing human trafficking as a public health issue provides a versatile approach to addressing social and structural factors associated with human trafficking.

Socioecological model

There are many frameworks by which to understand human trafficking through a public health lens, including the socioecological model, which captures the complex interactions among individual, relationship, community, and societal level factors. Specifically, the socioecological framework can be used to provide context between individuals' personal characteristics (e.g. a trafficked person's gender, sexuality, age, disability, health status, income level, education level, immigration/citizenship status), relationships with others (e.g. personal, professional and exploitative relationships), community factors (e.g. neighborhood, school, workplace, online), and societal factors (e.g. economic policy, social and cultural norms) (Centers for Disease Control and Prevention, 2015). Figure 10.2 portrays a socioecological framework specific to risk factors associated with the commercial sexual exploitation of children (Ijadi-Maghsoodi, Cook, Barnert, Gaboian, & Bath, 2016). Not limited to victims, a similar approach could also be used when assessing risk factors associated with perpetration of trafficking.

In parallel, the socioecological model frames potential prevention efforts in a broader context. Prevention can take on primary, secondary, and tertiary forms. Primary prevention involves preventing a disease or injury before it occurs (e.g. implementing school-based educational curriculums on healthy relationships); secondary prevention involves reducing the impact of a disease or injury that has already occurred (e.g. screening for trafficking in health centers); and tertiary prevention involves reducing the impact or burden of an existing and ongoing illness or injury with the aim of improving functional ability and quality and longevity of life (e.g. trauma

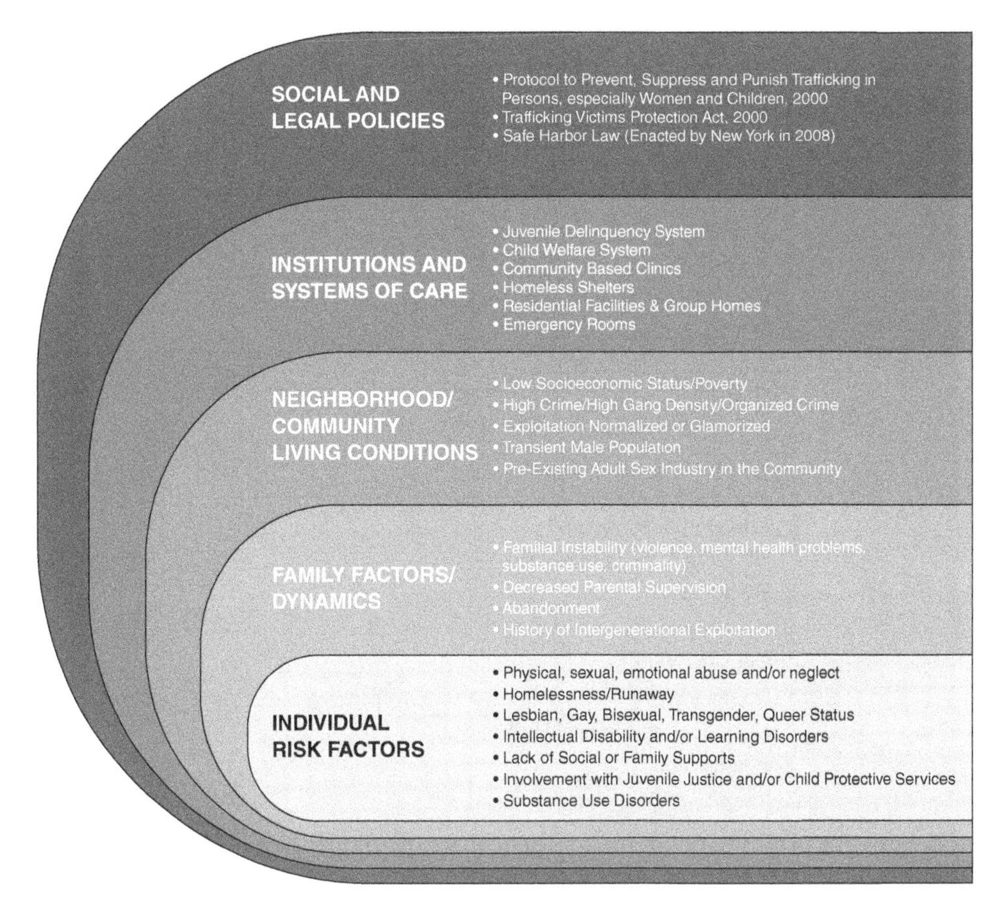

Figure 10.2 Socioecological framework contextualizing and conceptualizing commercial sexual exploitation of children

support groups) (Institute for Work & Health, 2015). The terms "upstream," "midstream," and "downstream" are sometimes used when describing primary, secondary, and tertiary prevention relative to each other. Upstream efforts aim to prevent harm before it occurs; midstream efforts aim to lessen the impact of harm that is already occurring; and downstream efforts aiming to address consequences of harm that has already occurred (Bharmal, Derose, Felician, & Weden, 2015; Coote, 2012).

Review the 26 typologies listed in Tables 10.1 *and* 10.2. *Select three from each table and then identify examples of primary, secondary, and tertiary prevention efforts for each type.*

Overlying socioecological factors are interactions across multiple sectors (e.g. housing, immigration, education, law enforcement, and healthcare) that impact human trafficking. These multi-sector interactions become apparent when reviewing the 26 "typologies" of human trafficking, created by Polaris Project, as listed in Tables 10.1 and 10.2 (Polaris, 2017). For example, physical and mental health issues related to hotel and hospitality-based trafficking may be linked to

Table 10.1 Typology of sex trafficking

Escort Services
Bars, Strip Clubs, and Cantinas
Pornography
Personal Sexual Servitude
Remote Interactive Sexual Acts
Residential
Illicit Massage, Health, and Beauty
Outdoor Solicitation
Primarily Labor Trafficking

Table 10.2 Typology of labor trafficking

Arts and Entertainment*
Health and Beauty Services*
Healthcare
Illicit Activities
Domestic Work
Restaurants and Food Service
Agriculture and Animal Husbandry
Construction
Recreational Facilities
Hotels and Hospitality
Commercial Cleaning Services
Landscaping
Forestry and Logging
Factories and Manufacturing
Travelling Sales Crews
Carnivals
Peddling and Begging

*May be categorized in sex trafficking in certain scenarios.

vulnerabilities created by education access, immigration policies, and occupational health considerations. Examining the ways in which various sectors intersect and influence each trafficking typology across socioecologic levels offers comprehensive, public-health-grounded ways in which to better comprehend and address each form of trafficking.

Here we will review two key frameworks that emphasize the multi-sector aspects of human trafficking: social determinants of health and trauma-informed care.

Social Determinants of Health

"Social Determinants of Health" (SDoH) are broadly defined as the non-medical conditions that affect the health risks and outcomes of places where people live, learn, work, and play (Centers for

Disease Control and Prevention, 2017). These may include environmental and structural factors such as neighborhood conditions, working conditions, education, income, and wealth, as well as individual factors such as race, gender, ethnicity, sexuality, and disability status. These factors have varying impacts throughout one's life course, from childhood to adulthood. An example of these intersectional concepts is illustrated in the Bay Area Regional Health Inequities Initiative's Public Health Framework for Reducing Health Inequities (BARHII) (see Figure 10.3).

---

*Review BARHII (*Figure 10.3*). In what ways do these initiatives address human trafficking–related issues? What changes would you consider to make this framework more applicable?*

Increasing awareness of SDoH has resulted in the development of interventions addressing these issues. In 2017, the Centers for Medicare and Medicaid Services Accountable Health Communities Model released a ten-item screening tool to identify the social needs of patients engaged in the healthcare system in five key domains: housing instability, food insecurity, transportation needs, utility needs (e.g. electric, gas, oil, water), and interpersonal safety. The importance and relevance of this information, which is not otherwise routinely collected in clinical settings in the United States, informs both medical treatment plans as well as integration with appropriate community services. These factors have all been identified as impacting trafficked people at various times in the spectrum of pre-, during, and post-trafficking related experiences (Perry & McEwing, 2013; Rollins, Gribble, Barrett, & Powell, 2017). This example of a "midstream" public health intervention demonstrates a bridge between medical care and SDoH, uniting the factors that ultimately impact an individual, the community, and the society's health.

Because SDoH both shape and are influenced by policy, campaigns such as the American Public Health Association's "Health In All Policies" promote awareness of the complex ways in which legislation can have a downstream impact on health (Health in All Policies, 2016). This approach holds accountable institutional policies and regulations across sectors including corporations, governmental agencies, schools, and non-profit agencies to be cognizant of the health impact of current and future policy. "Health in all laws" can be further applied to human trafficking–related risk and longevity factors, prompting stakeholders to reflexively ask, "how will this policy or practice impact the health of trafficked people?"

Trauma

A public health approach allows for the examination of human trafficking as a network of systems that dually perpetuate and address trauma (see Bloom and Brotherton, Chapter 8, this volume). Examples of traumatic events include abuse, bullying, assault, war, and natural disasters (Hodas, 2006) (refer to Table 10.3). Trauma is both an established risk factor for human trafficking as well as a long-term physical and mental consequence of it (Aberdein & Zimmerman, 2015; Hossain, Zimmerman, Abas, Light, & Watts, 2010; Oram, Stockl, Busza, Howard, & Zimmerman, 2012).

The Adverse Childhood Experiences (ACEs) study offers an example of significant public health research that can be applied to better understand the social risk factors and subsequent health consequences of some forms of human trafficking (Stevens, 2012). Led by Dr. Vincent Felitti, the ACE's study was initiated in 1995 and examined peoples' adverse childhood experiences in the forms of abuse, neglect, and household dysfunction (Table 10.3) and health diagnoses they had as adults, such as alcoholism, chronic obstructive pulmonary disease, and chronic depression (Felitti et al., 1998). The study, based in San Diego, enrolled

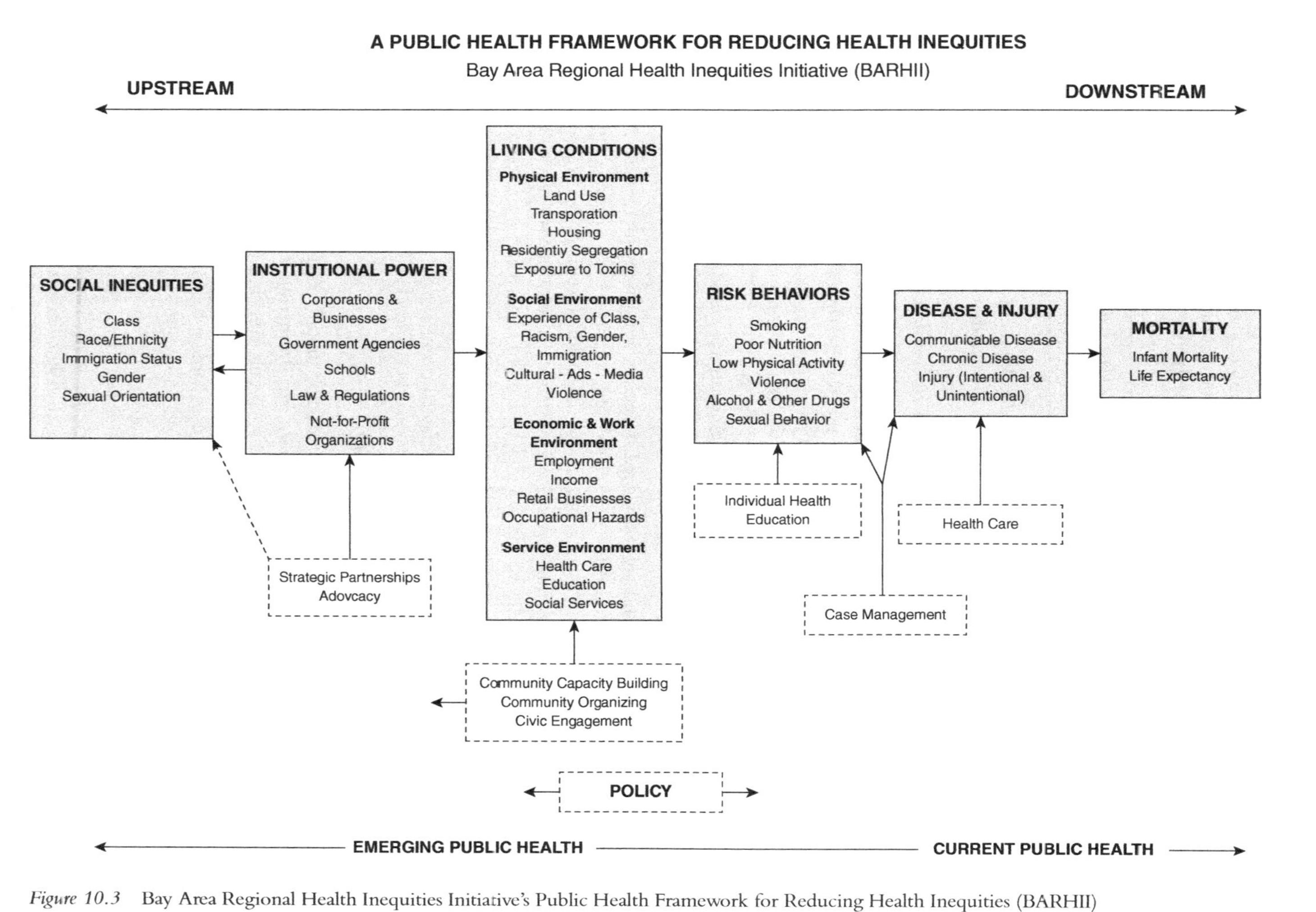

Figure 10.3 Bay Area Regional Health Inequities Initiative's Public Health Framework for Reducing Health Inequities (BARHII)

Table 10.3 Adverse childhood experiences (ACEs)

Abuse
Psychological
Physical
Sexual
Neglect
Emotional
Physical
Household Dysfunction
Substance abuse
Parental separation/divorce
Mental illness
Battered mother
Criminal behavior

17,421 participants who were followed longitudinally over 15 years. The results showed that the majority of participants had experienced at least two ACEs, that ACEs were additive, and furthermore, those with higher numbers of ACEs had long-term medical and social issues as adults, including chronic disease, mental illness, incarceration, and work absenteeism. The results also showed an association between biochemical coping methods, such as illicit substance use and increased food intake, to address symptoms of depression and anxiety.

ACEs can provide context for some of the health issues that trafficked youth face. A study by Reid et al. examining associations between human trafficking of minors and childhood adversity found that among a sample of 913 juvenile justice – involved boys and girls in Florida, the odds of human trafficking was 2.52 times greater for girls who experienced sexual abuse, and there was a 8.21 times greater risk for boys who had histories of sexual abuse when compared to a matched sample (Reid, Baglivio, Piquero, Greenwald, & Epps, 2017). ACEs also provide a means to comprehend how traumatic experiences that occur during youth can increase vulnerability to trafficking, the health issues that trafficked youth are at risk of developing as adults, and potential leverage points to incorporate prevention initiatives.

Recognizing the role of trauma in trafficking promotes the incorporation of trauma-informed care policies and practices across sectors as well. The four principles of trauma-informed care include (1) realizing the widespread impact of trauma; (2) recognizing signs and symptoms of trauma, including in patients and their families and in staff and clinical team members; (3) responding by fully integrating knowledge about trauma into policies, procedures, and practices; and (4) seeking to actively resist re-traumatization (Substance Abuse and Mental Health Services Administration, 2018). This fourth principle is especially relevant to service sectors, such as medicine and law enforcement, which though ideally designed to serve in the interest of trafficking victims can also result in additional trauma when not practiced sensitively.

The importance of trauma-informed care principles is being increasingly recognized, with efforts to address them at a federal level in the United States. In 2009, the U.S. Department of Health and Human Services' Office of the Assistant Secretary for Planning and Evaluation released a literature review of human trafficking into and within the United States (Clawson, 2009). In this review, six promising services and strategies to tackle human trafficking were identified, including requiring collaboration across multiple agencies and establishing trauma-informed programming – recommendations consistent with a public health approach to trafficking. On a legislative level, the "Trauma-Informed Care for Children and Families Act of 2016," introduced by U.S. Senator Heidi Heitkamp in an effort to incorporate ACE study related research into federal policy-making, also has the potential to benefit trafficking victims ("Trauma-Informed Care for Children and Families Act of 2016," 2016). The legislation includes trauma-informed training of law enforcement, provision of funding for schools to integrate mental health systems and trauma-informed clinician workforce development. As described by the Office of Victims Services' Human Trafficking Task Force e-Guide, such trauma-informed practices can mutually benefit law enforcement's tasks as well by leading to increased cooperation and more effective interviews with victims and witnesses (Office for Victims of Crime Training and Technical Assistance, 2017).

Key public health issues and human trafficking

Infectious disease

Infectious diseases, including those that are transmitted through sexual transmission and through intravenous drug use, is a significant pillar of public health that overlaps with human trafficking – particularly sex trafficking.

Infectious diseases associated with sex trafficking include sexually transmitted infections (STIs) such as HIV (Macias-Konstantopoulos, 2016). Public health research and interventions more broadly directed at populations involved in the sex industry have largely focused on harm reduction strategies. Harm reduction is a set of principles designed to reduce the negative consequences of risky behaviors by prioritizing the safety and the agency of affected individuals over condemnation and penalization (National Health Care for the Homeless Council, 2010). Examples include the use of needle exchanges to decrease the behavior of needle sharing and ultimately decreasing risk of associated infectious disease transmission (e.g. HIV, hepatitis C) and encouraging the use of condoms for people in situations where people have multiple or high-risk partners, such as in the pornography and brothel industries (Centers for Disease Control and Prevention, 2016c; Ghose, Swendeman, & George, 2011; Gupta, Raj, Decker, Reed, & Silverman, 2009).

Despite the negative health-related consequences of condomless sex, sex trafficked people face paradoxical pressures inflicted by traffickers regarding condom use (Gupta et al., 2009; Ravi, Pfeiffer, Rosner, & Shea, 2017a). Some traffickers threaten violence if victims have sex with buyers without using condoms (traffickers who use sexual intercourse to maintain control over victims sometimes perceive condomless sex with a buyer as a sign of infidelity), but also threaten violence if victims do not meet financial quotas set forth by traffickers (making condomless sex enticing as buyers are noted to pay more for condomless sex). Furthermore, victims face threats of violence from buyers who insist on condomless sex and from traffickers if a buyer injures them, as the financial profitability from an injured victim who is beaten, disfigured, and so forth decreases. Given these complexities, in order to design appropriate interventions for both victims and broader population health purposes, it is imperative that STI prevention efforts acknowledge and address the disincentives of condom use that trafficked people face.

The Zika virus illustrates a classic example of an STI with public health consequences for which human trafficking related complexities must be considered. Zika virus, a mosquito-borne flavivirus, can be transmitted through infected mosquito bites as well as through sexual transmission (World Health Organization, 2018). Complications of the virus include neurological disorders such as Guillain-Barre syndrome, and issues in pregnancy, including the potential for congenital fetal brain abnormalities. As a result, multiple public health organizations initiated guidelines for best and safe practices for virus prevention. The following is the World Health Organization's (WHO) advisory regarding the prevention of Zika virus through sexual transmissions (World Health Organization, 2018):

> For regions with active transmission of Zika virus, all people with Zika virus infection and their sexual partners (particularly pregnant women) should receive information about the risks of sexual transmission of Zika virus. WHO recommends that sexually active men and women be correctly counselled and offered a full range of contraceptive methods to be able to make an informed choice about whether and when to become pregnant in order to prevent possible adverse pregnancy and fetal outcomes. Women who have had unprotected sex and do not wish to become pregnant due to concerns about Zika virus infection should have ready access to emergency contraceptive services and counselling. Pregnant women should practice safer sex (including correct and consistent use of condoms) or abstain from sexual activity for at least the whole duration of the pregnancy.
>
> For regions with no active transmission of Zika virus, WHO recommends practicing safer sex or abstinence for a period of six months for men and women who are returning from areas of active transmission to prevent Zika virus infection through sexual intercourse. Sexual partners of pregnant women, living in or returning from areas where local transmission of Zika virus occurs should practice safer sex or abstain from sexual activity throughout the pregnancy.

The above is a classic example of the ways in which broader public health messaging of practicing safer sex or abstinence during pregnancy often overlooks the complexities of coercion that sex trafficked people face. Integral to this is the role of reproductive justice in infectious disease-related public health interventions. The formalization of the "reproductive justice" movement is often credited to a group of African American women who organized following the 1994 International Conference on Population and Development in Cairo, which had highlighted the important connection between reproductive health and achievement of global development goals (The Pro-Choice Public Education Project, 2007). To ensure that minority populations and intersectional issues (e.g. LGBTQ, disability, and immigration status) would be considered in reproductive-health-related policy and advocacy moving forward, the framework of reproductive justice was created. This framework includes the principles of women's right to manage their reproductive capacity (e.g. the right and access to safe, respectful, and affordable contraceptive materials and services), women's right to appropriate care with regard to pregnancy (e.g. the right and access to economic security, the right to physical safety) and a woman's right to be the parent of her child (e.g. the right to education and training in preparation for earning a living wage, the right to affordable and high-quality child care). These tenets include aspects of the socioecological model, social determinants of health, and upstream and downstream concepts of health and prevention.

When reviewing the WHO recommendations through the lens of reproductive justice – that sexually active women should be offered a full range of contraceptive methods, should be able to make an informed choice about pregnancy timing and intention, and should have the ability to engage in safer sex or abstinence – it becomes clear that these recommendations are not easily applied to the circumstances sex trafficked women face, given their limited access to routine healthcare and the decreased leverage to negotiate condom use. Recognizing that such recommendations do not incorporate the circumstances of sex trafficked women is critical in managing and preventing not only the Zika virus, but also other diseases that can be sexually transmitted, such as Ebola and HIV. Successfully preventing STIs requires consideration of the needs of the most marginalized populations, again highlighting the value of approaching human trafficking through a public health framework.

Substance use

Substance use encompasses the use of either or both alcohol or drugs (pharmaceutical and non-pharmaceutical). Opioids include forms of pain medication, as well as heroin. Heroin, typically used intravenously, has multiple health consequences, including risk for hepatitis C and HIV as mentioned in the previous section. In the United States, the opioid epidemic has been identified as the leading cause of death among adults (Centers for Disease Control and Prevention, 2016b). More globally, the World Health Organization identifies opioid misuse as a significant public health issue, with multiple initiatives to curb prescribing while increasing access to pain management and substance use recovery (World Health Organization, 2017a).

The opioid epidemic, along with other forms of substance misuse, impacts trafficked people in four main ways: drugs as a type of trafficking, substance use as a risk factor of being trafficked, substance use as a form of exerting control over those being trafficked, and substance use as a method of coping with trafficking-related trauma.

Drug trafficking can be a form of labor exploitation. This link was highlighted in a study among homeless youth in ten U.S. cities who have experienced trafficking (Center for the Human Rights of Children & The Young Center for Immigrant Children's Rights, 2016). Eighty-one percent of reported labor trafficking involved forced drug dealing, with 7% of the 641 youth interviewed reporting that they had been forced into working in the drug trade. Forced involvement arose from violence perpetration by suppliers and gangs and familial and cultural coercion. The public health consequences of this practice are numerous, particularly given the risk for and subsequent harms of incarceration among these trafficked youth, as will be described below.

Review one policy that has been passed in the last month at a federal level and identify how such policy may impact human trafficking.

Substance use, particularly drug addiction, is a risk factor for sex trafficking (Diaz, Clayton, & Simon, 2014; Institute of Medicine, 2013). The promise of drugs by traffickers to feed an individual's addiction results in exploitation of this vulnerability. In addition, review of the Power and Control Wheel in Figure 10.1 illustrates the way in which drugs can be used as a way to perpetuate long-term exploitation in the "physical abuse" section. The inherent trauma and violence in trafficking – both physical and psychological – results in ongoing substance use for both chronic pain management and trauma-related diagnoses such as depression, anxiety, and post-traumatic stress disorder, even post-trafficking (Macias-Konstantopoulos, 2016). Given that trafficked populations have experiences with both trafficking and non-trafficking associated trauma, they are at risk for long-term addiction. For example, a study of sex trafficking survivors incarcerated in New York City highlighted ways in which survivors relied on substance use to cope with sex trafficking-related trauma (Ravi et al., 2017b) This practice is also consistent with the previously discussed ACEs study indicating the use of biochemical substances to cope with trauma.

Framing the opioid epidemic as a public health issue highlights the complex interactions between trauma, substance use, and mental health diagnoses. Such conceptualization promotes essential public health informed practices in different sectors, such as incorporating trauma-informed care practices into substance use-related rehabilitation programs, and considering trafficking-related interventions at needle exchanges. These links also help in shifting substance use from exclusively a criminal justice issue to a public health issue, which, as discussed below, can ultimately benefit survivors, their families, and their communities.

Incarceration

Mass incarceration is established as a significant medical and public health issue worldwide, with the United States having the highest incarceration rate in the world (American Academy of Family Physicians, 2017). Due to current legal practices, both juvenile and adult survivors of trafficking are often criminalized due to crimes committed secondary to their being trafficked, including the practice of "forced criminality," increasing their risk for incarceration (Institute of Medicine, 2013; Serita, 2013). The health harms of incarceration have been extensively documented, impacting all levels of the socioecological model (American Academy of Family Physicians, 2017; National Research Council, 2013). Incarceration also negatively influences survivors' social determinants of health. For example, having a criminal record makes people ineligible for public housing, forms of public assistance including food and nutrition programs, and can limit the post-incarceration employment possibilities for victims (Alexander, 2010; "Criminal Justice, Homelessness, & Health, 2012 Policy Statement," 2012; Dennis et al., 2015). Approaching human trafficking as a public health issue instead of as solely a criminal justice issue highlights the health harms of incarceration and facilitates the creation of alternate solutions for the purposes of improved health outcomes.

At an individual level, incarceration increases victims' exposure to infectious disease, mental, physical, and sexual trauma, and self-harm (suicide is a leading cause of death among incarcerated persons), and incarceration decreases access to therapeutic services for chronic substance use, thereby increasing the risk both for withdrawal while incarcerated and overdose upon release (American Academy of Family Physicians, 2017; Ford, Kim, & Venters, 2017; National Research Council, 2013). Similarly, people seeking asylum from their native country, including those seeking asylum due to experiencing trafficking, may be held upon arrival to the United States in immigration detention centers, where they have been found to be at risk for multiple health issues, exacerbated by limited access to medical care (Center for the Human Rights of Children & The Young Center for Immigrant Children's Rights, 2016; Linton, Griffin, Shapiro, & Council On Community, 2017).

On relationship and community levels, incarceration can have adverse intergenerational impacts for the victims' families while also increasing victims' vulnerabilities to potential traffickers. The intergenerational health impact of incarceration for trafficked persons can begin from the time a survivor may have a pregnancy diagnosed in jail to their separation from their children while incarcerated. Having an incarcerated household member is categorized as an adverse childhood experience, thus putting that child at possible risk for future victimization (American Academy of Family Physicians, 2017; Davis & Shlafer, 2017; Turney, 2017a, 2017b). Furthermore, correctional settings are sometimes considered a "prison pipeline" for trafficking, as they become sites that traffickers can focus on to recruit new victims (Connolly, 2014; Meekins, 2017). Vulnerable women who appear to have poor external social support are sometimes targeted and lured into trafficking upon release by fellow women prisoners.

There has been, however, an increased recognition in the American legal system of trafficked people as victims and not criminals, allowing for the health-related impacts of trafficking to be considered when working with victims. In 2004, New York state piloted its first iteration of Human Trafficking Intervention Court (HTIC) (Serita, 2013). The court mostly handles the cases of people arrested on prostitution or loitering charges. Designed to be an alternative to incarceration, the court facilitates connecting victims with a broad range of services, including counseling, job training, education, housing, medical assistance, immigration services, and substance abuse and mental health treatment. As described in her HTIC overview paper "In Our Own Backyards," Judge Toko Serita, an HTIC Judge, states the following (2013, p. 655):

> All persons working in the HTIC recognize that prostituted women suffer a myriad of afflictions. These include long-term physical and psychological trauma, post-traumatic stress disorder, high rates of health problems and infections, and mental health and substance abuse issues.

HTIC recognizes the impact of social determinants of health, including unstable housing, social support network, and documentation status as trafficking-related risk factors. Furthermore, the court is cognizant of the complexity of alternatives of incarcerations that are offered, as some victims are still controlled by the trafficker throughout their court proceedings, and may face personal and logistical barriers in completing the mandated sessions.

While the focus of this chapter was largely on the impact of different sectors on victims and their families, the criminal justice system does also incorporate health-related messaging when addressing buyers of sex trafficked people. (Overview of John Schools and Justification for Further Research in Ohio, 2015) "John Schools," programs in cities across the United States, are designed for people arrested for illegal solicitation or the actual purchase of sex. In certain instances, buyers may pay a fine and complete the John School course in exchange for sealing a conviction, or they may be mandated to the program as part of their sentencing. While John Schools have varying, non-standardized curriculum content and length, a 2012 review of course content showed sex trafficking was incorporated as a topic to increase awareness of the issue among sex buyers (Shively, Kliorys, Wheeler, & Hunt, 2012).

Environmental health

Environmental health spans broad issues from climate change to individual protective factors in an occupational environment, such as worker safety equipment. Climate change can impact people's health as a result of more extreme weather, rising sea levels, increasing carbon dioxide levels, and rising temperatures (Centers for Disease Control and Prevention, 2016a). These trends are associated with environmental changes such as poor water quality and air pollution, which ultimately link with society level changes including migration and displacement, as well as individual impacts of acute, chronic physical, mental and infectious conditions. Examples of the intersection between environmental changes and health range from respiratory illnesses and mold exposure to post-traumatic stress disorder following increased hurricane activity. Table 10.4 lists the major U.S. climate trends noted across the country (Balbus, 2016).

From 2007 to 2009, the European Commission conducted the Environmental Change and Forced Migration Scenarios (EACH-FOR) multi-country research project, which provided additional insight on climate-related changes that perpetuate trafficking (United Nations University, 2017). A country study from Bangladesh noted four populations vulnerable to trafficking post–natural disaster. These include women, typically widows whose husbands either passed away during a cyclone or were away on temporary migration, who were then most commonly forced into sex trafficking due to economic circumstances. In addition, men in cyclone-destroyed areas were vulnerable to labor trafficking by human smugglers who promised men work in northern India, which was ultimately nothing more than working in sweatshop conditions. The other two populations included children who were forced into labor and sexual exploitation, and

Table 10.4 Major U.S. climate trends

Rising temperatures
Wildfires
Waves
Drought
Cold waves and winter storms
Sea levels increased
Extreme precipitation
Floods
Hurricanes

entire families that become involuntarily trapped in trafficking networks (Poncelet, 2009). Similar trends were noted in situations of both acute and long-term climate related changes, such as natural-disasters or draughts, in country studies of Vietnam, India, and Mali (Enarson, InFocus Programme on Crisis Response and Reconstruction, and International Labour Office. Recovery and Reconstruction Dept., 2000; Findley, 1994).

Go to www.justice.gov/usao-sdny/pr/bronx-sex-trafficker-sentenced-manhattan-federal-court-20-years-prison. What are all of the public health issues that you can identify in this case?

Climate change can cause situations that perpetuate "mixed flows," broadly defined as people who are on the move for different reasons but who share the same routes, modes of travel and vessels, and who do so without the required documentation upon arrival at their destination (International Organization for Migration, 2016). As per the International Organization for Migration (IOM), mixed flows can involve vulnerable populations, including trafficking victims. Furthermore, the IOM states "Perhaps the single most indeterminable factor in attempting to gauge the future extent of . . . mixed flows is the impact of climate change and environmental degradation" (International Organization for Migration, 2010, p. 9). "Environmental migrants" – those who are moving either within their countries or across borders, on a permanent or temporary basis, due to climate or environmental related changes – are vulnerable to trafficking. For example, repeated extreme or slow onset weather events can plunge rural families into extreme poverty. This, in turn, can result in the migration of younger women, typically daughters, including minors, placing them at risk for encountering people or circumstances that result in sexual exploitation or trafficking.

The aftermath of environmental-related disasters is rife for labor exploitation. The lawsuit against Signal International, LLC, coordinated by the Southern Poverty Law Center and a network of pro-bono attorneys across the United States, resulted in its being among the largest labor trafficking cases in U.S. history (Southern Poverty Law Center, 2008, 2015). The case highlights the intersection between environmental health and labor trafficking.

Signal is a shipbuilding company that was tasked with repairing oil rigs and related Gulf Coast facilities damaged from Hurricanes Katrina and Rita. Guest workers from India were lured under false pretenses, promised green cards and permanent U.S. residency for themselves and their families. Given these expectations, workers and their families went into deep debt or sold their property to pay these fees. However, upon arrival to the United States, they were informed that they would not be receiving green cards or a path to residency. Instead, they were subjected to threats of deportation if they did not comply with the mandated fees and rules during the course of their employment with Signal. They had mandated housing, described as racially segregated (non-Indians were not required to live in company housing), and the workers were forced to have $1,050 in rent deducted from their monthly paychecks. Kept under guard, the company also enforced strict rules (e.g. no visitors, no alcohol) and subjected workers to regular searches and fines for violations. Court documents showed that Signal's chief financial officer referred to the housing as "profit centers."

The health issues associated with the exploitation of these workers were noted throughout the case. For example, the housing units slept up to 24 people in a double-wide trailer, resulting in illnesses related to extensive overcrowding. A press release by the American Civil Liberties Union described the living conditions in which the workers were kept (Yachot, 2013):

> in conditions even Signal has acknowledged did not comply with the basic health and safety standards required by law. . . . Signal also admitted in internal emails that the dining facilities in which the workers ate were "disgusting" – so much so that the company "prayed" they would go undetected by health inspectors.

The Signal case represents a classic example of the ways in which trafficking intersects with multiple domains of public health. In this case study alone, environmental health, including climate change and worker safety, social determinants of health such as food and housing security, and psychological health influenced the circumstances and outcomes of this situation.

Unsafe labor or working conditions are another form of environmental health that is associated with human trafficking (Buller, 2015). Lack of access to protective equipment, such as when working with pesticides or harsh cleaning solutions, can have detrimental impacts on victims' health. Because workers have little recourse in reporting unsafe working, such employer perpetrated negligence and abuse can sometimes result in long-term negative health exposures.

Finally, in the broader context of the socioecological framework, consideration of secondary and tertiary prevention with regard to environmental health related issues tie in with the concept of resilience. As stated by the National Institute of Environmental Health Sciences: "Resilience also has a communal dimension, as governance, social capital, physical infrastructure, planning, and preparedness impact how a community will fare when stressed or shocked by climate change, particularly extreme events" (National Institute of Environmental Health Sciences, 2016).

Technology

The intersection of online, digital, and mobile technologies with human trafficking and public health exposes the vulnerabilities through which persons are exploited, and also offers potential ways to address the issue.

Technologies such as social media, mobile devices, and web-based advertisements and forums can fuel the social, economic, and political factors associated with sex and labor trafficking. For sex trafficking, it was well established that certain websites have been used to recruit victims through deceptive online advertising, to find buyers and to interconnect trafficker networks. In the United States, websites such as Backpage.com and Craigslist became the focus of sex trafficking interventions, primarily due to concerns regarding the promotion of child sex trafficking (Dixon, 2013; Harris, Morgester, Mailman, & Krell, 2017) The threat of releasing private digital photos in provocative or compromising sexual positions has also been used as a form of coercion and entrapment into sex trafficking. Further upstream, acts that impact children's and adolescents' self-esteem, including cyberbullying, can increase vulnerability to trafficking.

In contrast to sex trafficking, where advertisements are targeted towards buyers as described above, labor traffickers use technology to recruit and maintain control over the people they traffic. For example, some traffickers thrive on strategically placing job postings targeting vulnerable populations among other advertisements such that the postings cannot be readily identified as exploitative. In addition, a review of human trafficking cases and patterns involving technology by the University of Southern California's Annenberg Center on Communication Leadership and Policy on Human Trafficking Online found that the use of technology by labor traffickers tended to be limited to pay-as-you-go cellphones (Latonero, Wex, Dank, & Poucki, 2015). This study also found that isolation from technology and social networks increases migrant workers' vulnerability to trafficking.

Unintended consequences from other web-based databases in other sectors can also result in further exploitation of vulnerable populations. For example, the U.S. Department of Homeland Security implemented the Victim Information and Notification Exchange (VINE) in 2017 (Tahirih Justice Center, 2017). This was designed for victims and crime witnesses to be notified when a detained immigrant is released or moved. This database includes those booked for criminal offenses and minor crime violations, as well as those detained for immigration status and those applying for human trafficking visas under the U and T Visa program. Shortly after the program was implemented, the Tahiri Center for Justice noted that this database could be manipulated by exploiters to track their victims. Similarly, traffickers can use correction departments' public online database to find pictures, personal information, and potential release dates and addresses to find their victims or to prey on new ones (Meekins, 2017).

Technology advancements, however, are also aiding in interventions and the prevention of human trafficking. The interfaces and audiences of such initiatives vary, and include cloud-based and mobile phone apps. Examples of technology-based initiatives include those that provide resources for victim-centered services, including a route to reporting and gaining help while trafficked. The initiatives can also be useful to bystanders who suspect trafficking is occurring, to law enforcement, and to private and governmental actors associated with trafficking-related risk factors (Latonero et al., 2015). One example of intervention through technology is Polaris Project's (2018) National Human Trafficking Resource Center (NHTRC), which provides a toll-free hotline, email access, and an online tip reporting form for victims and community members and private sectors developing technological tools to acquire data on contractors and suppliers involved in employment supply chains (National Human Trafficking Hotline: https://polarisproject.org/national-human-trafficking-hotline).

Case study

Tasha Gardner was born in Jamaica. She lived there until the age of two, when her mother moved her and her sister to the United States to reunite with their father. Her father had moved to Queens, New York, a few years earlier to work in a construction company, and had been sending money home to support them. Shortly after Tasha's arrival to the United States, Mr. Gardner experienced an injury at a construction site, resulting in an extended hospitalization and recovery. Her mother had been working in a restaurant at night to help make ends meet and to pay medical bills. No longer able to afford their rent, Tasha's family moved in with her uncle, who also lived in Queens. In the process of taking care of Mr. Gardner, Tasha's family eventually overstayed their visa, leaving them without legal status in the United States. At the age of ten, Tasha's parents divorced, and Tasha, her mother and sister remained living with her uncle. Because her mother worked the night shift, Tasha's uncle was responsible for picking her and her sister up from school. A few weeks after he started doing this, however, he began molesting Tasha in their home. He threatened to hurt her sister if Tasha told anyone, leaving her scared and afraid to seek help. He continued perpetuating the abuse for the next two years.

During this time, Tasha began performing perpetually worse at school. She was not sleeping well, and had difficulty concentrating during classes and began had increasing absences from school. In tenth grade, Tasha met George, a 17-year-old boy who came up to her while she was shopping at the local mall. They began trading text messages and started dating shortly afterwards. George brought Tasha gifts, and saying that he missed her, would ask her to send him pictures of her posing in "sexy" ways. They became sexually active a few months later. As Tasha started spending more time with George, she spent less time at her home and eventually dropped out of school.

After four months of dating, George wanted to know if Tasha could help him pay their rent by doing a few favors for him. George began setting up "dates" for Tasha with his friends. Tasha did not like this, and told him that she was leaving and moving back in with her mother. But when she tried to leave, George reminded her that he knew where her sister lived, and said he would send the sexy pictures that she had sent him to her mother. Tasha did not want to hurt her family any further, and stayed with George. Soon Tasha was forced to sell sex out of hotels, cars, and on sidewalks to men who found her ads posted online, and had to turn all her money over to him. She was expected to bring in $5,000 on weekends and $1,000 on weekdays. George would buy her clothing and provide her with food on the days she met her quota. She also started using cocaine that George gave her, which helped her stay awake during the night to see enough buyers and to numb the pain she was experiencing during intercourse.

Because of her undocumented status, George created a new ID for her. During the next five years, Tasha was arrested multiple times on various charges: carrying a weapon (to keep her safe from buyers), petty theft (George would not purchase sanitary napkins for her, so she would end up stealing them from drug stores), and drug possession. She was frequently beaten and injured by George and by buyers, but was not permitted to seek healthcare, no matter how severe her injury. When Tasha was 26, George was arrested and incarcerated.

During this time, she learned she was pregnant. She continued to use cocaine and occasionally sold sex to make ends meet. A few months later, she re-connected with her mother and sister, and six months later, delivered a premature baby boy. George was released from jail one year later and found Tasha. He promised her that he had changed and they reunited. However, shortly afterwards, he began to traffic her again. She was eventually re-arrested for cocaine possession, but this time, while on Rikers Island, the public defender's office came in to explain the Human Trafficking Intervention Court (HTIC) to the women in jail. Tasha realized that she was eligible for the program, and connected with a lawyer who was able to divert her case to HTIC and assist her in connecting with services. During this time, her lawyer became aware of her undocumented status, and assisted her in meeting with an immigration lawyer so that she could apply for a T-visa – a visa for trafficking survivors. However, she was not able to connect with an outpatient rehabilitation program for her cocaine use, as she was uninsured.

Because she was not permitted to work until her T-visa was processed, Tasha took informal jobs such as hair braiding and nannying. One of her positions was as a housekeeper cleaning rooms at a local hotel chain. During this time, she began developing a cough and rash on her hands because of the strong cleaning chemicals she had to use. She was told not to complain about this issue to management or to request protective equipment, as she could risk losing her job.

One day, when she returned home from her shift, she saw that a Child Protective Services (CPS) agent was at her door. The CPS agent told her that that there had been a report that she was leaving her five-year-old son home alone at night while at work, which she had been doing as she was unable to afford formal childcare, and did not feel comfortable asking a relative to watch her son after her own experience with her uncle. Cocaine was also found on the premises. Her son was removed from her home and her visa status became endangered due to the family court case that was filed against her.

Cast study discussion questions

1. Apply the socioecological framework to Tasha's experience with regard to risk factors for trafficking and areas of prevention.
2. What are examples of social determinants of health that affect Tasha's life?
3. How have social determinants of health affected Tasha?
4. Describe adverse childhood events that Tasha has experienced.
5. How does the concept of reproductive justice intersect with Tasha's experience?
6. How has substance use affected Tasha's life?
7. How has incarceration impacted the life of Tasha and her family?
8. What has the role of technology played in Tasha's life?
9. In reviewing Tasha's case, what are ways in which the concepts of upstream and downstream prevention could be applied?

Media

The media plays a critical role in human trafficking. Editorial decisions can influence public perception and relevant stakeholders' understanding of human trafficking and its nuances. For example, trafficking experts have expressed frustration that labor trafficking is less frequently covered by the media as compared to sex trafficking, despite it being more prevalent (Chisholm-Straker & Stoklosa, 2017). This section highlights the ways in which language choice, image use, and approaches to interviewing survivors demonstrates the intersection of media, human trafficking, and public health.

The intentional or unintentional perpetuation of stereotypes or misconceptions is a critical component of a public health understanding of human trafficking. The University of North Carolina's School of Journalism and Mass Communication's Irina Project represents one such initiative that both monitors and advocates for responsible reporting regarding sex trafficking (DART Center for Journalism & Trauma, 2014). The project's team reviewed print, broadcast and online media over a five-year period from 2008 to 2012 to identify how sex trafficking was covered, how persons involved in sex trafficking were described, and the themes used to frame the issue (Johnston, 2015). In a content analysis, they found that while sex trafficking issues were commonly framed as a crime related issue ranging from 60% to 95% during the five-year study period, public health was among the least common frameworks discussed, peaking in 2010 at 20%, around the time when the World Health Organization reported that 2010 was "a year of public health challenges" following a series of worldwide natural disasters. The consequences of trafficking on public health were mentioned in 2.7%, 2.8%, and 3.2% of the frameworks of policy/legislation, crime, and human rights, respectively. The results of this study, and initiatives such as the "No Such Thing" campaign, advocate against the use of the term "child prostitute," as it implies that children can voluntarily consent to selling sex, something which they cannot legally do. In April 2016, the Associated Press recommended that writers avoid the term (Vafa, 2016).

Best practices in working with survivors are also necessary to decrease unintended health repercussions towards them. Lauren Wolfe, a journalist and photographer and director of the Women's Medical Center's "Women Under Siege" put forth a list of ten "Dos" and "Don'ts" when interviewing sexual violence survivors (Wolfe, 2017). Embedded in these recommendations, it becomes clear that the potential for re-traumatizing survivors during interviews is high and the downstream impact of these decisions can be ultimately detrimental. Beyond journalism, practices such as "Don't rush a survivor" can also be used by public health researchers and those conducting qualitative and ethnographic studies with survivors.

Conclusion

As you have likely seen throughout this chapter, multiple sectors intersect and overlap with various forms of trafficking, impacting health from an individual to a societal level.

While this chapter covered six main concepts that link with human trafficking through a public health framework, there are of course multiple other concepts of relevance such as education, immigration, and transportation. However, the larger goal is having the ability to consider the ways in which the concepts of health and human trafficking can be applied across sectors.

Also of note is that while the concepts of SDoH and trauma were largely discussed with the perspective of trafficking victims, the public health framework makes it clear that to truly eradicate human trafficking approaching this issue by addressing issues related to traffickers is necessary as well. Understanding the factors from an individual experience to broader policies that influence one's decision to sell and exploit a human being is essential when striving for trafficking-informed policy, interventions, and prevention.

And finally, while this chapter highlights ways in which appropriately approaching interactions with trafficking survivors, whether they be by trauma-informed practices or media sensitivity during interviews are essential, of equal importance is ensuring the protection of trafficked people in public health research. These practices are in light of histories of inhumane, exploitative research such as the Tuskegee Experiment, whereby African American men were enrolled in a syphilis treatment research study without informed consent. Among other injustices, some participants were also denied treatment for their illnesses. Such abuse has weakened the relationship between the public and health-related research ("U.S. Public Health Service Syphilis Study at Tuskegee," 2015). Cognizance of this issue and its downstream impacts, such as mistrust in the medical system among minority populations, is essential in avoiding re-exploitation of any and all vulnerable populations when pursuing public health research regarding human trafficking.

Supplemental learning materials

Documentaries

A Path Appears: Transforming Lives, Creating Opportunity. Retrieved from http://apathappears.org/

Altan, D., Cediel, A., & Bergman, L. (2013). *Rape on the night shift.* Frontline (PBS), Univision, Reveal from The Center for Investigative Reporting (CIR), the Investigative Reporting Program (IRP) at UC Berkeley, and KQED.

Half the Sky: Turning Oppression into Opportunity Worldwide. Retrieved from www.pbs.org/independentlens/half-the-sky/sex-trafficking/

Very Young Girls. Retrieved from www.gems-girls.org/get-involved/very-young-girls

Writing from survivors

Gray, M. (2016, March). *Why human trafficking is a public health problem.* Retrieved from www.cnn.com/2016/07/11/opinions/human-trafficking-health-margeaux-gray/

Woworuntu, S. (2016, March). *Shandra Woworuntu: My life as a sex-trafficking victim.* Retrieved from www.bbc.com/news/magazine-35846207

News articles

Allen, E. (2015, May). *Something rotten in New York city nail salons.* Retrieved from www.nytimes.com/times-insider/2015/05/07/something-rotten-in-the-state-of-nail-salons/.

McDowell, R., Mason, M., & Medoza, M. (2015, March). *Are slaves catching the fish you buy?* Retrieved from www.usnews.com/news/business/articles/2015/03/24/ap-investigation-are-slaves-catching-the-fish-you-buy

Winn, P. (2015, March). *The slave labor behind your favorite clothing brands exposed.* Retrieved from www.salon.com/2015/03/22/the_slave_labor_behind_your_favorite_clothing_brands_gap_hm_and_more_exposed_partner/

Webinars

Baldwin, S., Chaffee, T., & Greenbaum, J. Introduction to labor and sex trafficking: A health care & human rights challenge. Futures Without Violence: Webinar & PDF www.futureswithoutviolence.org/14599-2/

Public health and trafficking organizations

HEAL Trafficking: https://healtrafficking.org/

Polaris Project: http://polarisproject.org/

References

Aberdein, C., & Zimmerman, C. (2015). Access to mental health and psychosocial services in Cambodia by survivors of trafficking and exploitation: A qualitative study. *International Journal of Mental Health Systems, 9*, 16. Retrieved from https://doi.org/10.1186/s13033-015-0008-8

Alexander, M. (2010). *The new Jim Crow: Mass incarceration in the age of colorblindness.* New York [Jackson, TN]: New Press; Distributed by Perseus Distribution.

American Academy of Family Physicians. (2017). Incarceration and Health: A Family Medicine Perspective (Position Paper). *AAFP Policies.* Retrieved from www.aafp.org/about/policies/all/incarcerationand-health.html

Balbus, J. (2016). Climate change and health resilience: Overview and approaches. Retrieved from www.niehs.nih.gov/research/supported/translational/peph/webinars/climate_change/balbus_508.pdf

Bharmal, N., Derose, K., Felician, M., & Weden, M. (2015). *Understanding the upstream social determinants of health.* Retrieved from www.rand.org/content/dam/rand/pubs/working_papers/WR1000/WR1096/RAND_WR1096.pdf

Buller, AM, Vaca, V., Stoklosa, H., Borland, R., & Zimmerman, C. (2015). *Labour exploitation, trafficking and migrant health: Multi-country findings on the health risks and consequences of migrant and trafficked workers.* Retrieved from: https://publications.iom.int/system/files/pdf/labour_exploitation_trafficking_en.pdf

Centers for Disease Control and Prevention. (2015, March 25). *The social-ecological model: A framework for prevention.* Retrieved from www.cdc.gov/violenceprevention/overview/social-ecologicalmodel.html

Centers for Disease Control and Prevention. (2016a, July 26). *Climate effects on health.* Retrieved from www.cdc.gov/climateandhealth/effects/

Centers for Disease Control and Prevention. (2016b, December 16). *Drug overdose deaths in the United States continue to increase in 2015.* Retrieved from www.cdc.gov/drugoverdose/epidemic/

Centers for Disease Control and Prevention. (2016c). *Syringe services programs.* Retrieved from www.cdc.gov/hiv/risk/ssps.html

Centers for Disease Control and Prevention. (2017, May 11). Social determinants of health: Know what affects health. *Social Determinants of Health.* Retrieved from www.cdc.gov/socialdeterminants/

Center for the Human Rights of Children Loyola University Chicago, & The Young Center for Immigrant Children's Rights at the University of Chicago. (2016). *Alternative Report: An NGO response to the periodic report of the United States of America to the Un Committee on the rights of the Child Concerning the optional protocol to the Convention on the rights of the Child on the Sale of Children, Child prostitution and Child pornography.* Chicago, IL. Retrieved from http://luc.edu/media/lucedu/chrc/pdfs/OPSC%20Alternative%20Report.pdf

Chisholm-Straker, M., & Stoklosa, H. (2017). *Human trafficking as a public health issue: A paradigm expansion in the U.S.* Springer International Publishing. Retrieved from www.springer.com/us/book/9783319478234

Clawson, H., Dutch, N., Solomon, A., & Grace, L.G. (2009). *Human trafficking into and within the United States: A review of the literature.* Washington, DC. Retrieved from https://aspe.hhs.gov/report/human-trafficking-and-within-united-states-review-literature

Connolly, K. P. (2014, September 8). Sex slavers arrested in Orlando for trafficking women from prison, MBI says. *Orlando Sentienl.* Retrieved from www.orlandosentinel.com/news/breaking-news/os-sex-slaves-orlando-female-prisoners-20140918-story.html

Coote, A. (2012). *The wisdom of prevention: Long-term planning, upstream investment and early action to prevent harm.* 3 Jonathan Street, London SE11 5NH, United Kingdom. Retrieved from http://b.3cdn.net/nefoundation/b8278023a5b025649f_5zm6i2btg.pdf

Criminal Justice, Homelessness & Health: 2012 Policy Statement. (2012). Retrieved from www.nhchc.org/wp-content/uploads/2011/09/Criminal-Justice-2012.pdf

DART Center for Journalism & Trauma. (2014). Covering sex trafficking: The Irina project. Retrieved from https://dartcenter.org/blog/covering-sex-trafficking-irina-project

Davis, L., & Shlafer, R. J. (2017). Mental health of adolescents with currently and formerly incarcerated parents. *Journal of Adolescence, 54,* 120–134. Retrieved from https://doi.org/10.1016/j.adolescence.2016.10.006

Dennis, A. C., Barrington, C., Hino, S., Gould, M., Wohl, D., & Golin, C. E. (2015). "You're in a world of chaos": Experiences accessing HIV care and adhering to medications after incarceration. *Journal of the Association of Nurses in AIDS Care, 26*(5), 542–555. Retrieved from https://doi.org/10.1016/j.jana.2015.06.001

Diaz, A., Clayton, E. W., & Simon, P. (2014). Confronting commercial sexual exploitation and sex trafficking of minors. *JAMA Pediatrics, 168*(9), 791–792. Retrieved from https://doi.org/10.1001/jamapediatrics.2014.1002

Dixon, Herbert B. (2013). Human trafficking and the Internet* (*and other technologies, too). *The Judges' Journal- The American Bar Association, 52*(1).

Domestic Abuse Intervention Programs: Home of the Duluth Model. (2017). *FAQs about the wheels.* Retrieved from www.theduluthmodel.org/wheels/faqs-about-the-wheels/

Enarson, E. P., InFocus Programme on Crisis Response and Reconstruction, & International Labour Office. Recovery and Reconstruction Dept. (2000). *Gender and natural disasters.* Geneva: International Labour Office.

Felitti, V. J., Anda, R. F., Nordenberg, D., Williamson, D. F., Spitz, A. M., Edwards, V., . . . Marks, J. S. (1998). Relationship of childhood abuse and household dysfunction to many of the leading causes of death in

adults. The Adverse Childhood Experiences (ACE) Study. *American Journal of Preventive Medicine, 14*(4), 245–258.
Findley, S. E. (1994). Does drought increase migration? A study of migration from rural Mali during the 1983–1985 drought. *International Migration Review, 28*(3), 539–553.
Ford, E., Kim, S., & Venters, H. (2017). Sexual abuse and injury during incarceration reveal the need for re-entry trauma screening. *Lancet, 389*(10077), 1393. Retrieved from https://doi.org/10.1016/S0140–6736(17)30888–7
Ghose, T., Swendeman, D. T., & George, S. M. (2011). The role of brothels in reducing HIV risk in Sonagachi, India. *Qualitative Health Research, 21*(5), 587–600. Retrieved from https://doi.org/10.1177/1049732310395328
Gupta, J., Raj, A., Decker, M. R., Reed, E., & Silverman, J. G. (2009). HIV vulnerabilities of sex-trafficked Indian women and girls. *International Journal of Gynecology & Obstetrics, 107*(1), 30–34. Retrieved from https://doi.org/10.1016/j.ijgo.2009.06.009
Harris, K., Morgester, R., Mailman, R., & Krell, M. (2017). *People of the state of California, versus Carl Ferrer, Michael Lacey, and James Larkin.* (16FE024013). Sacramento, CA. USA. Retrieved from https://oag.ca.gov/system/files/attachments/press_releases/backpage%20redacted.pdf
Health in All Policies. (2016). Health in all policies report. Retrieved from www.ci.richmond.ca.us/2575/Health-in-All-Policies-HiAP
Hodas, G. (2006). *Responding to childhood trauma: The promise and practice of trauma informed care.* Retrieved from www.childrescuebill.org/VictimsOfAbuse/RespondingHodas.pdf
Hossain, M., Zimmerman, C., Abas, M., Light, M., & Watts, C. (2010). The relationship of trauma to mental disorders among trafficked and sexually exploited girls and women. *American Journal of Public Health, 100*(12), 2442–2449. Retrieved from https://doi.org/10.2105/AJPH.2009.173229
Ijadi-Maghsoodi, R., Cook, M., Barnert, E. S., Gaboian, S., & Bath, E. (2016). Understanding and responding to the needs of commercially sexually exploited youth: Recommendations for the mental health provider. *Child and Adolescent Psychiatric Clinics of North America, 25*(1), 107–122. Retrieved from https://doi.org/10.1016/j.chc.2015.08.007
Institute of Medicine. (2013). *Confronting commercial sexual exploitation and sex trafficking of minors in the United States. A guide for providers of victim and support services.* Washington, DC. Retrieved from www.ncjfcj.org/sites/default/files/IOM%20Report%20on%20Services.pdf
Institute of Medicine and National Research Council. 2013. *Health and Incarceration: A Workshop Summary.* Washington, DC: The National Academies Press. https://doi.org/10.17226/18372.
Institute for Work & Health. (2015). Primary, secondary, and tertiary prevention. *Atwork* (80), 1–8.
International Organization for Migration. (2010). Background paper WMR 2010: Irregular migration and mixed flows. Retrieved from http://publications.iom.int/system/files/pdf/wmr2010_irregular_migration_and_mixed_flows.pdf
International Organization for Migration. (2016). The climate change-human trafficking nexus. Retrieved from https://publications.iom.int/system/files/pdf/mecc_infosheet_climate_change_nexus.pdf
Johnston, A.F.B., & Sobel, M. (2015). Framing an emerging issue: How U.S. print and broadcast news media covered sex trafficking, 2008–2012. *Journal of Human Trafficking* (1), 235–254.
Latonero, M., Wex, B., Dank, M., & Poucki, S. (2015). *Technology and labor trafficking in a network society.* Retrieved from https://communicationleadership.usc.edu/files/2015/10/USC_Tech-and-Labor-Trafficking_Feb2015.pdf
Linton, J. M., Griffin, M., Shapiro, A. J., & Council on Community Pediatrics. (2017). Detention of immigrant children. *Pediatrics, 139*(5). Retrieved from https://doi.org/10.1542/peds.2017–0483
Macias-Konstantopoulos, W. (2016). Human trafficking: The role of medicine in interrupting the cycle of abuse and violence. *Annals of Internal Medicine, 165*(8), 582–588. Retrieved from https://doi.org/10.7326/M16–0094
Meekins, J. (2017). *Human trafficking in women's prisons (Vol. 2017): Chicago books to women in prison.* https://chicagobwp.org/2017/01/11/human-trafficking-in-womens-prisons/
National Health Care for the Homeless Council. (2010). *Harm reduction: Preparing people for change.* Nashville, TN. Retrieved from www.nhchc.org/wp-content/uploads/2011/09/harmreductionFS_Apr10.pdf
National Human Trafficking Hotline. (Updated: 2018). Retrieved from https://polarisproject.org/national-human-trafficking-hotline
National Human Trafficking Resource Center. (2010). *Human trafficking power and control wheel.* Retrieved from https://humantraffickinghotline.org/resources/human-trafficking-power-and-control-wheel

National Institute of Environmental Health Sciences. (2016). *Climate change and health: Partnerships for environmental public health.* Retrieved from www.niehs.nih.gov/research/supported/translational/peph/webinars/climate_change/index.cfm

Office for Victims of Crime Training and Technical Assistance. (2017). *Human trafficking task force e-guide: Strengthening collaborative responses.* Washington DC. Retrieved from www.ovcttac.gov/taskforceguide/eguide/

Oram, S., Stockl, H., Busza, J., Howard, L. M., & Zimmerman, C. (2012). Prevalence and risk of violence and the physical, mental, and sexual health problems associated with human trafficking: Systematic review. *PLOS Medicine, 9*(5), e1001224. Retrieved from https://doi.org/10.1371/journal.pmed.1001224

Overview of John Schools and Justification for Further Research in Ohio. Columbus, OH. (2015). Retrieved from http://humantrafficking.ohio.gov/links/John-Schools-Report.pdf

Perry, K. M., & McEwing, L. (2013). How do social determinants affect human trafficking in Southeast Asia, and what can we do about it? A systematic review. *Health and Human Right, 15*(2), 138–159.

Polaris. (2017). *The typology of modern slavery.* Retrieved from https://polarisproject.org/sites/default/files/Polaris-Typology-of-Modern-Slavery.pdf

Poncelet, A. (2009). *Bangladesh case study report.* Retrieved from https://proyectoambientales.files.wordpress.com/2011/05/csr_bangladesh_090126.pdf

The Pro-Choice Public Education Project. (2007). *Reproductive justice briefing book: A primer on reproductive justice and social change.* Retrieved from www.law.berkeley.edu/php-programs/courses/fileDL.php?fID=4051

Ravi, A., Pfeiffer, M. R., Rosner, Z., & Shea, J. A. (2017a). Identifying health experiences of domestically sex-trafficked women in the USA: A qualitative study in Rikers island jail. *Journal of Urban Health.* Retrieved from https://doi.org/10.1007/s11524-016-0128-8

Ravi, A., Pfeiffer, M. R., Rosner, Z., & Shea, J. A. (2017b). Trafficking and trauma: Insight and advice for the healthcare system from sex-trafficked women incarcerated on Rikers island. *Medical Care.* Retrieved from https://doi.org/10.1097/MLR.0000000000000820

Reid, J. A., Baglivio, M. T., Piquero, A. R., Greenwald, M. A., & Epps, N. (2017). Human trafficking of minors and childhood adversity in Florida. *American Journal of Public Health, 107*(2), 306–311. Retrieved from https://doi.org/10.2105/AJPH.2016.303564

Retrieved from https://innovation.cms.gov/Files/worksheets/ahcm-screeningtool.pdf

Rollins, R., Gribble, A., Barrett, S. E., & Powell, C. (2017). Who is in your waiting room? Health care professionals as culturally responsive and trauma-informed first responders to human trafficking. *AMA Journal of Ethics, 19*(1), 63–71. Retrieved from https://doi.org/10.1001/journalofethics.2017.19.1.pfor2–1701

Serita, T. (2013). In our own backyards: The need for a coordinated judicial response to 337 human trafficking. *N.Y.U. Review of Law & Social Change, 36*(4).

Shively, M., Kliorys, K., Wheeler, K., & Hunt, D. (2012, June 15). An overview of john schools in the United States. National Institute of Justice, Office of Justice Programs. Retrieved from: http://www.demandforum.net/wp-content/uploads/2012/01/john.school.summary.june_.2012.pdf

Southern Poverty Law Center. (2008). *SPLC lawsuit: Indian guest workers defrauded by recruiters, forced into slave-like conditions.* Montgomery, AL. SPLC Law Press Center. Retrieved from: https://www.splcenter.org/news/2008/03/10/splc-lawsuit-indian-guestworkers-defrauded-recruiters-forced-slave-conditions

Southern Poverty Law Center. (2015). *$20 million settlement agreement reached in labor trafficking cases coordinated by SPLC on behalf of exploited Indian guest workers.* SPLC Press Center. Montgovery, AL. Retrieved from: https://www.splcenter.org/news/2015/07/14/20-million-settlement-agreement-reached-labor-trafficking-cases-coordinated-splc-behalf

Stevens, J. (2012). The adverse childhood experiences study – The largest, most important public health study you never heard of – Began in an obesity clinic. *ACEStoohigh.com.* Retrieved from Aces Too High website: https://acestoohigh.com/2012/10/03/the-adverse-childhood-experiences-study-the-largest-most-important-public-health-study-you-never-heard-of-began-in-an-obesity-clinic/

Substance Abuse and Mental Health Services Administration. (2018). *Trauma-informed approach and trauma-specific interventions.* Retrieved from www.samhsa.gov/nctic/trauma-interventions

Tahirih Justice Center. (2017, May 25). *DHS'VINE database includes federally protected information on survivors of crime.* Retrieved from www.tahirih.org/news/dhs-vine-database includes-federally-protected-information-on-survivors-of-crime/

Turney, K. (2017a). The unequal consequences of mass incarceration for children. *Demography, 54*(1), 361–389. Retrieved from https://doi.org/10.1007/s13524-016-0543-1

Turney, K. (2017b). Unmet health care needs among children exposed to parental incarceration. *Maternal and Child Health Journal, 21*(5), 1194–1202. Retrieved from https://doi.org/10.1007/s10995-016-2219-2

United Nations University. (2017). Environmental change and forced migration scenarios (EACH-FOR). *Migration Network.* Retrieved from https://migration.unu.edu/research/migration-and-environment/environmental-change-and-forced-migration-scenarios-each-for-2.html#outline

U.S. Centers for Medicare & Medicaide Services (2017). Accountable Health Communities Model. Retrieved from https://innovation.cms.gov/initiatives/ahcm/

U.S. Public Health Service Syphilis Study at Tuskegee. (2015). Retrieved from www.cdc.gov/tuskegee/timeline.htm

Vafa, Y. (2016). There is no such thing as a child prostitute. *Rights4Girls.*

Wolfe, L. (2017, May 17). 10 do's and don'ts on how to interview sexualized violence survivors. *Women Under Siege.* Retrieved from www.womenundersiegeproject.org/blog/entry/10-dos-and-donts-on-how-to-interview-sexualized-violence-survivors

World Health Organization. (2017a). *Management of substance abuse.* Retrieved from www.who.int/substance_abuse/facts/opiates/en/

World Health Organization. (2017b). The VPA approach. *Global Campaign for Violence Prevention.* Retrieved from www.who.int/violenceprevention/approach/ecology/en/

World Health Organization. (2018, February 8). *Zika Virus.* Retrieved from www.who.int/news-room/fact-sheets/detail/zika-virus

Yachot, N. (2013). *Prestigious law firms join fight for guest workers' rights in major human trafficking case.* In A.C.L. Union (Ed.). Retrieved from www.aclu.org/blog/human-rights/prestigious-law-firms-join-fight-guestworkers-rights-major-human-trafficking-case

11

TRAFFICKING IN PERSONS FOR THE PURPOSE OF ORGAN REMOVAL

Ana Manzano

Abstract

Organ transplantation abroad is a global business that has contested legalities, since it can or cannot be related to criminal activity (see Siller, Chapter 7, this volume). Some people are trafficked for the purpose of removing their organs to sell for profit. In some cases, people are transferred from their place of residence to another location where one of their organs is removed and transplanted into another person. This chapter aims to clarify organ trafficking contextual complexities. In doing so, it starts with two cautionary notes, discussing first the confusing and loaded terminology used in the trafficking in human beings for the purpose of organ removal (THBOR) literature and second, critically analyzing the little evidence available. The chapter then examines the actions and actors involved in the process of THBOR, critically reflecting on why some people sell and why others buy human body parts. The role of brokers and whether coercion, deception and informed consent are present is then discussed. The final section explores how all these concepts are related to exploitation in the specific contextual circumstances of THBOR.

Learning Objectives

At the end of the chapter, readers will be able to:

1 Correctly apply key terms and concepts used in THBOR;
2 Understand the importance of the organ market debates and challenges to evidence-based policies in THBOR;
3 Identify some of the challenges of international and national legislation when approaching actions, means and purpose in THBOR;
4 Understand why and in what circumstances some people sell and some people buy human organs; and
5 Understand the role of a network of facilitators that support THBOR.

Key Terms: Organ trafficking; transplant tourism; organ trade; trafficking in human beings for the purpose of organ removal.

Introduction

People are trafficked worldwide every year. Some of those will be trafficked for the purpose of removing their organs to sell them for profit (see Siller, Chapter 7, this volume). Most commonly, people are transferred from their place of residence to another location (region/country), where one of their organs (e.g. a kidney or a portion of their liver) is removed and transplanted into another person. The reasons why this takes place are extremely complex but the overall drive for this phenomenon is that human organ transplantation has the potential to be the best treatment available for several chronic and terminal illnesses. However, this treatment, unlike many others, depends on the availability of donated human organs. These organs can be retrieved from deceased bodies (deceased organ donation) or living bodies (living organ donation), although organs from living donors are most likely to have the best post-transplant results. Trafficking in Human Beings for the Purpose of Organ Removal (THBOR) is included in the United Nations Palermo Protocol on Trafficking of 2000 but is one of the most unknown and least addressed forms of trafficking (OSCE, 2013).

Deceased organ donation provides a perfect example of a modern healthcare phenomenon – the intersection of advanced technology, medical science and the emotions, beliefs and customs that surround human decision-making at the moment of death. The process of identifying, assessing, maintaining, extracting, transporting and transplanting suitable organs from dead bodies is extremely complex and demands exacting logistics and an infrastructure to support it, which is absent or deficient in many countries. Whether this process succeeds depends essentially on consent and the wishes of a potential donor. These wishes may range from the unknown and implicit to the formal and explicit and they have to be reinterpreted by family members in conjunction with hospital staff. This intensely complex process is characterized by enormous international cultural diversity on the meaning of death, body integrity, altruism, religion, funeral practices and so forth (Manzano & Pawson, 2014). Making a diagnosis of brain death is not straightforward, and perceptions and definitions continue to be contested. For instance, brain death was only legally recognized as the end of human life in Japan – where organ donations rates continue to be extremely low – in 1997 and it is still unlawful in Germany. Linking medical practice to human expectations at this precise and fleeting moment is fraught with difficulties and has resulted in significant differences in donation rates throughout the world, with some countries having no or minimal deceased donation rates.

What possible clinical outcomes can be anticipated from people who have sold a kidney and those who had paid for a kidney?

In the meantime, the worldwide demand for donated human organs has increased exponentially in the last decade. Transplant-related technical innovations have proliferated in many forms. The list of organs that can be transplanted (kidney, liver, heart, pancreas, lung, bowels, hand, face, etc.) between humans keeps growing, and the associated technologies of organ preservation and avoidance of organ rejection have also been improving rapidly. With the demographic challenges of a worldwide aging population, more people develop chronic diseases than ever before and the age of candidates awaiting organ transplantation has also been steadily increasing. This is because the treatment approach for older people (over 70 years old) with kidney failure has experienced a significant transformation and there is now a consensus in the medical community that age is not a barrier for transplantation. In fact, in many countries, like the United States and Norway (Lønning et al., 2016), there is currently no upper age limit for access to kidney transplantation. Moreover, since the life expectancy of a transplanted kidney is 7–15 years (Azancot, Cantarell, Perelló, Torres, & Serón, 2011) and the worldwide average life expectancy is 71 years (WHO, 2016), the practice of re-transplantation (repeated kidney transplantations in the same person) is also expanding (Heldal et al., 2017). As a first step to understanding the global organ trafficking landscape, it is important to understand that these radical changes are here to stay, presenting opportunities for some and risks for others.

At the time of writing, there is only one country where it is legal to sell and buy organs: Iran (except for the province of Shiraz). This has not always been the case worldwide, and it is only in the last decade that there has been increased regulatory activity from global institutions to promote measures to deter the trade in human organs for profit. These include the United Nations (UN) and the Council of Europe (Caplan, Dominguez, Matesanz, & Prior, 2009), the World Health Organization (Noel, 2010), the European Union (EU) (European Union, 2010) and the international transplantation societies in the Declaration of Istanbul on Organ Trafficking and Transplant Tourism (Steering Committee of the Istanbul Summit, 2008), which established a set of principles to guide professional conduct and government policy.

The UN Protocol to Prevent, Suppress and Punish Trafficking in Persons, Especially Women and Children – also known as The Palermo Protocol – (United Nations, 2000b) in their Article 3 defines and criminalizes THBOR by specifically mentioning it when referring to the "purpose" element of trafficking in persons:

> "Trafficking in persons" shall mean the recruitment, transportation, transfer, harbouring or receipt of persons, by means of the threat or use of force or other forms of coercion, of abduction, of fraud, of deception, of the abuse of power or of a position of vulnerability or of the giving or receiving of payments or benefits to achieve the consent of a person having control over another person, for the purpose of exploitation. Exploitation shall include, at a minimum, the exploitation of the prostitution of others or other forms of sexual exploitation, forced labour or services, slavery or practices similar to slavery, servitude or *the removal of organs.* [emphasis added]

What assumptions underlie the UN legislation against human organ trade?

Other transnational legislations have also prohibited THBOR: the Council of Europe Convention on Action against Trafficking in Human Beings (Council of Europe, 2005); the Directive 2011/36/EU of the European Parliament and of the Council (European Parliament and the Council, 2011) and the Optional Protocol to the Convention on the Rights of the Child on the Sale of Children, Child Prostitution and Child Pornography (United Nations, 2000a). Although the purpose of "trafficking humans for their organs" is internationally accepted in the definition of human trafficking (the other two being sexual and/or labor exploitation), it is very difficult to assess the magnitude of this crime. As with the other types of human trafficking, a combination of complex factors means nobody knows how many organs are being traded across the world and it is not known either how many of those organs belonged to humans who were trafficked. There are also differences, misunderstandings and overlaps between the terms "organ trafficking" and "trafficking in human beings for the purpose of organ removal." Despite the reaffirmation of criminality used by numerous legal instruments, the United States and other developed countries' efforts against human trafficking seem to have focused on sex and labor trafficking (U.S. Department of State, 2005), with organ trafficking receiving little attention (Efrat, 2016).

There are three significant issues connected to how organ trafficking has been regulated until now by the UN. The first one relates to the consequence of conflating sex, labor and organ trafficking, in the same definition. Assembling them together in one legislative instrument (the UN Protocol) not only prevents the organ trafficking contextual complexities from being approached, but it can also misguide understandings of this complex issue (Efrat, 2016). Second, the focus on the three specifically defined elements of "action," "means" and "purpose" frames but also constrains future analysis and interpretations. These are specified as follows (Pascalev et al., 2013, p. 11):

> an action being recruitment, transportation, transfer, harboring or receipt of persons; a means by which that action is achieved: threat or use of force, or other forms of coercion, abduction, fraud, deception, abuse of power or abuse of a position of vulnerability, and the giving or receiving of payments or benefits to achieve consent of a person having control over another person; a purpose of the intended action or means: exploitation.

Except when the victim is a child, all of these three elements must be present to constitute "trafficking in persons." Finally, the UN protocol associates the purpose of trafficking with the exploitation of organ sellers – emphasizing that the consent of the victim to the intended exploitation is irrelevant if the consent has been obtained through threat or use of force, coercion, abduction, fraud, deception, abuse of power or vulnerability, or giving payments or benefits. As explained later in the chapter, "exploitation" is a contested and heatedly debated concept in the organ trade literature, with some arguing that not every person who sells an organ suffers exploitation. On that premise, this chapter aims to clarify what the organ trafficking contextual complexities and unique challenges are.

Cautionary note on organ trafficking terminology

There is a varied terminology used in the area of "organ trafficking." This generic term consists of different practices which can overlap and are used without distinction. Some of them refer to the general phenomenon. These are "trafficking in persons for organ removal," "organ sales," "black market of organs," "transplant commercialism" and "transplant tourism." Others refer to the actors involved in these occurrences: "sellers," "donors," "buyers," "recipients," "brokers" and so forth. Table 11.1 offers a comprehensive list and the definitions of this vocabulary.

This section demonstrates how language matters in THBOR because it conveys a form of knowledge through which the problem is understood and made sense of. It critically analyzes some of the common terms used in this area, taking into consideration that some scholars like Columb et al. (2017) have argued that these terminology conundrums have contributed to presenting the organ trade as a whole "as a serious organized crime that can only be tackled by a punitive response." This quote exemplifies how the inconsistent use of language not only reflects the complexity of how the trade in human organs operates but it also exposes the moral, legal and policy debates that embed this territory.

In organ trade debates, the choice of terms often denotes a position statement loaded with ideology. For example, calling people who sell their kidneys "victims" implies recognition of the exploitation that surrounds the purchase transaction cycle. Using the terms "sellers" or "suppliers" may exclude from the purchasing transaction any form of coercion or deception. The latter

Table 11.1 Organ trafficking terminology

Term	*Definition*
Human trafficking for the purpose of organ removal	Using coercive measures to recruit, transport or house another person with the purpose of removing that person's organs or having them removed (de Jong, 2015).
Organ trade	Offering to sell and actually selling an organ, buying an organ and acting as an intermediary with a profit motive and/or intentionally transplanting a trafficked organ, between the buyer and seller (de Jong, 2015).
Organ tourism/transplant tourism	Organ tourism/transplant tourism: traveling abroad to receive an organ for implantation involving the trade in human organs and/or commercial organ donation, or when the resources (organs, healthcare professionals and transplant centers) used by the foreign patient for transplantation undermines the capacity of the country in question to provide transplant services to its own population (de Jong, 2015).
Organ supplier	A person who supplies an organ (Pascalev et al., 2013).
Organ seller/vendor/commercial living donor/compensated kidney donor	A person who benefits financially and/or materially when an organ is removed from that person's body (Pascalev et al., 2013).
Victim-donor	The person whose kidney is the commodity of a THBOR network (de Jong, 2015).
Organ donor	A person who donates one or several organs, whether the donation occurs during lifetime or after death (European Parliament, 2010).
Organ advertising	Advertising the need for, or availability of organs or tissues, with a view to offering or seeking financial gain or comparable advantage (Pascalev et al., 2013).
Organ recipient Organ purchaser Organ buyer	A person who receives an organ transplant, also known as *patient* (Pascalev et al., 2013)
Organ broker Organ trafficker Recruiter International transplant coordinator Middlemen Connectors Agents Third parties	A person who facilitates and organizes the transactions of money and body parts both, making extensive profits in the process (Pascalev et al., 2013).
Organ trafficking	The recruitment, transport, transfer, harboring or receipt of living or deceased persons or their organs by means of the threat or use of force or other forms of coercion, of abduction, of fraud, of deception, of the abuse of power or of a position of vulnerability, or of the giving to, or the receiving by, a third party of payments or benefits to achieve the transfer of control over the potential donor, for the purpose of exploitation by the removal of organs for transplantation (Steering Committee of the Istanbul Summit, 2008).
Trafficked person	Victim of trafficking; any natural person who has been subject to trafficking in persons (Pascalev et al., 2013).

Term	*Definition*
Transplant tourism Organ tourism	Travelling abroad to receive an organ for implantation involving the trade in human organs and/or commercial organ donation, or when the resources (organs, healthcare professionals and transplant centers) used by the foreign patient for transplantation undermines the capacity of the country in question to provide transplant services to its own population (de Jong, 2015).
Black market of organs	An illegal market for organs, which market coexists with the legal systems for organ retrieval (Pascalev et al., 2013).
Transplant commercialism	A policy or practice in which an organ is treated as a commodity, including by being bought or sold or used for material gain (Steering Committee of the Istanbul Summit, 2008).
Travel for transplantation	The movement of organs, donors, recipients, or transplant professionals across jurisdictional borders for transplantation purposes. Travel for transplantation becomes transplant tourism if it involves organ trafficking and/or transplant commercialism or if the resources (organs, professionals, and transplant centers) devoted to providing transplants to patients from outside a country undermine the country's ability to provide transplant services for its own population (Steering Committee of the Istanbul Summit, 2008).

represents many scholar and lay views who see nothing wrong with the commercialization of human organs for profit and openly promote a legal human organ market. These lexical fights reflect a polarized scholarship: there are those who think that the commodification of human body parts for profit should not be promoted, arguing principles of social justice and avoidance of exploitation of the poor by the rich, and that only organ donation which is altruistically motivated should occur. In opposition are those who emphasize the principle of human autonomy and promote the right of persons to sell their body parts, free of state paternalism, arguing that financial transactions involving human organs should occur, albeit with diverse views on how regulated this market should be.

Against this contextual background, it is important to consider that the term "trafficking" is often associated with trading illegal goods like arms and drugs. When what is traded is a living human body part, there is an important distinction to be made between trading the body parts (which are not illegal goods) independent of their bodies and trading the whole living human body (which is an illegal act) that happens to have organs inside it that could be removed. The prevailing conflation of organ trafficking with trade or commercialism has two connected implications: it is premised on the assumption that organ sales only involve organs that are harvested from trafficked persons (Columb et al., 2017), and it implies that all organ transactions convey exploitation.

Organ sales, however, can happen with non-trafficked people. A number of individuals who pay for organs transplants do not travel or do not travel far as demonstrated in the Ambagtsheer, Jong, Bramer, and Weimar (2016) systematic review. This identified 15 articles reporting domestic organ commercialism supporting arguments that domestic trade rather than cross-border trade maybe the most widespread form of organ transactions. Trade in organs also takes place within national boundaries with people buying them from fellow citizens or from people who are in the country temporarily like migrant workers and refugees (Efrat, 2013). Since some argue that organ sales can also happen without exploitation, the terminological conflation trade/trafficking can lead to oversimplification of a very complex myriad of processes, with criminalities and liabilities embedding the purchasing transactions when living human body parts are involved.

Case study: Israel*

In 2003, South African police uncovered an Israeli-led international organ trafficking network, which arranged at least 109 illegal transplants for Israeli patients. Israeli "donors" were initially paid up to $20,000 per kidney before the brokers discovered that poor Romanians and Brazilians were willing to accept $3,000.

Case study discussion questions

1. What, if any, issues of exploitation are evident in the organ trafficking network?
2. Were the donors in this case trafficked? What vulnerabilities, if any, many have been exploited?
3. What difference, if any, does it make that the organ "donors" were Romanians and Brazilians?
4. What difference, if any, does it make that the organ "donors" were paid $3,000 rather than the purported $20,000?

*Taken from Ambagtsheer et al. (2014).

A market for organs: the debate

The idea of establishing a market for organs is not new and it attracts extraordinary support from different disciplines. On the clinical side, some physicians argue for a free market using principles of supply and demand but also of urgent health need: there is a shortfall in organs resulting in increased morbidity and mortality in the general population. This physician argument remains the same one that, in the eighteenth century, drove the surge and advancement in transplant technology when bodysnatching and grave-robberies were the source of body parts for early transplantation efforts. It is well known that the famous surgeon-anatomist John Hunter, who is often called "the father of scientific surgery" was a recipient of snatched corpses (Richardson, 2006). Nevertheless, in the eighteenth century medical ethics was not an established discipline as it is now and this clinician view is still strongly supported by some liberal bioethicists (Cherry, 2015; Radcliffe-Richards, 2012) who use the same moral argument – "the rich in question here are dying" (Radcliffe-Richards, 1996, p. 376) – on the demand side; and *laissez choisir* arguments on the supply side: individuals know what is best for them and it is paternalistic to impose our judgments on them. The opposing views argue that vendor "own judgment" is likely to be overshadowed by how informed their consent to this medical procedure is. Also, as a whole body of literature on global health inequalities (Marmot, 2005; Navarro, 2009) demonstrates, the poor in question die daily of curable diseases because of lack of means or insurance and few seem to be morally outraged by this. Those opposing a regulated organ market also clarify that transplanted organs do not necessarily save recipients' lives (in the case of kidneys) but have the potential to improve quality of life for a time-limited period. In doing so, the body of the seller is harmed and unnecessary health needs are generated but this time they are displaced towards the seller who, as a poor member of society, is less likely to overcome them (Koplin, 2014).

This insistence on using the bodies of the poor as a form of treatment to prolong the lives of the rich has been referred to as a novel form of bioviolence against them (Lock, 2000). The concept of bioviolence, which is "a blend of physical, structural, and symbolic violence, all of which are carried out to extract organs from the oppressed bodies of the poor" (Moniruzzaman, 2012, p. 72), illustrates the main analysis made by anthropologists and sociologists. That is, the transplant industry is insatiable and human body parts have become "commodities" because they have acquired a use-value subject to commercial exchange. This commodification is caused and reproduced by bioscience and medicine through the pursuit of new technologies that fragment and isolate body components to serve a variety of purposes. The potential for medical use makes the body a form of merchandise (Sharp, 2000), and hence the growth in for-profit traffic in human organs and tissues. Exploitation arguments are related to these views since an intrinsic characteristic of capitalism is systematic exploitation of the poor. Therefore, the narrative of "saving lives" becomes void when low tech solutions readily available are not accessible to the poor in many countries.

Bioethicists also question why motivational altruism is necessary rather than desirable in organ donation (Moorlock, Ives, & Draper, 2014). Social policy analysts use Titmuss's (1970) seminal work to prove that when altruism is corrupted by the presence of financial inducements, it is undermined and, therefore, deters altruistic donation. Applied researchers studying organ sales transactions warn that a large collection of elements tends to correlate in these situations: coercion, external or internal duress, shoddy standards, profiteering, deception, misinformation and lasting psychological, financial, social and health consequences for the sellers (Awaya et al., 2009; Budiani-Saberi & Karim, 2009; Tong et al., 2012; Zargooshi, 2001). Harms to vendors, however, do not seem to feature strongly in pro-market arguments because the value of personal autonomy (Dworkin, 1994) and self-ownership (Cherry, 2015) of body parts is considered greater. Personal autonomy values, inexorably and conveniently, cancel any social liabilities: it is the vendors' choice to harm their bodies. Risks to vendor well-being are only recognized as a justification for a decriminalized regulated market, which somehow would eliminate all those risks. This relates to idealized views of market rules (neoliberal "utopia"), where social relations are governed by market forces (competition and exchanges), which are assumed to operate according to immutable laws no matter the contextual circumstances in which they are placed (Brenner & Theodore, 2002). Although scholars still know very little about THBOR crimes, there is enough knowledge to confirm the phenomenal complexities in which the contextual circumstances of living organ donation for the purposes of transplantation occur; it therefore seems improbable that a regulated market would eliminate those risks.

Transplant tourism: a new phenomenon?

An archetype of viewing body parts purchasing transactions as free from exploitation is the proliferation of the term "transplant tourism," born on the back of the glamorized concept of "medical/health tourism," which is no more than a rebranding of the historical phenomenon of health-motivated cross-border travel. In the contemporary globalized world, the "tourism" discourse of health-driven "glittering makeover vacations advertised online" (Smith-Morris & Manderson, 2010, p. 33) disguises the enormous variations within this practice: who travels, why, under what circumstances, where and what kind of treatments they are receiving. It also conceals the fluid legalities, illegalities and liabilities in these processes. The most common reasons for healthcare mobility range from affordability to accessibility of consultations, treatments or drugs. Accessibility includes promptness of services but also less regulated and experimental healthcare. In the case of organ transplantation when the source of the organ occurs abroad, accessibility and deregulation are the two main factors driving the travel. Affordability also comes into play in countries with private healthcare systems. A bone marrow transplant costs ten times more in the

United States than in India (Alberti, Giusti, Papa, & Pizzurno, 2014), and these saving opportunities are also promoted by cost-conscious health insurers. For example, Bramstedta and Xu (2007) reported that in the United States, some medical insurance programs encouraged policy holders to travel to foreign countries for organ transplantation and then savings for "medical value" procedures abroad were passed to the employee as a bonus for lowering corporate healthcare expenses. In the Netherlands, the Dutch Healthcare Insurance Act reimbursed transplants outside the Netherlands with no exclusion clause for commercial transplantation until regulations were amended after a paid transplant in Pakistan was reimbursed by an insurer (de Jong, 2015).

"Medical tourism" is considered "a vexed term that was produced dialogically within a particular set of debates about globalization, mobility, neoliberalism and health care" (Roberts & Scheper-Hughes, 2011, p. 4). "Transplant tourism" is another such "vexed term" with the additional premise that the medical treatment purchased abroad is fundamentally made of body parts belonging to another human being (dead or living). In the case of the living, the organs removed are two (kidneys and liver) of the five (brain, heart and lungs) vital organs that are essential for survival. The key question is what part of this healthcare treatment is purchased when organ transplantation takes place abroad? Since purchasing organs is illegal, the practice can only be legal if people travel with another human being who is donating the organ for altruistic reasons to have the transplant in a centre of their choice (Budiani-Saberi & Delmonico, 2008). Illegal transplants tend to be concealed or disguised as altruistic donations since, despite measures in place, it is difficult to understand the true nature of the donor-recipient relationship. In this case, the United Network for Organ Sharing (UNOS), defined transplant tourism as "the purchase of a transplant organ abroad that includes access to an organ while bypassing laws, rules, or processes of any or all countries involved" (as cited in Budiani-Saberi & Delmonico, 2008, p. 926).

It must be noted that although these debates are mostly polarized, opposition to a complete prohibition of organ sales does not necessarily imply the support of a free market of organs. Some scholars oppose the punitive measures accompanying prohibition as a main strategy to resolve the organ black market. These views worry about the unintended consequences of punitive measures for the more vulnerable actors in this process: the sellers. If the seller is criminally liable, they are less likely to report abuse and can be exposed to further harm (Columb, 2015; Columb et al., 2017). Furthermore, it has become apparent that worldwide sellers are more likely to be prosecuted when organ trafficking cases are brought to justice. Organ trafficking is therefore no different from crimes such as drug trafficking where the criminalization of the vulnerable (i.e. drug mules) is likely (Manzano, Monaghan, Potrata, & Clayton, 2014). Measures to deter THBOR should therefore focus on the powerful structures and professionals behind the crime: doctors, brokers and other supporting services.

Cautionary note on the evidence for THBOR

There is no doubt that illegal paid organ donation occurs worldwide but, unsurprisingly, there is lack of hard data regarding the incidence of THBOR. Data scarcity is a typical feature of all organized crime–related evidence but in THBOR specifically, countries that promote, facilitate or do not patrol paid donations do not record or release data regarding, for example, the number of transplanted foreign patients in their hospitals (Budiani-Saberi & Delmonico, 2008). Furthermore, as the previous section has demonstrated, since THBOR is a heavily politicized and contested policy area, there is prevalence of what scholars call "mythical numbers" that could play to the advantage of both sides of the debate. This term, coined by Singer (1971) and developed by Reuter (1984) describes the tendency to cite numbers that are not supported by adequate research evidence without challenging them. Despite the inadequate empirical base, these numbers are accepted and repeated by policymakers, the media and scholars. Crime and organized crime are favourite fields for the purveyors of mythical numbers (Calderoni, 2014) and the organ trade is no exception. For example, in THBOR one of the commonly repeated figures is Shimazono's (2007) estimate that 5% of kidney transplants performed annually in the world are via organ trafficking.

There are several methodological problems with the estimation strategy employed by Shimazono who uses the disclaimer of "circumstantial evidence" before settling on " the total number of recipients who underwent commercial organ transplants overseas may be *conservatively* estimated at 5%" (2007, p. 959, italics added). In 2005, the world transplant activity was established at "around 66,000 kidney transplants (plus 21,000 liver transplants and 6000 heart transplants)" (Shimazono, 2007, p. 955). Although in 2005, there were 193 countries in the UN, only 91 of those collected kidney transplantation data and of those, only transplantation activity data from 12 countries is aggregated to obtain the 5% global figure. In this group of 12 countries, there is also over representation of one country, China with 12,000 cases, which produces a clear outlier effect (leaving the statisticians to wonder what would be the effect if China's data were excluded from the sample). It is unknown how many of the 12,000 transplants performed were from executed prisoners and how many were transplanted into foreign patients and therefore, there is possible conflation of commercialism with trafficking and of international with domestic commercialism.

Case study: Siong*

Siong has developed an extensive brokerage network primarily sending U.S. and Canadian citizens to China for transplantation. Many of his referrals come directly from kidney specialists, all of Chinese origin. Siong admits to knowing that these kidneys belonged to executed prisoners.

Case study discussion questions

1 What ethical issues arise in the global trade of organ trafficking from executed prisoners, if any?
2 Should organ recipients be notifed that an organ they receive is from an executed prisoner? Why/why not? What ethical and moral issues arise by telling (for the recipient)? By not telling?

*Taken from Fraser (2016, p. 104).

Reflecting on and exposing the presence of mythical figures in THBOR does not equate to the denial of its existence, but it should be understood as a recognition of the global complexities and dimensions of the organ trade. THBOR exists and is recorded in the scientific literature but there is also aggregation of anecdotal evidence observed by transplant physicians, law enforcers and prosecutors. THBOR has both a clandestine and a politicized nature and these can affect the lack of evidence and the type of evidence available. A review of the interdisciplinary literature suggests at least three possible explanations for the lack of "reliable" evidence in this area.

Hypothesis 1: there is little incidence of THBOR

Some authors support the view that there is a low incident of THBOR, which implies a high incident of "urban legends," false stories "commonly believed despite the total lack of evidence for it because it encapsulates, in story form, widespread anxieties about modern life" (Leventhal, 1994, p. 3). Typical legends that have never been verified despite media panics are the "child organ trafficking ring myth" based on rumours of children being kidnapped by organized criminal networks to remove their organs and use them in transplantation. There are also "kidney robbery" tales where victims awake in a hotel room or their car, discovering that one of their kidneys has been removed. In the United States, typical destinations quoted are New York and Las Vegas; in Europe, Amsterdam, Venlo, and Strausbourg. Other destinations include Western vacation favourites like Thailand, Brazil, Istanbul, the Balkans, North Africa, Venice and Spain (Leventhal, 1994). In the case of organ theft, scholars suggested that these anxieties are related to a combination of suspicion and resentment of rich foreigners with fear of mutilation and death but also encapsulated an ancestral fear of modern technology. Folklore analysts explain how in developing countries or continents, these legends seem to be more explanations (for missing children or foreign adoptions, for example) than narratives (Donovan, 2002). Although several national and international investigations of child organ trafficking and organ thefts have taken place, no credible evidence was ever obtained and investigations deemed them unsubstantiated.

The lack of scientifically documented and reliable data are common in the field of organized crime and therefore it is expected that this would be the case in THBOR. Some scholars, while recognizing that this crime is hard to monitor and prone to urban legend, clarify that the business of THBOR is very different from organ snatching tales. The folklore stories are based on an explicit lack of consent, while in THBOR, the issue mostly relies on how truly "informed" consent is. They also argue that the negation that THBOR exists is a form of promotion, calling it a "protected crime" (Scheper-Hughes & Boström, 2013) which is a well-described characteristic of crimes of the powerful (Meyer, 2006). Although prosecutions are scarce, we know THBOR exists because cases have been brought to justice in Brazil, India, Kosovo, South Africa, Turkey, Ukraine and the United States. Scheper-Hughes is the most prolific academic researcher who has reported THBOR incidents in multiple papers (Scheper-Hughes, 2000, 2001, 2003, 2006, 2011).

Others scholars point out "moral crusade" theories relying on the social constructionist perspective of crime where social events become "problems" only "because of "claims-making by interested parties, claims that may or may not reflect actual social arrangements" (Weitzer, 2007, p. 448). Problems are dramatized to alarm the public and policy makers, justifying prohibition and criminalization. The idea behind a crusade in THBOR is that if trading in organs is seen as violating human rights and dignity, states ratifying more international human rights instruments are more likely to pass legislation banning commercial transplantation (Fikrejesus, 2016). In the organ trade, medical communities have been identified as key moral actors to promote ethical practices and professional conduct but also to lobby for prohibitionist legislation. For example Efrat (2013) explained the persistent efforts of physicians as a fundamental explanation of Pakistan's *Transplantation of Human Organs and Tissues Act* (2010) and Israel's *Organ Transplantation Law* (2008). The same happened in recent transplant policies and laws in India and China (Delmonico, 2009).

Hypothesis 2: there is a high incidence of THBOR crimes, but they are not reported

This explanation is based on recognizing the inadequacy of official records to reflect the true extent of criminality in general and specifically, in areas like white collar crime or domestic violence. This well-known phenomenon has been described by criminologists as the "dark figure of crime"

(Muncie & McLaughlin, 1996) or the "tip of the iceberg crime theory" (Coleman & Moynihan, 1996) reflecting how the majority of crime is hidden and unrecorded. The complex, interrelated and multifaceted reasons why crime remains unreported can include victims' reluctance to accept their victim status for fear of embarrassment, stigmatization or fear of implicating themselves, absence of reliable witnesses, illicit goods being difficult to trace and the high status of the offenders.

In the case of THBOR, neither sellers nor buyers are interested in making the crime public because of the illegalities they may have committed, and some sellers may not be aware of the fact that they are violating transplantation legislations (Mendoza, 2011). The problem of gathering reliable data in THBOR results from the complex business itself which is integrated in legal healthcare institutions (normally private hospitals). Successful THBOR requires the involvement of medical staff and sophisticated cooperation between a range of licensed healthcare professionals and licensed health services providers (i.e. laboratories) because organ removal is a highly specialist technology. Crimes committed by high-status individuals are frequently unrepresented in official figures and medical professionals have a superior social status in most countries. The literature investigating crimes committed by healthcare professionals explains how this societal status is supported by four main mechanisms present in medical contexts that make staff more likely to escape prosecution: opportunity, lack of supervision, lack of accountability and healthcare industry idiosyncracy.

What research evidence supports and contradicts the existence of THBOR?

Health professionals have increased opportunity to commit crimes which are more difficult to detect (Stark, Paterson, & Kidd, 2001) because of a number of factors which include the intimate nature of the doctor-patient relationship, the vulnerability of the people in their care and the access afforded to such professionals. Lack of supervision and monitoring systems by their institutions and by external authorities are related to a global tradition of allowing the medical professions to regulate themselves. Healthcare corporations' crime has been identified as one of the most difficult white-collar crimes to prosecute (Bucy, 1988) because of the idiosyncratic features of the healthcare industry: the ambiguous and emotional nature of medicine, deference to the doctors, complex regulatory schemes and the small amounts of money involved in typical healthcare transactions. This is reflected in the fact that to date there are only two known prosecutions of hospitals in THBOR (South Africa and Bulgaria) for allowing facilities to be used and employees to conduct illegal transplantations (Allain, 2011; Pancevski, 2006). Finally, lack of accountability is a major consideration in crimes occurring in medical contexts, which is exacerbated by the great latitude in most countries for the medical profession to police itself and by the tendency of the law to make doctors a "special case" (Montgomery, 1997).

Furthermore, organs obtained illicitly can take on the veneer of a licit transaction when recipients travel back to their countries of residence because illegal transplants tend to be concealed or disguised as altruistic donations. How determined healthcare staff are to understand the true nature of the donor-recipient relationship is a key issue in this area. This is the case in the countries where transplants take place but also for clinical teams in the home countries. Although recipients should always be treated, professional guidelines that safeguard sellers and recipients are necessary. Manzano, Monaghan, Potrata & Clayton (2014) claim that home countries also perpetuate THBOR invisibility by "laundering" organs bought abroad in the healthcare systems of the purchaser's country, hindering accurate estimation of the problem.

Equally important, as will be demonstrated in the next section, is that crimes can be reported by victims but also by society. In countries where paid donation is an established practice and legislation prohibiting organs purchases does not exist or has not been implemented or monitored, communities do not police these events because they have become normalized activities. As Wong, Pawson, and Owen (2011) explained, quoting suffragette Carrie Chapman Catt, laws do not succeed without the support of public opinion: "*No written law has ever been more binding than unwritten custom supported by popular opinion.*"

Hypothesis 3: there is a high incidence of THBOR but when it is reported, current legislation is unhelpful

Numerous resolutions, guidelines, statements, declarations, initiatives and reports have been released over the past decades by multiple policy actors objecting to commercial transplantation (Fikrejesus, 2016) but this frantic regulatory activity is not enough to capture the crime. This hypothesis is supported by arguments that focus on the complexity or failings of the legislations that have been written. Poor drafting criticisms have been mentioned by several scholars; for example, Ambagstsheer, Zaitch, and Weimar (2013) point out how the Declaration of Istanbul (Steering Committee of the Istanbul Summit, 2008) – which is the only international document that defines transplant tourism – does not facilitate prosecutions because

> If a patient purchases an organ on the territory of another state (the destination state), he or she is criminally liable and can be persecuted under the law of the destination state and not of the (resident) state. [. . .] when the patient leaves a country after buying an organ that goes unnoticed or is ignored by local enforcement institutions, the legal consequences for the patient cease to exist. Consequently, whereas the purchase of organs is illegal, the purchase of organs will not (always) be punishable.
>
> *(Ambagtsheer et al., 2013)*

Equally not only the definition but other terms included in it are said to be ambiguous and eventually unhelpful:

> The parameters around what constitutes "trafficking" are not firmly established in the literature. Various definitions are given of "coercion," "abuse of a position of vulnerability," "exploitation" and other relevant terms. These definitions are broad and vague, adding to the complexity rather than clarifying the terms.
>
> *(Pascalev et al., 2013, p. 12)*

Columb et al. (2017) point out that legislative attempts to establish universal principles like the 2014 Council of Europe Convention against Trafficking in Human Organs added confusion to organ trade terminology and conceptualization by promoting several of these overlaps and defining "trafficking in organs" as the "illicit removal of human organs." Accordingly, even sales that occur with the consent of donors are considered to be "trafficking," regardless of the circumstances involved."

All these arguments need to be contextualized in the acknowledgement that even if legislations employ the adequate wording and terminology, they are not always enacted and, if they are implemented, they are not always enforced either. The intersection of the supranational, the national and the local comes heavily into place here. Social scientists know that there are multiple "threats" that impede legislation success and some of these are undoubtedly present in THBOR. Wong et al. (2011) proposed a framework to assess the challenges that legislations may encounter in unique contextual local circumstances. These are:

- Problem misidentification (is the severity of the problem sufficient to justify a law?)
- Criminalization and blame (will subjects pursued and prosecuted under new legislation become toughened in their attempts to pursue illegal behavior?)
- Unintended, compensating and displaced behavior (in case the legislation may lower the risk, will the risk be transferred to other risky behavior?)
- Lack of public support (is there likely to be public support for such a law?)
- Lobby group opposition (is there likely to be effective pressure group opposition?)
- Obfuscating the new regulations (will opponents pick and choose in the face of complex legislation and will "fake compliance" be a problem in these circumstances?) (Pawson, Owen, & Wong, 2010)
- Low perceived threat of enforcement (is the law enforceable?)
- Insufficient enforcement resources (is there sufficient resources like police, investigators, lawyers, medical inspectors to enforce the legislation?).

This list should remind the reader about the encounter of two extraordinary complexities: legislation implementation and THBOR in a myriad of countries operating in different cultures and across different jurisdictions. THBOR is often a transnational crime, the characteristics of which jeopardize possibilities of detection, prevention and prosecution. They span several jurisdictions and when confronted with cross-border crimes, nation states are still struggling to prosecute their citizens for crimes committed abroad. Police discretion and strategic decisions over which activities to prioritize are often based on chances of securing successful convictions. Prohibition may not, then, always be accompanied by rigorous enforcement when the police face both the challenges of international investigations and the logistical difficulties in proving that a transplanted organ was illegally bought (Manzano, Monaghan, Potrata & Clayton, 2014).

The action and the actors: recruitment, transfer and receipt of persons

THBOR is a complex process involving a number of key actors and varying relationships. These are: recipients, sellers, brokers, surgeons, nephrologists, transplant support healthcare professionals (nurses, lab technicians) and other facilitators (i.e. hospitals, service providers, translators, border officers, law enforcement officials). In this section, the actions of both the sellers and the buyers will be discussed.

Recruiting sellers: why some people sell their organs

The reasons why people sell and buy organs are complex and intertwined but they tend to be simplified with a narrative of a concurrence of two desperations: the financial desperation of those in need of money and the clinical desperation of those in need of better health. This explanation, however, focuses exclusively on individual motivation for embarking on body part selling/purchasing transactions. It does not consider that what seems an individual feeling (desperation) is, in fact, mediated by numerous contextual social and institutional circumstances. Since in today's society, pursuit of more money and better health is omnipresent, the complexity of these elements deserves a more nuanced understanding. A human body part transaction could not succeed without those colluding desperations but it could not progress without the involvement of those who notice that there are opportunities in those desperations to make profit. National transplant legislation and local policy also facilitate these events directly or indirectly.

It is not surprising that in the academic literature there is more information about sellers than about buyers. Organ sellers are not only more likely to be prosecuted than buyers; they are also easier to recruit as research participants. This is always the case of the poor who are more likely to become subjects of investigations than the rich across the natural, human and social sciences (Mann, 1996). According to the literature, poverty, debt and the inability to provide for their families are clear and constant reasons for people to sell one of their body parts with debt featuring heavily in the majority of the studies across numerous international settings (for example, 98% in Budiani-Saberi, Raja, Findley, Kerketta, & Anand, 2014; 93% in Naqvi, Ali, Mazhar, Zafar, & Rizvi, 2007; and 96% in Goyal, Mehta, Schneiderman, & Sehgal, 2002). The seller's financial need can be due to poverty in lower-middle-income countries (e.g. Vietnam, India, the Philippines), but also due to extreme wealth differential within and across countries – inequality in countries with higher incomes (e.g. Singapore, Hong Kong) but with high living expenses. The latter explanation based on income inequality and not just absolute poverty offers a more nuanced understanding of the cases were people have been prepared to sell body parts to purchase expensive or luxury objects, famously, the story of the 17-year-old who sold their kidney to buy an iPad (Neuberger, 2011).

Although it is difficult to establish a general profile, sellers tend to come from countries with a large proportion of the population living below the poverty line. There is also more information about the situation and experiences of organ sellers from some countries than others and the nationality varies as prohibitionist legislation has been implemented. A number of countries have been identified by Pascalev et al. (2013) in their systematic review as more likely to have organ sellers, namely India, China, the Philippines, Pakistan, Bangladesh, Kazakhstan, Ukraine, Russia, Iraq, Jordan, Egypt, Romania, Moldova, Kosovo, Turkey, Israel, Brazil, Colombia, Peru and Bolivia. The socio-demographic characteristics of vendors are not homogeneous either although they tend to be from a relatively young age and low-level education (Pascalev et al., 2013).

There is disagreement in the academic literature about which is the dominant gender of sellers. Pascalev et al. (2013) concluded that the vast majority of them are men and, in fact, men have been interviewed more for ethnographical studies in countries like Bangladesh, Moldova, Egypt, Pakistan, Colombia and the Philippines. Male sellers are also the ones who have been prosecuted in the few THBOR cases brought to justice. However, sociologists have long established how patriarchal power relations shape gender differences in crime related activities, with women being pushed into crime mainly through "victimization, role entrapment, economic marginality, and survival needs" (Steffensmeier & Allan, 1996, p. 470). Women suffer exploitation in different ways from men and this is also the case in THBOR. In a cross-sectional survey study with 305 kidney sellers in India of which 71% were female (Goyal et al., 2002), 31% of the married women reported they sold organs because their husbands were the breadwinners and two women said that they had been forced into doing so by their husbands. This phenomenon can be further understood with Tong et al.'s (2015) in-depth interview study with 53 transplantation staff across Asia. Professionals reported that the number of women donors appeared disproportionately high and related this to the extended practice of covert commercial transplantation in the form of illegitimate marriage arrangements and falsification of relationships. The occurrence of pseudo-marriage for transplantation is acknowledged by many policy instruments and deterrents are put in place to avoid it. For example, Hong Kong's living organ donation legislation stipulates that spouses from marriages that have lasted for fewer than three years are not considered as eligible living donors (Jingwei, Yu-Hung, & Ching, 2010). Similarly, in Taiwan living donation is restricted to spouses married for a minimum of two years or who have given birth to at least one child (Tong et al., 2015).

There are several strategies to initiate a purchasing transaction. People may develop an intention to sell on their own and start enquiring about or advertising their intentions or they are directly approached or indirectly influenced by others. Strategies vary from active searching to passive behaviour:

- Voluntary search strategies like self advertising in publicly displayed posters, word of mouth and internet postings;
- Knowledge of organ sales gained from a member of the community;
- Responding to an advertisement posted by a prospective buyer or a third party;
- Directly approached by third parties (some of them former organ sellers), which include brokers, syndicates/gangs, matching agencies, scouts and physicians;
- Recommendation by family members, friends and local officials to these third parties; and
- Living in an environment where body parts transactions are common. Some locations have been referred to as "kidney-villes," "villages of half men," "kidney towns/villages" and "no-kidney islets," where kidney sales have proliferated and are concentrated (Pascalev et al., 2013).

There are several ways in which organ purchasing transactions develop but most commonly, a third party is involved. These third parties can operate individually (including licensed doctors), or they are agencies and organized groups (e.g. syndicates) (Mendoza, 2011). How the recruitment of sellers and buyers occurs is significant not only to understand motivations and actor interrelations but also to ascertain whether THBOR is an organized crime since there is disagreement about this (Meyer, 2006). These discussions are contextualized in the politicized debates about the organ trade but also fuelled by the lack of international consensus on organized crime definition. Some define it according to crime typology of economic motives while others base it on the structure of the criminal group facilitating the operation. In THBOR, third parties act as mediators between the demand and the supply sides and they may have diverse roles. They can take the form of "professional" organ brokers, "brokerage firms," "fee-based organ scouts" hired by brokers (Pascalev et al., 2013), "matching agencies" or "syndicates/gangs" (Mendoza, 2011).

Recruiting buyers: why people buy human organs

Although the business of organ selling is demand driven and supposedly benefits from endless worldwide demand, there is scarce information about the customer profile. Little is known about their demographics (nationality, ethnicity or religion) with heterogeneity being the key characteristic. In 2007, Shimazono identified a number of "organ-importing countries" to refer to the most common countries of origin of the people going overseas to purchase organs for transplantation, naming and shaming Australia, Canada, Israel, Japan, Oman, Saudi Arabia and the United States. Other studies added countries to that list and the process of continuous reproach that followed by scholars had significant impact in some countries. Famously, Israel received strong criticism by the international medical community because, despite the small size of its population, its citizens were featured in numerous organ transplant abroad initiatives as buyers. One of the reasons for this was that this practice was state-sponsored, with authorization from the Ministry of Health; the Israeli Health Maintenance Organizations reimbursed patients for transplant organs sourced abroad regardless of origin (Efrat, 2013). The banning of this practice came into effect in 2008 in conjunction with other measures implemented at the same time to promote altruistic donation and this seems to have reduced transplantation abroad in Israelis (Danovitch et al., 2013). Another country where after the passing of such laws the incidence of THBOR seemed to decrease is the Philippines (Padilla, Danovitch, &

Lavee, 2013). Despite the lack of data about recipients, there are three clear areas of established academic knowledge about this population:

1 Buyers of organs (also known as recipients) are people with a chronic or sometimes terminal illness. Although dialysis is an alternative option to transplantation for people with renal failure, those with liver failure have no alternative treatment to resort to, although liver transplantation is a newer technology with significantly higher mortality risks (especially for the donor). People with renal failure are more likely to travel overseas than those with liver failure (Pascalev et al., 2013).

   Buyers or recipients are mostly referred to in the literature as "patients," deemed vulnerable with their offender status remaining ambivalent. It must be noted that organ sellers are also patients although they are never referred to (and hardly treated) as such. They are also patients about to embark in elective surgery with a number of short-term and long-term health risks; they may also be patients with undisclosed or unknown co-morbidities. They will be patients for several months after their organ has been removed, since four to six weeks of recovery time follows this major surgery.

   In the case of buyers, however, their patient status seems to legitimise the ends to which they resort and there is widespread disagreement as to whether their role in the purchasing transaction should be criminalized with convictions for purchasing being rare (Manzano, Monaghan, Potrata & Clayton, 2014). Pascalev et al. (2013) could not find any prosecutions and convictions of buyers specifically for THBOR. Their financially privileged position makes prosecutions harder, and this favor is aggravated by their clinical circumstances with some of them being already deceased by the time THBOR is brought to justice. The recipient, however, would have at some point during the purchasing and clinical process made false statements, claiming to be blood related to the seller or holding false documentation.

2 Buyers of organs have enough money, or manage to assemble enough money to pay for an organ transplantation procedure. Buyers are commonly referred to as "the rich," and they are in a significantly better financial situation than the sellers. They do not always pay for the surgery by themselves; they can get outside support taking the form of fundrasing or support through non-governmental organizations. They often also get help from their families or they succeed in getting the transplantation covered by their health insurance. Prices for transplantation abroad vary extensively and they are suggested to be as low as $2,800 and up to $160,000 for a "transplant package." This contrasts with the amounts that sellers get, which were suggested to be as a minimum of $1,000 and a maximum of $20,000 (Pascalev et al., 2013). Some studies (Mendoza, 2011) reported that sellers sometimes also receive various "gratuities" in addition to their payments (medical insurance, life insurance, livelihood assistance and/or payments in-kind like food baskets). Buyers have reported paying their fees to a variety of actors including donors, brokers, hospitals, companies and doctors.

3 Organ scarcity is not the only reason why people pay for an organ. Since scarcity of organs is the single most common explanation given for the existence of THBOR in the literature, a distinction must be made between scarcity, accessibility, choice and affordability. Scholars like Scheper-Hughes (2001) argue that there is a discourse of "invented scarcity," created and promoted by the medical community that should be replaced with increasing acknowledgement of excessive demand. Scarcity is clearly the key mechanism motivating the people who travel abroad because their countries of residence do not have established local transplantation programs (Ackoundou-N'Guessan et al., 2010; Majid, Al Khalidi, Ahmed, Opelz, & Schaefer, 2010). Scarcity of other treatments for kidney failure can also play a role

in some decisions, for example, there is only one dialysis center in Oman (Al Rahbi & Al Salmi, 2017). However, other more complex reasons only tangentially related with scarcity come into place for other buyers.

a Accessibility (related to eligibility criteria). Some people who are denied access to the transplantation waiting lists (Krishnan et al., 2010) in their countries, decide to challenge this clinical decision by sourcing an organ themselves. Reasons for refusal to add people to organ transplant lists are varied but in general relate to strict eligibility criteria that are not all based on economic demand management. These reasons are associated with scarcity but also with cost/efficiency and risk assessments and can include: not being considered fit for transplantation because of co-morbidities and clinical risk (i.e. moderate to severe ischaemic heart disease, overweight); refusal/inability to comply with the conditions imposed by transplantation centers (e.g. abstinence from alcohol for an established period of time); re-transplantation cases for those who have already had a previous transplant.

How would people from different socioeconomic backgrounds, ages and genders be affected by a legal market of human organs?

---

b Accessibility (related to health inequality for ethnic minorities). Larger proportions of ethnic minorities travelling to the region of their ethnicity to obtain transplantation have been identified in several countries. This is because they are less likely to be compatible with local organs (Ambagtsheer et al., 2012; Cronin, Johnson, Birch, Lechler, & Randhawa, 2011; Krishnan et al., 2010; Gill et al., 2008, 2011) in their countries of residence and waits are longer. There are considerable inequalities in the donation process based on ethnicity and geographical location. For example, organ allocation protocols tend to be based on matching two principal immunological characteristics between donor and recipient: blood groups and genetic type (called the tissue type or HLA-human leukocyte antigens-type). A "same blood group" rule matching donors and recipients is usually maintained in most countries. There are four main blood types in human populations: O, A, B and AB. In the UK, for instance, O is the most common. B and AB are particularly concentrated amongst South Asian, Chinese and Japanese communities. This means that these blood groups are also geographically concentrated. The distribution of HLA antigens also differs between ethnic groups. For complex reasons (Purnell et al., 2013), the majority of organs are donated from the white population, therefore access to organs can be particularly difficult for some communities with chances of being allocated an organ next to impossible.

c Choice (related to waiting). Some people buy organs because they choose not to wait or not to wait for too long, typically people who have been active on the waiting list for more than two years. There is also another group of buyers who refuse to be placed on dialysis and prefer to have a transplant before their kidney fails completely. This choice, called "pre-emptive transplant" (Gill et al., 2008), is preferred by some because it is supposed to have better outcomes than starting dialysis first and then proceeding with transplantation after a few years.

d Choice (related to organ supplier/recipient value). Some people refuse to have an organ transplanted that they perceive not to be valuable enough, for example, refusing an organ from deceased donation. In contrast, it is also common to refuse a living organ donation from a person who is perceived as being too valuable (a family member); the recipient would rather pay and risk the quality of life of a stranger (Al Rahbi & Al Salmi, 2017). In the case of buyer descendants being assessed as suitable living donors, they may be considered to be at higher risk of developing organ failure because of inherited/genetic conditioning.

e Affordability. As explained earlier, some medical insurance programs encourage policy holders to travel abroad for organ transplantation regardless of the organ source. Savings are then passed to the employee as a bonus for lowering corporate healthcare expenses.

Finally, it is important to note that the presence of recruiters and brokers in THBOR impacts the organ sellers and buyers. There are diverse reasons why a country/transaction/hospital/surgeon are chosen (Pascalev et al., 2013):

- The destination country is chosen because the buyers have an affinity with it (nationality, friends or family living there, used to work or live there)
- Recommendations from other patients
- Broker's recommendation
- Websites offering transplant packages.

In some cases, local agents also actively recruit organ buyers in their home countries. For example, Al Rahbi and Al Salmi (2017) explained how in Oman, local agents approach prospective buyers at the dialysis center directly, and there is also ongoing recruitment with agents educating recovered transplant patients to talk about their successful experience.

Transfer and receipt of persons

There is no doubt that human organ transplantation abroad is a complex endeavor that requires a network of facilitators and mediators. On a practical level, brokers act as price negotiators since in most instances they fix or negotiate the price which helps sustain low compensation for the sellers. They also act as mediators with matching agencies. Local agents seem to organize most of the logistics in the buyer's country, while there is another broker with a bigger role in the country of transplantation who organizes logistics with the donor, the medical staff and surgery venues.

In cases where sellers are transported to a different country, they have often flown "together with one or more family member and on the same flight as other suppliers and recipients" (Pascalev et al., 2013, p. 37). Transport and accommodation for sellers tend to happen in groups of varying sizes (up to ten in Moniruzzaman, 2012) sometimes in apartments privately rented by brokers, or in a hospital room or ward (Scheper-Hughes, 2003). The costs of accommodation, travel documents and medical tests are paid by brokers but eventually deducted from the seller's fee. The majority of organ recipients in the Al Rahbi and Al Salmi (2017) study explained that the actual surgery took place in a "sort of vacation accommodation that was prepared as a hospital," and a few said that they were operated on at a private residence.

Sellers only stay in their accommodation for a few days after the operation and according to the literature, they are always sent back home without receiving adequate post-operative care. This is aggravated by the fact that often in the countries of origin there is no universal healthcare insurance systems and follow-up is unlikely, expensive or unaffordable. Buyers tend to stay for longer periods of time (around a week), but they also seem to be sent back home with some medical complications (Al Rahbi & Al Salmi, 2017; Yakupoglu et al., 2010).

Case study: Netherlands*

In 2012, a Nigerian man was found in a hospital car park. He said that he had been brought to the Netherlands to sell his kidney. A man paid for a passport, visa and ticket for him to fly to Paris. In the Netherlands, a doctor told him he had diabetes and could not donate. He escaped. He provided insufficient evidence for a criminal investigation.

Case study discussion questions

1 Identify the moral and ethical issues involved in this case study.
2 To what extent, if at all, does this case represent "trafficking" according to the UN Protocol?

*Taken from de Jong (2015, p. 32).

Medical staff are key players in THBOR but most international legislations, with the exception of Switzerland which sets a higher penalty for health professionals, do not explicitly distinguish between medical staff and other actors. Doctors normally claim to not know or to have been tricked into believing that there was no financial exchange and defer responsibility to other bodies like ethics committees (Tong et al., 2015). Only in the Czech Republic, Iceland, Ireland, Panama and China is there a medical practice ban imposed for health professionals involved in THBOR. As explained earlier, the impunity of surgeons performing illegal extractions and transplants of organs may be exacerbated by their high status in many countries. As an example, in 2010, an organ trafficking network uncovered in South Africa included four surgeons and one nephrologist (Allain, 2011), and the country's biggest private hospital group admitted to 102 counts relating to illegal operations. In this network, Brazilians sold their kidneys to Israeli patients with transplantation taking place in South Africa. Although the kidney sellers were imprisoned in their home countries, the nephrologist was fined $15,000 and the four transplant surgeons, originally charged with assisting in 90 illegal transplant operations, had all charges against them withdrawn.

The means and the purpose: coercion, abduction, fraud, deception, abuse of power, consent and exploitation

The UN THBOR definition (United Nations, 2000b, p. 42) specifies the means by which the organ transaction takes place as "threat or use of force, or other forms of coercion, abduction, fraud, deception, abuse of power or abuse of a position of vulnerability, and the giving or receiving of payments or benefits to achieve consent of a person having control over another person." In this THBOR definition, it is assumed that at least directly, the organ buyers (because of their position of vulnerability) will not be able to enact this alone. The presence of brokers who facilitate the transaction, share illegalities and profit in THBOR is well described in the literature and it is a key factor to prove the exploitation of the sellers. Pascalev et al.'s (2013) systematic review demonstrated that the existence of brokers is correlated to organ seller exploitation because they abuse the seller's vulnerability (poverty and illiteracy) by means of deception, force or other forms of coercion, abduction or fraud.

Fraser (2016) reported that as in other forms of human trafficking, in THBOR there is a trend towards the smaller online brokerages. Brokers also seem to diversify trafficking activity with labour traffickers occasionally moving to THBOR because of the higher profit per person despite the lower volume of business. Fraser (2016) explained that traditional models of brokerage both in labor and organ sales have shifted. They used to be based on a "low number of well-established and well-known brokerage organisations" (Fraser, 2016, p. 111) who received large commissions from both buyers and sellers. In recent years, however, buyers and sellers have started to communicate directly via social media, the internet and the dark Web, which saves money for both sides. Brokerages are now smaller (micro-brokers) who "perhaps only deal with one employer (labor) or hospital (organs) and operate at a level sufficient for sustaining a living for their family, rather than making vast profits achieved by the traditional mega brokers" (Fraser, 2016, p. 111). For this reason, detection has become harder because the new micro-brokers are numerous and fragmented, dealing primarily online.

Even if the prospective sellers approached the brokers themselves, they are still likely to face exploitation, though this is not inevitable. A summary of the types of abuses committed by brokers identified by Pascalev et al. (2013, pp. 41–45) in their comprehensive review is summarized below:

- Organ sellers are not remunerated fairly or to the agreed amount. They are often given less than the promised amount, if anything at all.
- Deception on the availability and quality of health support. The promised post-operative and longer term care does not materialize; health checks and other follow up services are either not available or are of poor quality.
- Sellers are misled about the procedure of organ transplantation, risks and long-term consequences and need for follow-up care.
- Misleading and inadequate information to sellers by telling them the story of the "sleeping kidney" (one kidney sleeps and the other one works), presenting the "donation" as a medical procedure without any risks or harms involved.
- Sellers are misled about the psychological and lifestyle impact of donation because the medical procedure is trivialized.
- Some sellers are recruited by means of false promises of employment to work abroad.
- Portraying the "kidney donation" as a noble act that saves lives and will be performed by world-renowned specialists, emphasizing the desperation of the dying recipient.
- Threats to sellers by explaining that after costs are incurred from medical examinations and expectations on the part of the buyer are raised, they cannot change their mind.
- Brokers seize sellers' passports after they cross the border to ensure that they cannot return home before their kidney is removed.
- Sellers who change their minds are held captive, threatened and/or physically abused.
- Brokers instruct sellers and recipients how to deceive donation authorization or (ethical) committees. For instance, they familiarize suppliers and recipients with the questions that they will be asked, and instruct suppliers to deny that they received any payment for the organ.
- Sellers are asked to report false details of their place of residence to escape police inquiries.
- Brokers arrange a proxy "donor" to make statements on their behalf. They forge legal documents that indicate that the person is donating an organ to a relative and advise the supplier not to disclose his/her true identity, so healthcare personnel will not reject the case.

Mendoza (2011) explained that in the Philippines, brokers also manage the cash and other in-kind payments made to government officials. Brokers or scouts have local politicians and the local police as family members or friends so officials get involved directly or indirectly in the logistical support. When it comes to prosecution, if a broker is approached by an organ seller, it has proven difficult to prosecute the broker, even if exploitation was present (Yea, 2010). Although testimonies against brokers are rare (Lundin, 2012) because neither buyers nor sellers report them, prosecutions of brokers have taken place in Turkey, Israel, India, South Africa, the United States, Kosovo and Brazil (Pascalev et al., 2013).

What is the relationship between brokers and exploitation of the organ sellers?

Finally, criticisms of conflating trade with trafficking are mainly based on the idea that some people sell their organs without exploitation. The assumption here is that a seller could finalize a transaction without any of the abuses mentioned above. To be able to assess if that is the case, it would require a deeper understanding of "exploitation" both generally and within the human organ contextual circumstances. Exploitation is unsurprisingly a contested concept but it is generally understood to mean to take unfair advantage, which in itself can take several forms. The case of the poor selling their organs to the richer seems a straightforward case of structural exploitation based on class exploitation. The removal of a perfectly working human organ is expropriation of surplus (net) value (their organs) from the poorer person. The rules of the legal organ market unfairly and undoubtedly benefit one group of people – those who can pay – because of the promise of increased positive health outcomes. These benefits are always to the detriment of another's person health outcomes because the person who loses an organ will always encounter short-term negative health outcomes and an increased likelihood of negative long-term health outcomes. This is compounded by the reality that those with less means always have worse health outcomes than the rest of the population. The pro-organ market discourse unashamedly sees no essential moral problem in selling human organs. The ultimate question for those who do is, why do we care more about the body parts of the poor than about their whole bodies? The poor are exploited globally and locally on a daily basis without the corresponding moral outrage.

Conclusion

Organ transplantation abroad is a global business that has contested legalities since it can or cannot be related to criminal activity. It is also related to people being trafficked for the purpose of removing their organs to sell them for profit. Some people are transferred from their place of residence to another location where one of their organs is removed and transplanted into another person who has paid for it. The reasons why this takes place are extremely complex but the overall drive for this phenomenon is that human organ transplantation has the potential to be the best treatment available for several chronic and terminal illnesses. The terminology employed by the different international legislations available to prevent this crime can be confusing and most importantly, it can lead to oversimplification of a very complex myriad of global processes, criminalities, legalities and liabilities embedding the purchasing transactions when living human body parts are involved.

There is an ongoing debate about the need for a regulated free market which politicizes the little hard evidence available. There is no doubt that illegal paid organ donation occurs worldwide but, unsurprisingly, there is lack of hard data regarding the incidence of THBOR. The reasons why people sell and buy organs are complex but they tend to be simplified with a narrative of a concurrence of two desperations: the financial desperation of those in need of money and the clinical desperation of those in need of better health. Although a human body part purchase transaction could not succeed without these colluding desperations, it could not progress without the involvement of those noticing the opportunity to make profit. The presence of brokers who facilitate the transaction, share illegalities and profit in THBOR is a key factor in proving the inevitable exploitation of the organ sellers.

Supplemental learning materials

Podcasts

The Moral Maze- Organ Donation. Retrieved from www.bbc.co.uk/programmes/b01by7cz
Organ Donation – Flip Flops. Retrieved from www.bbc.co.uk/programmes/b00nfqzg

Websites

The HOTT Project, an international research project on "combating trafficking in persons for the purpose of organ removal" funded by the European Union. The project systematically collected THBO information and published nine reports and a book. Retrieved from http://hottproject.com/home.html

HOTT Project case study report examines in detail four cases of THBOR in South Africa, Kosovo, Israel and the U.S. Retrieved from http://hottproject.com/userfiles/Reports/3rdReportHOTTProject-TraffickinginHumanBeingsforthePurposeofOrganRemoval-ACaseStudyReport.pdf

A patient brochure for people thinking about buying a kidney, available in several languages can be downloaded here: www.declarationofistanbul.org/resources/patient-brochure-thinking-about-a-kidney

The website of The Declaration of Istanbul Custodian Group website offers updated world news on THBOR. Retrieved from www.declarationofistanbul.org/

Films

Tales from the Organ Trade directed by Ric Esther Bienstock. Retrieved from www.talesfromtheorgantrade.com

References

Ackoundou-N'Guessan, C., Gnionsahe, D. A., Dekou, A. H., Tia, W. M., Guei, C. M., & Moudachirou, A. M. (2010). Outcomes of renal patients from the Ivory Coast transplanted abroad: Time for a local kidney transplantation program. *Transplant Proceedings, 42*(9), 3517–3520.

Al Rahbi, F., & Al Salmi, I. (2017). Commercial kidney transplantation: Attitude, knowledge, perception, and experience of recipients. *Kidney International Reports* 2(4), 626–633.

Alberti, F. G., Giusti, J. D., Papa, F., & Pizzurno, E. (2014). Competitiveness policies for medical tourism clusters: Government initiatives in Thailand. *International Journal of Economic Policy in Emerging Economies*, 7(3), 281–309.

Allain, J. (2011). Trafficking of persons for the removal of organs and the admission of guilt of a South African hospital. *Medical Law Review, 19*(1), 117–122.

Ambagtsheer, F., Gunnarson, M., De Jong, J., Lundin, S., van Balen, L., Orr, Z., Byström, I., & Weimar, W. (2014). *Trafficking in human beings for the purpose of organ removal: A case study report.* Retrieved June 5, 2017, from www.hottproject.com

Ambagtsheer, F., Jong, J., Bramer, W. M., & Weimar, W. (2016). On patients who purchase organ transplants abroad. *American Journal of Transplantation, 16*(10), 2800–2815.

Ambagtsheer, F., Zaitch, D., & Weimar, W. (2013). The battle for human organs: Organ trafficking and transplant tourism in a global context. *Global Crime, 14*(1), 1–26.

Ambagtsheer, F., Zaitch, D., van Swaaningen, R., Duijst, W; Zuidema, W., & Weimar, W. (2012). Cross-border quest: The reality and legality of transplant tourism. *Journal of Transplantation, 2012*, 1–12.

Awaya, T., Siruno, L., Toledano, S. J., Aguilar, F., Shimazono, Y., & De Castro, L. D. (2009). Failure of informed consent in compensated non-related kidney donation in the Philippines. *Asian Bioethics Review, 12*, 138.

Azancot, M. A., Cantarell, C., Perelló, M., Torres, I. B., & Serón, D. (2011). Estimation of renal allograft half-life: Fact or fiction? *Nephrology Dialysis Transplantation, 26*(9), 3013–3018.
Bramstedta, K. A., & Xu, J. (2007). Checklist: Passport, plane ticket, organ transplant. *American Journal of Transplantation, 7*, 1698.
Brenner, N., & Theodore, N. (2002). Cities and the geographies of "actually existing neoliberalism." *Antipode, 34*(3), 349–379.
Bucy, P. H. (1988). Fraud by fright: White collar crime by health care providers. *North Carolina Law Review, 67*, 855.
Budiani-Saberi, A., & Karim, K. (2009). The social determinants of organ trafficking: A reflection of social inequity. *Social Medicine* (4), 48–51.
Budiani-Saberi, D. A., & Delmonico, F. L. (2008). Organ trafficking and transplant tourism: A commentary on the global realities. *American Journal of Transplantation, 8*(5), 925–929.
Budiani-Saberi, D. A., Raja, K. R., Findley, K. C., Kerketta, P., & Anand, V. (2014). Human trafficking for organ removal in India: A victim-centered, evidence-based report. *Transplantation, 97*(4), 380–384.
Calderoni, F. (2014). Mythical numbers and the proceeds of organised crime: Estimating Mafia proceeds in Italy. *Global Crime, 15*(1–2), 138–163.
Caplan, A., Dominguez, B., Matesanz, R., & Prior, C. (2009). *Trafficking in organs, tissues and cells and trafficking in human beings for the purpose of the removal of organs*. Directorate General of Human Rights and Legal Affairs, a joint study of Council of Europe and United Nations.
Cherry, M. J. (2015). *Kidney for sale by owner: Human organs, transplantation, and the market*. Washington, DC: Georgetown University Press.
Coleman, C., & Moynihan, J. (1996). *Understanding crime data*. Buckingham: Open University Press.
Columb, S. (2015). Beneath the organ trade: A critical analysis of the organ trafficking discourse. *Crime Law & Social Change, 63*, 21–47.
Columb, S., Ambagtsheer, F., Bos, M., Ivanovski, N., Moorlock, G., & Weimar, W. (2017). Re-conceptualising the organ trade: Separating "trafficking" from "trade" and the implications for law and policy. *Transplant International, 30*, 209–213.
Council of Europe Convention on Action against Trafficking in Human Beings. (2005). Warsaw, 16.V.2005. CETS 197 (2005).
Cronin, A. J., Johnson, R. J., Birch, R., Lechler, R. I., & Randhawa, G. (2011). Solving the kidney transplant crisis for minority ethnic groups in the UK: Is being transplanted overseas the answer? In W. Weimar, M. A. Bos, & J. J. Busschbach (Eds.), *Organ transplantation: ethical, legal and psychosocial aspects expanding the European platform* (pp. 62–72). Lengerich: Pabst Science Publishers.
Danovitch, G. M., Chapman, J., Capron, A. M., Levin, A., Abbud-Filho, M., Al Mousawi, M., & Jha, V. (2013). Organ trafficking and transplant tourism: The role of global professional ethical standards the 2008 declaration of Istanbul. *Transplantation, 95*, 1306–1312.
De Jong, J. (2015). *The trade in human organs and human trafficking for the purpose of organ removal. An exploratory study into the involvement of the Netherlands and Europe* Retrieved June 5, 2017, http://hottproject.com/userfiles/Reports/DeJong2015TradeinhumanorgansandtraffickinginhumanbeingsanexploratorystudyintotheinvolvementoftheNetherlandsandEurope.pdf
Delmonico, F. (2009). The implications of Istanbul declaration on organ trafficking and transplant tourism. *Current Opinion in Organ Transplantation, 14*, 116–119.
Donovan, P. (2002). Crime legends in a new medium: Fact, fiction and loss of authority. *Theoretical Criminology, 6*(2), 189–215.
Dworkin, G. (1994). Markets and morals: The case of kidney sales. In G. Dworkin (Ed.), *Morality, Harm, and the law*, 155–161. Boulder, CO: Westview Press.
Efrat, A. (2013). Combating the kidney commerce: Civil society against organ trafficking in Pakistan and Israel. *British Journal of Criminology, 53*(5),764–783.
Efrat, A. (2016). Global efforts against human trafficking: The misguided conflation of sex, labor, and organ trafficking. *International Studies Perspectives, 17*(1), 34–54.
The European Parliament and the Council. Directive 2011/36/EU on preventing and combating trafficking in human beings and protecting its victims, and replacing Council Framework Decision 2002/629/JHA, (2011).
European Union. Directive 2010/53/EU of the European Parliament and the Council of 7 July 2010 on standards of quality and safety of human organs intended for human transplantation. European Union 210. Retrieved from http://eurlex.europa.eu/LexUriServ/LexUriServ.do?uri=OJ:L:2010:207:0014:0029:EN:PDF.

Fikrejesus, A. (2016). Human rights and world culture: The diffusion of legislation against the organ trade, *Sociological Spectrum, 36*(3), 158–182.
Fraser, C. (2016). An analysis of the emerging role of social media in human trafficking: Examples from labour and human organ trading. *International Journal of Development Issues, 15*(2), 98–112.
Gill, J., Diec, O., Landsberg, D. N., Rose, C., Johnston, O., Keown, P. A., & Gill, J. S. (2011). Opportunities to deter transplant tourism exist before referral for transplantation and during the workup and management of transplant candidates. *Kidney International, 79*, 1026–1031.
Gill, J., Madhira, B., Gjertson, D., Lipshutz, G., Cecka, J. M., Pham, P. T., . . . Danovitch, G. M. (2008). Transplant tourism in the United States: A single-center experience. *Clinical Journal of the American Society of Nephrology, 3*, 1820–1828.
Goyal, M., Mehta, R. L., Schneiderman, L. J., & Sehgal, A. R. (2002). Economic and health consequences of selling a kidney in India. *Journal of the American Medical Association, 288*(13), 1589–1593.
Heldal, K., Hartmann, A., Lønning, K., Leivestad, T., Reisæter, A. V., Line, P. D., Holdaas, H., & Midtvedt, K. (2017). Should patients older than 65 years be offered a second kidney transplant? *BMC Nephrology, 18*(1), 13.
Jingwei, A. H., Yu-Hung, A. L., & Ching, L. (2010). Living organ transplantation policy transition in Asia: Towards adaptive policy changes. *Global Health, 3*(2), 1–14.
Koplin, J. (2014). Assessing the likely harms to kidney vendors in regulated organ markets. *The American Journal of Bioethics, 14*(10), 7–18.
Krishnan, N., Cockwell, P., Devulapally, P., Gerber, B., Hanvesakul, R., Higgins, R., & Baharani, J. (2010). Organ trafficking for live donor kidney transplantation in Indoasians resident in the West Midlands: High activity and poor outcomes. *Transplantation, 89*, 1456–1461.
Leventhal, T. (1994). *The child organ trafficking rumor: A modern urban legend.* Washington, DC: U.S. Information Agency, 18.
Lock, M. (2000). The quest for human organs and the violence of zeal. In V. Das, A. Kleinman, M. Ramphele, & P. Reynolds (Eds.), *Remaking a world: Violence, social suffering, and recovery* (pp. 271–295). Berkeley: University of California Press.
Lønning, K., Midtvedt, K., Leivestad, T., Reisæter, A. V., Line, P-D., Hartmann, A., & Heldal, K. (2016). Are octogenarians with end-stage renal disease candidates for renal transplantation? *Transplantation, 100*(12), 2705–2709.
Lundin, S. (2012). Organ economy: Organ trafficking in Moldova and Israel. *Public Understanding Science, 21*(2), 226–241.
Majid, A., Al Khalidi, L., Ahmed, B. Q., Opelz, G., & Schaefer, F. (2010). Outcomes of kidney transplant tourism in children: A single center experience. *Pediatric Nephrology, 25(1)*, 155.
Mann, K. (1996). Who are you lookin at? Voyeurs, narks and do gooders. In H. Dean (Ed.), *Ethics and social policy research.* Luton: ULP /Social Policy Assoc.
Manzano, A., Monaghan, M., Potrata, B., & Clayton, M. (2014). The invisible issue of organ laundering. *Transplantation, 98*(6), 600–603.
Manzano, A., & Pawson, R. (2014). Evaluating deceased organ donation: A programme theory approach. *Journal of Health Organization and Management, 28*(3), 366–385.
Marmot, M. (2005). Social determinants of health inequalities. *The Lancet, 365*, 1099–1104.
Mendoza, R. L. (2011). Price deflation and the underground organ economy in the Philippines. *Journal of Public Health* (United Kingdom), *33(1)*, 101–107.
Meyer, S. (2006). Trafficking in human organs in Europe. *European Journal of Crime Criminal Law and Criminal Justice, 14*(2), 208–229.
Moniruzzaman, M. (2012). "Living cadavers" in Bangladesh: Bioviolence in the human organ bazaar. *Medical Anthropology Quarterly, 26*, 69–91.
Montgomery, J. (1997). *Health care law.* Oxford: Oxford University Press.
Moorlock, G., Ives, J., & Draper, H. (2014). Altruism in organ donation: An unnecessary requirement? *Journal of Medical Ethics, 40*(2), 134–138.
Muncie, J., & McLaughlin, E. (1996). *The Problem of Crime.* London: Sage.
Naqvi, S. A. A., Ali, B., Mazhar, F., Zafar, M. N., & Rizvi, S. A. H. (2007). A socioeconomic survey of kidney vendors in Pakistan. *Transplant International, 20*(11), 934–939.
Navarro, V. (2009). What we mean by social determinants of health. *Global Health Promotion, 16*(1), 5–16.
Neuberger, J. (2011). Making an offer you can't refuse? A challenge of altruistic donation. *Transplant International, 24*(12), 1159–1161.

Noel, L. (2010). WHO Guiding principles on human cell, tissue and organ transplantation. *Transplantation, 90*, 29.
OSCE. (2013, July). *Office of the special representative and co-ordinator for combating trafficking in human beings, trafficking in human beings for the purpose of organ removal in the OSCE region: Analysis and findings*. Occasional Paper Series no. 6.
Padilla, B., Danovitch, G.M., & Lavee, J. (2013). Impact of legal measures prevent transplant tourism: The interrelated experience of the Philippines and Israel. *Medicine, Health Care and Philosophy, 16*(4), 915–919.
Pancevski, B. (2006). Bulgarian hospital admits role in illegal transplants. *The Lancet, 367*(9509), 461.
Pascalev, A., de Jong, J., Ambagtsheer, F., Lundin, S., Ivanovski, N., Codreanu, C., & Weimar, W. 2013. *Trafficking in human beings for the purpose of organ removal: A comprehensive literature review*. Retrieved June 5, 2017, from http://hottproject.com/userfiles/HOTTProject TraffickinginHumanBeingsforthePurposeofOrganRemoval-AComprehensiveLiteratureReview-OnlinePublication.pdf
Pawson, R., Owen, L., & Wong, G. (2010). Legislating for health: Locating the evidence. *Journal of Public Health Policy, 31*(2), 164–177.
Purnell, T.S., Powe, N.R., Troll, M.U., Wang, N.Y., Haywood, C., LaVeist, T.A., & Boulware, L. (2013). Measuring and explaining racial and ethnic differences in willingness to donate live kidneys in the United States. *Clinical Transplantation, 27*(5), 673–683.
Radcliffe Richards, J. (1996). Nephrarious goings on kidney sales and moral arguments. *Journal of Medicine and Philosophy, 21*(4), 375–416.
Radcliffe Richards, J. (2012). *The ethics of transplants. Why careless thought costs lives*. Oxford: Oxford University Press.
Reuter, P. (1984). The (continued) vitality of mythical numbers. *The Public Interest, 75*, 135.
Richardson, R. (2006). Human dissection and organ donation: A historical and social background, *Mortality, 11*(2), 151–165,
Roberts, E., & Scheper-Hughes, N. (2011). Introduction: Medical migrations. *Body & Society, 17*(2–3), 1–30.
Scheper-Hughes, N. (2000). The global traffic in human organs. *Current Anthropology, 41*(2), 191–224.
Scheper-Hughes, N. (2001). Commodity fetishism in organs trafficking. *Body & Society, 7*(2–3), 31–62.
Scheper-Hughes, N. (2003). Keeping an eye on the global traffic in human organs. *The Lancet, 361*(9369), 1645–1648.
Scheper-Hughes, N. (2006). Kidney kin: Inside the transatlantic transplant trade. *Harvard International Review, 27*(4), 62.
Scheper-Hughes, N. (2011). Tati's holiday and Joao's safari: Seeing the world through transplant tourism. *Body & Society, 17*(2–3), 55–92.
Scheper-Hughes, N.M., & Boström, D. (2013). The body of the enemy. *Brown Journal of Global Affairs, 19*(11, Spring/Summer).
Sharp, L.A. (2000). The commodification of the body and its parts. *Annual Review of Anthropology*, 287–328.
Shimazono, Y. (2007). The state of the international organ trade: A provisional picture based on integration of available information. *Bulletin of the World Health Organization, 85*, 955–962.
Singer, M. (1971). The vitality of mythical numbers. *The Public Interest, 23*, 3.
Smith-Morris, C., & Manderson, L. (2010). The baggage of health travelers. *Medical Anthropology*, 331–335.
Stark, C., Paterson, B., & Kidd, B. (2001). Opportunity may be more important than profession in serial homicide. *British Medical Journal, 322*, 993.
Steering Committee of the Istanbul Summit (2008). Organ trafficking and transplant tourism and commercialism: the Declaration of Istanbul. *The Lancet*, 372(9632), 5–6.
Steffensmeier, D., & Allan, E. (1996). Gender and crime: Toward a gendered theory of female offending. *Annual Review of Sociology, 22*(1), 459–487.
Titmuss, R.M. (1970). *The gift relationship: From human blood to social policy*. London: George Allen and Unwin Ltd.
Tong, A., Chapman, J.R., Kee, T., Li, P.K., Tsai, D.F., Wong, G., & Craig, J.C. (2015). Perspectives of transplant professionals on the values, ethics, and challenges of living kidney donor evaluation in Asia. *Transplantation, 99*(7), 1386–1395.
Tong, A., Chapman, J.R., Wong, G., Cross, N.B., Batabyal, P., & Craig, J. (2012). The experiences of commercial kidney donors: Thematic synthesis of qualitative research. *Transplant International, 25*, 1138–1149.
United Nations. (2000a). United Nations Optional Protocol to the Convention on the Rights of the Child on the Sale of Children, Child Prostitution and Child Pornography. Treaty Series, vol. 2171, p. 227 Doc. A/RES/54/263 (2000).

United Nations. (2000b). United Nations protocol to prevent, suppress and punish trafficking in persons, especially women and children, supplementing the United Nations Convention against transnational organized crime, United Nations Office on drugs and crime. Vienna. Treaty Series, vol. 2237 (2000).
United States Department of State. (2005, June). *Trafficking in persons report*. Washington, DC.
Weitzer, R. (2007). The social construction of sex trafficking: Ideology and institutionalization of a moral crusade. *Politics & Society*, *35*(3), 447–475.
WHO. (2016). Life expectancy increased by 5 years since 2000, but health inequalities persist. Retrieved June 5, 2017, from www.who.int/mediacentre/news/releases/2016/health-inequalities-persist/en/
Wong, G., Pawson, R., & Owen, L. (2011). Policy guidance on threats to legislative interventions in public health: A realist synthesis. *BMC Public Health*, *11*(1), 222.
Yakupoglu, Y. K., Ozden, E., Dilek, M., Demirbas, A., Adibelli, Z., Sarikaya, S., & Akpolat, T. (2010). Transplantation tourism: High risk for the recipients. *Clinical Transplantation*, *24*(6), 835–838.
Yea, S. (2010). Trafficking in part(s): The commercial kidney market in a Manila slum, Philippines. *Global Social Policy*, *10*(3), 358–376.
Zargooshi, J. (2001). Quality of life of Iranian kidney "donors." *Journal of Urology*, *166*, 1790.

SECTION IV

Social work

12

TRAINING SOCIAL WORKERS IN ANTI-TRAFFICKING SERVICE

Jacquelyn C.A. Meshelemiah

Abstract

As human trafficking is becoming recognized as an issue that needs social workers' attention, more social workers are expressing an interest in serving trafficked persons. This chapter examines human trafficking from a broad lens that incorporates an anti-trafficking training model for social work students and professionals. The author discusses human trafficking as a form of modern-day slavery and charges the social work professional with fostering a human rights approach to anti-trafficking service.

Learning Objectives

At the end of the chapter, readers will be able to:

1. Illustrate the need for social work professionals to turn to active participation in anti-trafficking work;
2. Describe empowerment and the values of the social work profession and discuss how they are embedded within a social justice mission;
3. Examine human trafficking from a human rights lens;
4. Discuss trafficking elements for social work students and professionals;
5. Apply knowledge gained throughout this chapter to illustrate critical elements of vulnerability and service provision using a human trafficking case study; and
6. Dissect contextual factors related to understanding and addressing human trafficking.

Key Terms: human trafficking; human rights; social work; empowerment; social justice.

Introduction

As a profession, social work is over a century old (Lesser & Pope, 2007; Tannenbaum & Reisch, 2001). It began under the auspice of the Charity Organization Society (COS) and the settlement house movement. Under the leadership of Mary Richmond (COS) and Jane Addams (settlement house), social work adopted an action-oriented stance (Segal, Gerdes, & Steiner, 2013). Jane Addams, in particular, is responsible for much of the action associated with social work. She is hailed as an activist before her time due to her unrelenting pursuit of justice (civil, social, political, legal, and economic) and empowerment for all (Gil, 2013; Meshelemiah, 2016). Despite the rich history of social workers explicitly serving and advocating on behalf of vulnerable groups of people, the profession of social work is slow in turning its attention and training to social problems of a human rights nature (Healy, 2008, 2015). This includes human trafficking. Human trafficking is a widespread form of modern-day enslavement that is grounded in preying on the vulnerable, stripping them of their human rights, and human profiteering (Alvarez & Alessi, 2012).

Human trafficking is a term that was officially coined and adopted in 2000 by the U.S. government through federal legislation with the enactment of the Victims of Trafficking and Violence Protection Act (refer to C.deBaca, Chapter 2, this volume). This Act is best known for its section on trafficking, which is known as the Trafficking Victims Protection Act (TVPA). Human trafficking activities primarily fall into two categories: sex trafficking and labor trafficking. Sex trafficking involves the inducement of others into commercial sex activities by force, fraud or coercion (without force, fraud or coercion for those younger than 18 years of age). Labor trafficking, through the use of force, fraud, and coercion, involves making a person provide labor services for free; for far less than what was agreed upon; or under terms that were not agreed upon (Okech, Morreau, & Benson, 2011; Public Law No. 106–386). The most comprehensive definition of trafficking, however, is the one adopted by the UN Office of Drugs and Crime in 2000, which is known as the United Nations Protocol to Prevent, Suppress and Punish Trafficking in Persons, Especially Women and Children, Supplementing the United Nations Convention Against Transnational Organized Crime (United Nations, 2000, p. 3):

Article 3 of the said Protocol reads as follows:

(a) Trafficking in persons shall mean the recruitment, transportation, transfer, habouring or receipt of persons, by means of the threat or use of force or other forms of coercion, of abduction, of fraud, of deception, of the abuse of power or of a position of vulnerability or of the giving or of receiving of payments or benefits to achieve the consent of a person having control over another person, for the purpose of exploitation. Exploitation shall include, at a minimum, the exploitation of the prostitution of others or other forms of sexual exploitation, forced labour services, slavery or practices similar to slavery, servitude or the removal of organs;
(b) The consent of a victim of trafficking in persons to the intended exploitation set forth in sub paragraph (a) of this article shall be irrelevant where any of the means set forth in sub paragraph (a) have been used;
(c) The recruitment, transportation, transfer, harbouring or receipt of a child for the purpose of exploitation shall be considered "trafficking in persons" even if this does not involve any of the means set forth in sub paragraph (a) of the article;
(d) "Child" shall mean any person under eighteen years of age.

These definitions have led to the increased awareness of human trafficking domestically and internationally. These are seminal pieces of legislation.

Due to the prevalence of human trafficking in the United States and across the globe, social workers must become more involved in the anti-trafficking movement through service at the micro, mezzo, and macro levels. Although prevalence is difficult to determine, approximately 600,000 to 800,000 persons are estimated to cross national and international borders annually for trafficking purposes (Okech et al., 2011). Reportedly, 14,500 to 17,500 people are estimated to be annually transported into the United States for these same reasons (Fedina, Trease, & Williamson, 2008). These statistics suggest that human trafficking is widespread and persistent. It epitomizes the gross violation of the human rights of millions around the globe, including in the

United States. Preparing social workers to address human trafficking is compulsory. It is critical for social workers to join the anti-trafficking movement due to the insidious relationship human trafficking has with human rights violations.

Intersection between human rights and human trafficking

The International Federation of Social Workers (IFSW) declared almost 30 years ago that social work is a human rights profession (IFSW, 1988). Unfortunately, still today, most social workers do not identify as champions of human rights. Social workers mostly identify with the charge to promote social justice (Healy, 2015). For instance, the profession of social work has always been inculcated with the belief that all humans deserve to be viewed and treated with dignity and worth and afforded access to basic necessities as commensurate with social justice. The National Association of Social Workers (NASW) Code of Ethics espouses that social workers must promote social justice (NASW, 1996, 2017a) and social work textbooks repeatedly echo the importance of promoting social justice (Lesser & Pope, 2007; Segal et al., 2013). Rarely, however, are social workers indoctrinated with the belief that knowing, understanding, and protecting human rights is also part of the profession's charge. Transitioning to the expectation that the social work profession will preserve human rights has been slow in coming (Healy, 2008, 2015; Reichert, 2001).

"Social justice is the view that everyone deserves equal economic, political and social rights and opportunities" (NASW, 2017a, para. 2) while human rights are broadly defined as the "basic rights and freedoms that all people are entitled to regardless of nationality, sex, national or ethnic origin, race, religion, language or other status" (Amnesty International USA, 2015, *Human Rights section*). Although the terms are related, the adoption of human rights requires specific actions related to a set of rights and freedoms as asserted in the United Nations Universal Declaration of Human Rights (UN UDHR). The intersection between human rights and human trafficking are explicated here (see Table 12.1). Before discussing anti-trafficking training of the student,

Table 12.1 Human rights and human trafficking

Human Rights Article	*Human Trafficking and Social Work*
Article 1. All human beings are born free and equal in dignity and rights. They are endowed with reason and conscience and should act towards one another in a spirit of brotherhood.	Slavery is abolished all across the world. All humans are born free.
Article 2. Everyone is entitled to all the rights and freedoms set forth in this Declaration, without distinction of any kind, such as race, colour, sex, language, religion, political or other opinion, national or social origin, property, birth or other status. Furthermore, no distinction shall be made on the basis of the political, jurisdictional or international status of the country or territory to which a person belongs, whether it be independent, trust, non-self-governing or under any other limitation of sovereignty.	These 30 articles apply to all people.

(Continued)

Table 12.1 (Continued)

Human Rights Article	*Human Trafficking and Social Work*
Article 3. Everyone has the right to life, liberty and security of person.	All people have the right to enjoy life, liberty and security of person. Social work interventions must consider this in treatment planning as part of the reintegration.
Article 4. No one shall be held in slavery or servitude; slavery and the slave trade shall be prohibited in all their forms.	This Article explicitly forbids human trafficking (modern slavery).
Article 5. No one shall be subjected to torture or to cruel, inhuman or degrading treatment or punishment.	Victims of trafficking are subjected to a range of abuses. Trauma-informed approaches are imperative.
Article 6. Everyone has the right to recognition everywhere as a person before the law.	All people are "persons" before the law. This includes victims of trafficking. Person-first language is critical in our interaction with trafficked persons.
Article 7. All are equal before the law and are entitled without any discrimination to equal protection of the law. All are entitled to equal protection against any discrimination in violation of this Declaration and against any incitement to such discrimination.	Trafficking victims have the right to be treated fairly before the law. Anti-trafficking legislation fights to ensure this protection. Social work documentation and testimonies in court must be pro-trafficking survivor.
Article 8. Everyone has the right to an effective remedy by the competent national tribunals for acts violating the fundamental rights granted him by the constitution or by law.	Trafficking victims have the right to be competently reviewed regarding their rights.
Article 9. No one shall be subjected to arbitrary arrest, detention or exile.	Trafficking victims are oftentimes arrested and detained as criminals during raids and busts. Social workers must be a part of teams interviewing people after a bust. Interpreters may be helpful with this.
Article 10. Everyone is entitled in full equality to a fair and public hearing by an independent and impartial tribunal, in the determination of his rights and obligations and of any criminal charge against him.	Trafficking victims have the right to a fair and public trial when charged with a crime. Social workers may have to serve as advocates in these cases.
Article 11. (1) Everyone charged with a penal offence has the right to be presumed innocent until proved guilty according to law in a public trial at which he has had all the guarantees necessary for his defense. (2) No one shall be held guilty of any penal offence on account of any act or omission which did not constitute a penal offence, under national or international law, at the time when it was committed. Nor shall a heavier penalty be imposed than the one that was applicable at the time the penal offence was committed.	Trafficking victims must be presumed to be innocent of crimes levied against them until proven guilty. For instance, sex trafficked women are often presumed to be prostitutes and subsequently charged with solicitation charges when in reality they are victims of a crime – human trafficking.

Human Rights Article	*Human Trafficking and Social Work*
Article 12. No one shall be subjected to arbitrary interference with his privacy, family, home or correspondence, nor to attacks upon his honour and reputation. Everyone has the right to the protection of the law against such interference or attacks.	Trafficking victims (and their family members) are routinely threatened with harm and/or death if they leave the trafficker. The law protects against such attacks.
Article 13. (1) Everyone has the right to freedom of movement and residence within the borders of each state. (2) Everyone has the right to leave any country, including his own, and to return to his country.	Trafficked persons do not have the freedom of movement and travel. Upon release, the survivor may need assistance in navigating her or his new found landscape.
Article 14. (1) Everyone has the right to seek and to enjoy in other countries asylum from persecution. (2) This right may not be invoked in the case of prosecutions genuinely arising from non-political crimes or from acts contrary to the purposes and principles of the United Nations.	Trafficking victims sometimes seek asylum (Stepnitz, 2012). Social work advocates may be needed to help victims with this process.
Article 15. (1) Everyone has the right to a nationality. (2) No one shall be arbitrarily deprived of his nationality nor denied the right to change his nationality.	Trafficking victims sometime are too embarrassed to return home (abroad) after being rescued due to shaming and rejection by family and friends who assert that people of their group do not work as sex workers. Social workers must work within these confines.
Article 16. (1) Men and women of full age, without any limitation due to race, nationality or religion, have the right to marry and to found a family. They are entitled to equal rights as to marriage, during marriage and at its dissolution. (2) Marriage shall be entered into only with the free and full consent of the intending spouses. (3) The family is the natural and fundamental group unit of society and is entitled to protection by society and the State.	Trafficking victims do not have the right to marry who they want or even at all. Upon release from trafficking, social workers will be needed to help survivors establish healthy relationships with others.
Article 17. (1) Everyone has the right to own property alone as well as in association with others. (2) No one shall be arbitrarily deprived of his property.	Trafficking victims do not have the right to own anything including their own bodies. Simple things like shopping for food and clothing may be need to be taught. Learning how to budget money will be important given that man y survivors will have little to no experience managing money.
Article 18. Everyone has the right to freedom of thought, conscience and religion; this right includes freedom to change his religion or belief, and freedom, either alone or in community with others and in public or private, to manifest his religion or belief in teaching, practice, worship and observance.	Trafficking victims do not have this right.

(Continued)

Table 12.1 (Continued)

Human Rights Article	*Human Trafficking and Social Work*
Article 19. Everyone has the right to freedom of opinion and expression; this right includes freedom to hold opinions without interference and to seek, receive and impart information and ideas through any media and regardless of frontiers.	Trafficking victims do not have this right.
Article 20. (1) Everyone has the right to freedom of peaceful assembly and association. (2) No one may be compelled to belong to an association.	Trafficking victims do not have this right. Resistance of any type is met with harsh consequences.
Article 21. (1) Everyone has the right to take part in the government of his country, directly or through freely chosen representatives. (2) Everyone has the right of equal access to public service in his country. (3) The will of the people shall be the basis of the authority of government; this will shall be expressed in periodic and genuine elections which shall be by universal and equal suffrage and shall be held by secret vote or by equivalent free voting procedures.	Trafficking victims do not have this right. Access to services and outsiders (beyond those whom services are being provided to and for) are limited to none.
Article 22. Everyone, as a member of society, has the right to social security and is entitled to realization, through national effort and international co-operation and in accordance with the organization and resources of each State, of the economic, social and cultural rights indispensable for his dignity and the free development of his personality.	Trafficking victims do not have this right.
Article 23. (1) Everyone has the right to work, to free choice of employment, to just and favourable conditions of work and to protection against unemployment. (2) Everyone, without any discrimination, has the right to equal pay for equal work. (3) Everyone who works has the right to just and favourable remuneration ensuring for himself and his family an existence worthy of human dignity, and supplemented, if necessary, by other means of social protection. (4) Everyone has the right to form and to join trade unions for the protection of his interests.	Traffickers determine choice of employment, payment (if any), pay schedule (if any), and hours of work. Post-trafficking, survivors may need assistance acquiring vocational skills.
Article 24. Everyone has the right to rest and leisure, including reasonable limitation of working hours and periodic holidays with pay.	Trafficking victims do not have this right. They are worked to capacity and beyond. Survivors will need to learn to enjoy life and leisure activities. This should be a part of the treatment plan.
Article 25. (1) Everyone has the right to a standard of living adequate for the health and well-being of himself and of his family, including food, clothing, housing and medical care and necessary social services, and the right to security in the event of unemployment, sickness, disability, widowhood, old age or other lack of livelihood in circumstances beyond his control.(2) Motherhood and childhood are entitled to special care and assistance. All children, whether born in or out of wedlock, shall enjoy the same social protection.	Trafficking victims do not have this right. They receive the bare minimum (if any) of everything available to free persons. This is the primary area of potential service delivery to trafficking victims/survivors by social workers. Upon release, in particular, is when these individuals will be free to access these services.

Human Rights Article	*Human Trafficking and Social Work*
Article 26. (1) Everyone has the right to education. Education shall be free, at least in the elementary and fundamental stages. Elementary education shall be compulsory. Technical and professional education shall be made generally available and higher education shall be equally accessible to all on the basis of merit. (2) Education shall be directed to the full development of the human personality and to the strengthening of respect for human rights and fundamental freedoms. It shall promote understanding, tolerance and friendship among all nations, racial or religious groups, and shall further the activities of the United Nations for the maintenance of peace. (3) Parents have a prior right to choose the kind of education that shall be given to their children.	Trafficking victims do not have this right. Education is not an option. Upon release, most trafficking survivors will need to acquire some degree of education or training.
Article 27. (1) Everyone has the right freely to participate in the cultural life of the community, to enjoy the arts and to share in scientific advancement and its benefits. (2) Everyone has the right to the protection of the moral and material interests resulting from any scientific, literary or artistic production of which he is the author.	Trafficking victims do not have this right. Their lives are centered around trafficking-related work. As a freed person, trafficking survivors should be introduced to their communities in a social and cultural way.
Article 28. Everyone is entitled to a social and international order in which the rights and freedoms set forth in this Declaration can be fully realized.	Some governments do attempt to allow for social order to take place after trafficking victims are rescued. Social workers must always approach and work with trafficking survivors in a way that protects their rights and freedoms.
Article 29. (1) Everyone has duties to the community in which alone the free and full development of his personality is possible. (2) In the exercise of his rights and freedoms, everyone shall be subject only to such limitations as are determined by law solely for the purpose of securing due recognition and respect for the rights and freedoms of others and of meeting the just requirements of morality, public order and the general welfare in a democratic society. (3) These rights and freedoms may in no case be exercised contrary to the purposes and principles of the United Nations.	Trafficking victims do not enjoy this right. Their personalities are fully suppressed. Released trafficked persons must learn what their rights and freedoms are.
Article 30. Nothing in this Declaration may be interpreted as implying for any State, group or person any right to engage in any activity or to perform any act aimed at the destruction of any of the rights and freedoms set forth herein.	These Articles are all applicable to trafficking survivors. Social workers must understand the relationship between human rights, human trafficking and social work as a profession.

social work intern, and social work professional, an examination of the human rights articles that directly apply to those persons who are trafficked is necessary. This examination sets the foundation for why and how social workers must be trained to provide services to trafficking survivors.

If social work education incorporated a human rights approach to addressing social injustices using explicit language as espoused in the definition of social justice and the United Nations (UN) definition of human rights, domestic and global social ills like human trafficking would garner more attention from social workers. For instance, the most definitive conceptualization of human rights is best articulated by the United Nations. The UN issued the Universal Declaration of Human Rights (UDHR) in 1948 in an attempt to bring attention to the inalienable rights of all people in all nations as agreed upon by its signatories (United Nations, 1948; see Ollus and Joutsen, Chapter 3, this volume). The UDHR contains 30 articles. These articles address civil, political, economic, social, and cultural rights (United Nations, 1948, Articles 1–30). As seen in Table 12.1, Article 1 of the UDHR states that all humans are equal in dignity and worth. Articles 2–15 address political and individual freedoms. Articles 16–27 address economic, social, and cultural rights. Articles 28 and 29 address collective rights among and between nations, and Article 30 states that no one can take away a person's human rights (United Nations, 1948).

Social work practice, by its mission and charge, aligns closely with the promotion of the Universal Declaration of Human Rights. Whether consciously recognized or not, social workers routinely work to ensure and provide access to basic needs like food, housing, education, healthcare, and employment for the people they serve. These service provisions are consistent with the promotion of human rights as stated in Articles 23 and 25 of the UDHR (Riches, 2002; United Nations, 1948). It often appears that social work professionals, however, view these activities as simply helping people. In reality, however, providing access to basic necessities like those just presented, exceeds helping (see Williamson and Roe-Sepowitz, Chapter 13, this volume). They are in direct accordance with imperatives of the Universal Declarations of Human Rights.

Anti-trafficking training

Learning how to engage in anti-trafficking work is a process. It is a continuation of the basic learning that goes into being a social work student at the generalist level, onto being a social work intern, and then a social work professional. It moves beyond the notion of just being a "do-gooder" who "helps" others. At the core, social workers are college educated, professionally trained and licensed women and men who are cultivated as social scientists to methodically engage, assess, plan, implement, evaluate, terminate, and follow-up – at minimum (Kirst-Ashman & Hull, 2002). Social workers simultaneously focus on the person and the environment in an intentional way unlike many closely related professions (Palmer, 2010). Social work, as formally charged by its founding mothers, along with the Council on Social Work Education's Educational Policy and Accreditation Standards (EPAS), expects social work professionals to embrace a framework and service model that boldly aligns with fostering and protecting human rights at all levels. Gil (2013) asserts that taking this charge seriously requires blatant attacks on oppressive infrastructures that induce suffering in others. Social work is primed to play a role in the attack on this oppressive global system.

Similar to social work expectations, anti-trafficking work is intentional, deliberate, and comprehensive. It is learned. Social work requires one to adopt a core set of beliefs that fundamentally abhor victim-blaming, oppression, ethnocentrism, predatory work structures, and human injustices. Starting with its first single-page Code of Ethics in 1960, the NASW articulated that social workers must dedicate their service to the welfare of others (NASW Code of Ethics, 1960). The revised and expanded NASW Code of Ethics in 1996 added social work values that include service, social justice, integrity, the importance of human relationships, competence, and the dignity and worth of all people (NASW, 1996). These values clearly indicate the need to serve, promote, and protect the rights of all people without prejudice and bias (Healy, 2008).

Empowerment

An element of promoting social justice and preserving human rights includes empowerment. Empowerment is an important goal when working with any client (Segal, Gerdes, & Steiner, 2007), but it is particularly important in the anti-trafficking arena where there is a need to empower survivors to take control of one's life. Empowerment strategies involve helping clients to gain individual power over one's self, one's actions, one's environment, one's rights, and one's freedoms. It allows for self-determination and a transferring of power from external players and the environment to the client. The adoption of empowerment requires the clinician to understand the biography of the client so that his or her thoughts and actions are properly understood in the context in which the individual has experienced the world (Payne, 1997). It allows the trafficked person to shift his or her language from "victim" to "survivor". In its best form, an empowerment framework equips clinicians with methods and tools that work to address inequities on the micro, mezzo, and macro levels. Reichert (2001) asserts that the impact of the environment on the person is fully taken into consideration when applying this model.

Social work requires an integration of social justice, human rights and empowerment in any model designed to serve human trafficking survivors. As shown in Figure 12.1, the social work student is introduced to the concept of social justice in the classroom. During this period, she or he is then introduced to human rights as an intern in the field placement. Social justice and human rights are often brought to life when working with clients for the first time. The student witnesses protecting and addressing human rights in practice. In doing so, she or he begins to understand the need for empowerment of oneself as well as those whom she or he is charged to work with. Van Voorhis and Hostetter (2013) found that graduate social work students felt that empowerment was an important belief for themselves as well as for oppressed groups. After graduation, a social work professional is afforded opportunities to work to impact systems of care at the micro (individual clients' day-to-day), mezzo (groups, communities, clients, and their families), and macro (laws and systems that need to change to address the client's needs) levels.

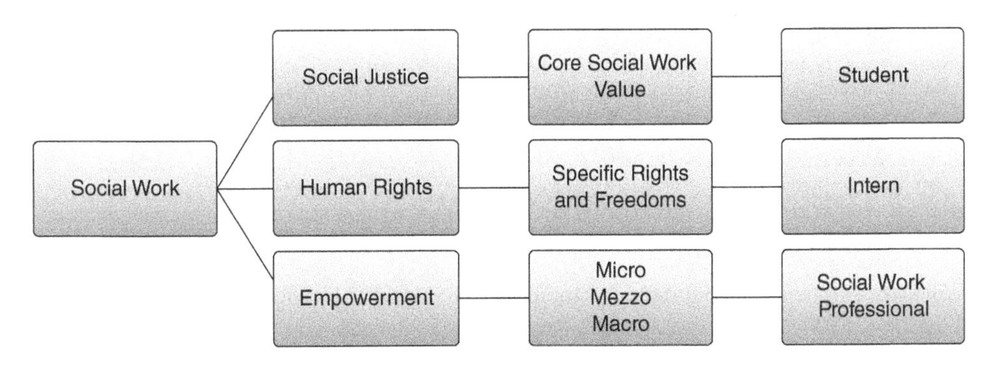

Figure 12.1 Anti-trafficking training model

Anti-trafficking activities

In what follows, ideal components of an anti-trafficking social work training program are presented. Specific learning opportunities within the classroom, field placement, and professional arenas are included.

Students in the classroom

The Council on Social Work Education (CSWE) accredits undergraduate and graduate level programs of social work throughout the United States and its territories. Accreditation of these institutions of higher learning is based on CSWE's Educational Policy and Accreditation Standards. All accredited programs must adhere to these standards as set forth by CSWE. Specific to recognizing and promoting human rights, the explicit curriculum requires programs to integrate a human rights perspective (as a component of its nine competency-based requirements). This must be evident in an institution's social work education (competency-based education) and the field practicum (field education) (CSWE, 2015; Meshelemiah, 2016).

CSWE requires that students work to *advance human rights and social, economic, and environmental justice*. Specifically, Competency 3 of the EPAS states:

> Social workers understand that every person regardless of position in society has fundamental human rights such as freedom, safety, privacy, an adequate standard of living, health care, and education. Social workers understand the global connections of oppression and human rights violations, and are knowledgeable about theories of human need and social justice and strategies to promote social and economic justice and human rights. Social workers understand strategies designed to eliminate oppressive structural barriers to ensure that social goods, rights, and responsibilities are distributed equitably and that civil, political, environmental, economic, social, and cultural human rights are protected. Social workers: apply their understanding of social, economic, and environmental justice to advocate for human rights at the individual and system levels; and engage in practices that advance social, economic, and environmental justice.
>
> *(CSWE, 2015, pp. 7–8)*

As articulated in this competency, social workers are charged with taking on injustices that interfere with one's civil, political, environmental, economic, social, and cultural human rights (Karger, 2015). Human trafficking victims are stripped of these rights as slaves. Therefore, confronting individuals, groups, organizations, and systems that perpetuate oppression and who deny basic human rights through trafficking should be a said priority of social workers. Additionally, providing services to trafficking survivors is a social work responsibility. Given these realities, anti-trafficking services must be grounded in a people centered human rights framework that includes empowering the disempowered (Alvarez & Alessi, 2012).

Human rights and human trafficking courses and workshops

Social work students are required to complete a fixed number of hours of social work courses guided by CSWE EPAS competencies related to professionalism/ethics; diversity; human rights and social, economic and environmental justice; human behavior/relationships; policy;

research/statistics; practice; and engagement, assessment, intervention, and competency with micro, mezzo, and macro systems (CSWE, 2015). Specific to human trafficking as it relates to human rights and justice, the most direct way for the student to learn this content would be to enroll in semester-long courses focusing on this content whenever available. These kinds of courses (in-class and online) are offered by universities and colleges across the country as well as through free online public formats that include iTunes and massive open online courses (MOOCs), for example. Taking these kinds of courses through a social work department is ideal given our unique approach to addressing social ills, but taking courses of this nature in other departments is also valuable.

A specific course on human trafficking, human rights, or justice is not the only way to learn the material. The content could be infused throughout the social work curriculum. Students should also pursue the content by attending trainings and professional conferences whenever possible. Understanding the complexities of human trafficking and its many forms requires repeated exposure. Students should also complete as many assignments as possible on the topic of human trafficking and human rights in courses. For instance, writing on human trafficking and human rights for a policy course would look very different than a paper on this same topic for a practice course. In order to be prepared to do the work with trafficked persons, the student needs to develop an in-depth understanding of what trafficking is from many angles.

NASW membership

The NASW was formed in 1955 and boasts of having the most members throughout the world (NASW, 2017b). Its purpose is to "enhance the professional growth and development of its members, to create and maintain standards for the profession, and to advance sound social policies" (NASW, 2017b, p. 3). NASW also serves as advocates for individuals, families, and communities (NASW, 2017b) and has taken a lead in addressing human rights by creating the Human Rights and International Affairs Department. This department's scope of practice is national and international and works in concert with the United Nations (Clark, 2003). NASW, the profession's signature organization, offers many benefits to its student members, including discount membership fees, chapter newsletters, communication about advocacy opportunities, free online continuing education units (CEUs) via webinars, admission to social work gala events, social work conference discounts, information on licensure updates, and access to liability insurance, to name a few (NASW, 2017b). Members of NASW also have access to human trafficking and human rights content.

Scope of practice competency: post-coursework and training

After a student takes a course or attends a training on human trafficking, the student should be able to educate others about what trafficking is and the most at-risk populations. Moreover, after taking a comprehensive course on human trafficking a student would be able to say that they:

1 Are familiar with the forms, severity, and extent of human trafficking including sex and labor trafficking;
2 Have explored the causes of human trafficking including the push and pull factors involved with it;
3 Have been exposed to the major political, social, and economic factors that contribute to human trafficking;

4 Are familiar with laws, anti-trafficking policies, and restoration efforts related to human trafficking;
5 Have explored the characteristics and special needs of trafficking victims (adults and children) and their life experiences;
6 Have acquired introductory knowledge of the role of social workers and/or other professionals, non-government organizations (NGOs), and others in the resolution of human trafficking from a social work, human rights, and social justice perspective (J. Meshelemiah, OSU, Human Trafficking Course Syllabus, Autumn, 2017).

Although coursework completion enables one to secure basic services for a client, additional training is necessary to reach the level of competency needed to provide clinical services of a counseling nature.

Students in a multi-site field practicum and human rights hours

In field placement, students are expected to be challenged. Many will be learning for the first time how to engage clients, develop treatment plans, receive supervision, advocate on the behalf of others, work with people from different ethnic and cultural backgrounds, and deal with professional and ethical dilemmas (Doskocil, 2017). Hessenauer and Zastrow (2013) found that practicing social workers identified student internships as the primary educational activity that connected the dots between the classroom and practice in the real world. While in placement, students are supervised and complete additional academic coursework that supplements the internship experience. In accordance with CSWE requirements, students must complete a specific number of hours in the field practicum (Doskocil, 2017).

The field placement is very structured and requires competencies to be met. According to CSWE (2015), these include:

- Competency 1: Demonstrate Ethical and Professional Behavior
- Competency 2: Engage Diversity and Difference in Practice
- Competency 3: Advance Human Rights and Social, Economic, and Environmental Justice
- Competency 4: Engage In Practice-informed Research and Research-Informed Practice
- Competency 5: Engage in Policy Practice
- Competency 6: Engage with Individuals, Families, Groups, Organizations, and Communities
- Competency 7: Assess Individuals, Families, Groups, Organizations, and Communities
- Competency 8: Intervene with Individuals, Families, Groups, Organizations, and Communities
- Competency 9: Evaluate Practice with Individuals, Families, Groups, Organizations, and Communities.

Given these parameters, to better prepare social work students to fight against human trafficking, an alternative multi-site model for the practicum is recommended. A field placement providing experience across multiple organizations would be extremely beneficial. Ideally, the student would split time across two or three closely connected agencies according to the needs of each organization. For instance, a MSWII student in placement could spend eight hours a day in each of three agencies in a 24-hour-a-week period (see Table 12.2).

Many of the organizations fighting human trafficking are relatively small. As a result, students may not have a wide range of opportunities at a single agency. Conversely, if agencies share an

Table 12.2 Multi-site placement

Clinical	*Administrative*	*Criminal Justice/Legal*
A safe haven (group home) for trafficking survivors	NASW local chapter	Courthouse: a specialty docket for trafficking survivors

intern, not only will the intern gain more experience, but agencies will not be burdened by having to fill the student's day when the workload is down. The University of South Carolina recognizes this, and as such makes a provision for students in a similar situation.

> There are instances when an agency may not possess the resources to provide all the required learning experiences. In such cases, a secondary placement site may be identified and used for the purpose of meeting the student's learning objectives and accumulation of Field Practicum hours. A large multidisciplinary placement agency site may also decide to broaden the student's experience by rotating to different departments to expand learning opportunities.
>
> (*Villaverde, 2017, p. 10*)

Lastly, student interns should be required to read the UN UDHR in placement and then be required to complete between 8 and 16 hours of Human Rights Activities (HRAs) while in the field placement (The Ohio State University [OSU], 2017). Human Rights Activities vary and are designed to offer the student opportunities to engage in advocacy work outside of the field placement site but as part of the hours for the practicum (OSU, 2017). Human Rights Activities are required of BSSW and MSW students at The Ohio State University College of Social Work. Examples include: political events; legislative events, homeless shelters, children services events, women's empowerment events, anti-trafficking advocacy, and so forth.

Scope of practice competency: post-field placement

Post-field placement, the student should be able to:

1 Identify trafficking victims;
2 Locate and refer survivors to basic social services;
3 Offer human trafficking trainings to general populations;
4 Be able to testify before legislators why new laws are needed for trafficking victims;
5 Know the key stakeholders in the anti-trafficking arena; and
6 Understand the connection between human rights and human trafficking.

While there are many benefits to an alternative multi-site model, there are also some challenges to engaging in this type of placement. A multi-site model does not allow for dedicated time to one specific agency. The student may feel stressed and rushed to complete tasks at each agency. It will also require lots of driving between agencies. Students may also feel overwhelmed by the demands of each agency. The challenges presented by this type of placement, however, could also be a strength given that it would require the student to be organized, mature, and dedicated. The diversity of experiences, nonetheless, will allow for increased experiences and readiness for practice.

Social work professional

Unlike the student taking courses and participating in internship hours, the social work professional has reached these milestones and earned at least one college degree and participated in at least one field practicum, ideally supplemented by anti-trafficking course work/internship experiences. Social work professionals are challenged to take his or her experience, practice, and advocacy to a higher level. With or without a general exposure to anti-trafficking work as a student, it is recommended that social worker professionals engage in the following activities in the anti-trafficking movement.

i Continuing Education
  a Given how the tactics of traffickers continue to change over time, social workers must stay abreast of the latest threats to the freedom of at-risk groups. One of the best ways to do this is to seek out human trafficking and human rights content through CEUs.
  b CEUs are widely available and required to maintain one's licensure as a social work professional (Counselor, Social Work, and Marriage and Family Therapist Board, 2017).
ii University Courses
  a As licensed/certified professionals, continuing education units are required. One of the quickest ways to obtain a large amount of CEUs is through university level courses.
  b Prioritizing human trafficking and human rights coursework are a must.
iii NASW and other professional conferences
  a Attendance at professional social work conferences is critical to professional development. It is also a potential venue in which to meet trafficking survivors (if it is a human trafficking or human rights conference); learn about the latest research on clinical interventions; learn how to use clinical therapeutic interventions in practice; and meet other social workers who share similar passions.
  b Attending presentations related to human trafficking and human rights is a necessary learning activity. Conferences are also a good place to pick up a wealth of information on trauma informed services, substance abuse treatment, mental disorders, trauma bonding, and the latest innovations related to treatment as a whole for trafficking survivors.
iv Rescue and Restore Coalitions
  a These task forces bring key anti-trafficking stakeholders to the table from a variety of like-minded agencies. Joining could serve as referral sources, information sharing outlets, and support systems to those in the anti-trafficking movement.
  b Rescue and Restore Coalitions tend to work to increase public awareness; address demand reduction; strengthen anti-trafficking legislation through advocacy; offer comprehensive services to trafficking survivors; and work with the centrally appointed law enforcement Anti-trafficking Task Force for the region (Salvation Army, 2016a).
v Legislative and Courtroom Testimonies
  a As a professional social worker in the anti-trafficking arena, one may find him or herself being asked to testify before legislators and/or judges on behalf of trafficked persons.
  b Only qualified, articulate, and experienced social work professionals should take on these tasks. In the case of judges, however, any social worker may be subpoenaed to appear. If that is the case, the social worker must be well-prepared to defend his or her documentation and/or to expound it when testifying before a judge. Cases involving trafficked persons can be complex and intimidating. The social work professional must be ready to advocate at all times.

Scope of practice competency: as a licensed social work professional

The social work professional is expected to be able to competently offer clinical interventions of a therapeutic nature as well as provide a trauma informed approach at the micro, mezzo, and macro levels to trafficking survivors. Knowing how and when to offer cognitive behavioral therapies, diagnose mental disorders, treatment plan, make referrals to substance abuse facilities, work in safe havens, serve as case managers, and advocate for policy changes that affect trafficking victims are all areas of work expected of professional social workers.

Knowing how to serve trafficking survivors comes best by exposure. Like the move from the classroom to the field practicum helps the student to apply learned material, so does the transition from learning about human trafficking as a social work practitioner to directly working with survivors. The real work starts as a front-line service provider. Working with survivors can be daunting, however. The horrors of trafficking are hard to digest at times.

Case study

As an illustration of sex and labor trafficking and anti-trafficking work, the story of Talia is shared here. The case depicts her childhood sexual abuse, grooming by a trafficker, parental neglect, forced commercialized sex, forced labor, an arrest, and subsequent contact with a social work provider in a safe haven. It also depicts the push and pull factors of trafficking. Push factors relate to those variables that make one vulnerable to being deceived and manipulated into a trafficking situation (poverty, few supports, homelessness, lack of knowledge, few employment opportunities, gender stereotypes, etc.) while pull factors relate to those variables that entice a potential victim (promises of a better life, attention, feigned love and support) (International Labour Organization (ILO), 2011; Krehbiel, 2016; Okech et al., 2011; Wooditch, 2011). Talia is a trafficking survivor. Her story, presented in the first person, is based on a composite of trafficking survivors.

Case study: the voice of a human trafficking survivor

Let me go back 20 years. That is when my nightmare began. It started with my cousin Alex. Well, he wasn't really my cousin. This is what I called him because he was my mother's boyfriend's son. At first we were close and he treated me like his little cousin. He walked me to school, microwaved me frozen dinners, and played video games with me. He was my favorite "cousin." I was eight when Alex moved in with us. He was 16. I didn't know what he was doing at the time when he did all of these nice things for me, but I now know that this is called grooming. Grooming takes place when a person does nice things in an effort to build trust and to get you to let your guard down. I didn't know this back then.

Alex stopped being my cousin the first time that he kissed me though. He kissed me like he kissed Sefina. She was his girlfriend. He went from wet tongue kisses, to holding me in his lap, to lifting my dress, to "touching" me. When I finally told my mom after he touched me for several months, she didn't believe me. She even accused me of being jealous of Sefina and wanting Alex's attention. Alex was the star shooting guard for his varsity basketball team and was popular with everyone in his elite high school. He was also very good looking with very white teeth. His hair was long and wavy as is for most men from Samoa. I am also Samoan American.

After my mom did not believe me, I didn't bring it up again. I thought that maybe what Alex was doing was not so bad. This went on for two years until Alex went off to college on a basketball scholarship. I was no longer close to my mom after this though. I eventually went on to live with my grandmother at age ten. My mother had a serious mental disorder and could no longer care for me. I got involved with the "wrong crowd" by the time I was 13. My grandmother was nice, but she couldn't keep up with me and all of the foster kids she had in the home. She also drank a lot and fell asleep early. This is how I met my first boyfriend. His name was Loto.

As an unsupervised teenager, I was often out in the community hanging out and smoking cigarettes. Loto frequently drove by the high school I eventually attended in his shiny red Ford Mustang. He kind of reminded me of Alex. He was tall, handsome, and had lots of money. He was 23 but he looked much younger. I was 15. We texted and talked all day the first week we met. By the second week of our talking, he asked me to meet him at the mall. We met and he was nicer than I could ever imagine. He held my hands and we kissed before I left the mall. We met every Friday for about a month before he asked me to be his girl. I was happy to be his girl. He had money, a nice car, and his own place. By our second month together, I had started to spend the night over at Loto's every Friday and Saturday. My grandmother didn't even miss me. On one Friday, Loto asked me to move in with him so that we could spend every day together. I told him that I had to think about it, but he told me that if I were not ready to be with him then he would get with a "real woman." I quickly told him that I would have my things packed by the next day.

Things went well for the first week when we lived together. All of sudden, he came home one day and told me to put on this tight short black dress. I put it on. A few minutes later a tall strange man knocked on the door. Loto looked at me and told me that I had to help pay the rent this month. This ended up being the first of many nights where Loto sold me. I ended up sleeping with Loto and anyone else who Loto brought home. This went on for almost two years. In addition to sleeping with men for Loto, he even loaned me out to people as a babysitter. I never got paid though.

At age 17, I got arrested for prostitution. Loto had set me up with a "date" that ended up being an undercover cop. At first I was frightened when the man put the handcuffs on me, but I immediately calmed down when he asked me to play along. He pretended to arrest me so that Loto could see me leave the hotel in handcuffs, but he actually took me to Child Protective Services. As we drove to Child Protective Services, the officer called me Talia. I froze and asked her how he knew my name. I had given him a fake ID with the name Zora Price. He went on to say, "I know about you and Loto. We have been watching you and Loto for a while now. He is not your boyfriend. He is a pimp." The word "pimp" hit me like a ton of bricks. I slowly said to myself in a trance like state, "Loto is a pimp? Well, if Loto is a pimp, I must be a p-r-o-s-t-i-t-u-t-e?" I can tell he read my face. "Yes, Loto is a pimp but you are not a prostitute. You are a victim of human trafficking. I will GET you some help," said the officer.

I had heard about CPS (that's what I call Child Protective Services) and social workers. The intake social worker asked lots of questions. After a very long interview, I was FINALLY transported to a safe haven – this beautifully painted lavender and pink home. I was assigned a social work case manager who understood trauma. I was put into a room with another survivor. The paint on the walls was soft and warm in our room and throughout the hallways. The house managers were very patient. My group counselor was soft-spoken. She allowed us to talk in a safe environment in small groups among all female survivors. There were empowering phrases all over the walls. I personally met the owner of the safe haven. She was a survivor too. She understood my trauma, hurt, pain, and rejection. After meeting with my social work case manager over several months, I was helped to access all of the social services that I needed to get on my feet. I got transitional housing, healthy food, clothing that fit, prep classes for the GED, a thorough physical examination, and even business clothing to wear to job interviews. More importantly, I received drug counseling and was helped to kick my habit of popping Xanax after having been made to do so before having sex with all of those men. With the help and support of the agency, I worked with the local prosecutor to convict Loto. He was given a 25-year sentence. Even my case manager had to testify. She explained to the judge what human trafficking was and how vulnerable teens are prime targets for domestic minor sex trafficking.

The social workers who worked with me understood my brokenness and connection to Loto even though he was bad for me. They did not judge me and they explained to me what trauma bonding was and how that kept me connected to Loto despite the abuse, rapes, and trafficking. I have been in therapy for a very long time and I don't regret it. I need it. It is part of my healing. As part of my healing, I am part of an agency's Speaker's Bureau. I get paid to tell my story as a human trafficking survivor. The social workers have taught me that freedom is a human right and that trafficking erodes away all of the freedoms of an individual. Now that I understand that I was a slave, I work to make sure that others understand what human trafficking is.

Case study discussion questions

1. How did Alex groom Talia?
2. What were the push factors for Talia?
3. What were the pull factors for Talia?
4. What made Talia a target for Loto?
5. How is it possible that Talia did not know that she was being trafficked?
6. How did the social worker help Talia?
7. What elements of the safe haven appeared consistent with an anti-trafficking agency?
8. How does Talia show evidence of connecting trafficking with the denial of human rights?

As one critically reflects on the upbringing and immediate environment of Talia as a child, one can easily identify the vulnerabilities of the home. These push factors, if known to Child Protective Services (CPS), would have been of grave concern and certainly resulted in quick action. Instead, Talia left her mother's home sometime after the sexual abuse began and ended up as a domestic minor sex trafficking (DMST) victim. Elevated risk emerged with the introduction of Loto, although a relationship with an older boyfriend appeared to have many perks (pull factors) from the perspective of a na ve teenager looking for love. After her arrest at age 17, Talia needed a safe space, a nonjudgmental environment, a competent social work case manager, and comprehensive services specific to a trafficking survivor. An anti-trafficking service model calls for such a trauma-informed approach and culturally competent service delivery. As illustrated in Talia's case, service providers who were knowledgeable about the psychology of human trafficking were imperative. They made a world of difference in Talia's outcome. At the micro level, Talia was placed in a safe haven and provided the necessary services to turn her life around. This included putting her in an environment with other survivors where community could be built. The mezzo level (group work) approach to treatment is common in social work practice. Macro level factors included sensitivity, attention to, and application of the human rights that Talia deserved to be afforded. Testimonies about situations like Talia have resulted in anti-trafficking legislation. Moreover, in an effort to advocate for Talia, her casemanager had to testify. Advocacy of this nature has implications for policy change given that it educates legal personnel on how they address and interact with survivors. Awareness has been shown to result in macro policy changes surrounding human trafficking (Polaris, 2018b).

Talia's case surpassed helping an abused child find a home. It required a methodical approach to situating her within a safe environment among providers who understood the complexities of human trafficking and the importance of trauma informed services (the physical building, decorations in the home, resisting of re-traumatization, gender specific services, peer support, empowerment approach, etc.). The agency approached Talia in a way that espoused an anti-trafficking mission; demonstrated core social work values; promoted social justice; and upheld the importance of human rights.

Anti-trafficking model

To adequately, ethically and competently address human trafficking as social workers, it is imperative to train and work in agencies that subscribe to an anti-trafficking model of service. An anti-trafficking model is multi-layered. It is intentional and deliberate. The author argues that any social work student or professional seeking to work in an agency or program offering anti-trafficking services should look for a framework that incorporates three main elements: (1) an anti-trafficking mission, (2) core social work values that include social justice, and (3) human rights as a framework.

Mission

The mission statement of the agency or program must speak to the commitment of the serving body to trafficking victims and/or survivors. According to Bresciani (2017), a mission statement must be brief and explicit. Brief mission statements keep the focus on the work of the agency or program. A mission statement related to serving survivors of trafficking must be backed up by services specific to trafficking survivors that include a trauma informed approach that is implemented by highly trained employees with skills and expertise related to anti-trafficking work (refer to Williamson and Roe-Sepowitz, Chapter 14, this volume).

Values

Trauma bonding refers to loyalty to a destructive person (Stines, 2015).

Values that are commensurate with the social work profession are imperative and need to be clearly articulated in an agency's/program's policies and practices. A commitment to service, integrity, the importance of human relationships, self-determination, and the dignity and worth of all people are important social work values (NASW Code of Ethics, 1996) to embrace when working with trafficking survivors. Service is what social workers offer as social service providers in the pursuit of justice. Providing services with the highest degree of honesty and ethics relate to the profession's integrity. This is particularly important to distrusting trafficking survivors who have been maltreated and deceived by many in the past. Understanding the importance of human relationships is also critical for service providers working with human trafficking survivors given the trauma bonding that often takes place between the perpetrator and the survivor. A highly skilled social worker would understand why a survivor expresses love and/or thanksgiving toward the trafficker despite his brutality towards him or her. The clinician would also understand why the victim may leave the agency or program and return to the trafficker. Granting the freedom to stay or to leave is a component of self-determination. As a member of a group of people denied basic freedoms in the past, it is critical to allow the victim to make decisions (even bad ones) after being informed of his or her options. Zimmerman (as cited by Krehbiel, 2016) passionately asserts that trafficking survivors must be afforded the agency to make choices. Last, in the face of challenges and successes when providing services to trafficking survivors, it is important to maintain the dignity and worth of all people despite how the general population may perceive trafficking survivors or blame them for what they may perceive as complicit behaviors (for more detail, refer to Torres, Nsonwu, Cook Heffron, and Busch-Armendariz, Chapter 13, this volume).

Social justice

Visit www.freedomalacart.org to learn how one company promotes economic empowerment to break the cycle of exploitation.

According to the National Association of Social Workers, "Social justice is the view that everyone deserves equal economic, political, and social rights and opportunities" NASW, 2017a, para. 2). Keeping in step with this value, many social service agencies address the social and economic dimensions of service delivery by directly offering or providing linkages to housing, food subsidies, mental health/drug counseling, case management, healthcare, Child Protective Services, interpreters, Adult Protective Services, job training, child care provisions, and so forth (James & Gilliland, 2005; Segal et al., 2013). These are the kinds of services needed by trafficking survivors. Upon interviewing law enforcement officers and service providers to trafficked minors, Clawson and Goldblatt Grace (2007) found that trafficking survivors needed housing, food, a safe place to sleep, a place to shower, intensive case management, mental health counseling, medical screening/routine care, life skills and job training, youth development programming (minors), educational programming, and family involvement/reunification. To further break down the need and priority of housing, Maney et al. (2011) found that diverse forms of housing were needed by trafficking survivors. Specifically, 64.9% needed emergency housing; 74.5% needed transitional housing, 86.6% needed long-term housing, and 22.2% needed independent housing. Service providers in this same study reported that they were somewhat or highly unsatisfactory in meeting the needs of survivors due to inadequate and insufficient housing options. Housing is a clear and present need of trafficking survivors. In terms of social services as a whole, it would be critical to advocate for trafficking survivors to access safe havens (which are far and few between) (Irazola, Williamson, Chen, Garrett, & Clawson, 2008; Kotrla, 2010) and the range of services set aside specifically for trafficking victims as stipulated in the Trafficking Victims Protection Acts (H.R. 898, 2013; H.R. 972, 2005; H.R. 2620, 2003; H.R. 7311, 2008; Okech et al., 2011; Pub. L. 106–386, 2000).

Beyond these services and those related to general benefits of a financial nature (TANF, WIC, SNAP, etc.), additional services should be considered. Financial literacy is one of them. Teaching the survivor about high-interest rates on predatory credit cards, inflated payday loans, and high-risk borrowing from pawn shops is critical to one's overall financial proficiency (Karger, 2015). Discussing gainful and fair employment options are critical as well. Assisting survivors with acquiring specific skills that enable them to earn a living wage is important (Krehbiel, 2006) as inadequate income may result in self-determination related to returning to the *familiar* or *quick money*. That is, he or she may return to a trafficking situation or another exploitive condition.

In pursuit of justice, Jane Addams fiercely took on the government with regard to political matters. For example, she widely protested World War I and denounced the government for not allowing women the right to vote (Addams, 1959). Her bravery was unparalleled at the time. As both a micro and macro level social work practitioner and activist, she understood the role of politics and the importance of participating politically to advocate for the disenfranchised. Political engagement remains an important facet of the social work profession. Political rights and opportunities vary for groups of people, but addressing social problems from a political lens is necessary for macro level change. Political advocacy can take many forms in the anti-trafficking movement, from helping survivors negotiate competing agendas when trying to start an NGO, to helping clients get their criminal records expunged, to lobbying for the rights of trafficking survivors through testimony and collaborative relationships with legislators. All of these activities lead to empowerment of survivors and are in step with promoting social justice.

Human rights

An anti-trafficking model is the cornerstone for agencies offering comprehensive services to trafficking survivors.

The discourse on human rights is visibly absent from social work jargon and the profession as a whole (Meshelemiah, 2016). It is essential, however, that any agency or program aspiring to be an effective change agent in the anti-trafficking movement swiftly and overtly adopt a human rights position and then proceed to articulate it as such. This adoption should be evident in practice and policy, as previously discussed, but it should also be prominent on an agency's website, via its social media accounts, and in all printed materials. For example, adopting a motto in addition to an anti-trafficking mission statement is important. An example like, "*Anti-trafficking work is human rights work*" or "*Protecting human rights is our #1 priority*" is a good addendum. This posture clearly associates preserving human rights with anti-trafficking work. Upholding human rights requires action. Consequently, it is important for anti-trafficking agencies and programs to act and to call others to action as well. One agency or discipline cannot do it alone (United Nations, 2017). Calling for action allows an agency or program to fulfill its mission and to offer the full range of services needed by trafficking victims and survivors. Calls to action include a range of activities and could include but are not limited to:

1 Social work internships
2 Volunteers who:
   a educate others about human trafficking
   b work as paraprofessionals
   c write grant proposals
   d arrange fundraising events
   e offer outreach in highly populated commercialized sex areas and distribute business cards and care packages
3 Donations in the form of:
   a money
   b clothing
   c shoes
   d furniture
   e household appliances
4 Mentoring to support victims on their journeys

5 A Speakers Bureau to increase knowledge of human trafficking among community members (should include a paid survivor if possible)
6 Collaboration with local law enforcement as first responders
7 Collaboration with local social service agencies
8 Monitoring a phone or email hotline to report trafficking related activities and/or working closely with the National Human Trafficking Hotline (1-888-373-7888 that is run by Polaris (Polaris, 2018a).

The Salvation Army is a prime example of a national organization that offers a comprehensive package of services to trafficking survivors that include all of the above elements. Additionally, they take on social work interns, hire social workers, and head a task force that brings together key anti-trafficking stakeholders to meet regularly (Salvation Army, 2016a). Social work casemangers employed with Salvation Army are first responders for trafficking victims in many cities and they work closely with law enforcement to provide assistance to trafficked persons (Salvation Army, 2016b).

Contextual framework

The mission, values, social justice, and human rights elements work in tandem in the proposed anti-trafficking model. They must all be attended to, however, in a larger context. This includes (1) the Westernization of globalization; (2) oppression; (3) capitalism in the form of predatory/criminalized work structures; (4) victim blaming; and (5) objectification (see Figure 12.2). That

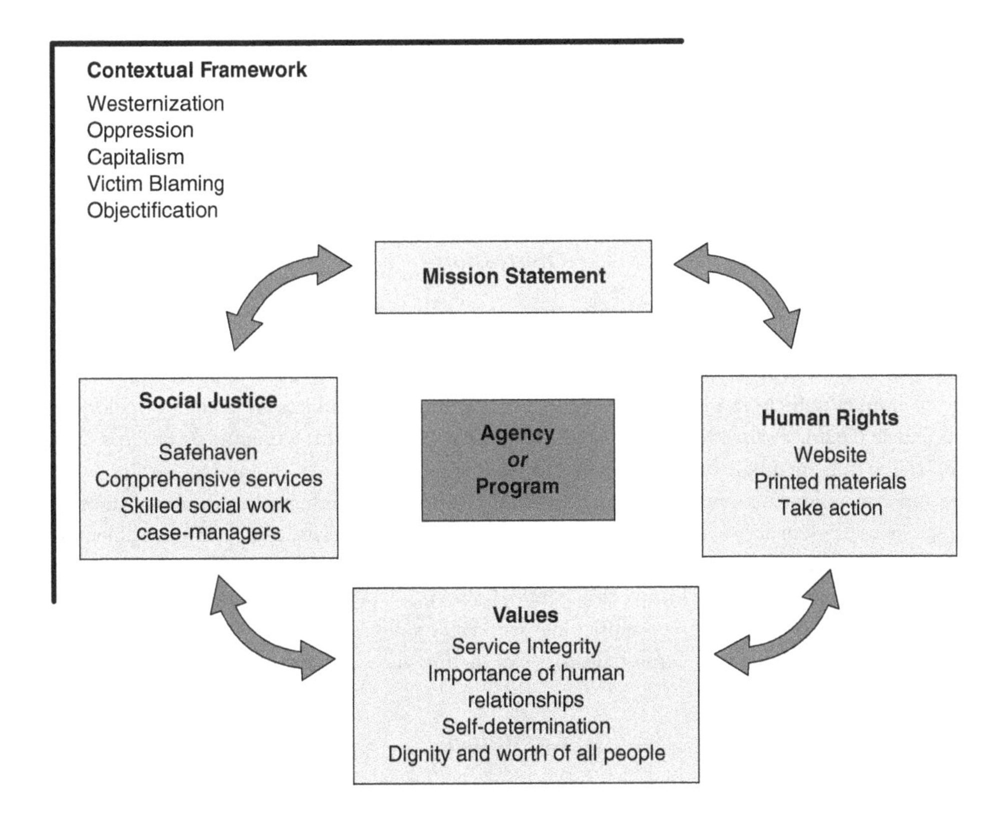

Figure 12.2 Anti-trafficking model

is, anti-trafficking agencies and programs must take into consideration the realities that these five elements play a major role in creating scenarios that allow for trafficking to take place and the vulnerable to be subsequently preyed upon. The social work student, intern, and professional must understand these dynamics in order to fully appreciate human trafficking as a long-standing oppressive institution throughout the world.

Westernization of globalization

Westernization of globalization refers to the unspoken presumption that globalization is destined to serve and benefit Westerners. There does not seem to be the expectation that mutual benefits will present as a result of the economic, technological, political, and social advances related to globalization (Alvarez & Alessi, 2012). Globalization has resulted in a global exchange that better serves the interests of the West but not the East, North, or South in the same manner (refer to Bravo, Chapter 1, this volume). For instance, globalization allows for faster and increased intercultural and international exchanges between people, food, products, businesses, and educational possibilities. Thus far, however, it appears that non-Westerners are experiencing massive dislocation of persons, deprived livelihoods, and little economic expansion from globalization while the West is experiencing massive consumption (Alvarez & Alessi, 2012). On a darker side, the West also benefits from sex and labor trafficking due to globalization. Faster and increased international exchanges have allowed for easier trafficking of people into the United States. The United States is a top destination country for trafficking victims (Jordan, Patel, & Rapp, 2013). Most persons trafficked to America come from Asia, Eastern Europe, Latin America, the Middle East, and Africa. Thus, most trafficked persons are people of color (Okech et al., 2011). Therefore, anti-trafficking social work professionals must mindfully consider culture, race/ethnicity, religion/spirituality, language, family connections, shame, guilt, and the intercultural impact of globalization. Social workers in America must remember that the Westernization of globalization has cultivated a breeding ground for the exploitation of others for sex and labor purposes. Considering this information as a service provider informs understanding of how immigrants fall victim to exploitation and trafficking.

Oppression

Oppression directly ties in with the Westernization of globalization. Oppression refers to systematic prejudice and discrimination based on class or group membership (Segal et al., 2007). Systemic racism, classism, and sexism, in particular directly impact social justice and human rights and are tied to human trafficking given that most victims of human trafficking are people of color, poor, and female (Fedina et al., 2008; Irazola et al., 2008; Okech et al., 2011; Raymond & Hughes, 2001). Oppression puts members of a group at a disadvantage. Disadvantages due to race/ethnicity, gender, and class result in a range of consequences related to poor health, increased mental disorders/substance use, lack of access, limited opportunities, little to no prosperity, and persistent vulnerability (Garcia & Sharif, 2015). These same disadvantages have been reported by sex trafficking victims and survivors (Fedina et al., 2008; Irazola et al., 2008; Rahman, 2011). Oppression leads to desperation and vulnerability. Viewing human trafficking from this contextual lens reveals the complexities of choices, impositions, and trafficking trajectories of victims and survivors.

Capitalism

Capitalism in itself is considered a good thing to many individuals living in capitalistic societies. In capitalistic societies, the goal is profit and the means of production are privately owned (Peavler,

2017). Profit is palatable, but it becomes insufferable when people are financially exploited while producing products or providing services to others. To illustrate, Peavler (2017) asserts that outsourcing customer service centers or factories to Asia where low wages can be paid is problematic and exploitative. Although job creation is perceived as beneficial to society, this is only true when both parties (the worker and the owner) mutually benefit from the relationship. Capitalistic work structures that are predatory, criminal, violent, and divorced from ethical execution are gross violations of human rights. This type of structure is labor trafficking. According to the International Labour Organization (ILO), labor trafficking is the most prevalent form of human trafficking in the world (ILO, 2011). Labor trafficking, by virtue of the elements of force, fraud, and coercion, signifies that the labor-related working relationship is not mutual. It is exploitive and criminal and undermines one's humanity and human rights. Anti-trafficking service providers must always default to the reality that capitalistic measures designed to garner excessive profits via labor trafficking exists. Labor trafficking is present in developing countries as well as across the United States. Human trafficking is estimated to generate $32 billion in profits annually around the world. Approximately 50% of that profit is estimated to be generated in the United States alone (Rahman, 2011). Although probably not intended to be so in its initial development, globalization and capitalism have resulted in an emergent and profitable trafficking market (Wooditch, 2011).

Victim blaming

Victim blaming results in internalized guilt and shame for the trafficking survivor.

Victim blaming distances perpetrators and co-conspirators from their role in afflicting pain and suffering onto others. It also absolves the guilt of bystanders, critics, and even professional helpers who do nothing. According to Segal et al. (2013), victim blaming refers to assigning the responsibility of one's condition to the victim. It serves as a moral compass for a person's hardship and struggle. It pontificates the limitations and deficits of the individual. It simply blames the person for all that is "wrong" or "bad" in his or her life. The harm in victim blaming is that it disempowers, paralyzes, and perpetuates a cycle of all that is damaging in one's life. Moreover, victim blaming fails to acknowledge the role of the physical and social environments (including oppression) and their impact on the individual.

Anti-trafficking service providers must avoid victim blaming. This includes the frequent occasions when victims blame themselves for being trafficked. Service providers must view trafficking holistically and in the context of the environment in which it was incubated and birthed – not on an individual level alone.

Objectification

The objectification of people as inanimate objects, animals, insects, sex objects, and inferior beings is complicit in the justification of human trafficking and all of the other atrocities afflicted on people around the world via slavery, genocide, and the Holocaust (Chappell, 2015). Trafficking perpetrators view victims as legal tender – the dollar in the United States, the birr in Ethiopia, the cedi in Ghana, the peso in Mexico, and the renminbi or yuan in China. Viewing others as objects absolves one of guilt, thereby facilitating their abuse and exploitation. The dehumanization of trafficking victims also results in the de-identification of the person as a trafficking victim. This results in challenges in trying to serve the trafficked population (Fedina et al., 2008; Irazola et al., 2008; Okech et al., 2011). Lack of self-identification stems from not knowing what trafficking is, fear of retribution, not knowing who to call, not knowing where one is physically located as a captured victim in a remote location, fear of deportation, and trauma (Lange, 2011). Objectification is a powerful tool in the human trafficking industry.

The trauma of being trafficked while not recognizing this abuse as such is well documented (Grant & Hudlin, 2007; Irazola et al., 2008; Okech et al., 2011). Trafficking victims often present with PTSD, dissociative disorders, anxiety disorders, depressive disorders, and substance use disorders (Clawson & Goldblatt Grace, 2007; Irazola et al., 2008; Palmer, 2010) – illnesses and disorders that often go undiagnosed and untreated. Furthermore, some of these mental disorders prevent the victim from thinking clearly or reacting to the depth of their abuse. PTSD, in particular, is common among trafficked persons. Post-traumatic stress disorder is a maladaptive response to a deeply disturbing or distressing stressor(s) or event(s) that manifests itself at least one month after exposure (APA, 2013). It manifests itself via a four-cluster symptomatology that includes intrusive symptoms, persistent avoidance of stimuli associated with the trauma, negative alterations in cognitions, and hyperarousal symptoms (APA, 2013; Meshelemiah, 2014).

Summary

This chapter examined human trafficking from a broad lens that incorporated steps to training the social work student, intern, and professional. It also included an anti-trafficking model of service for social workers. Specifically, the author discussed human trafficking as a form of modern day slavery and charged the social work professional with the task of fostering a human rights approach to anti-trafficking service and advocacy. These concepts were fleshed out with a case study of Talia – a survivor of sex and labor trafficking.

The importance of a clear and present anti-trafficking mission statement was evident in the anti-trafficking model. The additional emphasis on human rights, core social work values, and social justice was reiterated. Given the multilayered and complex nature of human trafficking, the author also discussed the outer layers of trafficking that include (1) the Westernization of globalization; (2) oppression; (3) capitalism; (4) victim blaming; and (5) objectification. It is critical for social work providers in the anti-trafficking arena to incorporate all of these tenets into their practice.

Supplemental learning materials

Brownlie, S. I., & Goodwin-Gill, G. S. (2010). *Brownlie's documents on human rights* (6th ed.). Oxford: Oxford University Press.

Brysk, A. (2000). *Globalization and human rights*. Berkeley: University of California Press.

Clifford, D., & Burke, B. (2009). *Anti-oppressive ethics and values in social work*. New York, NY: Palgrave Macmillan.

Dalla, R. L., Baker, L. M., Defrain, J. D., & Williamson, C. (2013). *Global perspectives on prostitution and sex trafficking: Africa, Asia, Middle East, and Oceania*. United Kingdom: Lexington Books.

Donnelly, J. (2013). *Universal human rights in theory and practice* (3rd ed.). Ithaca, NY: Cornell University Press.

Enrile, A. (Ed.). (2018). *Ending human trafficking & modern day slavery: Freedom's journey*. London: Sage.

Geist, D. (2016). From victim to healer: How surviving sex trafficking informs therapeutic practice. *Dignity: A Journal on Sexual Exploitation and Violence*, *1*(1), 9. Retrieved from https://doi.org/10.23860/dignity.2016.01.01.09

George, S. (2012). The strong arm of the law is weak: How the Trafficking Victims Protection Act fails to assist effectively victims of the sex trade. *Creighton Law Review*, *45*, 563–580.

Hafner-Burton, E. M., & Tsutsui, K. (2005). Human rights in globalizing world: The paradox of empty promises. *American Journal of Sociology*, *110*(5), 1373–1411.

Hodge, D. R. (2008). Sexual trafficking in the United States: A Domestic problem with transnational dimensions. *Social Work*, *53*(2), 143–152.

Lee, M. (2005). Human trade and the criminalization of irregular migration. *International Journal of the Sociology of Law, 33*(1), 1–15. Retrieved from https://doi.org/10.1016/j.ijsl.2004.09.004
Office to Monitor and Combat Trafficking in Persons. (2013). Civilian security, democracy, and human rights: Male trafficking victims. Washington, DC: United States Department of State.
Reamer, F.G. (2006). *Social work values and ethics: Foundations of social work knowledge.* New York, NY: Columbia.
Sabella, D. (2011). The role of the nurse in combating human trafficking. *American Journal of Nursing, 111*(2), 28–37.
Sen, A. (2005). Human rights and capabilities. *Journal of Human Development, 6*(2), 151–166.
Sherr, M. E., & Jones, J. M. (2014). *Introduction to competence-based social work: The profession of caring, knowing, and serving.* Chicago: Lyceum.
Simmons, B. A. (2009). *Mobilizing for human rights: International law in domestic politics.* Cambridge: University Press.
Van Wormer, C. S. (2012). *Confronting oppression, restoring justice: From policy analysis to social action* (2nd ed.). Alexandria, VA: Council on Social Work Education.

References

Addams, J. (1959). *Twenty years at Hull-House.* New York, NY: Macmillan Company.
Alvarez, M. B., & Alessi, E. J. (2012). Human trafficking is more than sex trafficking and prostitution: Implications for social work. *Affilia: Journal of Women and Social Work, 27*(2), 142–152.
American Psychiatric Association (APA). (2013). *Diagnostic and Statistical Manual of Mental Disorders* (5th ed.). Washington, DC: Author.
Amnesty International USA. (2015). *Human rights basic.* Retrieved from www.amnestyusa.org/research/human-rights-basics
Bresciani, A. (2017). *51 Mission statement examples from the world's best companies.* Retrieved from www.alessiobresciani.com/foresight-strategy/51-mission-statement-examples-from-the-worlds-best-companies/
Chappell, P. (2015). *Cosmic ocean: New answers to big questions.* New York, NY: Prospecta Press.
Clark, E. J. (2003, October). Social work and human rights. *NASW News, 48*(9), p. 1. Retrieved from www.naswdc.org/pubs/news/2003/10/clark.asp
Clawson, H. J., & Goldblatt Grace, L. G. (2007). *Finding a path to recovery: Residential facilities for minor victims of domestic sex trafficking* (Human Trafficking: Data and Documents. Paper 10). 11 pages.
Council on Social Work Education. (2015). *Educational policy and accreditation standards for baccalaureate and master's social work programs.* Alexandria, VA: Author.
Counselor, Social Work, and Marriage and Family Therapist Board. (2017). Laws and rules video. Retrieved from http://cswmft.ohio.gov/CELawsRulesExam.aspx
Doskocil, D. (2017). Preparing for placements, finding your true calling, and surviving as a student in the field. Retrieved from www.mswguide.org/schools/the-ultimate-field-education-guide/
Fedina, L., Trease, J., & Williamson, C. (2008). *A resource guide for social service providers.* Toledo, OH: Second Chance.
Garcia, J. J., & Sharif, M. Z. (2015). Black Lives Matter: A commentary on racism and public health. *American Journal of Public Health, 105*(8), e27–e30.
Gil, D. G. (2013). *Confronting injustice and oppression: Concepts and strategies for social workers.* New York, NY: Columbia University Press.
Grant, B., & Lopez-Hudlin, C. (2007). *Hands that heal: International curriculum to train caregivers of trafficking survivors.* Springfield, MO: Life Publishers.
H.R. 2620. (2003). *Trafficking Victims Protection Reauthorization Act of 2003,* H.R. 2620, 108th Cong., 1st Sess.
H.R. 7311. (2008). *Trafficking Victims Protection Reauthorization Act of 2008,* H.R. 7311, 110th Cong., 2nd Sess.
H.R. 972. (2005). *Trafficking Victims Protection Reauthorization Act of 2005,* H.R. 972, 109th Cong., 1st Sess.
H.R. 898. (2013). *Trafficking Victims Protection Reauthorization Act of 2013, H.R.* 898, 113th Cong., 1st Sess.
Healy, L. (2008). Exploring the history of social work as a human rights profession. *International Social Work, 51(6),* 735–748.
Healy, L. (2015). Exploring the history of social work as a human rights profession. *International Federation of Social Workers.* Retrieved from http://ifsw.org/publications/human rights/the-centrality-of-human-rights-to-social-work/exploring-the-history-of-social-work-as-a-human-rights-profession/
Hessenauer, S., & Zastrow, C. (2013). Becoming a social worker: BSW social workers' educational experiences. *Journal of Baccalaureate Social Work, 18*(1), 19–35.

International Federation of Social Workers. (1988). *Standards in social work practice meeting human rights: Executive summary*. Berlin. Germany: Author.
International Labor Organization. (2011). *Trafficking in persons overseas for labor purposes: The case of Ethiopian domestic workers*. Addis Ababa: ILO Country Office.
Irazola, S., Williamson, E., Chen, C., Garrett, A., & Clawson, H. J. (2008). *Trafficking of US citizens and legal permanent residents: The forgotten victims and survivors*. Fairfax, VA: ICF International. Retrieved from http://thehill.com/sites/default/files/ICFI_TraffickingofUSCitizens_0.pdf
James, R. K., & Gilliland, B. E. (2005). *Crisis intervention* (5th ed.). USA: Brooks/Cole.
Jordan, J., Patel, B., & Rapp, L. (2013). Domestic minor sex trafficking: A social work perspective on misidentification, victims, buyers, traffickers, treatment, and reform of current practice. *Journal of Human Behavior in the Social Environment, 23*(3), 356–369.
Karger, H. (2015). Curbing the financial exploitation of the poor: Financial literacy and social work education. *Journal of Social Work Education, 51*(3), 425–438.
Kirst-Ashman, K. K., & Hull, G. H. (2002). *Understanding generalist practice* (3rd ed.). Australia: Brooks/Cole.
Kotrla, K. (2010). Domestic minor sex trafficking in the United States. *Social Work, 55*(2), 181–187.
Krehbiel, S. (2016, February 24). *The victim narrative on sex-trafficking: An interview with Yvonne Zimmerman (Part 1)*. Our untold stories: World Press.
Lange, A. (2011). Research note: Challenges of identifying female human trafficking victims using a national 1–800 call center. *Trends in Organized Crime, 14*, 47–55.
Lesser, J. G., & Pope, D. S. (2007). *Human behavior and the social environment: Theory and practice*. Boston, MA: Pearson/Allyn & Bacon.
Maney, G. M., Brown, T., Gregory, T., Mallick, R., Simoneschi, S., Wheby, C., & Wiktor, N. (2011). *Meeting the service needs of human trafficking survivors in the New York city metropolitan area: Assessment and Recommendations*. New York, NY: Lifeway Network. Retrieved from https://lifewaynetwork.org/wp-content/uploads/2011/11/Hofstra-University-LifeWay-Network-Report-2011.pdf
Meshelemiah, J.C.A. (2014). Diagnosing posttraumatic stress disorder and adjustment disorders in adults using the DSM-5: What social workers and other mental health professionals need to know. *(NASW). Specialty Practice Sections.*
Meshelemiah, J.C.A. (2016). Human rights perspectives in social work education and practice. In *Encyclopedia of social work*. Washington, DC: National Association of Social Workers Press/Oxford University Press.
National Association of Social Workers. (1960). *NASW code of ethics*. Silver Springs, MD: Author.
National Association of Social Workers. (1996). *NASW code of ethics*. Washington, DC: Author.
National Association of Social Workers. (2017a). *Social justice*. Retrieved from www.socialworkers.org/pressroom/features/Issue/peace.asp
National Association of Social Workers. (2017b). Social workers stand up. *NASW Ohio Chapter Newsletter, 40*(2), 1–24.
Ohio State University (the). (2017). *Field education: Human rights activities*. Retrieved from https://csw.osu.edu/field-education/human-rights-activities/
Okech, D., Morreau, W., & Benson, K. (2011). Human trafficking: Improving victim identification and service provision. *International Social Work, 55*(4), 488–503.
Palmer, N. (2010). The essential role of social work in addressing victims and survivors of trafficking. *ILSA Journal of International & Comparative Law, 17*(1), 41–56.
Payne, M. (1997). *Modern social work theory* (2nd ed.). Chicago, IL: Lyceum Books, Inc.
Peavler, R. (2017). Differences between capitalism and socialism. *The Balance*, Business Finance section.
Polaris. (2018a). *National human trafficking hotline*. Retrieved from https://polarisproject.org/get-assistance/national-human-trafficking-hotline
Polaris. (2018b). *Policy & legislation*. Retrieved from https://polarisproject.org/policy-legislation
Public Law 106–386. (2000). *Trafficking Victims Protection Act of 2000*, H.R. 3244, (2000). 106th Cong., 2nd Sess.
Rahman, M. A. (2011). Human trafficking in the era of globalization. The case of trafficking in the global market economy. *Transcience Journal, 2*(1), 54–71.
Raymond, J. G., & Hughes, D. M. (2001). Sex trafficking of women in the United States: International and domestic trends. *Coalition Against Trafficking in Women.*
Reichert, E. (2001). Move from social justice to human rights provides new perspective. *Professional Development: International Journal of Continuing Social Work Education, 4*(1), 5–13.
Riches, G. (2002). Food banks and food security: Welfare reform, human rights, and social policy. Lessons from Canada? Social Policy & Administration, 36(6), 648–663.

Salvation Army. (2016a). *Central Ohio rescue and restore coalition.* Retrieved from http://swo.salvationarmy.org/rescueandrestore/getinvolved
Salvation Army. (2016b). *Combatting human trafficking.* Retrieved from http://co.salvationarmy.org/CentralOhio/combating-human-trafficking
Segal, E. A., Gerdes, K. E., & Steiner, S. (2013). *An introduction to the profession of social work: Becoming a change agent* (4th ed.). Belmont, CA: Thomson – Brooks/Cole.
Stepnitz, A. (2012, July/August). Human trafficking and asylum: Problematic overlap. *Women's Project at Asylum Aid*, (112), 1–16.
Stines, S. (2015). What is trauma bonding? *Psych Central.* Retrieved from https://pro.psychcentral.com/recovery-expert/2015/10/what-is-trauma-bonding/
Tannenbaum, N., & Reisch, M. (2001). *From charitable volunteers to architects of social welfare: A brief history of social work* (pp. 7–19). University of Michigan's Ongoing Magazine, Michigan.
United Nations. (1948). *United Nations universal declaration of human rights.* New York, NY: Author.
United Nations. (2000). *Protocol to prevent, suppress and punish trafficking in persons, especially women and children, supplementing the United Nations Convention Against Transnational Organized Crime.* New York, NY: Author.
United Nations. (2017). General assembly speakers call for stronger, more tailored responses to 'heinous' human trafficking crimes, especially those targeting children. Retrieved from https://www.un.org/press/en/2017/ga11957.doc.htm
Van Voorhis, R. M., & Hostetter, C. (2013). The impact of MSW education on social worker empowerment and commitment to client empowerment through social justice advocacy. *Journal of Social Work Education, 42*(1), 105–121.
Villaverde, V. (2017). *Field education manual.* USC Suzanne Dworak-Peck School of Social Work. Retrieved from https://dworakpeck.usc.edu/media/188/download
Wooditch, A. (2011). The efficacy of the trafficking in persons report: A review of evidence. *Criminal Justice Policy Review, 22*(4), 471–493.

13

UNIQUE CONTRIBUTIONS OF SOCIAL WORK IN COMBATING HUMAN TRAFFICKING

Melissa I. M. Torres, Maura Nsonwu, Laurie Cook Heffron, and Noël Bridget Busch-Armendariz

Abstract

Social workers, as global human rights advocates and agents of change, are uniquely poised to address international and domestic human trafficking through multidimensional systems of care. Social work values, based on universal human rights and the empowerment of those seeking assistance, are centered on the most vulnerable populations, which are also the most often exploited for human trafficking worldwide. An examination of risks faced by populations, a victim's removal from a trafficking situation, indicators for identification, and systems of care that work across these processes along with survivor rehabilitation is vital to deliver culturally competent and effective services to those affected by human trafficking. This chapter applies social work theory and international practice with the ecological perspective at mezzo and macro levels using a case study.

Learning Objectives

At the end of the chapter, readers will be able to:

1. Describe the unique contribution of the social work profession at the mezzo and macro levels to address human trafficking locally and globally;
2. Illustrate a multicultural perspective that depicts the "best practice" and intersecting role of social work that centers individuals and their communities;
3. Identify indicators of human trafficking and sex and labor exploitation to assist social workers in international settings;
4. Examine the intersection of systems of care in addressing needs of human trafficking victims;
5. Compare the principles central to social work such as social justice and aspects embedded in the field of human trafficking; and
6. Describe the unique role of the social worker in valuing the culturally relevant, community perspective of collectivism in combating human trafficking.

Key Terms: international social work; human trafficking; systems of care; community centered approach; ecological perspective; self-determination; victim centered; human rights approach; culturally competent system of care; multidisciplinary team; micro, mezzo, and macro social work interventions; humanitarian aid; cycle of violence; victim identification.

Introduction: the social work profession paradigm

Social work is a profession guided by intersectional frameworks to assist vulnerable populations and to right social injustices. The International Federation of Social Workers (IFSW) defines the essence as "the empowerment and liberation of people" guided theories, research, and practice. In 2014, IFSW defined the social work profession as

> a practice-based profession and an academic discipline that promotes social change and development, social cohesion, and the empowerment and liberation of people. Principles of social justice, human rights, collective responsibility and respect for diversities are central to social work. Underpinned by theories of social work, social sciences, humanities and indigenous knowledge, social work engages people and structures to address life challenges and enhance wellbeing.
>
> *(International Federation of Social Work, 2014)*

IFSW (2014) also recognizes that "one key principle of the social work profession is respecting the inherent dignity and worth of a person, a human rights and human dignity value, and further defines this principle as:

1. Respecting the right to self-determination – Social workers should respect and promote people's right to make their own choices and decisions, irrespective of their values and life choices, provided this does not threaten the rights and legitimate interests of others.
2. Promoting the right to participation – Social workers should promote the full involvement and participation of people using their services in ways that enable them to be empowered in all aspects of decisions and actions affecting their lives.
3. Treating each person as a whole – Social workers should be concerned with the whole person, within the family, community, societal and natural environments, and should seek to recognize all aspects of a person's life.
4. Identifying and developing strengths – Social workers should focus on the strengths of all individuals, groups and communities and thus promote their empowerment.

Given the profession's underpinning principles it is uniquely positioned to promote effective mezzo and macro interventions in human trafficking (Busch-Armendariz, Nsonwu, Cook Heffron, 2018), a contemporary, complex, global crisis (Hodge & Lietz, 2007; Nsonwu, Busch-Armendariz, & Cook-Heffron, 2014; Rafferty, 2013; Busch-Armendariz et al., 2018; Polaris Project, 2014; Bales, 2012). While it is understood that trafficking in people does not require the movement of individual(s) across borders or jurisdictions (Busch-Armendariz, 2012; Albanese, Donnelly, & Kelegian, 2004) evidence about globalization and migration trends suggests that marginalized and oppressed populations are at higher risk for exploitation and human trafficking around the world (ILO, 2012). It is important to remember that though we are addressing international human trafficking, domestic trafficking – the exploitation of citizens and residents within their own countries – also occurs in every country in the world. Though international social workers are, by definition, working in international settings, if the trafficking situation is occurring to nationals within that country, it is not an international case of human trafficking. Yet, human trafficking is also non-discriminating (Bales, 2009), and as such social workers must develop services, programs, and policies that are specialized and inclusive (Nsonwu et al., 2015; Busch-Armendariz, Nsonwu, & Heffron, 2014).

This chapter is framed by a human trafficking case study that depicts mezzo and macro social work interventions. The ISFW professional principles and accompanying social work roles and responsibilities are applied to this case in the context of an ecological perspective, human rights approach, and the inherent dignity and worth of a person.

Case study

Rebecca is a social worker whose career has taken various transitions. During her time as a BSW student, she worked as a resource manager at a charity organization that sent emergency supplies and deployed community care providers to sites of natural disasters and conflict to work with afflicted communities. She spent her time learning about different cultures in order to brief deploying staff about their new environment and way of life. She researched issues of injustice and oppression that may have been present in communities prior to the precipitating crisis that deployed community care providers. Rebecca also worked diligently to communicate effectively with current partners while establishing new affiliates in various regions. Often, she was asked to link staff to trainings on topics that would better serve the community. One day she received a request from staff members who had recently set up a camp at the site of a massive earthquake. Community care providers were told that several girls from the town had gone missing after the quake and the families were distraught because they had seen the girls alive after the quake, so it was assumed that they were trafficked for sex in the aftermath. The community care team requested more resources and information regarding prevalence of human trafficking in the area and any local resources for victims. As a result of needing to support her team, Rebecca began to learn more about human trafficking. She researched the ways in which social workers, health and mental health care providers, and the community care team as a whole could provide assistance and help identify victims. Rebecca even invited experts on trauma-informed care to her organization's training day in order to educate staff, practitioners, and volunteers about human trafficking and share best practices. One of the suggestions of the trainers was to create a protocol for the organization regarding identifying and reporting potential victims and having a set list of resources to offer. Rebecca led the initiative in developing these procedures and later began to volunteer with local anti-trafficking organizations – most of which focused on addressing sex trafficking.

After becoming so involved and meeting local survivors, Rebecca decided to study for her masters in social work (MSW) with the goal of becoming a mental health practitioner, focused on working with survivors of sexual abuse, trauma, and sex trafficking. While in her MSW program, her field placement was with local support groups for survivors of sexual assault and trafficking at a local shelter; she also continued her volunteer and agency work. After she obtained her license to practice clinical social work, Rebecca began to specialize in providing trauma-informed care for survivors of abuse and human trafficking who were in the rehabilitation process. She was hired at the agency where she interned and worked as a clinical social worker. Years of collaborations, trainings, professional, and volunteer work with survivors of trafficking contributed to Rebecca's expertise on human trafficking, and she was sought out as an expert. After many requests to speak on indicators of trafficking, available local resources, risks faced by exploited populations, and the long-term care of survivors, Rebecca registered for a train-the-trainer opportunity so that she could begin to train others on addressing trafficking in their organizations or settings. Her former employer contracted her to train staff about to be deployed; Rebecca was also sent to sites to train workers and meet local organizations working on the ground.

While on one site visit, Rebecca was approached by the community care team. They had concerns regarding possible trafficking but were met with resistance when they addressed it with the local community. Considering that this resistance was due to miscommunication, they used several interpreters, but were unsuccessful in discussing the topic of human trafficking and the community was unwilling to accept any resources. The team came together to discuss the situation with Rebecca, who questioned them about their concern that human trafficking was an issue in the community. The team reported that when assessing for missing persons, several locals mentioned family members had left the area and had not notified their families. One service provider mentioned that another outside group had come into the community offering resources – food, water, and blankets – as well as recruiting for job opportunities in the bordering country. Rebecca and the team assessed that this outside group served as a front for traffickers who exploited the vulnerability of the community, recruiting their daughters into sex work; therefore, the community was untrusting of "outsiders." The team determined that the community needed to be educated about human trafficking while the team needed to work to develop trust and began to help families in reporting and finding their daughters; they continued providing service provision to the community. After a few days, Rebecca was walking through the community, meeting people and offering vouchers for the food pantry and community closet. Through an interpreter, she approached community members to inquire about their children. A few of them responded with abrupt answers, but she was able to surmise that the majority of the missing family members were men and that some left with their wives. After further discussion with the community, Rebecca began to theorize that recruiters came to the community for the purpose of labor trafficking. She and the team then compiled translated information and handouts about labor trafficking and labor rights. When the team returned to the community to provide education, they described the risk of human trafficking during a time of natural disaster or crisis; one example was when recruiters promise better jobs in another country, despite lacking legal permission to allow workers to migrate or work in another country. The team then solicited the community to report concerning relatives or share information about potential recruiters with the team so they could begin the reporting and search process. Though the team prepared for nearly 20 families to come forward, only one arrived – a mother of two missing sons.

Unable to figure out how to gain more trust in the community or what other factors contributed to their resistance, Rebecca and the team reached out to a gatekeeper – a community member who has the trust of both their community and of the team and serves as a liaison between the two – to ask for guidance on how to collaborate with the community in a culturally relevant manner. The next day, the gatekeeper met with the team and shared the community's perception that it was common for family members to go missing after an earthquake or crisis and that many would eventually return. The team further explained human trafficking to the gatekeeper stating that it is not guaranteed that missing persons will return. The gatekeeper in turn explained that many people in the community left to work in a neighboring country, often without permission to migrate or work there, and that some eventually call to say they are okay while others are never heard from again; some migrants return to the community only to leave later. Rebecca clarified to the gatekeeper that human trafficking is different from leaving to work in another country and returning, or notifying family when they please. But the gatekeeper insisted that the community may not listen to the team if they tried to educate them.

The gatekeeper further expounded on the community's cultural viewpoint: the majority of the population was of indigenous origins and had experienced extreme poverty, discrimination, ostracism from government representation or assistance, and has had a history of state and societal violence. Over time, they have witnessed the fading of their indigenous language and culture as oppressive structures have strengthened and circular migration had increased among the population. Some community members seeking job opportunities and secure futures for their children had migrated to the nearest metropolitan area or crossed the border, leaving their cultural traditions, customs and values behind. Younger community members had begun to view migration as the only option to advance. Therefore, the community was left with few younger members to learn about their culture and maintain their language and traditions. Some of community members return – either through forced deportation, a family emergency, or because they had earned enough money to secure housing for them and their family – which further complicated the preservation of their culture as these members returned to the community with different experiences, another learned language, foreign customs, a pace and way of life that drastically differed from their native community, and were lacking knowledge of their indigenous traditions and language. They shared stories of the bigger cities or foreign country with other community members, influencing others' decisions to migrate, or minimizing the importance of the local way of life. The same goes for community members who have left but remained in touch with family – their distance and differing experiences created a divide that oftentimes impressed the youth who hoped to leave. It is often assumed that those who are not heard from again have turned their back on their community in order to start a modern life rather than questioning if they are unable to communicate due to being in danger or had even died during their migration. Outsiders often passed through the area and recruited those willing to migrate for work, often to be offered cheap labor working in inadequate or dangerous conditions. Most who leave like it, but say it's better than what's offered back home. Some even returned as recruiters themselves, either working with someone else, or merely because they wanted someone from back home to go back with them to serve as both financial and emotional support. This cycle has happened for decades, though it has intensified since the changes in government in the last few years. As this region was prone to disaster and increased violence, communities were used to receiving support and service from deployed temporary community care teams during periods of crisis. Previous community care teams had arrived and offered resources such as hotlines to report missing persons. But the rate of circular migration had changed local perceptions of who was really missing and who had "forgotten where they come from." Along with charity and service agencies arriving at times of crisis, so do traffickers who take advantage of marginalized communities and their precarious situation and the traffickers are prepared to recruit large groups of people who are vulnerable because they have nowhere to live, no source of income, no resources, and who feel hopeless and helpless about their future. Because of this history of crisis, circular migration, and poverty, the emergency response to human trafficking fell flat.

The community had seen that the crisis response, though helpful for immediate needs in disaster aftermath and breakdowns in infrastructure due to violence, was temporary. Their concern was not to identify and report exploitation, as they did not necessarily believe that outsiders were the biggest threat to their community. Their focus was to preserve their community and find resolutions and responses to the oppression that they faced, which was what traffickers exploit, and what, ultimately, threatens their existence. Their first priority was the preservation of the community as a whole, with individuals' needs coming second; a collectivist perspective. Though identifying and reporting trafficking are immediately helpful, that alone was inadequate in addressing the issues most distressing to the local community – namely, poverty, instability, and the extinction of their traditions. The exploitation the community faces was seen as a consequence and not the main problem. Therefore, Rebecca and the team took what they have learned from this information and decided they needed to reframe their focus on working with the community in order to address both their immediate needs, along with the exploitation and trafficking in their population, while respecting and valuing a collectivist perspective.

Case study discussion questions

1 What were the various systems that Rebecca worked with in her role as a social worker? What strengths and challenges did each system exemplify? How did these systems intersect to impact individual and community vulnerabilities for exploitation?
2 How can Rebecca integrate or leverage a human rights approach in her work with the community?
3 How do workers' impulses to act as liberators or rescuers play out? What conflicts does this create?
4 What were the challenges to community participation with the outreach initiatives by Rebecca and the team?
5 What are the consequences of limited self-awareness and lack of culture-specific knowledge on behalf of Rebecca and the team? What power imbalances existed and in humanitarian aid in general, and what is the social worker's role to define and correct power and power imbalances?
6 How could the team apply the strengths-based perspective in helping the community learn about human trafficking and the vulnerabilities being exploited by labor traffickers?
7 What alerted Rebecca and the team to the possibility of human trafficking? What factors might play into disclosure of victimization and help-seeking by the community?
8 How do natural disasters and conflict crises impact communities and correlate with human trafficking? What roles can social workers play in prevention, disaster preparedness, humanitarian aid, and crisis response?
9 What are the differences in goals, implementation, and impact between international humanitarian aid, international social work, and social justice? How does the social worker keep the victim centered in these intersecting systems?

Ecological perspective

The social work profession draws heavily from the ecological perspective to address its commitment to social and economic justice (Siporin, 1980). Microsystems, mezzosystems, and macrosystems engage marginalized and oppressed individuals and families, and partner with communities, to implement policy that end human trafficking. While not unique to social work, the ecological perspective reflects and supports a core component of social work practice. That is, in addressing social and economic justice, social work moves beyond the consideration and analysis of an individual's experience. Using an ecological approach, social workers examine the relationships and exchanges between individuals and their social, political, and physical environments (Gitterman, 2009).

In the context of human trafficking, social workers utilize an ecological frame to engage multidiscipline stakeholders while putting the victim at the center of the practice (Busch-Armendariz et al., 2018). This perspective recognizes that the social environment is multidimensional (Hutchinson, 2010) and is comprised of a series of nested structures (Bronfenbrenner,

1979). The ecological perspective highlights the interconnection and interdependence between these nested structures, or systems, as well as the fit between an individual and her/his environment. Germain (1973) described a process that involves the "adaptive fit of organisms and their environments and with means by which they achieve dynamic equilibrium and mutuality" (p. 326). Its usefulness is the cognitive scaffolding about the nature of human trafficking, as well as the social work response. This chapter describes mezzo and macro systems relevant to human trafficking and the role of the social worker to assess and identify change initiatives. The micro system is also an important change initiative as it relates to an individual and her or his characteristics in relation to their family and close social groups. The mezzo system involves institutions, organizations and larger communities. These may include anti-trafficking coalitions, interdisciplinary taskforces, law enforcement, social service agencies, legal service providers, school systems, health departments, and faith groups (Busch-Armendariz et al., 2018). The broader cultural and political realm constitutes the macro system and may be impacted by policies, social norms, attitudes and ideologies that make exploitation possible and/or that hinder the prevention of and response to human trafficking (such as those influenced by racism, sexism, homophobia, xenophobia, and nativism) (Busch-Armendariz et al., 2014).

Although presented separately, their interaction and dependency is equally important. These systems are fluid and dynamic and as Mary (2008) coined the "web-of-life." Finally, temporal and chronological perspectives are important to note due to changes over time (Busch-Armendariz et al., 2014). Regardless of whether or not these complex interactions are overtly recognized by those affected, social workers are often strategically placed to view and assess the nested environments of survivors and/or professionals. In fact, some argue it is the explicit role and responsibility of the social worker to "analyze these structures and bring harmony through the increased understanding and coordination among coalition members and between survivors and professionals" (Busch-Armendariz et al., 2014, p. 16).

By employing an ecological approach, social workers can better understand how the experiences and needs of those impacted by exploitation interact with the micro system (their children, parents, and traffickers), the mezzo system (such as the criminal justice system and legal, social and medical service providers), and the macro system (for example current social and political movements related to immigration) (Busch-Armendariz et al., 2014). Finally, this perspective allows social workers to examine impacts over time and to prepare for how the needs of those impacted change over time due to age and developmental stage, employability, changes in legal status, and reunification with family, among other factors (Busch-Armendariz, Nsonwu, & Cook Heffron, 2017).

The role of the social worker

Any efforts aimed at effectively addressing human trafficking and assisting its victims and perpetrators must include the many factors that contribute to the vulnerabilities that are exploited to traffic a person. Systems which marginalize people such as increasing poverty, inequality, lack of education, improper responses to crisis and disasters, and the like serve as impetus for those seeking to exploit another person. Identities such as race, gender, age, citizenship, disability, and sexual orientation also factor into the greater systems. Framing these core issues are deeply rooted in the mission, ethics, and functioning of social work. Social workers are, then, in unique positions to witness and contribute to understanding what human trafficking looks like and how it occurs (Nsonwu et al, 2015; Ross-Sheriff, 2011; Roby, 2005).

Logistically, the many roles of social workers are vital in identifying and reporting victims, rehabilitating survivors, advocating for policies and services at the micro, mezzo, and macro levels on behalf of the survivors and the profession that serves them, and researching the issue from a human rights perspective. Social work practitioners play a key role in the rehabilitation of survivors from working through the trauma, offering new opportunities to build a self-sufficient life and a more secure future, and being a constant support after an exploitive situation. Social work case managers connect survivors to emergency and long-term services that are vital to a survivor's rehabilitative and recovery processes such as shelter and housing, nutrition, education, job placement, individual and group counseling, legal assistance, and daily functions such as translation or accessibility.

Though most expect social workers to be present in direct practice and in roles such as case managers or therapists, other settings vital to these processes include social workers in the legal, medical, law enforcement, and legislative settings. Social workers in the legal settings can work as victim advocates, or they may provide evaluations or written reports and amicus briefs on behalf of the prosecution. Medical social workers and nurses tend to spend more time with patients than doctors and have unique access across the care spectrum by being present in primary, secondary, and tertiary care. Many major U.S. cities now employ mental health units to attend certain emergencies or crime scenes with law enforcement and are able to evaluate certain cases of abuse. Being able to differentiate between scenes of a mental health episode, abuse, and trafficking could help in the identification process. Along with policy research, social workers also serve as legislative aides or assistants and help draft bills, reports, and testimonies for social justice issues. Social workers play a critical role in raising awareness, education, and prevention in communities, assisting survivors, and advocating for social justice.

Human rights approach to human trafficking

Human trafficking is a global issue that affects every population and includes various systems of oppression. Social work is a field that functions in various roles and works to be inclusive of all marginalized peoples and addresses all injustices. Anti-trafficking efforts should therefore be tantamount in the field of social work due to its ethics and human rights based approach. Human trafficking functions by removing a person's agency and exploiting, or robbing them, of their most basic human rights. Because social workers are trained, educated, and grounded in defending and advocating for the rights of all, the social work ethics and human rights based approach is poised to address and respond to the issue of human trafficking. As shown in the systems approach, social workers are able to work in the intersecting spheres such as the local and global. As such, social workers must be aware of the global context of trafficking as well as the local *and* across the micro, mezzo, and macro practice frameworks, because when an individual is trafficked, there are always greater exploitive systems at play. Though anyone can be exploited, the vast majority of victims of human trafficking are marginalized or oppressed populations. The preamble to the National Association of Social Workers (NASW) Code of Ethics begins:

> The primary mission of the social work profession is to enhance human well-being and help meet the basic human needs of all people, with particular attention to the needs and empowerment of people who are vulnerable, oppressed, and living in poverty.

People who are vulnerable, oppressed, and living in poverty are largely represented in those at risk of exploitation and those who have been victimized by human trafficking. Because the social work profession is founded on a code of ethics which is based on human rights, social justice, and empowerment, it is the duty of social workers to recognize that their work with vulnerable populations overlaps with the factors which cause exploitation and trafficking. Human trafficking feeds off of injustices such as poverty, gender-based discrimination and violence, and displacement – all of which relate to the foundation of social work. The exploitation and trafficking of a person cannot happen without a process of gross abuses and violations of basic human rights and the stolen human dignity that occurs as a consequence can continue far beyond the trafficking experience. Trafficking does not have to happen by blatant abuse and physical threats to be a human rights violation. Traffickers exploit oppression and marginalization such as lack of economic or stability opportunities by promising good jobs or a new life. They can exploit displacement caused by poverty, political instability, natural disaster, or violence by pretending to offer an opportunity for room and board in exchange for labor – whether skilled or unskilled. Regardless of how the exploitation or trafficking occur, while empowerment says that the victim is more than their situation, the human rights based approach says that the victim also has a right to not be in this situation.

A human rights approach understands that any type of force, fraud, or coercion used to exploit a victim is a violation of basic human rights and that no one right is greater than another, echoing the Universal Declaration of Human Rights by the General Assembly of the United Nations. Its preamble asserts the "recognition of the inherent dignity and of the equal and inalienable rights of all members of the human family is the foundation of freedom, justice and peace in the world" (United Nations, 1948). In fighting for equity and social justice, social workers can only be effective by advancing human dignity and welfare.

Understanding and applying the inherent dignity and worth of all people

The NASW Code of Ethics states that social justice is the foundation of the profession's purpose (see Meshelemiah, Chapter 12, this volume). Peace and social justice are a focal point for the NASW practice agenda as social workers are guided to advocate for justice and peace. According to the NASW, "Key aspects of promoting peace and social justice, and topics of concern to NASW, are the prevention of human trafficking, poverty alleviation, and prevention of torture" (NASW, 2008). The NASW practice agenda for human trafficking provides a background, identification and assistance recommendations, news articles, education on global initiatives and anti-trafficking policy, and a list of resources and agencies working on the issue and with survivors. This resource exemplifies the various ways in which social workers can work and advocate in anti-trafficking efforts.

International Federation of Social Workers provides a guide for resolving ethical dilemmas. IFSW gives the following examples of ethical dilemmas that social workers may experience:

- Conflicts of loyalty in human trafficking;
- When providing safety, social workers may also find themselves controlling victims of human trafficking; and
- Conflicts arising between the duty of social workers to protect the interests of the people with whom they work and societal demands for efficiency and utility.

Inherent dignity and worth of a person

Aid versus care: applying systems of care to human trafficking

As we shift towards globalized responses to international problems, we must be aware and critical of the lens and framework from which we approach social work throughout the various systems. In particular, in addressing human trafficking, the *distinction between international social work and international humanitarian aid* should be addressed as the missions of meeting basic human needs intersect in a global context (Ross-Sheriff, 2007). Human trafficking thrives off of vulnerabilities of oppressed and marginalized populations, of which some exploit for profit. Because international humanitarian aid, by definition, occurs in insecure settings and times of crisis or conflict, the overlapping of communities receiving aid and those at risk of exploitation and trafficking requires a careful understanding of both the immediate and long-term risks and needs of the population. Protected by international humanitarian law as defined by the International Committee of the Red Cross, humanitarian aid is an immediate response to those affected by natural or man-made disaster and conflict with the end goal being to meet the vital needs of individuals in crisis (Bernard, 2015). Social work, as led by principles of social justice, responds to the person in the environment while intersecting with needs beyond the individual. These two frameworks for response and care often employ similar models of service provision and both engage with the issue of human trafficking or in populations where it is occurring.

How does the contemporary global influx of refugees and asylum seekers impact the social problem of human trafficking? What specific knowledge and skill set do social workers need to address this vulnerable population?

The training and education of social workers (for details, refer to Meshelemiah, Chapter 12, this volume) has also evolved in parallel to these globalized models. In assessing the development of social work education and its connection to working with foreign-born populations or working abroad, Richard Estes (2010) states,

> over time, social work professionals have been increasingly confronted with the challenges of immigrants and refugees or have traveled to assist in humanitarian and reconstruction efforts during or after major catastrophic events such as disasters and war. Consequently, social work education has embraced a global perspective on many fronts: curriculum transformation, study abroad, student and faculty exchange, and collaborative overseas research, among others.
>
> *(p. 5)*

One of the cornerstones of social work is that the work be client-centered and the acknowledgment that all work must start with those in need, or to "meet the client where they are," rather than setting goals without the individual's or community's input. In cases of community or mezzo social work, the client would be the community or population. Using our case study as an example, when assessing an issue that preys on vulnerabilities, such as human trafficking, this community-centered approach helps us to see what is the crisis (i.e. disaster and missing persons) and what are the underlying roots which intersect with that crisis (i.e. poverty, mistrust, cultural marginalization, unstable migratory practices). These distinctions are crucial in helping systems of care deliver services more effectively. Even when having the best of intentions to help, administering – or even offering – assistance incorrectly can be detrimental to the goals and cause more harm. In offering emergency resources or humanitarian aid, communities can receive assistance for immediate needs in crisis. In providing services for individuals in need of long-term assistance with issues that have existed after and before crisis, clients can work more intently on the consequential effects of their experience and their response. Social workers are present throughout both humanitarian aid and service provision and are trained to start from where those in need are starting.

How does the social work perspective of "meeting the client where they are" function in anti-trafficking work in cases where victims of human trafficking are not willing or ready to be removed from their exploitation? How do social workers balance the professional value of their clients' right to self-determination with the risk for continued harm?

Right to self-determination

To understand exploitation and trafficking, it is critical to understand violence and explore it beyond acts of abuse or assault. Violence is a community issue (National Academies of Sciences, Engineering, and Medicine, 2017). Other than self-harm, violence is often inflicted by an external perpetrator (Pickard, 2015). The perpetrator can be an individual such as a partner, an entity such as a government, or system such as food insecurity (Allen, 2001). Though a trafficker is an individual or group perpetrating the exploitation of others for profit, trafficking can happen by and within these sectors. By definition, human trafficking is perpetrated by a trafficker as a willing individual would not be forced, defrauded, or coerced into exploitation. An understandable intention to help someone in an abusive situation is complicated by the reaction of trying to rescue them. The cycle of violence, used in research and practice with survivors of domestic violence and abuse, states that perpetration of violence is based on power and control through various physical, emotional, mental, and economic methods. Force, fraud, and coercion are methods of gaining power and control for the purpose of exploitation and trafficking (Busch-Armendariz, Nsonwu, & Cook Heffron, 2011; Potocky, 2010). Although the cycle of violence model is most often used for intimate partner violence, it can also be applied in sex and labor trafficking since traffickers use many of the same tools as perpetrators of intimate partner violence such as isolating victims, using coercion and threats, and inflicting economic and emotional abuse. If exploitation for labor or commercial sex are present in these acts of violence, it is possible that it is a case of human trafficking.

Beyond the cycle of violence model, research has shown us that violence, itself, is a cycle, which means that those who inflict violence on others have more than likely had it inflicted on themselves prior to their own perpetration (Mercy, Butchart, Farrington, & Cerdá, 2002; Reilly, Muldoon, & Byrne, 2004). Knowing this, social workers should examine their role in anti-trafficking work. Past the point of a victim being removed from their exploitation – liberation or rescue – the experience and effects of violence remain and work must be done to prevent the cycle of violence to self or others from continuing, both with survivors and perpetrators.

Like intimate partner violence, human trafficking is often portrayed as occurring through physical acts of violence. Film, ads, and campaign material (see Ollus and Joutsen, Chapter 3, this volume) frequently portray a chained, bruised, and seemingly hidden young girl as a visual to describe the issue, though this type of human trafficking is not the norm (Laczko & Gozdziak, 2005). These images are used to portray an urgent need of a population that is in desperate need of rescuing. This supplements the liberation and rescue reaction, which, then, justifies the need for a rescuer, as the victim is portrayed as not able to liberate themselves. What is important to include in this examination of social work and human trafficking is how these systems and perspectives intersect with differing cultures, policies, and systems of oppression. Particularly in situations of migration and international trafficking, using such images stereotypes victims and constructs human trafficking as a blight in need of rescue interventions, which is a disconnect from intersecting factors which frame the international migrant experience (Lindquist, 2010). Understanding human trafficking based on what is usually seen in images – that the majority of victims are females trafficked for sexual exploitation – frames the public discourse which, in turn, guides the identification processes of assumed victims. Such a narrow framework of human trafficking at the international level stifles the identification of other types of trafficking (i.e. labor, child soldiers) and further stigmatizes other victims (i.e. males) (Vijeyarasa, 2013). Social workers have the unique ability to see past these images in their direct service work, which allows for more in-depth discussion of exploitation experiences within the context of the victim's overall experience and its intersecting issues. Such information compliments the understanding of human trafficking from a numbers (prevalence) discussion to a lived experience in need of assessment an assistance (Lindquist, 2010).

Promoting the right to participation

The social work motto "meeting the client where they are" is crucial to addressing human trafficking, much more so on a global scale. Social workers practicing within both systems of international humanitarian aid and international social work, should note that individuals or communities receiving assistance – whether immediate or long term – will not be successful in achieving goals set by others. This is particularly critical to understand when it comes to anti-trafficking initiatives.

Though we've stated that international social work was somewhat based on the practice of international humanitarian aid, when it comes to social work addressing human trafficking, it should be noted that one of the developments on which international humanitarianism began was the development of antislavery initiatives worldwide (Barnett, 2013). As many view human trafficking as "modern-day slavery" (Sigmon, 2008) (for details, refer to Bravo, Chapter 1, this volume), this context is worth exploring in terms of how we approach anti-trafficking responses. The antislavery frameworks of liberation and rescue are prevalent in today's anti-trafficking initiatives worldwide. Similar perspectives have shaped some of the work within international humanitarian aid (Barnett, 2013) and international social work systems (Estes, 2010). While the acts of liberation and rescue may be warranted in some cases of human trafficking, the need for a liberator or rescuer are prevalent in current anti-trafficking rhetoric. Fundamentally, this is contrary to the ethics of social work practice, though necessary in much of humanitarian aid. Promoting an individual's or community's right to participation in addressing their own needs or during their service provision within systems of care centers on the individual or community rather than focusing on the actions of the social worker.

This distinction is also helpful to those working with individuals or communities who have experienced violence. Remaining aware of the power imbalances between providing aid in crisis and working on long-term needs within systems of care; both might employ social workers, but providing aid puts the aid worker in a position of giving something that is needed and lacking, while care work is a partnership between the social worker and those in need by utilizing the strengths they already have to reach attainable goals that go beyond crisis. In particular, those who have experienced violence or human trafficking have faced a situation where others have obtained power and control over them and may require time, examination of cultural competence, and trauma-informed care in order to build trust for that collaborative partnership with a social worker to be effective (Nickson, Dunstan, Esperanza, & Barker, 2011).

Treating each person as a whole

International policies regarding human trafficking, though lacking uniformity, mostly define human trafficking as the force, fraud, or coercion for the purpose of labor or commercial sexual exploitation. Underlying vulnerabilities and intersecting factors, however, are often not understood in the same ways. This is important to remember when examining anti-trafficking efforts and the needs of the individual or community at risk. What may be determined to be exploitation to some may not be understood as such by those at risk. This should also be taken into consideration when determining which system of care would be most effective within the culture of the individual or community with which the social worker is interacting, as it cannot be assumed that these definitions or perspectives are universal. Culture is multidimensional and can intersect with systems of care at every level of interaction with the social worker and to different degrees. In developing his model for a Culturally Competent System of Care, Cross (1989) states,

> the culturally competent system values diversity, has the capacity for cultural self-assessment, is conscious of the dynamics inherent when cultures interact, hainstitutionalized cultural knowledge, and has developed adaptations to diversity. Further, each of these five elements must function at every level of the system. Attitudes, policies, and practices must be congruent within all levels of the system.
>
> (p. 19)

In valuing diversity, what does the social worker need to be cognizant of when working with foreign-born victims versus domestic-born victims? What considerations does the social worker need to be sensitive to when working with gender specific victims of trafficking, victims whose gender identity do not correspond with their biological sex, and LGBTQ victims of human trafficking?

The value base for a culturally competent system of care parallels the values and ethics of social work as both frameworks address the diversity, difference, intersecting factors, and respect of different experiences and perspectives inherent in international social work. In terms of applicability to issues of social justice, a culturally competent system of care must be accessible, adaptable, and available to marginalized populations (Cross, 1989). This model addresses the broadening of base values across the micro, mezzo, and macro social work systems of care across cultures and helps us to understand cultural relevance in each country as the ethics have the same appreciation for diversity, differences, and self-determination. Human rights and social justice unite us globally though the varying systems of care in which social workers are involved and may be implemented differently due to cultural, social, or political stratification and the history of the population.

Further examining the approaches utilized in addressing human trafficking on a global scale, a social worker's interaction with potential victims or at-risk populations benefit from the three critical elements in Cross's (1989) model of cultural competence: (1) self-awareness; (2) culture-specific knowledge; and (3) skills promoting effective socio-cultural interactions by an individual. Applying these elements to international social work with potential victims and survivors of human trafficking further help social workers to best meet the client where they are in terms of human trafficking – whether that is at risk of exploitation, in a trafficking situation, or seeking rehabilitation.

Cross's framework for cultural competence addresses the multidimensional nature of culture with the intersection of various systems of care and their respective applications. The framework (see Figure 13.1) defines a spectrum of cultural competence spanning from dangerous practices towards individuals and communities of a differing culture to practices which respect and include them within a system of care. The following is an abridged list of the spectrum: (1) cultural destructiveness – attitudes and practices towards a culture that is destructive and irreverent due to lack of knowledge or lack of consideration; (2) cultural incapacity – extreme bias and superiority, acting paternally or as a savior; (3) cultural blindness – superficially unbiased, blind to differences and assumption that practices and beliefs are universal; (4) cultural pre-competence – aware of weaknesses and trying to diversify capacity, but with a false sense of accomplishment; (5) cultural competence – characterized by acceptance and respect for difference, constantly self-assessing regarding culture and adaptation of service models; and (6) cultural proficiency – respecting

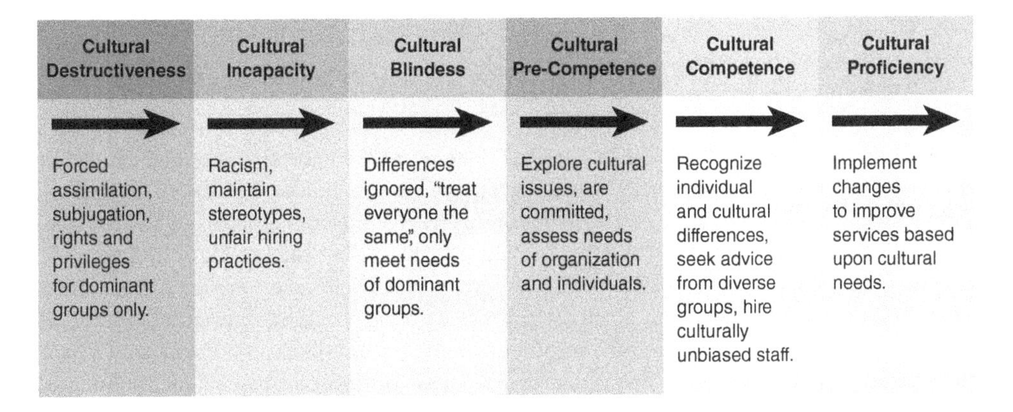

Figure 13.1 Continuum of cultural competency

Source: Adapted from Cross, 1989.

culture at all levels, seeks to add to knowledge, capacity, and practice of cultural respect and competence (Cross, 1989).

This framework encompasses the principles needed in examining the goals and methods social workers implement in international settings as assuring themselves that the human rights approach and respecting the individual's or community's cultural identity are taken into consideration during service provision. It is crucial to recognize that the degrees to which a social worker can either harm or help an individual can occur whether they intend to or not.

In working internationally, what culturally relevant considerations does the social worker need to be respectful of? What should social workers consider when examining their cultural competence, bias, and overall role?

Human trafficking operates by commodifying an individual for the profit of the trafficker. Addressing the most critical needs of survivors is critical for their rehabilitation (Busch-Armendariz et al., 2014) though meeting the immediate needs in crisis is only the first step in assisting the individual, or community, as a whole. Knowing that traffickers exploit vulnerabilities of their victims, long-term care in addressing vulnerabilities such as healthcare, legal services, mental and emotional well-being, financial stability, and family/support system reunification helps the rehabilitative and restorative processes in a holistic manner (Busch-Armendariz et al., 2014). Cross's framework and spectrum for cultural competence guides social workers and sets a precedent for the systems of care in which they work which takes the individual's or community's whole personhood and culture into consideration.

Identifying and developing strengths

Focusing on the individual or community and having a victim-centered framework is an important part of social work practice. Research has shown that survivors of human trafficking benefit from services provided from ecological, strengths-based, and victim-centered perspectives in collaborative rehabilitative service provision with social workers (Busch-Armendariz et al., 2014). Addressing the legal, cultural, emotional, and socioeconomic factors which are exploited by traffickers and help to sustain the trafficking situation requires a human rights approach (Rijken,

2009) and the practice of doing so can be addressed at every level of the ecological perspective while remaining victim-centered.

Building on strengths, or the strengths-based approach, positions the social worker to guide an individual or community focused on their "capacities, talents, competencies, possibilities, visions, values, and hopes, however dashed and distorted these may have become through circumstance, oppression, and trauma" (Saleebey, 1996, p. 297). This perspective guides the collaborative process with the social worker in working with victims or survivors of human trafficking, who have faced a violation of their human rights and loss of their agency, as they assist in navigating resources and accessing other necessary services within systems of care. Focusing on strengths, accomplishments, and tools which the victim or survivor brings with them in their interactions with social workers is also a way in which to empower those who have faced disempowerment with a focus on their own capabilities rather than those of the social worker (Saleebey, 1996). Building on the victim's or survivor's strengths through their experience removes the focus from the overall problem which aids in helping the individual or community in taking steps towards progress without being overwhelmed by what they cannot yet answer (Saleebey, 1996). The strengths-based approach goes hand in hand with self-determination, promoting the right to participation, and treating the person as a whole. The belief that individuals who have faced oppression or trauma are just as capable of identifying their own needs as those who haven't (Fast & Chapin, 1997) relies on self-determination while promoting the right to participation. This approach also takes the person as a whole into account since their attributes, identities, and perspectives are viewed as strengths which have contributed to their process of identification and rehabilitation (Heffernan & Blythe, 2014).

Improve victim accessibility by including identification and ensuring rehabilitation

---

What are indicators of exploitation and trafficking and how can they differ between types of trafficking, by population, and within different settings of interaction with a social worker? How can social workers value and respect cultural sensitivity when working with individuals and communities who are vulnerable to and at risk of exploitation and trafficking?

Though several gaps exist within and across systems, the secretive and often hidden nature of human trafficking increases the difficulties in identifying victims and making rehabilitation to survivors accessible. Yet the various roles and methods in which social workers can engage with victims gives them a unique and critical opportunity to intervene once social workers learn how to best identify, engage, and help victims seeking assistance. Awareness of human trafficking is not enough. It is critical that social workers be trained in proper victim identification and have the ability and resources to then respond to victims' needs as one of the major challenges in assisting victims is not only the lack of identification, but misidentifying victims in general (Hardy, Compton, & McPhatter, 2013). Indicators of exploitation and human trafficking have been understood and embedded within training for social workers and other professionals for some time. Many social workers are not prepared to consider or encounter human trafficking in their daily service provision. Clarity about the scope, risks, or lack of training on indicators of victimization can lead to misidentifying trafficking as symptoms of other types of abuse, mental health issues, relationship problems, health concerns, or may be ignored overall. When not trained to actively look for the warning signs among their clientele or community, victims might be entered into ineffective or improper services or be ignored. Several studies have addressed this in assessing the likelihood that social workers are able to identify victims of human trafficking. Though varied, results have demonstrated that because of the clandestine nature of the crime and its hidden populations, most social workers:

- Did not understand the risk prevalence in their clientele (Pierce, 2012);
- Were unable to assess the criminal factors associated with child trafficking as juvenile justice matters (Kotrla, 2010); and
- Fewer than half of medical social workers at a large U.S. city's leading hospital were able to correctly identify a trafficking victim with even fewer able to distinguish between a child who was trafficked or abused (Beck et al., 2015).

How could the social worker consider the differences and similarities between labor and sex trafficking cases? Elements to consider: prevention, identification, and intervention.

Actual numbers of trafficking cases are difficult to gauge because it's a hidden crime, though even more challenging is confirming the number of victims who have yet to be identified. An important issue in determining how prevalent human trafficking is and how to identify it is how it is defined. Social workers that are social scientists and social and human service providers across multilateral systems have not agreed on a uniform definition of human trafficking or even on common terminology when identifying it (Chuang, 2014). Examples of how this has aided in the lack of identification and misidentification of potential victims include the conflation of sex trafficking and human trafficking; sex trafficking and prostitution; sex trafficking and sexual assault; labor abuse and labor trafficking; intimate partner violence and human trafficking, and so forth. Lack of uniformity in understanding these terms leads to varying approaches and perpetuated gaps in effectively combating human trafficking while the different terms also contribute to the lack of understanding of the crimes (Chuang, 2014). An example of lack of uniformity in the United States is the current question of whether "child sex trafficking" is interchangeable with "commercial sexual exploitation of minors." Beck et al. (2015) also found that the majority of service providers surveyed (63%) had not received training on victim identification and human trafficking. There are still challenges, however, in training social workers to properly identify victims, and providing training founded on sound research privy to local concerns, risks, cases, and systems: social workers are not immune to misperceptions, misinformation, or misguided processes.

Another concern in victim identification, which is one of the most difficult to overcome, is self-disclosure on the part of the victim. Social workers who suspect potential trafficking should consider their approach and take careful measures to assure the safety of all involved, especially the potential victim. Confronting a potential victim without thinking through the process first could cause more harm than good, especially if the victim is unlikely to immediately disclose. In cases of therapeutic relationships, the ongoing work could be irreversibly altered if the victim is not ready to self-disclose and accept assistance (Kalergis, 2009). In situations of primary care or emergency situations where trust has not been developed with the social worker, victims might be dependent or bonded with their trafficker and not fully comprehend their exploitation or feel that they need to be helped. There are some practice and research methods, such as the stages of change and motivational interviewing (Knowles, 2012), which could help to make the potential victim more aware of their situation and able to make decisions regarding their situation (Walker, 2013). These processes can also help to build rapport with social workers until the victim is ready to self-disclose and seek assistance, in which case the social worker can facilitate a safety and treatment plan with the victim. Regardless, the imperative is to always meet the victim where they are and remain nonjudgmental without imposing values on one who is not seeking help (Vakharia & Little, 2017). In these cases, it is best to help ensure that the victim remains as safe as possible and knows that they have options.

While working with children, some of these measures may have to take legal issues into consideration. Social workers should be informed on possible mandated reporting laws in their region and how child welfare and law enforcement might play a role in identifying a child trafficking situation. Other barriers could include convincing the greater systems that the problem exists. Communities that do not believe the problem exists, lack legislation that allows for a proper response post-identification, or even organizations that either do not allow for training of their staff on the matters or lack funding for service provision, create barriers for a holistic response after proper victim identification. Therefore, it is imperative that social workers at the various levels – direct services, community work, administration, legislation, research, government, and education – continue to advocate for closing gaps and creating more collaboration within these systems.

How might a multidisciplinary network assist in efforts to identify and address human trafficking? Who would be important to include in engaging and establishing such networks to offer rehabilitative assistance to those identified as victims of human trafficking?

In any case, social workers can effectively address the situation of human trafficking and best assist victims if they prepare adequately (see Meshelemiah, Chapter 12, this volume). Best practices for these preparations include trauma-informed care (Greenbaum, 2016), a human rights–based approach (Schwarz et al., 2016), and having a network of care providers and resources in place to assist the victim in creating a safety and treatment plan (Greenbaum, 2016). No matter how training or education occurs, once a social worker learns how to properly identify and assist victims of human trafficking, they should take into consideration how to work within their agencies to increase internal awareness and prepare for screening and response. If the agency does not have internal guidance on these matters past acquiring training, the practice of having an external network helps to build community for the service providers and resources for the victim. Having a broader network that is multidisciplinary can include task forces, issue committees, and advisory boards led by service providers and survivors (see Williamson and Roe-Sepowitz, Chapter 14, this volume). These networks should include all stakeholders who can add to the resource access for survivors such as law enforcement agents, lawyers and possibly judges, both mental and public health professionals, educators, and others. Such networks could assist alleviating gaps within and across systems as well as establishing a uniform definition, understanding, and approach towards a continuum of care for survivors. Because assisting victims of human trafficking is, by nature, an interdisciplinary process, such an approach provides another service to survivors as it allows for a coordinated community response that offers intersecting resources in the rehabilitation process (Van Impe, 2000). Likewise, networks of care can also address prevention efforts for the community. In these networks, social workers bring and provide an important perspective in service provision and survivor rehabilitation. It is necessary that social workers advocate to bring survivors to these opportunities for leadership, as well as provide a social justice, empowering, and human rights based approach to the function of these coordinated care and task force efforts (Busch-Armendariz et al., 2014; Roby, 2005). In addition to these functions, service provision networks also serve as a source to draw support for those who face these difficult matters and choices daily.

Conclusion

Social work examines the person-in-environment, current and historical intersecting policies while acknowledging injustices. Multidisciplinary teams are at the center of social issues, particularly issues of human rights, and are poised to address human trafficking as a multidimensional problem. The unique framework of meeting the client where they are focuses on the immediate and long-term needs of individuals and communities and is, therefore, applicable to any situation worldwide. It is the implementation of *how we meet the client* that must constantly be examined and revised so that all efforts are made to remove bias and risk of the social worker imposing their own views through any interaction or throughout systems of care. Human trafficking continues to develop as the risks of victimization change, the methods of force, fraud, or coercion become more hidden, and the opportunities for exploitation increase with globalization. Anti-trafficking efforts worldwide would benefit from social workers trained in molding and adapting the tools they have learned to the environment in which they enter. So long as this continues to be respectful of the culture, victim identification, survivor rehabilitation, trafficking prevention, and intervention efforts will be more effective as they focus on the individuals whose human rights have not been centered during these injustices. Whether a social worker is focused on an individual, community, or a problem, their values, ethics, and frameworks help them to see how human trafficking is present and intersecting at each level where the social worker is present.

Supplemental learning materials

Readings

Bales, K. (2000). *New slavery: A reference handbook*. Santa Barbara, CA: ABC-CLIO.

Bales, K. (2012). *Disposable people: New slavery in the global economy, Update with a new preface* (3rd ed.). Berkeley: University of California Press.

Bales, K. (2016). *Blood and earth: Modern slavery, ecocide, and the secret to saving the world*. New York, NY: Spiegel & Grau.

Bales, K., & Soodalter, R. (2009). *The slave next door*. Berkeley: University of California Press.

Busch-Armendariz, N. B., Nsonwu, M., & Heffron, L. C. (2018). *Human trafficking: Applied research, theories, and case studies*. Thousand Oaks, CA: Sage Publications, Inc.

International Organization for Migration: Counter-Trafficking. Retrieved from www.iom.int

Kara, S. (2009). *Sex trafficking: Inside the business of modern slavery*. New York, NY: Columbia University Press.

Kara, S. (2011). Supply and demand: Human trafficking in the global economy. *Harvard International Review, 33*(2), 66.

Kristof, N., & WuDunn, S. (2010). *Half the sky*. New York, NY: Knopf Doubleday Publishing Group.

Lloyd, R. (2010). *Girls like us: Fighting for a world where girls are not for sale, an activist finds her calling and heals herself*. New York, NY: HarperCollins.

Policies: Trafficking Victims Protection Act 2000, 2003, 2005, 2008, and 2013.

Shelley, L. (2010). *Human trafficking: A global perspective*. New York, NY: Cambridge University Press.

The United Nations. (1948). *Universal declaration of human rights*. Retrieved from www.un.org/en/universal-declaration-human-rights/index.html

United Nations Global Initiative to Fight Human Trafficking. Retrieved from www.ungift.org

UNHCR. (2008). Refugee protection and human trafficking. Retrieved from www.unhcr.org/trafficking

U.S. Department of State. (2016). Trafficking in persons report. Retrieved from www.state.gov/j/tip/rls/tiprpt/2016/

Wahab, S., & Panichelli, M. (2013). Ethical and human rights issues in coercive interventions with sex workers. *Work, 28*(4), 344–349.

Websites

(1976) www.ohchr.org/EN/ProfessionalInterest/Pages/CCPR.aspx
British Association of Social Workers Code of Ethics. Retrieved from http://cdn.basw.co.uk/upload/basw_112315-7.pdf
British Association of Social Workers Victims of Modern slavery – Competent Authority guidance. Retrieved from www.basw.co.uk/resource/?id=5195
British Association of Social Workers Victims of Modern slavery – frontline staff guidance. Retrieved from www.basw.co.uk/resource/?id=5194
Caring for trafficked persons: Guidance for health providers. (2009). International Covenant on Civil and Political Rights, 16 December 1966. International Covenant on Economic, Social and Cultural Rights, 16 December 1966 (1976). Retrieved from www.ohchr.org/EN/ProfessionalInterest/Pages/CESCR.aspx
International Federation of Social Workers. Retrieved from http://ifsw.org/
International Human Right Conventions:
National Association of Social Workers Code of Ethics. Retrieved from www.socialworkers.org/pubs/code/default.asp
Polaris Project: www.polarisproject.org
Retrieved from http://publications.iom.int/bookstore/free/CT_Handbook.pdf
Shared Hope International www.sharedhope.org
Slavery Footprint: www.slaveryfootprint.org
UNICEF: www.unicef.org
United Nations Human Rights Office of the High Commissioner. Retrieved from www.ohchr.org/EN/Pages/Home.aspx
United Nations Human Rights Office of the High Commissioner Fact Sheet on the International Bill of Human Rights. Retrieved from www.ohchr.org/Documents/Publications/FactSheet2Rev.1en.pdf
United Nations Office on Drugs and Crime on Human Trafficking and Migrant Smuggling. Retrieved from www.unodc.org/unodc/en/human-trafficking/index.html?ref=menuside

Films

Born into Brothels: Calcutta's Red Light Kids. Director: Zana Briski, Ross Kauffman.
Call + Response. Director: Justin Dillon.
The Dark Side of Chocolate. Directors: Miki Mistrati, U. Roberto Romano.
The Day My God Died. Director: Andrew Levine.
Don't Shout Too Loud. Director: Courtney Campbell.
Food Chains. Director: Sanjay Rawal.
Half the Sky: Turning Oppression into Opportunity for Women Worldwide. Retrieved from www.halfthesky movement.org/pages/film
The Price of Sex. Director: Mimi Chakarova.
The Price of Sugar. Director: Bill Haney.
Very Young Girls. Directors: David Schisgall, Nina Alvarez.

Game

Half the Sky Movement: The Game. Retrieved from www.facebook.com/HalftheGame/

References

Albanese, J., Donnelly, J.S., & Kelegian, T. (2004). Cases of human trafficking in the United States: A content analysis of a calendar year in 18 cities. *International Journal of Comparative Criminology, 4*, 96–111.
Allen, J.V. (2001). Poverty as a form of violence: A structural perspective. *Journal of Human Behavior in the Social Environment, 4*(2–3), 45.
Bales, K. (2009). *The slave next door: Human trafficking and slavery in America today.* Berkeley: University of California Press.

Bales, K. (2012). *Disposable people: New slavery in the global economy*. Berkeley: University of California Press.

Barnett, M. N. (2013). *Empire of humanity: A history of humanitarianism*. Ithaca, NY: Cornell University Press.

Beck, M. E., Lineer, M. M., Melzer-Lange, M., Simpson, P., Nugent, M., & Rabbitt, A. (2015). Medical providers' understanding of sex trafficking and their experience with at-risk patients. *Pediatrics, 135*(4), 895–902.

Bernard, V. (2015). Principles guiding humanitarian action. *International Review of the Red Cross, 97*(897/8, Spring/Summer), 7–18.

Bronfenbrenner, U. (1979). *The ecology of human development: Experiments by design and nature*. Cambridge, MA: Harvard University Press.

Busch-Armendariz, N. B. (2012). The Trafficking Victim's Protection Act (TVPA) and the Trafficking Victim's Protection Reauthorization Act (TVPRA). In S. Loue & M. Sajatovic (Eds.), *The encyclopedia of immigrant health*. New York, NY: Springer.

Busch-Armendariz, N. B., Nsonwu, M. B., & Heffron, L. C. (2011). Human trafficking victims and their children: Assessing needs and vulnerabilities and strengths and survivorhood. *Journal of Applied Research on Children: Informing Policy for Children at Risk, 2*, 1–19.

Busch-Armendariz, N. B., Nsonwu, M. B., & Heffron, L. C. (2014). A kaleidoscope: The role of the social work practitioner and the strength of social work theories and practice in meeting the complex needs of people trafficked and the professionals that work with them. *International Social Work, 57*(1), 7–18. Retrieved from https://doi.org/10.1177/0020872813505630

Busch-Armendariz, N., Nsonwu, M.B., & Heffron, L.C. (May 2017). Human Trafficking: Applying Research, Theory and Case Studies. Thousand Oaks, California: Sage.

Chuang, J. A. (2014). Exploitation creep and the unmaking of human trafficking law. *The American Journal of International Law, 108*(4), 609–649.

Cross, T. L., & Georgetown University Child Development Center, Washington, DC. CASSP Technical Assistance Center. (1989). *Towards a culturally competent system of care a monograph on effective services for minority children who are severely emotionally disturbed*. Washington, DC: Distributed by ERIC Clearinghouse. Retrieved from www.eric.ed.gov/contentdelivery/servlet/ERICServlet?accno=ED330171

Estes, R. J. (2010). United States-based conceptualization of international social work education. Retrieved from http://repository.upenn.edu/spp_papers/181

Fast, B., & Chapin, R. (1997). The strengths model and critical practice components. In D. Saleebey (Ed.), *The strengths perspective in social work practice* (2nd ed., pp. 115–131). White Plains, NY: Longman Publishers.

Germain, C. B. (1973). An ecological perspective in casework practice. *Social Casework, 54*(6), 323–330.

Gitterman, A. (2009). The life model. In A. R. Roberts (Ed.), *Social workers' desk reference*. New York, NY: Oxford University Press.

Greenbaum, J. (2016). Identifying victims of human trafficking in the emergency department. *Clinical Pediatric Emergency Medicine, 17*(4), 241–248.

Hardy, V., Compton, K., & Mcphatter, V. (2013). Domestic minor sex trafficking: Practice implications for mental health professionals. *Journal of Women and Social Work, 28*(1), 8–18.

Heffernan, K., & Blythe, B. (2014). Evidence-based practice: Developing a trauma-informed lens to case management for victims of human trafficking. *Global Social Welfare, 1*(4), 169–177.

Hodge, D. R., & Lietz, C. A. (2007). The international sexual trafficking of women and children: A review of the literature. *Affilia: Journal of Women and Social Work, 22*, 163–174. Retrieved from https://doi.org/10.1177/0886109907299055

Hutchinson, E. D. (2010). *Dimensions of human behavior: The changing life course*. Thousand Oaks, CA: Sage.

International Federation of Social Workers. (2014, August 6). *Global definition of social work*. Retrieved from http://ifsw.org/policies/definition-of-social-work/

International Labour Organization (ILO). (2012). ILO global estimate of forced labour: Results and methodology. Retrieved from www.ilo.org/global/topics/forced-labour/publications/WCMS_182004/lang – en/index.htm

Kalergis, K. I. (2009). A passionate practice: Addressing the needs of commercially sexually exploited teenagers. *Affilia, 24*(3), 315–324.

Kotrla, K. (2010). Domestic minor sex trafficking in the United States. *Social Work, 55*(2), 181–189.

Laczko, F., & Gozdziak, E. (Eds.). (2005). Data and research on human trafficking: A global survey. Offprint of the Special Issue of *International Migration, 43*(1–2). Geneva, Switzerland: International Organization for Migration.

Lindquist, J. (2010). Images and evidence: Human trafficking, auditing, and the production of illicit markets in southeast Asia and beyond. *Public Culture, 22*(2), 223–236.
Mary, N. L. (2008). *Social work in a sustainable world.* Chicago, IL: Lyceum Books, Inc.
Mercy, J. A., Butchart, A., Farrington, D., & Cerdá, M. (2002). *Youth violence. World Report on Violence and Health* (pp. 23–56). Geneva: World Health Organization.
National Academies of Sciences, Engineering, and Medicine. (2017). *Community violence as a population health issue: Proceedings of a workshop.* Washington, DC: The National Academies Press. Retrieved from https://doi.org/10.17226/23661
National Association of Social Workers. (2008). *Practice. Peace and Social Justice.* Retrieved from www.naswdc.org/practice/intl/issues/peace.asp
Nickson, A., Dunstan, J., Esperanza, D., & Barker, S. (2011). Indigenous practice approaches to women, violence, and healing using community development: A partnership between indigenous and non indigenous workers. *Australian Social Work, 64*(1), 84–95.
Nsonwu, M.B., Busch-Armendariz, N.B., & Cook Heffron, L. (2014). Human Trafficking. In L. Cousins (Ed.), *The Encyclopedia of Human Services and Diversity.* Thousand Oaks, California: Sage. doi:http://dxdoi.org/10.4135/9781483346663.n287
Nsonwu, M. B., Welch-Brewer, C., Heffron, L. C., Lemke, M., Busch-Armendariz, N., Sulley, C., . . . Li, J. (2015). Development and validation of an instrument to assess social work students' perceptions, knowledge, and attitudes about human trafficking questionnaire PKA-HTQ: An exploratory study. *Research on Social Work Practice*, 1–11. Retrieved from https://doi.org/10.1177/1049731515578537
Pickard, H. (2015). Self-harm as violence: When victim and perpetrator are one. In *Women and violence: The agency of victims and perpetrators* (pp. 71–90). London: Palgrave Macmillan.
Pierce, A. (2012). Vulnerability to sex trafficking intervention strategies. *American Indian and Alaska Native Mental Health Research, 19*, 37–56.
Potocky, M. (2010). Social work practice with victims of transnational human trafficking. In N. Junko Negi & R. Furman (Eds.), *Transnational social work practice* (pp. 111–123). New York, NY: Columbia University Press.
Rafferty, Y. (2013). Child trafficking and commercial sexual exploitation: A review of promising prevention policies and programs. *American Journal of Orthopsychiatry, 83*, 559–575. Retrieved from https://doi.org/10.1111/ajop.12056
Reilly, J., Muldoon, O. T., & Byrne, C. (2004). Young men as victims and perpetrators of violence in Northern Ireland: A qualitative analysis. *Journal of Social Issues, 60*(3), 469–484.
Rijken, C. (2009). A human rights based approach to trafficking in human beings. *Security and Human Rights, 3*, 212–222.
Roby, J. L. (2005). Women and children in the global sex trade: Toward more effective policy. *International Social Work, 48*(2), 136–147. Retrieved from https://doi.org/10.1177/0020872805050206
Ross-Sheriff, F. (2007). Globalization as a women's issue revisited. *Affilia, 22*(2), 133–137. Retrieved from https://doi.org/10.1177/0886109907302582
Ross-Sheriff, F. (2011). Global migration and gender. *Affilia, 26*(3), 233–238. Retrieved from https://doi.org/10.1177/0886109911417692
Saleebey, D. (1996). The strengths perspective in social work practice: Extensions and cautions. *Social Work, 41*(3), 296–305.
Schwarz, C., Unruh, E., Cronin, K., Evans-Simpson, S., Britton, H., & Ramaswamy, M. (2016). human trafficking identification and service provision in the medical and social service sectors. *Health and Human Rights, 18*(1), 181–192.
Sigmon, J. N. (2008). Combating modern-day slavery: Issues in identifying and assisting victims of human trafficking worldwide. *Victims & Offenders, 3*(2–3), 245–257.
Siporin, M. (1980). Ecological systems theory in social work. *Journal of Sociology and Social Welfare,* 7(4), 507–532.
United Nations. (1948). *United nations universal declaration of human rights.* New York, NY: Author. Retrieved from www.un.org/en/universal-declaration-human-rights/
Vakharia, S. P., & Little, J. (2017). Starting where the client is: Harm reduction guidelines for clinical social work practice. *Clinical Social Work Journal, 45*(1), 65–76.
Van Impe, K. (2000). People for sale: The need for a multidisciplinary approach towards human trafficking. *International Migration, 38*, 113–191.

Vijeyarasa, R. (2013). Stigma, stereotypes and Brazilian soap operas: Road-blocks to ending human trafficking in Vietnam, Ghana and Ukraine. *Gender, Place & Culture, 20*(8), 1015–1032.
Walker, K. (2013). *Ending the commercial sexual exploitation of children: A call for multi-system collaboration in California*. California Child Welfare Council. https://www.chhs.ca.gov/wp-content/uploads/2017/06/Committees/California-Child-Welfare-Council/Council-Information-Reports/Ending-CSEC-A-Call-for-Multi-System-Collaboration-in-CA-February-2013.pdf
Wirsing, K. E. (2012). Outreach, collaboration and services to survivors of human trafficking: The salvation army STOP-IT program's work in Chicago, Illinois. *Social Work & Christianity, 39*(4), 466–480.

14

HOW TO WORK ACROSS MULTIPLE SECTORS TO RESPOND TO HUMAN TRAFFICKING

Values, leadership, alliances, and program models

Celia Williamson and Dominique Roe-Sepowitz

Abstract

This chapter focuses on how to work across multiple sectors to effectively respond to human trafficking. Using an anti-trafficking coalition as the vehicle for collaboration, we first focus on the values and ethics needed to work with a vulnerable and victimized population. Next, we discuss how to set the coalition on the right course by providing solid leadership, focusing on the mission, working to establish shared ownership, and ensuring that leadership grows with its coalition. Inclusivity breeds success. We emphasize the need for coalition members that are ethnically, professionally, and experientially diverse and that allow its members to contribute from various perspectives, experiences, and knowledge bases. Critical to the chapter is the discussion regarding the need for transparent communication from the leadership to the membership and vice versa (vertical communication) and across membership (horizontal communication), as well as clear logistical (where, when, and how often to meet) and structural components (bylaws and a strategic plan). The chapter delves into various pitfalls and barriers that impede the success of an anti-trafficking coalition. Two successful models of a multi-sector response to human trafficking are presented.

Learning Objectives

At the end of the chapter, readers will be able to:

1. Provide components needed to effectively respond to human trafficking using a multi-sector approach;
2. Describe the values, knowledge, and skills necessary for a successful multi-sector anti-trafficking response that avoids common pitfalls and barriers; and
3. Present an example of two successful multi-sector anti-trafficking programs.

Key Terms: coalition; comprehensive services model; horizontal versus vertical communication; incentivized program; Office of Victims of Crime (OVC); PATH Model; trauma-informed care; victim versus survivor versus thriver.

Introduction

The U.S. government calls on advocates to rescue and restore victims of human trafficking. While "rescue" falls largely under the purview of criminal justice, "restoration" requires a long-term, multi-sector approach that involves diverse providers. We define multiple sectors as social service, healthcare, and criminal justice entities along with faith-based communities, universities, and survivors, among other groups. Because human trafficking consists of an effective complex web of unscrupulous players and networks, it requires a community response that is consistent, diverse in type, and unified in mission. Service providers should be guided by a set of values, led by effective leaders, who engage in the implementation of comprehensive, coordinated, transparent, data-driven, and accountable services. We offer this chapter based on the authors' combined 38 years (to date) of anti-trafficking work. As such, many of our suggestions are based on our shared experience as organizers, direct service providers, and researchers. This chapter focuses on what we consider to be the guiding values anti-trafficking providers should have, leadership skills of anti-trafficking champions, and those elements of effective coalitions that serve as the foundation for a successful community-wide response. In addition, we offer two models, the Phoenix, Arizona, 1st Step Drop-In Model of effective engagement and linkage, and the PATH Model of a data-driven, transparent, and accountable continuum of care model in Toledo, Ohio, as examples of effective interventions with trafficking victims and survivors.

To offer more effective responses, traditional helping organizations will be required to alter their practices to meet the needs of human trafficking victims and those at risk. Perhaps nowhere is this most evident than in the main institutions where victims are likely to intersect. It is no surprise that in many communities around the U.S. social service organizations would prefer to continue to offer a generalized menu of services to a population of trafficking victims that have highly specialized needs. A traditional counseling and mental health program may provide weekly counseling, typically lasting an hour, or may facilitate a youth group that consists of two hours of focused weekly programming. In turn, traffickers offer services 24 hours a day, seven days a week to vulnerable youth, which often includes meeting a young person's basic living and emotional needs. In only offering traditional intervention services, advocates are outmatched by their competition. Healthcare communities may interact with victims as they are treating and triaging them in their emergency rooms and clinics. Unaware of their trafficking status, they may patch them up and send them back into their dangerous and underground lives. The criminal justice system may be continuing to arrest and hold youth victims accountable for adult perpetrated crimes and treat foreign victims as illegals. The criminal justice system also gives access to new traffickers who view them online on arrest websites and recruit them directly from jails and prisons. Various child welfare systems may consider adolescent commercial sex to be a juvenile justice issue instead of a child abuse issue, the ramifications of which criminalize youth victims. Overall, both a change in service provision as well as a paradigm shift in thinking (see Bravo, Chapter 1, this volume) must occur to adequately respond to human trafficking and/or the prevention of trafficking.

Community-wide involvement in anti-trafficking efforts can create positive and lasting change as well as build an awareness of needed services instead of continued service gaps and duplications. Using the connections of strong community collaborations and alliances allows for effective prevention and intervention methods to be implemented. An African saying summarizes this perspective, "If you want to go quickly, go alone. If you want to go far, go together" (Damanaki, 2016). The ability to adequately address the fourth "P" of what the U.S. Department of State (n.d.) refers to as "prevention," "protection," "prosecution," and "partnership" is the focus of this chapter. An effective multi-sector approach enhances the legitimacy of the cause, increases access to resources, and improves community relations overall (Whitley, 2003).

Guiding values for serving victims of human trafficking

It should be noted that the authors of this chapter are social workers. Therefore, we approach this issue from a social work perspective. As such there are guiding principles and values we use to work with human trafficking victims and the community. The Office of Victims of Crime (OVC) outlines the core ethical principles of which we espouse. First, the recognition and respect for both clients' and collaborators' rights and dignity (Office of Victims of Crime, n.d.). This is in line with a social worker's belief in the inherent dignity and worth of every person, as well as a client's right to self-determination (National Association of Social Workers [NASW, 2017] Code of Ethics, n.d.). Social workers see clients as "the experts in their lives and over their own lives" and therefore professional helpers, whether they be social workers, counselors, peer-supporters, or para-professionals, must respect and honor that inherent autonomy (Office of Victims of Crime, n.d.). Clients also have the right to their own privacy and for their provider to hold all information as confidential as legally and ethically possible (Office of Victims of Crime, n.d.; NASW Code of Ethics, n.d.). For a discussion on when information can no longer be held in confidence, please see the NASW Code of Ethics (for a discussion of social worker training, see Meshelemiah, Chapter 12, this volume).

It is incumbent upon each provider or professional helper to make themselves aware of power differentials, racial/ethnic differences, gender identity, class differences, immigration status, and religious differences, to name a few. In acknowledging this awareness, helpers must work on their own biases, and be sensitive to the nature of the relationship they have with a client who is or was a victim of human trafficking. In addition, providers should be sensitive to the barriers clients face when interfacing with organizations and should work to advocate for clients and empower them to successfully intervene on their own behalf whenever possible (Office of Victims of Crime, n.d.).

Further, providers that work with victims of trafficking should recognize their limitations and act within their level of competence. They should regularly seek out training to improve their knowledge and skills and mentor personal wellness and self-care to their clients (Office of Victims of Crime, n.d.). Providers working with victims of trafficking should act with integrity and have genuine concern for the welfare of others. They should explore and become aware of their biases, opinions, and experiences regarding human trafficking. Finally, advocates should assume professional, legal, and social responsibility and apply their knowledge to fight injustice as well as support policies that are in the best interest of victims and communities (Office of Victims of Crime, n.d.)

Effective leadership for anti-trafficking coalitions

What, if any, anti-trafficking coalitions exist in your community or state?

In addition to the guiding values needed to serve clients, possessing specific principles regarding leadership for building and/or facilitating coalitions is important. The establishment of formal anti-trafficking networks typically represent a diverse array of occupations and backgrounds. These entities may be large or small and operate as a state, region, county, or city-wide collaboration. They may involve government as well as non-governmental members. Throughout this chapter we refer to these networks as coalitions, although they may be known as task forces, commissions, or collaborations. Working with multiple sectors requires that an advocate assume the role of coalition leader(s). Coalition leaders bring people together to fight a common cause. Being an effective coalition leader requires that the leader be a person that people want to follow. Because people are typically self-interested or motivated by the mission of their particular agency, a good coalition leader finds common interests across people and connects their organization to human trafficking in ways that furthers their mission and/or even their particular career (Office of Victims of Crime, n.d.).

Leaders in the movement are often those that not only bring human trafficking awareness to the community via an anti-trafficking coalition, but who use the coalition as a mechanism to provide coordinated community-wide responses. Human trafficking advocates assuming the role of leader can emerge from anywhere. Leaders may come from the faith-based community, universities, from sex workers and trafficking survivors, government entities, or the front lines of direct service work. No matter from where a leader emerges, we believe the most effective leaders share common attributes. Those common attributes are outlined below.

Productive leadership

Community organizers start with a vision and a passion. They enable people with a common interest to come together to work on a common cause. Effective leaders work with their collaborators to identify needs and work in concert to move their coalition agendas forward.

However, not all collaborators are productive. If an inordinate amount of processing occurs at coalition meetings, then very little actual activity will move forward. This could be because: critically important people in power are not a part of the coalition, organizations or individuals come to the table with hidden agendas that usurp the meeting, or there is historical conflict among the coalition members. The bottom line is the leadership must identify the barriers that inhibit the coalition towards action, establish a shared desire, and harness the power to move the coalition forward, because action is the hallmark of productive leadership.

Effective leaders stay focused on the mission

Effective leaders are individuals with personalities that are able to both build relationships and motivate a diverse set of people with divergent personalities. Leaders are focused on the mission in almost everything they do. When confronted with tasks, the effective leader first asks themselves if what they do, or agree to do, will advance the mission. Successful leaders work across the aisles of ideology or purpose to determine ways that others can contribute. They recognize, appreciate, and use agreed-upon strategies to advance the mission. In times of conflict, they determine the value and importance of the issue, the players, and how the conflict will affect the mission, and then act accordingly. Effective leaders choose conflict for specific purposes to advance the mission. They worry less about their ego and more about the mission. They work with people they don't like or don't agree with on all issues if it serves the mission. They put their fear, shyness, ego, and emotion second to the mission. Leaders work to have all collaborator voices heard.

Effective leaders create shared ownership

In the beginning of any effort, leaders have to take ownership and be responsible for growing a coalition and then stabilizing it. The leaders develop the agenda and engage in the heavy lifting, while orienting, educating, and motivating others to believe in the cause. Once the coalition is stable enough, it is the leaders' job to grow additional leaders. This may be done by creating committees or otherwise passing responsibilities to various leaders that have agreed to take ownership of various components of the coalition. The original leader(s), if needed, may assist and mentor new leaders to learn to move agenda items forward. However, when new leaders have taken competent hold of their various positions, it's time for the progenitor(s) to step back, trust, and let go of the reins. In fact, it could be argued that it is a necessary process that allows coalitions to thrive when the leader(s) allow true and genuine ownership of the coalition to belong to the membership.

Leaders have limitations in that they don't always have the answers or know the path to take, but wise leaders know enough to get the individuals with the right knowledge and skills into the room and at the decision table. Leaders recognize, validate, and appreciate what members bring to the coalition. They understand that others must take ownership in order to buy-in to the cause for the multi-sector approach to be successful. Leaders reward others, highlight them, and lift them up for the job they did, are set to do, or have agreed to do.

What type of knowledge and skills are needed on your coalition?

However, in some coalitions the initial champions continue to run the meeting, even after potential community leaders have tried to step up and assume responsibility for various components or tasks. This is a critical juncture in the coalition's trajectory, as members that want to be more involved will not continue to come to meetings to watch a few people do the work. Each member of the coalition will need to feel included and necessary to sustain their interest and involvement.

Some possible problems that exist with coalitions include that over time the coalition may become populated with members ordered by their agency to participate or motivated to attend by their career goals. These members may not be genuinely invested. Other potential issues arise when leadership is not passed on clearly. Some coalitions do attempt to transition leadership, but this is a façade as the new leadership becomes a puppet for the original leadership. In these cases, some of the members will continue to reach out to the original leadership, bypass the new leader(s), and stifle the change.

Effective leaders grow with the coalition or organization

Much like people, organizations are born, grow, and die (Daft, 2013). Obtaining the right leader at the right time is critical. For instance, grassroots organizers may be great when a coalition or organization is just starting. They are bold, sometimes fearless, well-known and trusted, and may be well suited for the beginning role of leadership within a coalition. Grassroots organizers have skills that are suitable for organizing a unified voice and developing and coaxing a shared vision among coalition partners. Grassroots organizers have skills that are suitable for the time, however as the coalition grows, if the organizer is not growing in leadership skills alongside the coalition they will soon become ill-suited to serve the needs of the coalition.

This is especially true for coalition leadership that comes from the direct service organizations that work with human trafficking victims. When a grassroots organization grows and becomes more complex and/or has significantly more funding, leaders must be able to take on the responsibilities of developing and adhering to policies and procedures, designing reporting mechanisms, and protecting the coalition or organization against liability. A leader skilled in grassroots advocacy may be left behind by an ever-growing and complex organization.

Effective elements of anti-trafficking coalitions

We spend a considerable amount of time devoted to presenting the formal structure of a coalition as we regard a coalition as the best mechanism through which to provide a multi-sector approach that is coordinated, collaborative, and has the best opportunity to provide effective services to clients that have been victims of human trafficking.

What type of diverse members should you seek out that would enrich your coalition?

Anti-trafficking focused coalitions are best if they use a diverse community to achieve several objectives, including but not limited to, advocating for relevant laws and institutional policies, assisting agencies to understand, identify, and report trafficking, develop response protocols, engage in prevention, enable agencies to collaborate for the benefit of victims, bring perpetrators to justice, and prevent further victimization of individuals. The most inclusive coalitions ensure that there is an equitable and diverse membership and no one member is more important than another. Each member has a vote and can take ownership within the collective body and make an impact on the human trafficking in the area of their coalition.

Human trafficking–focused ideas may be brought forward by coalition members and decided upon to ensure that the majority of members agree with the proposals, opportunities, or strategic plan ("Consensus Building," 1998). When there is a wider array of groups, there is an increased abundance of ideas, resources, and solutions to be shared. This structured and inclusive approach centralizes all of the members' voices, energies, and resources into one body (Whitley, 2003).

The members most critical to an anti-trafficking coalition are criminal justice professionals including law enforcement and prosecutors, survivors and survivor-led programs, social service providers, healthcare professionals, sex workers, policy makers, education professionals, university professors and students, researchers/evaluators, municipal personnel, members of the private sector, ethnic-focused organizations, faith-based communities, advocacy groups, and private citizens. We discuss each in more detail below.

Criminal justice professionals such as law enforcement agents (i.e. police, probation, juvenile corrections, and prosecutors), court officials, and other members of the criminal justice field have an important role as members of the coalition. These members seek to legally assist victims and hold perpetrators accountable. They are often the point of first contact for victims and their involvement in actions by the community for awareness building, prevention, and connecting victims to services is critical.

Survivors and survivor-led groups are critical to combating human trafficking. These individuals and groups should be recruited and honored for what they bring in serving the mission. They serve as the living embodiment of the mission of collaboration groups. Further survivors bring an authenticity, lived experience, knowledge, and skills needed to move the mission forward. In some cases, all of the members of the coalition are paid by their jobs to attend while the survivor(s) volunteers their time. Consider this when assigning tasks or seeking funding to support the group's activities.

As important as criminal justice representatives and survivors are to the cause, social service providers and agencies, especially those that work directly with human trafficking victims or who address the risk factors associated with trafficking are essential. Both front-line workers, advocates, and administrators play a vital role in the developing awareness, and the prevention or restoration of individuals victimized by trafficking. Receiving participation from key social service representatives can significantly improve the identification and recovery process for trafficked individuals and the prevention of trafficking of high-risk and vulnerable individuals.

Of equal importance are healthcare professionals. By being present on coalitions, they learn to identify, treat, and report human trafficking victims to the appropriate places (e.g. child welfare, law enforcement) as well as meet the comprehensive healthcare needs of victims and those at risk without re-victimization.

Sex workers who may or may not have been victimized add critical value as they bring the passion, lived experience, and knowledge and skills that are highly valued. Attention to diverse sex workers (LGBT, race/ethnicity, age) adds to the resources and skill sets available to contribute to the mission.

Policymakers create policies that affect the lives of trafficking victims and bring perpetrators to justice. Involvement of local, state, and/or federal lawmakers or municipal staff on the coalition can be a valuable asset that may serve mutually beneficial goals. They are able to see and learn about the needs of the community and in turn, the coalition is able to have a collective political voice.

Education professionals who work with the K-12 population should be recruited because of the impact and influence they have on minors. Teachers and school administrators have the unique opportunity to potentially be the first group of people to introduce age-appropriate anti-trafficking messages to minors. They may also serve to identify at-risk youth.

University professors, researchers, and students can be a valuable resource to coalitions. Coalition members looking to recruit professors might first appeal to "assistant" professors, who most often are looking for meaningful projects in which they can be of service to the community, as well as publish articles. Professors bring the ability to conduct research and lend the skills related to their particular disciplines. They can bring students to the table to complete independent studies, internships, and/or service learning projects, all for the benefit of the coalition. Various student groups can play an important role in a coalition as they bring together motivated and enthusiastic students that can take on and accomplish salient and important tasks for a coalition.

Members of the faith community should be recruited for involvement in anti-human trafficking coalitions. The faith community can be a strong partner regarding dissemination of prevention and identification materials, the collection of needed items for victim services, and to create community action for a purpose. The involvement of faith-diverse groups in the coalition will positively add to the scope and capacity of the group.

Members of the private sector can serve key roles as members of coalitions. Entrepreneurs, union leaders, tourism leaders, and other members of the community are essential to combating both sex and labor trafficking. Being able to identify those businesses that take a stand against labor trafficking can encourage other companies to improve their labor practices. Banks, agriculture, hotels, restaurants, beauty and nail salons, and the trucking industry, among others, may be included on the coalition. As each of these industries become more aware of the existing problem, the more likely these issues can be spotted, reported, and rectified. Having representatives from these communities on the coalition is vital to alerting the proper authorities and ending the cycle of human trafficking.

What process can be used to equip the coalition with members that will work hard, bring wealth of resources, as well as the wisdom and expertise needed to serve the mission?

Coalitions should not be limited to the groups identified above. Members of other community groups should be sought out and included on the coalition. When contemplating new members, consider those that bring work, wealth, or wisdom to the coalition. Those that bring "work" are those that are known to work hard and complete tasks successfully. Potential members that bring "wealth" to the coalition may bring financial wealth, but alternatively they may bring the ability to open doors, remove barriers, or make critical connections that benefit the coalition. Those that bring wisdom bring special skills needed by the coalition such as accounting, legal advice, and more (Johnson, n.d.).

Ethnic-focused organizations that serve various minority groups should be prioritized, sought after, and successfully recruited. With an extensive history of abuse, oppression, and discrimination experienced by many ethnic groups in the United States, knowledge, sensitivity, and trust is needed to effectively collaborate. Organizations that work with historically oppressed populations are knowledgeable and sensitive. They have spent time building the trust of those they serve. Collaborating on effective and trustworthy strategies to educate and develop protocols so that members of these communities can safely report suspected trafficking without risk of deportation or retaliation will need to be addressed. This effort may first require that the coalition build trust with these critical organizations and that may depend greatly on who is approaching them and their current relationship with various existing members of the coalition.

Being inclusive and recruiting members from various non-governmental and governmental entities, advocacy groups, and private citizens that have a passion to help allows the coalition to be diverse and take ownership of the issue. The result is an extended reach into professional and lay communities, which brings opportunities to reach wider audiences. Recruiting professionals and para-professionals may require that the coalition leadership frame anti-trafficking work to be one of the critical social justice issues of our lifetime and emphasize the value their participation brings to the issue. The coalition leadership should assist each professional to recall the reasons they went into their various helping fields, the difference they wanted to make, what they hoped to accomplish, and what they would like to leave as their legacy. Helping the vulnerable to live free and have the opportunity to achieve the American Dream is often at the heart of helping professionals and indeed most American citizens.

Where to begin

Starting and maintaining a human trafficking coalition requires an enthusiastic community and meticulous organization. In building a coalition, providing the proper organizational structure is the foundation for a well-run and successful operation. There are useful resources, provided by groups such as Coalitions Work (2007), that founding members should review to understand how to specifically form a coalition.

In general, the coalition should have written bylaws and structured meetings. Every member should have the opportunity to voice their opinions and ideas (Whitley, 2003). Coalition committees may be formed to delegate the workload and provide the due diligence necessary to conduct effective business. These committees need to have diverse membership.

Coalitions should also have a strategic plan. The individual(s) who are delegated the task of strategic planning should be knowledgeable about the steps needed to complete a strategic plan. There are various ways to engage in strategic planning and the coalition should choose a method with which the founding members are comfortable. One simple approach to strategic planning is to (1) determine the current number of active members; (2) identify what is important to the coalition; (3) clearly define what the coalition expects to accomplish; (4) assign accountability to members or committees in order to meet expectations; and (5) review the plan on a consistent basis (Aileron, 2011). The strategic plan should include expectations and timelines that will guide the completion of the work.

Coalitions should develop a set of rules to establish membership. Membership, meetings, and minutes should be available to the membership, and unless sensitive information is discussed, to the community at large.

In establishing the meeting time and place, the leadership should choose a day and time that maximizes the capacity for as many potential members to attend as possible. Choosing the location for regular coalition meetings is critical in that the meeting location sets the tone for the coalition. For example, having meetings in a church seems innocent enough, but may provide an unspoken and subliminal message to others that may seem welcoming to some but not to others. Hosting meetings at a university may communicate an academic vibe that may be perceived by some as respectful of those with degrees and less honoring of those without degrees. It may set the tone that we are interested in focusing our work on activities recognized by universities, such as research and rationale, to the exclusion of practice and passion. We suggest the coalition leadership be cognizant of the tone they set and choose a location that conveys the most neutral message and increases the perception of being a welcoming place to all.

Once a location, time, and day has been established, the coalition leadership should provide easy access for potential members to find out when and where each meeting will take place. This information may be disseminated through social media and formal invites, as well as the coalition's website. Meetings should reoccur in the same location, on the same day, and at the same time. Consistency allows busy members to plan their schedule around the meeting thereby increasing attendance.

Meetings should begin and end on time, be organized, and stay on task. The most effective way to accomplish this is by having an agenda, a facilitator, and minutes distributed to members after meetings and before the next meeting (Whitley, 2003). There should also be written notes on who will be following up on each specific agenda item mentioned at the coalition meeting. Accountability is crucial to ensuring the success of a coalition.

The next step is to create communication protocols. A clear line of communication where all coalition and community members can locate and distribute information is a critical step to having a high functioning coalition (Whitley, 2003). We suggest the use of an online service that allows information to be disseminated to members and/or stored for member access.

Emphasis should be placed on publicity, especially when the coalition is in its beginning stages. There should be an outline of the coalition's mission, as well as a clear message of the goals the coalition expects to accomplish. The coalition may opt to have a functional website, as well as active social media accounts. Community members outside of the coalition should be encouraged to get involved in the coalition and each meeting or event in which the coalition is involved should be advertised (Whitley, 2003).

All of the logistical and structural components of a coalition will not mean much until all members are knowledgeable about all forms of human trafficking, including labor and sex trafficking as well as domestic and foreign victims. Founding members should seek out and obtain a comprehensive education of human trafficking and then work to ensure other members receive the same.

Finally, the coalition should work to achieve maximum vertical and horizontal communication. Vertical communication traditionally means communicating within the same organization from the top to the bottom. In this case, it also may mean communicating with your state level anti-trafficking coalition, if one exists; as well as local, county, state, and federal offices and policy makers. Horizontal communication is communication between separate coalitions in different communities. The hope with horizontal communication is that there can be a meeting of the minds, where ideas can be shared and implemented across communities. Having clear vertical and horizontal communication within and between coalitions can be beneficial to the implementation of consistent practices and policies throughout the state.

Barriers to effective interventions with human trafficking victims

Anti-human trafficking coalitions should work from a victim-centered viewpoint. While this may involve including the voices of survivors, it must also include recognizing the rights of the victims to determine their involvement in their recovery and the actions against their traffickers (refer to Torres, Nsonwu, Cook Heffron, and Busch-Armendariz, Chapter 13, this volume). Victim-centered work with trafficking victims includes the commitment to inform victims of all actions on their behalf, allowing the decision to participate in the court actions against their perpetrator(s) to be theirs, and to support their unique pathways out of the trafficking situation. Possessing the appropriate values, obtaining suitable leaders, and growing a thriving coalition sets the stage for the important work ahead; the task of enabling the multi-sector coalition to benefit victims of human trafficking. Even with these components successfully in place, barriers may still exist. It behooves us to understand those elements that may render attempts unsuccessful. Those barriers include making the mistake of treating all victims of human trafficking the same, having no continuum of care plan in place, no identified model of intervention, not addressing the trauma victims face, having great ideas but access to a few clients, too much awareness raising and not enough direct client intervention, and a lack of a coordinated, transparent, and accountable system of care.

Formal one-size-fits-all approaches to assist victims

Victim experiences are diverse; therefore, services should not be neatly packaged in a one-size-fits-all response. Every client will not need housing or substance abuse treatment. Not only might the type of services needed be different, but how a service should be provided may be different. For instance, substance abuse treatment groups may serve those clients with a substance abuse disorder, but one of the hallmarks of treatment is to share the past, and through sharing, as well as learning, processing, reflecting, and growing, recovery is possible. However, if a victim is in a group with others that have not been victimized through a human trafficking situation, they are not likely to share those aspects of their victimization. Deciding not to share and work through such traumatic events may threaten sobriety. Therefore, it may be most appropriate to offer some group experiences with other victims of trafficking, or at minimum, victims of other crimes.

Lack of a continuum of care plan

The goal of any intervention with victims of trafficking is to assist in moving them from victim to survivor with improved well-being. Yet, the literature remains stagnant in identifying the needs of victims and the needs of survivors along the domains of housing, legal services, mental health and more (U.S. Department of Health & Human Services, 2008; Potocky, 2010; National Sexual Violence Resource Center & Pennsylvania Coalition Against Rape, 2012). In addition, there is little understanding or agreement on the characteristics or milestones of a survivor as opposed to a victim. As a result, practitioners may be largely unable to identify when/if their client moved from being a victim to being a survivor. Of those that do document movement from victim to survivor, many service providers may close the case once a victim becomes a survivor. Agencies should assist in helping victims become thrivers, defined as a move beyond survivorship to economic empowerment and full integration back into conventional society. Long-term support is an important component of long-term recovery.

No identified model of practice: informal organic approaches

Informal organic approaches seem to consciously strike back at the formal system. In an attempt not to apply the same system of service to everyone, these programs offer organic methods that appear to boil down to what feels right. The problem is these organizations are so loosely run, that no one can explain if or when a victim became a survivor and beyond and the markers that identify movement. Victims may enjoy the nonjudgmental and trusting relationship built in these grassroots, organic-styled organizations, but the helping professional has difficulty objectively identifying outcomes in a measurable manner. Programs such as these are likely living a very sparse existence with little funding. Some may be very effective, but if it's not measurable, it's often not fundable. These types of programs are wonderful at building relationships with clients, but have difficulty scaling up to help a larger number of victims over the long term, which is what is needed for human trafficking victims. Further these types of programs may be at risk once their donors realize they cannot demonstrate sufficient outcomes.

Unrecognized or ill-treated trauma

It's important for interveners to recognize that almost all victims of human trafficking have suffered some form of trauma, whether it be physical, mental, or emotional and thus need some form of trauma treatment (Clawson, Salomone, & Goldblatt-Grace, 2008). Trauma from trafficking experiences can affect physical, emotional, and mental health. In fact, trauma may affect every part of one's being including cognition, behavior, and affect (National Child Traumatic Stress Network, n.d.).

What are the differences between trauma treatment and mental health counseling?

Providing trauma informed care means adopting the understanding that victims have experienced trauma and may be re-traumatized in the agencies where they seek help (see Torres et al., Chapter 13, this volume). Agencies that are trauma informed and work to increase human trafficking victims' feelings of safety, are driven by compassion and responsiveness, and avoid coercive practices to build resiliency and empowerment in clients receiving services. Trauma-focused treatments are specific therapeutic modalities used to address the trauma clients have experienced (Trauma Informed Care, 2013). Many providers assume that attending counseling is indeed the road to psychological recovery, and while that is true for many with a mental health issue, victims that attend mental health treatment that does not involve an effective trauma treatment modality may not reap the benefits of mental health counseling, and in fact may decide that mental health counseling is not something that works for them. Therefore, it is recommended that victims engage trauma treatment counselors as opposed to obtaining general mental health counseling.

Great ideas, few clients

Exceptional, well-thought-out models for assessment and intervention may exist, but without clients it's just a great plan. Human trafficking victims rarely fit into a mold of "perfect client" and due to exposures to traumatic experiences and the rigidity of most trafficking experiences, are often resistant to following exact pathways. Potential interventions may consist of mind maps and complex treatment plans, but there is often a failure to execute the plan because of a lack of an adequate number of clients that meet the advanced criteria of the programs. When this happens, it may be because there are many great minds at the planning table, but a lack of the recognition and importance of the voices direct service providers, survivors of sex and/or labor trafficking, and grassroots programs that may have been engaging this population.

Imbalance between awareness raising and direct service intervention

Communities that have thriving coalitions but focus on awareness building may soon find themselves with an abundance of victims, in absence of a coordinated response to effectively serve them. These coalitions lack infrastructure to care for the victims they teach the community to identify.

Lack of coordinated, transparent, and accountable system of care

Identifying and serving victims requires a multi-sector, coordinated approach. However, instead of coordinating programs based on what is needed, some programs use what is available in the agency or interact only with a few choice agencies that they already have an established relationship. Accompanying a coordinated system of care should be a data-driven process of service delivery. This will illuminate what is working and not working in terms of movement toward healing and well-being. Data-driven work makes successes clear, exposes barriers, and makes outcomes evident. It also increases accountability to clients, funders, and the community.

Emerging models of human trafficking practice

Below we present three models of practice that address the issues above. They are transparent, accountable, data-driven, and lead to effective recruitment, identification, and care for victims of human trafficking. We begin with the Comprehensive Services Model (CSM) as it provides some standards of care to which all providers should adhere. This is followed by the PATH Model which serves as a pathway to providing comprehensive services to human trafficking victims for coalitions. The Phoenix 1st Step Model is then presented as an innovative action of a human trafficking coalition to provide the collective services directly to human trafficking victims.

Comprehensive services model

The Office of Victims of Crime offers the Comprehensive Services Model as an example of how to work with victims of all forms of crimes, including human trafficking. Their model provides three standards of care, which provides agencies and advocates with a guide consisting of program standards, competency standards, and ethical standards each should strive to meet. Each standard is then organized into five separate sections to provide detailed information on how to identify the scope of services, coordinate with the community, provide direct services, protect privacy, confidentiality, data security, and assistive technology, and effectively administrate and evaluate the program. While what the CSM provides is indeed comprehensive in scope, it still falls short in that it lacks acknowledgement of the need for a healing focused continuum of care toward recovery. The OVC Model doesn't provide instruction, standards of care, or best practices that promote movement toward healing, or indictors such as common milestones to identify emotional, mental, or physical healing and growth.

However, critical components of the CSM include the need to provide case management services, which is a collaborative process between the client, case manager, and other providers to assess, plan, and facilitate care coordination, evaluation, and advocacy to meet a client's comprehensive needs (Case Management Society of America, n.d.).

An Individualized Service Plan (ISP) is another important component. ISPs consist of a written and detailed plan of the supports, activities, and resources required for the individual or family to achieve his/her/their goals. The Individualized Service Plan articulates decisions and agreements made between clients and provider(s).

A Coordinated System of Care provides for certain needs and involves a knowledgeable and responsive community that offers a broad array of flexible and responsive services at multiple levels that are culturally and linguistically competent (Families Helping Families, n.d.). Providing wraparound services is a process that involves communication among a client's direct service providers. It is an efficient way to develop and implement an individualized service plan and to coordinate and manage services for the benefit of clients (National Wraparound Initiative, n.d.).

Partners Against Trafficking in Humans (PATH)

The Toledo project, Partners Against Trafficking in Humans (PATH), incorporates all elements of the Comprehensive Services Model as well as a project called the Pathways Model. The Pathways Model is a project in Toledo that is used to improve the birth outcomes of low-income, high-risk, African American babies by addressing low birth weight. When implemented, the model significantly improved the birth outcomes of high-risk women in Toledo (Hospital Council of Northwest Ohio, 2016). In merging the CSM, Pathways Model, and two additional elements, The PATH Model was born. Our eight-element framework is depicted in Figure 14.1.

The overall goal of the PATH Model is to enhance the quality and quantity of services available to assist all victims of human trafficking in achieving their goals in a documented, data driven, evidenced-informed manner that moves victims to survivors and survivors to thrivers. The focus is on increasing autonomy, self-sufficiency, and feelings of safety and well-being. The basic premise of the PATH Model is to meet clients where they are, assess client needs, and walk the pathways with clients to link them with targeted services and resources that increase healing

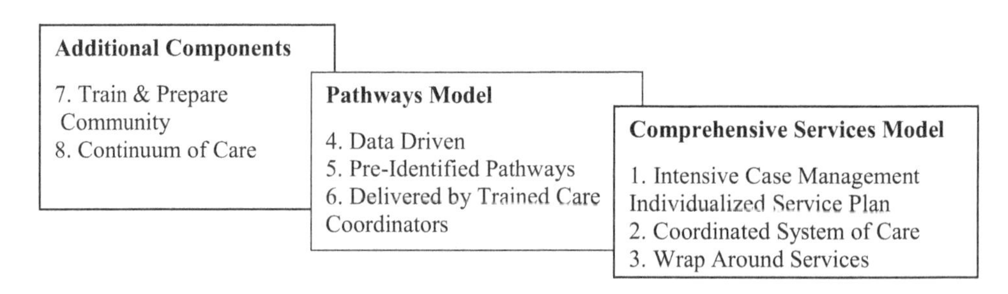

Figure 14.1 Eight elements of the PATH Model

and well-being. In short, communities work to implement the PATH Model using the following steps:

Step 1: Develop an active coalition populated with social service, healthcare, and criminal justice professionals along with survivors, the faith-based community, university members and others.

Step 2: Become trained in implementing PATH and develop agency connections to pathways that are specific to the community.

Step 3: Train professionals in human trafficking, trauma-informed care, and the PATH Model and provide each the designation of being PATH Approved.

Step 4: Educate the general public to increase their ability to identify and report trafficked clients.

Step 5: Identify agencies that can provide care coordinators and train them to assess and intervene with clients.

Step 6: Set up Core Clusters and a Leadership Committee as a part of the coalition

Step 7: Produce high quality Individualized Service Plans and services that address the individualized needs of trafficking victims, survivors, and thrivers.

Step 8: Document and identify barriers (What's not working) and strengths (What is working) of services and service delivery for trafficked clients using a data-driven process of evaluation and feedback response.

Step 9: Through continued data analysis and feedback, identify trajectories of continuums of care for victims to move to survivors and survivors to move to thrivers.

Definitions

Before we discuss PATH in detail, we offer definitions of victims, survivors, and thrivers. Conceptual definitions were born out of the literature and a collective consciousness of those providing direct services to victims, those who were victims, and data from qualitative research with victims in Toledo, Ohio.

Victim

A victim of human trafficking is a person who experienced destructive or injurious, acute and/or chronic, emotional, mental, and/or physical victimization, derived from real or perceived threats or action, and because of these circumstances suffers from trauma. A victim may continue to be involved in trafficking or may no longer be involved, but continues to suffer trauma manifested in some or all of the following ways: continued dysfunctional professional or personal relationships or moving into other dysfunctional relationships, living in or experiencing reoccurring crises, continued necessity for basic needs, lack of adequate attention to health, an unwillingness or inability to engage in reflection or insight into their life and situation, a lack of meaningful movement toward recovery or change, significant deficits in positive and prosocial informal and/ or formal support systems. A helping professional/peer advocate's primary focus in assisting victims should be on increasing safety.

Survivor

A survivor is a person who suffered from destructive or injurious, acute or chronic, emotional, mental, and/or physical victimization, derived from real or perceived threats or action, and because of these circumstances suffers from trauma. Survivors may be identified with one or more of the following characteristics. S/he is actively involved in recovery but is fragile and may be re-traumatized and/or re-injured emotionally. A survivor may shift in and out of victimization and victim-survivor status as they may return to their trafficker and/or other situations involving exploitation. Survivors may be involved in some or all of the following:

- Some relationships in their lives are dysfunctional and some are positive;
- Survivors recognize their circumstances and issues and are actively working on them;
- S/he experiences a periodic crisis and basic needs may be occasionally needed;
- Acute conditions are resolved immediately and chronic conditions are addressed under the care of a professional;
- There is meaningful reflection and/or insight by a survivor about his/her life and situation, and meaningful movement is occurring toward recovery; and/or
- There are positive and/or prosocial informal and/or formal support systems in his/her life.

A helping professional/peer advocate assisting a survivor should primarily focus on increasing feelings of safety and well-being.

Thriver

A thriver is a person who experienced destructive or injurious, acute or chronic, emotional, mental, and/or physical victimization, derived from real or perceived threats or action. A thriver no longer suffers or minimally suffers the trauma related to the reasons they became involved in services. S/he may or may no longer be involved in recovery services, however s/he continues to work to maintain emotional, mental, spiritual, and physical health. Thrivers feel empowered to make healthy decisions about their lives and people involved in their lives. S/he actively pursues and is engaged in positive and prosocial informal and formal support systems and works toward goals with attainable objectives. Thrivers may be identified with some or all of the following.

- Most meaningful relationships in their lives are positive;
- Thrivers consciously monitor their emotional mental, physical and spiritual health and attend to it;
- Thrivers live their lives intentionally and purposefully because they chose to;
- Thrivers experience periodic crisis, but can recover using the resources they have or the knowledge they have on how to obtain the resources they need;
- Thrivers engage in meaningful reflection and/or insight into their lives and situations and make plans to maintain or enhance those positive aspects;
- Recovery is something a thriver holds dear; s/he puts time in on it and places importance to it;
- Thrivers empathetically reach out to others in need because they can do it without being easily re-wounded or triggered; and/or
- Thrivers understand boundaries and balance and work to achieve both.

A helping professional/peer advocate's primary focus should be to assist in increasing a healthy interdependence and self-sufficiency. The needs of victims may be different than the needs of survivors. Further, the needs of survivors may be different from the needs of thrivers. Movement along the continuum from victim to thriver requires understanding that if needs are different, then services are different. An example of the mental health needs of a potential client that

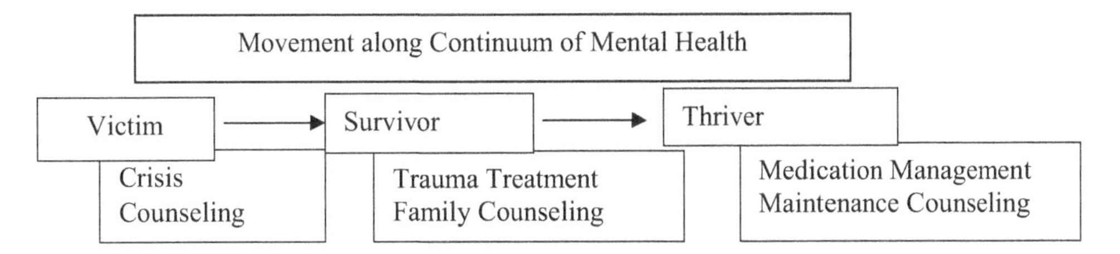

Figure 14.2 Movement along continuum of mental health

has been involved as a victim of some form of human trafficking, is presented below (see Figure 14.2). Whereas victims may need immediate crisis counseling, a survivor may need trauma treatment. However, a thriver may need mental health maintenance, counseling and/or medication management.

In another example, a victim may need immediate shelter, whereas a survivor who is no longer in immediate crisis may need transitional housing, while a thriver may desire permanent housing. Finally, a victim may need immediate basic needs assistance to secure necessary items to live, whereas a survivor may need the assistance of Medicaid and food stamps, while a thriver may be seeking a job, training, or education to pursue the career of their choice.

Of course movement is not always linear with clients moving toward improved well-being, autonomy, and self-sufficiency. Victims may move from survivor to victim, as they return to their trafficker or replace the elements of their victimization with an abusive intimate relationship. In turn, thrivers may return to survivor status or victimhood. In implementing PATH, services/service providers move in tandem with the needs of clients in supportive ways.

Preparing the community to become PATH approved

Using the collective experiences of survivors and helping professionals, along with the literature, the PATH Model was developed. Agreement had to be reached among Toledo stakeholders in order to include a particular path. Led by the PATH Coordinator, the group in Toledo revised the original Pathways assessment to capture the needs of trafficking victims, survivors, and thrivers. The group identified ten critical pathways that victims, survivors, and thrivers need to be "restored" to the individuals they may have been had tragic experience(s) not occurred. To implement PATH, the group identified the agencies to provide services, along with a personal point of contact.

The ten critical pathways are provided in Figure 14.3 and include enrollment, basic needs, legal needs, mental health, health care, empowerment, support systems and lifeskills, substance abuse, services for dependents, and injury, impairment, and supports.

The PATH Coordinator trains each identified agency and provides the designation of "PATH Approved" to these agencies that have received a three-hour training. During the training, agencies learn about human trafficking, trauma-informed care, and the PATH Model. Trained healthcare, social services, and criminal justice focused agencies receive a pre- and post-test to measure learning. Each trained agency provides the coalition with a new member who will serve as the point of contact and who will assist in navigating referred clients through their system. Referring clients to our "in-network" agencies, or PATH Approved agencies, is preferred. However, it is acceptable to use outside agencies that meet a need. Newly identified agencies are sought out by the PATH Coordinator to become PATH Approved.

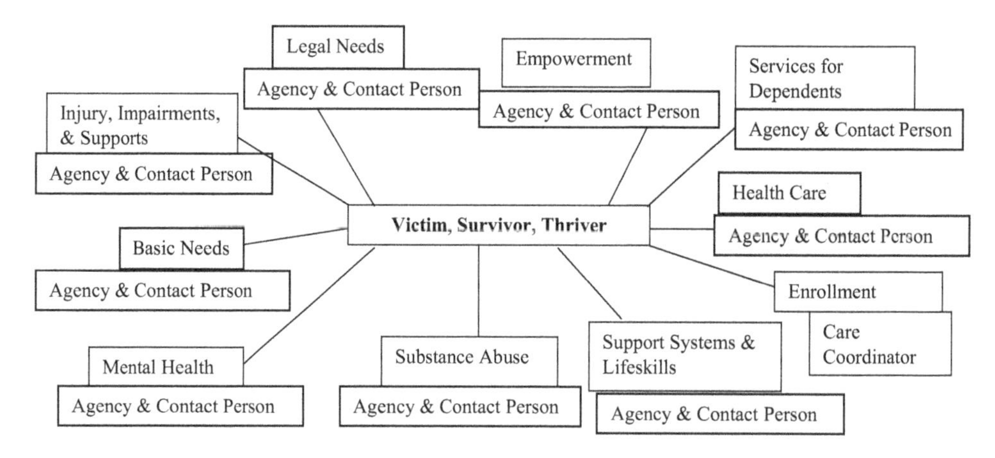

Figure 14.3 Ten critical pathways for restoration

Implementation of the PATH model

There are nine critical features of successful implementation of the PATH Model; each is described in detail below.

Care coordinators and referrals

Clients enroll in PATH via referrals to identified Care Coordinators. Care Coordinators are highly knowledgeable about both trafficking and local resources. They are chosen because of their experience working with victims and/or desire and preparedness because they are thrivers. Care Coordinators may receive referrals from local task forces, child protection agencies, ethnic organizations, juvenile courts, LGBTQ-focused organizations, or may self-refer. It is estimated that each Care Coordinator may serve an estimated ten clients or less at one time. A viable referral is one in which a client reports in the assessment they had/have an experience as a victim of any form of trafficking.

Engagement, assessment, and intervention

Once a Care Coordinator receives a referral, she/he will contact the client, work to build rapport, and complete a PATH Initial Comprehensive Assessment to identify client needs. Assessment questions are designed to identify the ten common needs of victims, survivors, and thrivers and align with the ten identified intervention pathways. Responses will lead Care Coordinators to open particular pathways. Depending on the client's needs, for example, the Care Coordinator and client may choose to open and work on pathway 1, 4, and 7, while another may work on pathway 2, 6, and 10. This allows for an Individualized Service Plan within a structured model of effective service provided by trained Care Coordinators and prepared agencies. Care Coordinators also provide transportation and/or bus tokens when needed to remove transportation barriers.

Clients may enter the PATH project at any time along their continuum of care. Thus, they may enter as a victim, survivor, or beginning thriver, as the assessment will allow Care Coordinators to better understand where each client is along the continuum of care. Care Coordinators and clients complete a PATH Initial Comprehensive Assessment, and periodically a PATH

Ongoing Assessment and may be involved in interventions that consist of any number of the ten pathways for victims, survivors, and thrivers. PATH consists of conducting assessments (Initial Comprehensive Assessment, Ongoing Assessment, and Tools) and engaging in interventions (Open Pathways). Each is defined below.

Initial comprehensive assessment, ongoing assessment, and tools

Overall assessments include the Initial Comprehensive Assessment, Ongoing Assessment, and Tools (called Checklists). The Initial Assessment is performed when each client is enrolled. This assessment identifies those pathways that need to be opened. Thus, based on the initial assessment, the client and Care Coordinator identify which of those ten key pathways the client would like to work on. The assessment covers information related to the ten pathways including basic needs, legal needs, mental health, health care, empowerment, support systems and lifeskills, substance abuse, services for dependents, and injury, impairment, and supports. Enrollment is also a pathway that consists of the assessment, orientation to PATH, education on human trafficking, and assessment of safety as well as the establishment of a safety plan. Each pathway is designed with victims, survivors, and thrivers in mind. For example, a victim may want to attend to immediate legal needs related to safety such as obtaining a restraining order or continued presence, while a survivor may request the pursuit of a criminal case against a trafficker, child support, or a divorce from her trafficker, and a thriver may be ready to sue his/her traffickers in civil court.

An Ongoing Assessment may be done at any time by a Care Coordinator but should be completed at least every 90 days. The purpose is to re-adjust and determine the current needs of clients. Tools consist of specific assessments that are particular to specific pathways. While the comprehensive and ongoing assessments allow for Care Coordinators to determine client needs, tools allow Care Coordinators to delve deeper into an issue and conduct a more thorough screening to properly link clients to appropriate services.

Tools may be well established screening tools such as the PTSD Checklist, Trauma History Screen, Lifeskills Inventory or NIDA quick screen Drug Use Questionnaire, or may consist of our Basic Needs Tool, Support Systems and Lifeskills Tool, and the Empowerment Assessment Tool. Once successful linkages are made, the Care Coordinator may re-administer a tool at any time to assess improvement but are required to re-assess every 90 days.

Interventions: open pathways

While assessments provide for a more thorough understanding of a client situation, an open pathway is the "intervention" or "action" part of the process. Thus once a pathway is opened, Care Coordinators work to link clients to services that respond to their needs. Completed appointments leading to progress is emphasized. For example, a client with an open mental health pathway is encouraged to complete their initial mental health appointment and each appointment thereafter. Care Coordinators will call, meet clients at appointments, provide transportation, or arrange for transportation to encourage clients to complete appointments.

Assessments and interventions that every client receives

Based on the literature (Federal Strategic Action Plan for Services of Victims of Human Trafficking, 2013–2017; National Violence Resource Center, 2012), and our collective experiences in Toledo, there are responses that every client will receive. Every client will receive a screening for safety and a safety plan. Each Care Coordinator will educate their client on trafficking in general, the law and ways the law can protect victims, and the PATH Model Program. Finally, every client will receive a screening for post-traumatic stress disorder (PTSD) and traumatic brain injury (TBI). Those that screen positively for potential PTSD will have a mental health pathways opened, while those that screen positively for a TBI will have a healthcare pathway opened.

Incentives

PATH is an incentivized program, meaning clients, Care Coordinating agencies, and Care Coordinators are incentivized. Providing incentives can be controversial with many wondering why an organization would submit to providing incentives to helping providers that are already being paid to do their job and why clients would be incentivized to work on their own healing. Our efforts are rooted in the framework of the social work profession, which is to "start where the client is." Our clients are often unable to see the long-term results of their work in trauma treatment for example, or even see the value in counseling, opting instead to focus on how to survive today or tomorrow. Thus, there is often a disconnect between what the helping provider knows to do and the where the client is focused. Providing a direct incentive encourages the client to move down a path that will ultimately aid in their healing and well-being. It provides the motivation for client engagement beyond their immediate vision to just survive. The original pathways project documented the savings of preventing premature and sick infants from spending time in the neonatal intensive care unit. We project that the cost of saved lives, restored families, productivity, reduced jail stays, and emergency room visits, will also outweigh the cost of incentives. In fact, in a study completed by Martin and Lotspeich (2014) it was found that for every $1 spent in preventing the sex trafficking of minors, $34 is saved.

In incentivizing Care Coordinators, we challenge them to put in the extra effort that is otherwise not required. Care Coordinators have extra motivation to work that much harder to connect their client to services. Care Coordinator's monthly meetings are focused on training, support, collaboration, and how to produce outcomes. Unlike traditional case management, based largely on time spent with clients in ways that translate to billable hours, the focus for PATH is not on spending time and billable hours, but on relationship building and completing outcomes.

Similar to original Pathways, Care Coordinators are contracted from other agencies to use PATH. In exchange, each agency, Care Coordinator, and their clients are incentivized. Each time a client *completes* an appointment, meeting, session, training, or class, both the client and Care Coordinator receive an incentive. Clients may receive up to $20 gift card for a local grocery store, clothing store, movie theatre, and more. Care Coordinators are incentivized to go the extra mile in assisting their clients. For each completed small or large outcome, the Care Coordinator's agency may receive up to $20. Because the project consists of a coordination of existing services, Care Coordinators receive their base pay from their existing direct service organizations. In addition, Care Coordinators and their home agency supervisors are required to receive training, attend coalition meetings, and monthly Care Coordination meetings. To replace the time lost, Care Coordinator agencies are provided an initial incentive to make up for lost traditional activity and implement the PATH Model.

Supports and feedback loop to improve success

Support and feedback are necessary to any intervention. Three elements have proven particularly effective in successful implementation of the PATH model, including the Core Cluster, Care Coordinator Collaboration, and Leadership Committee.

CORE CLUSTER

The Core Cluster, similar to wraparound services, are monthly meetings made up of Care Coordinators and the direct service providers that clients work with. The purpose of Core Cluster meetings are to discuss cases, develop Individualized Service Plans, and to implement, monitor, and alter plans when needed to benefit clients. Members of the Core Cluster will change depending on the client being reviewed and the agencies involved.

CARE COORDINATOR COLLABORATION

Monthly Care Coordinator meetings occur for three reasons: (1) for Care Coordinators to be trained on issues related to human trafficking, the PATH Model, or community resources; (2) for Care Coordinators to ask and answer questions and discuss the strengths, barriers, and opportunities of the project with the PATH Coordinator; and (3) to have Care Coordinators discuss, bond and share resources and information.

The most important initial agenda item is to work through the barriers of confidentiality, HIPAA, and legal privilege so that limited, but necessary, client information may be shared among agencies working with clients. Client written approval will be needed before information is shared among agency providers and each Care Coordinator. In Toledo we secured a federal Certificate of Confidentiality to protect information and protect those involved in providing services from being subpoenaed to court.

LEADERSHIP COMMITTEE

The Leadership Committee of the Coalition exists to identify and remove barriers to effective care. The Leadership Committee is made up of the leaders of various identified pathways (e.g. mental health, substance abuse etc.). Representatives will change depending on the problem to be resolved. For instance, in resolving barriers to housing, directors of the various housing programs or their designee come together to meet consistently until any identified housing barriers for victims of human trafficking is resolved. Once there is eligibility and access to immediate housing, transitional housing, and permanent housing, the committee can invite new representatives and move to work on the next barrier and so on. Care Coordinators participate in the process so they can describe the barriers to the leadership committee and ensure that the new barrier-free process established works.

Data driven process

Assessment and intervention data is de-identified and sent to one central location known as the "Hub." The Hub analyzes data patterns and trajectories that outline movement from victim to survivor to thriver. Analyzed data in the form of de-identified user-friendly charts and findings are provided to Care Coordinators, the coalition, the Core Cluster, and the Leadership Committee. One purpose of this feedback loop is so that the Leadership Committee, charged with removing barriers, can address and remove barriers and increase and expand those services and resources that promote well-being and movement toward thriverhood.

Outcomes

PATH emphasizes outcomes. Outcomes may be small or large. Small outcomes consist of completed appointments. Large outcomes create significant changes in someone's life and result in completed and closed pathways. For instance, a housing pathway that results in the type of housing a client wanted and needed concludes the need for that pathway to be opened. However, a pathway may be reopened when/if a client would like to move from transitional housing to permanent housing, indicating movement from survivor to thriver.

Phoenix 1st Step Drop-In Center

How might your community develop and implement a pop-up direct service fair?

The Phoenix 1st Step Model is an innovative action of a human trafficking coalition to provide the collective services directly to human trafficking victims. Phoenix 1st Step is a bi-annual intervention coordinated and provided with members of the City of Phoenix Human Trafficking Task Force. The City of Phoenix Human Trafficking Task Force has an engaged group of city personnel, law enforcement, city and county prosecutors, advocacy groups, faith community leaders, academics/researchers, court personnel, and service providers (including medical, housing, homeless youth and families, and mental health). The task force collectively recognized the limited access to necessary services within the community for sex trafficking victims, particularly in areas in Phoenix with high rates of arrests for street-level prostitution. Specific needs identified by the task force include crisis housing, medical services, crisis detoxification services, drug and alcohol abuse treatment, mental health services (both long and short term), public defenders, and basic needs (e.g. showers, clothing, and hygiene items). Task force members are invited to participate in a community event that provides direct services to meet needs. Events are designed by a small group of task force members including academics/researchers, survivor leaders, and staff from direct service organizations. Each event is developed through planning meetings including the design, location, hours of operation, security, targeted marketing, survivor involvement client flow through, service provider inclusion, and the identification of items needed to be collected for the project. The event became a pop-up direct service fair only for sex trafficked and prostituted persons. The use of a walk-in model was chosen to allow for self-determination of the clients to self-identify as ever having been sex trafficked or prostituted. Services were not offered to persons who attended but didn't meet the criteria of having ever experienced sex trafficking or prostitution. This was decided by the group to ensure the confidentiality and safety of the clients.

For one of the events, event-site requirements for the event space were developed and a site was identified and donated by the City of Phoenix at no cost. The site was a large and spacious senior center, unused on Saturdays, and in the center of the city where the most street prostitution had been identified as well as the greatest needs. There were four large private areas where agencies could work and have confidential conversations with clients and one very large community room where more general services were offered. Through discussion with law enforcement, survivor leaders, and community members, the peak hours of street prostitution activity were identified, agency staffing and volunteer abilities were considered and the event occurred from 10:00 a.m. to 8:00 p.m.

Security concerns were shared among the planning committee members and it was decided that an undercover vice officer would provide security. They were to be available when needed but were not to initiate any contact with clients unless there was a safety concern for the staff or volunteers. Items brought into the event were placed in a large reusable bag with their names on it and placed in a locked room. This prevented clients from bringing in items that could pose a risk for the staff and volunteers.

Marketing materials were created including a flyer (see Figure 14.4) made from a word cloud of words used by the committee designing the event to describe what the services would include. The committee decided on using the line "Are you in the life and want help?" as the indicator that this event was for persons who had been in the "life" of prostitution.

The flyer was sent to the juvenile and adult courts in the region, persons posting ads on sex selling websites, and distributed to halfway houses and drug and alcohol programs, juvenile and adult probation, city and county prosecutors, as well as many of the police departments in the area, the victim advocate programs throughout the region, and large medical centers. Calls were made by social service providers to current and former clients who had identified as having experienced prostitution and flyers were posted in and around hotels and convenience stores in the area around the event site.

Survivor leaders were integral to the development of the event and they participated in every design and decision. The design of the event included having the first person each walk-in client meet be a survivor leader who would give them a brief screening to determine if they met the criteria for the event; the client was then given to another survivor leader, who served as a "tour guide" and guided and stayed with him/her through the entire event. Survivor leaders were recruited through the local survivor networks and one survivor leader screened all potential survivor leader volunteers related to readiness to provide support services considering their time since exiting prostitution, substance use status (i.e. how long they had been clean and sober), and their ability to support others at the event without being triggered or experiencing overwhelming feelings. The survivor leaders on the planning committee co-developed a training for the survivor "tour guides" to prepare them for the experience. The training included how to have smart boundaries (i.e. when and if to share your phone number), how to advocate for your clients, and information about the services provided at the event.

Walk-in clients were asked basic demographic questions by their tour guides and then were given an intake by one of the three survivor leaders. The intake included life history questions (including childhood maltreatment), education, work experience, mental health, experiences with domestic violence and sexual exploitation, their current medical and housing needs, and their hopes for the future. This intake provided the basis for the services to be offered at the event

Figure 14.4 Phoenix 1st Step Drop-In Center

and a check sheet was completed by the intake worker and given to the survivor tour guide who then used it as a road map through the services provided at the event.

The planning committee identified a number of criteria for service provider inclusion in the event. The criteria included:

1. Client possesses self-determination and they are able to decide what is best for them.
2. Service providers must act from a victim-centered and trauma informed lens. In action, this means that each agency doesn't ask prying questions about a client's history of prostitution and that each group has been well informed and are understanding of the risk factors, experiences, and the possible resulting behaviors and experiences that victims of sex trafficking/ prostitution may experience.

The items needed to hold the event were collected through community drives including within the local community colleges and university, the municipal offices, and multiple faith communities. The following items were collected and distributed at the event:

Kids backpacks filled with school supplies
Clothing (casual) lightly used for all genders and ages
Shoes (all genders and sizes)
Bras, underpants, and tank tops
Hygiene kits including hotel-size toiletries
Gift cards for super markets
Gift cards for medical prescriptions
Meals for the event (hot breakfast, lunch, and dinner)
Dry food goods to give to clients to take (granola bars, small canned food)
Over the counter medical supplies (bandages, pregnancy tests, gauze, antiseptic, wound cleaning/suture kits).

Services provided to the clients at Phoenix 1st Step included connections to basic needs services (e.g. immediate temporary housing, access to showers, food, clothing, and hygiene kits) along with additional services such as access to a medical services, drug and alcohol treatment with detoxification options, immediate and long-term mental health services, free legal services including access to public defenders, and staff to assist with applications to seek financial assistance. Those most utilized included immediate housing, showers, clothing, hygiene items, medical services, drug and alcohol abuse detoxification and treatment, mental health services, and the use of public defenders.

Each event of Phoenix 1st Step has involved more than 20 service agencies and over 125 volunteers including students, faith-based community members, and survivor leader volunteers. The planning committee offered each participating staff and volunteer training to build their awareness of sex trafficking and prostituted persons. The impact of the event is difficult to measure but an average of 50 clients drop in each event and the experiences of the participants and the agency staff and volunteers have been very positive.

Conclusion

The authors discuss those important issues that may affect the ability of a community to provide a successful multi-sector response. Two provocative community-based multi-sector anti-trafficking programs were described. These programs complement each other and may be implemented simultaneously. In applying the Phoenix 1st Step approach, advocates have an opportunity to engage and link a number of victims to services. In implementing the PATH Model, victims may receive quality, data-driven, and accountable services from trained providers ready to receive them.

Supplemental learning materials

Coalitions work: Tools and resources. Useful materials to help you in your work. Retrieved from http://coalitionswork.com/resources/tools

Office of Justice Programs. Office of Victims of Crime. Guiding values for serving victims of crime. Retrieved from www.ovc.gov/model-standards/guiding_values.html

References

Aileron. (2011). Five steps to a strategic plan. *Forbes*. Retrieved from www.forbes.com/sites/aileron/2011/10/25/five-steps-to-a-strategic- plan/#42df5e4361af

Case Management Society of America. (n.d.). *What is a case manager?* Retrieved from www.cmsa.org/Home/CMSA/WhatisaCaseManager/tabid/224/Default.aspx

Clawson, H. J., Salomone, A., & Goldblatt-Grace, L. (2008). *Treating the hidden wounds: Trauma treatment and mental health recovery for victims of human trafficking*. Retrieved from https://aspe.hhs.gov/report/treating-hidden-wounds-trauma-treatment-and-mental-health-recovery-victims-human-trafficking

Coalitions Work. (2007). *Coalition work tools*. Retrieved from http://coalitionswork.com/resources/tools/

Consensus Building. (1998). Retrieved from www.colorado.edu/conflict/peace/treatment/consens.htm

Daft, R. L. (2013). Organization size, life cycle, and decline. In R. L. Daft (Ed.), *Organizational theory and design* (11th ed., pp. 348–388). Canada: Cengage Learning.

Damanaki, M. (2016, March 1). *If you want to go quickly, go alone. If you want to go far, go together*. Retrieved from www.huffingtonpost.com/maria-damanaki/if-you-want-to-go-quickly_b_9352480.html

Families Helping Families. (n.d.). *Coordinated system of care*. Retrieved from http://fhfjefferson.org/resources/online-resources/behavior-health-mental-health/coordinated-system-of-care-csoc

Federal Strategic Action Plan on Services for Victims of Human Trafficking in the United States. (2013–2017). *Coordination, collaboration, capacity*. Retrieved from www.ovc.gov/pubs/FederalHumanTrafficking StrategicPlan.pdf

Hospital Council of Northwest Ohio. (2016). *Care coordination systems*. Retrieved from http://carecoordinationsystems.com/case-studies/community-health-access-project-chap-2/

Johnson, J. (n.d.). *Work, wisdom, and wealth: Creating opportunities for board members*. Retrieved from https://ravsak.org/work-wisdom-and-wealth-creating-new-opportunities-board-members

Martin, L., & Lotspeich, R. (2014). A benefit-cost framework for early intervention to prevent sex trading. *Journal of Benefit-Cost Analysis*, *5*(1), 43–87. Retrieved from https://doi.org/10.1515/jbca-2013-0021

National Association of Social Workers. (2017). *NASW: Code of ethics*. Retrieved from www.socialworkers.org/pubs/code/default.asp

National Child Trauma Stress Network. (n.d.). *Effects of complex trauma*. Retrieved from www.nctsn.org/trauma-types/complex-trauma/effects-of-complex-trauma

National Sexual Violence Resource Center & Pennsylvania Coalition Against Rape. (2012). *Assisting trafficking victims: A guide for victim advocates*. Retrieved from www.nsvrc.org/sites/default/files/publications_nsvrc_guides_human-trafficking-victim-advocates.pdf

National Violence Resource Center. (2012). *Assisting trafficking victims: A guide for victim advocates*. Retrieved from www.nsvrc.org/sites/default/files/publications_nsvrc_guides_human-trafficking-victim-advocates.pdf

National Wraparound Initiative. (n.d.). *Wraparound basics*. Retrieved from http://nwi.pdx.edu/wraparound-basics/#whatisWraparound

Office of Victims of Crime. (n.d.). *Guiding values for serving victims and survivors of crime*. Retrieved from www.ovc.gov/model-standards/guiding_values.html

Potocky, M. (2010). The travesty of human trafficking: A decade of failed U.S. policy. *Social Work*, *55*(4), 373–375.

Trauma Informed Care. (2013). *Trauma informed care vs trauma treatment.* Retrieved from https://alamedacountytraumainformedcare.org/trauma-informed-care/trauma-informed-care-vs-trauma-specific-treatment-2/

U.S. Department of Health and Human Services. (2008). *Addressing the needs of victims of human trafficking: Challenges, barriers, and promising practices.* Retrieved from https://aspe.hhs.gov/report/addressing-needs-victims-human-trafficking-challenges-barriers-and-promising-practices

U.S. Department of State. (n.d.). *3Ps: Prosecution, protection, prevention.* Retrieved from www.state.gov/j/tip/3p/index.htm

Whitley, J. R. (2003). *Strength in numbers: A guide to building community coalitions.* Retrieved from www.communitycatalyst.org/doc-

INDEX

Note: Page numbers in *italics* indicate figures or images, and page numbers in **bold** indicate tables.

3P/4P paradigm: anti-trafficking efforts and 21, 36, 41–42, 53; as framework 99, 191–192; human rights focus of 41–42; international policy and 36; Palermo Protocol and 39, 53, 162, 192; rhetoric and 59; rights-based approach of 67; TVPA and 39, 41, 51, 53, 56–57, 67; *see also* prevention; prosecution; protection
1926 Slavery Convention 168
2030 Sustainable Development Agenda 169, 180–181

abolition 12, 18, 20, 29, 31n1, 82
Abraham, I. 28, 30
abuse of a position of vulnerability (APOV) 196, 208n3
abuse of power 195–196
"action element" 193–194, **194**, 195
Addams, Jane 315, 334
Administration for Child Services (ACS) 252, 257
Adverse Childhood Experiences (ACEs) 267, 269, **269**, 270, 272
Africa 17, 19–20, 77, 178
African Americans: civil rights and 44–46; debt bondage and 45, 48–50; domestic terrorism and 44; Jim Crow laws 18, 20, 44, 63; migrant agricultural crews 50; police brutality and 44–46; public health research and 280; reproductive justice movement and 271
African American women 45, 48, 271
African Union 77
Agbu, O. 107
alcohol abuse 226, 228, 230; *see also* substance abuse
alexithymia 227
Allain, J. 206
Alliance 8.7 181
Al Rahbi, F. 304
Al Salmi, I. 304
Ambagtsheer, F. 289, 291, 298, 300, 302, 305, 306
American Academy of Pediatrics 252
American Civil Liberties Union 276
American College of Emergency Physicians 252
American College of Obstetrics and Gynecologists 252
American Medical Women's Association 252
American Public Health Association (APHA) 252
Amnesty International: bandwagoning and 106–107, 111–112, 117; corrupt officials narrative 111; exploitation of women narrative 111; human trafficking narratives and 104, 110–113, **115**, 116–118, **119**, 122, **122**, 124; organ markets narrative 111; poverty and migration narrative 111–112; refugee crises narrative 117; refugee narrative 112; sex worker narrative 117–118, 121; sub-Saharan narrative 112; victim support services narrative 112
Andreas, P. 21, 29
Annenberg Center on Communication Leadership and Policy on Human Trafficking Online 277
anti-corruption efforts 48, 176–177
anti-discrimination 50
anti-peonage societies 49
Anti-Slavery International 87
anti-slavery laws 44–46, 49, 57, 72
anti-trafficking coalitions: barriers to effective interventions in 373–375; communication protocols for 372; community-based 386–387; Comprehensive Services Model (CSM) and 375–376; continuum of care in 373; coordinated system of care in 375–376; criminal justice professionals and 369; education professionals

and 370; effective elements of 369–370; effective leadership for 366–368, 372; ethnic-focused organizations and 371; faith community and 370; formation of 371–372; guiding values for 366; healthcare professionals and 370; horizontal communication in 372–373; informal organic approaches in 374; membership of 369–371; PATH model and 376–384; Phoenix 1st Step Model and 384–386; policymakers and 370; service for trafficking victims and 365–366; sex workers and 370; social services and 369; survivor-led groups in 369; trauma-informed response and 374; vertical communication in 372; victim-centered approach in 373–375
Anti-trafficking Coordination Teams 52
anti-trafficking discourse: developing countries blame in 17–18; distancing in 18–19; emotional language in 13–15; expanded responsibility in 39; innocent victims in 22; liberation and rescue reaction 352–353; morality-based stories in 42; neo-abolitionist model 29; nomenclature of 38; righteousness in 16–18; sexual exploitation focus in 26; trans-Atlantic slave trade in 12–18, 20, 27; white slavery in 23–24
anti-trafficking efforts: 3P/4P paradigm and 21, 36, 41–42, 53; action plans for 96; business role in 179; community-wide involvement in 365; criminalization focus in 20–21; economic solutions for 20–21, 29; interagency 51–52, 64; international conventions and 10–11, 160; international policy and 23–24, 28, 38; justice-seeking approach 67; morality-based stories in 42; racialized hierarchy in 25–28; responsibility and 67; sexual exploitation focus 25–28; technology and 65; transparency and 62–63; U.S. legislation and 10, 39–42, 46–52; victim-centered approach 52–55, 66
anti-trafficking laws: civil law and 58–59, 61; criminal law and 57–58, 92; definitional confusion and 206–207; hard law instruments 72; international 76, 191–193, 206–207; prevention and 53–55, 62–64; protection and 55–57; safe harbor 65; soft law instruments 72, 77–78; United States 10, 39–42, 46–52; *see also* international conventions; Palermo Protocol
anti-trafficking model: capitalism and 336–337; contextual framework of 335, *335*, 336; human rights and 334–335; mission 332; objectification and 337–338; oppression and 336; social justice and 333–334; social work and 332–338; values 332–333; victim blaming and 337; Westernization of globalization and 336
anti-trafficking movement 37–39, 50, 64–66
anti-trafficking training: curriculum and 324; empowerment strategies in 323; field placement in 326–327; human rights courses in 324–325; model for *323*; post-coursework and training 325–326; social work and 322–327
anti-vice crusade 41
Arab Initiative for Building National Capacities to Combat Human Trafficking (2010) 78
Aristotle 142, 154n3
ASEAN Trafficking in Persons Handbook on International Cooperation 78
Association of South East Asian Nations (ASEAN) 78
ATEST Coalition 42
Athens Ethical Principles against Human Trafficking of 2006 84
Australia 62, 170
Australian Modern Slavery Act 179
awareness-raising campaigns 78–79, *80*, 81

Bachrach, P. 108
Baglivio, M. T. 269
Bales, K. 15
bandwagoning: definition of 106; European Parliament (EP) and 115–116; human rights narratives and 106–107; human trafficking narratives and 111; nongovernmental organizations (NGOs) and 106–107, 111–112, 116–117
Baratz, M. S. 108
Barner, J. R. 107
Barry, K. 141
Barzilai-Nahon, K. 109
Batabyal, P. 300
battered woman syndrome 50
Bay Area Regional Health Inequities Initiative's Public Health Framework for Reducing Health Inequities (BARHII) *267*, *268*
Beattie, Charlton 48
Beck, M. E. 357
Beckman, M. D. 22–23
begging 75, 207
Belgium 91
Benita case study 219
betrayal trauma 228
Biddle, Francis 49
binge-purge behavior 228
bioviolence 293
"blackbirding" 19
Bob, C. 109
Bos, M. 289, 298
Bramer, W. M. 291
Bramstedta, K. A. 294
Brazil 12, 31n1
Brewer, D. D. 146
Brinkley, J. 41
British Empire 12, 19–20
Brooks, Desley 138
Brown, T. 333
Brownback, Sam 25, 31n8

Bruch, E. M. 26
Burmese fisherman case 170–171
Busby, J. W. 107
Bush (G.W.) administration 40, 42, 51
Bush, George W. 13, 18–19
business enterprises: anti-trafficking efforts and 179, 370; corporate social responsibility (CSR) and 62–63; forced labor and 179, 370; greenwashing and 63; prevention of trafficking in 84–85; supply-chain transparency and 62–63

Californians Against Sexual Exploitation Act 180
California Supply Chain Transparency Act 62, 85, 179
Cambodia 14
Camp, M. A. 107
capitalism 336–337
Catt, Carrie Chapman 298
Centers for Medicare and Medicaid Services Accountable Health Communities Model 267
Chapman, J. R. 300
Charity Organization Society (COS) 315
Charter of Fundamental Rights in the European Union 74
chattel slavery 43–44
Chen, L. 142
Child Abuse Prevention and Treatment Act (CAPTA) 252
child labor 38, 47, 62, 75, 181
child maltreatment: disorganized/disoriented attachment patterns and 226; fear conditioning and 225; mandated reporting of 252; moral injury and 229; risky sexual behavior and 216, 226; self-destructive eating behavior and 228; self-harming behavior and 228; traumatic memory and 225–226
Child Protective Services (CPS) 331, 333
child trafficking: criminal law and 92; health impacts of 175; international conventions **73**, 74–75, 175; sex trafficking and 59, 64–65, 152, 175, 218–219, 243–244; UNICEF and 77
child trafficking victims: chronic stress and 223–224; complex trauma and 233; consent and 280; criminal justice response to 175–176; fear conditioning and 225; mental health symptoms in 223–226; needs of 175–176; organ trafficking and 296; physical abuse and 218–219, 223, 225; prevention of 165; psychological abuse and 218–219; rights of 89; risk factors for 216, 244; sexual abuse and 218–219, 223, 247; social media and 244; social workers and 358; socioecological model and *265*; specific needs of 164, 175–176; state-dependent learning and 224–225, 235; trauma-informed response and 223, 226; use of technology by 244
Cho, S.-Y. 149
Chong, D. 106
chronic stress 223–224
Citizenship and Immigration Services (CIS) 65
civil law 58–59, 61
Civil Liberties Unit 49
Civil Rights movement 49
Civil Rights Section (Justice Dept.) 49
Clawson, H. J. 333
Clayton, M. 297
climate change 274–275, **275**
Clinton, Hillary Rodham 51, 65
Clinton, William J. 40, 51
Clinton administration 39–41, 191
coalition leadership 366–368
Coalition of Immokalee Workers (CIW) 52, 63
coalitions 366–372; *see also* anti-trafficking coalitions
Coalitions Work 371
codification 190–191
Codreanu, C. 298, 300, 302, 305, 306
coercion: consent through 92–93, 151–153, 192, 208, 243, 289, 305; debt bondage and 243; forms of 173–174; human trafficking and 173–174, 242–244; *juju* and 173–174; psychological 50–51, 55
cognitive-behavioral therapy (CBT) 233
cognitive restructuring (CR) techniques 233
Cohen, A. 144
Columb, S. 289, 298
common law 190–191
Commonwealth of Independent States Agreement on Cooperation in Combating Trafficking in Persons, Human Organs and Tissues (2005) 76
communication 104, 106, 109, 145–147
COMP.ACT (European Action Pact for Compensation for Trafficked Persons) project 87
complex PTSD (CPTSD) 222–223, 230, 235
complex trauma 222–223, 233
Comprehensive Arab Strategy for Combating Trafficking in Human Beings (2012) 78
Comprehensive Services Model (CSM) 375–376
conceptual justice 136, 150–153
conflict 178
consent: abuse of power and 195; child victims and 175, 243, 280; coercion and 92–93, 151–153, 192, 208, 243, 289, 305; forced labor and 202; interpretational issues and 191; irrelevance of 49, 55, 74, 77, 152, 167, 193; medical experiments and 280; organ removal and 201, 287, 292, 296, 298; proof of trafficking and 242
contraception 270–271
Convention Against Transnational Organized Crime (CTNOC) *see* UN Convention
Convention for the Protection of Human Rights and Fundamental Freedoms 74
Convention for the Suppression of the Traffic in Persons and of the Exploitation of the Prostitution of Others 23

Convention on Action against Trafficking in Human Beings (2005) *see* Council of Europe Convention 2005
Convention on the Protection of Children against Sexual Exploitation and Sexual Abuse (2007) 75
Convention on the Rights of the Child (CRC) 74, 175
corporate social responsibility (CSR) 62–63
corrective justice 136, 142–143
corruption: anti-trafficking efforts and 160; criminalization of 162–163; government 111, 113–114, 119, 125, 165; immigrant organizations and 107; police and 45, 124; policy formation and 53–54; reduction of 176–177; urban areas and 48; *see also* anti-corruption efforts
corrupt officials narrative 111
Council of Arab Ministers of Justice 78
Council of Europe 74–76, 86, 288
Council of Europe Convention 2005: child exploitation and 75, 164; comparison of **76**; forced begging and 207; human trafficking and 76, 162; organ trafficking and 288; partnerships and 95; prosecution and 93; trafficking law and 206; victim assistance 87–89, **90**, 91; victim protection in 174–175
Council of Europe Convention against Trafficking in Human Organs 298
Council on Social Work Education (CSWE) 322, 324, 326
court-mandated recovery 233
Craig, J. 300
criminal justice: anti-trafficking coalitions and 369; armed conflict and 178; child victims and 175–176; communication and 145–147; complexity of trafficking and 166–171; conceptual justice and 150–153; corrective justice and 142, 153; corruption and 176–177; data collection and 171–172; forced marriage response 169–170; health issues and 274; human-rights based approach and 161; injustice and 136, 153; international conventions **73**, 75–76, 92; international police 94; natural disasters and 178–179; online exploitation and 180; organized crime and 173; prevention and 165–166; procedural justice and 153; prosecution and 162–163; protection and 164–165; response components 160–161; retributive justice and 139–141, 153; situational crime prevention theory and 160, *161*; substantive criminal law 190; therapeutic justice and 143–144, 153; trafficking risk factors 177; transformative justice and 145–150, 153; transnational crime and 172–173; victim-centered approach and 161
criminal networks narrative 119, 121, 124
criminal offenses 190–191
Cross, N. B. 300
Cross, T. L. 354–355
Culturally Competent System of Care 354–355, *355*
cyberbullying 277
cycle of violence model 352

Dahre, J. 105–106
Dalla, R. L. 125
Danish Centre against Human Trafficking 85
"Deaf Mexicans" case 51, 61
debt bondage 45, 48–50, 205, 220, 243
decision-making 108
Declaration Against Trafficking in Persons, Particularly Women and Children (2004) 78
Declaration of Istanbul on Organ Trafficking and Transplant Tourism 288, 298
Declaration of the Economic Community of Western African States on the Fight against Trafficking in Persons (ECOWAS) (2001) 77
defendants 190
de Jong, J. 298, 300, 302, 305, 306
demand 82–83
Demleitner, N. 22
Denmark 85
deportation threats 50–51, 174, 246, 248, 276, 338, 371
depression 174, 247, 267, 269, 272
DESNOS (disorders of extreme stress, not otherwise specified) 223
DeStefano, A. 41
detention centres narratives 116
devastation of societies narrative 113
developing countries 17–18
Diagnostic and Statistical Manual (DSM) 223
Diego-Rosell, P. 177
disorganized/disoriented attachment patterns 226
dissociation 218, 222, 224, 227
domestic minor sex trafficking (DMST) 331
domestic trafficking 343; *see also* human trafficking
domestic violence 140, *263*, 352
domestic workers 243
Donnelly, J. 106
Douglass, Frederick 37
downstream interventions 265, 267
Dozema, J. 150–151
Dreher, A. 149
drug abuse 144, 228; *see also* substance abuse
drug trafficking 272
Duff, R. A. 145
Duty of Vigilance Law (France) 179

ecological perspective 347–348
Economic Community of Western African States 77
economic inequality 72, 79, 99, 104, 300, 348
economic sanctions 204
economic systems: human trafficking and 11, 20–22, 27–29, 79, 81–82; structural transformation of 20–21; white slavery and 22, 28

ECPAT International 86
Educational Policy and Accreditation Standards (EPAS) 322, 324
education and assistance narratives 116
education professionals 370
Efrat, A. 296
Emancipation Proclamation 20
emotional numbing 226–227
empowerment: human rights and 323; legalization of prostitution and 148; prevention and 63–64; social justice and 323, 333–334; social work and 316, 323; strategies for 323; women and 176
End Child Prostitution, Child Pornography, and Trafficking for Sexual Purposes (ECPAT) 176
enslavement *see* slavery
Environmental Change and Forced Migration Scenarios (EACH-FOR) 274
environmental health 274–276
environmental migrants 275
Epps, N. 269
Estes, R. 351
ethnic-focused organizations 371
EU Directive 2011/92/EU 75–76, **76**
EU Directive 2014/95/EU 179
European Parliament (EP): bandwagoning and 115–116; criminal networks narrative 119, 121; devastation of societies narrative 113; European Union narrative 114; fishing narrative 114; gatekeeping and 123; gender-based violence and children narrative 120; gender-based violence narrative 113–114; human rights narratives and 104; human trafficking narratives and 113–115, **115**, 119–121, **121**, 122, **122**, 123–124; identification and victim services narrative 120; missing support services narrative 114; natural disasters narrative 114; surrogacy and adoption narrative 114–115; technology narrative 120; trafficking in sports narrative 115
European Union (EU) 105, 178, 288
European Union narrative 114
European Women's Lobby 150
EU Victims Directive of 2012 86–89, **90**, 93, 95
exploitation: definition of 198, 200–201; forced begging as 207; forced marriage as 169–170; involuntary servitude and 205; removal of organs as 201; sexual 200–201; types of 206–207; U.S. federal law and 205
exploitation of women narrative 111
exposure therapy 234
eye movement desensitization reprocessing (EMDR) 234

Fair Food Program 63
Fair Food Standards Council 63
faith community 370
fear conditioning 225
Felitti, Vincent 267
fight-flight-freeze response 218, 223–224
"Fighting the Crime of Trafficking in Persons, especially Women, Adolescents, and Children" (OAS, 2003) 78
Fight Online Sex Trafficking Act (FOSTA) 180
Finland 95–96
Finn, P. 145–146
First Offender Program (FOPP) 145–146
fishing narrative 114, 125
Flores, Miguel 52, 63
Flygare, C. 145–146
FM case study 240–242, 247–250, 252–253, 257
food industry, forced labour, and corrupt officials narrative 116–117
forced begging 207
forced labor: African 19–20; British Empire and 19–20; business role in preventing 179; child labor and 75; criminalization of 38; definition of 201–202; international conventions 72, **73**, 74; slavery statues and 48; as violation of rights 39; women and girls in 170
Forced Labour Convention *see* ILO Convention No. 29 (Forced Labor)
forced marriage 169–170
Forced Marriage Protection Orders (FMPOs) 169
Framework Act on Combating Trafficking in Persons of the League of Arab States (2008) 76
framing 104–107, 125
Fraser, C. 306
Freedom Network 42
Freeman, Calvin 140
Freud, Sigmund 227

Gallagher, A. 11
Gallagher, A. T. 160–161, 166, 197
gatekeeping 109, 123
gender-based violence and children narrative 120
gender-based violence narrative 113–114, 121, 125
gender inequality 123, 125, 148, 150
George, Vincent, Jr. 140
George, Vincent, Sr. 140
Gerdes, K. E. 337
Germain, C. B. 348
Gil, D. G. 322
girls *see* women and girls
Global Estimates of Modern Slavery (GEMS) 170
globalization 336, 343
Global North 107, 336
Global Slavery Index 162–163, 177
Global South 107, 336
Global Survival Network 24
Goldblatt Grace, L. G. 333
Golden, Michael 138
Goode, Paula 26
Grant, Ulysses S. 45
Grant administration 44–45
Greenwald, M. A. 269
greenwashing 63
Gregory, T. 333

grooming 217–220, 245
Group of Experts on Action against Trafficking in Human Beings (GRETA) 75, 162
Gruber, A. 144
Guttenplan, D. D. 106

Hafner-Burton, E. M. 106
Han, Kim 140
Handbook on Direct Assistance for Victims of Trafficking (IOM) 86
hard law instruments: comparison of **76**; definition of 72; international conventions 72, **73**, 74–76, **76**; prevention measures in 78–79, 81–85; prosecution measures in 91–94; protection measures in 85–90, **90**, 91
harm minimisation model 148–149
healthcare corporation crime 297
healthcare professionals: advocacy by 257; digital information-sharing in 252; education and 251–252; follow-up appointments 249, 251; healthcare protocols and 249–250; identification of victims by 249–250, **250**, 253; labor trafficking identification 251; mandated reporting and 252–253; organ trafficking and 294, 297, 305; patient confidentiality and 248–249, 253–254; resources for 254, **255–256**; sex trafficking identification 251–252; trafficking victims and 247–254, 256, 370; trauma-informed response by 249–251, **251**, 253; victim resources and 250–251, 254, 256
health issues: confidentiality and 248; destination phase and 245; incarceration and 273; inequities and *268*; labor trafficking and 275–276; organ donation and 287; physical exams and 242, 247–248; pre-trafficking phase and 245; trafficking victims and 242, 245–249; transportation/harboring phase and 245; *see also* mental health; public health
Heitkamp, Heidi 270
Herman, Judith 230, 233–234
Hessenauer, S. 326
HIV 270, 272
Hobbs, D. 173
Holmes, P. 160–161
horizontal communication 372–373
Hostetter, C. 323
"house rules" 246
Huda, S. 136
humanitarian aid 350–351, 353
human rights: 3P/4P paradigm and 41–42; awareness training 94; culture and 105–106; definition of 317; empowerment in 323; international conventions **73**, 74; issue arenas and 126; narratives and 104; social work and 316–317, 322, 334–335, 343; trafficking and 9, 11, 161, 316–317, **317–321**, 322, 349–350; victimization and 107–108; violations of 125–126
Human Rights Activities (HRA) 327
human rights narratives 104–106, 108
Human Rights Watch (HRW): bandwagoning and 111–112; corrupt officials narrative 111; detention centres narratives 116; education and assistance narratives 116; exploitation of women narrative 111; fishing narrative 114; food industry, forced labour, and corrupt officials narrative 116–117; human trafficking narratives and 104, 110–113, **115**, 116–118, **119**, 122, **122**, 124; poverty and migration narrative 111–112; refugee narrative 112; sub-Saharan narrative 112; victim support services narrative 112; vulnerable people narrative 118
human trafficking: armed conflict and 178; causes of 20; climate-related changes and 274–275; complexity of 170–171; criminalization of 192, 203, 207–208; criminal justice response to 41, 160–181, 274; cycle of violence model 352; data collection on 98, 171–172; definition of 10, 39, 67, 107, 166–167, 191, 242–243; ecological perspective and 347–348; economic systems and 11, 20–22, 27–30; evidence-based policy and 180–181; human rights and 316–317, **317–321**, 322, 349–350; indicators of **217**, **242**; inequality and 104; investigative measures 93–94; issue salience and 125–126; media reports and 24–25; multiple systems estimation (MSE) and 171; multi-sector interactions in 265–266; national security and 11, 30; nomenclature of 38, 43; perception of 9–11, 30, 60; policy suggestions and 124–126; prevalence of 8–10, 243, 316; profit and 244; public consciousness of 9–11; public health approach and 262–267, 269–277, 279–280; pull factors for 72, 82, 244, 329; push factors for 72, 244, 329; race and 24–25; recruitment trope and 59–60; risk factors for 177, 244, 343; root structural contributors to 29, 41–42; scope of 16, 71; social determinants of health (SDoH) and 266–267; socioecological model of 264–266; systems of care and 350–351; training for 126; trans-Atlantic slave trade analogy 12–18, 20, 27–30; transnational elements of 172–173; violence and 352; white slavery analogy 11, 21–22; *see also* labor trafficking; sex trafficking; trafficking in persons; trafficking in women
human trafficking case study 203
Human Trafficking Intervention Court (HTIC) 273–274, 278
human trafficking narratives: context of 108; European Parliament (EP) and 113–115, **115**, 119–121, **121**, 122, **122**, 123–124; framing of responsibility and 111–113, 123–124; nongovernmental organizations (NGOs) and 110–113, **115**, 116–119, **119**, 121–122, **122**, 123; power relations in 108; research methods 110; social practices and prejudices in 113; understanding in 106

Hunter, John 292
Hyland, K. 10
hyperarousal 218, 224–225, 228

Ibhawoh, B. 105
identification and victim services narrative 120
ideological power 108–109
illegal, unreported and unregulated (IUU) fishing 114
ILO Abolition of Forced Labour Convention of 1957 74
ILO Convention No. 29 (Forced Labor) 74, 167, 201–202
ILO Convention No. 97 (Migration for Employment) 74
ILO Convention No. 143 (Migration in Abusive Conditions) 74
ILO Convention No. 182 (Worst Forms of Child Labour) 75, 175
ILO Minimum Age Convention, 1973 75
ILO Protocol on Forced Labor (2014) 84, 167
immigrants 11, 50, 65; *see also* migrants
immigration policy 65, 177–178, 277
incarceration 273–274
indentured servitude 19
Individualized Service Plan (ISP) 376
inequality: economic 72, 79, 99, 104, 300; gender 123, 125, 148, 150; health 303; marginalization and 348; social 108, 115; trafficking and 79, 99, 104
infectious disease 270–273
Inter-Agency Coordination Group against Trafficking in Persons 98
Interagency Council on Women 51
International Agreement for the Suppression of the White Slave Trade (1904) 23, 74, 150
International Committee of the Red Cross 351
International Conference on Population and Development 271
International Convention for the Suppression of the Traffic in Women and Children (1921) 74
International Convention for the Suppression of the Traffic in Women of Full Age (1933) 74
International Convention for the Suppression of White Slave Traffic (1910) 23, 74
International Convention on the Protection of the Rights of All Migrant Workers and Members of Their Families 74
international conventions: anti-trafficking efforts 10–11, 160, 162; child exploitation **73**, 74–75; criminal justice **73**, 75–76, 92; forced labor 72, **73**, 74; hard law and 72; human rights **73**, 74; human trafficking and 75–77; influence of 76; migration **73**; organized crime and 75; partnerships and 94–98; prosecution and 92–94; prostitution **73**, 74; regional 75–76; sanctions and 92–93; slavery and 72, **73**; soft law and 72; on trafficking **73**; victim assistance 75, 85, 87–90, **90**, 91
international coordination mechanisms 97–98, 166
International Covenant on Civil and Political Rights of 1966 74
International Federation of Social Workers (IFSW) 317, 343, 350
International Labour Organization (ILO) 74, 167, 202, 243, 244, 337
international law: on exploitation 198; on forced labor 201–202; human trafficking and 202–203; sex trafficking definition in 204; trafficking definition in 204; *travaux préparatoires* in 193
International Organization for Migration (IOM) 11, 79, *80*, 98, 172, 178, 275
international police 94
international policy: 3P/4P paradigm and 36, 53–55; anti-trafficking efforts and 10–11, 23–24, 28, 37–38; best practices in 55; responsibility and 67; rights-based approach of 66; sexual exploitation focus 25–28; white slavery and 23–24, 28; *see also* policy formation
international social work: client-centered approach to 351; cultural competence and 354–355, *355*; humanitarian aid and 350–351, 353; right to participation and 353; right to self-determination and 352; systems of care and 353–355; *see also* social work
International Society for Traumatic Stress Studies (ISTSS) 233
internet 146, 180, 306; *see also* technology
intervention strategies 232–233
intimate partner violence 352; *see also* domestic violence
involuntary servitude: African Americans and 44–45; American South and 44, 49; enforcement of 44, 46; freedom from 61–62; immigrants and 50; migrant agricultural crews and 50; psychological coercion and 50–51; U.S. federal law and 205
Involuntary Servitude and Slavery (ISS) 38–39, 43, 50–52
Iran 288
Irina Project 279
Israel 292, 301, 305
Israeli Health Maintenance Organizations 301
Israeli organ trafficking case study 292
issue arenas 106, 108–109, 126
Italy 91, 172
Ivanovski, N. 289, 298

Jalbert, S. K. 145–146
Janet, Pierre 227
Jim Crow laws 18, 20, 44, 63
Joachim, J. 105
John schools 145–148, 274
Johnston, R. 173
Jones, Anne Marie 144
Jong, J. 291
Jordan, A. 146

Joudo Larsen, J. 177
judicial precedent 190
juju 173–174
Jungels, A. 145
justice: conceptual 136, 150–153; corrective 136, 142–143; criminal law and 67, 135–136; procedural 136–139; retributive 136, 139–141; therapeutic 136, 143–144; transformative 136, 145–148, 150
Justice for Victims of Trafficking Act of 2015 252

Kangaspunta, K. 198
Kapstein, E. B. 15, 18–19
Keck, M. 108
Kempadoo, K. 17–18
Kennedy, H. 125
Kling, R. 145–146
Krehbiel, S. 333
Kristof, Nicholas 14
Ku Klux Klan 18, 46

labor movement 63
labor trafficking: capitalism and 337; civil lawsuits and 61; definition of 316; demand and 83; deportation threats and 50–51, 246, 248, 276; drug trafficking as 272; environmental health and 275–276; health issues and 245, 275–276; power and control wheel 246, *246*, 264; prevalence of 242–243, 337; prosecution and 57–58, 243; under-reporting of 243; sex trafficking and 52, 243; use of technology in 276–277; victim identification in 251; Western policy and 48; *see also* forced labor
La Strada International 87
law enforcement: anti-trafficking coalitions and 384; front-line 163; proactive investigative techniques in 163, 173; reactive investigative techniques in 163, 173; response to trafficking by 160, 163; specialist 163; trauma impacts and 174; unwillingness to cooperate with 174–175; *see also* police
leadership 366–368
League of Nations 23, 72
learned helplessness 220, 225
legislation: anti-trafficking discourse and 42; criminal justice response to trafficking and 162–163, 170; monitoring in 162–163; online exploitation and 180; UN Convention and 162; U.S. anti-trafficking efforts and 10, 39, 41–42, 46–52, 190; *see also* international law
Levine, E. 146–147
Levy, A. 142
Lewin, K. 109
liberation and rescue reaction 352–353
Libya 117–118, 178
Lineer, M. M. 357
Lotspeich, R. 382
Louisa case study 217–218, 231
Lovell, R. 146
Lukes, S. 108
Lundin, S. 298, 300, 302, 305, 306

macro level interventions 316, 323, 325, 329, 331, 343, 348
Maedl, A. 108
Maiti Nepal 81
Mallick, R. 333
Manasurangkun, Auntie Suni 52
mandated reporting 252–253
Maney, G. M. 333
Mann, James 48
Mann Act 23, 46–49, 52–53, 60
Manzano, A. 297
Marcin, Steve 140
Margaronis, M. 106
Martin, L. 382
Mary, N. L. 348
May, Theresa 14, 19, 21
McCarthy, L. A. 207
McClean, D. 194, 197, 201
"means" element 195–196, **196**, 197–198
media reports: human trafficking and 24–25, 279–280; public health and 279–280; race and 24; sex trafficking and 279–280; sexual exploitation focus of 41; victimization stories in 41–42
medical profession *see* healthcare professionals
medical tourism 293–294
Melzer-Lange, M. 357
Mendoza, R. L. 306
mental health: chronic stress and 223–224; continuum of *379*; depression and 174, 247, 267, 269, 272; dissociation and 218, 222, 224, 227; hyperarousal and 218, 224–226, 228; post-traumatic stress syndrome (PTSD) and 222, 224–227, 247; self-harming behavior and 226, 228; trafficking victims and 222, **222**, 223–231, 235–236, 247, 264, 338
Meyer, J. M. 106
mezzo level interventions 316, 323, 325, 329, 331, 343, 348, 351
micro level interventions 316, 323, 325, 329, 332, 348
midstream interventions 265, 267
migrants: climate change and 274–275; debt bondage and 50; deportation threats 50–51; environmental 275; forced labor conventions 74; international conventions **73**; involuntary servitude and 50; mixed flows of 275; protections for 50–51; Thailand 178
migratory prostitution 22, 47
Miller, John 13–14, 20, 25, 27
missing support services narrative 114
Mittelman, J. H. 173

mixed flows 275
modern slavery: anti-trafficking efforts 36; definition of 18, 20, 167–169; extent of 164; race and 25; situational crime prevention theory and *161*; transparency efforts and 62; as umbrella term *168*; *see also* human trafficking
Modern Slavery (UK) Act 14, 62, 84, 169, 179
Mogulescu, K. 144
Monaghan, M. 297
Moorlock, G. 289, 298
moral injury 229
morality-based stories 42
multiagency cooperation mechanisms 96–97
multiple systems estimation (MSE) 171
Murad, Nadia 64
Murdie, A. 105
Muth, S. Q. 146

Nadelman, E. A. 21, 29
narratives: bandwagoning in 106–107; communication and 104; criminal networks 119, 121, 124; gender-based violence 113–114, 120–121, 125; human law 105; human trafficking 106, 108; issue arenas and 106; policy formation and 104, 122–125; selective framing and 104–107; *see also* human rights narratives
Nash, K. 106
NASW *see* National Association of Social Workers (NASW)
NASW Code of Ethics 317, 322–323, 349–350, 366
National Academy of Medicine (NAM) 252
National Association of Social Workers (NASW) 317, 322–323, 325, 333, 349, 366
national coordination mechanisms 94–95, 165
National Human Trafficking Resource Center (NHTRC) 277
National Rapporteur on Trafficking in Human Beings 95–96, 98
National Referral Mechanism (NRM) 96–97, *97*, 98
national security 11, 30
National Worker Exploitation Task Force (WETF) 51–52
natural disasters 178–179
natural disasters narrative 114
naval stores industry 44–45, 48
neo-abolitionist model 29
Netherlands organ trafficking case 305
Newmayer, E. 149
NGOs *see* nongovernmental organizations (NGOs)
Nicholson, S. 106
Niger 178
Nigerian trafficking victims case 172
non-citizen visas 254, 256
non-decision-making 108
nongovernmental organizations (NGOs): bandwagoning and 111–112, 116–117; child victims and 176; data collection and 98; framing of responsibility and 111–112; gatekeeping and 123; human rights narratives and 105; human trafficking narratives and 110–115, **115**, 116–119, **119**, 121–122, **122**, 123–124; international policy and 10; on modern slavery 20; multiagency cooperation mechanisms and 96; national coordination mechanisms and 95; policy formation and 105; power relations in 108; social media and 109; victim assistance and 86–87
Nordic Model 148–149
"No Such Thing" campaign 280
Nugent, M. 357

Obama administration 40, 42, 52
objectification 337–338
O'Connor, Sandra Day 51, 55
Office of the United Nations High Commissioner on Refugees (UNHCR) 77
Office of Victims of Crime (OVC) 366, 375
Office on Trafficking in Persons (TIP) 79, *80*
Office to Monitor and Combat Trafficking in Persons 13, 26, 51, 54
Okech, D. 107
online exploitation 180
opioid epidemic 272
oppression 336
Optional Protocol to the Convention on the Rights of the Child on the Involvement of Children in Armed Conflict 175
Optional Protocol to the Convention on the Rights of the Child on the Sale of Children, Child Prostitution and Child Pornography 175, 288
organ brokers 305–308
organ buyers: accessibility and 303; affordability and 304; choice and 303–304; demographics of 301–302; ethnic minorities and 303; fear of implication by 297; financial means of 302; as patients 302; post-operative care and 304; prosecution of 299, 302; recruitment of 301, 304; scarcity and 302–303
Organization for Security and Cooperation in Europe (OSCE) 78, 179
Organization of American States 78
organized crime 48, 75, 107, 173
organ markets narrative 111
organ sellers: demand for 287, 292, 301; exploitation of 306–307; fear of implication by 297; financial need and 292–293, 299–300, 307; gender of 300; health outcomes and 307; nationality of 300; post-operative care and 304; prosecution of 299–300; recruitment of 299–301; transaction strategies 300–301
organ trafficking: brokers in 305–308; children and 296; concealment of 297; estimates of 295–296; evidence of 296–297; financial need and 291–293, 299–300; normalization of 298; organ theft and 296; social media and 306;

terminology in 289, **290**, 291, **291**; third party involvement in 301, 305–306; victims of 111; *see also* Trafficking in Human Beings for the Purpose of Organ Removal (THBOR)
Organ Transplantation Law (2008) 296
organ transplants: affordability and 293–294; bioviolence and 293; concealment of illegal 297; debate over 292–293, 307; definition of 289; demand for 287–288; domestic trade and 291; donation for 287–288, 293; excessive demand for 302–303; as exploitation 201, 243, 291, 293, 306; ideology and 289, 291; market for 292–294; mediators and 304–305; organ buyers and 293, 299–304; organ sellers and 299–301; regulation of 288–289; transplant tourism and 293–294, 298
"Other" 18, 24, 27, 42
Ouagadougou Action Plan to Combat Trafficking in Human Beings, Especially Women and Children (2006) 77
Outland, R. 45
Owen, L. 298

Palermo Protocol: 3P/4P paradigm and 39, 53, 162, 192; abuse of a position of vulnerability (APOV) and 196; abuse of power and 195; adoption of 10–11, 36, 39, 191; child victims in 175; comparison of **76**; criminal law and 57, 162; demand-reduction and 82; denial of liberty in 51; exploitation in 169, 198, 200, 206–207; forced labor and 202, 208n6; implementation of 49, 65; organ trafficking and 201, 287–288; partnerships in 94–95; prosecution and 75; recognition of coercion in 51; regional laws and 77; State Party requirements of 202; trafficking approach and 55; trafficking definition in 151–153, 166–167, 191–193, 198, 203–206, 208, 243, 316; victim assistance 86–89, **90**, 91, 94
Pallas, C. L. 104
Pape, Pierrette 150
Partners Against Trafficking in Humans (PATH) 376
partnerships 94–98; *see also* anti-trafficking coalitions
Pascalev, A. 298, 300, 302, 305, 306
PATH model: assessment and intervention 380–382; care coordinators in 380–383; collaboration and 383; Core Cluster 382–383; critical pathways for 379, *380*; elements of 376, *376*; implementation of 377, 380; incentives in 382; Leadership Committee 383; mental health continuum and *379*; outcomes and 383–384; PATH coordinator and 379; survivors and 377–378; thrivers and 378–379; victims and 377–379
Pathways Model 376
Pawson, R. 298
PEACE model for interviewing 56–57
Peavler, R. 337
penitential communication 145–147
peonage 45, 48–50, 63
Pettigrew, A. M. 104
Philippines 301, 306
Phoenix 1st Step Model 384–385, *385*, 386
Piquero, A. R. 269
Pliley, J. 48
Polaris Project 243, 277
police: arrests of prostituted persons 112, 117, 140–141; brutality and 44–46; detention centres narratives 116; international 94; procedural justice and 136–139; sex trafficking and 137–138; sexual contact with prostituted persons 137–139; sexual violence and 138–139; victim distrust of 56, 86, 88, 138; *see also* law enforcement
Policing Sexuality (Pliley) 48
policy formation: agenda setting in 106; consensus in 104; corrupt officials and 125; human trafficking narratives and 122–125; implementation and 127; limitations in 127; narratives and 104–106, 122–125; nongovernmental organizations (NGOs) and 105; process of 123, *123*; training and 126; value framing in 107; victim support services and protocols 126–127
post-trafficking life: adaptation to 220–221, 235; assessment in 230, **230**, 231; barriers to service in 234; intervention strategies 232–234; mental health symptoms in 222, **222**, 223; recovery in 221–223, 233–234; sequenced approach in 233–234; stages of change in 231–232, **232**; trauma-informed response and 223–230
post-traumatic stress syndrome (PTSD) 222, 224–227, 247, 338
Potrata, B 297
Potterat, J. J. 146
poverty and migration narrative 111–112
Power and Control Wheel 246, *246*, 263, *263*, 264, 272
power relations: abuse in 92, 195–196, 229, 305; child trafficking victims and 175; decision-making and 108; gatekeeping and 109, 122; human trafficking and 104–105, 107–108, 152, 243, 289; ideological 108–109; issue arenas and 108–109; non-decision-making and 108; patriarchal 300; police and 138; policy formation and 105, 109, 123; political actors and 105, 107; victimization and 107, 120
preparatory works *see travaux préparatoires*
President's Interagency Task Force 51
prevention: awareness-raising campaigns 21, 54, 78–79, *80*, 81; definition of 191; demand-reduction 82–83; downstream interventions 265, 267; economic opportunity and 79, 81–82; international coordination mechanisms 166; midstream interventions 265, 267; national coordination mechanisms 165; partnerships in 94; private sector role 83, 85; public

health approach and 262–267, 269–270; socioecological model of 264–266; survivor inclusion and empowerment in 63–64; technology-based initiatives for 277; training for 86; transparency efforts and 62; upstream interventions 265; U.S. foreign policy and 53–55; victim-centered approach and 53–55; worker-led social responsibility (WSR) and 63
primary source of law 190
proactive investigative techniques 163, 173
procedural justice 136–139
Progressive Era 22, 45–48
Project Dawn Court 143–144
prolonged exposure (PE) 233
prosecution: civil law and 58–59; criminal law and 57–58, 92–93; definition of 190, 192; international conventions and 92–94; judicial cooperation and 94; law enforcement and 163; legislative frameworks for 162–163; offender identification in 91; prosecutorial/judicial response in 163; specialist law enforcement 163; trafficking victims and 88; victim assistance and 92; victim-centered approach and 57–59, 163
prostitution: anti-trafficking rhetoric and 42; decriminalization of 148–150; demand-reduction 82–83; drug addiction and 144; harm minimisation model 148–149; international conventions **73**, 74; John School and 145–148, 274; legalization of 148–149; migratory 22, 47; morality-based policy 46, 48; neo-abolitionism and 29; organized crime and 48; police sexual contact with 137–139; prosecution of 112, 117, 140–141, 147–148; regulation of 27, 46, 148; sting operations and 61; Swedish model and 82–83; as trafficking 136, 141, 149; victim-centered approach and 86; violence and 148–149; *see also* sex trafficking; sex work
protection: commerce lens and 56; definition of 192; slavery lens and 55; trauma-informed response and 56; victim-centered approach and 55–57, 85–90, **90**, 91, 164–165; victim identification in 164
psychoeducation 234
psychological coercion 50–51, 55
PTSD *see* post-traumatic stress syndrome (PTSD)
public health: environmental health and 274–276; incarceration and 273–274; infectious disease and 270–272; labor trafficking and 275–276; media and 279–280; multi-sector issues and 263, 265–266; opioid epidemic and 272; research and 280; substance use and 272–273; technology and 276–277; trafficking prevention and 262–267, 269–270; trauma and 267, 269–270; unsafe working conditions and 276; *see also* health issues
pull factors 72, 82, 177, 244, 329
"purpose" element 198, **199**, 200–202
push factors 72, 177, 244, 329

Quackenbos, Mary Grace 45

Rabbitt, A. 357
race: media reports and 24; natural enslavement and 27; sex tourism and 27; sex trafficking and 24–25; white slavery and 23–24, 30; *see also* African Americans
Rassam, A. Y. 29
Raymond, J. 151
reactive investigative techniques 163, 173
Reagan administration 50
Recommended Principles and Guidelines on Human Rights and Human Trafficking 162
recruitment trope 59
refugee crises narrative 117
refugee narrative 112
Reichert, E. 323
Reid, J. A. 269
repetition compulsion 227
reproductive justice 271–272
resilience 276
responsibility 67, 234
restrictive immigration policies case 177–178
retributive justice 136, 139–141
Reuter, P. 294
Rhodes, W. 145–146
Richmond, Mary 315
righteousness 16–18
Rijken, C. 196–197
Roberts, J. M., Jr. 146
Roosevelt, Franklin D. 45–46, 49
Roosevelt, Theodore 45–46
Roth, V. 75

SADC Strategic Plan of Action on Combating Trafficking in Persons, Especially Women and Children 77
safe harbor laws 65
Salvation Army 335
Satre, L. J. 19
Scheper-Hughes, N. 296, 302
Scully, E. 22, 23, 24
secondary source of law 190
Segal, E. A. 337
self-destructive eating behavior 228
self-determination 352, 356, 366, 384
self-harming behaviors 226, 228, 235
sequence approach 233–234, 236
Serita, Toko 274
service neutrality 66
settlement house movement 315
Sewell, Paul 139
sex tourism 9, 27
sex trafficking: children and 59, 64–65, 152, 175, 243–244; coercion in 276–277; compelled service under 38; conceptual justice and 150–153; consent and 55, 152; corrective

justice and 142–143; criminalization of 39; debt bondage and 220; definition of 151–153, 153n1, 204, 316; as domestic violence 140; drug addiction and 272; enforcement strategies 53; grooming in 245; health issues and 245; hierarchical systems in 108; infectious disease and 270–272; international 9; labor trafficking and 52, 243; legalization of prostitution and 149; Mann Act and 52–53; media coverage of 279–280; mental health and 222; "Other" and 24; Palermo Protocol and 151–152; power and control wheel 246, *246*, 264; procedural justice and 136–139; process of victimization in 219–221; profit and 244; prosecution and 57–58, 61, 243; prostitution as 136, 141; punishment of victims 140–141; racialized hierarchy in 24–25; recruitment trope and 59; under-reporting of 243; retributive justice and 139–141; risk factors for 216, **216**; social media and 244, 276; technology use in 276–277; therapeutic justice and 143–144; transformative justice and 145–150; typology of **266**; U.S. federal law and 204–205; victim identification in 251; victimization process in 217–218; Western policy and 25–27, 48; white slavery as 47
sexual exploitation 200–201
sexually transmitted infections (STIs) 270, 272
Sexual Offences Act 2003 92
sexual violence: children and 218–219, 223, 247; police and 138–139; risk of trafficking and 269; self-harming behavior and 228; sex work and 148–149
sex work: anti-trafficking coalitions and 370; conceptual justice and 151; legalization of 148–149; prohibition on 26; racial hierarchy in 22; violence and 148–149; *see also* prostitution
sex worker narrative 117–118, 121
Shay, Jonathan 229
shelters 64–65
Shimazono, Y. 295, 301
Shively, M. 145–146
Shonte case study 221
Signal International, LLC 275–276
Sikkink, K. 108
Simoneschi, S. 333
Simpson, P. 357
Singer, M. 294
Siong case 295
situational crime prevention theory 160, *161*
slavery: alternative forms of 19–20, 31n8; chattel 43–44; compelled service under 38; definition of 20, 168; distancing from 18–19; economic systems and 22; extent of 9; forced labor and 19–20; international conventions 72, **73**; nomenclature of 38, 43; "Other" and 27; trans-Atlantic trade and 9, 11–12, 15–18, 27–30; white slavery and 11; *see also* modern slavery
Slavery, Servitude, Forced Labour and Similar Institutions and Practices Convention 72
Slavery Convention of 1926 20
Smith, C. J. 198
social determinants of health (SDoH) 266–267, 271, 273–274
social inequality 108, 115
social justice: anti trafficking model and 333–334; empowerment and 323, 333–334; social work and 317, 322, 333–334, 350–351
social media: labor trafficking and 276; organ trafficking and 306; sex trafficking and 244, 276; social issues and 109; trafficking and 180; *see also* technology
social services organizations 365, 369
social work: action orientation of 315; anti-trafficking activities and 328, 348–349; anti-trafficking model in 332–338; child trafficking victims and 358; client-centered 351; Code of Ethics in 317, 322–323, 349–350, 366; cultural competence and 354–355, *355*; definition of 343; ecological perspective and 347–348; ethical dilemmas in 350; history of 315–316; humanitarian aid and 350–351, 353; human rights and 316–317, 322, 343, 349–350, 355–356; international 350–354; intersectional frameworks in 343; macro level interventions 316, 323, 325, 329, 331, 343, 348, 354; mezzo level interventions 316, 323, 325, 329, 331, 343, 348, 351, 354; micro level interventions 316, 323, 325, 329, 332, 348, 354; multidisciplinary networks in 358–359; peace promotion and 350; social justice and 317, 322, 333–334, 350–351; strengths-based approach 356; trauma-informed response and 329, 331–332, victim-centered approach 355–356; victim identification in 356–358
social work case study 344–347
social work education: anti-trafficking training 322–327; competencies in 324–325; empowerment and 323; field placement in 326–327; globalized models for 351; Human Rights Activities (HRA) 327; human rights approach in 322, 324; human rights courses in 324–325; multi-site placement 326–327, **327**; post-coursework and training 325–326; post-field placement 327; professional membership and 325
socioecological model 264–265, *265*, 266
soft law instruments 72, 77–78
South Africa 305
South Asian Association for Regional Cooperation Convention on Preventing and Combating Trafficking in Women and Children for Prostitution (2002) 76
Southern African Development Community (SADC) 77
Southern Poverty Law Center 275
Soviet Union 9, 11
Specter, M. 15, 25

state-dependent learning 224–225, 235
statutory laws 190–191
Steiner, S. 337
Stockholm syndrome 50, 217, 229, 247
Stop Enabling Sex Traffickers Act (SESTA) 180
stress 218, 223–224, 228; *see also* post-traumatic stress syndrome (PTSD)
sub-Saharan narrative 112
substance abuse: alexithymia and 227; drug abuse and 144, 228; public health and 272–273; sex trafficking and 272; stress and 228; trafficking victims and 226–228, 230; trauma and 272
substantive criminal law 190
Supplementary Slavery Convention 205
surrogacy and adoption narrative 114–115
survivor-led groups 369
survivor mission 230
survivors 377–379
Sustainable Development Goals (SDG) 169, 181
Sweden 82–83, 149–150
Swedish model 82–83, 148–149; *see also* Nordic Model
syncope 240

Taft, William Howard 45
Taft administration 45–46, 49
Tahiri Center for Justice 277
Talia trafficking case study 329–331
Tasha Gardner case study 277–279
technology: children and 244; criminal justice use of 180; digital information-sharing and 252; online exploitation and 180; public health and 276–277; trafficker use of 180, 276–277; trafficking prevention and 277; *see also* social media
technology narrative 120
Thai Community Development Center (Los Angeles) 52
Thailand 116–117, 178
THBOR *see* Trafficking in Human Beings for the Purpose of Organ Removal (THBOR)
therapeutic justice 136, 143–144
Thirteenth Amendment *see* United States Constitution
Thorn 180
thrivers 378–379
TIP report *see* Trafficking in Persons (TIP) report
Todros, J. 27
Tong, A. 300
trafficking chain 193
Trafficking in Human Beings for the Purpose of Organ Removal (THBOR): brokers and 305–308; definition of 305; deterrence measures for 294; estimates of 294–296; evidence of 296–297; ideology and 289, 291; legislation for 298–299; medical profession involvement in 294, 297, 305; Palermo Protocol and 287–288; recruiting sellers for 299; terminology in 289, **290**, 291, **291**; third party involvement in 301, 304; transnational elements of 299; *see also* organ trafficking
trafficking in persons: "action element" in 193–194, **194**, 195, 208; criminalization of 192–195; definitional ambiguity in 193; definition of 192, 208; elements constituting 192–193; "means" element in 195–196, **196**, 197–198, 208; "purpose" element in 198, **199**, 200–202, 208; sexual exploitation and 200–201; trafficking chain in 193; U.S. federal law and 204; *see also* human trafficking
Trafficking in Persons (TIP) report 39, 51, 53–54, 65, 162, 204
trafficking in sports narrative 115, 125
trafficking in women: economic beneficiaries of 22; forced labor and 170, 244; forced marriage and 170; prevalence of 176, 243; racialized hierarchy in 24–25, 27; sex/labor trafficking intersection 52; Western policy and 25; white slavery and 22–23, 47; white women and 24–26; *see also* trafficking victims; women and girls
trafficking process: grooming in 217–220, 235; physical abuse and 218–219, 235; psychological abuse and 218–219; taking control stage in 219–220; traumatic experience and 225–226
trafficking prosecutions 57–59, 61
Trafficking Protocol *see* Palermo Protocol
trafficking victims: assessment of trauma in 230, **230**, 231–232; blaming 337; chronic stress and 223–224; comparison of protections for **90**; compelled service and 38, 61; complex PTSD and 222–223; court-mandated recovery 233; critical pathways for 379–380, *380*; definition of 377; deportation fears 174, 248; dissociation and 218, 222, 224; effective responses to 365; emergency services for 86–87; emotional response in 226–227; empowerment and 333–334; escape planning by 250, 254; fear of authorities by 86, 88; gender and 170; guiding values for serving 366; healthcare treatment and 247, 249–254; health issues and 242, 245–249; "house rules" for 246; housing for 333; hyperarousal and 218, 224–226, 228; identification of 56–57, 85–86, 126, 164, 170, 230, 247–250, **250**, 251, 356–358; interviewing 56–57, 280; law enforcement cooperation and 174–175; learned helplessness in 220, 225; legal options for 87–89; liberation and rescue reaction 352–353; mental health continuum *379*; mental health symptoms in 222, **222**, 223–231, 235–236, 247, 264, 338; models of practice for 375–379; multidisciplinary network of care for 358–359; needs of 89, 254; non-citizen visas 254, 256; objectification of 337–338; PATH model and 377–384; Phoenix 1st Step Model and 384–385; power and control of 246, *246*; privacy protections for 88, 92, 94; punishment of 141, 174; recovery/reflection period for 90–91,

221; recruitment of others by 245; reintegration programmes for 81, 89; resources for 254, 277, 333–334; restitution for 87, 142–143; right to participation by 353; risk factors for becoming 244; safe harbor laws 65; sanctions and 93; self-determination and 352, 356, 366, 384; self-disclosure and 357–358; self-harming behavior and 226, 228; self-identification as 174, 230–231; service-neutral approach to 66; shelters and 64–65; stereotypes of 352; substance abuse and 226–228, 230; support systems for 164–165, 233; as survivors 64, 230, 377–379; technological controls and 252; threat of violence and 246; as thrivers 378–379; trauma bonding and 228–230, 235; trauma-informed response and 143, 269–270, 358; traumatic memory in 225–227; universality and 66; voluntary return/repatriation 91; willingness to prosecute 88, 91–92; *see also* child trafficking victims; post-trafficking life

Trafficking Victims Protection Act (TVPA): 3P/4P paradigm and 39, 41, 51, 53, 56–57, 67; abolition underpinnings of 19, 43–44; adoption of 10, 36, 39, 41, 204; debt bondage and 205; economic sanctions and 204; gender/nationality neutrality in 51; human trafficking and 67, 204; involuntary servitude and 205; labor trafficking and 57; monitoring of government action in 162–163; morality-based stories in 42; psychological coercion standard in 51; restitution and 142; sex trafficking and 57, 204; sexual exploitation focus 21, 25; standards in 54, **54**, 55; trafficking definition in 242–243, 316; victim-centered approach 52–54; *see also* Trafficking in Persons (TIP) report

Trafficking Victims Protection Reauthorization Act of 2003 58

training 86, 94, 122, 126; *see also* social work education

trans-Atlantic slave trade: in anti-trafficking discourse 12; diminishing of 15–16, 27; economic systems and 11–12, 19; emotional legacy of 8, 13–15, 27–28; exploitation forms in 16; extent of 12, 15–16; legal prohibition on 8; modern trafficking analogy 9, 12–18, 20, 27–30; modern trafficking and 11

transformative justice: criminal justice and 145–150; definition of 136; John School and 145–148, 274; legalization of prostitution and 148–149; Nordic Model and 148–150; sex trafficking and 145–150

transparency efforts 62–63

Transplantation of Human Organs and Tissues Act (2010) 296

transplant tourism 111, 293–294, 298

trauma: assessment of 230, **230**, 231–232; betrayal 228; complex 222–223, 233; cumulative 223–224, 235; emotional processing and 226–227, 229; fight-flight-freeze response 223–224; hyperarousal and 225–226, 228; intervention strategies 232–233; public health approach and 267, 269–270; reenactment of 227; self-harming behavior and 228, 235; substance abuse and 228, 272; trafficking victims and 174, 222–230

trauma bonding 228–230, 235, 247

trauma-informed care: child trafficking victims and 223; medical profession and 249–251, **251**, 253; post-trafficking life 223–230; principles of 269; protection and 56; trafficking victims and 143, 269–270

Trauma-Informed Care for Children and Families Act of 2016 270

traumatic memory 225–227, 235

traumatic reenactment 227

travaux préparatoires 190, 193

Trump, Ivanka 17, 19, 30

Trump administration 19, 40, 42, 65

Tsutsui, K. 106

turpentine camps 44–45, 48, 50

Tuskegee Experiment 280

TVPA *see* Trafficking Victims Protection Act (TVPA)

UN Convention: criminal law and 92, 94, 162; development of 10; human trafficking and 166–167; implementation of 191; investigative measures and 94; organized crime and 75, 162; ratification of 162

UN General Assembly 13, 77, 191

UN.GIFT (United Nations Global Initiative to Fight Human Trafficking) 98

UN Global Compact 83–84

UN Guiding Principles on Business and Human Rights 84, 179

UNICEF 77

United Kingdom: abolition and 12; anti-trafficking efforts 14, 47–48; forced criminality cases in 65; forced marriage in 169; labor trafficking and 61; National Referral Mechanism (NRM) in 97; slave trade and 17; transparency efforts and 62

United Nations (UN) 288–289

United Nations Commission on Human Rights 77

United Nations Convention Against Transnational Organized Crime (CTOC) *see* UN Convention

United Nations Declaration of Basic Principles for Victims of Crime and Abuse of Power 92

United Nations Global Plan of Action to Combat Trafficking in Persons 77, 161

United Nations International Children's Emergency Fund (UNICEF) 77

United Nations Office on Drugs and Crime (UNODC): anti-corruption efforts 177; on exploitation 202; organized crime and 191; on

organ removal 201; Palermo Protocol and 191, 193; PEACE model for interviewing 56–57; pillars for action in 161; "Work Abroad" PSA campaign 78, *79*
United Nations Protocol against the Illicit Manufacturing of and Trafficking of Firearms, their Parts and Components and Ammunition 191
United Nations Protocol against the Smuggling of Migrants by Land, Sea, and Air 162, 191
United Nations Protocol to Prevent, Suppress and Punish Trafficking in Persons, Especially Women and Children *see* Palermo Protocol
United Nations Special Rapporteur on Trafficking in Persons 152, 163
United Network for Organ Sharing (UNOS) 294
United States: 3P/4P paradigm and 53; abolition and 12, 18, 20; anti-slavery laws 44–46, 49, 57; anti-trafficking efforts 20–21, 37, 39–43, **43**, 47–55, 64–65; anti-trafficking statutes 58, 64; civil rights in 44–45; Civil War and 17–18, 20; contradictory policy in 19, 30, 42; Emancipation Proclamation 20; enforcement agendas in 61; federal trafficking law in 204–205; immigration policy in 65; incarceration rates in 273; involuntary servitude in 44–46; Jim Crow laws 18, 20, 44, 63; labor trafficking lawsuits 61; mantle of righteousness and 16–18; organ transplants in 301; policy agenda of 39–40; policy legacies **43**; safe harbor laws 65; sex trafficking law in 61, 204–205; slave trade and 12, 17–18; trafficking definition in 204, 207; transparency efforts and 62; transplant tourism and 294; white slavery policy in 23, 47; women's suffrage 48
United States Constitution: Fifteenth Amendment 46; Fourteenth Amendment 46; Thirteenth Amendment 12, 18, 20, 37, 43–44, 46, 48–50, 52
United States v. Bradley 57–58
United States v. Cadena 51–53
United States v. Flores 52, 63
United States v. Ingalls 49
United States v. Kozminski 50–51, 57
United States v. Lewis 142
United States v. Manasurangkun 51–52
United States v. Paoletti 51
United States v. Shackney 50–51
United States v. Venters 45, 48
Universal Declaration of Human Rights 37, 74, 125, 317, 322, 327, 350
universality 66
University of North Carolina 279
University of Southern California 277
UNODC *see* United Nations Office on Drugs and Crime (UNODC)
UNODC Model Law 196–197
UN Organized Crime Convention and Trafficking Protocol 10
UN Regional Action Plan for MENA against Trafficking in Persons and the Smuggling of Migrants (2006) 78
UNTOC *see* UN Convention
UN Working Group on Contemporary Forms of Slavery 9
upstream interventions 265
Urpelainen, J. 104
U.S. Advisory Council 64
U.S. Congress 105
U.S. Department of Homeland Security 79, 277
U.S. Department of Justice 38
U.S. Executive Order on Strengthening Protection Against Trafficking in Persons in Federal Contracts of 2012 85

value framing 106–107
van den Anker, C. 15
Vandenberg, M. 142
van Schendel, W. 28, 30
Van Voorhis, R. M. 323
Vera Institute of Justice 230
vertical communication 372
victim blaming 337
victim-centered approach: *Cadena* case and 52–53; criminal justice and 161; *Flores* case and 52; international conventions and 75; interviewing victims in 56–57; prevention and 53–55; prosecution and 57–59, 163; protection and 55–57, 85–90, **90**, 91, 164–165; social work and 355–356; survivor testimony and 52–53, 56; worker-led social responsibility (WSR) and 63
Victim Information and Notification Exchange (VINE) 277
victimization 107–108; *see also* trafficking victims
victim narrative videos 109
victim support services 126–127
victim support services narrative 112
violence: as community issue 352–353; cycle of 352; domestic 140, *263*, 352; fight-flight-freeze response to 218, 223–224; gender-based 113–114, 121, 125; hyperarousal and 218; police and 44–46, 138–139; repetitive exposure to 218; sexual 138–139; sex work and 148–149; threat of 246
vulnerabililty characteristics 196–197
vulnerable people narrative 118

Walk Free Foundation 98, 163
Wallace, Bob 148–149
Waltman, M. 150
Warsaw Convention *see* Council of Europe Convention 2005
Weimar, W. 289, 291, 298, 300, 302, 305, 306
Weitzer, Ron 42
Wellstone, Paul 21, 25, 31n8
Westernization of globalization 336

Wheby, C. 333
Wheeler, K. 145–146
whiteness 8, 27, 30, 47
white slavery: economic systems and 22, 26, 28; history of 21–23; international conventions 74; international policy and 23–24, 26, 28; modern trafficking analogy 11, 21–22; public perception of 22–23, 25, 30; racialized efforts against 23–24, 30–31, 150–151; regulation of commerce and 46–47; as sex trafficking 47; Western women and 22–23, 74, 150
White Slave Traffic Act (Mann Act) *see* Mann Act
Wiktor, N. 333
Wilberforce, William 37
Wolfe, Lauren 280
women and girls: African American 45, 48, 271; anti-corruption efforts and 176–177; debt bondage and 49; empowerment of 176; experience of sex/labor trafficking 52; exploitation narratives 111; forced labor and 170; forced marriage and 169–170; ISIS enslavement of 64; as majority of trafficking victims 170, 176, 243; as organ sellers 300; re-victimization prevention 81; white slavery and 22–24, 26, 47, 150; *see also* trafficking in women
Women's Medical Center 280
women's suffrage 48
"Women Under Siege" 280
Wong, D. 11
Wong, G. 298, 300
"Work Abroad" PSA campaign (UNODC) 78, *79*
worker-led social responsibility (WSR) 63
World Health Organization (WHO) 262, 271–272, 280, 288

Xia, Y. 125
Xu, J. 294

Zaitch, D. 298
Zastrow, C. 326
Zika virus 270–271